Planning and Administering Early Childhood Programs

Fifth Edition

CELIA ANITA DECKER
Northwestern State University

JOHN R. DECKER
Sabine Parish, Louisiana, School System

Merrill, an imprint of
Macmillan Publishing Company
New York

Maxwell Macmillan Canada
Toronto

Maxwell Macmillan International
New York   Oxford   Singapore   Sydney

**To Kelcey and Keith, our twin sons, and Kristiana, our daughter, who have
helped with the clerical and computer aspects of the writing of this book.**

Cover photo copyright © David Young-Wolff, PhotoEdit
Editor: Linda A. Sullivan
Production Editor: Constantina Geldis
Production Buyer: Pamela D. Bennett

This book was set in Palatino by Carlisle Communications, Ltd. and was printed and bound by New
England Book Components. The cover was printed by New England Book Components.

Macmillan Publishing Company
866 Third Avenue
New York, NY 10022

Macmillan Publishing Company is part of the
Maxwell Communication Group of Companies.

Maxwell Macmillan Canada, Inc.
1200 Eglington Avenue East, Suite 200
Don Mills, Ontario M3C 3N1

Library of Congress Cataloging-in-Publication Data

Decker, Celia Anita.
    Planning and administering early childhood programs / Celia Anita
Decker, John R. Decker.—5th ed.
        p.   cm.
    Includes bibliographical references and index.
    ISBN 0-02-327965-6
    1. Early childhood education—United States.   2. Educational
planning—United States.   3. Day care centers—United States–
Administration.   4. Instructional systems—United States–
I. Decker, John R.   II. Title.
LB1139.25.D43   1992
372.21'0973—dc20   91-20961

Printing: 1 2 3 4 5 6 7 8 9   Year: 2 3 4 5

Preface

Planning and Administering Early Childhood Programs, Fifth Edition, is built on the conviction that thoughtful planning and administration are essential to the success of early childhood programs. Our main priority is to present the rationale for this thoughtful planning and administration. The more administrators know about factors influencing quality programs, the better equipped they will be to plan and administer programs. From our perspective, each child, parent, staff member, and sponsor deserves nothing less.

We know how important planning is. So we are committed to helping new and experienced administrators and students of administration make sense of what they are doing.

The text is organized to suggest how early childhood administrators must structure their thinking as they make decisions about their local programs. Thus, following a brief overview of the current status of early childhood education, the text is divided into three sections. Part I is concerned with the framework for program planning such as choosing the program rationale and abiding by regulatory constraints. Part II is focused on the operational aspects of the program, the more purely administrative component. Staffing, housing, equipping, and financing decisions must stem from the selected program rationale. Part III is centered on the program's services. Services for children involve: planning for their activities; meeting their nutritional, health, and safety needs; and assessing, recording, and reporting their progress. Services for parents include: involvement through communication between staff and parents and through parent participation; and provisions for parent education and family resource and support programs. Each program service for children and parents must mirror the selected program rationale. And finally, to be truly professional, administrators must contribute to their own profession in direct ways.

NEW FEATURES

The fifth edition of the text reflects a balanced concern for all types of early childhood programs with their varying purposes, sponsorships, and ages of children. Early childhood is becoming a more broadly based field and this text reflects that outlook on early education and child care aspects.

The perspective of this new edition is that administrative decision making must be based on a chosen psycho-philosophical position. Several of these positions are discussed. Because the diversity of views has been reduced to two basic program orientations, these views are the focus of the book: (1) to nurture the total development of the young child (i.e., primarily the interactionist position), and (2) to help the child master cultural literacy demands (i.e., primarily the behavioral-environmental position). Throughout the text there are discussions on how a chosen psycho-philosophical view affects decisions in all areas of program planning.

There are two major focuses of this new edition. First, there is a focus on the growing need for affordable, quality early childhood programs for children from infancy through the primary grades (levels). Thus, the new edition has an expanded emphasis on infant/toddler programs, primary grade (level) programs, and school-age child care programs. Second, there is a focus on the professional concern over the heavy academic emphasis which led to various position statements by professional associations. The reasons for the call for "appropriate practices" are explained in Chapter 2 and developed throughout the text.

This fifth edition also offers the following new features:

1. Examples of inside and outside arrangements and equipment needed for infant/toddler programs, primary-age programs, and school-age child care programs in addition to the housing and equipping needs for programs serving three- through five-year-old children.
2. Broad outlines of "appropriate" curriculum practices for the entire range of children's programs.
3. A more comprehensive treatment of informal methods of assessment.

All text and resource information has been thoroughly updated. The "Notes" and "For Further Reading" sections at the end of each chapter also refer to the most current information.

PEDAGOGICAL FEATURES

Readers will find the three subdivisions of the book helpful, because these parallel the planning processes of an administrator—namely, deciding on the program's framework, operationalizing the program, and implementing the children's program. The summaries of each chapter will also help readers focus on the main themes of the book.

We have raised issues to stimulate early childhood leaders to reexamine their own beliefs and then take another look at their program's rationale and practices. Thus, relevant studies are included throughout. Cookbook formulas are omitted and options are given, because single solutions are obviously not appropriate for everyone.

The text provides information needed by all early childhood programs. The field is diverse, but there is a great deal of overlap of the types of competencies needed in various programs. We have attempted to provide a balance among research and supported statements, applied ideas for implementation, and resources for further thought and consideration.

Like the four before it, this edition will aid in initial planning of early childhood programs and be a source of helpful information after programs are under way. The purpose of this book will be fulfilled when the reader makes wiser judgments about planning and administering early childhood programs.

We thank the following reviewers of this edition for their helpful comments: Patricia Bence, Tompkins Cortland Community College (Dryden, NY); Kim Madsen, Chadron State College (NE); and Beverly Schumer, Mercy College of Detroit.

Celia A. Decker
John R. Decker

Brief Contents

Contents

Chapter 1
Overview of Early Childhood Programs

The momentum for early childhood programs has been building for the last two decades and shows no signs of abatement. Among the extensive and varied programs concerned with the total development of human potential, early childhood programs are in the forefront. Demographic data detail an ever-increasing need for high-quality early childhood programs. Professionals agree on many factors that make for effective programs, and research extols the benefits of high-quality programs and the damaging effects of poor ones. The importance of high-quality early childhood programs to families has resulted in a ripening awareness in political and economic circles. This growing political and economic will is seen in the numerous child- and family-related bills recently introduced in Congress and state legislatures,[1] the National Governors' Association reports on children,[2] and activity of the business-led Committee for Economic Development.[3]

In spite of the obvious need for high-quality early childhood programs, the empirically based rationale for planning programs, the promising data confirming such programs' benefits for young children and their families, and the seeds of political and economic support, complex challenges lie ahead. As an unprecedented number of groups and individuals in both the public and private sectors set off to implement programs for our young children, the need for adequate planning and administration seems self-evident; yet, judging by the frequent absence of a rational, conceptual, and systematic approach, planning and administration are often considered irrelevant to program quality. Careful attention to planning and administration can prevent costly, frivolous, and counter-productive mistakes and can protect program growth in the face of far-outstretched resources, so that program quality is maintained and enhanced.

NATURE AND EXTENT OF PROGRAMS

Effective planning and administration begin with some perspective on the nature and extent of early childhood programs. An overview of the influential factors and the status and types of programs for young children will provide a setting from which to view the nature of their planning and administration.

Factors Influencing Early Childhood Programs

Early childhood programs are the products of their exciting heritage and an expression of our society's determination to provide the best for its young. Several factors appear to influence the nature and extent of today's programs. First, literature reveals a growing conviction that a child's early years are highly important to the remainder of development. Because of evidence that early life experiences, including those of the newborn, influence later development, the quality of early childhood experiences is believed to determine, to a large extent, how effective later development can be. Consequently, programs designed to meet the needs of young children are receiving high priority.

Further, there have been major changes in the ecology of childhood. There is more divorce, more single-parent families, fewer extended families, and more teenage parents. Zimiles calls these changes in family life style the **diminishing mothers** factor.[4] Today, one in five of all children living in the United States lives with a single parent, and by the year 2000, one in four will live with a single parent. Over half of all births are to teenagers, and four out of five of these mothers are unmarried. Over a quarter of a million children are living apart from their families in foster care and institutional settings.[5] The number of poor children under six years of age increased by 35 percent between 1968 and 1987. The 23 percent poverty rate for children under six years of age is more than double the rate for children six to eighteen years of age. Almost half of these children live in urban areas, and the remaining numbers are almost equally divided between suburban and rural areas. The largest group of poor children is white (42 percent), but minority children have a much higher likelihood of living in poverty (48 percent of black children live in poverty, 42 percent of Hispanic, 29 percent of other minorities, and 13 percent of white children excluding Hispanic).[6] These social and demographic trends are likely to continue and even rise, partially because of popular beliefs about children and families in poverty that impede more adequate social policies.[7]

More and more children need care in productive group environments while their mothers work. Over half of all preschool children have mothers in the work force, and by the year 2000, 70 percent of all preschool children will have working mothers. Only 30 percent of employed mothers work part-time (33 percent of married mothers and 26 percent of unmarried mothers).[8] And the largest increase in employed mothers in the last decade is in the proportion of children under age one with mothers in the work force.[9]

Finally, against the background of today's social problems, early childhood programs are seen as support systems for families. In some ways, these programs have come full circle. They are seen today as they were seen under the leadership of Jean Oberlin, Friedrich Froebel, Elizabeth Peabody, Susan E. Blow, Kate Wiggin, Patty S. Hill, Maria Montessori, and Rachel and Margaret Mc-Millan, as the best hope of reducing poverty of mind and body.

Even today's advantaged families often feel inadequate in trying to meet the demands of our rapidly changing society. Thus, universally available early childhood programs are now considered worthwhile to provide an essential service to families and an enriched, productive environment for young children.

Status of Early Childhood Programs

Early childhood programs come in all sizes, shapes, and philosophies, and, like most things, with various degrees of excellence. Young children and early childhood programs are big business from almost every standpoint. Early childhood programs, which came into their own about thirty years ago, are no longer the additional service of a more affluent public school system, the special project of a philanthropic organization, an undertaking of a state welfare agency, or the result of a federal program. Currently, all states provide moneys for universal public school kindergartens; since 1980, there has been a movement for public education of economically disadvantaged four-year-olds. More and more children from infants to school age are in day-care programs—the federal government funds projects such as Head Start; corporations operate early childhood programs; and resource and referral centers provide needed services.

Universities are bombarding the scholarly market with research about young children and their programs, producing professionals and paraprofessionals for child service programs. Programs have encouraged a burgeoning commercial market for educational toys, equipment, and books.

Although early childhood programs have greatly expanded, the body of data for the whole field is incomplete.[10] Figures inadequately reflect care by relatives, children in multiple care arrangements, and school-age child care. Several trends are evident, however. Universal education for all five-year-olds is, for all practical purposes, a reality. On the other hand, infant/toddler and school-age child care are very scarce. Programs for children in low-income families are expanding with Head Start enrollments and public school programs for pre-kindergarten at-risk children (especially four-year-olds). However, this expansion lags further and further behind the growing numbers of poor children in the United States.

TYPES OF EARLY CHILDHOOD PROGRAMS

One of the first problems encountered in attempts to differentiate among the various types of early childhood programs was that the term **early childhood** was not precisely defined. Educators, child psychologists, and others used vague synonyms or different chronological ages or developmental milestones.

The National Association for the Education of Young Children defines early childhood as birth through age eight.

One simple classification of early childhood programs is by their source of funding. Generally, early childhood programs are under the jurisdiction of one of the following: (1) public schools (e.g., kindergartens); (2) private control (e.g., nurseries, kindergartens, parent cooperatives, business-operated day-care programs, and programs for young children sponsored by churches, service organizations, and charities); (3) federal programs (e.g., Head Start and Parent and Child Center Program); (4) national private agency programs (e.g., American Montessori schools); and (5) university laboratory programs (e.g., nursery, kindergarten, and primary-level schools). Closely paralleling the sources of funding are the legal forms of organization: proprietorships, partnerships, corporations, and public agencies. (For details on these legal forms of organizations, see Chapter 3.)

Early childhood programs may also be described according to their origin. The following types can be historically traced: day-care, Head Start and Follow Through, kindergartens, Montessori schools, nursery schools, and primary schools.

Day-Care

The term **day-care** generally refers to programs that operate for extended hours (often twelve hours) and offer services for children from birth through school age. Most programs for young children are of the day-care type because they involve the care and education of children separated from their parents for all or part of the day. The exception to this is the night-care program.

The forerunners of day-care centers in the United States were the Infant Schools of Europe. Although these schools were conducted by social reformers in an attempt to help the poor, educators in the United States saw them as important for all young children. These Infant Schools, based on the writing of Comenius, Rousseau, and Pestalozzi, hoped to take advantage of the fact that young children learn rapidly and retain easily, to develop character, and to lay the foundation for good mental health.[11]

Medical discoveries of the mid-1800s aroused greater concern for children's sanitation and health. In 1854, a Nursery School for Children of Poor Women was established in cooperation with the Child's Hospital of New York City. It was patterned after the 1844 French crèche, which was designed as day-care for working French women and as a method of reducing infant mortality rates. Concern for physical well-being soon broadened to include concern for habits, manners, and vocational skills.[12]

As immigrants settled in urban areas, settlement-house day nurseries opened (e.g., Hull House nursery in 1898). These day nurseries were considered necessary to counter many social evils (such as the exploitation of women and children in the labor force) and to help alleviate immigrants' cultural assimilation problems. Education was deemed essential for true social reform. Thus, some day nurseries added kindergartens, and some were sponsored by boards of education and opened in public schools (e.g., Los Angeles). Parent education became a component of the day nursery's educational program. Parents were taught various household skills and management, and the care of children.[13]

In time, however, some social reformers began to feel the day nurseries might supplant the role of the family in child rearing. Consequently, emphasis was placed on the importance of mothering (i.e., nurturing), and mothers were encouraged to remain in the home. In order to help mothers "afford" to stay in the home, the Mother's Pension Act was enacted in 1911. Enthusiasm for day nurseries further declined when the National Federation of Day Nurseries drew attention to the poor quality of some programs. Concern over the appropriateness of day nurseries stimulated the development of nursery schools in the 1920s.[14] (The history of nursery schools is discussed later in this chapter.)

Day nurseries regained their status during the Depression, when the government for the first time subsidized all-day programs in order to aid children and unemployed school teachers. Although they were called Works Progress Administration (WPA) nursery schools, they are included here because of their all-day schedule. Early childhood nursery school educators associated with the National Association of Nursery Education, the Association for Childhood Education, and the National Council on Parent Aid formed an advisory committee to assist in supervising and training teachers for WPA nursery schools and in developing guides and records.[15]

Federal funds for all-day child care were again provided in 1942 by P.L. 137 (the Lanham, or Community Facilities, Act). The purpose of the funds was to provide for the child's physical needs, and nursery school educators again assisted. Outstanding examples of such centers were the two Child Service Centers established by Kaiser Shipbuilding Corporation in Portland, Oregon, and directed by Lois Meek Stolz and James L. Hymes, Jr.[16] These centers also provided such support services as precooked meals for parents and children, on-site grocery stores, and clothes mending, to ease the burden of working parents. Support ended with termination of the Act in 1946. During the Korean War, appropriation of funds under the Defense Housing and Community Facilities and Services Act (1951) was negligible.[17]

The Economic Opportunity Act (1964) funded Head Start, day-care services for migrant workers, and day-care for children whose parents were involved in the various manpower projects. The Housing and Urban Development Act, Title VII (1965), The Model Cities Act (1966), and the Parent and Child Centers (funded with Head Start moneys) also assisted the day-care efforts.

In the 1980s, federal funds for various types of day-care programs decreased. Today, government support for day-care is seen in The Child Care and Dependent Care Tax Credit begun in 1975–76 and expanded in 1982–83, and in the Title XX Social Services Block Grant, which provides funds to states to cover a wide range of social services. Thus day-care has shifted back to state and local control for the most part. For primary child care, about half of all children are cared for by relatives and the other half are almost equally split between center

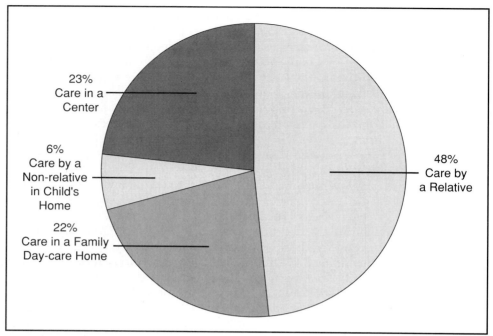

FIGURE 1–1

Primary Child Care Providers

Based on: S.L. Hofferth, *Child Care in the United States, Testimony before the House Select Committee on Children, Youth, and Families. Hearing on American Families in Today's Economy* (Washington, D.C., July 1, 1987).

care and family day-care homes, as shown in Figure 1–1. These figures exclude school-age children.

Basic Types of Day-Care

The two basic types of day-care are **center care** and **family day-care.** A **day-care center** is defined as an out-of-home program and facility serving children who need care for a greater portion of the day. Usually the schedule fits the working hours of families who use the center. There are also drop-in centers that provide occasional, part-time care. Day-care centers are regulated by state licensing requirements and other standards and may be licensed to serve children from infancy through school age. For-profit centers are usually owned and operated by individuals or family corporations, but about 10 percent are operated as large chains or franchises.[18] Not-for-profit centers are sponsored by state and local governments, religious groups (which sponsor half of all group child care for three- and four-year-old children[19]), women's organizations, and parent cooperatives. The federally funded Head Start program (which may not be classified as day-care by some professionals, although it falls under its broad definition) operates on a not-for-profit basis.

Family day-care is defined as nonresidential care provided in a private home other than the child's own. Usually the group of children is small—approximately six children, including the caregiver's own children. About half the states also define a **private home** in which seven to twelve children are cared for and additional staff are hired to meet adult-child ratios as a **group home.** Group homes are also called **large homes** or **mini-centers** under some licensing laws; these group homes are licensed as centers rather than as family day-care. Family day-care may consist of **unregulated family homes** and **regulated family homes.** "The National Day-Care Home Study"[20] found relative care especially common among unregulated caregivers. Children cared for by relatives often entered the home in infancy and remained there longer than other children. School-age children are also commonly cared for by relatives in the after-school hours. In contrast, over half of regulated family homes operate as independent businesses. The remaining family day-care homes are part of three systems. Systems include: (1) **sponsored homes,** in which a local agency assumes administrative control of homes and organizes services (e.g., recruits caregivers, screens children, aids in licensing the home, collects fees, and keeps financial records; (2) **limited affiliates,** in which a local agency provides an organizational structure for licensed, independent homes to qualify for the United States Department of Agriculture (USDA) Child Care Food Program; and (3) **provider networks** in which caregivers form a network for informal exchange or support (e.g., go together when purchasing supplies). Government agencies would rather monitor public subsidies for child care with one system than negotiate with and monitor each individual home. The "National Day-Care Home Study" also found the quality of child care was better in agency- or group-related homes than in unregulated homes.

Trends in Day-Care
In addition to the increased enrollment in day-care programs, trends can be seen in the groups of children served and in the providers of services.

Groups of Children Served. As already noted, most five-year-olds are now in kindergarten programs. Three- and four-year-old children form the bulk of the enrollment for all programs combined. However, there are trends in *extending the age* of the children served (i.e., infants/toddlers and school-age) as well as including mildly ill children.

Infant/toddler day-care usually refers to care given to children from birth to age three years. There has been some concern about infant programs. For years infant/toddler programs were thought of as usurping family rights or breaking apart the family unit, and stressing the common good of all children over individual needs. There was also some concern that the positive attachment between the mothering figure and baby would be prevented, possibly leading to Bowlby and Spitz's Institutionalized Child. However, Klimer's extensive review of research led to the summary statement that there were few differences between infants and toddlers attending group day-care and peers who stayed home with their mothers.[21] Characteristics of the infant/toddler programs, especially adult-child ratio, staff turnover, and staff training, have been strongly implicated in the outcomes for infants and toddlers.[22, 23] (See Appendix 1 for program planning.) Although the number of infant/toddler programs is increasing, they still constitute one of the most difficult forms of day-care to find. Many infants and toddlers are cared for in their own homes by relatives, babysitters, and nannies. Other infants and toddlers are placed in family day-care homes, and more and more infants and toddlers are being placed in center care. The need for high-quality infant/toddler care will continue to increase, given the fact that 52 percent of mothers return to their jobs within the child's first year.[24]

A second trend is what is referred to as **after-school care** or **school-age child care** (SACC) programs. **SACC** is a more encompassing term defined as nonparental care of the five- to sixteen-year olds during periods when school is not in session—before and after school, on holidays or vacations during the school term, and during the summer. School-age children make up the bulk of children (two to seven million or more[25]) who are referred to as **latchkey children,** or **children in self-care,** an alternative label many feel is a linguistic "cop-out" for such a serious problem. (Being unsupervised after school is believed to contribute to childhood fear, depression, loneliness, depressed school achievement, crime, and increased sexual activity.[26]) SACC is growing. The most common form of day-care for school-aged children is family day-care, serving all ages of school children, followed by add-on programs to preschool centers, often serving children in the primary grades. A few organized programs, sponsored by parent cooperatives, religious groups, and community organizations, are especially designed for school-age children. School-based programs, sponsored directly by school districts or by parental groups or other agencies and operated in school facilities, are growing in number and appear to be the most logical way to provide care for elementary children of all ages. However, concerns have been expressed over schools entering the day-care business, including the extent of school liability, charges for building use and maintenance, and costs of providing programs on an already tight budget.[27] Regardless of sponsorship, the basic goals of school-age programs are: (1) supervision (i.e., protection, shelter, food, and guidance); (2) recreation (i.e., supervised play to specific skill development); (3) diversion (i.e., crafts, drama, field trips, etc.); and (4) stimulation (i.e., formal lessons or practices). (See Appendix 1.)

There has been a growing need to find **special alternative care for mildly ill children** who attend day-care centers and other programs, including elementary schools, but are either too ill to attend their regular program or are prohibited from attending by policy. At least three types of alternative care are being used. One type includes centers specializing in the care of sick children (e.g., "Chicken Soup" in Minneapolis, Minnesota). A second type is infirmary care in pediatric wards of hospitals (e.g., Heights General in Albuquerque, New Mexico). A third alternative form of care is to send trained workers into homes to care for ill children (e.g., Sick Child Home Health Care Program, Tucson Association for Child Care, Inc., Tucson, Arizona). Work/Family Direction publishes an excellent guide, *A Little Bit Under the Weather: A Look at Care for Mildly Ill Children*, which describes prototype programs, gives criteria for programs, and provides an annotated list of currently operating programs.[28]

Providers of Services. Recently, there has been a great expansion in sponsorship of day-care services. Individuals, groups of individuals, corporations, local school districts, community organizations, religious groups, and private not-for-profit agencies may sponsor day-care. Three providers of services are becoming more common: these are day-care chains, employer-supported day-care, and the employment of nannies.

A growing segment of the proprietary market includes **chains and franchises.** Of the seventy thousand child care centers in the United States, half are for-profit; the one hundred largest chains account for 10 percent of all the for-profit centers.[29] Although the for-profit industry is dominated by owner/operators of one or two centers, the three largest chains (Kinder-Care, LaPetite Academy, and Children's World) showed an average expansion rate of 26 percent per year from 1980 to 1985 and 12 percent per year from 1986 to 1988. A slowdown continued in 1989, with only a 3 percent combined annual expansion, and is predicted for the future because of several factors: (1) increases in licensing standards; (2) increases in costs of developing new sites; (3) more competition among chains; (4) aging of centers requiring remodeling of facilities or closure due to population shifts; and (5) a decline in the rate of increase of women entering the job market. Compared with the large chains, which grew at an average rate of 7 percent from 1987 to 1989, regional mid-size chains grew at an average rate of 12 percent.[30] Chains have made a major impact in day-care with their often twelve-hour-per-day operation, services available to all age groups, convenient locations, and their expert help in meal/snack planning and curriculum development. In addition to the direct operation of centers, several companies are now managing centers established by employers. Businesses being served by these managing companies range from hospitals to office parks. Some of the companies may only manage centers (e.g., Developmental Day Schools with headquarters in Liberty, Utah) while others own some centers and manage others (e.g., Kinder-Care Learning Centers, Inc.).[31]

Because the need for child care continues to escalate, labor and business are now taking a more active role in what is called **employer-supported day care.** Prior to World War II, business and labor involvement in child care was primarily limited to the health profession and a few industries. With mothers entering the work force during World War II, public day-care and child-care programs in defense plants (e.g., Kaiser Shipbuilding Corporation) served thousands of children. After the war, however, industry-sponsored day-care declined sharply. A 1978 survey identified nine day-care centers sponsored by industries, seven sponsored by the Amalgamated Clothing and Textile Workers Union, fourteen sponsored by government agencies, and seventy-five sponsored by hospitals. A 1985 survey estimated that there were twenty-five hundred employer-supported child-care initiatives. In 1988, only thirty-three hundred of the forty-four thousand employers with one hundred or more workers provided child-care assistance.[32] However, a 1988 survey by the American Society for Personnel Administration found that almost one-half of these large companies were considering actually planning child-care initiatives.[33] Companies most likely to be involved in child care are banks, insurance companies, hospitals, or high-tech firms that: (1) have a local labor shortage; (2) have a local culture of community involvement; (3) are located in areas where high-quality care is available; (4) hire many women; (5) are in good financial health or are not in good financial health and want to recruit employees); and (6) employ one or more individuals who have taken up child-care issues. Employer-supported day-care may take one of a variety of forms. These include:

1. **Multibusiness center or consortium,** in which several firms share responsibility and costs for a center.
2. **Single-business center,** in which a corporation owns and operates an on-site facility.
3. **Family satellite program,** in which employers assist neighborhood families to become day-care providers.
4. **Corporate reserve slots,** given to employees in local day-care agencies at a rate less than the employer paid or perhaps free.
5. Corporation use of a **voucher system** in which the corporation reimburses the employees for all or part of their expenses.
6. Employer-provided **resource and referral services.** (See later section in this chapter.)
7. Employer-provided assistance through a **tax savings** under the firm's flexible benefit package, whereby salary reductions are used to fund child care.[34]

Figure 1–2 shows the major ways in which large companies offer child-care services. In small companies, work schedules are more often adjusted for employees with children than through other means of assistance. These work schedule adjustments include **flextime** (i.e., employees have core work hours with flexible starting and stopping times); **compressed time** (i.e., work more hours per day but fewer days); **task contracting** (i.e., assigned tasks to be completed within a given time frame, but need not specify time worked); **flexiplace** (i.e., location of where worked performed is flexible, such as in one's home); and, **job sharing** (i.e., two or more employees share one job and the salary/profits).

Similar to employer-supported day-care are programs operated on military bases, colleges and universities, and secondary schools. The military services are upgrading facilities, hiring early childhood coordinators, and training staff members through formal courses and staff development programs. Additional information may be obtained from the Military Early Childhood Alliance (see

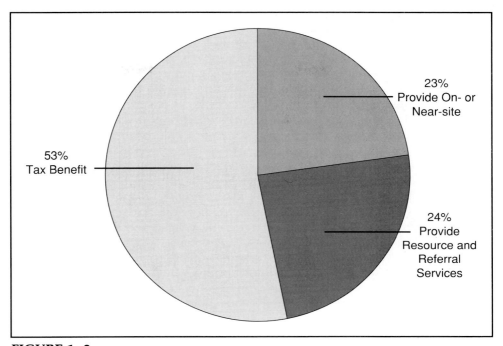

53%
Tax Benefit

23%
Provide On- or
Near-site

24%
Provide
Resource and
Referral
Services

FIGURE 1–2
Child-care Services Offered by Large Companies
Based on: Congressional Caucus for Women's Issues, "Results of the Child-Care Challenge on Employer-Sponsored Child-Care Services," *Young Children* 43, 6 (1988): 60–62.

Appendix 4). Many colleges and universities are offering campus day-care programs that provide care for students and sometimes have openings for children of faculty or from the community. For information, write the National Coalition for Campus Child Care, Inc. (Appendix 4). Some secondary schools also have on-campus child-care programs. These programs are designed to introduce students to child-care principles and practices and may serve as support services to the growing numbers of teenage mothers.

Trained in-home child-care specialists, called **nannies** or **parenting partners,** are increasing in numbers. Children of at least one-quarter million mothers are cared for in their own homes by a nonrelative, including the nanny. Nannies are employed most frequently by two-career families from the business and professional community. Fewer nannies are employed by the wealthy or by single parents. Many see the nanny movement as not only providing quality in-home child care for a growing number of families, but also view the movement as making a professional contribution to early childhood care because nannies are screened before training, undergo competency testing for certification, and receive wages commensurate with a professional service rendered.[35]

Nursery Schools

The term **nursery schools** is difficult to define because these programs are a loose array of individual facilities. It is often applied to programs for three- and four-year-old children although some nursery schools serve younger children.

Nursery schools developed in the twentieth century. Rachel and Margaret McMillan worked in the slums of London several years prior to the passage of the Education Act of 1918, which provided tax money for services to children aged two to five years. These nursery schools, as they were named by the McMillan sisters, attempted to meet the basic needs of impoverished children and establish cooperation between home and school.[36]

With the advent of nursery schools came the decline of day nurseries and the beginning of scientific child study. Day nurseries declined when mothers were encouraged to keep their children home. However, those involved in scientific child study felt that parents at all socioeconomic levels failed to provide the "best" for their children. In contrast to day nurseries and even to the English nursery schools, nursery schools in the United States were a middle- and upper-class institution. Common philosophies of these nursery schools were: (1) Young children have a developmental need for group association with peers; (2) play is beneficial for investigation of environment and for alleviating emotional stress; (3) children should begin the process of social weaning, that is, becoming detached from parents; (4) routine bodily functions of sleeping, eating, and eliminating should be managed; and (5) teachers should provide guidance and guard against emotional stress.[37] Parent education and participation, often an admission requirement, emphasized child development and observation in home and school.[38] Because the scientific child study movement attracted people from many different disciplines, nursery schools established in various institutions had somewhat different objectives.

Montessori Schools

Maria Montessori, the first woman to graduate from an Italian medical school, became interested in children with mental disabilities as a result of her medical practice at the psychiatric clinic at the University of Rome. She worked with these children, who were institutionalized with the insane children. Montessori studied the works of two French physicians, Jean Itard and his student Edoward Séguin, who worked to educate persons with disabilities. Montessori's lectures on persons who are disabled led to the creation of an orthophrenic school in Italy, which she directed. She actually taught the children enrolled in the school; and, at night, she analyzed the results and prepared new curriculum ideas, methodology, and materials. Almost from the beginning, Montessori felt that normal children learn in the same way. After two years of directing the orthophrenic school, she resigned and enrolled in philosophy and psychology courses.

In 1906, a building concern backed by the principal banks of Italy constructed some apartments in a slum area of Rome. While the parents who occupied the building were away at work, their children, too young for school, damaged the property. The property owners decided that it was more economical to provide group day-care for these children than to repair the damage they were doing. Montessori was asked to oversee the program housed in a room in the apartment complex. Thus, the *Casa dei Bambini* (Children's House) was founded in Rome in 1907. Slum children, between the ages of two and one half and seven years, attended the all-day program. Some of Montessori's contributions included: (1) parents should be given training in child development and regulations for extending the principles taught to their children; (2) parents collectively owned the "Children's House"; (3) children taught themselves through self-correcting materials with minimal guidance from adults; (4) children worked with Montessori-designed didactic materials (i.e., materials of various graded stimuli, such as weighted wooden tablets), engaged in reality-oriented practical-life exercises (i.e., care of the environment and of self), and were instructed in the skill areas of language, reading, writing, and mathematics; and (5) children could grasp academic-type learning.

Although Montessori's ideas met with sudden death in the United States in the 1920s, an Americanized version was introduced with the opening of the Montessori School in Greenwich, Connecticut (1958), and with Rambusch's publication *Learning How to Learn: An American Approach to Montessori* (1962).[39] The Americanized Montessori approach included some of the content of other early childhood programs such as creative art, dramatic play, science activities, and large muscle play on playground equipment, as well as the traditional Montessori content. Much debate stemmed from these new practices; the dispute later led to a division of thinking within the Montessori ranks. Those who hold to the traditional Montessori method are members of the Association Montessori Internationale, and those who support innovations join the American Montessori Society (see Appendix 4).

Head Start

In 1964 the federal government asked a panel of child-development experts to develop program guidelines to help communities overcome the handicaps borne by disadvantaged preschool children. The report became the blueprint for Project Head Start, which was launched as an eight-week summer program, and soon became a full-year program.[40] Head Start currently serves more than 450,000 children in all fifty states, the District of Columbia, and the U.S. Territories and has served almost eleven million children and their families since 1965.[41] Head Start is locally administered by community-based not-for-profit organizations and school systems. Grants are awarded by the Health and Human Services Regional Offices (i.e., ten regional offices, American Indian Program Branch, and the Migrant Program Branch). Head Start legislation states that the federal grant to operate a local Head Start program shall not exceed 80 percent of the approved costs of the program, with 20 percent to be contributed by the community either in cash or services.

There are four major components in Head Start: education, health care (i.e., medical and dental care, nutritional, and mental health), parent involvement, and social services. In 1975, performance standards were adopted to ensure that every Head Start program provides the services necessary to meet the goals of each of the components.[42] In carrying out its goal of providing comprehensive developmental services to children of low-income families, Head Start provides children with a center-based or home-based program. Head Start experience has shown that the needs of children vary considerably among communities and that programs should be individualized to serve local needs most effectively. Therefore, Head Start permits and encourages local sponsors to develop and implement various options.

Although Head Start is designed to serve children from age three to school entry, Parent and Child Center programs (PCCs) were initially launched in 1967 to provide comprehensive services to families below the Federal Income Guidelines with children from birth to three years of age, including services to parents in the prenatal stage. The thirty-eight PCCs emphasize the prevention of a variety of developmental deficits. The Human Services Reauthorization Act of 1990 authorized doubling the number of PCCs.[43]

Research on Head Start indicates that high-quality intervention for infants and preschool children has lasting effects (see Chapter 2). According to Mallory and Goldsmith,[44] Head Start has been successful because it (1) has provided comprehensive services to children and their families; (2) involved parents in parent education classes, in policy-making bodies, and as program volunteers and paid staff; (3) was designed to meet local community needs and use the most feasible delivery system; (4) was supported by training and technical assistance; and (5) has used a collaborative approach with other organizations at the national and local levels. Pizzo[45] indicates that future directions for Head Start must be in-service to infants through more PCCs and Child and Family Resource Programs (CFRPs). There is also a need to expand Head Start family day-care initiatives in which family day-care homes are developed as satellites to a Head Start Center that can offer training and technical assistance and support services (e.g., preventive health care and nutrition).

Public School Early Childhood Programs

Public schools have had considerable experience in early childhood education. Not only has primary education been an integral part of our public schools since their inception, but kindergartens became part of many public schools before the turn of the century. Now many public schools are incorporating programs for children below kindergarten age.

Programs for Pre-Kindergarten Children

Although public schools have only recently begun programs for pre-kindergarten children, these programs are rapidly expanding. In 1979, only seven states funded pre-kindergarten programs, and only four states contributed to Head

Start programs.[46] A 1987 study of 2,800 school districts of the program found that 33 percent of districts serve special education students, 11 percent are Head Start programs, 16 percent are pre-kindergarten programs funded by the state, 8 percent are locally funded pre-kindergarten programs, 9 percent are Chapter 1 pre-kindergarten programs, 6.5 percent are child-care programs, 2 percent are child-care programs for teenage parents, 3 percent are preschool programs operated by high school students, 3 percent are parent education programs, and 8 percent are magnet schools or summer programs.[47] In 1989, twenty-seven states funded pre-kindergarten programs that were mainly part-day programs for at-risk four-year-olds. Eleven states contributed to Head Start programs.[48]

Many early childhood leaders have voiced concern about public school pre-kindergarten programs. These leaders have said that the public schools had not appropriately served five- to eight-year-old children and expressed fears that pre-kindergartens would have inappropriate curricular content and teaching strategies and would also harm the enrollments of privately sponsored programs.[49, 50] The Public School Early Childhood Study,[51] which compared public school-operated programs and community-based programs, found that: (1) the range of practices in both went from very appropriate to not appropriate; (2) although public school programs were well-equipped, equipment was often not used well; (3) public school programs neglected large muscle play; and (4) public school programs were good if the program administrators were well-grounded in early childhood education and child development and were influential with the district superintendent. The study found that public school programs competed with community-based programs for children if the community-based program served at-risk children (e.g., Head Start), and for staff if the community-based programs offered low salaries. (Staff competition was only seen during the original staffing of the public school program.) However, without careful planning, service may be over-represented for one age group or for high-risk children, and ignored for other groups.

Kindergartens

Kindergartens are publicly or privately operated programs for four- and five-year-old children. More specifically, the term **kindergarten** is used to define the unit of school which enrolls five-year-olds prior to entrance into the first grade.

Historically, the kindergarten (children's garden) was an 1837 German institution that enrolled children three through seven years and provided teaching suggestions to mothers of infants. As the founder of the kindergarten, Friedrich Froebel's farsighted contributions included: (1) freedom of movement for the child; (2) a planned sequence of activities centered on the "gifts" (i.e., small blocks for building, developing mathematical concepts, and making designs), reinforced by the "occupations" (i.e., craft work) as well as other activities, and surrounded by a verbal "envelope" (i.e., poems, songs, storytelling, and discussions); (3) the emphasis on the relationship and order of ideas; (4) the education of mothers, nurses (babysitters), and prospective kindergarten teachers; and (5) the desire that the kindergarten become a state-supported institution.

Kindergartens came to the United States in 1855 via a German immigrant, Margarethe Meyer (Mrs. Carl) Schurz. Although many kindergartens became English-speaking institutions, following the endeavors of Elizabeth Peabody, the kindergartens were philosophically a Froebelian transplant. When the progressive child study movement began in the early 1900s under the direction of G. Stanley Hall, a divisive debate ensued between the conservative Froebelian kindergarten leaders (under the direction of Susan E. Blow) and the progressive kindergarten leaders (headed by Patty S. Hill). The progressives gained control of the kindergarten leadership and replaced the Froebelian curriculum with a more nonstructured curriculum virtually unchanged until the emphasis on more academic-type programs for young children in the 1960s.

The first public school kindergarten was opened in St. Louis in 1873. A few other public school kindergartens followed although major expansion did not occur until 1890. The Depression was devastating to the growth of the public school kindergarten. Since the 1940s, however, enrollment in public school kindergartens has steadily increased. Today every state provides financial support for its public kindergartens. Several states make kindergarten attendance compulsory. In addition, there is a trend toward replacing half-day kindergartens with full-day kindergartens.

Even as early as the 1930s, there was concern about the role of kindergarten in primary education. Headley has stated that the use of the letter "K" has made the kindergarten appear to be an "integral part of the education program" and yet somewhat different from grade school education."[52] Kindergartens vary in the amount of emphasis on academic skills, but academic programs have increased since the 1960s. Professional associations have voiced concerns (see Chapter 2).

Primary Schools

The original purpose of primary schools in America was to instruct children in the "3 R's," especially in reading. This purpose was expounded in the Preamble to the Puritan School Law of 1647 (commonly referred to as the "Old Deluder Satan Law"). The methodology was rote memorization and recitation. During the eighteenth century, the schools were seen as a unifying force for the emerging America. State support of education and the concept of free, universal education were born during this century. Curriculum and methodology changed in the primary schools of the nineteenth century. The schools began to add aesthetic education, nature study, geography, and physical education to the 3 R's curriculum. The Pestallozzian system of an activity-oriented methodology was accepted and the still frequently used unit-system of teaching evolved from the nineteenth century Herbartian method. *Normal schools* began teacher training programs as the need for trained teachers emerged. Although primary schools have continued to change with the demands of the times, many people still consider them the level at which skill subjects of reading, writing, and arithmetic must be mastered and content subjects (e.g., science and social studies) introduced in a more structured atmosphere than is found in most preprimary programs.

Home Visiting Programs

The **home visiting programs** are strategies for supporting the development of young children by professional home visits. These programs maximize the principle that effective care and education services "begin where the client is." Home visiting programs played a major role in the intervention programs of the 1960s and 1970s. Today, these programs operate through health departments, mental health agencies, and schools.

Home visiting programs vary in their approach. Powell[53] has discussed three ways in which they may differ:

1. The content of the visit may focus on the child only[54] or on the child and the family.[55] It is argued that unless family's needs are met, children's needs will be unfulfilled. Conversely, child's needs may go unmet if family needs are too pressing, or the general quality of services may diminish when home visitors attempt to provide a broad range of services.
2. The relations between the parent and home visitor differ from program to program. Because the visitor is on the "parent's turf," the home visitor is the one who adapts. In some programs, parents are very actively involved, but in other programs, parents assume a spectator role. Programs also differ in the ways they attempt to get parents involved; in some programs, the professionals develop and model the activities for the parent, while in other programs, parents assume the planning and executing roles gradually.
3. Individualization of the home visit differs from program to program. Some professionals individualize program services as they feel the need. Others individualize the content of the curriculum (i.e., sequencing activities in the order that seems most appropriate for a parent/child; selecting activities from a predetermined range of options; or encouraging parents to adopt the activities).

Home visiting is one method of working with young children that has not reached its potential. Even with its many possibilities, however, home visiting is not a panacea for improving the lives of children within the family context.

Resource and Referral Centers

Resource and referral centers are counseling services designed to assist parents in locating and selecting child-care services that are suited to their needs, preferences, and ability to pay. These agencies must:

1. Collect and analyze data on community child-care supply and demand.
2. Recruit new child-care providers and offer training opportunities and technical assistance to providers.
3. Maintain a computerized data base with detailed information on all licensed child-care providers in the area.
4. Provide consumer education and referrals (often by telephone with a follow-up mailing).

Resource and referral centers refer parents to a range of choices rather than to a specific program. Thus, parents' rights to select appropriate care are protected and liability for child-care choices rests with parents.

QUALITY PROGRAMS: MEETING NEEDS OF THE WHOLE CHILD

There is a growing recognition that high-quality early childhood education programs are good for young children. However, many see education and care as two different entities. This misunderstanding perhaps emanates from the fact that the development of kindergartens and nursery schools was separate from the development of day-care. Some writers indicate that in the 1930s, day-care was an essential part of child welfare programs. Efforts were made to differentiate between day-care as a philanthropic activity and nursery school as an educational activity, as noted in the following statement: "This purpose (care and protection), the reasons for which a family and child may need it, and the responsibilities shared with parents distinguish a day-care service from educational programs."[56] Conversely, others believe that nursery school thinking was assimilated by workers prior to World War II, in that day-care programs, in keeping with nursery school philosophy, see the teacher as assisting the child in each developmental stage, use play as the core of their curriculum, and seem to rank language and intellectual development slightly behind children's physical and affective well-being.[57]

Today there is a growing sense of urgency about meeting the needs of the whole child within the ecological context (i.e., interdependence of parent, child, and community). Kagan[58] has pointed out that three forces have mandated an interdependence between care and education. These are: (1) the mandates of equal educational opportunities (e.g., *Brown v. Board of Education* decision, Title I of the Elementary and Secondary Education Act of 1965, and P.L. 94-142); (2) research that underscores the interdependence of parent, child, and community; and (3) policy makers' concern about the state of our children and the ineffectiveness of delivering public services in uncoordinated ways.

Caldwell[59] believes that through these artificial distinctions between *care* and *education* and our devotion to labels, we exclude rather than include. Similarly, Kagan[60] states that such a differentiation leads to "undervaluing our profession" and to inappropriate practices by those who are trying to prove they *teach.* Thus Caldwell[61] has proposed the term **educare** as a way to enhance the field conceptually (i.e., to embrace the many services provided). Hymes[62] has proposed the term **publicdaycareandschooling,** "all mixed up in one."

NATURE OF PLANNING AND ADMINISTERING EARLY CHILDHOOD PROGRAMS

Variety among the early childhood programs is commonplace, although there is a general consensus regarding the importance of the child's early years and the need for early childhood programs. It becomes the administrator's responsibility to select an appropriate program base and to organize the program—the choice of goals, policies, content of the curricula, methodology, types of equipment, housing specifications, personnel matters, and evaluation, recording, and reporting practices—in ways consistent with the chosen philosophical stance.

Adequate planning and administration will mean that the environment provided and the services rendered are in keeping with the program's goals, are consistent with the legal funding agency's regulations, and are stimulating and supporting to those involved. Planning and administering local early childhood programs must be commensurate with contemporary needs and available resources. Planning entails the following five-step process: (1) identifying legitimate goals for the local early childhood program; (2) communicating these goals to those who will help in planning and administering the program; (3) determining the process by which these goals will be met; (4) operationalizing the means for their achievement; and (5) providing for feedback and evaluation. The remaining chapters of this book consider each step in the process.

The first step in planning an early childhood program is to develop a philosophical foundation and incorporate its goals into the curriculum. From this point, there is no linear progression in planning an early childhood program. In fact, all other aspects of planning should be considered simultaneously because all facets influence each other. In short, there should be congruity between the philosophy and each of the other aspects of the local program.

SUMMARY

Early childhood programs have experienced growth unlike any other American enterprise except the computer industry. The increased demand for child care and education in a society whose work force involves and will continue to involve more women and greater ethnic/racial diversity has fostered this growth, as has the desire to help children in poverty with a better start in life, and the expanding body of research that shows the benefits of quality programs for all children.

Early childhood programs, taken collectively, constitute a diverse, rather uncoordinated system contributed to by various individuals and by public and private organizations with differing historical roots. Professionals are becoming keenly aware of the need to achieve two goals. First, establish a national policy that promotes a greater collaboration among the many agencies that serve children and their families (e.g., health, human services, and education). Such a collaboration would increase the quantity and quality of available programs and help ensure the equitable distribution of program services. Second, drop the *care* and *education* labels and recognize that these are inextricably bound components in all effective programs for young children.

In an effort to meet the needs of the whole child within an ecological context, it becomes crucial for administrators to select an appropriate program base. The administrator must then plan and implement the administrative, pedagogical, and evaluation components in keeping with the chosen program stance.

NOTES

1. National Conference of State Legislatures, *State Issues 1989: A Survey of Priority Issues for State Legislatures* (Denver: Author, 1989).
2. National Governors' Association, *America in Transition: Report of the Task Force on Children* (Washington, D.C.: Author, 1989).
3. Committee for Economic Development, *Children in Need: Investment Strategies for the Educationally Disadvantaged* (New York: Author, 1987).
4. H. Zimiles, "The Social Context of Early Childhood in an Era of Expanding Preschool Education," *Today's Kindergarten: Exploring the Knowledge Base, Expanding the Curriculum*, ed. B. Spodek, 1–14. (New York: Teachers College Press, Columbia University, 1986).
5. Children's Defense Fund, *A Vision for America's Future* (Washington, D.C.: Author, 1989).
6. National Center for Children in Poverty, *Five Million Children: A Statistical Profile of Our Poorest Citizens* (New York: Columbia University, 1990).
7. J. A. Chafel, "Children in Poverty: Policy Perspectives on a National Crisis," *Young Children* 45, 5 (1990), 31–37.
8. Children's Defense Fund, *A Vision for America's Future.*
9. S. L. Hofferth and D. A. Phillips, "Child Care in the United States, 1970 to 1995," *Journal of Marriage and the Family* 49 (1987): 559–571.
10. S. L. Hofferth, "What Is the Demand and Supply of Child Care in the United States?" *Young Children* 44, 5 (1989): 28–33.
11. A. L. Kuhn, *The Mother's Role in Childhood Education: New England Concepts 1830–1860* (New Haven: Yale University, 1947), 27.
12. I. Forest, *Preschool Education: A Historical and Critical Study* (New York: Macmillan, 1927), 311–12.
13. G. M. Wipple, ed., "Preschool and Parental Education," *The Twenty-Eighth Yearbook of the National Society for the Study of Education* (Bloomington: Public School Publishing, 1929).
14. Forest, *Preschool Education*, 266–309.

15. M. D. Davis, "How NANE Began," *Young Children* 20, 2 (1964): 106–9.
16. J. L. Hymes, Jr., "The Kaiser Answer: Child Service Centers," *Progressive Education* 21 (1944), 222–23, 245–46.
17. V. Kerr, "One Step Forward, Two Steps Backward," *Child Care: Who Cares?* ed. P. Roby (New York: Basic, 1973), 166.
18. R. Neugebauer, "Child Care 1989: Status Report on For-Profit Child Care," *Child-Care Information Exchange* (February, 1989), 19–23.
19. B. Caldwell, " 'Educare': A New Professional Identity," *Dimensions* 16, 4 (1990): 4.
20. J. H. Stevens, Jr., "The National Day-Care Home Study: Family Day-Care in the United States," *Young Children* 37, 4 (1982): 59–66.
21. S. Klimer, "Infant-Toddler Group Day-Care: A Review of Research," *Current Topics in Early Childhood Education*, vol. 2, ed. L. G. Katz (Norwood, N.J.: Ablex, 1979), 69–115.
22. C. Howes and J. Rubenstein, "Determinants of Toddlers' Experiences in Day-care: Age of Entry and Quality of Setting," *Child Care Quarterly* 14 (1985): 140–151.
23. D. A. Phillips, S. Scarr, K. McCartney, "Dimensions and Effects of Child-Care Quality: The Bermuda Study," *Quality in Child Care: What Does Research Tell Us?*, ed. D.A. Phillips (Washington, D.C.: National Association for the Education of Young Children, 1987), 43–66.
24. E. Galinsky, "Government and Child Care," *Young Children* 45, 3 (1990): 2–3, 76–77.
25. Select Committee on Children, Youth, and Families. U.S. House of Representatives, *Families and Child Care: Improving the Options* (Washington, D.C.: U.S. Government Printing Office, 1984).
26. J. Merrow, "Viewpoint: Self-Care," *Young Children* 40, 5 (1985): 8.
27. M. Seligson, "Child Care for the School-Age Child," *Phi Delta Kappan* 67, 9 (May, 1986): 637–640.
28. Write: Work/Family Directions, 9 Galen Street, Suite 230, Watertown, MA 02172 (617–923–1535).
29. R. Neugebauer, "How's Business? Status Report #6 on For-Profit Child Care," *Child-Care Information Exchange* (February, 1990): 31–34.
30. Ibid.
31. Ibid.
32. Congressional Caucus for Women's Issues, "Results of the Child-Care Challenge on Employer-Sponsored Child-Care Services," *Young Children* 43, 6 (1988): 60–62.
33. E. Galinsky, "Update on Employer-Supported Child Care," *Young Children* 44, 6 (1989): 2, 75–77.
34. Ibid.
35. C. A. Readdick, "Schools for the American Nanny: Training In-Home Child-Care Specialists," *Young Children* 42, 4 (1987): 72–79.
36. E. Bradburn, *Margaret McMillan: Portrait of a Pioneer* (London: Routledge, 1989).

37. I. Forest, *Preschool Education: A Historical and Critical Study* (New York: Macmillan, 1927), 301–2.

38. M. D. Davis, *Nursery Schools: Their Development and Current Practices in the United States, Bulletin No. 9* (Washington, D.C.: Department of the Interior, Office of Education, 1932).

39. N. McCormick Rambusch, *Learning How to Learn: An American Approach to Montessori* (Baltimore: Helicon, 1962).

40. P. Greenberg, "Before the Beginning: A Participant's View," *Young Children* 45, 6 (1990): 41–52.

41. Head Start Bureau, *Head Start: A Child-Development Program* (Washington, D.C.: Government Printing Office, 1990).

42. Head Start Bureau, *Head Start Performance Standards*, 45–CFR, 304, DHHS Publication No. (OHDS) 84–31131 (Washington, D.C.: Government Printing Office, 1986).

43. Human Services Reauthorization Act of 1990, (H. R. 4151), *Congressional Conference Report of the 101st Congress, Committee on Education and Labor* (Washington, D.C.: U.S. Government Printing Office, 1990).

44. N. J. Mallory and N. A. Goldsmith, "Head Start Works! Two Head Start Veterans Share Their Views," *Young Children* 45, 6 (1990): 36–39.

45. P. A. Pizzo, "Family-Centered Head Start for Infants and Toddlers: A Renewed Direction for Project Head Start," *Young Children* 45, 6 (1990): 30–35.

46. A. Mitchell, "Old Baggage, New Visions: Shaping Policy for Early-Childhood Programs," *Phi Delta Kappan* 70, 9 (1989): 665–672.

47. D. B. Strother, "Preschool Children in the Public Schools: Good Investment? Or Bad?" *Phi Delta Kappan* 69, 4 (1987): 304–308.

48. Mitchell, "Old Baggage, New Visions: Shaping Policy for Early Childhood Programs."

49. G. Morgan, "Programs for Young Children in Public Schools? Only If . . ." *Young Children* 40, 4 (1985): 54.

50. National Black Child Development Institute, *Child Care in Public Schools: Incubator for Inequality* (Washington, D.C.: Author, 1985).

51. F. Marx, and M. Seligson, *The Public School Early-Childhood Study: The State Survey* (New York: Bank Street College, 1988).

52. N. E. Headley, *Education in the Kindergarten* (New York: American, 1966), 42.

53. D. R. Powell, "Home Visiting in the Early Years: Policy and Program Design Decisions," *Young Children* 45, 6 (1990): 65–73.

54. P. Levenstein, "The Mother-Child Home Program," *The Preschool in Action*, eds. M. C. Day and R. K. Parker (Boston: Allyn and Bacon, 1987), 27–49.

55. S. L. Kagan, D. R. Powel, B. Weissbourd, and E. F. Zigler, eds., *America's Family Support Programs* (New Haven: Yale University Press, 1987).

56. Child Welfare League of America, *Standards for Day-Care Service* (New York: Author, 1960), 2.

57. K. H. Read, *The Nursery School: Human Relationships and Learning*, 6th ed. (Philadelphia: W. B. Saunders, 1976), 32.

58. S. L. Kagan, "Early Care and Education: Beyond the Schoolhouse Doors," *Phi Delta Kappan* 71, 2 (1989): 107–112.

59. B. M. Caldwell, " 'Educare': A New Professional Identity," *Dimensions* 16, 4 (1990): 3–6.
60. S. L. Kagan, "Current Reforms in Early-Childhood Education: Are We Addressing the Issues?" *Young Children* 43, 2 (1988): 27–32.
61. Caldwell, " 'Educare': A New Professional Identity."
62. J. L. Hymes, Jr., "Public School for 4-Year-Olds," *Young Children* 42, 2 (1987): 51–52.

FOR FURTHER READING

Bradburn, E. *Margaret McMillan: Portrait of a Pioneer* London: Routledge, 1989.

Bureau of National Affairs. *The National Report on Work and Family.* Washington, D.C.: Buraff, 1988.

Cahan, E. D. *Past Caring: A History of U.S. Preschool Care and Education for the Poor, 1820–1965.* New York: National Center for Children in Poverty, Columbia University, 1989.

Elkind, D. "Montessori Education: Abiding Contributions and Contemporary Challenge." *Young Children* 38, 2 (1983): 3–10.

Fernandez, J. P. *Child Care and Corporate Productivity: Resolving Family/Work Conflicts.* Lexington: Lexington Books, D.C. Heath, 1986.

Friedman, D. *Child Care Makes It Work—A Guide to Employer Support for Child Care.* Washington, D.C.: National Association for the Education of Young Children, 1986.

Friedman, D. *Family-Supportive Policies: The Corporate Decision-Making Process.* New York: The Conference Board, 1987.

Halper, R. "Major Social and Demographic Trends Affecting Young Families: Implications for Early-Childhood Care and Education," *Young Children* 42, 6 (1987): 34–40.

Jaisinghani, V. T., and Morris, V. G. *Child Care in a Family Setting: A Comprehensive Guide to Family Day-Care.* Cheltenham: Family Care Associates, 1986.

Lombardi, J. "Head Start: The Nation's Pride, A Nation's Challenge." *Young Children* 45, 6 (1990): 22–29.

Maynard, F. *The Child-Care Crisis: The Thinking Parents' Guide to Day-Care.* New York: Penguin, 1986.

Reeves, C., Howard, E., and Grace, C. "A Model Preschool: London's Rachel McMillan Nursery School." *Dimensions* 19, 1 (1990): 10–13.

Strother, D. B. "Latchkey Children: The Fastest Growing Special Interest Group in the Schools." *Phi Delta Kappan* 66, 4 (1984): 290–294.

Thorman, G. *Day-Care . . . An Emerging Crisis.* Springfield: Charles C. Thomas, 1989.

Washington, V., and Oyemade, U. J. *Project Head Start: Past, Present, and Future Trends in the Context of Family Needs.* New York: Garland, 1987.

Part 1

Constructing the Early Childhood Program's Framework

Chapter 2
Planning, Implementing, and Evaluating the Program

D irecting program planning, implementation, and evaluation is the major task of the early childhood administrator. Every aspect of a program—staff, housing, equipment, assessment practices, parent education programs—must be designed to contribute to children's development.

The last three decades have seen a concentrated effort to improve program planning, implementation, and evaluation due in part to the fact that more people are concerned about the care and education of young children. Certain standards have been met by high-quality early childhood programs. All effective programs have staff who are concerned for the children in their care and for their families. All meet the health and safety needs of children in their care. All have housing and equipment which are more or less designed with children in mind. And all provide activities for children.

Beyond these basic features, however, high-quality programs vary enormously. There is no consensus as to what goals are the "best" for the children (i.e., what type of intellect, skills, knowledge, and values should be fostered); how educators should achieve these goals (i.e., the type of pedagogical method to be used); where to conduct the program (i.e., the home or group setting, the public- or privately operated); when to time the experiences (i.e., age at which children will be involved); or how to evaluate the results. Therefore, implicit or explicit individual perspectives form the basis for each program's practice. Such a viewpoint that is well-constructed may be referred to as a **program base.** Simply defined, a program base is a statement about the experiences of learning and teaching and the choices educators make to control these experiences.

Administrators must determine or select a program base and use this base to develop program rationale. Administrators are responsible for making implementation decisions consistent with the rationale. Figure 2–1 depicts the role of the administrator in planning, implementing, and evaluating the program.

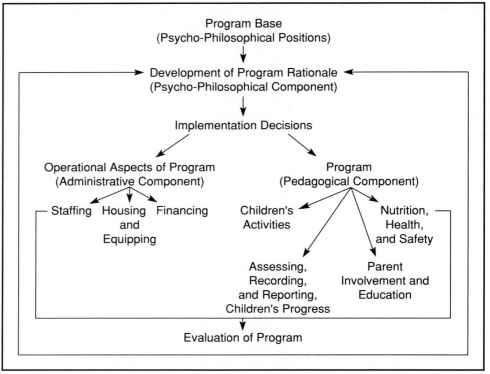

FIGURE 2–1
Framework for Program Planning, Implementation and Evaluation

FACTORS DETERMINING THE PROGRAM BASE

Few early childhood educators have a systematic program base from which they determine practice. Without such a base, problems and confusions arise. And all too often, the reverse happens; namely, theories and value statements are used to justify current practices.

Proper Sources

The two most relevant sources for determining program base are theoretical and philosophical positions. The theoretical position comes from psychological theories and helps answer questions about "what children can learn." The philosophical position comes from values for children individually and collectively, both now and in the future, and thus is concerned with "what children ought to know."

Psychological Theories

Three major psychological theories have influenced early childhood education. The first school is the **maturational** view, in which development is seen as the result of the maturation of structures within the individual. According to this view, the dominant aspect of development is genetic construction. Maturationists maintain that humans are alike in many ways because they are members of the same species; differences can also be accounted for by genetic makeup. Although the genes guide the process of maturation, teaching or nurturing determines the specific content of what an individual learns (e.g., naming colors, riding a bicycle, or using proper table manners) and influences to some degree the rate and extent of learning. The maturational view holds that teachers should provide educative experiences when the child shows interest or should provide instruction when the child is ready. This theory, formulated by Gesell[1], permeates the literature from the 1930s through the 1950s. In the 1950s, the integration of assumptions from the analytic theory with the maturational theory brought about the child development approach.[2]

The second school of thought, which was initially implemented in a laboratory setting, is the **behavioral-environmental** view.[3] In this approach development is viewed as environmental inputs and behavioral outputs. In short the environment, rather than genetic construction, has the dominant role in development. The focus is not on mental processes, but upon eliciting and reinforcing verbal, perceptual, and motor behaviors. Two teaching approaches are based on this view. One technique is to wait for desired behaviors to occur and then reinforce them with praise or object-type rewards. The second method is to communicate the desired behavior verbally, or physically model the behavior, and reinforce the child for making the appropriate response following the cue. It should be noted, however, that there are two limitations on using the behavioral-environmental view in teaching: (1) what is reinforcing to one individual may not be so to another, and consequently, adults may be rewarding (or punishing) behavior without being aware of it; and (2) because there is a variety of reinforcement sources, there may be a stronger reinforcement for certain responses outside the program setting.

The third school of thought, the **interactionist,** was a direct challenge to the behaviorist. Interactionist theorists see genetic makeup and environment, nature and nurture, as more or less equal in shaping development. Interactionists believe development is the result of experience coupled with the way the human interprets, recognizes, or modifies experience. Five main influences that shape an individual's interactions throughout his development are: (1) maturation or mainly genetic factors; (2) experience or environmental input; (3) developmental tasks through which an individual interacts with his environment; (4) consultation with other people; and (5) the interaction of all the foregoing influences.[4] Piaget began developing the interactionist theory in the 1920s, but the theory was not generally received until the 1960s.

Bronfenbrenner believes that most interactionists have not spent enough time studying the dynamic impact of the environment on behavior. Bronfenbrenner suggests that an ecological perspective be applied to all behaviors—that is, consideration of the interrelationship of the organism and the setting in which a behavior is observed.[5] The essence of an ecological system is that behaviors are not only influenced by the environment but also influence the environment. In addition, the environment closest to us (e.g., day-to-day activities at home and school) influences our behaviors to a greater degree than more distant ecological systems (e.g., values and customs).

Philosophical Positions

Schools are designed to meet social purposes. This has been recognized since the time of Plato, who describes education in *The Republic*[6] as preparation of children to do the state's bidding. Like Plato, Dewey believed that education is the fundamental lever of social progress.[7] Even more recently, Hymes, who supported the child development approach, also understood the necessity of a philosophical position; he characterized himself as "trying to be something of a bridge between child development and children's experiences in school."[8]

During the 1960s, the emphasis on psychological theories almost overshadowed philosophical positions. In the early 1970s there was a voiced recognition that psychological theory alone cannot be the sole basis for determining program design. Kohlberg and Mayer,[9] as well as Shapiro and Biber[10] felt that philosophical views must be made explicit. Kohlberg and Mayer stated that philosophically desirable ends must be rooted in the "facts of development." Furthermore, "philosophical principles cannot be stated as ends of education until they can be stated psychologically."[11] They also saw psychological theories as having either implicit or explicit values and stated that when theories are used as the basis for program design they become an ideology.[12] Kohlberg and Mayer believed that neither the "romanticism" of Rousseau, Freud, and Gesell (seen in the child development view) nor the "cultural-transmission ideology" of Thorndike and Skinner (seen in the behavioral-environmental view) is adequate for today's education. They felt that the interactionist view of Dewey and Piaget is most adequate for today. In this approach the child is not seen as a "plant" (romanticism) or as a "machine" (cultural-transmission) but as a "scientist-poet" with development as the educational goal. In short, Kohlberg and Mayer saw the role of the educator as a facilitator in the child's movement through various levels of adequacy.[13]

In Shapiro and Biber's viewpoint, Erikson, Werner, Piaget, and Dewey are all credited with providing insights.[14] A basic tenet of their developmental-interaction approach is that cognitive functions (e.g., acquiring and organizing information, using symbols) cannot be separated from the growth of the personal and interpersonal processes (e.g., development of self-esteem, internalization of impulse control). Educators must choose methods for fulfilling the first goal that never violate the second goal, and must find methods for fulfilling the second goal that make the first goal more realizable.[15] Shapiro and Biber's approach derives from a humanist position; that is, the goal is the optimal development of the individual and the enhancement of social organization. In sum, the optimally educated person balances the experiences of satisfying the self and "yields" (not "exchanges") the self for the pleasures of social mergence.[16]

Consideration of these viewpoints led to a questioning of values. Caldwell[17] pointed out that the current generation is seemingly afraid to specify what it wants for its children. According to Caldwell, Americans say they want their children to become "what they are capable of becoming"; however, we know that what they are capable of becoming depends to a great extent on experiences chosen for them by adults. Similarly, Americans say the school's purpose is "to let children find out who they are," and it is unfashionable "to say we teach them anything." Caldwell believes that this lack of specific educational goals is due to a vague national ideology or to a voiced national ideology inconsistent with what is observed (e.g., ethics in high places). She concludes that our schools must be based on articulated values—values considered good for society.

Educational values are discussed in the conference proceedings of the Joint Bank Street–Wheelock College Conference on the "Developmental-Interaction Point of View"[18] and by Spodek.[19] Although most program designers see the need for a close connection between psychological and philosophical viewpoints, Eagan[20] does not. In fact, he believes that the dominance of psychological theories has led to ineffective educational practice.

The need for a philosophical position as a base for program design seems clear. Whether the lack of a philosophical basis is due to a vague ideology,[21] dominance of psychological theories,[22] or other causes, the dilemma posed by this gap in value-base is pinpointed by Sommerville, who states, "Children are going to school for an ever-longer period, but we seem less and less sure about what they should be getting from it."[23]

Improper Sources

Several improper sources have been used for program design. Later school content, assessment items, and policies of funding agencies are the most common improper sources.

Later School Content

Generally speaking, objectives of the present program should be consistent with programs that children will be involved in later. For example, the Follow Through program was initiated to continue the work of Head Start because children who went into a traditional program from the Head Start program soon lost the advantages they had gained. Also, Miller and Dyer found that participation in one type of preschool program may interfere with learning in a later program if the programs are greatly disparate in approach.[24]

On the other hand, the goals of any program should center on the child's present benefit and not merely on preparation for the future. For many years the term **readiness** had been applied to many activities of the early childhood program (e.g., reading readiness and mathematics readiness) and even to the names of some of the assessment devices used with young children (e.g., *American School Reading Readiness Test* and the *Metropolitan Readiness Tests*). These readiness skills were considered necessary to prepare children for later schooling. For example, some intervention programs, such as Bereiter-Englemann, were based on a philosophy of overcoming specific "readiness deficits." Although some "readiness skills" may be worth learning, and continuity between present and future programs is valuable, planning a program solely on the basis of future content is compromised: (1) readiness skills are not goals in themselves, but means to goals; (2) the advantages gained in "crash" preparation may be lost; (3) formal readiness training may be detrimental in itself[25]; and (4) the use of later school content as a source for early childhood program design is circular reasoning that avoids assessing value.

Assessment Items

Assessment of children's progress in a program is essential. If the content of the assessment instruments and the techniques used in the assessment process relate closely to a program's objectives, assessment results may be used to add to or revise content or methodology to help meet stated objectives. However, one must avoid the pitfall of using assessment instruments that do not match a program's goals and of letting those instruments determine content or methodology.

Policies of Funding Agencies

Funding agencies have a great deal of control over a program:

1. Legislative control over curricular content of public school programs exists via legislation of what may or may not be taught and regulations regarding textbook adoptions.
2. The local school board or the board of directors/advisers can control program content and methodology by determining what may or may not be taught, what equipment will be used in the program, what curricular assistance will be given to teachers, and how the program will be staffed, as long as they stay within the restrictions and authorizations of federal, state, and local laws, directives, and guidelines.
3. Some federal programs have established goals for their programs, such as the "Performance Objectives" of the Head Start program.
4. Program content may also be determined by a State Task Force. Usually the state board of education and/or the superintendent of education, with approval of the state legislature, asks a committee of early childhood professionals to write a master plan for statewide early childhood education. The recommendations and implementation guidelines are then presented to the state legislature for approval.

5. Printed information, such as a curriculum guide, from the state education agency or the department that licenses child-care facilities, often affects program content.
6. A program seeking funding must follow the agency's guidelines, including program guidelines, in order to be funded.

Program design must be in the hands of the professional. When funding agencies alone determine program design, it is similar to test items being used for program design (i.e., the "tail wagging the dog").

OVERVIEW OF CURRICULUM MODELS

A **curriculum model** is the psycho-philosophical, administrative, and pedagogical components of an educational plan. The model is presumed valid for achieving certain outcomes.[26]

Models Based on Psychological Theories

Fein and Schwartz contrast theories of development with theories in practice. A **theory of development** offers general statements about factors affecting children's behaviors.[27] Such theories do not offer principles for modifying or generating those factors. In contrast, a **theory of practice** describes what a practitioner must do to encourage particular behaviors. The following section discusses how three theories of development have been applied to early childhood programs—that is, have become theories of practice.

Application of Maturational Theory
Until the 1960s most early childhood programs serving middle-class populations were based on concepts stemming from the **maturational** theory. Programs following this model were referred to as "permissive-enrichment programs,"[28] "child-centered curriculum,"[29] "child-development model,"[30] and "developmental-maturationist."[31] Table 2–1 gives a synopsis of the three components of the maturational models. Additional information on specific programs is located in Appendix 1.

Application of the Behavioral-Environmental Theory
Programs following the **behavioral-environmental** theory aim to teach facts and skills the program designers consider necessary for future functioning in the culture, but lacking in the children served. Programs applying the behavioral-environmental theory have been referred to as "structured-information,"[32] "programmed approach,"[33] the "verbal-didactic model,"[34] and "behavioristic theoretical."[35] Table 2–2 gives a synopsis of three components of the behavioral-environment models. Additional information on specific programs is located in Appendix 1.

TABLE 2–1
Maturational Model

Psycho-Philosophical Component

Based on theories of Gesell, Freud, and Erikson.

Considers children to be born with a genetic blueprint for certain patterns of behavior. Sees behavioral changes occurring as a result of physiological maturation (readiness) and environmental situations that encourage certain behaviors (developmental tasks).

Administrative Component

Housing	Roomy environment calculated to give maximum mobility. Learning centers are only somewhat defined.
Equipment	Rich assortment of multidimensional materials that serve many modes of expression (e.g., language, mathematics, motor, aesthetic) are chosen. Developmental levels of children served are considered.
Staff	Provides a warm, supportive environment. Does few, it any, prescribed learning activities, but "enriches" on-going activities when children need to expand their understanding/skills.
	Sets limits and redirects unacceptable social behaviors.

Pedagogical Component

Activities	Units and broad themes based on studies of children's interests are introduced; children are free to "sample" activities as they wish.
	Activities based on the theme are carried out by play with materials located in the learning centers and by field trips.
	Activities are almost completely child-selected rather than adult-prescribed.
Motivational strategy	Verbal extrinsic motivation (e.g., praise).
Grouping	Heterogeneous grouping (i.e., family grouping) is most common. Occasional loosely defined homogeneous groups based on age/stage.
Scheduling	Flexible schedules are designed to fit children's needs and interests.
	Large blocks of time in which a child may work on a single activity or change activities are typical.
Assessment of children	Attempts are made to observe the whole child (physical, cognitive, and affective), primarily using naturalistic observations.

Program Evaluation

Program is seen as successful if children progress according to physical, cognitive, and affective norms. Allowances are made when children are seen as having hereditary or environmental constraints placed on their development.

TABLE 2–2
Behavioral-Environmental Model

Psycho-Philosophical Component

Based on theories of Skinner, Baer, Bijou, and Bandura.

Considers children to be born with a "blank slate"; passive children's behaviors are shaped by the environment.

Sees behavioral changes occurring as a result of reinforcing planned or unplanned events.

Administrative Component	
Housing	Less roomy environment calculated to focus child's attention and to avoid distractions. Areas within the room are clearly defined—often with high dividers.
Equipment	More narrowly focused and unidimensional materials, which meet program-selected objectives and serve one mode of expression (e.g., language).
Staff	Plans and controls the environment. Almost all activities are adult-prescribed. Does much direct (expository) teaching of small units of materials that have been broken down from larger tasks and sequenced.
	Uses principles of behavior modification to prevent and control deviant behavior.

Pedagogical Component	
Activities	Goal-oriented activities designed to achieve specific cultural learnings, usually academic in nature, are provided; same learnings are often expected of all children.
	Activities are conducted by direct teaching, often in a "drill" format.
	Activities are adult-prescribed (rather than child-selected).
Motivational strategy	Incentive systems with extensive sources of motivation—token-economy systems.
Grouping	Homogeneous ability-grouping dominates.
Scheduling	Brisk-paced program presented on a "tight" schedule (i.e., "clock-bound").
	Blocks of time are short, with all children in a group staying "on task" throughout the lesson.
Assessment of children	Instructional levels are sequenced. Initial instructional levels are diagnosed by formal evaluation. As children meet the objectives at a given level, they progress to the next "rung on the instructional ladder."

Program Evaluation

Program is seen as successful if children have achieved specific learnings, which are often academic (i.e., a preparation for later school learnings).

Application of the Interactionist Theory

Programs under the umbrella of **interactionist** theory usually follow an "open-framework" curriculum, in which the teacher initiates ideas and responds to the child's activities.[36] Some interactionist models are based on the Montessori-type program and are often referred to as the "structured-environment" or "prepared-environment approach,"[37] "sensory-cognitive model,"[38] and "cognitive-interactionist."[39] Other interactionist models follow Piagetian theory and are referred to as "structured-cognitive programs,"[40] the "verbal-cognitive model,"[41] the "cognitive-interactionist,"[42] and the "constructivist."[43] Still another interactionist model bases its theory on that of Piaget, Erikson, and Werner and is referred to as the "developmental-interaction" approach.[44] Table 2–3 gives a synopsis of the three components of the interactionist model. Additional information on specific programs is located in Appendix 1.

Differences within a Theory

Models that derive their program rationale from the same theoretical base often differ in many essential ways, because some elements of theory get discarded and other parts are added. For example, Forman and Fosnot[45] analyzed six Piagetian programs in relationship to four propositions that undergird Piagetian theory. Each of these six programs focused on these propositions in a different way in their pedagogical design. Under the behavioral-environmental theoretical umbrella, the Behavioral Analysis Program of Project Follow Through focuses on a set of narrow goals[46] in comparison with the goals set forth by Bijou.[47]

Within-theory differences also occur in model programs because of the ages of children served. Honig and Brill[48] utilized the sensory motor stage theory of Piaget to enhance the development of infants during their first year of life. On the other hand, the Early Childhood Education Project[49] in Buffalo, New York, used Piagetian theory on representational knowledge (i.e., noting real "things" can be represented in two- and three-dimensional forms) as the pedagogic component for two- and three-year-old children.

When more than one theoretical base is combined in a model program, the pedagogical design differs from single-base programs. For example, Biber's[50] initial foundation for the Bank Street program was the educational philosophy of John Dewey. Later Piaget's and Erikson's psychological theories were used to give a firmer foundation for the Bank Street program's pedagogical component. In fact, Biber[51] questions the use of one theory as the foundation for practice. She calls for a broader theoretical base achieved by combinations of theories which have a common ideological base but differ in substantive ways.

Summary of Programmatic Research

Most of the programmatic research in early childhood education dates from the mid-1960s. Because of the impetus of compensatory programs, research was limited primarily to the economically disadvantaged. However, some studies

TABLE 2–3
Interactionist Model

Psycho-Philosophical Component

Based primarily on theory of Piaget.

Considers children to be a product of heredity and environment.

Describes development as occurring when a person's self-organization (denoted by stage that is qualitatively different from other stages) is challenged to an optimal degree by experiential events.

Administrative Component

Housing	Roomy environment designed to give the child opportunities to be actively involved. "Learning centers" are more defined than in the maturational model, but children's interaction among learning centers is encouraged.
Equipment	Multidimensional materials that encourage exploration and problem-solving and that are arranged in a way to convey the idea of a conceptual order.
	Children's needs for concrete and representational materials are considered.
Staff	Arranges activities that challenge the current level of development. At times the adult is active (giving new challenges) and at other times the adult is passive (waiting for the child's new learnings to be stabilized). Adults often emphasize language that accompanies the children's developing concepts.
	Plans and guides children toward self-discipline.

Pedagogical Component

Activities	Emphasis is placed on the heuristics of learning (e.g., problem-solving strategies, elaboration skills, and questioning techniques); academic content, often presented in units or themes, is seen as a means to an end, not an end in itself.
	Planned activities are provided and the children are encouraged to be actively involved. Adults interact in ways to help structure children's activities (e.g., ask open-ended questions).
	Activities are adult-arranged for their potential to engage and challenge; children select among the activities.
Motivational strategy	Intrinsic motivation (e.g., epistemic curiosity).
Grouping	Heterogeneous grouping dominates; much individual work.
Scheduling	Sequenced activities are felt to aid the children's temporal concepts; however, there is built-in flexibility.
	Large blocks of time are provided in order that children may explore.
Assessment of children	Progress is noted if thinking skills change (i.e., if a child moves to a more advanced stage of development).

Program Evaluation

Program is seen as successful if children progress to higher stages of development in terms of Piaget's theory (e.g., physical knowledge, logico-mathematical knowledge, spatio-temporal knowledge, social knowledge, and representation).

have been done on the effects of preschool for advantaged children. Furthermore, because of interest in cognitive development, and because the most reliable assessment devices measure cognitive functioning, program evaluations were primarily based on cognitive variables.

Compensatory Program Research

In the 1960s, many early childhood programs were designed to break the cycle of poverty. It was assumed that family poverty led to scholastic failure and to subsequent poverty as an adult. Many types of models were tried and compared. Some of these early programs were thought to develop the whole child; but most were designed to correct perceived language, perceptual, and conceptual deficits. Proponents of academically oriented programs argued that their programs were most important in enhancing intellectual and school achievement. Discovery, or informal method, supporters saw social skills and autonomy as areas of major importance to young children. Taking a midpoint view were those who looked to Piagetian theory as a basis of curriculum design. These programs tried to influence children's thinking and processing skills. Programs were also extended upward (e.g., Follow Through) and downward (e.g., infant and toddler programs).

Now, two decades later, researchers are seeking the link between short-, mid-, and long-term effects. The model for linking the effects is as follows:

1. Children from impoverished families who attend a quality preschool program are better prepared for school cognitively and affectively.
2. This results in greater school success (i.e., fewer grade retentions and less need for special education placements).
3. Greater success in school leads to greater life success (i.e., lower rates of delinquency, teenage pregnancy, and welfare usage, and higher rates of school completion[52, 53]).

The major effects of early childhood education may be organized according to the major outcomes in each period of the children's lives.

1. *Short-term effects.* Program evaluation of short-term effects has resulted in a wealth of information about specific programs, along with some generalizations and methodological problems involved in programmatic research. A comprehensive summary of specific studies was provided in the third edition of *Planning and Administering Early Childhood Programs.*[54] In general, Schweinhart and Weikart found that data attest to the positive effect of early childhood programs on intelligence quotients.[55] Four studies reported a maximum effect of between one-half and one standard deviation on the *Stanford-Binet;* however, statistically significant group differences disappeared by age eight. More support for the positive, short-term effects comes from the Milwaukee Study, which provided full-time, year-round developmental child care for children ranging in age from a few months to six years.[56] The Milwaukee

program had a maximum effect of two standard deviations on the *Stanford-Binet*, and statistically significant group differences still exist with the children at age ten. Ramey and others, who reviewed eleven experimental studies, found that in every study the average intelligence quotient of children who participated in the experimental programs was as good as or better than the average intelligence quotient of children in control groups.[57] The experimental programs had an average effect of one-half a standard deviation on the *Stanford-Binet*.

2. *Mid-term effects.* Schweinhart and Weikart found that the rate of special education placements was reduced by half, in four of the five studies that included data on these placements.[58] Two studies reported statistically significant reductions in retentions, too. Ramey reported similar findings on scholastic placements.[59] In terms of scholastic achievement, the Perry Preschool Project found differences consistently favoring the preschool group over the control group at ages seven, eight, nine, ten, eleven, fourteen, and nineteen.[60] The Early Training Project found a positive impact of preschool on achievement at age eight, but no effects at ages seven, ten, or eleven.[61] The Consortium for Longitudinal Studies found statistically significant positive effects on arithmetic at ages ten, eleven, and twelve but not at age thirteen.[62] In reading, the consortium found statistically significant positive effects of preschool at ten only.

3. *Long-term effects.* Schweinhart and Weikart summarized these long-term effects from several programs.[63] Neither the Perry Preschool Project of Ypsilanti, Michigan, nor the Rome Head Start Program of Rome, Georgia, found a difference between participants and nonparticipants in preschool programs and the number of persons referred to juvenile courts. However, the Perry Preschool Project found reduced delinquency among participants. Teenage pregnancy rate was less for Perry Preschool Project participants than for the control group; conversely, the Early Training Project reported no between-group differences in teenage pregnancies. School drop-out rates were lower for those attending preschool programs than for their nonparticipating peers in the Rome Head Start Program (17 percent lower), Early Training Project (21 percent lower), and Perry Preschool Project (18 percent lower). The Perry Preschool Project also reported positive effects of their program on employment; at age nineteen, 50 percent of the preschool group and 32 percent of the nonpreschool group were employed.

Kagan challenges the "continuity" in the child's maturation.[64] Citing several longitudinal studies, he points out that these studies show variation in psychological qualities during the first three years of life and were not substantially predictive of variation in "culturally significant" and "age-appropriate" characteristics later. He found the greatest predictor of a child's intelligence quotient and reading skill is the family's educational level and social class.

Noncompensatory Program Research

The tacit assumption of the deficit hypothesis so commonly used in compensatory programs is that middle-class children are likely to receive adequate stimulation at home and thereby experience only minimal benefits from preschool. Yet others feel few homes provide adequate stimulation. There are also disagreements as to the appropriate focus of learning experiences. There is concern for intellectual functioning and for social competence, which is defined as success of the person in meeting societal expectancies and in self-actualization or personal development.[65] Larsen and Draper studied the effects of a preschool program on children from child-oriented Mormon families who were well-educated and had a high socioeconomic status.[66] Using the *California Preschool Social Competency Scale,* they showed that these children were more competent at the end of the preschool term and at the end of kindergarten than the control group. In kindergarten, ratings of social competence for girls who had not attended preschool paralleled those of both boys and girls who had attended preschool, but such was not the case for boys. The researchers concluded that a preschool experience may be of particular importance in helping young boys develop socially.

Problems in Programmatic Research

Research problems are a major reason for the lack of definitive answers as to the effects of different programs in early childhood education. According to Ball and Bogatz[67] and Cooley,[68] some of the research's major shortcomings include assessing program implementation, inadequate measuring instruments, establishing comparable experimental and control groups, and limitations in interpretation of data. Attrition rates have minimized the effectiveness of many longitudinal studies. Seitz et al. have argued that most of these studies "have had such serious methodological shortcomings that they have been virtually uninterpretable in regard to evaluating either the short-term or long-term effectiveness of intervention."[69] Aside from methodological problems, perhaps even the idea of comparing early childhood models has its limitations. Hanson argues that we should not be testing models by comparing them.[70] She believes researchers should test each model by manipulating various parameters within the model (e.g., small group versus large group). Goodman suggests that drawing conclusions on positive effects of preschool programs is questionable, considering that available data primarily come from high-quality programs such as the Ypsilanti study.[71]

More research is needed to study the relationship between process variables (e.g., teacher behavior, child behavior, and classroom environment) and child outcomes, to assess curriculum areas other than reading and math, to measure specific rather than global achievement, and to develop more assessment devices for the affective domain. As those interested in education reflect on past and plan future research, they must also remember that statistically significant differences cannot necessarily be equated with educational or social significance.

PROGRAM ISSUES ON THE CONTEMPORARY SCENE

Since the beginning of formal education, various conceptual frameworks have been proposed. In the 1960s, leading psychologists and educators were encouraged to apply conceptual curriculum alternatives in programs for young children. Programmatic research was generated from these diverse psycho-philosophical positions. Although three major psycho-philosophical positions (i.e., maturational, behavioral-environmental, and the interactionist) were identified, today the diversity is, to a great extent, reduced to two program orientations. These are (1) to nurture the total development of the young child (i.e., primarily the interactionist position) or (2) to help the child master cultural literacy demands (i.e., primarily the behavioral-environmental position).

Main Issue

The main issue has centered on curriculum content and teaching methodology. During the last three decades, kindergartens and other early childhood programs have moved from the conceptual heritage of Froebel, Montessori, and Piaget, who saw children as learning by direct encounters with their world (i.e, an interactionist approach), to the conceptual positions of the behaviorists, who use didactic instruction to teach abstract symbolic systems in order that children may develop "cultural competence." The following statistics from the Educational Research Service survey provide data on this trend. The survey found that 22 percent of the principals surveyed have "academics" (i.e., skills and achievement) as the primary focus of their kindergarten programs and 63 percent have "preparation" (i.e., academic and social readiness) as the primary focus. Only 8 percent have developmental goals as their primary focus. In 85 percent of the kindergartens, principals reported that their program goals ignored two or more of these areas of development—physical, social, and emotional; conversely, cognitive development was not ignored in any of the programs.[72] A somewhat similar trend is occurring in pre-kindergarten programs. A decade ago, only four states funded pre-kindergartens,[73] and today twenty-eight states are committed to such funding.[74] Half of the state programs are required to have comprehensive developmental goals, but the other states either have no curriculum requirements or primarily focus on cognitive development.[75] And all early childhood professionals have seen many privately funded early childhood programs that have an academic focus.

Causes of Trend

Elkind[76] has described political, social, and economic pressures as responsible for this trend. Until the 1960s, early childhood education was out of the spotlight—and therefore insulated from outside pressures. At this time, three pressures converged, putting early childhood programs in the center arena. First, in the late 1950s, education was criticized when the U.S.S.R. launched *Sputnik I* and moved ahead in the space race. The demise of progressive education was bemoaned, and it was claimed that children were not learning (e.g., publications such as *Why Johnny Can't Read* were popular). Children were considered to be poorly *prepared* for school, and thus, rigorous early childhood programs were desired.

Second, civil rights of minorities had become an issue. Minority children were experiencing inferior quality education in segregated schools. Some rationalized, however, that the schools were providing sound education and that the problem was the minority student was not prepared for school. Hence, Head Start and other early childhood programs were funded with the idea of young minority children "catching up" with their middle-class cohorts.

Third, the conception of the **competent** child was fostered by the emotions of these political and social movements. No new data surfaced that suggested changes in the competence of children, but rather the "selection and interpretation" of psycho-philosophical theory supported notions of competence (e.g., J. Bruner's *The Process of Education*, J. McV. Hunt's *Intelligence and Experience*, and B. S. Bloom's *Stability and Change in Human Characteristics*). Furthermore, the competent-child idea was in keeping with the changing life styles of families (i.e., especially working mothers) who needed to feel that their children were competent to withstand the stresses and even profit from early education, including the academically oriented programs. And finally, some people felt that children's competence had grown as a result of the influence of high technology.

Major Areas of Disagreement

The interactionist and the behavioral-environmental approaches are radically different in terms of their perceived aims of education and in the curriculum content and methodology deemed necessary to achieve these aims. The interactionists believe the primary goal of education is to develop individuals who are "creative, inventive, and discoverers," and believe the secondary goal of education is to develop critical minds that question rather than merely accept information.[77] And, in order to help children "want to know,"[78] teachers choose curriculum materials that are age-appropriate. These materials are then matched to the level of each child's total developmental abilities, because there are wide age variations in any age-homogeneous group. More complex materials are introduced as each child attains the optimum developmental level for its use. The materials are real and relevant for the child's present life (as opposed to future school content).

Proponents of the behavioral-environmental approach, on the other hand, believe the primary aim of education is to help children achieve the facts and skills possessed by culturally literate adults (e.g., as expounded in *Nation at Risk: The Full Account*,[79] *The Closing of the American Mind*,[80] and *Cultural Literacy: What Every American Needs to Know*[81]). This "derived" type of knowledge[82] is then analyzed to determine the level of mental ability that is required for its mastery. (Other aspects of development are at least secondary to mental development and may be totally ignored.) The children are then ability-matched to the curriculum. Learning consists of the acquisition of a set of isolated skills (often the three R's) accomplished primarily by direct teaching and reinforcement. Children come to "know what we want."[83]

In practice, the traditional early childhood program with its holistic view of the child and its play orientation has become, at least in many places, more and more academic—that is, it has become difficult to distinguish the early childhood curriculum from that of the later elementary grades and secondary schools. The following practices illustrate this trend:

1. Curricular content is often adult-prescribed, at least one year more difficult (i.e., traditional first-grade curriculum) and divided into separate subjects, with each subject taught for a prescribed number of minutes.
2. Activities are conducted via paper-and-pencil tasks in workbooks and worksheets, referred to as "seatwork" in the elementary grades, and aptly named because the tasks require a "sit still" attention span.
3. There is a focus on the academic product, the achievement of prescribed objectives, as evaluated by standardized tests.

Associated Issues

Outgrowths of the controversy centering on the academic curriculum content and expository teaching methods are three associated issues—namely, age of entrance, placement and retention practices, and the length of the daily session. These practices were thought to be pragmatic ways of protecting some young children from a too-difficult academic program.

Age of Entrance

Some proponents of the more academic early childhood programs believe that raising entrance age is the easiest way to handle the problem of the "not ready" child. For example, it was estimated that using entrance-age cutoffs of five by December, January, or February, programs could expect 54 percent of the males and 25 percent of the females to be developmentally "not ready." Programs using September, October, or November cutoffs should expect 33 percent of the males to be developmentally "not ready."[84] Some studies show that older kindergarten children do better than younger kindergarten children in initial academic achievement.[85, 86] This is called the **birth date effect.** Thirty states now require a child to be five by September or October,[87] and Missouri requires a July birth date.[88] There is a trend toward moving back enrollment dates.

There are several reasons why later entrance is not really a viable policy. These are:

1. A more comprehensive review of the research shows that younger children's problems are not as severe as once thought. For example, on achievement tests given in the first grade, there were only six or seven percentile points separating the two groups. And there were no differences in older and younger first graders who were above the 75 and 50 percentile ranks of their respective age intervals. In short, major differ-

ences in older and younger children are seen only in those who are below the twenty-fifth percentile. Furthermore, the differences in achievement have totally disappeared by third grade.[89, 90]

2. Holding a child back who is "ready" may result in negative consequences.[91]

3. Raising entrance age by three months denies schooling for one year to one-fourth of age-eligible children. The increased numbers of children in preschool services result in an additional burden to the already short supply of available spaces for pre-kindergarten children (e.g., Head Start serves only one-fifth of the eligible children) and in an additional year of day care expenses for families whose children do not attend government-sponsored programs.

4. There are always younger and older children in a group with any entry age. The effects of age are not due to absolute age, but the relative position of a child within the group. The teacher will soon adjust to the average ability of this older group, too, and the younger ones will once again be behind.

5. Parents are discouraged from enrolling their age-eligible children because of their anxiety over the difficulty of the program.[92] Unfortunately, being the oldest does not ensure success.

6. The "gift of time" (as delayed entrance is supposed to ensure) denies kindergarten to children who could benefit the most from an appropriate curriculum and the social interaction with age-mates.

Placement and Retention Practices

Again, in an effort to protect the "not ready" child from the academic program, screening practices are being used to determine placement. Screening was popularized by the Gesell Institute,[93] and the *Gesell School Readiness Test* became one of the most widely used tests for screening children for placement purposes. The Gesell test battery contains tasks such as copying forms, writing one's name, writing numerals, and naming animals. If a child scores low on the screening test and/or other measures, the age-eligible child is said to be "at risk" for failure in the regular kindergarten program, and the early childhood program provides one or both of these options:

1. The child is placed in a pre-kindergarten, usually called **developmental kindergarten** (i.e., a program with traditional kindergarten curriculum content and teaching methodology) the first year, then promoted to kindergarten (i.e, an academic program) the second year, and then to the first grade at age seven if successful. In a few cases, the at-risk child may test out of the academic kindergarten after the year in the developmental program, but this is rare because the more abstract academic skills were not taught in that program.

2. If no developmental kindergartens are available, the parents are asked to keep their child out of kindergarten for another year. Because the

child is expected to mature during the calendar year, this practice is referred to as the **gift of time** for the child.

These placement policies have many flaws, such as:

1. There are many problems with the tests and the testing process. For example: (a) tests are often used for purposes other than those for which they were designed; and (b) studies of certain tests' reliability and validity are meager or nonexistent.[94, 95] None of the available tests are accurate enough to screen children into special programs without a 50 percent error rate.[96] Even if appropriate tests could be selected, children have many difficulties in taking tests.[97] (Chapter 10 provides a more in-depth description of the problem.)
2. Children who attended developmental kindergarten show almost no advantage over equally at-risk children who were placed in the kindergarten. Furthermore, there are emotional costs associated with staying back.[98]
3. Children who are given the "gift of time" may have the same disadvantages as the later-entrance child, except these age-eligible at-risk children will be even older.
4. Developmental placement often implies failure to parents and to the children themselves before schooling begins.

Testing, with all of its problems, is often conducted in the spring of the kindergarten year to determine whether children will be retained in kindergarten, will enter a pre-first class, often called a **transitional class** (a form of retention), or will be promoted to first grade. The academic kindergarten programs have increased the risk of kindergarten failure; more than 300,000 kindergarten students were retained in 1988.[99] The common remedy for dealing with low achievement in the elementary school is retention, and this trend now seems to be supported by kindergarten teachers. For example, Smith and Shepard[100] found that teachers feel that student careers should be determined by "competence" (or "readiness") and not "social promotion," and they act according to these beliefs. Other reasons for retention are children's general cognitive abilities, behavior, gender, socioeconomic status, and minority status.[101] Retention policies, including placement in the transitional classes, have these problems:

1. There seem to be no academic advantages gained by retention. For example, Shepard and Smith[102] found no differences at the end of first grade between children who had been retained and those in matched control groups who were recommended for retention but not retained. Another study found that transitional-class children fall below or at best perform equally to children eligible for transitional class who were placed in a regular classroom.[103] In an effort to explain why retention does not work, Smith and Shepard's studies have led them to conclude that retention lowers expectations of parents and teachers and, thus, decreases the possibility that retained children will attain their potential.[104]

2. Many teachers feel that early retention does not have the same negative effects as later retention. Contradictory evidence is found in the literature.[105] Some educators feel that retention removes stress, but in reality it produces trauma.[106] For example, in one study over one-fourth of the children interviewed would not admit to having been retained. Children rated the idea of retention as most stressful next to blindness and the death of a parent.[107]

3. Retention is associated with misconduct. Moran[108] feels that retention and misconduct have a synergistic effect—that is, aggressive students are more apt to be retained than nonaggressive students, and retained students are more apt to become delinquent than promoted students.

4. There is a significant increase in the drop-out rate of retained students as compared with promoted students.[109]

5. Retention brands students as failures, and minorities, low-income children, and males are disproportionately represented among children retained.[110]

Length of the Daily Session

Session length of kindergartens is only an associated issue when the all-day kindergarten is seen as a tool to enhance the learning time for academic subjects. Learning cannot be rushed. Certainly, one does not make an inappropriate curriculum appropriate by simply extending the length of instruction.

The "Backlash" Effect

Raising entrance ages, placing at-risk kindergarten children in developmental kindergartens, retaining kindergarten children by having them repeat kindergarten or attend a transitional class, or increasing the length of the day and, thus, the length of time spent on teaching/learning academic subjects were all designed to protect the "immature," the "unready," or the "at-risk" child, but in reality, these practices exacerbate the problem of academic curriculum content and didactic teaching methods. Once these "immature" children (by whatever name they are called) are no longer in the kindergarten program, curriculum planners and teachers are given license to further increase the academic demands of the curriculum. However, as demands increase, even the brightest children may be injuriously stressed. And there are always the less mature children in any given group. What happens to them—even later school entrance ages imposed? more stringent placement requirements? an even longer day of academic training?

These practices (i.e., the associated issues) are at best only short-term solutions for educators who want to match the child to the curriculum, rather than the curriculum to the child. This has left many educators asking the most serious long-term question: What price will our young children and their families pay for *miseducation* (as Elkind refers to this academic push[111])?

Professional Reactions

Many educators have been concerned about program issues. Teachers are reporting **philosophy-reality** conflicts (i.e., discrepancies between their beliefs and required instructional practices).[112] Teachers report that they have "little control over what they are being asked to do," and this reality conflicts with "their views of what is best for children."[113]

The source of the problem is always identified as parents, administrators, or legislators.[114] Today's parents are influenced by "toys" that promise early achievement, publications about raising smarter children (e.g., Glen Doman's *Teach Your Baby to Read*, Sidney Ledson's *Teach Your Child to Read in 60 Days*, and Peggy Eastman and John L. Barr's *Your Child Is Smarter Than You Think*), and other parents' claims of their children's achievements.[115] Parents may even be misled by their own children's knowledge of "bits and pieces" (e.g., ability to sing the alphabet song at age three). Thus, parents insist that their children be taught more—especially expecting their children to learn to read before first grade. And, in their focus on cursory academic skills, they fail to see how other aspects of the curriculum (e.g., the arts, block building, dramatic play) contribute to the overall learning experience.[116, 117]

Administrators are also pressuring early childhood teachers. In some cases, this attitude is a result of their lack of knowledge about young children.[118] Administrators are also influenced from the "outside" by public demand for more stringent educational standards, which are often measured by children's achievement on standardized tests and from the "inside" by pressures from primary teachers who, in turn, are feeling pressures due to escalating standards.

As previously discussed, there have been pressures from social and political critics concerning the nation's educational system. During the last decade at least three major publications have outlined new demands and reforms for education. These publications are: the National Commission on Excellence in Education's *A Nation at Risk*, the Carnegie Forum on Education and the Economy's *A Nation Prepared*, and the National Governors' Association's *Time for Results*. Demands such as these have been translated by state legislative bodies into legislation for policy statements that dictate when children may be legally enrolled in public school programs, what they should learn, and how they should be taught and assessed. Although everyone wants excellence, unfortunately most of the legislative planning is essentially a "top-down" experience.[119] And it was this lack of attention to young children's unique learning styles that, to a great extent, was the origin of program issues on the contemporary scene.

Early childhood teachers themselves are also unwittingly responsible for the academic trend. For example, teachers often *say* young children learn best by direct encounters with materials and events, and then, in practice, eschew the dramatic play, music, and art materials in favor of workbooks/worksheets. Durkin[120] reported that most teachers said that reading should *not* be taught in kindergarten, but considered the drill work in phonics "readiness," not "reading." As noted, teachers have been in favor of raising entrance age, screening for placement, retention, and full-day kindergarten for academic purposes, because they wanted to relieve the stress placed on "at-risk" children and free themselves from accountability for academic achievement, as measured by their groups' assessment scores.

Professional associations began to see the need to take a stand on the issues. Thus, position statements were issued on behalf of young children. Because pre-first-grade reading instruction was an early academic issue, the following was one of the first issued:

> Early Childhood and Literacy Development Committee of the International Reading Association. *Literacy Development and Pre-First Grade: A Joint Statement of Concern About Present Practices in Pre-First Grade Reading Instruction and Recommendations for Improvement.* Adopted by Association for Childhood Education International, Association for Supervision and Curriculum Development, International Reading Association, National Association for the Education of Young Children, National Association of Elementary School Principals, and National Council of Teachers of English. Newark, Del.: International Reading Association, 1985.

In July 1984, the National Association for Young Children's governing board created a commission for the purpose of developing a position statement on appropriate education for young children. The commission, chaired by Bernard Spodek, worked from July 1984 to July 1985. A statement was first published in 1986 and expanded in 1987 under this title:

> Bredekamp, S. (Ed.). *Developmentally Appropriate Practice in Serving Children from Birth through Age 8* (expanded ed.). Washington, D.C.: NAEYC, 1987.

The statement was widely read, with more than 120,000 copies sold, and soon the term **developmentally appropriate practice** appeared everywhere in speeches and written materials. Other position statements soon followed, including:

> Association for Supervision and Curriculum Development. *A Resource Guide to Public School Early Childhood Programs.* Alexandria, Va.: Author, 1988.

> National Association of Early Childhood Specialists in State Departments of Education. *Unacceptable Trends in Kindergarten Entrance and Placement.* Lincoln, Neb.: Author, 1987.

> National Association of Elementary School Principals. *Standards for Quality Programs for Young Children.* Alexandria, Va.: Author, 1990.

> National Association of State Boards of Education. *Right from the Start. The Report of the NASBE Task Force on Early Childhood Education.* Alexandria, Va.: Author, 1988.

> National Black Child Development Institute. *Safeguards: Guidelines for Establishing Programs for 4-Year-Olds in the Public Schools.* Washington, D.C.: Author, 1987.

Besides these, numerous state organizations have issued position statements. Finally, statements are being issued on certain aspects of early childhood program implementation (e.g., testing). These will be discussed in other chapters.

IMPLEMENTING THE PROGRAM

After carefully considering all the factors that determine a program, an early childhood administrator, along with board members, staff, and prospective parents, must develop a preference for a particular psychological-philosophical stance. The "ideal" program they choose is one suited to their children's needs. Personal beliefs, whether articulated or maintained as a preconscious set of values, influence decision making. (Spodek has an interesting discussion of how **implicit theories** affect teachers' professional behaviors.[121]) For starters, administrators need to think through questions pertaining to the pedagogical component such as:

1. What are the goals and objectives of your early childhood program—to provide an environment conducive to the development of the whole child? to teach young children academic skills? to provide intensive instruction in areas of academic deficits and thinking skills? to develop creativity? to build a healthy self-concept? to spur self-direction in learning?
2. What provisions for children's individual differences are consistent with your program's philosophy—as children develop at their own rates, should you expect the same or varying levels of achievement? Are individual differences accepted in some or in all academic areas? in some or all developmental areas (psychomotor, affective, cognitive)? Are activities child-chosen and appropriate to his own interest and developmental level or staff-tailored to meet individual differences? activities presented for one or several learning styles?
3. What grouping strategy is in accord with your program's rationale—homogeneous (chronological age, mental age, achievement, interest) or heterogeneous groups? fixed or flexible? staff-determined or child-interest? large or small?
4. What schedule format is needed to facilitate your program's philosophy and objectives—a full- or a half-day schedule? same session length for all children or length of session tailored to each child's and/or parent's needs? a predetermined or flexible daily schedule based on children's interests?

Administrators must also consider questions pertaining to the operational components of the program such as:

1. What staff roles are necessary to implement the learning environment as set forth in the philosophy of your program—persons who dispense knowledge, resource persons, or persons who prepare the environ-

ment? persons who use positive or negative reinforcement? group leaders or individual counselors? academic content specialists or social engineers? persons who work almost exclusively with young children or who provide parent education?

2. What staff positions (director, caregivers, teachers, aides, volunteers) are needed to execute your program? what academic or experiential qualifications are required or desired? what type of orientation or in-service training is needed? what child-staff ratio is required?

3. What equipment and materials are required—items and materials that are self-correcting or that encourage creativeness? equipment and materials designed to stress one concept (color paddles) or many concepts (blocks)? which require substantial or minimal adult guidance? are designed for group or individual use? provide for concrete experiences or abstract thinking?

4. What physical arrangement is compatible with the educational philosophy and goals of your program—differentiated or nondifferentiated areas of specific activities? fixed or flexible areas? outside area used primarily for learning or for recess? equipment and materials arranged for self-service by the child or for teacher distribution?

And then the crucial question must be answered: Is there a supportable rationale for the answers? Relevant and irrelevant beliefs, appropriate and inappropriate values, and timely and outdated information can be recognized as one considers the alternatives. Bowman has stated that the tremendous increase of knowledge from interdisciplinary sources provides us with a rich base to plan for children, but it also encourages us to "tolerate faddism, quackism, and just plain foolishness."[122]

EVALUATING THE PROGRAM

Administrators are held accountable for the programs under their leadership and direction. With a constant demand for excellence, evaluation has become one of the administrator's most significant responsibilities. Funding and legal sources require evaluation reports. Accreditation in self-evaluation is based on standards set by the accrediting agencies, such as professional groups. The staff objectively and subjectively makes judgments as its members work in the program. Parents question program quality, and there is heightened public interest, especially on the part of taxpayers, in program value. Administrators must answer to each of these groups.

A discussion of evaluation leads to classification of the types of evaluation. Dopyera and Lay-Dopyera identified two types of evaluation—**intuitive** and **formal.** And they sub-divided *formal* into objectives-based evaluation, standards-based evaluation, and evaluation research.[123]

Intuitive Evaluation

Intuitive evaluation might be called a **personal construct** by a researcher or **practical knowledge** by others. **Intuitive evaluation** is an unexamined, internal map, or a notion about what constitutes the right way to achieve something. Unlike formal evaluation, which is planned, implemented, and analyzed, intuitive evaluation concerns how we survive on a minute-by-minute basis. Intuitive evaluation is used when a person chooses to take an umbrella to work because "it looks as if it may rain" or when a person seasons food because "it tastes as though it needs . . ."

Similarly, early childhood teachers and administrators have notions about their professional practice. Although these notions guide their day-to-day practice, they are difficult to articulate. These notions come to light when there is a clash between one's own ideas or actions and those of another who is respected or when the outcomes of what one expects and what ensues differ.

Studies of intuitive evaluation are rather recent.[124, 125, 126] However, two points seem to be established:

1. Early childhood educators take their book-learned knowledge and guided observations and integrate these with their values and practical knowledge. For example, Spodek states that **values** are what we desire for children now and in the future and practices we believe are professionally ethical[127] and Elbaz identifies **practical knowledge** as knowledge integrated by each individual teacher from his or her theory-based knowledge, accumulated experience, and understanding of milieu and self.[128]
2. Intuitive evaluation is important, because educators must often make judgment calls so quickly that they do not have time to reflect on theory and empirical findings; thus, intuitive evaluation guides practice.

Formal Evaluation

Formal evaluation had its roots in concern over accountability to the funding agencies. With an increasing number of mandates for evaluation, the evaluation profession grew and activities involving formal evaluation increased. Many educational endeavors required formal evaluation such as the needs and demands for certain services (i.e., **needs assessment**), analysis of the components of a program such as staff, curriculum, and materials (i.e., **program analysis**), and the effectiveness of a program as it relates to cost per child (i.e. **cost effectiveness**) or to positive changes in children or families which impact on society (i.e., **program impact**).

Administrators must determine the appropriate type of evaluation to serve their needs. **Objectives-based** and **standards-based** evaluation are both concerned with accountability. Evaluation research is concerned with the interplay of various aspects of a given program related to outcomes.

Objectives-Based Evaluation

Objectives-based evaluation is the most common form of formal evaluation. It focuses on what children achieve as a result of participation in a specific program. Thus, the criteria used for evaluation are program-specific (i.e., developed by examining the program's goals/objectives). The analyses of evaluation data provide information on the degree to which program goals/objectives are met.

Evaluation may be conducted at two different points in the program. **Formative evaluation** is used to determine the effectiveness of various aspects of the program (e.g., grouping practices) while program changes are still being made. **Summative evaluation** determines the effectiveness of the overall program at some ending point.

Standards-Based Evaluation

Standards-based evaluation is an appraisal of a program based on a set of standards (criteria) developed outside of any specific program. These standards may be deemed worthwhile by a professional association (e.g., National Academy of Early Childhood Programs' accreditation), the monitoring agency (e.g., Head Start Performance Objectives, licensing regulations for day-care), or a researcher (e.g., *The Early Childhood Environment Rating Scale*).

Several standards-based evaluations are:

1. *Day-Care Environmental Inventory.* The *Inventory* was developed by Prescott and her associates.[129] Prescott references the developmental stages defined by Erikson[130] and Cumming and Cumming.[131] Prescott's environmental inventory includes an observational recording system for collecting information about children's behavior and physical space. The behavior schedule provides a description of the child's experiences within the larger setting of the center—each activity is described in terms of whether it was within a free-choice or teacher-directed structure; the physical setting in which the activity took place; equipment and props used; degree of mobility; people with whom the activity occurred; and the teacher influence. The *Inventory* provides a description of the center and its effects upon children. The administrator/staff can then determine whether what they saw happening was what they wanted for the children. To use the *Inventory*, trained evaluators are needed, several children must be observed for various periods of time under different situations, and computer analysis of data is required.

2. *Naturalistic Evaluation for Program Improvement.* The *Evaluation* is built on the philosophical position of Bronfenbrenner[132] that one must not only examine the effects of program and staff on the children but also the effects of the children on program and staff.[133] The *Evaluation* is also based on the research of Day and Sheehan.[134] Day and Sheehan concluded that children's behavior in an early childhood program was a function of their interactions with three environmental factors: (a) extent to which the staff had considered the importance of the physical

environment and how it was arranged, (b) use of materials, and (c) amount and kind of teacher-child interactions. Children's natural behaviors during their day in the program are observed. Observations are made on a total of thirty-four behaviors in seven areas: task involvement, cooperation, autonomy, verbal interaction, materials, maintenance, and consideration.

3. *The Early Childhood Environment Rating Scale (ECERS).* The *Scale* was developed by Harms and Clifford, who see an early childhood program as an ecological system with more parts than just the individual within the program.[135] ECERS is used to examine thirty-seven attributes that cover seven areas of quality: personal care routines, furnishings and display, language/reasoning experiences, fine and gross motor activities, creative activities, social development, and adult needs. Ratings are given for each area and a total rating can be calculated for each group. Scores on all the groups within a center may be compiled to get a quality score for a center. Kontos and Stevens field tested ECERS.[136] They noted that (a) directors saw ECERS useful for improvement of center and for providing the focus of staff training; (b) staff began making changes; (c) staff resistance to change was minimized; and (d) staff liked the idea that "adult needs" must be met in quality programs.

4. *The Family Day-Care Rating Scale (FDCRS).* The FDCRS was developed by Harms and Clifford and follows the same pattern as their ECERS.[137] FDCRS is used to examine thirty-two attributes that cover six areas of quality: space and furnishings for care and learning, basic care, language and reasoning, learning activities, social development, and adult needs. Each item is described in four levels of quality: inadequate, minimal, good, and excellent. Eight **Supplementary Items** are provided when a child with special needs is included in the child care home.

5. *Infant/Toddler Environmental Rating Scale (ITERS).* The ITERS was developed by Harms, Cryer and Clifford and follows the same pattern as their ECERS and FDCRS.[138] The ITERS consists of thirty-five items for the assessment of the quality of center-based child care for children up to thirty months of age. These items are organized under seven categories: furnishings and display for children, personal care routines, listening, talking, learning activities, interaction programs structure, and adult needs. Each item is presented on a seven-point scale, with descriptors for 1 (inadequate), 3 (minimal), 5 (good), and 7 (excellent). ITERS items correspond with the Child Development Associate competency goals.

6. *The Instrument-Based Program Monitoring Information System (IPM) and Indicator Checklist for Child Care (IC).* In most states, licensing workers make an on-site visit and prepare a summary of observations along with interpretive and evaluative comments. This is not only a laborious task for the licensing agency, but centers are expected to be in total compliance for licensing. The Children's Services Monitoring Consortium (CSMC), representing California, Michigan, Pennsylvania, West Vir-

ginia, and New York City, developed a system model for the purpose of focusing on exemplary day-care regulations. The IPM, designed by Fiene, is a system of assigning weights to items in the state's day-care regulations so scores reflect the relative importance of the regulations. An IC is a questionnaire or checklist that contains selected, predictive items (e.g, director qualifications, health appraisal of staff, adult-child ratios, hazard-free environment, nutrition, emergency contact information, medication, safety carrier, supervision of children, program observation) from the comprehensive instrument that a state uses in licensing.[139] Not only does the IC increase the licensing agency's efficiency in checking centers, but the state's policy may be made even more effective from a regulatory point of view (i.e., identifying the better-quality programs as opposed to low-quality programs).[140]

Other standards-based assessments such as licensing, certification, and accreditation are discussed in Chapter 3.

Evaluation Research

Evaluation research examines how various aspects of a program impinge on outcomes for children or families. The purpose of such research is to better understand the interplay of variables. Researchers are concerned about all effects generated by program components; thus, they go beyond specific program goals/objectives and standards that have been deemed worthwhile. Evaluation research studies are often longitudinal, and all are rigorous in their research methodologies. Evaluation research studies on early childhood programs were discussed under the heading "Summary of Programmatic Research" on pages 36, 38.

An Important Consideration

Evaluation generates program changes mandated by external commands (e.g., regulatory agencies) and or stimulated by internal visions or problems. The most meaningful evaluations are most often those stimulated by internal factors rather than those resulting from external mandate. Flaherty found that evaluations mandated by external sources were perceived as useful only when data were also used for internal center purposes.[141] Changes affect programs in different ways, such as (1) change is more difficult if program restructuring rather than program enriching is required; (2) change is more difficult when the entire staff is involved rather than just a few employees; (3) fast change is as difficult as slow change with staff turnover; and (4) change is difficult under staff resistance. Cronbach and his associates stated that to overcome the negative effects of evaluation, the following points must be addressed:

1. Staff must acknowledge the interdependent cumulative effects of all program components.
2. Evaluation must include all components.
3. Evaluation must be ongoing.
4. Evaluation must include all those involved in a program.[142]

Pressures for answers from within and without the program will not seem so unbearable, or the difficulties involved in overcoming content and methodological problems so insurmountable, if one keeps in mind the major purpose of program evaluation. If evaluation is seen as a means for program improvement, it becomes a continuous process, and its results become starting points for future planning.

SUMMARY

The administrator's main task is providing leadership in program planning, implementation, and evaluation. The administrator, as a first step, must understand various program bases and curriculum models. The factors that should determine a program base are psychological theories and philosophical positions. A curriculum model consists of the psycho-philosophical base and the administrative and pedagogical components emanating from the base (Figure 2.1). Three curriculum models (i.e., maturational, Table 2.1; behavioral-environmental, Table 2.2; and interactionist, Table 2.3) have been used for early childhood programs; since the 1960s, the interactionist and the behavioral-environmental models are the most commonly used. Because these later two approaches are diametrically opposed, there has been much controversy over curriculum practices and the associated policies of admission, placement, retention, and length of the daily session. This controversy has led to the professional associations' position statement that favored the interactionist point of view.

After considering the curriculum models and understanding the controversy, the administrator must choose a curriculum model as a second step. Implementation of the program is developed in keeping with the model.

Because of accountability, program evaluation is an important aspect of administration. Thus, the making of evaluation plans is a third step. There are two types of evaluation—intuitive and formal. Unplanned, intuitive evaluation is constantly functioning; thus, attempts should be made to understand the criteria being used by all involved in the local program. Formal or planned evaluation may be objectives-based, standards-based, or research evaluation. The administrator and staff should jointly determine the reasons for evaluation (e.g., needs assessment, program analysis), the appropriate type of evaluation, the specific instrument to be used, and the timing of the implementation for both formative and summative. And as shown in Figure 2.1, evaluation results should provide feedback into future program planning.

NOTES

1. A. Gessell, "Maturation and Patterning of Behavior," *A Handbook of Child Psychology,* ed. C. Murchinson (Worchester: Clark University Press, 1931), 209–235.

2. A. T. Jersild, *Child Development and the Curriculum* (New York: Bureau of Publications, Teachers College, Columbia University, 1946).

3. B. F. Skinner, *The Behavior of Organisms: An Experimental Analysis* (Englewood Cliffs: Prentice-Hall, 1938).

4. *Early Childhood Education: How to Select and Evaluate Materials* (New York: Educational Products Information Exchange Institute, 1972), 13–14.

5. U. Bronfenbrenner, *The Ecology of Human Development* (Cambridge: Harvard University Press, 1979).

6. Plato, *The Republic*, book 2, trans. by B. Jowett (New York: Random House, 1941).

7. J. Dewey, "My Pedagogic Creed," *The School Journal* 54 (1897): 77–80.

8. M. J. E. Senn, "Insights on the Child Development Movement in the United States," *Monographs of the Society for Research in Child Development*, serial no. 161, 40 (1975): 8.

9. L. Kohlberg and R. Mayer, "Development as the Aim of Education," *Harvard Educational Review* 42 (1972): 449–496.

10. E. Shapiro and B. Biber, "The Education of Young Children: A Developmental-Interaction Approach," *Teachers College Record* 74 (1972): 55–79.

11. Kohlberg and Mayer, "Development as the Aim of Education," 485.

12. Ibid., p. 463.

13. Ibid., p. 456.

14. Shapiro and Biber, "The Education of Young Children: A Developmental-Interaction Approach," 55–79.

15. B. Biber, "Goals and Methods in a Preschool Program for Disadvantaged Children," *Children* 17 (1970): 16.

16. Shapiro and Biber, "The Education of Young Children: A Developmental-Interaction Approach," p. 68.

17. B. M. Caldwell, "Child Development and Social Policy," *Current Issues in Child Development*, ed. M. Scott and S. Grimmett (Washington, D.C.: National Association for the Education of Young Children, 1977), 80–81.

18. B. Spodek, "The Knowledge Base of Kindergarten Education," ERIC ED 280 569 (Paper presented at the Five-Year-Olds in School Conference, Michigan State University, East Lansing, Mich., January 9, 1987).

20. K. Egan, *Education and Psychology: Plato, Piaget, and Scientific Psychology* (New York: Teachers College Press, 1983).

21. Caldwell, "Child Development and Social Policy."

22. Egan, *Education and Psychology: Plato, Piaget, and Scientific Psychology.*

23. C. J. Sommerville, *The Rise and Fall of Childhood* (Beverly Hills: Sage, 1982), p. 16.

24. L. B. Miller and J. L. Dyer, "Four Preschool Programs: Their Dimensions and Effects," *Monographs of the Society for Research in Child Development*, serial no. 162, 40 (1975): 5–6.

25. M. Stephen, *Policy Issues in Early Childhood Education* (Menlo Park: Stanford Research Institute, 1973), 336.

26. B. Spodek, "Curriculum Models in Early Childhood Education," *Early Childhood Education*, ed. B. Spodek (Englewood Cliffs: Prentice-Hall, 1973), 27–34.
27. G. Fein and P. M. Schwartz, "Developmental Theories in Early Education," *Handbook of Research in Early Childhood Education*, ed. B. Spodek, (New York: Free Press, 1982:), 82–104.
28. J. S. Bissell, "The Cognitive Effects of Preschool Programs for Disadvantaged Children," *Revisiting Early Childhood Education*, ed. J. L. Frost (New York: Holt, Rinehart, and Winston, 1973), 223–241.
29. D. P. Weikart, "Relationship of Curriculum Teaching and Learning in Preschool Education," *Preschool Programs for the Disadvantaged: Five Experimental Approaches to Early Childhood Education*, ed. J. C. Stanley (Baltimore: Johns Hopkins Press, 1972), 22–66.
30. R. S. Mayer, "A Comparative Analysis of Preschool Curriculum Models," *As the Twig Is Bent*, ed. R. H. Anderson and H. G. Shane (New York: Houghton Mifflin, 1971), 286–314.
31. D. Ellis, "Focus on Philosophies for Educating Young Children," ERIC ED 142 283 (Paper presented at the annual convention of the International Reading Association, May 2–6, 1977).
32. Bissell, "Cognitive Effects," 223–41.
33. Weikart, "Relationship of Curricular Teaching."
34. Mayer, "Contemporary Analysis," 286–314.
35. Ellis, "Focus on Philosophies."
36. Weikart, "Relationship of Curricular Teaching."
37. Bissell, "Cognitive Effects," 223–41.
38. Mayer, "Comparative Analysis," 286–314.
39. Ellis, "Focus on Philosophies."
40. Bissell, "Cognitive Effects," 223–41.
41. Mayer, "Comparative Analysis," 286–314.
42. Ellis, "Focus on Philosophies."
43. R. DeVries and L. Kohlberg, *Constructivist Early Education: Overview and Comparisons with Other Programs* (Washington, D.C.: National Association for the Education of Young Children, 1987).
44. B. Biber, "A Developmental-Interaction Approach: Bank Street College of Education," *The Preschool in Action*, 2nd ed., ed. M. C. Day and R. K. Parker (Boston: Allyn and Bacon, 1977), 423–460.
45. G. E. Forman and C. T. Fostnot, "The Use of Piaget's Constructivism in Early Childhood Education Programs," *Handbook of Research in Early Childhood Education*, ed. B. Spodek (New York: Free Press, 1982) 185–211.
46. D. Bushell, Jr., "The Behavior Analysis Classroom," *Early Childhood Education*, ed. B. Spodek (Englewood Cliffs: Prentice-Hall, 1973), 163–175.
47. S. W. Bijou, *Child Development: The Basic Stages of Early Childhood* (Englewood Cliffs: Prentice-Hall, 1976).
48. A. Honig and S. Brill, *A Comparative Analysis of the Piagetian Development of Twelve-Month-Old Disadvantaged Infants in an Enrichment Center with Others*

Not in Such a Center (Syracuse, N.Y.: Syracuse University Children's Center, 1970).

49. I. Sigel, A. Secrist, and G. Forman, "Psychoeducational Intervention Beginning at Age Two: Reflections and Outcomes," *Compensatory Education for Children, Ages Two to Eight*, ed. J. Stanley (Baltimore: Johns Hopkins Press, 1973), 25–62.

50. M. C. Day, "A Comparative Analysis of Center-Based Preschool Programs," *The Preschool in Action*, 2nd ed., ed. B. Spodek (Boston: Allyn and Bacon, Inc., 1977), 466.

51. B. Biber, *Early Education and Psychological Development* (New Haven: Yale University Press, 1984).

52. L. J. Schweinhart and D. P. Weikart, *Young Children Grow Up: The Effects of the Perry Preschool Program on Youths Through Age 15*, Monographs of the High/Scope Educational Research Foundation, no. 7 (Ypsilanti: High/Scope, 1980).

53. J. R. Berrueta-Clement el al., *Changed Lives: The Effects of the Perry Preschool Program on Youths Through Age 19*, Monographs of the High/Scope Educational Research Foundation, no. 8 (Ypsilanti: High/Scope, 1984).

54. C. A. Decker and J. R. Decker, *Planning and Administering Early Childhood Programs*, 3rd ed. (Columbus: Merrill, 1984).

55. L. J. Schweinhart and D. P. Weikart, "Evidence that Good Early Programs Work," *Phi Delta Kappan* 66, 8 (1985): 545–51.

56. H. L. Garber and R. Heber, "The Efficacy of Early Intervention with Family Rehabilitation," *Psychosocial Influences in Retarded Performance, Vol. 2: For Improving Competence*, ed. M. J. Begab, H. C. Haywood, and H. L. Garber (Baltimore: University Park, 1981).

57. C. T. Ramey, D. M. Bryant, and T. M. Swarez, "Preschool Compensatory Education and the Modifiability of Intelligence: A Critical Review," *Current Topics in Human Intelligence*, ed. D. Detterman (Norwood, N.J.: Ablex, 1984).

58. Schweinhart and Weikart, "Good Early Childhood Programs."

59. Ramey, Bryant, and Swarez, "Preschool Compensatory Education."

60. Berrueta-Clement, Schweinhart, Barnett, Epstein, and Weikart, *Changed Lives*.

61. S. W. Gray, B. K. Ramsey, and R. A. Klaus, *From 3 to 20—The Early Training Project* (Baltimore: University Park, 1982).

62. Consortium on Longitudinal Studies, *Lasting Effects After Preschool*, DHEW Publication No. OHDS 79-30178 (Washington, D.C.: Administration for Children, Youth, and Families, 1978).

63. Schweinhart and Weikart, "Good Early Childhood Programs."

64. J. Kagan, *The Nature of the Child* (New York: Basic, 1984).

65. E. Zigler and P. K. Trichett, "IQ, Social Competence, and Evaluation of Early Childhood Intervention Programs," *American Psychologist* 33 (1978): 789–98.

66. J. M. Larson and T. W. Draper, *Does Preschool Help the Educationally Advantaged Child? Preliminary Findings From a Longitudinal Study,* ERIC ED 247 001 (Provo: Brigham Young University, 1984).

67. S. Ball and G. A. Bogatz, *A Summary of the Major Findings in "The First Year of Sesame Street": An Evaluation* (Princeton: Educational Testing Service, 1970).

68. W. W. Cooley, "Evaluations of Evaluation Programs," *Evaluation of Educational Programs for Young Children: The Minnesota Round Table on Early Childhood Education II* (Washington, D.C.: CDA Consortium, 1975).

69. V. Seitz, N. H. Apfel, and C. Efron, *Long Term Effects of Intervention: A Longitudinal Investigation* (Paper presented at the Meeting of the American Psychological Association, Washington, D.C., 1976).

70. B. Hanson, *Trends and Problems in Comparison Studies of Early Childhood Education Models* (Washington, D.C.: Department of Health, Education, and Welfare, National Institute of Education, November 1973).

71. P. W. Goodman, *Are the Long Term Effects of Early Childhood Education Effective Even Though the Short Term Effects Seem Ineffective?*, ERIC ED 251 170 (El Paso: University of Texas at El Paso, 1982).

72. D. S. Cheever, Jr., and A. E. Ryder, "Quality: The Key to Successful Programs," *Principal* 64 (1986): 18–23.

73. C. Morado, "Prekindergarten Programs for 4-Year-Olds: State Involvement in Preschool Education," *Young Children* 41, 6 (1986): 69–71.

74. F. Marx and M. Seligson, "Draft Notes on State Findings from Public School Early Childhood Study" (Wellesley: College Center for Research on Women, 1987).

75. Ibid.

76. D. Elkind, "Formal Education and Early Childhood Education: An Essential Difference," *Phi Delta Kappan* 67, 9 (1986): 631–636.

77. R. E. Ripple and V. E. Rockcastle, eds., *Piaget Rediscovered: A Report of the Conference on Cognitive Studies and Curriculum Development* (Ithaca: School of Education, Cornell University, 1964), p. 5.

78. D. Elkind, "Developmentally Appropriate Practice: Philosophical and Practical Implications," *Phi Delta Kappan* 71, 2 (1989): 116.

79. National Commission on Excellence in Education, *Nation at Risk: The Full Account* (Washington, D.C.: The Commission, 1984). [U.S.G.P.O., distributor].

80. A. Bloom, *The Closing of the American Mind* (New York: Simon and Schuster, 1987).

81. E. D. Hirsch, Jr., *Cultural Literacy: What Every American Needs to Know* (Boston: Houghton Mifflin, 1987).

82. Elkind, "Developmentally Appropriate Practices," 115.

83. Ibid., 116.

84. P. Langer, J. M. Kalk, and D. T. Searls, "Age of Admission and Trends in Achievement: A Comparison of Blacks and Caucasians," *American Educational Research Journal* 21 (1984): 61–78.

85. J. K. Uphoff and J. Gilmore, "Pupil Age at School Entrance: How Many Are Ready for Success?" *Young Children* 41, 2 (1986): 11–16.

86. N. Karweit, "Quantity and Quality of Learning Time in Preprimary Programs," *Elementary School Journal* 89 (1988): 119–133.

87. Ibid.

88. D. J. Walsh, "Changes in Kindergarten: Why Here? Why Now?" *Early Childhood Research Quarterly* 4 (1989): 377–391.

89. L. A. Shepard and M. L. Smith, *Boulder Valley Kindergarten: Retention Practices and Retention Effects* (Boulder: Boulder Valley Public Schools, 1985).

90. L. A. Shepard and M. L. Smith, "Synthesis of Research on School Readiness and Kindergarten Retention," *Educational Leadership*, 44 (1986): 78–86.

91. T. B. Proctor, K. N. Black, and J. F. Feldhusen, "Early Admission of Selected Children to Elementary School: A Review of Research Literature," *Journal of Educational Research* 80 (1986): 70–76.

92. L. G. Katz, J. D. Raths, and R. T. Torres, *A Place Called Kindergarten* (Urbana: ERIC Clearninghouse on Elementary and Early Childhood Education, 1987).

93. L. B. Ames, *Is Your Child in the Wrong Grade?* (Lumberville: Modern Learning Press, 1978).

94. S. J. Meisels, "Uses and Abuses of Developmental Screening and School Readiness Testing," *Young Children* 42, 2 (1987): 4–9.

95. M. E. Grave and Shepard, "Predictive Validity of the Gesell School Readiness Tests," *Early Childhood Research Quarterly* 4 (1989): 303–315.

96. Shepard and M. L. Smith, "Synthesis of Research on School Readiness and Kindergarten Retention," 80.

97. Meisels, "Uses and Abuses of Developmental Screening and School Readiness Testing," 68–73.

98. Shepard and Smith, "Synthesis of Research on School Readiness and Kindergarten Retention," 85.

99. J. Merrow, "Repeating a Grade," *Children* 4 (1988): 23.

100. M. L. Smith and L. A. Shepard, "Kindergarten Readiness and Retention: A Qualitative Study of Teachers' Beliefs and Practices," *American Educational Research Journal* 25 (1988): 307–333.

101. P. Mantzicopoulos, D. C. Morrison, S. P. Hinshaw, and E. T. Corte, "Nonpromotion in Kindergarten: The Role of Cognitive, Perceptual, Visual-Motor, Behavioral, Achievement, Socioeconomic, and Demographic Characteristics," *American Educational Research Journal*, 25 (1989): 107–121.

102. L. A. Shepard and M. L. Smith, "Effects of Kindergarten Retention at the End of First Grade," *Psychology in the Schools* 24 (1987): 346–357.

103. G. R. Gredler, "Transition Classes: A Viable Alternative for the At-Risk Child?" *Psychology in the Schools* 21 (1984): 463–470.

104. M. L. Smith and L. A. Shepard, "What Doesn't Work: Explaining Policies of Retention in the Early Grades," *Phi Delta Kappan* 69, 2 (1987): 129–134.

105. Shepard and Smith, "Synthesis of Research on School Readiness and Kindergarten Retention," 78–86.

106. Shepard and Smith, "Effects of Kindergarten Retention at the End of First Grade," 346–357.
107. D. A. Byrnes and K. Yamamoto, "An Inside Look at Academic Retention in the Elementary School," *Education* 106 (1985): 208–214.
108. J. J. Moran, "Professional Standards for Educators Making Retention Decisions," *Education* 109 (1989): 268–275.
109. N. B. Schuyler and B. O. Turner, "Retention or Promotion: Have Policies Passed or Failed?" ERIC ED 288 904 (Austin: Independent School District, Office of Research and Evaluation, 1986–87).
110. National Association of Early Childhood Specialists in State Departments of Education, *Unacceptable Trends in Kindergarten Entry and Placement: A Position Statement of the NAECS/SDE,* (Lincoln: Author, 1987). [Available from the early childhood specialist in each state's department of education]
111. D. Elkind, *Miseducation: Preschoolers at Risk* (New York: Knopf, 1987).
112. J. A. Hatch and E. Freeman, "Kindergarten Philosophies and Practices: Perspectives of Teachers, Principals, and Supervisors," *Early Childhood Research Quarterly* 3 (1988): 151–166.
113. T. W. Hills, "Children in the Fast Lane: Implications for Early Childhood Policy and Practice," *Early Childhood Research Quarterly* 2 (1987): 265–273.
114. C. Seefeldt and N. Barbour, " 'They Said I Had to . . .' Working with Mandates," *Young Children* 43, 4 (1988): 4–8.
115. B. Simmons and J. Brewrer, "When Parents of Kindergartners Ask 'Why?' " *Childhood Education* 61, 3 (1988): 177–184.
116. Ibid.
117. Hills, "Children in the Fast Lane: Implications for Early Childhood Policies and Practices."
118. L. J. Schweenhart, J. J. Koshel, and A. Bridgman, "Policy Options for Preschool Programs," *Phi Delta Kappan* 68, 7 (1987): 527.
119. E. D. Evans, "Curriculum Models and Early Childhood Education," *Handbook of Research on Early Childhood Education,* ed. B. Spodek (New York: The Free Press, 1982), 110.
120. D. Durkin, "A Classroom Observation Study of Reading Instruction in Kindergarten," *Early Childhood Research Quarterly* 2 (1987): 275–300.
121. B. Spodek, "Implicit Theories of Early Childhood Teachers: Foundations for Professional Behavior," *Professionalism and the Early Childhood Practitioner,* eds. B. Spodek, D. N. Saracho, and D. L. Peters (New York: Teachers College Press, 1988), 161–172.
122. B. Bowman, "Birthday Thoughts," *Young Children* 41 (1986): 6.
123. J. E. Dopyera and M. Lay-Dopyera, "Evaluation and Science in Early Education: Some Critical Issues," *Continuing Issues in Early Childhood Education,* ed. C. Seefeldt (Columbus: Merrill, 1990), 285–299.
124. L. G. Katz, "The Professional Preschool Teacher," *More Talks with Teachers* ed. L. G. Katz (Urbana: ERIC Clearinghouse on Elementary and Early Childhood Education, 1984), 27–42.

125. C. M. Clark and P. L. Peterson, "Teachers' Thought Processes," *Handbook of Research on Teaching*, 3rd ed., ed. M. C. Wittrock (New York: Macmillan, 1986), 255–296.

126. B. Spodek, "Thought Processes Underlying Preschool Teachers' Classroom Decisions," *Early Child Care and Development* 28 (1987): 197–208.

127. Ibid.

128. F. Elbaz, *Teacher Thinking: A Study of Practical Knowledge* (London: Croom Helm, 1983).

129. E. Prescott, *Assessment of Child-Rearing Environments: An Ecological Approach* (Pasadena: Pacific Oaks College, 1975).

130. E. Erikson, *Childhood and Society* (New York: W. W. Norton, 1950).

131. J. Cumming and E. Cumming, *Ego and Milieu* (New York: Atherton, 1967).

132. U. Bronfenbrenner, *The Ecology of Human Development* (Cambridge: Harvard University, 1979).

133. D. E. Day, E. Phyfe-Perkins, and J. A. Weinhaler, "Naturalistic Evaluation for Program Improvement," *Young Children* 34, 4 (1979): 12–24.

134. D. E. Day and R. Sheehan, "Elements for a Better School," *Young Children* 30, 1 (1974): 15–23.

135. T. Harms and R. Clifford, *The Early Childhood Environment Rating Scale* (New York: Teachers College, 1980).

136. S. Kontos and R. Stevens, "High Quality Child Care: Does Your Center Measure Up?" *Young Children* 40, 2 (1985): 5–9.

137. T. Harms and R. M. Clifford, *Family Day Care Rating Scale* (New York: Teachers College Press, Teachers College, Columbia University, 1989).

138. T. Harms, D. Cryer, and R. M. Clifford, *Infant/Toddler Environment Rating Scale* (New York: Teachers College Press, Teachers College, Columbia University, 1990).

139. R. Fiene, "The Instrument Based Program Monitoring Information System and the Indicator Checklist for Child Care," *Child Care Quarterly* 14 (1985): 198–214.

140. R. J. Fiene, *State Child Care Regulatory, Monitoring and Evaluation Systems as a Means for Ensuring Quality Child Development Programs, Licensing of Services for Children and Adults: A Compendium of Papers* (Richmond: Virginia Commonwealth University, School of Social Work, 1986.)

141. E. W. Flaherty, "The Boundaries of Government Intervention in Federally Funded Services," *Evaluation News* 17 (1980): 22–27.

142. L. J. Cronback et. al., *Toward Reform of Program Evaluation* (San Francisco: Jossey-Bass, 1980).

FOR FURTHER READING

Bredekamp, S., ed., *Developmentally Appropriate Practice in Early Childhood Programs Serving Children from Birth through Age 8* (exp. ed.). Washington, D.C.: National Association for the Education of Young Children, 1987.

Campbell, B. "From National Debate to National Responsibility." In *Early Schooling: The National Debate,* edited by S. L. Kagan and E. F. Zigler, 65–82. New Haven: Yale University Press, 1987.

Crain, W. C. *Theories of Development: Concepts and Application.* Englewood Cliffs: Prentice-Hall, 1980.

Goldbaber, D. "Does a Changing View of Early Experience Imply a Changing View of Early Development?" In *Current Topics in Early Childhood Education,* Vol. 2, edited by L. G. Katz, 117–140. Norwood: Ablex, 1979.

Hill, P. S. "The Function of the Kindergarten," *Young Children* 42, 5 (1987): 12–20.

Moyer, J., Egertson, H., and Isenberg, J. "The Child-Centered Kindergarten," *Childhood Education* 63, 4 (1987): 235–242.

Peck, J. T., McCaig, G., and Sapp, M. E. *Kindergarten Policies: What Is Best for Young Children?* Washington, D.C.: National Association for the Education of Young Children, 1988.

Puleo, V. T. "A Review and Critique on Full-Day Kindergarten," *Elementary School Journal* 88 (1988): 427–437.

Robinson, S. L. "The State of Kindergarten Offerings in the United States," *Childhood Education* 64, 1 (1987): 23–28.

Spodek, B. "Using the Knowledge Base." In *Today's Kindergarten: Exploring the Knowledge Base, Expanding the Curriculum,* edited by B. Spodek, 137–143. New York: Teachers College Press, Teachers College, Columbia University, 1986.

Weber, E. *Ideas Influencing Early Childhood Education: A Theoretical Analysis.* New York: Teachers College Press, Teachers College, Columbia University, 1984.

Chapter 3
Considering Regulations and Establishing Policies

The continuing growth of early childhood programs has required greater emphasis on regulations designed to ensure not only that minimum standards are met, but that existing quality standards for care and instruction are raised. Some consider maintaining affordability more important than maintaining quality. These people argue that regulating high standards further limits program availability and that program quality will improve as a result of the free enterprise system. On the other hand, early childhood professionals note that families may not understand the implications of lack of quality, may not have the expertise or time to monitor programs carefully, and may not have the income to pay for high-quality programs.[1] Thus, parents should have a right to expect that the state will assure them and their children a minimum level of protection just as it assures a minimum level of safety in other areas (e.g., foods and drugs, water supply, and police protection). Furthermore, high-quality programs benefit all segments of society—the children whose lives are enhanced, the parents who are assured of quality and are thus better employees, and the populace at large, which profits from its self-sufficient members.

Regulations are the rules, directives, statutes, and standards that prescribe, direct, limit, and govern early childhood programs. The following characteristics are generally representative:

1. Regulations cover all aspects of a program—administrative organization, facilities, personnel, funding, and services.
2. Various regulations apply to different types of early childhood programs. Some regulations govern private programs, for example, licensing and incorporation; others may affect federal and state programs—for example, direct administration and Head Start Performance Objectives; and some regulations must be met by virtually all programs—such as those concerning fire safety, sanitation, zoning, transportation, staff qualifications, the Civil Rights Act, and local board regulations.

3. Regulations vary in comprehensiveness; for example, licensing regulations cover the total program, but certification requirements affect only the educational preparation of the staff.
4. Most regulations are mandatory; an exception is accreditation, which is self-regulation.
5. Regulations come from various sources. Federal agencies regulate some early childhood programs because they provide funds through various grants and subsidies. In the 1960s, federal programs often dealt directly with community agencies; today, most federal programs do not bypass state administration. There is thus more control at the state level. State agencies regulate some early childhood programs they fund as public education is a state responsibility. Local governments regulate other programs through community ordinances and health and safety codes. The judiciary system regulates still other early childhood programs through decisions affecting civil rights and the responsibilities of agencies and schools. It is not easy to determine which of several agencies has jurisdiction over programs.

The various regulatory agencies assume protective roles by assuring parents that the early childhood program meets at least minimum standards. Although this protective role is essential, there are at least five problems with regulations:

1. Regulations can keep early childhood programs at minimum levels. The overriding question should not be whether harm or risk has been prevented, but whether a child's development is enhanced.
2. Regulations may deter innovation. Regulations are often too concerned with uniformity.
3. Most states do not have a single agency or legislative committee responsible for early childhood programs. Often there are gaps in regulations or regulation jurisdictions collide. Establishing state offices of child development may help remedy this situation.
4. Some regulations are simply "on record" with little or no enforcement such as registration of family day-care homes.
5. Continuous consultation is often omitted. Continuous in-service training opportunities are necessary for providing and maintaining high quality in programs.

In an effort to ensure that children will be served in high-quality programs, many administrators are assuming an active role in influencing social policy on regulations. Advocacy is discussed in detail in Chapter 12.

The remainder of the chapter will be a discussion of the regulations governing all programs (i.e., private and public), private programs, public programs, and accreditation. In some cases, these regulations do not perfectly fit the category in which they are placed; for example, P.L. 94–142 is financed with public moneys, but the law affects children with disabilities in private as well as public schools.

REGULATIONS GOVERNING ALL EARLY CHILDHOOD PROGRAMS

Various types of minimum regulations are common to all programs. These regulations include health and safety, fiscal concerns, child-rights, and staff regulations. There is some overlap in regulations imposed by various agencies of the federal, state, and local governments. When there are regulations of a similar nature under more than one jurisdiction, an early childhood program must be in compliance with each. For example, a private early childhood program is subject to the fire safety standards of the local city code and the state licensing law. Furthermore, to help make sure both standards are met, most state licensing agencies require an application for licensure of an early childhood program to include proof of compliance with all applicable city ordinances.

Health and Safety Regulations

Health and safety regulations are among the most stringent affecting all early childhood programs. These include zoning, fire safety and sanitation, and transportation. (Other health regulations are discussed in Chapter 9, and housing regulations for meeting the needs of children and adults with disabilities are discussed in Chapter 5.)

Zoning Regulations

Zoning regulations restrict the use of land. Each city and town is enabled by a state zoning law to divide its land into districts. Within those districts, it can regulate the use of the land itself and the erection and use of buildings. The regulations are stated in the form of local zoning ordinances, bylaws, and zoning codes. Generally, zoning regulations become more stringent as population density increases.

Zoning regulates the location of early childhood facilities. Day-care facilities, unlike elementary schools, are often not included as a permitted use within a zoning plan. They are treated as "problem use" (i.e., excluded from both residential sections because of noise and commercial areas because such areas are not considered good places for children).

Fire Safety and Sanitation Requirements

The statutory basis for fire safety and sanitation requirements rests in public safety and health laws. These may be municipal ordinances or state regulations with local enforcement. The Life Safety Code of the National Fire Protection Association provides guidelines for appropriate fire codes for centers, group homes, and family day-care.

Transportation Requirements

In each state, whichever agency regulates matters pertaining to motor vehicles has the legal mandate to protect children transported in buses and private vehicles. Some states have devised special regulations for day-care transportation in addition to those required for licensure.

Federal Occupational Safety and Health Act of 1970
This Act requires all employers to provide a work environment free from any recognizable hazards that could cause death or serious harm. Records must be kept in programs employing seven or more staff members.

Fiscal Regulations

Many fiscal regulations are specific to given programs. However, most contracts and Internal Revenue Service (IRS) regulations must be complied with by all early childhood programs. IRS regulations applying to certain legal program categories will be discussed in later sections and mandatory state unemployment insurance and the Federal Insurance Contributions Act (Social Security) will be described in Chapter 10. Fraud or failure to comply with fiscal regulations results in serious consequences.

Contracts
Contracts are legally enforceable agreements that may be oral or written (e.g., insurance policies; employment contracts; contracts with parents for fees; contracts for food, supplies, and personal services; contracts with funding sources; and leases). There are three elements in a contract: (1) the **offer**—the buyer's proposal to the seller or the seller's invitation to the buyer to purchase a given object or service at a stated price (i.e., money or service); (2) **acceptance**—the buyer's acceptance of an offer or seller's acknowledgment of the buyer's willingness to accept offer; and (3) **consideration**—the legal term for the price or value of what each party exchanges (e.g., a subscription to a professional journal for forty dollars per year). Breaking a contract is called a **breach** and the potential penalty is referred to as **damages.**

IRS Regulations
Many Internal Revenue Service regulations apply to all early childhood programs:

1. *Employer Identification Number.* Each organization employing people on a regular salaried basis is required to obtain a federal employer identification number. A program cannot file for a tax-exempt status without first having obtained this number, using IRS Form SS–4.
2. *Tax returns.* Employers file quarterly tax returns, IRS Form 941. This form is filed with the regional IRS service center. There is a penalty for late filing.
   Salaried employers of public early childhood programs file the appropriate schedule on IRS Form 1040. All private programs must file tax returns. Sole proprietors and partnerships with other incomes file the

appropriate schedule on Form 1040; partnerships without other incomes file IRS Form 1065; for-profit corporations file Form 1120; and not-for-profit corporations file Form 990.

3. *Withholding Exemption Certificates and IRS Form 1099.* Withholding Exemption Certificates, IRS Form W-4, are required for each employee. The certificates are used for determining the amount to withhold for federal, state, and city income taxes. The form indicates marital status and number of dependents and must be completed before the first paycheck is issued. Employees must sign new forms if marital status or number of dependents changes or if employees desire more of their wages to be withheld. Annual statements of taxes withheld from an employee's earnings (W-2 forms) are sent to each employee no later than January 31 of the year following the year in which the employee was paid.

Occasionally, early childhood programs hire someone to do a temporary job, such as plumbing or electrical work. Because withholding taxes would not have been deducted from the wages, all centers paying six hundred dollars or more to any individual who is not a regular employee must file IRS Form 1099.

Children's Rights and Protection Regulations

Historically, children's rights were viewed in moral and ethical terms rather than legal. In 1979 the United Nations produced a list of moral and ethical rights that focused on children's right to be nurtured (e.g., right to affection, right to adequate nutrition, and right to be a more useful member of society). Children's legal rights are primarily in the form of "protection," rather than rights concerning freedom of choice. Today there are movements to both expand and restrict children's rights.[2] Protection rights for children are primarily assumed by parents who have rights of guardianship (e.g., determine level of financial support, provide religious and moral teachings, make choices regarding services such as education and health care). In some cases, society, through the law, protects children from the results of their own lack of judgment (e.g., children are not held responsible for their contracts), develops laws on behalf of children (e.g., school attendance and child labor laws), and intervenes between parents and children when the courts feel the children need more protection—the concept of *parens patriae* (e.g., foster care and the administration of health services in life-threatening situations). Children have recently been given some direct legal rights (e.g., due process and fair treatment in schools and juvenile courts).

Protection rights of children implies responsibilities on the part of all those involved—parents, society, and even children themselves. A triadic model of these rights and responsibilities has been developed by Caldwell.[3] Early childhood administrators are responsible for providing high-quality programs (i.e., meeting standards of licensing codes, fiscal monitoring, or accreditation), as discussed in later sections of this chapter, and for protecting children who are involved in custody disputes or are victims of child abuse.

Handling Custody Issues

Custody issues arise when two adults have a right to some degree of legal or physical custody of a child. **Legal custody** is the right and responsibility of an individual or agency to make a decision on behalf of a child; **physical custody** is the right and responsibility of an individual to provide immediate care. Custody issues arise more frequently when children are from single-parent families or under the legal custody of the state and in the physical custody of foster parents.

All early childhood programs need to protect children involved in custody disputes. Children can be protected if administrators follow this procedure:

1. Clarify custody of all children at or prior to time of enrollment. (Information must be in writing, dated, signed, and kept current.)
2. Name(s) and address(es) of those authorized to pick up the child must be given in writing.
3. Administrators should provide a statement to each person enrolling a child that the child will be released only to those persons named on the forms as being authorized to receive the child.
4. If an unauthorized party attempts to receive a child, follow these steps: (*a*) tell the person he is unauthorized, regardless of theoretical rights; (*b*) show him a copy of the authorization; (*c*) notify the authorized person of the problem; and (*d*) if the unauthorized person does not leave, call the police.

Reporting Suspected Child Abuse

State laws govern reports of suspected child abuse. Early childhood educators certainly desire protection for children, and there may be criminal or civil penalties, loss of a job, or loss of a license for not reporting. All programs should establish written policies regarding the reporting requirements and internal processes. Policies may include responsibilities for reporting, definitions of reportable cases, descriptions of the internal processes (e.g., who will make the report), and statements about liability. (Prevention of child abuse in centers will be discussed later in this chapter.)

Staff Regulations

Staff regulations involve prevention of discrimination, wage-law compliance, board regulations, and staff qualifications.

Title VII of the Civil Rights Acts of 1964 and as Amended by the Equal Opportunity Act of 1972

Fair employment practices are mandatory for organizations, companies, and individuals having a contract with the federal government. The practices are also mandatory for any entity employing or composed of fifteen or more individuals. Employees subject to this Act and its amendment must not discriminate against any individual on the grounds of race, creed, color, sex, national origin, or age.

Employment practices must be based on relevant measures of merit and competence. The employer must also develop job qualifications upon bona fide occupational qualifications (BFOQ); thus, job descriptions must clearly specify the tasks to be performed. (More specific information on recruiting and employing staff is given in Chapter 4.)

Fair Labor Standards Act
The Fair Labor Standards Act of 1938 as amended applies equally to men and women. Employers subject to this Act and its amendments must pay employees the current minimum wage; overtime (hours worked over the forty-hour week) at the rate of one-and-a-half times the employee's regular rate of pay; regular wages and overtime pay for attendance at training sessions, whether the sessions are conducted at the place of work or at another site; and equal wages for equal work. The Act does not apply to members of one's immediate family.

Local Board Regulations
Each faculty and staff member employed by an early childhood program is governed by the regulations of its governing board, which must be in keeping with the restrictions and authorizations of federal, state, and local laws, directives, and guidelines. The governing board's regulations may cover such items as (1) educational requirements in addition to state certification requirements; (2) salary and related benefits; (3) absences and leaves granted; (4) promotions; (5) evaluations of staff; (6) grievance policies; (7) housing of program; (8) equipment used in program; (9) curricular assistance given to teachers, in the way of detailed course outline, in-service training, resource personnel, or no curricular assistance; (10) plan of staffing for instruction whether self-contained classroom, team teaching, or departmentalized staffing; (11) teaching and nonteaching duties; (12) nature of communication with the public, through publicity, citizens' visits, or participation in schools; (13) administrative, instructional, and discipline requirements to be employed in working with children, such as attendance regulations, methods of determining and reporting children's progress, and discipline, including punishment guidelines; and (14) each administrative and supervisory employee's responsibility in giving direction to faculty and staff.

Regulations Concerning Administrator Qualifications
Administrators of public school early childhood programs must hold a state administrator's certificate that grants legitimate authorization to administer a school program. Administrators of private early childhood programs need not hold an administrator's certificate unless the program is educational in nature. The state education agency issues various types of administrator certificates, such as an elementary principal's certificate, secondary principal's certificate, general principal's certificate, and superintendent's certificate. Several states are working toward certification requirements for an early childhood education administrator's certificate. Generally, administrators must have for certification:

1. Teaching experience (usually three years)
2. From fifteen semester hours of graduate work to a master's degree in school administration, with courses in curriculum, supervision, general administration, and specialized fields of administration such as school law and school finance
3. Two or three years of school administrative experience (for a superintendent's position only)

Administrators must meet any other qualifications established by the local board or accrediting agency to which the program belongs.

Directors of private early childhood programs must meet the educational and experience requirements of their state's licensing law. In some states, the minimum educational requirement for a director is a high school diploma, but other states require two or more years of college work. Minimum experience requirements range from no experience to two years of successful experience in an early childhood program.

Regulations Concerning Teacher Qualifications

A teacher of young children performs many roles every day, including those of language model, arouser of artistic sensitivity and creativity, relater of knowledge, questioner, stimulator of curiosity, learning diagnostician, guidance counselor and mediator of conflicts, diplomat with parents, classroom administrator, and more. Because the teacher also has total responsibility for all that happens to children in the school setting and for the quality of education, regulations help ensure that qualified teachers are placed with young children. A clear picture of the standards for professionalism is emerging from the National Association for the Education of Young Children's work on the "Model for Professional Development." (This position statement will replace the position statement on "Nomenclature, Salaries, Benefits, and the Status of the Early Childhood Profession."[4])

Certification of Teachers in Public School Early Childhood Education Programs. Certification is the function of granting authorization to teach. Certificates may be standard or provisional and are limited to special fields and levels of instruction. In most states, the legislature delegates certification responsibilities to the state Department of Education (see Appendix 2). These responsibilities usually include the power to issue, renew, or revoke a certificate; the task of writing minimum requirements for each type of certificate; and the task of developing guidelines for colleges and universities to follow in planning a program for prospective teachers. Although the bases for certification are left to each state, most certification standards specify United States citizenship, age and health requirements, earned college degree with special course requirements, and possibly a recommendation from the college or university. Some states also require additional tests of competency.

Education of early childhood teachers has a long history. When American kindergartens were first established, prospective kindergarten teachers received their training in Germany and other European countries. The growing kindergarten movement, however, necessitated establishing kindergarten training schools in the United States. The first training institution was founded in Boston in 1868. These schools offered instruction in Froebelian theory and methods and on-the-job training in kindergarten classrooms. "The training given emphasized the kindergarten as a unique form of education apart from and having nothing in common with the school."[5] In the decade from 1890 to 1900, many public schools adopted kindergartens. The kindergarten training schools were continued as private, self-supporting institutions because the normal schools were not able to supply the increasing demand for trained teachers.

Many educators realized the desirability of employing state-certified kindergarten teachers rather than having the kindergarten work "carried on by people who play a piano and love dear little children."[6] Consequently, many colleges and universities reorganized their curriculum to meet the needs of students preparing to teach kindergartens. By 1925, in the forty states that had kindergarten legislation, all states had teacher certification laws for kindergarten except Alabama, Kentucky, Louisiana, Oklahoma, and Tennessee. Most of the certificates were based upon a high school diploma and a two-year professional program and were special subject certificates valid only for teaching in the kindergarten. In California, Illinois, Michigan, Ohio, and Wisconsin, however, a kindergarten-primary certificate, based on a two-year professional program, was issued.[7] Today a majority of states accept an elementary certificate or an elementary certificate with an additional endorsement (i.e., two or three courses and student teaching in addition to the requirements for an elementary certificate).

With the growth of pre-kindergarten public school programs, state policy makers are realizing the need for specialized training leading to early childhood certification. The Public School Early Childhood Study[8] found that teachers trained in early childhood education and child development were more likely to carry out appropriate practices than teachers with no early childhood background whose previous teaching experience was with older children. Although the National Association for the Education of Young Children cites standards for early childhood certification, among the twenty three states (and the District of Columbia) that specifically offer "early childhood certification," there is a great range in the definition of "early childhood."[9] Some states offer an early childhood certificate as nursery-kindergarten certification (Pre-K–K or N–K). Other states use a broader certification such as nursery through the primary grades (N–2, N–3, K–2, K–3, K–4, N–K–4). In addition to the above certification patterns, seven states now offer certification that recognizes training in both early childhood education and special education.[10] The inclusion of special education training was due to the passage of P.L. 99–457, which will be discussed later in this chapter.

In an effort to meet the ever-increasing demand for teachers in the 1980s while ensuring standards of quality for teaching (i.e., decreasing or eliminating "emergency certificates"), almost half the states developed "alternative certification" programs.[11] **Alternative certification programs** generally enroll individuals with a bachelor's degree, usually in the arts and sciences, and offer a curricular shortcut to teaching. Most of the alternative certification programs specified that only secondary teachers and those needed for critical areas (e.g., bilingual education) can use this nontraditional route. McKibben[12] noted that only New Jersey allows this route for prospective early childhood teachers.

As knowledge expands, and demands that teachers be more knowledgeable increase, teacher-preparation programs have faced many issues. Some of these issues include:

1. What general education coursework should be required? In 1986, two reports[13] called for abolishing the undergraduate degree in education. Under these plans, the prospective teacher would receive a liberal arts undergraduate degree and a professional education graduate degree. Several states have moved in this direction (e.g., Texas, Virginia, and New Jersey) by abolishing the undergraduate education major. Although an individual may receive a certificate after completion of a baccalaureate degree, "education hours" are limited and a major is required in the arts and sciences. Other states elected to increase the general education requirements in an effort to provide a broader liberal arts base for prospective teachers. Additional courses are often in economics, computers, English, and music.[14] Shulman[15] states that it is highly important to restore subject matter knowledge as an integral component if teachers are to help children make connections among the disciplines.

2. What professional education coursework should be required? McCarthy[16] has described pedagogical knowledge currently considered important as: the philosophical, psychological, and historical foundations of early childhood education; home, school, and community relations; curriculum; organization and management of the learning environment; mainstreaming children with disabilities; infant and toddler programs; health, nutrition, and safety; assessment and evaluation; legal rights and responsibilities; and professionalism. These will be discussed in appropriate chapters in this book.

3. Is one philosophical orientation better than another? Barbour[17] describes these three models of teacher education:

   a. **Competency-based teacher education** focuses on the technical aspect (i.e., a body of professional content to be learned and specific teaching skills to be mastered) of teacher education. In these programs, the predetermined objectives are stated in behavioral terms and are sequenced. Prospective teachers are pretested for level of competency and then follow standardized procedures for accomplishing the program's goals.

   b. **Humanistic teacher education** is based on perceptual and developmental psychologies. While developing psychological maturity, prospective teachers are encouraged to try out a number of different approaches and techniques and to discover the method of teaching that best suits their unique personalities.

c. **Inquiry-oriented teacher education** prepares teachers as critical-thinkers. The teacher is challenged to relate theory of the college classroom to the reality of early childhood programs. Prospective teachers are encouraged to examine issues and to determine the consequences of their own and others' actions. Most teacher training programs are eclectic in nature.[18]

4. How important are field experiences? There is a trend toward increasing both the number and length of these experiences.[19] There are both positive and negative aspects (positively, prospective teachers connect university knowledge with the reality of the classroom and, negatively, the experience can encourage teachers simply to become technicians who support the status quo).[20] Research indicates that prospective teachers use field experiences to learn the technical aspects of teaching rather than to develop reflective attitudes about their experiences.[21] Henderson[22] states that students should engage in reflective interplay between their values and beliefs and the professional knowledge base.

5. What should performance testing measure? By 1986, only four states did not require performance testing for certification. The most popular paper-and-pencil test is the *National Teacher Examination* required in eighteen states. On-the-job performance tests are required in addition to the paper-and-pencil tests in about two-fifths of the states.[23]

Approximately a decade ago, the National Association for the Education of Young Children (NAEYC) developed objectives and standards for undergraduate early childhood teacher education programs from a survey of existing program descriptions and from position papers prepared by the members of the Early Childhood Teacher Education Guidelines Commission. The *Guidelines* were then reviewed by several hundred teacher educators at over a hundred institutions. The revised *Guidelines* were discussed at a public hearing at NAEYC's 1981 annual conference. Further revisions were made in the *Guidelines* which were approved by the Governing Board of NAEYC in December 1981. In July 1982, the National Council for the Accreditation of Teacher Education (NCATE) gave official approval to the *Guidelines* and agreed to a separate listing for early childhood education in its listing of accredited teacher education programs. The *Guidelines* became the standards for NCATE accreditation in early childhood education in September 1983. In 1986, the National Association of Early Childhood Teacher Educators (NAECTE) and NAEYC agreed to work cooperatively on developing "Advanced Degree Guidelines in Early Childhood." The NAECTE Task Force prepared a first draft of the *Guidelines*. These *Guidelines* were then reviewed and revised by NAEYC's Teacher Education Guidelines Panel. This draft was also reviewed at an open hearing by participants at the Early Childhood Teacher Education Colloquium sponsored by

NAEYC in Miami in January 1988. Revisions were based on comments made at the hearing and received by mail. The *Guidelines* were endorsed by NAECTE and approved by the NAEYC Governing Board in April 1988. The *Guidelines* received approval by NCATE in September 1988.

The *Early Childhood Teacher Education Guidelines* contain program objectives and standards for both basic (undergraduate studies) and advanced (graduate studies) in these components: curriculum, instructional methods, resources (e.g., professional materials, faculty-candidate ratio, availability of field experiences), faculty qualifications, professional relationships, cultural diversity (i.e., sensitivity to cultural pluralism), enrollment (i.e., acceptance and retention of candidates), administrative structure (i.e., structure that facilitates the work of all those involved in the program), and evaluation and constituent responsiveness (i.e., assessment of candidate's performance and program effectiveness in producing the competent teacher).[24]

Teacher Qualifications in Day-Care Settings and Head Start. In addition to meeting standards for public school early childhood programs, teachers must also meet qualifications for work in day-care settings, nursery schools, private kindergartens, and Head Start programs. The educational qualifications for personnel employed in day-care settings are determined by each state's licensing regulations. Head Start teacher qualifications are determined by the U.S. Department of Health and Human Services. For the most part these day-care teachers must have a high school certificate; a few states require some college education with course work in child development, curriculum and materials, organization and administration, and teaching strategies.

In an effort to upgrade these teachers' qualifications, many institutions of higher learning offer associate degree programs. Generally, these consist of thirty hours of general education and thirty hours of professional studies and field experience. *Guidelines for Early Childhood Education Programs in Associate Degree Granting Institutions* were adopted by the Governing Board of the National Association for the Education of Young Children in July 1985. These *Guidelines* will set the standards for associate degree work.

Another effort to maximize their performance was the founding of the Child Development Associate Consortium, a not-for-profit organization, in 1972. Program managers were awarded federal grants. The Consortium's goals were to establish competencies needed for working in early childhood education, to develop methodologies for assessing such competencies, and to issue appropriate credentials. On March 25, 1975, the board of directors formally adopted the Credential Award System and authorized the awarding of the Child Development Associate (CDA) credential to anyone who could demonstrate competence by completing the requirements of the Consortium. Because of federal funding cutbacks, the Consortium disbanded in 1979, and credentialing was shuffled around. In 1985, the National Association for the Education of Young Children (NAEYC) took responsibility for credentialing, establishing a separate, not-for-profit corporation, the Council for Early Childhood Professional Recognition.

From 1985 to 1988, through a cooperative agreement between the federal government (represented by the Administration for Children, Youth, and Families) and the early childhood profession (represented by the National Association for the Education of Young Children), the Council worked to develop a new training program leading to a CDA credential and to revise procedures for direct assessment of candidates who received their CDA training by other means. Once the training program and direct assessment plans were approved, the Council became an independent entity in 1989. The Professional Preparation Program consists of these three phases: (1) fieldwork guided by an early childhood adviser who uses Council-designed manuals; (2) seminars, conducted in higher-education settings, that cover the knowledge base of early childhood education; and (3) integration of field experiences and course work, with candidates completing a series of exercises and performance-based assessments and a Council representative conducting a series of interviews and receiving documentation. Direct assessment will include a competency-based evaluation and a written assessment of the candidate's knowledge. For more information contact:

Council for Early Childhood Professional Recognition
1718 Connecticut Ave., N. W., Suite 500
Washington, DC 20009
1-800-424-4310

Teacher Qualifications in American Montessori Schools. Because the American Montessori Society, Inc., is a national private agency, the instructional staff of a Montessori school would have to meet the licensing code requirements of the state or, in some states, the requirements of the state board of education. In addition to the state's regulations, the American Montessori Society has its own certification requirements:

1. A degree from an accredited four-year college or equivalent foreign credential is required, but no specific field of study is stipulated.
2. About three hundred clock hours of academic work are required. This may include workshops or seminars in the historical and philosophical foundations of American education and the relationship of Montessori education to current knowledge of child development; knowledge of Montessori theory, philosophy, and materials for instruction as presented in seminars and as seen in observation of laboratory classes; and training in language arts, mathematics, science, art, music, social studies, and motor perception.
3. An internship of nine months is required. This must be on a site approved by the course director under the approved American Montessori Society supervisor during which the intern is observed by a training program representative.[25]

Potential Vulnerability to Legal Actions

Three legal principles often apply in legal actions involving any business. They are:

1. An employee is hired to perform certain types of duties with certain expectations as to how these duties will be performed. When an employee's actions are consistent with those expectations, an employee is said to be "acting within the scope of authority." An employee is not liable when acting within the scope of authority, but is liable when acting beyond it.
2. Except for "negligence" of employees, employers are responsible for all torts (i.e., civil wrongs) committed by employees. The legal phrase used for this principle is *respondent superior*—the boss is responsible. This principle does not apply to independent contractors who are responsible for their own torts.
3. Principals (e.g., boards of directors) are responsible for torts committed by their agents (e.g., directors) acting on the business of the principal and within the scope of employment.

Liabilities vary, depending on the form of organization. Programs fully liable are sole proprietorships, partnerships, and for-profit corporations. Liability is limited in some states by the "charitable immunity doctrine" for programs operated as not-for-profit corporations. In the past, public agency programs, such as public school early childhood programs and Head Start, have generally been immune from suits as provided by Section 1983 of the Civil Rights Act.[26] However, recent judicial decisions have held that public programs are not immune from full liability.[27] Even under the Civil Rights Act, immunity was not extended to these three types of suits: (1) intentional injury (e.g., corporal punishment resulting in lasting injury to body or health; restraint of a person, such as physically enforcing the time-out technique; and defamation, such as implying a student's lack of ability in nonprofessional communication); (2) negligence (e.g., failure to give adequate instruction, failure to take into account child's abilities, improper supervision, inadequate inspection of equipment); and (3) educational negligence (i.e., careless or incompetent teaching practices).[28]

Several implications can be drawn concerning the potential vulnerability to legal action. First, all employees should have job descriptions spelling out their scope of authority. Second, adequate staffing, safe housing and equipment, administrative diligence, staff awareness and training in care of children, and documentation will do much to reduce risks of torts. And third, the realization by all involved in programs that situations leading to liability are ever-present concerns and all employees are vulnerable to legal actions.

REGULATIONS GOVERNING PRIVATE EARLY CHILDHOOD PROGRAMS

There are many types of private programs for young children. A private early childhood program may be a single class conducted by an individual or a multiclass school staffed by a large faculty. The private program may be not-for-profit or for-profit with all varieties or combinations of financial support possible. And as described in Chapter 1, there are many typologies of private early childhood programs, each with its own historical origins and present goals. Certain regulatory procedures are unique to private programs. Some create the legal existence of a private program (i.e., sole proprietorships, partnerships, and corporations). Others pertain to the level of quality of a private program (i.e., licensing and registration). Each state determines what is meant by a private early childhood program/facility and establishes the regulations by which the program is operated as a sole proprietorship, a partnership, or a for-profit or not-for-profit corporation. Each state also provides the means, through licensing and registration regulations, for meeting the minimum standards for programs not funded or regulated by government agencies.

Proprietorships, Partnerships, and Corporation Regulations

Proprietorship, partnership, and corporation are legal categories for three types of private ownership. Legal requirements for operating an early childhood program under one of these categories vary from state to state; this discussion will focus on common features of the laws. Legal assistance should be sought before establishing a private early childhood program.

Proprietorship

Under a **proprietorship** a program is owned by one person. This individual has no partners and is not incorporated. Sole proprietorships may have a one-person owner and operator, or a larger staff with one person as owner.

The legal requirements are simple: to create a proprietorship, the owner must file with the city clerk a True Name Certificate, or, if she is not going to use her real name, a Fictitious Name Registration, such as "Jack and Jill Center." The Assumed Name Law informs clients and creditors of true ownership of the business. In a sole proprietorship, the owner has full decision-making authority as long as decisions are consistent with government regulations (e.g., owner must file a personal tax form). The owner may sell, give away, or go out of business with no restrictions except the payment of outstanding debts and the completion of contractual obligations. The owner, however, assumes full personal liability for debts, breaches of contract, torts, taxes, and regulatory fees; the liability is not limited in amount and may even exceed the owner's personal funds.

Partnership

In a **partnership** two or more individuals usually join together for purposes of ownership. However, a partnership may involve minor children, a sole proprietorship, or a corporation as a partner. (The sole proprietor and the corporation would be involved in their own business as well as the business owned by the partnership.) A partnership has limited transferability. A partner may sell or give away his interest in the partnership only if all other partners consent. If one partner dies, the partnership is dissolved. The law recognizes two types of partnerships:

1. **General partnership.** In this partnership, each partner is a legal coequal. Each partner has the right to make equal, but not necessarily the same kind of contributions to the program. Since contribution is a right and not an obligation, it may be worked out in reality on an equal or unequal basis. A general partnership can be risky because each partner has full authority to make binding decisions independently of other partners, sharing equally in any financial obligations including full personal liability. As with a proprietorship, the partners must file a True Name Certificate. Although partners have individual tax obligations, they also file an information return IRS Form 1065.

2. **Limited partnership.** In this type, there must be one or more general partners and one or more limited partners. Each general partner faces risks identical to those of a general partnership. Each limited partner is responsible and liable to the extent of his financial or service contribution calculated on a monetary basis at the time the center was created. Partners must file a True Name Certificate and a Limited Partnership Certificate that spells out the limitations of responsibility and liability. The limited partnership document is written and filed with the secretary of state or publicized according to the state's laws. Many partnerships find it desirable, though not mandatory, to prepare a partnership agreement, a document containing facts about how a program is to be operated and terminated. Because of limited liability, a limited partner participates only in decisions involving finances.

Corporation

A **corporation** is a legal entity established on a for-profit or not-for-profit basis. Corporations exist as legal entities forever unless dissolved by the board or a court. Most private early childhood programs legally organized as corporations are independent (i.e., not part of other businesses). However, work-site day-care programs may be organized as a division of the parent corporation, a subsidiary corporation, or an independent, not-for-profit corporation.

The corporation protects individuals from certain liabilities by creating a decision-making and accountable board of directors. Although the board may delegate decision-making power to a director, it is still responsible. Individual board members can be held personally liable in certain areas, such as failure of the corporation to pay withholding taxes on employees' salaries and fraud. In short, personal financial liability is greatly diminished in a corporation as compared with the proprietorship or partnership.

In addition to diminished personal financial liability, regulations governing taxation may provide incentive to operate a program as a corporation. There is often a monetary advantage in paying corporate taxes rather than paying all the taxes on the program's profits as personal income. Furthermore, not-for-profit centers must be incorporated to be eligible for tax-exempt status; proprietorships and partnerships are not eligible for a tax-exempt status.

Because the corporation is a legal entity, several documents are required. The forms are usually somewhat different for for-profit and not-for-profit corporations. Three documents required in the process of incorporating are:

1. **Articles of Incorporation** or **Certificate of Incorporation.** The organization's legal creators, or incorporators, give information about the corporation, such as the name and address of the agency; its purposes, and whether it is a for-profit or not-for-profit corporation; its powers—for example, to purchase property and make loans; membership, if the state requires members; names and addresses of the initial board of directors; initial officers; and the date of the annual meeting.
2. **Bylaws.** The Internal Revenue Service requires bylaws if the corporation is seeking tax-exempt status. Bylaws simply explain how the corporation will conduct its business, its power structure, and how the power may be transferred.
3. **Minutes of the Incorporator's Meeting.** After the incorporators prepare the aforementioned documents, an incorporator's meeting is held. The name of the corporation is approved, and the Articles of Incorporation and Bylaws signed. The incorporators elect officers and the board of directors, who will serve until the first meeting of the members. In for-profit corporations, they vote to authorize the issuance of stock. Formal minutes of the incorporator's meeting, including votes taken, are written and signed by each incorporator.

These documents, along with payment of a fee, are filed with the secretary of state or publicized according to state laws. Once the state approves the proposed corporation, a corporate charter is issued. The incorporators no longer have power. Board members carry out the purposes of the organization, and the members own the organization. When corporations dissolve, they must follow state law if they are for-profit corporations, or federal regulations if they are not-for-profit corporations.

Early childhood programs may operate either as **for-profit** or **not-for-profit** corporations. Although the titles are somewhat descriptive, they are often misleading, particularly when incorrectly called profit-making and nonprofit corporations, respectively.

For-profit corporations are organized for purposes of making a profit. Early childhood programs in this category, as well as proprietorships and partnerships, are businesses. A for-profit corporation may be a closed corporation, in which members of a family or perhaps a few friends own stock, or an open corporation, in which stock is traded on exchanges. If the corporation makes a profit, it pays taxes on the profits; individual stockholders file personal income tax forms listing items such as salaries and dividends received from the corporation. In a closed corporation with a subchapter "S" status, granted by the

Internal Revenue Service, the corporation may distribute its profits or losses in accordance with the proportion of stock held by each individual, who in turn pays taxes or files a depreciation schedule.

The main purpose of *not-for-profit* corporations is other than to make a profit, but they are permitted to make a profit. However, any surplus, or profit, must be used to promote the purposes of the organization as set forth in the Articles of Incorporation. In other words, the profit may be used for housing, equipping, or merit raises in the present or future. Proprietory operators have also organized not-for-profit corporations, which gives them certain advantages such as rent money for the facility, a salary for directing the program, and free surplus food for children in the program. Under child care, there are two types of not-for-profit corporations: those organized for charitable, educational, literary, religious, or scientific purposes under section 501(c)(3) of the Internal Revenue Code; and those organized for social welfare purposes under section 501(c)(4) of the Internal Revenue Code. Tax-exempt status is not automatic. The not-for-profit corporation must file for and be granted tax-exempt status at both federal and state levels.

Besides incorporation regulations, several additional regulations should be noted. Separate bank accounts should be obtained for any early childhood program. Corporations are required to have separate accounts, and some government agencies will not send funds to a program that does not have a separate account. Also, a Banking Resolution, stating the name of the individual authorized to withdraw funds, is required of corporations (and in some states of partnerships). Not-for-profit corporations with a certain income level, and other programs receiving moneys from certain funding sources, are required to have an audit. In most states, not-for-profit corporations are required to file an annual Financial Report following the audit.

Franchises and chains may fall under any of the three legal categories of private organizations but are most often corporations. Franchises and chains are differentiated as follows:

1. A **franchise** is an organization that allows an individual or an entity to use its name, follow its standardized program and administrative procedures, and receive assistance (for example, in selecting a site, building and equipping a facility, and training staff), for an agreed-upon sum of money and/or royalty.
2. A **chain** is ownership of several facilities by the same proprietorship, partnership, or corporation. These facilities are administered by a central organization. Kinder-Care is an example of a chain.

Licensing: Minimal Quality Regulations

Licensing is the procedure by which an individual, association, or corporation obtains from its state licensing agency a license to operate or continue operating a private child-care facility. A private, licensed facility is recognized by the state agency as having met only minimum standards of child care; that is, licensing is a regulation reflecting the criterion of preventing harm to children rather than providing exemplary care.

Licensing does not concern some child-care facilities. Nonlicensed facilities may include the following:

1. Programs operated under public auspices such as public school programs and Head Start. Public agencies are expected to implement their own standards and exercise supervision of their own facilities.
2. Day camps as defined by the various state codes.
3. Nurseries or other programs in places of worship during religious services. In a few states, other types of church-related child-care services are exempted from licensing.
4. Babysitting services as defined by the various state codes. (The minimum number of children not related to the provider and the place of operation are used to make a distinction between day-care and babysitting services.)

Licensing originated in New England when a board of charities was created in 1863 to inspect and report on various child-care facilities. In 1873, the National Conference of Charities and Correction was created. The Conference urged state regulation of private agencies, including those concerned with child care.[29] The first licensing law was passed in Pennsylvania in 1884; however, general interest in licensing did not begin until the early 1900s when public scandals arose over the abuse of children in some child-care facilities. This concern led to regulations for minimum standards of care and supervision of the publicly subsidized agencies. The first White House Conference on the care of dependent children (1909) recommended that each state regularly inspect all agencies dealing with minor children and regulate the incorporation of new agencies.[30] Three years later, the U.S. Children's Bureau was created. The Bureau urged the establishment of standards for child-care agencies. The Child Welfare League of America, established in 1920, developed such a set of standards.[31] By then most states had some regulation of child care. As a result of the federal grant-in-aid funds of 1935, state child welfare departments were able to procure better-qualified personnel; day-care facilities were brought under child-care licensing statutes; social workers took an active interest in protective services; and licensing was identified as a state child welfare function.[32]

The Licensing Agency

Licensing of child-care facilities is the responsibility of a particular state department (see Appendix 2). According to Class, the licensing agency is a regulatory agency with both quasi-legislative and quasi-judicial authority. The quasi-legislative powers include responsibility for establishing standards, and the quasi-judicial powers include responsibility for making decisions to issue or deny a license application and for conducting hearings in grievance cases. The major tasks of the licensing agency are (a) interpreting the fact that child care is an activity affecting public interests and is therefore recognized by the state as an area of regulation; (b) formulating and reformulating licensing standards which will reduce the risk of improper care; (c) evaluating each applicant's situation to decide whether or not to issue the license; and (d) supervisory activity to maintain conformity to standards and, usually, consultation to upgrade care.[33]

Features of Day-Care Licensing Laws.
The different types of child-care facilities may be covered by a general or differential licensing law. Differential licensing laws have varying standards for these types of programs: day-care (family day-care homes, group day-care homes, and day-care centers); educational facilities (private kindergartens and programs that carry the term *school* in their title); foster care (foster homes and group foster homes); child-placing institutions; residential facilities; children's camps; and centers for children with disabilities. (This section will be concerned only with the licensing of day-care centers; regulation of family day-care is discussed later.)

The content of licensing regulations originates with an advisory group comprising interested persons, child development and early childhood education experts, politicians, and consumers. Those with concerns regarding licensing laws look to this task force for action. Public hearings are held on the draft. The agency then issues a legal statement, which becomes the law.

Regulatory laws governing day-care centers differ widely from state to state. To learn specific regulations of a state, contact the state's licensing agency and request a copy of the regulations. (See Appendix 2.) Some areas covered in most licensing codes are:

1. **Licensing laws and procedures.** This section covers the following: terms such as *day-care*, programs that must be licensed, obtaining and submitting an application for a license, fees, application approval, duration of license, revoking a license, posting of license, and conditions requiring notification of licensing agency.
2. **Organization and administration.** State licensing laws require an applicant to indicate purposes and sponsorship of the organization, whether the program is for-profit or not-for-profit, the ways in which administrative authority is placed (e.g., boards, director), policies concerning children (e.g., admission, termination, nondiscrimination provision, fees), child-staff ratio, and financial solvency for immediate and continuous operation.
3. **Staffing.** Regulations concerning staffing usually include categories of personnel (i.e., director, primary program personnel, and support program personnel); age, education, health, character, and temperament characteristics of staff members; personnel records to be kept; and child-staff ratio. Several trends in staffing requirements include:
   a. A shift from states requiring a B.S./B.A. degree for at least one category of center staff to a requirement for the CDA credential.[34]
   b. The protection of children from abuse. Congress enacted P.L. 98–473 to provide supplementary funding to the Social Services Block Grant

program for training, including prevention of child abuse in day-care centers. States must screen specified child-care personnel for employment history, background, and nationwide criminal checks.[35]

c. Several states dropped their child-staff ratio requirements or opted for less favorable ratios. And there has been little progress in regulating group size, although the National Day-Care Study showed that "group composition" had a major impact on quality of care.[36]

4. **Plant and equipment.** Licensing codes require applicants meet local zoning, health, and fire standards and state health department standards before applying. The majority of states have regulations concerning the indoor housing (e.g., size, type, and number of rooms needed), environmental control, drinking water sources, sanitary facilities, kitchen facilities, and outdoor space needed. Some equipment regulations are common, such as equipment for naps. Specific regulations on other equipment may not be given but may be listed as "suggested" equipment.

5. **Health and safety.** Health and safety requirements concerning physical facilities, health forms, and nutrition are very specific. Two areas receiving more attention are: (a) sexual abuse as previously discussed, and (b) concern over infectious diseases in all day-care and especially infant programs (see Chapter 9).[37]

6. **Program.** Some states have detailed program specifications. Because child care is not considered educational but a public welfare service in some states, program regulations tend to be more lax than most other licensing regulations. Others desire minimum regulation or feel parents and staff should have a great deal of autonomy and control over program content and scheduling.

7. **Discipline.** Many states stipulate "no harsh discipline" and give suggestions for guidance of children. The outlawing of corporal punishment in state codes is the issue behind much effort by certain religious groups to exempt church-operated day-care from licensing.

8. **Parent involvement.** Most states require that parents be involved in the day-care program. Suggested means include serving on boards of advisors, visiting the facility during hours of operation, having parent-staff conferences, and being given materials on the program's goals and policies. Approximately one-half of the states guarantee parents the right to make unannounced visits to the child-care program.

Improving Licensing Laws

Morgan states that licensing laws can be judged in terms of whether (1) standards are high or low; (2) the state code covers all forms of child care—infant/toddler programs, family day-care homes, and group day-care homes; (3) the standards are implemented fully; (4) the licensing system has a broad base of support in the state; and (5) the state has adequate numbers of trained workers in the licensing agency.[38]

During the 1960s and 1970s, when federal funding of early childhood programs was plentiful, the Federal Interagency Day-Care Requirements (FIDCR) were instituted to ensure a higher quality of standards for programs receiving federal funds. Many states patterned their licensing codes after the FIDCR. These requirements were replaced in 1980 with the more stringent Department of Health and Human Services Day-Care Requirements (DHHSDCR), which then were eliminated in 1981. Licensing codes in many states eroded following the elimination of all federal standards, resulting in non-enforcement and/or movement to exempt certain programs.

Professionals see a need for strong licensing laws. According to Morgan, providers must be willing to meet standards, parents must be willing to pay for higher quality, and the general public must support enforcement. She also notes that the history, values, and cultures of a state influence what can be done in regulatory policy, and, in some states, deregulation (e.g., voluntary licensing and registration) is most attractive to policy makers.[39] These suggestions have been made for the improvement of licensing:[40]

1. Reflect current research in developing standards (e.g., Fiene's *State Child Care Regulatory, Monitoring and Evaluation Systems as a Means for Ensuring Quality Child Development Programs;* Howes' *Keeping Current in Child Care Research;* the National Academy of Early Childhood Programs' *Accreditation Criteria and Procedures;* and the National Association for the Education of Young Children's *Regulating Child Care Quality*).
2. Have mandatory regulation of all types of programs serving children.
3. Set standards that are appropriate for various types of settings and the number of children served.
4. Write standards in clear and reasonable terms.
5. Make the licensing agencies highly visible (i.e., agencies are known about and accessible to parents and providers).
6. Interface with referral programs, resource networks, and training/technical assistance programs to meet the needs of parents and providers.
7. Fund at levels necessary for full implementation of the regulatory and service aspects of the agency.

Registration and Other Forms of Regulation

Although the number of licensed centers doubled from 1976 to 1986, the trend did not hold true for family day-care. Approximately 50 to 90 percent of family day-care programs are not licensed.[41] Caldwell states that the lack of regulation of the family day-care system "is one of the factors responsible for the field's slow climb to legitimacy."[42] The main problems in regulating family day-care programs are the increasing numbers of these programs and the high turnover rate of the homes serving children.

There are several options for regulating family day-care homes. In addition to traditional licensing, registration is becoming a popular approach. **Registration** is a process by which a state's licensing agent publishes regulations, requires the provider to certify that he has complied with the regulations, and maintains records on all family day-care homes. In order for registration to be effective, it must be mandatory and about one-fifth of the homes must have a routine inspection each year.[43] Another regulatory model is the **supervisor model** in which an early childhood professional participates in the licensing of a home and in enforcement by frequent visits (e.g., twice a month). **Accreditation** (which will be discussed later in this chapter) may also be used when other forms of regulation are nonexistent or insufficiently provided by state government.[44]

REGULATIONS GOVERNING PUBLIC EARLY CHILDHOOD PROGRAMS

A public agency is an organization that is part of the federal, state, or local government. Publicly funded early childhood programs are not subject to licensing. Instead, all publicly funded programs, such as public school and federally supported early childhood programs, are regulated by a state or federal agency, respectively. A specified state or federal agency is required by law to prepare regulations. Some of these regulations are deemed inadequate by many professionals. For example, public school pre-kindergarten programs are exempt from child-care regulations in nearly every state; state codes, written with school-age children in mind, rarely include specific provisions for young children. Furthermore, because publicly funded programs are self-monitoring or answerable only to elected officials, program quality depends on citizen involvement.

Public School Regulations

Legally, public schools are public agencies. Public school education in the United States is a state function. The organizational structure is similar in each of the states.

In most states, the chief state school officer is the superintendent of public instruction or the commissioner of education, who is either elected or appointed. Early childhood education programs in the public schools fall under this officer's jurisdiction. The chief state school officer along with the state board of education, composed of elected or appointed board members, comprise the policy-making group for public education in the state. With the state board's approval, the chief state school officer selects the personnel and operates the department of public instruction or state education agency. Within the department of public instruction is a bureau concerned with early childhood education programs. Duties of the bureau may include approving requests for state aid, evaluating teacher certification applications, responding to requests for information or assistance, supervising programs in the local school districts, appraising legislative proposals that affect early childhood programs, and publishing information on regulations or trends in early childhood education.

The local school district may be, according to each state's law, a large urban district, a small community district, a cooperative arrangement among several communities, or a county district. The board of education or trustees, an elected group that represents the district's interests, is the policy-making group. As authorized by state laws, the board approves all school expenditures, plans for building projects, makes personnel appointments, and determines the services offered to students and parents. The superintendent, appointed by the school board, is the administrative officer for the school district. His function is to execute, within limits of state law, the board's actions.

Directly superior to the early childhood education teacher is the building principal, who is the instructional leader and administrator of the school physical plant, records, and personnel. Supervisors or supervisor-administrators may be assigned by the superintendent's office to supervise and assist early childhood education teachers. The early childhood education teacher is responsible for caregiving and instruction of the children assigned to him, for the management of the classroom, and for any assistant teachers or aides placed under his direction.

Fiscal Monitoring

When the government buys or creates a service through a grant or contract, it establishes specifications for quality. Based on contract law, the relationship of the government to the provider is that of purchaser or contractor. Specifications for quality are simply administrative accountability via fiscal monitoring. Some states require the public program to meet the standard used in licensing while others require a level of quality higher than licensing. One example of fiscal monitoring is the Head Start Performance Standards that local Head Start programs must meet for future funding. The Performance Standards are found in the *Federal Register* dated June 30, 1975, Volume 40, Number 126, Part II. These standards cover the areas of education, health, nutrition, social services, and parent involvement.

Individuals with Disabilities Education Act

The Individuals with Disabilities Education Act, Public Law 94–142, was signed in November 1975. The formula for financial assistance to state educational agencies and school districts was implemented in the 1978 fiscal year. The scope and comprehensiveness of this act make it the most significant piece of legislation enacted to meet the needs of children who are disabled.

History of Education of Children Who Are Disabled

Education of the disabled has a long and varied history. The first school for the mentally disabled was established in 1848. Samuel Howe, director of the Perkins Institution for the Blind, opened an experimental school for "idiot children."

Other residential schools followed. The federal government became involved in special education in 1864, with the establishment of Gallaudet College for the Deaf in Washington, D.C.

In 1896, the first special education class for mentally disabled was opened in the public schools of Providence, Rhode Island. The federal government established a Section on Exceptional Children and Youth in the Office of Education in 1930. Because parents saw the need to educate their disabled children, and because the federal government has provided matching funds to state and local agencies and has supported special education with moneys for research, dissemination of information, and consultative services, there has been a rapid increase in the number of special education classes in public schools since World War II.

Special education began to receive extensive federal support in 1965 with passage of Public Law 89–10, the Elementary and Secondary Education Act (ESEA), a bill for the "educationally disadvantaged." Three amendments to ESEA, Public Law 89–313 (1965), Public Law 89–750 (1966), and Public Law 90–247 (1967), provided more aid to exceptional children in state-operated and state-supported institutions. Public Law 90–538, Handicapped Children's Early Education Assistance Act of 1968, authorized experimental preschool programs for children with disabilities to demonstrate that disabling conditions might be eliminated or alleviated in over half the cases by early and comprehensive help.

Litigation has also been an important part of the history of publicly supported education for children with disabilities. The constitutional right of extending equal educational opportunities to all children, including the disabled, was settled by the United States Supreme Court in the case of *Brown* v. *Board of Education* (1954). More recent litigation has been concerned with methods of extending "equal educational opportunity." In *Madera* v. *Board of Education, City of New York* (1967), *Arreola* v. *Board of Education* (1967), and *Covarrubias* v. *San Diego Unified School District* (1970), parents were to participate (with legal counsel, in the *Madera* case) in and be informed of placement decisions. As a result of *Diana* v. *California State Board of Education* (1970), children must be tested in their primary language and in English, reevaluated within a specified length of time, and additional services must be provided to those students returning to the regular class following special class placement.

Two precedent-setting cases were decided in the early 1970s. In a federal district court action, *Pennsylvania Association for Retarded Children (PARC)* v. *Commonwealth of Pennsylvania*, parents invoked the equal protection clause of the Fourteenth Amendment.[45] The clause requires that, if the state provides a publicly supported program of education, it must be made available on an equal basis. PARC showed that inappropriate assessment instruments and labels led to incorrect placement or exclusion of children from school, and that it was more economical to educate mentally disabled children in the public schools than to provide special institutions or welfare assistance. As a result of this case, the Pennsylvania State Board of Education agreed to provide students who were disabled with equal educational opportunity and to implement due process hearings concerning a child's placement. The outcome of the second especially significant judicial decision, *Mills* v. *Board of Education*,[46] was similar to that of the Pennsylvania case. In this case, however, the plaintiffs included not only mentally disabled but all children with special needs.

Provisions of P.L. 94–142

The specific provisions of P.L. 94–142 are the culmination of a long history of legislation and litigation, but the provisions are so comprehensive and significant that they go beyond their history. P.L. 94–142 is a revision of Part B of the Individuals with Disabilities Education Act. The law is administered through the Office for Special Education and Rehabilitation Services. If certain stipulations are met, children in private as well as public schools may receive assistance under this Act. These are some of the major details and stipulations of the Act:

1. Children with disabilities are defined as mentally retarded, hard of hearing, deaf, speech impaired, visually handicapped, seriously emotionally disturbed, orthopedically impaired, and other health impaired, or children with specific learning disabilities, who by reason thereof require special education and related services. (Section 602)
2. All children aged three to twenty-one years are included under this Act. There is also provision for federal moneys for early identification and screening. Free public education was to be made available to children with disabilities aged three to eighteen by the beginning of the school year in 1978, and to all children with disabilities aged three to twenty-one by September 1, 1980. For children in the three-to-five and eighteen-to-twenty-one age ranges, such mandate does not apply if such a requirement is inconsistent with state law or practice or any court decree. Some state laws mandate special education services from birth.
3. Priorities will go to children who are not receiving an education and those with the most severe disabilities who are inadequately served. These priorities must be adhered to by both state and local education agencies.
4. To prevent "over-counting" of children for entitlement purposes, the law requires that the total number of children should not be greater than 12 percent of the total school-age population between the ages of five and seventeen inclusively. No more than one-sixth of those deemed disabled (or 2 percent of the total school population) may be children with specific learning disabilities (SLD).
5. Extensive child identification procedures are required.
6. Evaluation must not be culturally or racially discriminatory. More specifically, tests must be conducted in the child's primary language, administered by a qualified individual, validated for the specific purposes for which it was intended, and given in conjunction with other assessment devices.

7. Parents must be informed and give their permission for evaluation of their child. The state education agency must guarantee maintenance of due process procedures for all children with disabilities and their parents or guardians with respect to all matters of identification, evaluation, and educational placement, whether for initiation or change of such placement, or for refusal to initiate or change.

8. An individualized program for each child must be developed. The law specifies that the program be based on (a) a statement of the present levels of educational performance of such child; (b) a statement of annual goals, including short-term instructional objectives; (c) a statement of the specific educational services to be provided to such child, and the extent to which such child will be able to participate in regular educational programs; (d) the projected date for initiation and anticipated duration of such services; and (e) appropriate objective criteria and evaluation procedures and schedules for determining, on at least an annual basis, whether instructional objectives are being achieved. [Section 4(a)(19)]

9. Special education must be provided in the "least restrictive environment." This simply means that children who are disabled must be integrated into regular classes—the "mainstream" of education. Mainstreaming is thus the organizational answer to the mandate. Special classes and schools may be used for educating disabled when integration is not best for the child.

10. Related services must be provided for the child who is disabled. These are comprehensive, and include transportation, and such developmental, and other supportive services (including speech pathology and audiology; psychological services; physical and occupational therapy; recreation, medical, and counseling services, except such medical services shall be for diagnostic purposes only) as may be required to assist a child to benefit from special education, and includes the early identification and assessment of disabling conditions in children. [Section 4(a)(17)]

11. A document must be developed at the state level in the form of an annual state plan to meet the specific mandates of P.L. 94–142 and submitted to the U.S. Commissioner of Education. The state education agency monitors compliance by its local school districts with respect to the stipulations, and the U.S. Commissioner monitors the degree of compliance by the state education agency. The Commissioner may cut off funds to a state education agency if that agency is in substantial noncompliance with any of the major stipulations. Noncompliance may result in termination of funds for special programs for children with disabilities.

12. The U.S. Commissioner of Education will evaluate the impact of the Act on an annual basis and provide a complete report to Congress on the effectiveness of individualized instruction, educating children with

disabilities in the least restrictive environment, and procedures to prevent erroneous classification of children.

P.L. 94–142 established a payment formula based upon a gradually escalating percentage (5 percent, FY 1978, to a permanent 40 percent, FY 1982) of the national average expenditure per public school child times the number of children with disabilities served in the school districts of each state. Of course, actual appropriations are determined by Congress.

Amendment of 1986

Amendment of 1986, Public Law 99–457, is a companion piece of legislation to Public Law 94–142. Public Law 99–457 extends the population originally targeted by Public Law 94–142 by direct legislation for children with disabilities from birth to age three. Public Law 99–457 is thus the fulfillment of specific concern for young children that began with the 1968 Handicapped Children's Early Education Assistance Act (P.L. 90–538) and which provided grant moneys for the purposes of developing model programs for young children with disabilities.

The provisions of Public Law 99–457 (Part H) include:

1. Professionals organize multidisciplinary and multi-agency programs for young children with disabilities and their families.
2. Families are to be included very directly in planning for their infants and toddlers who are disabled.
3. New ways of delivery services are to be developed (e.g., professional supervision of paraprofessionals).

Prior to 1990, three- through five-year-old children who were disabled received services only at each state's discretion. Title II of Public Law 99–457 mandates full service for these children with disabilities by the 1990–91 academic year. Parents may elect part- or full-time day-care or home-based care as well as training for themselves under the law's provisions.

ACCREDITATION

Accreditation is defined as a process of self-regulation; thus, regulations governing programs (e.g., certification of staff, licensing, registration) differ from accreditation in several ways. Regulations are mandatory minimum standards requiring 100 percent compliance, are determined or set by government or funding agencies, and often are imposed at the local and state levels, although some regulations have federal scope (e.g., IRS regulations, Civil Rights Acts, P.L. 94–142). Conversely, accreditation standards are voluntary high-quality standards requiring substantial compliance, sponsored by professional organizations, and operated at the national level. Failure to meet regulation standards means legal sanctions, but failure to become accredited signifies failure to gain professional status. Early childhood programs accredited by a particular association or agency are not necessarily superior to other programs, although they are often superior because staff members have voluntarily pursued a degree of excellence.

Accreditation, as a process of self-regulation, involves three major steps. The first step involves an application and fee payment to the accrediting association followed by a **self-study** in which the program attempts to meet the accreditation standards as delineated by interpretive statements, usually called criteria. (See Appendix 3.) The self-study is submitted in a specified written format to the sponsoring association. Traditionally, associations have used, and most still use, a rather voluminous description of the program's compliance with each criterion. However, the National Academy of Early Childhood uses a 3-point rating scale (criterion fully met, criterion partially met, criterion not met) for its "Program Description." The second step involves on-site **validation,** which is a visit to the program by a team of validators (i.e., highly qualified professionals with association training to interpret the accreditation standards and procedures). As their title suggests, these validators verify that the written information is an accurate reflection of daily program operations. The validators then report their findings to the accrediting agency. The final step is the **decision-making process** by the accrediting agency. Programs are informed in writing concerning their accreditation status along with their strengths and weaknesses. For accredited programs, there is a term of accreditation; in order to stay accredited, program officials must reapply and successfully complete the entire process before the term expires. Furthermore, most associations now require annual reports on their accredited programs regarding each program's current status and maintain the right to revoke accreditation if the program does not maintain quality standards or fails to comply with any procedures. For deferred programs, there are appeal procedures and also association assistance plans for helping these programs meet the standards and become accredited.

There are several accreditation agencies involved in early childhood programs. In 1982, the National Association for the Education of Young Children (NAEYC) began developing an accreditation system for early childhood programs serving a minimum of ten children within the age group of birth through five, in part- or full-day group programs and five- through eight-year-olds in before- and after-school programs. No home-based day-care programs are included at this time. To accomplish the goals of accreditation, NAEYC established a new organization—the National Academy of Early Childhood Programs (the Academy). Programs working toward accreditation join the Academy as "candidate programs" and become members when accredited.[47] The self-study consists of four parts: an *Early Childhood Classroom Observation,* an *Administrative Report,* a *Staff Questionnaire,* and a *Parent Questionnaire.* The criteria are centered on these ten components of group programs for children: interactions among staff and children, curriculum, staff-parent interaction, staff qualifications and development, administration, staffing, physical environment, health and safety, nutrition and food service, and program evaluation.[48]

Recently the Academy completed two follow-up studies. Analysis of data from the annual report submitted on programs one year after their accreditation revealed that the high standards were not only maintained but were being improved upon.[49] And data from a survey of reaccredited programs completed three years after their original accreditation, suggest that because of changes in programs, a complete self study/validation leading to reaccreditation every three years is appropriate.[50]

In an effort to give family day-care programs an opportunity to gain professional recognition, the National Association for Family Day-Care developed an accreditation program in 1988. Family day-care providers rate their programs using the *Assessment Profile for Family Day-Care* to measure 186 criteria, which fall into seven categories: indoor safety, health, nutrition, interaction, indoor play environment, outdoor play environment, and professional responsibility. *Parent Questionnaires*, *Parent Observation*, and *Validator Observation* are also used.[51]

The Child Welfare League of America provides accreditation to child welfare agencies such as Child Day-Care-Center Based, Child Day-Care-Family Based, and Child Protective Services through its Council of Accreditation of Services for Families and Children. The accreditation process begins with the completion of a checklist. If no major questions are raised, the agency may begin the accreditation process.[52]

Public schools are necessarily accredited by the state education agency. Because early childhood programs in public schools are considered part of the elementary school, these programs are accredited with the elementary schools in a local school district. In addition to the various state education agencies, early childhood programs that are part of elementary schools may be accredited by the Southern Association of Colleges and Schools. (Among the six regional accrediting associations, only the Southern Association of Colleges and Schools has an arrangement for accrediting elementary schools.)

Teacher preparation institutions may be accredited by the National Council for the Accreditation of Teacher Education (NCATE). As has been discussed, the *Guidelines* prepared by the National Association for the Education of Young Children are the standards for NCATE accreditation of early childhood programs (i.e., a four- or five-year teacher preparation curriculum for those who want to be teachers of children from birth through age eight). In 1985, the National Association for the Education of Young Children completed its *Guidelines* for early childhood education programs in associate degree granting institutions.

ESTABLISHING POLICIES

After local program planners have considered regulations and accreditation that affect their program, they should establish policies. **Policies** are judgments that express a program's intentions for achieving certain purposes (e.g., in-service education of staff, budgetary priorities, and program evaluation). Although practices exist in any early childhood program regardless of whether or not written policies exist, policies establish the bases for authoritative action. The phrase "rules, regulations, and procedures" describes a specific course of action based on policies.

Reasons for Policy Establishment

There are several reasons for establishing a policy. They are as follows:

1. In many states, the state licensing agency and the state board of education require that programs under their respective jurisdictions have written policies covering certain aspects of the local program; and these policies must be in keeping with the restrictions and authorizations of state law.
2. Policies provide guidelines for achieving the program's goals. Inadequate policies or their absence result in (a) hesitancy on the part of the director because he never knows whether his decisions will result in endorsement or admonishment; (b) running from emergency to emergency; and (c) inconsistency in making decisions.
3. If policies are constant and apply equally to all, they assure fair treatment. Policies thus protect the program, staff, children, and parents.
4. Policies provide a basis for evaluating existing plans and for determining the merit of proposed plans and are usually required by various funding agencies.
5. Policies may be requested by auditors.

Formulation of Policies

The board of directors is the policy-making and governing body of an early childhood program. Members of the board may change periodically as new members are elected or appointed. Regardless of the program's organizational pattern, the board of directors usually performs these functions under its bylaws:

1. Formulates major policies for achieving overall goals of the program. The board must develop or adopt the program's basic philosophy and provide an outline of services.
2. Adopts all proposed policies planned by the director. Usually the director formulates policies, but the board must adopt all policies prior to execution.
3. Supports the annual budget. Usually the director formulates the budget, and the board approves it before implementation. The board can also authorize expenditures exceeding the specified limits of the budget.
4. Approves all personnel hired. The director selects staff within the guidelines set by the board, and the board acts on the director's recommendations and issues the contracts.
5. Develops criteria for evaluating the program. The director is expected to inform the board of various assessment instruments. Once the assess-

ment instrument is selected by the board, the director implements the evaluation.

6. Participates in community relations. The board represents the program in the community.

The execution of policy is the responsibility of the program's director or local superintendent of schools in the public school system. The director is selected and hired by the board. The director, who has specialized knowledge in early childhood programs and administration, is charged with furnishing necessary information to the board, relating and interpreting information and policies back to the staff, and serving as the administrator of the staff. The board determines the degree of decision-making power delegated to the director and, in turn, the director can be empowered by the board to further delegate responsibility.

There is a great deal of interchange between the board and the director. For example, the director should inform the board of needs for additional policies or changes in existing policies, of inconsistencies in policies, and of the community's attitudes and values; the board should provide adequate written and verbal reasons for and explanations of policies to facilitate execution and should suggest methods of executing policy.

Characteristics of Viable Policies

Developing viable policies requires that boards examine their potential to achieve a program's goals, overcome the tradition of operating a program by expediency, understand the technique of policy making, and devote the time required for planning and evaluating policy. Some of the characteristics of viable policies are as follows:

1. Local program policies must conform to state law, to the policies of the funding agency, and the policies of any other regulatory agency. The autonomy of local programs in providing care for an education of young children (i.e., developing local policy) has given way, in varying degrees, to policy and regulations of federal and state agencies. Some of these regulations may provide a needed protective role, but they also place serious constraints on the local program. For example, assessing children's progress with a specified assessment device shapes the program accordingly, or limiting funds for staff and equipment makes it impossible to operate "the best" program. (Additional discussion of how programs are affected by the policies of funding agencies is included in Chapter 7; some of the ways in which early childhood leaders can affect public policy are discussed in Chapter 12.)

2. Policies should cover all aspects of the local program, or at minimum, those situations which occur frequently.

3. Internally consistent (noncontradictory) policies should be developed for the various aspects of the program. There is greater likelihood of

consistency among policies if the philosophy and goals have been previously determined.

4. Generally speaking, policies should be followed consistently. When exceptions are necessary, they should be stated or allowed for in the
policy. Many requests for exceptions often indicate a need for policy
changes.

5. Policies should not be highly specific, as they are guidelines for establishing administrative consideration and action. The administrator
should be allowed discretion in solving the day-to-day problems. Furthermore, if policies are specific, they must be changed frequently. The
"specifics" should be stated in the rules, regulations, and procedures
developed from the policies. For example, the fee policy should indicate
criteria for assessing fees, and the fee regulation should state the specific
amount charged.

6. Policies should be written and made readily available, so they can be
interpreted with consistency by those concerned. A written policy minimizes the probability of sudden changes. Because the board formulates
policy, it can make changes at its discretion; however, the board feels the
necessity for explanations more frequently when policies are written
than when they are not.

7. Policies should be relatively constant. Policy should not change with
changes in the membership of the board. As has been noted, the "specifics" (rules, regulations, and procedures) can change without resulting
in a change of policy.

8. Local program policies should be subject to review and change, as their
validity rests on current state laws and regulations of other agencies.
Because of the necessity of having adequate and current policies, a
procedure requiring periodic review of all policies may be written, or
certain policies may be written containing a stipulation that they be
reviewed by the board a year from the date they go into effect.

Policy Categories

As mentioned, policies should cover all aspects of the local early childhood
program. Because of variations in programs, the categories of policies and especially the specific areas included in each category differ from program to
program. Most early childhood programs have policies in these categories:

1. **Program service policy.** The primary program services to be provided
(e.g., care and education), along with other services (e.g., food, transportation, social services, and parent involvement).

2. **Administrative policy.** Some specific areas included are the makeup of
and procedures for selecting or electing members to the board of directors, advisory group, parent council, or other councils or committees,
the appointment and functions of the director and supervisory person-

nel; and the administrative operations, such as the "chain of command" and membership and functions of various administrative councils and committees.

3. **Staff-personnel policy.** Areas covered often involve qualifications; recruitment, selection, and appointment; job assignment; staff training/development; supervision (e.g., statement of purpose of supervision and use of data, steps in supervision sequence, copy of observation and/or rating forms, and guidelines for corrective actions); tenure; promotion; termination process (e.g., circumstances for, procedures, and documentation involving firings, along with fair hearings); salary schedules and fringe benefits; payroll dates; absences and leaves; personal and professional activities; and records policies.

4. **Child-personnel policy.** This category may comprise requirements for service eligibility including government and agency rules for the determination and documentation of family needs, maximum group (class) size, child-staff ratio, attendance, program services and provisions for child welfare (e.g., accidents and insurance), assessing and reporting children's progress, and termination of program services.

5. **Health policy.** This category may cover evaluation of children before admission, daily admission, care or exclusion of ill children, medication administration, management of injuries, health services (e.g., screening and immunizations), management of injuries and emergencies, nutrition, and food handling, provision for rest/sleep, health and safety education, staff training in health and safety, and surveillance of environmental problems.

6. **Business policy.** Some areas included are sources of funding, nature of the budget (e.g., preparation, adoption, and publication), procedures for obtaining funds (e.g., fees), guidelines and procedures for purchasing goods and services, persons responsible for financial management and fiscal record keeping, persons involved in disbursement of money, and a system of accounts and auditing procedures.

7. **Records policy.** Some areas included are the types of records to be kept, designation of "official" records versus "staff members" notes, place where records are kept, which official will be responsible for records, and basic procedures for handling provisions of P.L. 93–380, Family Educational Rights and Privacy Act of 1974.

8. **Parents policy.** This category may comprise ways of meeting parents' needs for participation and education, staff involvement with parents, and basic procedures for parents to follow in making contact with the director or staff for various purposes (e.g., children's admission or withdrawal, obtaining progress reports, participation in the program, parent education, and suggestions or complaints).

9. **Public relations policy.** This category relates to participation by the public (e.g., citizens' advisory committees and volunteers), use of program facilities, relations with various agencies and associations, and communication with the public.

SUMMARY

Regulations are the rules, directives, statutes, and standards that prescribe, direct, limit, and govern early childhood programs. The regulations, which are mandatory, come from government and funding agencies.

Regulations covering health and safety, fiscal matters, protection of children's rights, and staff govern all early childhood programs. Because early childhood programs differ in various ways (e.g., have different purposes; are private or public; are private not-for-profit or are private for-profit), different regulations apply. Private early childhood programs are seen as having a legal existence and are thus governed by each state's laws regarding proprietorships, partnerships, and corporations. Because these private programs are in a child-care business, they are also subject to minimum standards such as the state's licensing codes or registration requirements. On the other hand, public early childhood programs such as those operated as part of the public school system or the federally-supported Head Start programs receive their governance directly from the state or federal agency, respectively. Unlike mandatory regulations, accreditation is a non-mandatory form of self-regulation which simply means that programs which underwent self study/validation and received accreditation have achieved a high level of quality.

In addition to regulations and accreditation, local early childhood programs need to develop policies that are the guidelines for achieving local program goals effectively and efficiently. The board of directors (or board of education), with the help of the director or superintendent, is responsible for local policy formulation.

NOTES

1. B. Willer, "Quality or Affordability: Trade-Offs for Early Childhood Programs?" *Young Children* 42, 6 (1987): 41–43.
2. R. K. Kerckoff and J. McPhee, "Receptivity to Child Rights Legislation: A Survey," *Young Children* 39, 2 (1984): 58–61.
3. B. M. Caldwell, "Achieving Rights for Children," *Childhood Education* 66, 1 (1989): 6.
4. "NAEYC Position Statement on Nomenclature, Salaries, Benefits, and the Status of the Early Childhood Profession," *Young Children* 40, 1 (1984): 52–55.
5. M. C. Holmes, "The Kindergarten in American Pioneer Period," *Childhood Education* 13 (1937): 270.
6. "Marked Kindergarten Progress in the Northwest," *Childhood Education* 1 (1925): 303.
7. N. C. Vandewalker, "Facts of Interest about Kindergarten Laws," *Childhood Education* 1 (1925): 325.
8. A. Mitchell, *The Public School Early Childhood Study: The District Survey* (New York: Bank Street College Press, 1988).

9. J. McCarthy, *State Certification of Early Childhood Teachers: An Analysis of the Fifty States and the District of Columbia* (Washington, D.C.: National Association for the Education of Young Children, 1988).

10. Ibid.

11. E. C. Feistritzer, *Teacher Crisis: Myth or Reality?* (Washington, D.C.: National Center for Educational Information, 1986).

12. M. D. McKibben, "Alternative Teacher Certification Programs," *Educational Leadership* 46, 3 (1988): 32–35.

13. The two reports were: Carnegie Forum on Education and the Economy, *A Nation Prepared: Teachers for the 21st Century* (New York: Carnegie Forum, 1986); and, Holmes Group, *Tomorrow's Teachers: A Report of the Holmes Group* (East Lansing, Mich.: Michigan State University, 1986).

14. B. Spodek; M. D. Davis; and O. N. Saracho, *Early Childhood Teacher Education and Certification,* ERIC ED 227 946 (Champaign, Ill.: Author, 1982).

15. L. Shulman, "Those Who Understand: Knowledge Growth in Teaching," *Educational Researcher* 15, 2 (1986): 8–9.

16. J. McCarthy, "The Content of Early Childhood Teacher Education Programs," *Early Childhood Teacher Preparation,* ed. B. Spodek and O. N. Saracho (New York: Teachers College Press, Columbia University, 1990), 82–101.

17. N. Barbour, "Issues in the Preparation of Early Childhood Teachers," *Continuing Issues in Early Childhood Education,* (Columbus: Merrill, 1990), 153–171.

18. K. M. Zeichner and B. Tabachnick, "The Belief System of University Supervisors in an Elementary Student Teaching Program," *Journal of Education for Teaching* 8, 1 (1982): 34–54.

19. Spodek; Davis; Saracho, *Early Childhood Teacher Education and Certification.*

20. K. M. Zeichner, "Alternative Paradigms of Teacher Education," *Journal of Teacher Education* 43, 3 (1983): 3–9.

21. M. Maberman, "Research on Preservice Laboratory and Clinical Experiences: Implications for Teacher Education," *Education of Teachers: A Look Ahead* (New York: Longman, 1983), 98–118.

22. J. Henderson, "A Curriculum Response to the Knowledge Base Reform Movement," *Journal of Teacher Education* 39 (1988): 13–17.

23. McCarthy, *The Content of Early Childhood Teacher Education Programs.*

24. *Early Childhood Teacher Education Guidelines—Basic and Advanced: Position Statement of the National Association for the Education of Young Children* (Washington, D.C.: National Association for the Education of Young Children, 1991).

25. *Approved Teacher Training Programs* (NY: American Montessori Society, 1973).

26. J. B. Mancke, "Liability of School Districts for the Negligent Acts of their Employees," *Journal of Law and Education* 1 (1972): 109–27.

27. C. B. Salowitz, "Immunity of Teachers, School Administrators, School Board Members, and School Districts from Suit under Section 1983 of the Civil Rights Act," *University of Illinois Law Forum* (1976): 1129–56.

28. L. C. Scott, "Injury in the Classroom: Are Teachers Liable?" *Young Children* 38, 6 (1983): 10–18.

29. N. E. Class, *Basic Issues in Day Care Licensing* (Washington, D.C.: Department of Health, Education, and Welfare, Office of Education, 1972), 58.
30. Children's Bureau, Department of Health, Education, and Welfare, *Spotlight on Day-Care* (Washington, D.C.: Government Printing Office, 1966), 4–5.
31. Class, *Basic Issues*, 58–59.
32. N. E. Class, *Licensing of Child Care Facilities by State Welfare Departments* (Washington, D.C.: Department of Health, Education, and Welfare, Children's Bureau, 1968), 56–60.
33. Ibid., 9.
34. L. Johnson and Associates, *Comparative Licensing Study: Profiles of State Day Care Licensing Requirements* (Washington, D.C.: Department of Health and Human Services, Office of Program Development, 1982).
35. N. Zimlack, *Preventing Sexual Abuse in Day Care Programs: National Program Inspection*, ERIC ED 260 836 (Seattle: Department of Health and Human Services, Region 10, 1985).
36. Johnson and Associates, *Comparative Licensing Study*, 1982.
37. G. Morgan et al., "Gaps and Excesses in the Regulation of Child Day Care: Report of a Panel," *Reviews of Infectious Diseases* 8 (1986): 634–43.
38. G. Morgan et al., *Quality in Early Childhood Programs: Four Perspectives, High/Scope Early Childhood Policy Papers, no. 3*, ERIC ED 264 944 (Ypsilanti, Mich.: High/Scope, 1985).
39. Ibid.
40. "NAEYC Position Statement on Licensing and Other Forms of Regulation of Early Childhood Programs in Centers and Family Day Care Homes," *Young Children* 42, 5 (1987): 64–68.
41. S. L. Hofferth and D. A. Phillips, "Child Care in the United States, 1970 to 1995," *Journal of Marriage and the Family* 49 (1987): 559–571.
42. B. Caldwell, "Educare: A New Professional Identity," *Dimensions* 16, 4 (1990): 4.
43. Morgan et al., *Quality in Early Childhood Programs*.
44. D. A. Corsini; S. Wisensale; and G-A. Caruso, "Family Day Care: System Issues and Regulatory Models," *Young Children* 43, 6 (1988): 17–23.
45. *Pennsylvania Association for Retarded Children v. Commonwealth of Pennsylvania*, 344 F. Supp., 1275 (E. D. Pa. 1971).
46. *Mills v. Board of Education of D.C.*, 348 F. Supp., 866 (D.D.C. 1972).
47. For more information, write National Academy of Early Childhood Programs, NAEYC, 1834 Connecticut Ave., N.W., Washington, DC 20009.
48. S. Bredekamp, ed., *Accreditation Criteria and Procedures* (Washington, D.C.: National Association for the Education of Young Children, 1984).
49. S. Bredekamp and J. Berby, "Maintaining Quality: Accredited Programs One Year Later," *Young Children* 43, 1 (1987): 13–15.
50. M. Mulrooney, "Reaccreditation: A Snapshot of Growth and Change in High Quality Early Childhood Programs," *Young Children* 45, 2 (1990): 58–61.
51. For more information, write National Association for Family Day Care, 725 Fifteenth St., N.W., Suite 505, Washington, DC 20005 (202-347-3356).

52. For more information, write Director of Standards and Field Consultation Services, Child Welfare League of America, 440 First Street, N.W., Suite 310, Washington, DC 20001 (202-638-2952).

FOR FURTHER READING

Bredekamp, S. *Regulating Child Care Quality: Evidence From NAEYC's Accreditation System.* Washington, D.C.: National Association for the Education of Young Children, 1990.

Bredekamp, S., and Apple, P. "How Early Childhood Programs Get Accredited: An Analysis of Accreditation Decisions." *Young Children* 42, 1 (1986): 34–38.

Bryant, D; Clifford, R; and Peisner, E. *Best Practices for Beginners: Quality Programs for Kindergarteners.* Chapel Hill: Frank Porter Graham Child Development Center, 1989.

Council for Early Childhood Professional Recognition. *The Child Development Associate Credential.* Washington, D.C.: The Author, 1990.

Feeny, S., and Chun, R. "Research in Review: Effective Teachers of Young Children." *Young Children* 41, 1 (1985): 47–52.

Goodlad, J. I. "Better Teachers for Our Nation's Schools." *Phi Delta Kappan* 72, 3 (1990): 185–194.

Isenberg, J. P. "Teachers' Thinking and Beliefs and Classroom Practice." *Childhood Education* 66, 5 (1990): 322, 324–327.

Iverson, T. J., and Segal, M. *Child Abuse and Neglect: An Information Reference Guide.* New York: Garland, 1990.

Kuykendall, J. "Child Development: Directors Shouldn't Leave Home Without It." *Young Children* 45, 5 (1990): 47–50.

McCarthy, J. *Early Childhood Teacher Certification Requirements.* Washington, D.C.: National Association for the Education of Young Children, 1988.

Peters, D. L. "The Child Development Associate Credential and the Educationally Disenfranchised." In *Professionalism and the Early Childhood Practitioner,* edited by B. Spodek; O. N. Saracho; and D. L. Peters. New York: Teachers College Press, Teachers College, Columbia University, 1988.

Phillips, D., ed. *Quality Child Care: What Does Research Tell Us?* Washington, D.C.: National Association for the Education of Young Children, 1987.

Spodek, B., and Saracho, O. N., ed. *Yearbook in Early Childhood Education, Vol. 1, Early Childhood Teacher Preparation.* New York: Teachers College Press, Columbia University, 1990.

Vandell, D.; Henderson, V.; and Wilson, K. "A Longitudinal Study of Children with Day Care Experiences of Varying Quality." *Child Development* 59, 5 (1988): 1286–1292.

Weiner, R. *P.L. 94–142: Impact on the Schools.* Arlington, VA: Capital Pub., 1985.

Whitebook, M.; Howes, C.; Phillips, D. *Who Cares? Child Care Teachers and the Quality of Care in America.* Oakland: Child-Care Employee Project, 1989.

Part 2

Operationalizing the Early Childhood Program

Chapter 4
Leading and Managing Personnel

The quality of the staff determines, to a great degree, the excellence of an early childhood program. To most people, a job is more than a means of earning money, it is a work situation in which an individual feels secure and accomplished. To ensure job satisfaction for staff as well as program quality, three criteria must be met in staffing: (1) the personnel must meet at least minimal qualifications for their specific duties, although an employer hopes to select employees who seem to have the most potential; (2) those selected must be willing to work within the psycho-philosophical framework of the program; and (3) personnel must believe in the program's rationale in order to work together effectively and harmoniously.

TRENDS IN STAFFING

Advocacy efforts have resulted in an increased recognition of the importance of early childhood education. In addition to the acceptance of kindergartens and primary programs as an integral part of public education, there is a growing consensus that there should be enough high-quality infant/toddler and preschool programs to meet the developmental needs of these children as well as the child care and support needs of the family, all at a cost families and society can afford.

All of the characteristics of high-quality programs depend upon adequate numbers of well-trained staff members. Early childhood programs need increasingly larger staff for several reasons. First, more early childhood programs are becoming comprehensive in nature, which necessitates additional staff members to provide educational, nutritional, health, and social services to children and their families and to assess programmatic results. Second, an adequate staff-child ratio based on the ages and needs of children served and a small group size are major factors in program quality. Unfortunately, as a result of today's economic problems, there is a tendency toward fewer staff and larger groups. And third, as more children with disabilities are mainstreamed, support staff are needed for screening and identifying such children and helping to integrate them into regular classrooms.

The demographic data on early childhood program staff are not encouraging. However, more complete data are needed. Problems include: (1) an inaccurate count of the number of early childhood program personnel—especially those employed in private centers and family day-care homes; (2) job titles that no longer reflect the field; (3) inaccurate salary data due to the failure to classify twelve-month versus nine-month positions; (4) the need for job categories that reflect differences in education and experience; and (5) data on enrollment in training programs and final job choices for students.[1] Despite these inconsistencies, demographics do give a somewhat appropriate view of two trends in staffing.

Staff Shortage: A Professional Precipice

There is a staffing crisis. The greatest problem is not in public school early childhood programs. Rather, the problem is primarily in day-care programs and Head Start. However, public school programs cannot afford to stay unconcerned for these three reasons: (1) pre-kindergarten children are headed for the public schools; (2) there is a growing pressure for public schools to offer pre-kindergarten programs; and (3) there is a decreasing interest in education careers among college students at a time when half of our nation's teachers are approaching retirement age.[2]

The day-care and Head Start programs are facing a current staffing crisis which is now identified as "the most difficult problem" facing the nation's early childhood programs.[3] With a labor shortage, recruiting is a problem. Six out of ten early childhood day-care and Head Start employees are between the ages of eighteen and twenty-four years. (The number of people in this age range decreased by approximately five million between 1980 and 1990.)[4]

Retention of staff especially affects program quality. Staff are leaving day-care and Head Start programs at alarming rates, as shown in the following retention data (as measured by turnover, separation, and tenure).

1. The **turnover rate** (i.e., number of teachers who leave a program during the year) has been extremely high. Whitebook and Granger reported an annual turnover rate between 40 and 60 percent.[5] This rate was confirmed in the National Child Care Staffing Study which reported an annual turnover rate of 41 percent and noted a 37 percent turnover rate just six months after the initial study.[6]
2. The **separation rate** (i.e., the percentage of workers who leave an occupation during a year) is also high. The Bureau of Labor Statistics data show separation rates are 35.2 percent for the category "Child Care

Worker, Except Private Household."[7] This rate is lower than the turnover rate because it measures individuals who have changed job categories rather than those who have simply changed employers. Thus, separation rates are highly critical to the staffing crisis, for these rates represent a total loss of individuals to the profession.

3. The **tenure rate** (i.e., amount of time individuals are in a given position or in a given field) is not good. The Bureau of Labor Statistics data on tenure show 2.7 years for the job category "Child Care Worker, Except Private Household" versus 6.6 years for the average of all jobs.[8] Tenure rates may be improving, however. The National Child Care Staffing Study found that two-thirds of the staff members viewed child care as a career rather than a temporary job. This view showed in the tenure. Although 29 percent of the teachers and 58 percent of the assistants had been employed in early childhood programs for less than three years, 19 percent had been involved for ten years or more (as compared with the 5 percent involved ten years or longer in 1977).[9]

The staffing crisis is not due to job dissatisfaction. The National Child Care Staffing study found that teachers expressed very high levels of satisfaction with their work.[10] The most important predictor of staff turnover was wages. Almost three-quarters of those who left for better-paying jobs in early childhood or other fields left due to inadequate compensation.[11] Other causes of the staffing crisis include the lack of benefits (e.g., health, retirement), lack of a career ladder, and a low social status as well as the general labor shortage previously mentioned. (Needed benefits and career ladders will be discussed in later sections of this chapter; compensation will be discussed in Chapter 7; and the social status of the profession will be reviewed in Chapter 12.)

The staffing crisis is detrimental to all those involved. Children are affected by the change in rituals and by the loss of people associated with the rituals. These less-secure children spend less time involved with peers and more time in "aimless wandering" and show drops in cognitive activities.[12] It also takes time for parents to feel comfortable with new staff members. And, of course, staff members are affected, too. For example, directors try to teach and still handle administrative responsibilities. Some centers violate licensing regulations by using unqualified personnel. The National Child Care Staffing Study reported that 55 percent of the infant/toddler rooms and 57 percent of the preschool rooms had only one teacher available for the bulk of the day[13]—an impossible situation if young children's lives are to be enriched.

Vanishing Breeds: Men and Minorities

The presence of men is advocated more in theory than in practice.[14] During the 1940s and 1950s, men could not teach in early childhood programs because people believed that a man was out of his element in the kindergarten and the lower grades.[15] In the 1960s and 1970s, men were recruited for early childhood staff positions to ameliorate some effects of father absence in the home for both boys and girls and to prevent children from viewing the school as a feminine environment. There is little research to justify these expectations.[16] Then in the late 1970s and early 1980s, much research was conducted on the development of sex roles and androgyny (i.e., the blending of both conventional masculine and feminine traits into one personality). Men were encouraged to take positions in early childhood programs for the balance they would provide rather than for the more "macho" image. Research supports that men in early childhood programs do indeed downplay their conventional masculine behaviors and that there are no sex-specific differences in how men and women work with young children.[17] However important men may be to children's development, relatively few enter and stay in early childhood programs. This may be due to poor salaries and to a general prejudice against them by female administrators and teachers. Today only about 5 percent of early childhood personnel are men.[18]

Many professionals believe that the quality of programs can be improved when the staff reflects the cultural and racial diversity of the United States. This diversity provides opportunities for all children to see representatives of their own and other groups in various staff roles. Since the 1960s the number of minority staff members has waxed and waned. The National Child Care Staffing Study found that twice as many of the teaching staff were minorities in 1988 (32 percent) than in 1977 (15 percent).[19] However, the pool of minority teachers is growing smaller in relation to the population in public school programs. Minorities have grown to 30 percent of the child population and the percentage of teachers has shrunk to 5 percent.[20] Fewer minority students are entering teacher education programs due to failure on college qualifying examinations and on state teacher competency tests.[21]

STAFFING AN EARLY CHILDHOOD PROGRAM

After developing a psycho-philosophical framework and program rationale on paper, an administrator is faced with the task of determining the staff needed and of matching job requirements with staff members. This task is a continual one; staffing patterns change as a program expands or vacancies occur.

Roles and Qualifications of Personnel

Although all staff members must be in good physical and psychological health and have the personal qualities necessary to work with young children, an individual's needed qualifications depend upon his specific roles. And even roles with the same title may vary from program to program.

Personnel may be classified as either primary program personnel or support program personnel. *Primary program personnel* have direct, continuous contact with children; these include teachers, associate teachers, and assistant teachers. *Support program personnel* provide services that support or facilitate caregiving and instructional program; these include dietitians, medical staff, psychologists, caseworkers, and maintenance staff. Although a staff member is classified by her major role, she may occasionally function in another capacity. For example, a teacher may occasionally clean the room or serve food, or a dietitian might discuss good eating habits with children or console a child who drops a carton of milk.

Director

A **director** is someone who may or may not be in charge of the total program. Directors of early childhood education programs in public schools are often supervisors, helpers, or resource personnel. In Montessori programs, teachers are traditionally given the title of director or directress. The title of director is frequently given to the person legally responsible for the total program and services, be it the operation of a public or private day-care center, a private nursery school or kindergarten, a university or college laboratory nursery school or kindergarten, or a Head Start program.

Role. Directors may function as (1) a director-teacher who moves between two roles as needed, (2) someone whose functions resemble a building principal's in public school and who has immediate contact with and control over staff, or (3) someone whose functions are similar to business managers, who delegates authority to midlevel management. More specifically, the director's responsibilities may include: providing professional assistance to the board of directors or advisory board by supplying needed information, by recommending changes in policy, and by assisting in program evaluation; developing program philosophy and goals and providing leadership for program planning; planning school policies that concern children and parents; demonstrating awareness of current laws and regulations that affect children, families, and education, and insuring that regulatory standards are maintained; recruiting, employing, supervising, and training staff members; delegating responsibility to and terminating employment of staff members; supervising building maintenance and managing the program and auxiliary services; representing the institution in the community; establishing and maintaining school records; and preparing an annual budget for the board's consideration, keeping the board informed of financial needs, and operating within the budget.

Professional Qualifications. The professional qualifications of directors vary depending on the program's organizational pattern. As you read in Chapter 3, directors of private early childhood programs must meet their state's licensing requirements. Education requirements are established by public agencies for those programs they monitor, such as directors of Head Start programs. Public school directors (e.g., superintendents, assistant superintendents, and building principals) must hold the administrator's certificate of their state and meet any other qualifications as established by the state department of education, the local school board, or the accrediting agency to which the school belongs. Directors must also know how to conduct their specific early childhood program. This knowledge may include understanding and communicating the program's philosophy, along with implementing the program and the procedures supporting it (e.g., community contacts).

Personal Characteristics. Regardless of the program, personal characteristics of effective directors are similar. These characteristics include physical and mental stamina, openness to new ideas, flexibility of expression and thought, ability to learn from mistakes, cheerfulness, warmth and sensitivity to both children and adults, personal sense of security, desire to succeed, and honesty.

Primary Program Personnel

As discussed in Chapter 1, distinctions between *care* and *education* should not be made. Similarly, distinctions between *child-care workers* and *teachers* are no longer useful. In 1982, a Long Range Planning Task Force of the National Association for the Education of Young Children established an ad hoc committee to recommend appropriate job titles and descriptions. The following was approved by the Governing Board in 1984:

1. *Early childhood teacher assistant* is a preprofessional with no specialized early childhood preparation who implements program activities under direct supervision.
2. *Early childhood associate teacher* is a professional with minimal early childhood preparation (i.e., holds a CDA credential or an associate degree in early childhood education/child development) who independently implements activities and may be responsible for a group of children.
3. *Early childhood teacher* is a professional with an undergraduate degree in early childhood education/child development and is responsible for a group of children.[22]

Role. The role of professional teachers will vary depending on education and experience and on the type of program. It may include the following responsibilities: (1) serve in a leadership capacity with other staff members; (2) implement the program's psycho-philosophical base by observing and determining children's needs in relation to program goals and by planning activities; (3) communicate verbally and sympathetically with children; (4) respond effectively to children's behavior; and (5) model and articulate practices in keeping with the program's rationale to parents and other staff members. Teachers must also be acquainted with, accept, and use differences in children's cultures.

Professional Qualifications. Professional qualifications of early childhood teachers in various programs were discussed in Chapter 3. Responsibilities of teachers, teacher associates, and teacher assistants in early childhood day-care centers and Head Start programs are very similar, as suggested by the National

Association for the Education of Young Children's nomenclature statement. Although the formal education and the compensation may vary, the duties performed by each are essentially the same.[23] In public school programs inexperienced certified teachers and teachers on "emergency-type certificates" are immediately given total responsibility for a group of children.

According to many professionals, the lack of a career ladder, which allows individuals to move through stages to higher levels of professionalism, has a negative effect on staffing in early childhood programs.[24] The goal of the National Association for the Education of Young Children is to develop a model for early childhood professional development that would define professional categories and delineate the pre-service and in-service qualifications for each. Such a model could be used to establish career ladders and staffing patterns. Similarly, for certified public school early childhood teachers, an internship program in which individuals could gradually assume full responsibilities as well as teacher and master-teacher levels could be used to establish career ladders.

Spodek and Saracho have indicated some problems with the career ladder approach to enhancing staff qualifications. First, vocationally-oriented courses taken in community colleges often cannot be transferred to baccalaureate programs. Second, individuals who enter the field with the lowest levels of training are less likely to complete additional training as compared with individuals who entered the field with higher levels of training. This is the opposite of what would be required to establish a career ladder.[25]

Personal Characteristics. Personal characteristics associated with an effective teacher are difficult to define. Opinion varies as to what constitutes a good teacher of young children. In addition, teaching styles (i.e., personality traits, attitudes) are interwoven with teaching techniques (i.e., methodology).[26] Seifert and Lyons found elementary school principals were less concerned with specialized skills and training than with personal qualities.[27] Characteristics and skills often associated with effective early childhood teachers include warmth, flexibility, integrity, sense of humor, physical and mental stamina, vitality, emotional stability and confidence, naturalness, and the ability to support development without being overprotective.[28]

Rosen found that the content of what college students recalled about their relations with their parents can predict their ability to relate to children and effectiveness in working with children of different ages. For example, the most effective teachers of the youngest children described their own joy and sense of security during those years. Those judged most effective with the five- to eight-year-olds recalled their desire for independence and the early need to achieve basic skills. The college students judged most effective with older children remembered adults and older siblings who had stimulated a love of learning in them.[29] Another study suggests that the majority of college students entering early childhood education are people-oriented rather than idea-oriented.[30] In addition to the foregoing characteristics, teachers who work with infants should be able to develop very close bonds with infants, "read" behavioral cues (e.g., distinguish among cries) and make long-term commitments to programs so infants are provided with continuity. Because teaching is so complex and multifaceted, more research needs to be conducted on personal characteristics and effectiveness.

Support Program Personnel

The major role of support program personnel is to furnish services that support or facilitate the program. This group includes dietitians and food-service personnel, medical staff, psychologists, caseworkers, maintenance staff, general office staff, transportation staff, and volunteers. Support program personnel must have the qualifications of their respective professions. They must also be knowledgeable about age-level expectations of young children. Personal qualifications include the ability to communicate with children and to work with all adults involved in the program.

Dietitians and Food-Service Personnel. The dietitian is responsible for all food service, including recommending the quantity, quality, and variety of food to be purchased; directing work assignments and schedules of all dietary personnel; and providing inservice training to employees responsible for preparing and serving the food and for cleaning the food area. Other food service personnel carry out, under supervision, some of the dietitian's responsibilities. If a registered dietitian is not employed on a full-time basis, the program should seek such services from a consultant.

A registered dietitian must have undergraduate education in dietetics and clinical experience in the form of a dietetic internship.* Other food service personnel should have some training and experience.

Medical Staff. Most medical services are supplied on an "as needed" basis or through contractual arrangements. Preferably, physicians should be pediatricians and should have backgrounds in public health. The physician's duties may include acting as a consultant to the institution in formulating and carrying out its policies for health care and planning, and supervising the medical staff's services.

Depending on the number of children in a program, a nurse may be employed as a full- or part-time staff member. Duties of the nurse may include inspecting the children as they enter the program each day, referring children who need special medical attention, conferring with other staff members and parents about the children's health, administering medical care during the day, and keeping health records.

In addition to a physician and a nurse, a dentist should be retained. Services may include a dental inspection of children and conferences with other staff members and parents about the children's dental needs.

Psychologist. The services of a qualified child psychologist should be available. Most early childhood programs employ a psychologist who has specialized in

---

*More information can be obtained from The American Dietetic Association, 216 West Jackson, Suite 800, Chicago, Illinois 60606.

school, educational, or clinical psychology. A person with a doctoral degree in psychology is eligible for license after examination by a board of examiners of a state psychological association, and a person who has a master's degree in educational or school psychology may be certified by a state board of education in some states. Duties of the psychologist may include psychological evaluation of children and the promotion of guidance techniques.

Caseworkers. Some institutions hire persons trained in social work or use caseworkers from a local government agency. Their services include explaining to parents the problems children may face upon entering day-care programs; helping a mother with finding a job or assuming her role as a full- or part-time mother; explaining to the parents the agency's requirements for admitting a child to a program and the opportunities offered; introducing the mother to the day-care staff; and helping the family understand the child.

Maintenance Staff. Staff members must be employed for housekeeping and maintaining the building and grounds. At least one staff member should be on duty throughout the day for any work that must be done immediately. Major cleaning and maintenance are performed when the children are not present.

General Office Staff. Office staff members perform secretarial and clerical duties, including maintenance of records, correspondence, and bookkeeping. The size of the staff and the specific skills needed will vary according to the size of the program.

Transportation Staff. Programs offering transportation services must employ persons in this area. A transportation staff may include drivers and mechanics.

Volunteers. Besides serving as program personnel, volunteers provide support services such as securing equipment, interpreting the program to the community, working with the office staff, and providing transportation services. Volunteers may be needed on either a regular or an irregular basis.

Substitute Personnel
Substitute personnel should have the same professional qualifications and personal characteristics as the regularly employed personnel whom they replace. In order to ensure program continuity, careful plans should be made. Such plans are most essential where substitute personnel will be working alone (e.g., in a self-contained classroom) rather than in a team approach. Because substitute teachers are the most often-hired substitute personnel, the following is a discussion of how plans for these teachers can be made. However, planning for any substitute would use the same methods.

Substitute teachers should have the same professional qualifications and personal characteristics as regular teachers. However, regular teachers or directors should make plans for substitute teachers to ensure program continuity. Such plans are most essential in a self-contained situation and in programs where special-subject teachers are hired. They are not as necessary in programs using a team teaching approach or paraprofessional assistance.

Directors of early childhood programs must develop a list of potential substitute teachers who meet the same qualifications as the teachers for whom they will be working. Each program must establish a procedure for obtaining substitute personnel; usually, the absent teacher contacts the director who, in turn, secures the substitute.

The teacher has an important responsibility in planning for substitute personnel. Because there are few advance warnings of impending illness or emergency, plans must be made soon after the teacher begins employment; the plans must be kept current. Some suggestions for planning for substitute personnel are:

1. As soon as the children are secure in the early childhood program, prepare them for the possibility of a substitute. Young children are often frightened of a substitute teacher unless they are prepared in advance. One way to do this is have prospective substitutes visit (or even employ them for work) before they are needed. The visitation can also serve as an orientation of the prospective substitute to the program or as a check to determine whether this person seems to fit into the program.

2. In as much detail as possible, have the procedures for the following in writing: for greeting the children, such as where to meet them and the greeting ritual; for meals, snacks, and toileting; for types of activities planned in each major block of time on the schedule; for moving the children from one activity to another within the room, such as a verbal, light-blinking, or musical signal; for moving children outdoors and to other parts of the building; for emergencies, such as evacuation of the building and illness of the child; for conducting the administrative functions, such as attendance or meal counts or sending notes home to parents; and for departure of the children, such as the method of getting home and to the exit door.

3. Write plans for a minimum of two or three days. Plans should be ideas appropriate any time of the year and should not burden substitute personnel by requiring extremely careful supervision or extensive preparation or cleanup time.

4. Provide a shelf or cabinet for the specific equipment and materials needed for the plans, such as a storybook and record for rhythmic activities. Large pieces of equipment like record players and playground balls may be left in their usual places. Because substitute personnel do not know the children's names, name tags should be placed with the equipment and materials.

5. Keep an up-to-date list of the children and note those with special problems—physical, intellectual, or emotional—and procedures to follow with these problems.

6. Keep a note taped to your desk or in some other obvious place telling where to find the information and materials for substitute personnel.

7. Leave on the desk the schedule of semiregular activities such as library time, special duty, or times for special-subject teachers or other personnel to work with children.
8. If the substitute did a good job, call and express appreciation. The substitute should relate any special problems that occurred. Inform the director or building principal of the quality of the substitute's work so a decision can be made about rehiring the substitute.

Assessing Needs and Recruiting Staff Members

The director must first assess the staff needs and desires for particular services. Since the budget is usually limited, the director must also determine priorities. Other considerations may include the potential staff available, the amount of space needed for staff offices and other facilities, and the amount of training and supervision to be conducted. The necessary positions must then be translated into job descriptions (discussed earlier in this chapter).

The director or personnel administrator is responsible for advertising the positions. Programs must follow affirmative action guidelines in recruiting and hiring. *Affirmative action* entails identifying and changing discriminatory employment practices and taking positive steps to recruit and provide an accepting working environment for minorities and women. There are manuals available on affirmative action programs.[31] Some possible steps in recruiting staff members are developing/gathering recruitment materials, advertising, having applicants complete job application forms, obtaining documentation of credentials, interviewing, and hiring for a probationary period.

Developing/Gathering Recruitment Materials

Recruitment materials must include job descriptions that list duties, responsibilities, and authority and give qualifications and skills required. Public relations brochures and policy manuals are also good recruitment materials.

Advertising

The director should first notify persons already involved in the program of an opening and then make the advertisement public. The advertisement should be in keeping with the job description and state all nonnegotiable items, such as required education and experience, so unqualified applicants can be quickly eliminated. It should also include the method of applying and deadline for application. Figure 4–1 is an example of a newspaper advertisement.

The method of applying and the acceptance of applications will depend on the abilities and experiences of applicants and the director's time. Thus, the method of application may vary from a telephone call or completion of a simple to a lengthy application form, a résumé, and a letter requesting transcripts and credentials. A simple application form is given on pages 118–119 as an example.

After the deadline for application, the director or other staff member in charge of hiring will screen applications to eliminate unqualified applicants. The

Early childhood teachers wanted for a college-sponsored child development center. Responsibilties include planning and implementing developmentally appropriate activities for a group of twelve three-year-old children. A.A. degree in Child Development/Early Childhood Education or a C.D.A. certificate required; teaching experience preferred. Write for an application to Mrs. Jones, Director, Johnson County Community College Child Development Center, 123 Alexander Rd. 43147 or call (614) 555-4689 Monday through Thursday from 2:00 to 4:00 p.m. Deadline for applications, August 1. We are an Equal Opportunity Employer.

FIGURE 4–1

administrator is required by affirmative action guidelines to list reasons for rejection and to notify applicants.

Obtaining Documentation of Credentials and Interviewing
The director can legally contact all references given on the application and all former employers concerning work history and character. These references are aids in seeing how the applicant performed in the eyes of others. A sample application letter and accompanying reference form are shown in Figures 4–2 (pages 118–119) and 4–3 (page 120).

A second type of documentation needed is a criminal history records check. Since 1985, many states have passed laws requiring national criminal records checks for day-care center employees. These laws were implemented to comply with federal legislation.[32] There is still much confusion as to whether some of the laws are in contradiction to equal employment opportunity laws. However, criminal history records checks are the only way to defend against a claim of negligent hire (i.e., employer is held responsible for injuries to a third party if the injury was foreseeable or if the employer did not investigate before hiring).

Following the screening of applications, reference checks, and criminal history records checks, all promising applicants should be interviewed. These steps should be followed in the interview process:

1. The director must follow established board policies concerning the nature, setting, and person conducting the interview, along with determining who will make the final decision regarding selection of the candidate.
2. Directors must be careful to follow Title VII of the 1964 Civil Rights Act prohibiting discriminatory hiring practices. The rule of thumb is that there must be a "business necessity" for any question asked of the applicant. Some questions to avoid are date of birth or age, marital status, spouse's occupation, pregnancy issues and number of children, child-care arrangements, religious affiliation (although inquiry may be made as to whether the scheduled work days are suitable), membership in organization (except those pertaining to the position), race or national origin (except for affirmative action information), arrest record, type of discharge from military, union memberships, and disabilities (only ask if person can perform job specific functions).[33] Inquiring about citizenship is not considered discriminatory; the administrator may ask to see a 1–151 Alien Registration Card or a 1–94 Arrival-Departure Card.
3. The interview should reveal the applicant's philosophy and attitudes toward children. Leak has developed an interesting approach to assessing applicants during a personal interview.[34]
4. The interviewer should also discuss and answer questions about the program and its philosophy, the ages of enrolled children, the guidance and discipline practices, how children are evaluated, the degree of parent involvement, salary, length of day and school year, complete description of job, opportunities for promotion, fringe benefits, sick leave and retirement plans, consulting and supervisory services, and the nature and use of evaluation to determine job performance and advancement. (For future reference, a staff handbook containing such information should be made available to those hired.)

Hiring

The applicants are informed about the selection at a given date and in a specified manner. The person who is hired must usually sign a contract and other required personnel papers. If no applicant is hired, the recruitment process is repeated.

Many programs give the "hired" applicant a trial work period in which the director or hiring committee tries to see how compatible the person is with program practices. The conditions of the probationary period must be clearly communicated to the new employee before hiring. The trial period should last six months or less, and pay should be slightly less than full salary.

WORKING WITH STAFF MEMBERS

The function of administration is to mobilize and coordinate ideas, resources (i.e., material things), and people to achieve the program's goals with effective-

Application For Teacher Position

JOHNSON COUNTY COMMUNITY COLLEGE CHILD DEVELOPMENT CENTER

Name of Applicant _____

Address _____
           Last   First   Middle or Maiden

Telephone Number ( ) _____ Zip _____

RECORD OF EDUCATION

High School(s) Attended

Name of School	School Address	Years Attended	Years Completed (check)
1. _____	_____	From _____ to _____	Fr. ____ Soph. ____ Jr. ____ Sr. ____ Graduated ____
2. _____	_____	From _____ to _____	Fr. ____ Soph. ____ Jr. ____ Sr. ____ Graduated ____

Colleges Attended

Name of College	Address	Years Attended	Level Completed
1. _____	_____	From _____ to _____	No Degree: _____ Degree received: _____ Major: _____
2. _____	_____	From _____ to _____	No Degree: _____ Degree received: _____ Major: _____

Teaching certificates: _____

_____
(Name of certificate)

RECORD OF WORK EXPERIENCE

Name and Address of Employer	Date of Employment	Nature of Work (Describe)
1. _____	From ____ to ____	_____
2. _____	From ____ to ____	_____
3. _____	From ____ to ____	_____

List names and address of three references who are familiar with your educational progress and/or work experiences.

1. _____
2. _____
3. _____

I understand that my signature on this application legally permits authorized administrators of the Johnson County Community College Child Development Center to contact all former employers concerning my work history and character as it pertains to the position for which I have applied.

_____   _____
(Signature)   (Date)

FIGURE 4–2
Application for Teacher Position

119

Johnson County Community College Child Development Center

TO:

FROM:

RE: _____

     (Name of Applicant)

The applicant has given your name as a person who can provide a reference on his or her qualifications. We want to select teachers whose professional preparation, experience, and personality can be expected to produce the best results at our Child Development Center. Please give your full and frank evaluation. Your reply will be kept in strict confidence. Please assist both us and the applicant by replying promptly.

Teaching Position Reference

How would you describe the applicant's ability in each of the following areas?

1. Knowledge of young children's development:
2. Ability to plan developmentally appropriate activities to enrich and extend children's development:
3. Ability to implement planned activities to enrich and extend children's development:
4. Ability to use positive guidance including disciplining techniques with children:
5. Ability to evaluate children's progress:
6. Ability to organize a physical setting:
7. Ability to work with parents:
8. Ability to work with other staff members as a team:
9. Capacity for professional and personal growth:

Based on your present knowledge, would you employ this applicant in a program for which you were responsible?
Please explain:
What opportunity have you had to form your judgment of this applicant?
Additional Remarks:

_____   _____   _____
        (Date)   (Signature)   (Title)

FIGURE 4–3
Sample Application and Reference Form

ness and efficiency. Working with staff members requires both leadership and management skills. *Leadership* involves making decisions that mold future goals of the program. All programs must function smoothly on a day-to-day basis. *Management* involves providing continuity for program functioning.

Educational administration has begun taking advantage of some of the theories, models, and tools of leadership and management from the business world. Educational administration is moving away from forms of organization referred to as *mechanistic organizations* (i.e., organizations that stress differentiation between line and staff personnel with precise specifications of the jurisdictions of each) to more *organic organizations* (i.e., organizations with more leadership and management by consensus).[35] In order to achieve a truly functioning organic organization, educational administrators have begun to make use of *management science* (also called *operations research* and *systems management*) in which organizational and administrative problems are dealt with in a scientific manner (i.e., formulating hypotheses, collecting data, and interpreting results). Other concepts from the business world are also utilized.

In working with staff members, several principles are appropriate. These principles include: (1) keeping the program's philosophy in the forefront; (2) making decisions through a team approach; (3) stating plans in terms of objectives; and (4) developing a plan for action.

Keep the Program's Base in the Forefront

In Peters and Waterman's research, three of the eight attributes characterizing excellent, innovative companies dealt with the organization's program base.[36] For example, they referred to one attribute as companies that *stick to knitting*, that is, companies do best when they stay close to the business they know. As stated earlier in this book, careful selection of an early childhood education psycho-philosophical base is important and, once it is chosen, all components of the program must fit the base. Another quality attribute was that a company had *tight properties*. This type of company has core values that administrators use for all decision making and for evaluation criteria. These values are the focal point for operations; thus, the company is *value driven*. Early childhood programs would do well to look at the research of major quality indicators such as that of Fiene. Fiene, in examining compliance on licensing standards, found that quality early childhood programs had a high level of compliance on certain major standards but did not necessarily show compliance on less important standards.[37]

Make Decisions through a Team Approach

Data from a San Francisco study of early childhood programs revealed that only 18 percent of the teaching staff were included in major decision making. Most staff members found themselves in a hierarchial decision-making structure, and over half said they were dissatisfied with the arrangement.[38] On the other hand, Peters and Waterman allude to group decision making in terms of these quality attributes: staying "close to the customer" (i.e., listening to one's clients), fostering "autonomy and entrepreneurship" (i.e., fostering leaders and innovators throughout the organization), believing in "productivity through people" (i.e., thinking of the rank and file as the root source of quality and productivity gain), and having "loose properties" (i.e., becoming decentralized by pushing autonomy down to nonadministrators).[39] The effectiveness of group decision making is seen in Japanese management systems using "quality control circles" to identify, analyze, and solve companies' problems.

In an early childhood program, staff members working together can generate novel ideas, innovative proposals, and new strategies. Many of these ideas may come during informal exchanges. However, there may be gaps in the sharing of ideas unless a more formal method of communication is established. Staff meetings are thus essential for planning. Effective staff meetings must be carefully planned and executed, and the following tips kept in mind:

1. Have a purpose for calling a staff meeting. Don't call meetings unless there is a need for discussion. Routine announcements may be made in other ways.
2. If decisions to be made pertain only to a few staff members, do not call a general staff meeting.
3. Schedule meetings at times suitable to the staff. Generally, a regular time should be set aside during work hours.
4. Prepare and distribute an agenda a few days before the scheduled meeting. Certain materials to be discussed should be available prior to the meeting. The agenda should indicate the name of the person presenting an item and the amount of time allocated for the presentation. Additional time for discussion and voting should be included.
5. Stay within time limits. (Agenda items may be omitted or added and time allocations changed with group consensus.)
6. Listen to each staff member's ideas during a discussion.
7. Start and stop the meeting on time.
8. Distribute minutes of the meeting to staff members. Minutes should be read and approved before sending them to the board of directors and/or filing them.

State Plans in Terms of Objectives

Once plans are made, they need to be stated in terms of objectives. From management science comes a strategy called *Management by Objective and Results (MBO/R)* based on the assumption that people perform better and are more productive if they know what is expected and if the expectations are considered to be realistic and achievable. MBO/R begins with defining the program's goals, then establishing objectives in keeping with the goals, identifying performance indicators, and setting standards for individuals. Thus, MBO/R places emphasis upon a sense of achievement based on knowing one's contribution to an organization.

Develop a Plan of Action

Much time and effort are lost without a plan of action. Peters and Waterman refer to an important attribute of successful companies as a "bias for action."[40] Two tools coming from management science for developing a plan of action are: (1) **Gantt Milestone Charts,** which show significant events and measure the estimated time required to complete each activity, and (2) **PERT,** the acronym for Program Evaluation and Review Technique, which shows the breakdown of a complex project into simple components, a flow plan for the work to be accomplished, the *network* or the sequence from one stage to the next, the established times for each step, and the means for monitoring the schedule. The PERT approach is more elaborate than the Gantt for planning, because it shows the sequence for completing and relationships among events.

IMPROVING QUALITY OF PERSONNEL

Analyses of a program's strengths and weaknesses provide a basis for improving the quality of personnel. All personnel need to refresh present skills and learn new ones. Because early childhood programs and personnel differ in many ways, methods of improvement also differ. Six methods for improving the quality of personnel are formal education, staff development, membership in professional organizations, supervision, alleviation of job stress, and performance evaluation for improvement.

Formal Education

The founder and early leaders of the kindergarten movement required a course of study for prospective teachers. As kindergartens and other early childhood programs became part of the public schools, teachers were required to obtain teaching certificates (discussed in Chapter 3). Local boards of education also required refresher courses or work toward an advanced degree for renewal of a contract and/or pay raises. Katz indicates that teachers in the stages of renewal and maturity (after three to five years of experience) are in need of college work.[41]

Teachers working in programs that must meet state licensing requirements (such as day-care centers) and public programs (such as Head Start) are taking college courses and seeking degrees. The National Child Care Staffing Study found that while less than half of the women in the civilian labor force have attended college, more than half of the assistant teachers and almost three-quarters of the teachers in the study had some college. However, fewer of the teaching staff had received a college degree in 1988 than in 1977. The National Child Care Staffing Study also found that formal education, not experience, was the strongest predictor of appropriate behavior (i.e., behavior defined as "sensitive," "less harsh," and "less detached"). Specialized training emerged as an additional predictor in infant classrooms.[42]

Staff Development

Another method for improving the quality of personnel is staff development. Concern over the facts that adults in day-care and Head Start programs often begin working before receiving adequate training and that staff in all settings often work in isolation without the benefits of sharing ideas and problems with others has led to the awareness that staff development programs are essential.[43,44]

The value of staff development appears to be obvious. As previously discussed, the National Child Care Staffing Study found that education, not experience, was the predictor of appropriate teacher behavior. However, research findings on the effects of training on program quality are inconsistent. Unlike the National Day-Care Study, the National Child Care Staffing Study found that the greater the amount of formal education, the more appropriate the teaching behavior.[45, 46] Furthermore, Clarke-Stewart and Gruber found that teachers with specialized training in early childhood education focused on cognitive development to the detriment of children's total development.[47] Similarly, Logue, Krause-Eheart, and Miles found that teachers with specialized knowledge showed more interest in directing structured lessons and less positive affect with children.[48]

Content of Staff Development

To be effective, staff development activities must meet the individual needs of staff members and the collective needs of the staff for improving the quality of the program.

Individual Needs. In thinking about individual needs of staff members and the type of support each needs, two excellent resources are available. First, Katz has identified four stages of development and the training needs of in-service teachers at each stage. The stages are:

1. Survival. The first year of teaching is filled with self-doubt. Teachers need on-site support and technical assistance.
2. Consolidation. During the second and perhaps third year, teachers consolidate the gains they have made and focus on specific skills. They need on-site assistance, access to specialists, and advice from colleagues.
3. Renewal. During the third and fourth year, job stress is eliminated by assistance in analysis of teaching and by participation in professional associations.
4. Maturity. After the fifth year, teachers benefit more by additional formal education, by professional conferences, and through contributions to the profession (e.g., journal writing).[49]

Instead of using experience stages, Arin-Krump has identified staff needs and training needs for seven age-stages. She has based her ideas on the work of Erik Erikson, Robert Havighurst, Roger Gould, and Gail Sheehy. For example, Arin-Krump states that teachers in their twenties are in the stages of identity and intimacy. Marriage and parents are key concerns, and family life creates much stress. At this age, teachers also want to demonstrate job competence. Thus, staff development for this age group is most successful if it (1) creates a climate that permits discussion of life stresses and (2) defines the parameters of the job and discusses means for effecting change in areas of deficit.[50]

Collective Needs. Orientation to a specific program is needed by all staff members. Orientation should always cover the program base. Staff members cannot work as a team if they do not understand and accept the rationale of the program base and the objectives stemming from the rationale. Other items that orientation should cover include the clientele served, the services of the program, the physical facility, and regulations and local program policies.

Development should continue throughout a staff member's tenure. To be effective, it must be seen as an active process of growing and learning and not a product (e.g., a workshop presented by someone else). In order for staff development to be effective, group needs must be identified. Abbott-Shim has recommended the use of data from individual evaluations, needs assessment surveys, and program evaluations.[51] Data can be collected in the following ways:

1. *Staff evaluations* show the strengths and weaknesses of individual staff members. A summary of strengths and weaknesses of staff members can be used to determine potential training areas.
2. *Needs assessment surveys* are surveys in which staff members check topics of perceived needs. The administrator summarizes the responses and identifies training needs. A simple needs assessment survey is given in Figure 4–4 (pages 126–127).
3. *Program evaluation measures* provide comprehensive evaluation. Several program evaluation measures were described in Chapter 2. Benham, Miller, and Kontos developed a way of identifying training needs using the **Early Childhood Environment Rating Scale (ECERS).** Quantitative data can be obtained using subarea profiles of the ECERS.[52]

Finally, research on other centers can be used for identifying training needs if one feels that the research pinpoints needs that are representative of needs in the local program. For example, Benham, Miller, and Kontos in their study of twenty-one centers, noted these four weak areas: (1) providing for privacy, comfort, and relaxation for children and adults in the physical facility; (2) developing a sensitivity to, and planning for, individual differences, differences in needs for group participation and quiet times, and needs of exceptional children; (3) promoting children's experimentation with, and exploration of, materials; and (4) translating developmental knowledge into goals/objectives and translating objectives into activities.[53]

Techniques Used for Staff Development
Techniques used in staff development should fit staff members' abilities, skills, and interests as well as possessing appropriate training content. The method of presentation should be varied to hold interest. And, most importantly, staff members must be involved and able to see direct application to their professional responsibilities.

Needs Assessment Survey
of
Johnson County Community College
Child Development Center

We need some information regarding your specific needs for training. After reading the entire list below, check six topics (from the forty-eight listed) that you would like to have covered in in-service training. After checking, rank the topics in order of importance with "1" being the most important to you.

Child care

_____ Regulations/Legal Issues

_____ Evaluation of Children

_____ Mainstreaming Exceptional Children

_____ Health and Safety

Child Development

_____ Physical Development (general)

_____ Social Development

_____ Cognitive Development

_____ Emotional Development

_____ Morals/Values Development

_____ Language Development

_____ Motor Skill Development

Curriculum (Preschool through Primary)

_____ Art

_____ Oral Language

_____ Writing

_____ Literature

_____ Pre-Reading Skills

_____ Mathematics

_____ Social Studies

_____ Science

_____ Music

_____ Gross Motor Play

_____ Fine Motor Play

_____ Incorporating Computers

_____ Incorporating Multicultural/Multilingual Learnings

_____ Cooking Experiences

_____ Sand/Water/Mud Play

_____ Woodworking Experiences

_____ Block Building Experiences

_____ Dramatic Play Experiences

FIGURE 4–4

Needs Assessment Survey

Organization and Management
_____ Arranging Physical Environments
_____ Use of Indoor Equipment/Materials
_____ Use of Outdoor Equipment/Materials
_____ Scheduling Problems
_____ Transitions
_____ Grouping
_____ Encouraging Effective Child-Child Interactions
_____ Encouraging Effective Child-Adult Interactions
_____ Encouraging Effective Child-Material Interactions
_____ Guiding Children's Behavior (Discipline)

Staff Needs
_____ Credentials/Training Requirements
_____ Communication Skills
_____ Team Teaching
_____ Evaluation
_____ Policy Development

Families
_____ Parent Education
_____ Parent Involvement
_____ Parent Support
_____ Meetings Needs of Special Families (e.g., single parents)

FIGURE 4–4   *(con't.)*

Many techniques for staff development are used. Some examples include:

1. *Teaching observations.* Modeling can be helpful if the person learning is free to observe and if the trainer sees himself in a teaching role (e.g., giving background information concerning classroom practices) and follows up with discussions of the practices observed.
2. *Discussions.* Staff can learn through discussing and solving problems. The trainer's role is to describe how principles of child development relate to the problem under discussion.
3. *Child observations.* Observing children and discussing observations with the trainer can provide insight into age-appropriate behaviors of children and/or specific behaviors (e.g., temper tantrums, altruistic behaviors).
4. *Individual conferences.* The director provides feedback to the staff member following an observation and discusses ways in which the staff member may grow and the director can be supportive.

5. ***Workshops.*** Workshops may be provided through outside sources (e.g., professional organizations) or developed by the staff members themselves. Workshops often center on one topic.
6. ***Consultation.*** Consultants must be viewed as resource people and not as "experts" hired to solve problems if consultation is to yield lasting results.[54] There are at least three consultation models. In the ***traditional model,*** the consultant is helped to understand the nature and cause of the problem and finds possible solutions.[55] The second model is called the ***enabler approach.*** The consultant is referred to as an "enabler" who comes to know the program and people and helps staff find their own solutions.[56] And, in the ***Yale Psycho-Educational Clinic Approach,*** the consultant goes beyond the problem presented by applying knowledge, skills, and/or resources not available to the program in an effort to improve the total program.[57]
7. ***Professional resources.*** All programs can benefit from professional journals, books, and audiovisual materials. These materials lend themselves to both group and individual development.

If consultant work is to be secured, the administrator must identify potential resource people, identify and describe (in writing) training needs, and provide a format to be completed by potential resource people. Figure 4–5 is an example of a format.

An evaluation of both proposed presentations and the selected presentation is essential. Figure 4–6 is an example of a format.

Workshop Proposal

The following information must be submitted for consideration as a resource person for the Johnson County Community College Child Development Center.

Name, address, day and evening phone numbers of individual submitting request.

Main presenter resume (title, academic and professional background).

Names and addresses and resumes of other presenters.

Objectives of presentation.

Outline of presentation.
Concept:
Delivery Stategy:
Time Required:

Method to be used to evaluate workshop effectiveness.

Resource materials provided by consultant.

Special requests (e.g., observation in center before presentation or audio-visual equipment).

FIGURE 4–5

Evaluation of _____

Johnson County Community College Child Development Center

Rank each item on a three-point scale: 1 (excellent), 2 (satisfactory), and 3 (poor).

	Proposal	*Presentation*
Objectives related to training needs	_____	_____
Content related to training needs	_____	_____
Content applicable to work with children	_____	_____
Content organized	_____	_____
Content clearly presented	_____	_____
Delivery strategies held interests of participants	_____	_____
Delivery strategies encouraged give and take among staff members and between staff and resource person(s)	_____	_____
Evaluation seemed effective	_____	_____
Resource materials seemed practical	_____	_____

Comments: _____

_____

_____

_____

FIGURE 4–6

Membership in Professional Organizations

Membership in professional organizations offers various opportunities for personnel to improve their qualifications. Unfortunately, the National Child Care Staffing Study found only 14 percent of the teaching staff belonged to a child-related professional group, and the ones who belonged to the professional organizations were the most educated.[58]

Professional organizations publish literature such as journals, position papers, and other materials aiding members in professional growth and competence. Almost all professional organizations have regular national, regional, and state meetings that provide a means for hearing and seeing the "latest" and for sharing ideas with others. Professional organizations serve as public representation—advocacy—of members' views to local, state, and national governing bodies. Some organizations offer opportunities for travel and study, research assistance, and consultation. Others provide personal services to members, such as insurance policies and loans. Finally, membership in a professional association says to parents and the community in general, "I am joining with others in an effort to provide the best for our children." See Appendices 4 and 5 for listings of many professional organizations concerned with the development of young children.

Supervision

Supervision is generally viewed as a component of administration and, thus, is executed by administrators. Because supervisors have been called upon to do many jobs—provide leadership in program planning and implementation; work with teachers, including beginning and student teachers; and evaluate teachers—supervision has been defined in various ways, such as program leadership and personnel development. Just as supervisors' job descriptions vary, titles also vary. The supervisor may be called a director, a principal, or a program or curriculum consultant.

Educational supervision was traditionally seen as an adjunct of administration, the primary purpose of which was the inspection of the schools. Improvement of instruction was recognized as an additional objective of supervision in the 1920s. In a differing theory under the democratic supervision of the Progressive Movement, supervisors and teachers were viewed as equal partners in policy formulation.

Supervision is in an embryonic stage of development; it has only recently become a discipline in its own right. Because of the recentness of supervision as a distinct field, many myths about supervision abound. Caruso and Fawcett[59] give examples of these myths such as "almost anyone can be an early childhood supervisor," "there is one best supervisory approach to use with everyone," "supervisors have all the answers," and "good teachers do not need supervision."

Functions of Supervision

In just over half a century, supervision of education has progressed from an inspection role to a highly sophisticated leadership role. There are ambiguities and voids in our knowledge of supervisory functions; such functions are not restrictive in nature. Because supervisors are educational leaders, their leadership role may be exercised in many ways and with many people, such as officials of state and federal regulatory and funding agencies, board members of the local program, the director, specialists involved in the program, support personnel and other supervisors. Keeping in mind the dynamic role of supervision, present literature suggests that supervision is composed of three functions: (1) improving the quality of instruction; (2) mutual growth of supervisor and teacher; and (3) evaluation.

Improving the Quality of Instruction. Improving the quality of instruction is the most important function of supervision, because the only purpose of any program is to help the children and their parents. The quality of any program is determined by content and staff. Supervision should become the pivotal activity around which to manage program and staff development. Program development requires specific training or retraining of staff members because new knowledge, methodological techniques, and even attitudes are required for implementation and maintenance of program changes. Staff development itself can cause changes in the program, too. Thus, supervisors must be involved in program and staff development in order to change the quality of instruction for the better.

1. *Program development.* The close relationship between supervision and program development is implied in the title of one of the major professional organizations for supervisors, the Association of Supervision and Curriculum Development. Supervisors are needed to help establish the direction of an early childhood program. The last two decades have seen a proliferation of new curricular ideas and model programs. Supervisors may keep abreast of new ideas, try some of these ideas as pilot projects with a few teachers or in demonstration centers, and serve on committees that choose from among alternatives that seem best for the local program. After program decisions are made, supervisors must provide professional assistance while the staff develops knowledge and skills for implementing the new program. More importantly, supervisors must help the staff develop a commitment to a particular action. (An example of the assistance needed in mainstreaming was given earlier in this chapter.)

2. *Staff development.* Programs are not "teacher proof." When new programs are developed, all staff members must have assistance and support in the implementation process. Continuous supervisory assistance is needed even when new program development is not being undertaken (e.g., note the assistance described by Katz in the four states of preschool teachers as previously described in this chapter).

Mutual Growth of Supervisor and Teacher. Developing programs and working out implemental problems should be an experimental process for both supervisor and teacher. This process will result in improving not only the quality of instruction, but also the supervisor's and teacher's mutual growth. Supervisors are not all-knowing authorities, nor are teachers "blank slates" to be written upon. Both must be committed to a relationship that fosters growth, learning, and exchange of ideas. Caruso and Fawcett[60] have addressed the growth of the supervisor and those supervised.

Evaluation Conducted by Supervisor. There is some disagreement as to whether supervision and evaluation can be successfully accomplished by the same person. Some feel that one cannot be both a helping hand and a judgmental figure—that is, the evaluative function breaks the lines of communication between supervisor and teacher. On the other hand, others argue that if the supervisor evaluates, the teacher will most likely perform to his maximum ability.

Regardless of the pros and cons of the supervisor's evaluative function, supervisors are usually called upon to evaluate because protection of the client (in this case, child and parents) justifies the evaluation. Evaluation takes on even greater importance when one considers that the standards for entry into early childhood education vary so much between various programs and from state to state. (Performance evaluation will be discussed later in this chapter.)

Finally, one hopes the process engaged in during supervision will be continued by the teacher beyond the period of formal supervision. An effective teacher must continue to evaluate his own teaching process. Both creativity and self-reliance are facilitated when self-evaluation is primary and evaluation by others is secondary.[61] Thus, supervisors should help teachers become self-supervising by serving as role models for the evaluative process.

Methods of Supervision

Supervisors may work with teachers as part of a training session or as an analysis of teachers' on-the-job performance. Both of these methods can be effective depending on the teacher's needs and on the purposes of the evaluation.

Supervision in a Training Session. If the purpose of supervision is to provide training, the supervision may follow this format:

1. The supervisor and the teacher should discuss, demonstrate, and practice ways to reinforce and extend the children's learning experiences in a training session.
2. The supervisor should observe the teacher's performance to compare it with the training session.
3. In the supervisory conference, the teacher and the supervisor should discuss the teacher's perceptions of his interactions with the children. If the interactions were successful, the teacher should be praised; if not, a plan of action should be developed.

Supervisors also work with teachers in groups. Orientation and in-service are examples of group supervision. There are also group supervisory conferences, identical to the individual supervisory conferences, except that the teacher usually discusses his own teaching first, followed by analyses from other teachers and the supervisor, all of whom have observed the teaching. Group supervision permits multiple perspectives to be introduced and is especially effective when support professionals, such as physicians or psychologists, are included.

Supervision as an On-the-Job Analysis. For an on-the-job analysis, the most common method of supervision involves observation of the teacher, followed by an individual conference. Certainly, the way the conference is conducted depends on the teaching situation and the level of functioning for both supervisor and teacher. Nonetheless, certain pointers can make a supervisory conference worthwhile:

1. The supervisor and the teacher should plan together prior to the teaching. Planning should include:
   a. Rethinking lesson objectives, content, and methodology. (It is assumed that the teacher has preplanned.)
   b. Proposing other strategies (by both supervisor and teacher) and predicting how children will respond.
   c. Choosing a final teaching strategy.
2. The supervisor should observe the teacher and record in detail both the presentation and the children's responses.
3. The children's responses should be studied by both supervisor and teacher prior to the conference. Questions may include:
   a. How did the children respond to the lesson objectives?
   b. Was classroom management smooth or disorganized?
   c. What was the affective relationship between teacher and children?
4. The conference should not be held immediately after observation. The teacher's feelings may be too sensitive, and both parties need time to think about what went on in the classroom.
5. The conference should focus on patterns that tend to recur during the teaching period. Two prerequisites are essential:
   a. The supervisor should have extensive evidence to document a problem.
   b. He should be able to summarize the problem in language devoid of vague emotional jargon.
6. Most of the conference time should be spent with supervisor and teacher presenting alternate ideas for solving each problem, keeping in mind that:
   a. The supervisor should elicit and accept the teacher's ideas and feelings and positively reinforce the teacher.
   b. The teacher should be allowed to make the final decision among the alternatives discussed.
7. The next lesson should be planned on the basis of the conference.
8. The following practices should be observed:
   a. Only four or five topics should be discussed in a conference, of which the first and last should be the teacher's strong points.
   b. A teaching technique should not be referred to as "bad" or "good," but rather as "appropriate" or "inappropriate" for the objectives and for the children.
   c. Successful teaching techniques should be reinforced with praise. Praise not only makes the teacher feel more adequate but will cause her to repeat the successful techniques. (The absence of criticism is not praise!)

Problems in the Supervisor-Teacher Relationship

Regardless of the structure of the classroom or the method of supervision, supervisors need to help teachers reach two broad goals:

1. Teachers must learn to consider the relationship between their actions and children's learning. Teachers must develop a style that is both effective with children and appropriate to their own personality.
2. Teachers must become more and more self-reliant. They should draw on their own resources, rather than see the supervisor as a "bearer of gifts" in the form of materials or an assistant teacher.

Both supervisor and teacher bring their respective knowledge and assumptions, skills, and attitudes to their relationship. Although the relationship is complex, communication between supervisor and teacher is essential to effective supervision. Sharing knowledge and attitudes to arrive at common understanding is a two-way process. The essence of supervision is communication, yet the literature is replete with hints at and discussions on the barriers and problems in the supervisor-teacher relationship. The relationship can be more effective when both parties recognize some of these barriers and problems.

Prescriptive Supervision. Traditionally, supervision of teachers has been an authority-subordination relationship. The idea between this relationship was that through innate qualities and experience (but rarely special training), the supervisor knew best, and all the teacher needed to do was follow directions. Prescriptive supervision, which often involves on-the-spot judgments, is usually of negative value. The objective was apparently to oversee the teacher and use competition with other teachers as a stimulus.

The attitude toward supervision now is of collaboration in a problem-solving effort. In order to have collaboration, the supervisor-teacher relationship must be collegial rather than hierarchial. In this partnership, alternatives are sought by each professional, and both assume responsibility for decisions. Thus, in a nonprescriptive relationship, there is heavy emphasis on the teacher's responsibility for analysis of and solutions to the instructional process. Teachers feel free to discuss their problems with supervisors as colleagues. Once the teacher sees the supervisor as a source of help, he will be more willing to understand and accept the analysis of his teaching, which in turn should result in more effective teaching.

Time Spent in "Telling." Closely related to prescriptive supervising is the amount of time supervisors spend in "telling." Blumberg and Cusick[62] analyzed fifty separate supervisor-teacher tape recorded conferences involving total conference time of over eleven hours. Analyses of the tapes indicated that supervisors spent only .04 percent of their talking time (1.2 minutes out of 5 hours) questioning teachers as to how they would solve their instructional problems and that teachers spent only .06 percent of their talking time (2.2 minutes out of 6 hours) asking the supervisor any kind of question. These analyses show that the bulk of the supervisor's behavior was "telling" in nature. Supervisors seldom ask teachers for ideas about how to solve problems, and teachers rarely ask supervisors questions. Teachers sometimes see supervisors' questions as attempts to "box them in" rather than to help them. Negative behavior on the part of the teacher was met in kind 13 percent of the time. Supervisors should listen a lot, for when teachers have been heard, they are better able to hear.

Alleviation of Job Stress

More and more teachers are becoming victims of job stress. *Burnout* can be defined as "a syndrome of emotional exhaustion and cynicism that can occur in individuals who spend much of their time working closely with other people."[63] Stress comes from several conditions: (1) the unexpected is common because of the age of the children and the fact that the curriculum designs in many programs are not highly structured; (2) undesirable working conditions often plague teachers such as unpaid overtime, inability to take scheduled breaks due to staff shortage, and the lack of fringe benefits including medical coverage; (3) early childhood positions are not considered high status jobs by some persons who see play activities as less than real teaching; (4) early childhood teachers are so indoctrinated in the importance of the early years of the child's life that they often feel let down when they do not achieve their lofty goals regardless of the underlying cause (e.g., the teacher, the child, the parents' lack of follow-through, the teaching-learning situation such as lack of equipment or space, or problems in scheduling); and (5) teachers are unable to maintain a detached concern (i.e., they see themselves as surrogate parents.)[64]

Most susceptible to burnout are teachers in day-care and Head Start programs. For the most part, these teachers are in the lowest status jobs in the early childhood field, and they receive the least compensation for their work. Stress may come from these teachers' personal lives. Research from the National Day-Care Study found that 30 percent of the caregivers were the sole support of their families and 69 percent provided more than half of their family's income.[65] On the other hand, the National Child Care Staffing Study found high job satisfaction.[66]

As a way to help alleviate some stress, Jorde-Bloom[67] has defined ten dimensions of organizational climate. When these dimensions are positive within a program, much stress is avoided. These dimensions are (1) collegiality (i.e., supportive, cohesive staff); (2) professional growth (i.e., emphasis placed on growth); (3) supervisor support (i.e., facilitative leadership); (4) clarity (i.e., clear policies and job descriptions); (5) reward system (i.e., fairness in pay and fringe benefits); (6) decision making (i.e., staff involved in decisions); (7) goal consensus (i.e., staff agreement on goals/objectives); (8) task orientation (i.e., emphasis placed on good planning and efficiency in job performance); (9) physical setting (i.e., spatial arrangement helps staff); and (10) innovativeness (i.e., organization finds creative ways to solve problems. Jorde-Bloom developed an *Early Childhood Work Environment Survey*[68] which measures the organizational climate.

Some stress conditions may be stimulating unless the "unexpected" approaches chaos. Realizing that some stress is all right, even helpful, may assure some teachers. Other things may help: (1) being informed about the developmental stages of young children and the specific characteristics of the children served in the local program; (2) being prepared with flexible plans; (3) using a schedule although some adaptation of the schedule may be occasionally needed; (4) keeping records of children's development, so one can see progress in all areas; (5) detaching one's emotions from situations which cannot be changed; (6) staying in good physical and mental health with proper diet, exercise, rest, leisure activities, and medical attention; and (7) finding others who may help by providing the "shoulder to cry on."

Performance Evaluation for Improvement

Performance evaluation for improvement, the method by which a person's performance is evaluated, is another way to improve the quality of personnel. In the area of evaluation, there seem to be only two points of consensus: (1) the practice of evaluation is almost universal; and (2) evaluation of personnel effectiveness is recognized as a complex task.

Purpose of Evaluation

The first question in considering a personnel evaluation program is, "What is the ultimate goal of evaluating personnel?" Evaluation may be formative or summative. **Formative evaluation** is focused on the diagnostic (i.e., reflects the strengths and weaknesses of a staff member) and is thus used to promote growth. Formative evaluation is usually focused on one problem or group of related problems at one time (e.g., planning or arranging the physical facility).

Summative evaluation, on the other hand, lets persons know how they perform against certain predetermined criteria. Summative evaluation "sums up" performance in that it looks at overall performance. Thus, summative evaluation is used for such decisions as continuance of employment, offering tenure, and advancing merit pay.

For our purposes, only formative evaluation will be considered. Performance evaluation for improvement is the most important because all other purposes of evaluation, such as tenure and merit pay, should be based on performance.

Selection of Evaluation Criteria

The next question that arises is, What are the steps to follow in initiating a program of evaluation? The first step is to determine whether all personnel should be evaluated by the same criteria and what criteria should be used. Generally, personnel who provide similar services should be evaluated according to the same criteria, but personnel serving in dissimilar roles should be evaluated according to different criteria, although some evaluation items might be the same.

Each early childhood program should develop its own criteria for evaluating personnel performance, rather than secure criteria developed for another program. In developing criteria, the policy-making body should keep in mind the philosophy and policies of the program, the roles of the personnel, and the staff member characteristics constituting a successful performance. Characteristics frequently evaluated are (1) physical characteristics—the physical health and vitality conducive to the effective performance of the position; (2) mental ability—the ability to conceptualize the philosophy of the program, the needs of the children and adults involved, and the employee's role and the roles of others as they relate to the position; (3) professional qualifications—knowledge of methods and materials used in performing one's role; and (4) personal attributes—enthusiasm, poise, ability to adjust to frustrations, ability to cooperate with colleagues, and ability to accept constructive criticism.

In addition to using criteria based on teacher characteristics, the appraisal of teacher performance may be linked to the growth and development of children in a program. Several problems arise when a program uses the assessment of children as a means of appraising teacher effectiveness. First, some aspects of growth and development may occur during a given period but are not the result of effective teaching. Rather, these changes could be the result of other factors (e.g., age). Second, as Spodek and Saracho point out, many of the goals of early childhood education—especially those in the psychomotor and affective domains—are too problematic to assess in young children.[69] And third, teachers may be more apt to design their curriculum based directly on the chosen children's assessment instrument in order to get a high accountability rating.

Care must be taken so all evaluation items closely relate to employees' responsibilities. In short, directors should use the same care in selecting evaluation items as in hiring. Criteria for evaluation should always be given with the job description or at the time of employment. Remind the employees of the upcoming evaluation a few weeks beforehand.

Selection of Evaluation Instrument

A second step in performance evaluation is to ascertain the type of instrument to be used. When criteria for evaluating personnel performance have been determined, they must be incorporated into an appraisal instrument. Locally devised evaluation procedures may include narratives, portfolios, interview procedures, check sheets, and rating scales.

Narratives are based on observations. These observations may be open-ended or may focus on specific areas such as guidance of children or planning. During observations, the evaluator observes the staff member and notes specific strengths and weaknesses of the performance based on the criteria selected for that particular job category. Sometimes a staff member is asked to make a self-evaluation based on personal recollections. Videotapes are also becoming a popular means of affirming the evaluator's observations and/or the staff member's self-evaluation. Videotapes can also identify facial expressions and body movements.

Portfolios are also being used in some programs. The portfolio is a collection of materials (e.g., written work, tapes, photographs) that teachers collect and assemble to represent their performance. Thus, portfolios are an extension

	Yes	No	Not Applicable
Was prepared for lesson	_____	_____	_____
Used a variety of teaching materials	_____	_____	_____

FIGURE 4–7

of narratives. Portfolios allow evaluators to see what teachers value in terms of both content and pedagogy.

Interview procedures may be developed as evaluation instruments. Interviews may take the form of an open-ended discussion concerning strengths, performance areas needing improvement, and discussions on how to make needed improvements. On the other hand, some interview forms may be, in actuality, verbal rating scales.

Check sheets and **rating scales** usually list evaluation criteria in categories of characteristics, such as physical characteristics and professional qualifications. Many check lists and rating scales also include an overall evaluation for each category of characteristics and/or for total performance evaluation. Although check sheets and rating scales are written evaluation instruments, each instrument has a distinctive style, as shown in the following examples:

1. The check sheet is used to indicate those behaviors satisfactorily completed by a staff member. The evaluator may check "yes," "no," or "not applicable" (see Figure 4–7).
2. A rating scale, a qualitative evaluation of performance, represents successive levels of quality along an inferior-superior continuum.
   a. Levels of quality may be described in words as shown in Figures 4–8 and 4–9.
   b. Levels of quality may be indicated with numerals (see Figure 4–10). Directions given on the rating scale must indicate whether numeral "1" is the most inferior or the most superior evaluation.
   c. Levels of quality may be described in words and numerals (see Figure 4–11). Cohen and Brawer discuss problems in using rating scales for measuring staff performance.[70]

Use of step-by-step presentation

Excellent	Good	Fair	Poor

FIGURE 4–8

a Excellent
b Above average
c Average
d Below average
Creative in teaching   a b c d

FIGURE 4–9

Kept the children's attention

1   2   3   4   5

FIGURE 4–10

Lesson was organized

1   2   3

Usually   Never

Overall evaluation

Superior		Excellent		Good		Average		Fair	
10	9	8	7	6	5	4	3	2	1

FIGURE 4–11

Frequency of Evaluation

Informal evaluation, especially self-evaluation, should be conducted continuously; however, the policy-making body should plan, determine the frequency of, and schedule formal evaluation. Formative evaluation should be conducted several times per year. Inexperienced teachers often need more formative evaluations than do experienced teachers. Summative evaluations are most often conducted annually.

Selection of an Evaluator

Another step is to decide who should evaluate. In most early childhood programs, the director, supervisor, or building principal evaluates all personnel, although in some large programs, a personnel director is charged with the responsibility. There is a growing trend towards self-evaluation. If individuals were able to evaluate themselves objectively and decide on target areas for improvement, self-evaluation might be the most effective means of improving performance. However, self-evaluation has not been successful.[71]

PERSONNEL SERVICES AND RECORDS

The state board of education and licensing agency require that certain personnel services be provided and records kept by early childhood programs under their respective jurisdictions. In addition to those mandated personnel services and records, the local board of education or the board of directors may provide additional services and require other records permitted by state law.

For the most part, public school early childhood programs have more complete services and records than do day-care centers. The National Child Care Staffing Study reported that 70 percent of the teaching staff in day-care centers worked without a written contract, 40 percent had no written job description, and 96 percent had no collective bargaining agreement. Furthermore, only 40 percent had health coverage and 20 percent had a retirement plan.[72] These working conditions should be changed, because they affect job satisfaction.

All early childhood programs should write an employee handbook that contains information on personnel services and records. Perreault and Neugebauer[73] suggest that handbooks should include information such as (1) history of the program, (2) program philosophy, (3) organization structure, (4) terms of employment, and (5) expectations of employees.

Contract and Terms of Employment

A **contract** is an agreement between two or more parties. In early childhood programs, a contract is an agreement between each staff member and the board of education or board of directors specifying the services a staff member must provide and the specific sum of money to be paid for services rendered. All contracts should conform to the following guidelines:

A written agreement as opposed to an oral one
Specific designation of the parties to the contract
Statement of the legal capacity of the parties represented
Provision for signatures by the authorized agents of the board of education or board of directors, and by the teacher or child-care worker

Clear stipulation of salary to be paid
Designation of date and duration of contract, and the date when
service is to begin
Definition of assignment[74]

In signing a contract, an employee indirectly consents to obey all rules and regulations in force at the time of employment or adopted during the period of employment. Policies that most directly affect employees may include hours per day and days per week; vacation; specific requirements, such as a uniform or driver's license; sick, emergency, and maternity leaves; substitutes; insurance; salary increases and fringe benefits; and retirement plan. Potential and present employees should have a written copy of all current policies.

The employee may receive a contract for some specified period of time, perhaps an annual or a continuing contract. Contracts for a specified period of time must be renewed at the end of such time period. The two types of continuing contracts are **notification** and **tenure.** An individual having a *notification* continuing contract must be notified on or before a given date if the contract is not to be renewed. A tenure contract guarantees that an employee cannot be dismissed except for certain specific conditions, such as lack of funds to pay salaries, neglect of duty, incompetency, failure to observe regulations of the board, and immorality; furthermore, a dismissed, tenured employee has the right to a hearing in which the board must prove "just cause" for the dismissal. Boards offering tenure require that an employee serve a probationary period of a given number of years (usually three or five) before receiving a tenure contract.

Special service contracts must also be written when a limited service is to be performed by a temporary employee such as a consultant for a workshop. This type of contract must clearly specify the services to be rendered; the date(s) services are to be performed, including any follow-up services; any special arrangements such as materials to be supplied by a temporary employee (or by the employer); and the fee. The signatures of the temporary employee and the requester should be affixed to the contract and the transaction should be dated.

Job Description

A job description for each personnel category should be written and kept current, and should include the following: (1) job title, (2) minimum qualifications, (3) primary duties and responsibilities, (4) working conditions, (5) additional duties, (6) reporting relationships and limits of authority, and (7) benefits. Job descriptions should be specific to the particular early childhood program and position, rather than adopted from another program. A potential employee should review the job description before signing a contract; all employees should keep their job descriptions in their files. A sample job description is shown in Figure 4–12.

Johnson County Community College Child Development Center

Title: Teacher

Qualifications: A teacher shall have at least an A.A. degree in Child Development/ Early Childhood Education or hold a Child Development Associate certificate. A teacher must also meet licensing regulations concerning minimum age and health status.

Primary duties and responsibilities: A teacher shall: (1) plan and execute developmentally appropriate activities; (2) observe and evaluate children's progress; (3) provide a written report (on the forms provided) to the director and parents at least two times per year; (4) be available for informal parent-teacher contacts at the beginning and end of each session; and (5) other duties particular to the program.

Working conditions: A teacher is paid for an eight-hour working day. Reporting time is 7:15 a.m. Monday through Friday. A teacher should be prepared to receive children at 7:30 a.m. A teacher will eat at the noon meal with the children and will have two fifteen minute breaks during the six-hour day. The teacher's planning period is from 1:30 until 3:15 p.m. daily.

(The director must be notified in the event of illness or emergencies. Paid vacation periods must be planned three months in advance and approved by the director.) Other optional benefits include a group health insurance plan, employee retirement fund, and others particular to the program.

Additional duties: A teacher is expected to attend staff development activities on the first Tuesday of each month from 3:30 until 5:30 p.m. and a monthly parent function usually held in the evenings from 7:00 until 9:00 p.m. on the third Thursday of each month.

Reporting relationships and limits of authority: A teacher reports directly to the director of the program. *Prior commitment from the director must be obtained* for purchasing any item, approving additional or terminating any services for children, and releasing information on center activities to the media. A teacher *may take action but must inform* when releasing a child to an authorized adult during normal attendance hours, administering authorized medications, and informing a parent about a child's nonsevere illness. A teacher *may take action without informing* when developing new activities in keeping with program's philosophy, changing sequence of daily activities except for snack and meal times, and talking with parents about children's development.

Benefits: Sick and emergency leave without loss of pay is twelve days for a twelve-month period of employment. A two-week paid vacation plus Thanksgiving and other national holidays are observed.

FIGURE 4–12

Insurance and Retirement Plans

Various kinds of insurance and retirement plans protect employees and organizations. Adequate coverage is expensive but essential. Some types of insurance and retirement plans may be mandated by state or federal laws, whereas other types may be voluntary.

Federal Insurance Contributions Act (FICA)

Most centers are required to pay the FICA, or Social Security, tax. The FICA tax is generally used for retirement purposes. Tax rates are set at a percentage of the employee's salary. The employer deposits quarterly the amount of the employee's contributions collected as payroll deductions, plus an equal amount from the employer. (This money is deposited in a separate account, because commingling of federal funds is prohibited by law.) A quarterly report on FICA taxes is also required. Even tax-exempt corporations should keep in close contact with the District Office of the Internal Revenue Service. Laws change and all organizations are responsible for keeping up with current tax laws.

Workman's Compensation Insurance

Workman's compensation insurance is liability insurance compensating an employee injured by an accident in the course of and arising out of employment. (Independent contractors are not covered. Directors should insist that any contractors doing work for a program certify they are adequately insured so they cannot later claim to have been acting as an employee.) Workman's compensation insurance is required in most states, but many states have exceptions for certain classes of employers such as an organization with a small number of employees or organizations wishing to self-insure. The insurance company pays 100 percent of all workman's compensation benefits required by state law. Injured employees, and, in the case of death, their dependents are eligible for one-half to two-thirds of their weekly wages plus hospital and medical benefits. Employees, in turn, give up their rights to sue employers for damages covered by the law except in the rare states where such actions are permitted.

State Unemployment Insurance

State unemployment insurance is required in most states and varies considerably from state to state. A questionnaire must be completed about the employees' activities and the tax status of the early childhood program. The insurance rates are figured as a percentage of total wages and will be different for for-profit and not-for-profit corporations.

Liability Insurance

Liability insurance protects the organization or employee from loss when persons have been injured or property damaged as a result of negligence (rather than accident) on the part of the institution or its employees; however, almost any "accident" that occurs is usually considered the result of negligence. The extent to which an institution or its employees can be held liable varies from state to state, and a liability policy should cover everything for which an institution is liable.

In the past, the insurance industry has benefited from high interest rates that produced high returns on their investment. Insurance companies are now canceling or not renewing policies or are renewing policies with less coverage and premium hikes ranging from 100–600 percent, with 300–400 percent as the norm. This is due to the tremendous number of costly law suits (e.g., medical) and sensationalistic headlines about child abuse in a few day-care settings. Steps to lower rates and find insurance companies willing to provide coverage are being taken by groups such as Committee on Children, Youth, and Families and the National Association for the Education of Young Children.[75]

In most states, programs providing transportation services are required to have vehicle insurance. One type is liability insurance, which is coverage of liability for injury to persons or damage to property. Minimal auto liability insurance should be from $50,000 to $100,000.

Health Insurance and Hospital-Medical Insurance

Health insurance, whether fully or partially paid for by the employer or taken on a voluntary basis and paid for by the employee, may assume any of three forms: (1) medical reimbursement insurance; (2) medical service or prepaid medical care; and (3) disability income benefits. Hospital-medical plans fall into three groups: (1) basic hospitalization and medical coverage; (2) major medical insurance; and (3) closed-panel operation (i.e., service available from a limited number of physicians, clinics, or hospitals).

Crime Coverages

Protection against loss resulting from dishonesty of employees or others is available under four forms of coverage: (1) fidelity bonds; (2) board-form money and securities policy; (3) "3-D policy" (dishonesty, disappearance, and destruction); and (4) all-risk insurance.

Retirement Programs

Federal Social Security coverage, FICA tax, is usually mandatory. Generally, the tax is used as a federal "retirement program." Most public school program personnel are also under state retirement programs, paid on a matching fund basis by employer and employee. Private institutions may have retirement programs in addition to federal Social Security coverage.

Personnel Records

Personnel administration involves keeping records and making reports in accordance with state laws, the program's governing body requirements, and federal legislation concerning privacy of personal information. Public and private schools must keep personnel records on each regulation pertaining to employees—both program and support personnel. In most cases, personnel records are kept by the local programs and reports are submitted to their respective state governing boards (licensing agency or state board of education); however, the governing board may inspect locally kept records.

Personnel records is a collective term for all records containing information about employees. Although these records vary from program to program, they usually embody these details:

1. Personnel information records are kept by all early childhood programs. Most of the personal information is given by a potential employee on the application form, and the information is kept current. Personal information includes name, age, sex, address, telephone number, citizenship, Social Security number, and names and addresses of those who will give references.

2. Personal health records signed by an appropriate medical professional are required by all early childhood programs. These records may be detailed, requiring specific medical results of a physical examination, or may be a general statement that the employee is free from any mental or physical illness that might adversely affect the health of children or other adults. In addition to records on general health, an annual tuberculosis test is required by most programs.

3. Emergency information is required by many programs. This information includes names, addresses, and telephone numbers of one or more persons to be contacted in an emergency; name of physician and hospital; and any medical information deemed necessary in an emergency situation, such as allergies to drugs or other conditions.

4. Records of education and other qualifications are required by all programs. They must include the names of schools attended, diplomas or degrees obtained, transcripts of academic work, and the registration number and type of teacher's or administrator's certificate or any other credential needed by an employee (such as a chauffeur's license).

5. Professional or occupational information records are kept by all programs, including the places and dates of employment, names of employers, and job descriptions.

6. Professional or occupational skill and character references are included in the personnel records. In most cases, these references are for confidential use by the employer.

7. Service records are kept by some programs. These records contain information concerning date of present employment, level or age of children cared for/taught or program directed, absences incurred or leaves taken, in-service education received and conferences attended, committees served on, salary received, and date and reason for termination of service.

8. Insurance records are kept by all programs involved in any group insurance.

9. Evaluation records are placed on file in many programs. However, they should not be kept after they have fulfilled the purposes for which they were intended.

Because an individual's legal right to privacy must be guarded, administrators must keep abreast of the laws pertaining to record keeping and record security. For example, The Privacy Act of 1974 (P.L. 93–579) requires federal agencies to take certain steps to safeguard the accuracy, currentness, and security of records concerning individuals and limit record keeping to necessary and lawful purposes. Individuals also have a right to examine federal records containing such information and to challenge the accuracy of data with which they disagree.[76] In accordance with The Privacy Act, the Office of the Federal Register has published a digest of the names of various record systems maintained by the federal government; categories of individuals about whom individual record systems are maintained; and procedures whereby an individual can obtain further information on any record system covered by The Privacy Act.[77] Personnel of many early childhood programs, such as Head Start and others receiving federal funding, are covered under The Privacy Act of 1974.

SUMMARY

The factors that influence the effectiveness of early childhood programs are incredibly multifaceted and hence complex. All research studies support the contention that the behavior of adults in early childhood programs does have an important impact on children.

Qualities of effective staff members have been studied. Although there is not a simple, single response to the question concerning what professional qualifications (i.e., knowledge and skills) and personal characteristics (i.e., personality traits and values) individuals need to work effectively with young children, there is some consensus.

The consensus of personnel competencies should serve three functions. First, competencies should guide the staffing of early childhood programs as boards assess their needs and then recruit and hire directors, primary program personnel, and support program personnel who can, in turn, perform certain roles based on their professional qualifications and personal characteristics. Second, these competencies should be used as a director mobilizes the staff into providing the program's services. And third, competencies should be used as criteria for improving staff performance via formal education, staff development, membership in professional organizations, supervision, alleviation of job stress, and performance evaluation for improvement.

Certain personnel services and records are required by various regulatory agencies. Personnel services and records also serve to make working conditions better for staff, which aids job satisfaction.

NOTES

1. D. Phillips and M. Whitebook, "Who Are Child Care Workers?" *Young Children* 41, 4 (1986): 14–20.
2. M. Whitehead, "The Teacher Shortage," *Young Children* 41, 3 (1986): 10–11.
3. E. Galinsky, "The Staffing Crises," *Young Children* 44, 2 (1989): 2–4.
4. Ibid., 2.

5. M. Whitebook and R. C. Granger, "Assessing Teacher Turnover," *Young Children* 44, 4 (1989): 11.

6. M. Whitebook, C. Howes, and D. Phillips, *Who Cares? Child Care Teachers and the Quality of Care in America: Executive Summary National Child Care Staffing Study* (Oakland: Child Care Employee Project, 1989), 12.

7. Bureau of Labor Statistics, *Current Population Survey, 1986 Annual Averages and Occupational Proportions and Training Data* (Washington, D.C.: United States Government Printing Office, January, 1987).

8. Ibid.

9. Whitebook, Howes, and Phillips, *Who Cares: Child Care Teachers and the Quality of Care in America*, 9.

10. Ibid., 11.

11. Ibid., 12.

12. Ibid.

13. Ibid., 13.

14. B. Robinson, "Changing Views on Male Early Childhood Teachers," *Young Children* 36, 5 (1981): 27–48.

15. E. V. Tubbs, "More Men Teachers in Our Schools," *Schools and Society* 63 (1946): 394.

16. K. Seifert, "Men in Early Childhood Education," *Professionalism and the Early Childhood Practitioner*, ed. B. Spodek, O. N. Saracho, and D. C. Peters, 105–116 (New York: Teachers College Press, Columbia University, 1988).

17. B. E. Robinson, "Vanishing Breed: Men in Early Childhood Programs," *Young Children* 43, 6 (1988): 54–58.

18. K. Seifert, "Men in Early Childhood Education."

19. Whitebook, Howes, and Phillips, *Who Cares? Child Care Teachers and the Quality of Care in America*, 8.

20. W. Whitehurst, E. Witty, and S. Wiggin, "Racial Equality: Teaching Excellence," *Action in Teacher Education: 10th Year Anniversary Issue*, ed. J. Sikula, 159–167 (Reston: Association of Teacher Education, 1988).

21. C. Fields, "Poor Test Scores Bar Many Minority Students from Teacher Training," *Chronicle of Higher Education* (November 2, 1988): A1.

22. "NAEYC Position Statement on Nomenclature, Salaries, Benefits, and the Status of the Early Childhood Profession," *Young Children* 40, 1 (1984): 52–55.

23. M. Whitebook, C. Howes, R. Darrah, and J. Friedman, "Caring for the Caregivers: Staff Burnout in Child Care," *Current Topics in Early Childhood Education, Vol. 4*, ed. L. G. Katz, 211–235 (Norwood: Ablex, 1982).

24. Galinsky, "The Staffing Crisis."

25. B. Spodek and O. N. Saracho, "The Preparation and Certification of Early Childhood Personnel," *Handbook of Research in Early Childhood Education*, ed. B. Spodek, 399–425 (New York: Free Press, 1982).

26. S. Kohut, Jr., "Research and the Teacher: Teacher Effectiveness in Early Childhood Education," *Aspects of Early Childhood Education: Theory To Research To Practice*, ed. D. G. Range, J. R. Layton, and D. L. Roubinek (New York: Academic, 1980).

27. K. Seifert and W. Lyons, *Attitudes of Principals about Early Childhood Teachers*, ERIC ED 178 172 (Winnipeg: Manitoba University, 1981).

28. K. Read and J. Patterson, *The Nursery School and Kindergarten*, 7th ed. (New York: Holt, Rinehart and Winston, 1980).

29. J. L. Rosen, *Perceptions of the Childhood Self and Teacher-Child Relationships. Final Report of the National Institute of Education* (New York: Bank Street College Research Station, 1975).

30. M. H. McCauley and F. L. Natter, *Psychological Type Differences in Education* (Gainesville: Center for Application of Psychological Types, 1980).

31. For specific information, contact: U.S. Equal Employment Opportunity Commission, Office of Communications and Legislation, 201 East Street, N.W., Washington, D.C. 20507. (1-800-USA-EEOC)

32. P.L. 98–473, Title IV, 401.98 Stat. 2195–2197, Oct. 12, 1984.

33. The Federal Age Discrimination in Employment Act of 1967 (29 USC 621–634) prohibits discrimination against persons age 40–70.

34. M. W. Leak, "An Experimental Approach to Staff Selection," *Child Care Information Exchange* (1982): 1–6.

35. T. Burns and G. M. Stalken, "Mechanistic and Organic System," *Classics of Organizational Theory*, ed. J. M. Shafritz and P. W. Whitebeck, 207–211 (Oak Park: Moore, 1978).

36. T. J. Peters and R. H. Waterman, Jr., *In Search of Excellence: Lessons from America's Best Run Companies* (New York: Harper and Row, 1982).

37. R. Feine, *National Child Care Regulatory, Monitoring and Evaluation Systems Model* (Washington, D.C.: National Association for the Education of Young Children, 1986).

38. M. Whitebook, "Profiles in Day-Care: An Interview with Millie Almy," *Day Care and Early Education* 8 (1981): 29–30.

39. Peters and Waterman, *In Search of Excellence*.

40. Ibid.

41. L. Katz, "Developmental States of Preschool Teachers," *Elementary School Journal* 73 (1972): 50–54.

42. Whitebook, Howes, and Phillips, *Who Cares? Child Care Teachers and the Quality of Care in America*, 8–9.

43. M. E. Logue, B. K. Eheart, and R. L. Leavitt, "Staff Training: What Difference Does It Make?" *Young Children* 41, 5 (1986): 8–9.

44. S. J. Rosenholtz and S. J. Kyle, "Teacher Isolation: Barrier to Professionalism," *American Educator* 8 (1984): 10–15.

45. R. Ruopp, et al., *Children at the Center: Final Report of the National Day-Care Study*, Vol. 1 (Cambridge: Abt Associates, 1979).

46. Whitebook, Howes, and Phillips, *Who Cares? Child Care Teachers and the Quality of Care in America*, 9.

47. A. Clarke-Stewart and C. Gruber, "Day-Care Forms and Features," *The Child and the Day Care Setting*, ed. R. Anslie (New York: Praeger, 1984).

48. M. E. Logue, B. Krause-Eheart, and J. Miles, *The Influence of Training and Choice on Teacher Behavior in Toddler Day-Care* (Paper presented at the Fifth Biennial International Conference of Infant Studies, Los Angeles, April, 1986).

49. Katz, "Developmental States of Preschool Teachers."
50. J. Arin-Krupp, *Adult Development: Implications for Staff Development* (Manchester: Adult Development and Learning, 1981).
51. M. S. Abbott-Shim, "In-Service Training: A Means to Quality Care," *Young Children* 45, 2 (1990): 14–18.
52. N. Benham, T. Miller, and S. Konton, "Pinpointing Staff Training Needs in Child Care Centers," *Young Children* 43, 4 (1988): 9–16.
53. Ibid.
54. S. F. Louchs, "At Last Some Good News from a Study of School Improvement," *Educational Leadership* 41 (1983): 4–5.
55. D. J. Keister, *Consultation in Day-Care* (Chapel Hill: University of North Carolina, Institute of Government, 1969).
56. B. Holt, *The Enabler Model of Early Childhood Training and Program Development* (Ames: Iowa State University, Child Development Training Program, 1977).
57. S. B. Sarason, et al., *Psychology of Community Settings: Clinical, Educational, Vocational, Social Aspects* (New York: John Wiley and Sons, 1966).
58. Whitebook, Howes, and Phillips, *Who Cares? Child Care Teachers and the Quality of Care in America*, 9.
59. J. J. Caruso and M. T. Fawcett, *Supervision in Early Childhood Education: A Developmental Approach* (New York: Teachers College Press, Teachers College, Columbia University, 1986).
60. Ibid., 70–91.
61. C. Rogers, *Freedom to Learn for the '80s* (Columbus: Merrill, 1983).
62. A. Blumberg and P. Cusick, "Supervision Teacher Interaction: An Analysis of Verbal Behavior," *Education* 91 (1970): 126–134.
63. A. Pines and C. Maslach, "Combating Staff Burn-Out in a Day Care Center: A Case Study," *Child Care Quarterly* 9 (Spring, 1980): 6.
64. R. H. Needle, et al., "Teacher Stress: Sources and Consequences," *Journal of School Health* 50 (1980): 96–99.
65. R. Ruopp, J. Travers, F. Glantz, and C. Coelen, *Children at the Center, Vol. 1 of Final Report of the National Day-Care Study* (Cambridge: Abt Associates, 1970), 224.
66. Whitebook, Howes, and Phillips, *Who Cares? Child Care Teachers and the Quality of Care in America*, 11.
67. P. Jorde-Bloom, *A Great Place to Work: Improving Conditions for Staff in Young Children's Programs* (Washington, D.C.: National Association for the Education of Young Children, 1988).
68. Ibid., 63–71.
69. B. Spodek and O. N. Saracho, "The Preparation and Certification of Early Childhood Personnel," *Handbook of Research in Early Childhood Education*, ed. B. Spodek, 412–413 (New York: Free Press, 1982).
70. A. M. Cohen and F. B. Brawer, *Measuring Faculty Performance* (Washington, D.C.: American Association of Junior Colleges, 1969).
71. G. Solomon and F. J. McDonald, "Pretest and Posttest Reactions to Self-Viewing One's Teaching Performance on Video Tape," *Journal of Educational Psychology* 61 (1970): 280–286.

72. Whitebook, Howes, and Phillips, *Who Cares? Child Care Teachers and the Quality of Care in America*, 11.

73. J. Perreault and R. Neugebauer, "An Ounce of Prevention: How to Write an Employee Handbook," *Child Care Information Exchange* (1988, January): 21–24.

74. W. S. Elsbree and E. E. Reutter, Jr., *Staff Personnel in the Public Schools* (Englewood Cliffs, N.J.: Prentice-Hall, 1954), 421–422.

75. "NAEYC Position Statement on the Liability Insurance Crises," *Young Children* 41, 5 (1986): 45–46.

76. *Title v. Section 522a, U.S. Code 1976 Edition: Containing the General and Permanent Laws of the U.S., In Force on January 3, 1977, vol. 1* (Washington, D.C.: U.S. Government Printing Office, 1977).

77. Office of the Federal Register, *Protecting Your Right to Privacy—Digest of Systems of Records, Agency Rules, and Research Aids* (Washington, D.C.: Government Printing Office, 1977).

FOR FURTHER READING

Ayers, W. *The Good Preschool Teacher: Six Teachers Reflect on Their Lives.* New York: Teachers College Press, Columbia University 1989.

Bernstein, G. S., and Halaszyn, J. A. *"Human Services? . . . That Must Be So Rewarding"—A Practical Guide for Professional Development."* Baltimore: Paul H. Brookes, 1989.

Caruso, J. J., and Fawcett, M. T. *Supervision of Early Childhood Education: A Developmental Perspective.* New York: Teachers College Press, Columbia University, 1986.

Greenman, J., and Fuqua, R., eds. *Making Day-Care Better: Training, Evaluation, and the Process of Change.* New York: Teachers College Press, Columbia University, 1984.

Jorde, P. *Avoiding Burnout: Strategies for Managing Time, Space, and People in Early Childhood.* Washington, D.C.: Acropolis, 1982.

Jorde-Bloom, P. *A Great Place to Work: Improving Conditions for Staff in Young Children's Programs.* Washington, D.C.: National Association for the Education of Young Children, 1988.

Katz, L. "The Professional Early Childhood Teacher." *Young Children* 39, 5 (1984): 3–10.

Klass, C. S., and Nall, S. W. "Accessible Professional Development: A Community Based Program for Early Childhood Educators." *Childhood Education* 65, 4 (1987): 224–227.

Schon, D. A. *The Reflective Practitioner: How Professionals Think in Action.* New York: Basic, 1983.

Yonemura, M. V. *A Teacher at Work: Professional Development and the Early Childhood Educator.* New York: Teachers College Press, Columbia University, 1986.

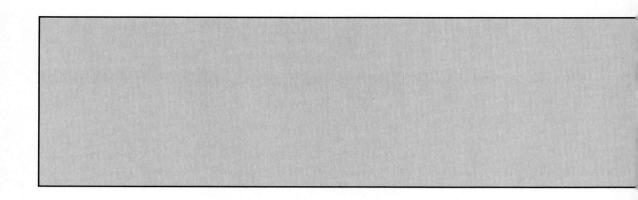

Chapter 5
Housing

Many adults may have a fixed image of a school facility—long corridors lined with doors leading to classrooms; desks facing the teacher's desk with a chalkboard behind; green- or brown-painted, closed storage cabinets; clanging radiators; high windows; coat hooks; a gritty, asphalt playground almost surrounding the building with swings, slides, climbing equipment, and ball areas; and a high fence enclosing the sea of asphalt and its island building.

In most facilities for today's young children, such a gloomy atmosphere no longer exists. Environments have changed as a result of a more profound understanding of how children develop and more accurate interpretations of child-child, child-material, and child-adult interactions. Despite differences in the psycho-philosophical bases of early childhood programs, most facilities are physically and psychologically comfortable. The homelike atmosphere of today's facilities comes about because children move around, rather than sit in the same work place all year; staff members move among the children rather than sit or stand behind a permanent station in front of the room; furnishings and equipment are more like the rugs, couches, and tools of home; and there is more floor and ground space because of curricular expansion and a greater variety of opportunities for learning.

Before contemplating the specifics of housing, one must remember that:

1. Location of the building is an important aspect of planning, because local zoning regulations may include restrictions.
2. Regardless of the type of program, most of the occupants will be young children, so the facility should be child oriented.
3. Safety of the children and staff members is of maximum importance and is discussed later in this chapter.
4. Housing is an important consideration in planning for the disabled. Programs receiving direct or indirect federal assistance of any kind must be accessible to children and employees who are disabled. Zoning laws

in many areas also require that buildings accommodate the disabled. Special architectural plans and room arrangements are needed for the physically disabled and visually impaired. Also, noise and activity levels must be controlled when learning disabled and hyperactive children are integrated into the regular classroom. Brooks and Deen found that some of the standards, as established by the American National Standards Institute, are appropriate for the disabled adults and older students but are hazardous for young children. They developed a checklist for facilities serving both children and adults.[1] Section 504 of P.L. 93–112 deals with making programs accessible to the disabled. P.L. 94–142 authorizes Congress to appropriate moneys for awarding grants to pay all or part of the costs of remodeling existing buildings to eliminate architectural barriers for children with disabilities.

5. Variations in arrangement of space and materials contribute to the effectiveness of housing. There should be differences in the placement of objects in space (such as high, eye-level, and low); size of areas, such as large areas for running and small areas for squeezing through; sound levels, such as noisy places and quiet areas; and light and color, such as cheerful, busy color schemes and quiet, relaxing hues. In short, design should be aesthetically pleasing.

6. Flexibility is essential. Housing should be planned to accommodate both individual and group pursuits. "The early childhood program requires that the site and the space, as well as the furniture and equipment, be so adaptable as to permit activities to expand, shrink, and disappear completely or even move outdoors."[2] Day and Sheehan, however, advocate somewhat closed rather than open settings for young children, because (1) activity stays within the room with less noise distractions; (2) children can find quiet, private places; and (3) closed areas encourage small group activities.[3]

7. Costs must be considered. The building or physical facilities require a large initial investment; however, when good facilities are amortized over forty years, the investment represents only eight to twelve cents of the total dollars spent on the program.[4]

Determining the specifics of housing begins with the program's psychophilosophical base. Objectives must be defined in terms of environmental features that make the program possible. Barker refers to the "essential fittingness" between environment and behavior of its inhabitants.[5] This is extensively elaborated on by Day's discussion of an ecological approach to early education.[6] Programs that adhere to the interactionist point of view (i.e., coming from maturational and transactional views) need a roomy environment—calculated to give maximum mobility. The room is often divided into learning centers with the size of each work space compatible with the number of children in the area at one time and the space required for both use and storage of equipment/materials. Facilities designed for programs adhering to the behavioral-environmental view have smaller, more enclosed (e.g., with high dividers) areas in which teacher-directed activities take place. There may be some less enclosed centers available for children's use during "free" times. (Because of the "appropriate practice" position statements described in Chapter 2, this chapter will focus on suggestions for housing programs holding the interactionist point of view.)

There are several logical steps in planning a facility for an early childhood program: (1) a committee, or several committees, must be appointed to investigate special needs and consider preliminary plans; (2) specific needs of the program must be outlined, including maximum enrollment, ages of children, special needs of children, and program objectives; (3) input should be obtained from individuals and organizations specializing in housing programs (a contact list is shown on p. 195–96) and trips should be planned to facilities housing similar programs; (4) preliminary plans should be submitted to the board of directors (or local school board) for action; and (5) evaluations of the housing plans should be continual, and the committee(s) planning housing may want to adapt an evaluation device for local use, such as the *Early Learning Environment Rating Scale*[7] or use criteria established by one of the professional accrediting associations.

Not every early childhood program will be so fortunate as to have a new building. Many will be housed in old structures, or in new additions to an older building. Renovated buildings are fine if they meet the needs of the program and are not just hand-me-downs or cast-offs. Many of the foregoing steps for planning new buildings are equally appropriate when planning an addition to an existing building. Some early childhood programs must share their children's activity room or building with other groups, such as a church or civic group. A major problem in a shared facility is that of cleaning the room or building, storing equipment, and setting up again. Vergeront gives many ideas for managing housing in programs that must share facilities.[8]

ENTRY-EXIT AREA

Because the entry-exit area serves as the first and last picture of the facility that children and parents see every day, the area may be a major factor in communicating the attitude, "It's nice here!" or, "This is a good place for my child!" The entry-exit area is also the view most often seen by the public, and its opinion of a program may be based on what it sees—even from street distance.

An entry-exit area should be a bright, welcoming area, because blind corners and dimly lit places are frightening to the young child. The entry-exit area could be a mall, with views of indoor and outdoor activity areas, a porch, a courtyard, or a gaily decorated interior room. This area should provide a view of the activity room and have a transition space (i.e., a place to say good-bye to parents and to watch from) so that young children can gradually join the activities of the program. Such a view also enables parents, returning for their children, to make a quick scan of the activity room in order to locate their children.

Because the acclimatized child will want to enter on his own, the entry door should operate easily. There should be a parking lot near the entry-exit area for parents who drive and a shelter for walking parents to watch until their children enter the building or outdoor activity area. To accommodate young children with disabilities, there should be a ramp to the building. The ramp should be located near the parking lot. (The curb must be cut to enter the parking lot or the ramp should lead directly from the street.) Other specifications for the ramp include a slope of no less than twelve feet for each foot of drop, a thirty-six-inch minimum width for wheelchairs and handrails. Thresholds to entrances should be no higher than three inches. Doors should open readily and have a thirty-two-inch clearing.

INDOOR SPACE

The amount and types of indoor space vary from program to program. Most public school kindergartens are housed in a single activity room with an emergency-use restroom. The kindergarten shares the cafeteria, main restrooms, isolation area, and other facilities with elementary-age children also housed in the building. A day-care center is usually housed in a separate building, so some of the following suggestions are not equally applicable to all early childhood programs.

Activity Room

Space affects the quality of living and learning within a center:

> the higher the quality of space in a center, the more likely teachers were to be sensitive and friendly in their manner toward children, to encourage children in their self-chosen activities, and to teach consideration for the rights and feelings of self and others. Where spatial quality was low, children were less likely to be involved and interested, and teachers more likely to be neutral and insensitive in their manner, to use large amounts of guidance and restriction, and to teach arbitrary rules of social living.[9]

The children's activity room is perhaps the single most important area of the building, because it is in this room that children work and play for most of their day.

Room-Directional Orientation
Generally, a southern or eastern exposure is better than a western exposure. A northern exposure is not recommended by most building planners although a northern exposure may be preferable in hot climates where there is no air conditioning. Of course, programs housed in renovated buildings will not have a choice as to directional orientation; however, if the orientation is incorrect, the

resulting light-reflection problems can be partially overcome by use of certain color schemes.

Room Size

Many states use thirty-five square feet per child as the minimum square footage in licensing regulations.[10] Thirty-five square feet per child is considered adequate for infants and toddlers.[11] For older children, especially those in programs that require extra "activity places," forty to sixty square feet per child would be more adequate.[12] Thirty-five square feet can be very workable if the area is exclusive of the space occupied by sinks, lockers, and storage cabinets. Limited indoor space may be offset by sheltered outdoor space where climate permits. If the group of children is small, the space per child should be increased. If a nap period is planned for an all-day program, as much as thirty square feet per child may be needed in addition to the suggested forty to sixty square feet. Regardless of the number of children or length of the session, the children's activity room should be a minimum of nine hundred square feet of clear floor space, exclusive of restrooms, dining area, and separate napping area.

There is a marked increase of negative and idle behavior in situations with a high density of children and few resources, or equipment. On the other hand, positive and constructive behavior was prevalent in day-care centers with low density (of at least forty-eight square feet per child) and plentiful resources. The quality and quantity of resources should be increased if high density is unavoidable.[13] Arrangement becomes very important in low density situations. Shapiro found that some lower density centers (over fifty square feet per child) had poor arrangements.[14]

When floor space is small and ceilings are high, space can be stretched vertically. Balconies with railings or cargo nets can be built over cot storage or other storage; they can be the second floors of two-story houses; or housekeeping centers can be arranged on balconies with block centers below. A balcony built against a wall, particularly corner walls, is most stable and economical. On the other hand, free-standing platforms give more freedom of placement. Various apparatus, such as stairs, ladders, and ramps, can be installed for ascending and descending. For safety purposes, a railing should be provided for stairs greater than three steps. Stationary ladders are safer than rope ladders, and ladder rungs should extend above a platform for easy mounting and dismounting. Ramps covered with friction material and with railings are safer than stairs or ladders, but ramps can be used only with platforms less than four feet high.

Room Arrangement

The room arrangement should have no hidden areas, for these cannot be supervised. Children still have privacy and staff members can supervise as long as dividers and storage cabinets are not over four feet high. When two rooms are joined by a wall, or when a small room opens off the main room, glass panels or openings in the wall at adult height facilitate supervision. An activity room slightly longer than it is wide is less formal looking and easier to arrange. Long, narrow activity rooms encourage running and sliding. The tunnel-like appearance can be minimized by (1) placing learning centers at each end, (2) conducting activities in the center of the room, and (3) using equipment (e.g., tables, shelves) to break straight pathways. Square rooms often have "dead space" in the center, because activity areas are placed along walls instead of being moved towards the center of the room.

A well-organized activity room cuts down on time loss by children and staff and reduces confusion and discipline problems. Room organization also helps communicate the general atmosphere of the program to the child; for example, in early childhood programs where staff members are engaged in direct instruction of children, small spaces defined by walls should be utilized. Conversely, for child-initiated activity programs, there should be a maximum amount of open space. (Specific suggestions for organizing the floor space are covered later in this chapter.) Regardless of the program, however, children need privacy areas—especially children in all-day programs. Prescott and her colleagues measured privacy using a continuum of seclusion-intrusion features (i.e., insulated units—protected areas for small groups, "hiding" areas—places that cozily house one or two children, and softness measures—rugs, cushions, and pillows).[15] Day and Sheehan observed chaotic and frantic child behaviors associated with centers not having privacy areas.[16]

Many building planners recommend covering the floor space with furniture and equipment; for example, Kritchevsky and Prescott state that good space organization is found where the surface is between one-half and two-thirds covered.[17] However, children may not prefer the covered floor surface. In one study of room arrangement, nursery school children were permitted to arrange their activity room as they pleased and leave the equipment in the main classroom or in the adjoining room or hall. This way, children could structure their own environment rather than adjust their activities to the prearranged environment. Instead of choosing a covered-floor arrangement, the children returned equipment and materials to the adjoining room and hall after each activity. They seemed to enjoy roominess and openness.[18]

The needs of children with disabilities should be considered when a room is being arranged. The physically disabled child requires more space for movement. Wheelchairs require an aisle of thirty-six inches and corners of forty-two inches minimum.

Floors, Ceilings, and Walls

These components must be both functional and durable. The materials used on their surfaces coordinated so they are aesthetically pleasing and comfortable.

Young children are accident prone; they get floors wet from play activities, spilling, and bathroom accidents. When choosing floor covering, keep in mind that floors must be kept dry, sanitary, and warm for children's play. Flooring materials should be easy to clean, suited to hard wear, and soundproof. Because children enjoy working on the floor, good floor covering can reduce the number of tables and chairs needed. In fact, floors should be viewed as part of the furniture.

Resilient flooring and carpet are the most prevalent materials used. Resilient flooring includes various types of vinyl floors and linoleum. Carpeting is superior to resilient flooring in softness, noise absorption, and minimizing injuries and breakage. However, carpeting presents problems, such as cleaning up spills, retaining germs and static electricity, moving cabinets or bins equipped with casters, using toys with wheels, and affecting children allergic to carpet fiber. High pile, shag, or even thickly padded carpeting causes problems for children in wheelchairs. Of the soft floor coverings, wall-to-wall carpeting is probably the most desirable, but large carpets, area rugs, throw rugs, carpet remnants joined together with tape, artificial grass, or astroturf may be suitable. To temporarily cover wall-to-wall carpeting, staff members can lay down plastic sheeting, then inexpensive boards such as one-by-twelve's or four-by-eight-foot plywood sheets. Boards should be free of splinters.

Carpeting is best for infant-toddler rooms. Carpeting with large pillows offers a safe floor environment for nonwalkers and toddlers. Toddlers may need a little play space on resilient flooring for block building and play with wheel toys. Resilient flooring is preferred under feeding and diapering areas. Similarly, programs for older children use resilient flooring for areas that get wet or have rugged use and carpet for areas that have passive or noisy, nonwet activities.

Many programs use platforms or wells to facilitate the floor as a place to work and play. Some infant and toddler rooms use a few-inch raised area with a low fence and gate both of transparent mesh or wooden bars (similar to a baby's playpen). This protects nonwalkers from the more active toddlers. Older children enjoy learning centers created by raised and sunken areas, but such areas are less flexible in use. Platforms or wells can be built into the activity room during its construction; less permanent structures can be built with wooden boxes attached to a plywood base and carpeted, or a platform can be built on rollers. If platforms or wells are used, consider the following recommendations: raised or lowered areas should be out of the main flow of traffic; changes in floor levels should not exceed two or three feet and the steps should not be steep—five or six steps for a well two feet deep; in some cases, a railing may be needed to partially surround the well if the well is used in programs for the very young child or if wells are located near areas of fast-moving traffic; and electrical outlets should be provided near the wells or platforms if electrical teaching equipment will be used.

A final problem is keeping floors warm and free from drafts. Radiantly heated floors have been used, but this kind of heat does not solve draft problems. A perimeter wall system as a supplementary heating source provides floor warmth and freedom from drafts.

Ceilings should be of differing heights, to accommodate equipment of various heights. Variation in ceiling height helps with noise control and is aesthetically pleasing. Seven-foot ceilings are too low, unless the space is for children only. Low ceilings make staff members appear excessively large because of the nearness of the adult to the ceiling. Such an illusion makes children feel dominated by the adult, and may cause more aggression by the children.[19] The recommended ceiling height would be ten to eleven feet. In order that the adult provide supervision yet further minimize his presence during free play times, there should be some play areas with low-ceilinged spaces, approximately four feet, that exclude the adult. Low-ceilinged areas may be created by building a two-story playhouse, by using a balcony along an entire wall with learning centers on and under the balcony, or by hanging a canopy.

Although permanent walls provide acoustical privacy, fewer interior walls give greater flexibility in room arrangement. Supervision becomes less of a problem when dividers and storage units delineate space rather than floor-to-ceiling walls. Just as low ceilings make an adult appear excessively large, so do nearby walls. If program planners desire to minimize the adult's presence, they should include fewer walls.

The amount of light in the area is one criterion for choice of wall colors. For example, soft pastels may be chosen for a southern or western exposure, but a northern exposure may need a strong, light-reflecting color such as yellow. Color has also been found to influence academic achievement. For example, red is a good choice for areas planned for gross motor activities and concept development activities; yellow is good for music and art activities; and, green, blue, and purple are effective in reading areas. The use of various colors may be most important in infant and toddler programs, because children have a perception of color over form until four years of age.[20] Equipment, art work, and the children themselves add to the room's brightness.

Walls may be covered with various types of materials other than paint. Wall finishes of soft porous materials can deaden sound, tackboard finishes can permit the use of walls for display, and various wall treatments can be aesthetically pleasing.

Storage and Display Facilities

Every early childhood program facility must have storage. Prescott noted that the amount of storage was positively associated with the richness of the program.[21] Some items always need to be in closed and/or secure storage, such as cleaning supplies, medicines, professional library items, teaching aids, records on children and staff, business records, and personal items of staff.

There needs to be a balance between open and closed storage areas for children's items. Open storage gives children some choices, and closed storage allows staff to regulate choices. Generally speaking, there is more open storage in programs housing older children and those following the interactionist psycho-philosophical view. On the other hand, there is more closed storage in programs housing infants and toddlers and those following the behavioral-environmental view. It is interesting to note that in programs for preschool children, if children were allowed to get things out of closed storage, even with a key, they were less destructive as compared to situations in which only teachers could get closed-storage items.[22]

For infant programs, storage shelves four feet high can hold items safe from reach of infants and toddlers. However, unless doors and drawers are secured with a standard lock or a child-proof device, items may be within the reach of a climbing toddler. Two-foot high shelves are appropriate for open storage, but they must be very sturdy as babies pull themselves up on them.

For preschool and primary programs, shelf height should be approximately three feet for open storage items. Shelves without or with removable doors are excellent, but bins are unsuitable for children. Shelves or racks should be placed near the area where they will be used to aid the flow of traffic and eliminate unnecessary additional steps. The design and materials used in storage units should be compatible with their purpose, such as steeply slanted shelves for books, resting-cot cupboards with louvered doors to allow air circulation, and shelf materials resistant to water damage in water play centers. Different storage designs (slanted vertically and horizontally partitioned cabinets, drawers and shelves of varying depths) help in arranging, finding, and protecting materials and equipment; they are also aesthetically pleasing.

Equipment and materials should be displayed like wares in a market so that children can "window shop" or "buy." How materials are arranged and their accessibility are almost as important as the materials themselves. For infants, items should be placed on the walls near the floor. These include low bulletin boards covered with simple pictures with few details or even household objects that contrast between object and field, unbreakable mirrors, and texture/color boards. For older children, too, an abundance of "pinning space" near eye level is desirable. Backs of storage units may be covered with corkboard or pegboard for displaying children's work. Chalkboards should be on a level children can reach. For children with disabilities, the lower edge of chalkboards, bulletin boards, and mirrors should be one-half foot from floors. Portable chalkboards are more functional than permanent ones.

General Criteria for Learning/Activity Centers
Certainly, the age of the children served and the psycho-philosophical view of a program determine whether learning activity centers are to be used. Most early childhood programs use some centers. Programs housing infants and toddlers and primary-grade children do not use centers as frequently as do programs housing three- through five-year-old children. Programs following the interactionist view often use learning/activity centers as the basis for room arrangements. Conversely, programs following the behavioral-environmental view might use centers to a lesser degree.

Learning/activity centers are a series of working areas that have a degree of privacy but are related to the whole activity room. Their distinctiveness and integrity can be maintained by:

1. Defining space. Shapiro notes the importance of organizing space and making clear boundaries between activity areas.[23] The space should remain flexible, but there should be enough definition to provide a feeling of place. This definition of space may be accomplished by placing dividers or storage units in *L, U,* or other configurations, or by using

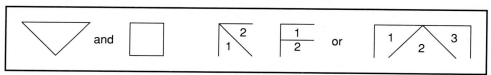

FIGURE 5–1
Using Dividers or Storage Units with Corners and Walls

dividers or storage units in conjunction with corners and walls to create two or more areas as shown in Figure 5–1. Such configurations permit traffic flow but also provide containment. Space can also be defined by differences in colors or shades of wall paint or carpet in adjoining centers, by differences in light intensity in adjacent centers, and by manipulation of the floor planes with wells, pits, or platforms. Adjoining centers can also be visually separated with dividers. (A four-foot high divider will provide enclosure to a standing or sitting child, and a two-foot high divider will provide enclosure to a sitting child.)

Before deciding how to define space for a learning/activity center, one must decide whether or not the space is to be permanent. Differences in colors or shades of wall paint, carpet colors, and manipulation of floor plane are somewhat permanent, but placement of movable dividers or storage units and light intensity are not. There are advantages in being able to change centers; for example, a center may be infrequently used and should be eliminated or made more attractive to the children. The teacher may wish to create an activity/learning center to fit a new curriculum topic, a popular center may need to be enlarged, or a similar center may be created to accommodate additional children. There may also be problems with traffic flow or storage, or the activity room may be too small to house all activities at one time and may need to be re-arranged during the day.

2. Allowing sufficient space. There should be sufficient space for the type of activity that a particular center is intended to accommodate. More space is required in centers with group play, large items of equipment or materials to spread out, or materials or equipment tending to cause aggressive acts among children.

3. Providing acoustical isolation. Noise levels from one center should not interfere with activities in another. Seclusion may be achieved by using adequate acoustical materials on the floors, walls, or ceilings; by providing headsets; by locating centers with similar noise levels, such as library and concept centers adjacent to each other; and by placing extremely noisy centers, like the workshop, outside. Most of the literature suggests separating noisy and quiet areas. However, Nilsen recommends mixing areas to more accurately resemble a real-life situation and

to help prevent areas of the activity room from appearing to be more "for boys" or "for girls."[24]

The types and arrangement of centers must be in keeping with the local program's objectives. Although there are many ways to think about centers in relation to program objectives, one way is through Jones and Prescott's seven dimensions of activity settings as shown in Table 5–1.[25]

In addition to the objectives of the program, other factors enter into the arrangement of learning/activity centers in the room and equipment and materials within each center, such as type of floor covering required; size and quantity of equipment and materials; special requirements, (e.g., a water source, an electrical outlet, a specific intensity of light, or a certain type of storage); the level of noise; and the maximum number of children working in each center at one time. To prevent problems of overcrowding, popular centers may be widely separated to distribute children throughout the room. Furthermore, pathways throughout the activity room should be clear and wide enough to prevent congestion. The edges of pathways can be defined by furniture or changes in floor covering. There should be one entrance per center.

The following comments are not intended as specific solutions on the arrangement of centers (or even a comprehensive list of all centers). Rather, the statements are a mixture of pertinent factors to consider in arranging centers.

Activity Centers for Infants and Toddlers

Infants and toddlers need a room organized into distinct areas that reflect a range of activities. Several principles need to be kept in mind:

1. Bins and toy boxes are inappropriate. Not only is safety a factor but the amount of play time decreases and the amount of toy-selecting time increases when toy boxes and bins are used rather than shelves.[26] Movable shelves aid staff members' response to developmental changes in children and correspond with new program demands. New arrangements are also enjoyed by children.
2. Smaller activity centers for one or two children are more appropriate than the larger centers typical of programs for older children.
3. Activity centers can surround a large play area that becomes the center of action. It is developmentally inappropriate to expect infants and toddlers to play exclusively in the activity areas. By two or three years of age, children recognize differences in space and know what types of behaviors are expected in certain areas. Toddlers who are ready to play in centers must have spatial areas sharply defined if order is to be maintained.
4. Activity centers need to house items in multiple quantities, for children this age rarely share and spend most of their time playing alone in the presence of others.
5. Infants and toddlers need many secluded places. A portable crib or an elevated and fenced area may protect infants from active toddlers for

TABLE 5–1
Dimensions of Activity Settings

Dimension	Explanation	Example
Dimension 1: Open/Closed	Open activity involves the use of materials with no correct outcome and no set stopping point, encourages creative experimentations, and supports interaction.	Sand play and art activities
	Closed activity involves the use of materials with "correct" outcomes and involves right-wrong feedback with a possible sense of accomplishment.	Puzzles and lotto
Dimension 2: Simple/Complex	Simple activity involves the use of usually one material with only one possible use.	Swings
	Complex activity involves the use of two or more play materials with the potential for active manipulations and alteration by children.	Sand table with digging equipment, sifters, sand molds, and water
Dimension 3: High/Low mobility	High mobility activity requires large muscle mobility.	Climbing equipment
	Low mobility activity requires little to no mobility.	Puzzles
	Intermediate mobility activity requires moderate mobility using both large and small muscles.	Blocks
Dimension 4: Social structure	Individual activity Small group activity Intermediate group activity Whole class activity	Looking at a book Blocks Music activity Listening to a story
Dimension 5: Soft/Hard	Softness is based on the presence of soft textures.	Malleable materials: sand lap to sit on single sling swings grass rug/carpet water messy activities (finger paints) cozy furniture dirt to dig in animals to be held
	Hardness is based on the presence of hard textures.	Lack of the above
Dimension 6 Intrusion/Seclusion	Intrusion is "interruption" by other children.	On a climbing apparatus a child may show off skills to another child by saying, "See me" or "Watch."
	Seclusion is the lack of intrusion by others.	"Reading" a book while sitting in a chair off the "beaten path" does not invite intrusion
Dimension 7: Risk/Safety	Risk activity tests the child's skills; child sees apparent risks.	Climbing activity
	Safe activity involves no risks.	Finger painting

short periods of time. Toddlers need couches, low sturdy shelves, barrels, and other secluded places.

6. Infants and toddlers especially need an activity room that permits high mobility, has mainly open activities, and provides materials for complex activities (as defined in Table 5–1).
7. Infants and toddlers need an aesthetically pleasing environment of beautiful colors, sounds, forms, textures (especially softness), and patterns.
8. Adults need comfortable places to sit while playing or holding young children. Thus, adult-sized couches, upholstered chairs, and rocking chairs should be placed throughout the activity room.

Cataldo lists these centers for infants and toddlers: block and vehicle, small manipulative toy area, quiet area, and art.[27] Adams and Taylor suggest these activity areas: listening, seeing, touch, fantasy, water and sand, quiet, gross motor, creativity, and construction.[28] Stewart adds a music area.[29]

Figure 5–2, a floor plan of an infant/toddler activity room, illustrates some of the principles discussed. Napping, feeding, and changing/toileting areas are discussed later in this chapter. Figure 5–2 is only an example, because administrators need to fit their plan to their program.

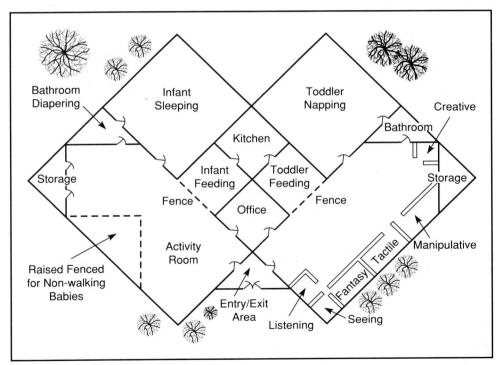

FIGURE 5–2
Infant/Toddler Center

Learning/Activity Centers for Older Children

As previously discussed, learning/activity centers are common in preschool programs and in kindergarten and primary level (or grade) programs using the interactionist psycho-philosophical view.

Several common learning/activity centers for preschool and kindergarten children are listed below along with a few statements about planning the center and locating it within the activity room. The comments are not intended as specific solutions on the arrangement of centers (or even a comprehensive list of all centers); rather the statements are simply some pertinent factors associated with each center.

Block Center. In block play, there is a tendency toward expansive aggression and solitary retreat; therefore, the block center should accommodate a child who wants to work alone, with another child, or with a group of four or five children. The working areas in the block center should be fluid enough to encourage a regrouping of children. There are several ways of accommodating various group sizes. Block centers may be housed both inside and outside, on a terrace or other firm, flat surface or can be divided into large or small areas. A center should be twenty-five square feet to accommodate one or two children; for three to five children, seventy-five square feet are necessary. These block center sizes can be created by subdividing a large block center with dividers or shelves, by placing block centers throughout the room (perhaps a small center near the entrance for a timid child and a larger center adjacent to the dramatic play center), and by using a raised platform or pit for small centers and open floor space for large centers.

Since block constructions are easily knocked over by fast-moving traffic, centers should be placed in areas where traffic moves at a slower pace. They should have protection via storage units or dividers almost enclosing the centers in configurations such as ⌐￣⌐ or ⌐￣￣. Finally, the block center requires acoustical materials to lessen the noise of falling or banging blocks. A dense, low-pile carpet should cover the floor, and block shelves could be carpeted to reduce noise.

Dramatic Play Center. The most common type of dramatic play center is the housekeeping corner. Because of the size of the furniture (stoves, doll beds, chairs, and tables), it requires approximately seventy-five to one hundred square feet of floor space. If a dress-up area is included, additional space is required. Carpeting is not needed for acoustical control in this area and should not be used if children use water in their miniature kitchen. Although the housekeeping corner needs to be enclosed to give a homelike atmosphere, the openings should be wide enough to accommodate doll buggies. Alcoves often serve as housekeeping centers.

Some early childhood programs attempt to expand dramatic play beyond prestructured areas. Staff members provide basic materials, such as boxes, bottles, cans, pillows, ropes, wheels, and hardware gadgets, and encourage children to dramatize any experience they wish. Unless prestructured areas are desired, there are two solutions for housing the dramatic play center: do not provide a specific center, instead, permit children to play in other centers or in a multipurpose area; or provide a specific space and equip it with materials conducive to many types of dramatic play.

Art Center. The art center should have places for individual and group work. Work surfaces include the wall (chalkboards and murals), tilted surfaces (easels), and flat surfaces (tables). Movable stand-up tables should be approximately twenty inches high and sit-down/stand-up tables about eighteen inches high. Built-in work surfaces should be twenty inches high and between two and three feet deep.

A sink in the art center or in an adjacent restroom with plenty of counter space on both sides is essential for mixing paints and cleanup. The sink should have a faucet twenty-three inches above the floor and should be equipped with a disposal drain for catching clay and paste. The sink counter and the wall behind the sink should be covered with an easily cleaned surface.

Surfaces in the art area should be impervious to water, paint, paste, and clay and be easy to clean. Floors should not be slippery when wet, and all surfaces should dry quickly. Linoleum, Formica, or a vinyl cloth should cover the tables; ceramic tile, vinyl-coated wallpaper, or waterproof paint should cover the walls; and the floor should have a vinyl covering.

The art center needs many storage shelves for supplies. To protect poster and construction paper from light and dust, these storage shelves should have doors, although other storage shelves may be open. Drying art products will require lines and racks for paintings and mobiles, and shelves for three-dimensional products.

The art center should be appropriately located where ample light is available from lighting fixtures or windows that provide sun-free directional light. When weather conditions permit, art activities can be taken outdoors.

Music Center. Children can listen to music in any of the quiet areas with the listening stations and headsets; however, the area for dancing and singing should be physically separate or acoustically treated to contain sound. Carpeting the rhythm/dance area does not permit as much freedom of movement as vinyl flooring, but it minimizes danger from falls. The piano should not be placed near windows, doors, or heating or cooling units.

Sand Play Center. A stand-up sand table should be twenty-two inches high and a sit-down sand table should be sixteen inches high. Because there may be many conflicts at the sand table, provide a flat working surface, such as an eight-inch wide board down the center of the table, from end to end, and station the children about two feet apart. Sand tables may be permanently installed or movable; a movable unit can be pushed out of the way when not in use or taken outdoors. Because sand tracks and is slippery underfoot, the sand play center should be carpeted (and sand removed by a heavy-duty vacuum), or a metal grate with a collecting pan installed flush with the floor. In addition to sand, other materials such as dirt, gravel, or styrofoam pieces may be used effectively in the sand table. A supply of containers for the sand when other materials are being used is needed.

Water Play Center. The indoor water play center should be close to a water source and drain, out of the main flow of traffic, and somewhat enclosed. Water table height should be between twenty and twenty-four inches. Children should be stationed about two feet apart; if both sides of the table are to be occupied, the table should be three feet wide. For toys, shelving should be made of material unaffected by water and adjacent to the water play area. The water play center should have a slip-proof surface—an indoor/outdoor carpet or a rubber mat with tapered edges.

Concept and Manipulative Centers. Concept and manipulative centers is a generic term used for areas where children engage in activities, such as reading readiness, mathematics, social studies, and fine motor skills (e.g., lacing cards, working puzzles, and stringing beads). In some programs, several concept and manipulative centers are set up and maintained separately as a math center, a reading center, and so on. In other programs, one center houses all of the materials for the various types of activities. Regardless of the specific housing arrangements, the concept and manipulative centers are characterized by quietness and by children working alone or in groups with staff members' assistance. For individual or small-group work, quietness can be created by using a corner with tables, using built-in alcoves, or creating alcove-like spaces. The teacher can arrange shelves or screens to give a sense of enclosure, use study carrels modified to accept audiovisual machines, or have special lighting, acoustical, or other design treatments. If a separate room is used for group sessions, the room should be no larger than one hundred square feet and unaffected by outside sounds.

Microcomputer Center. Similar to the concept and manipulative center, the microcomputer center is characterized by quietness and by children working alone or in groups with staff members' assistance. Although the center may be small, microcomputers usually require three or more electrical outlets for operation. Security for microcomputers may also be a problem when schools are not in operation. A large closet with heavy doors that lock may allow for some security. The closet may be used as the microcomputer center if adjustable shelves provide space for keyboards and video terminals. With the doors open, the closet would serve as a divider to provide quietness and some privacy.

Places for Animals and Plants. Many programs for young children include the keeping of animals and plants. A major problem in this is that young children disturb living things. Places for living things should be carefully planned to provide for their safety and for children's learning. Such planning requires housing each animal and plant on an appropriate table; placing animal homes out of the flow of traffic; providing a sturdy table (preferably child-sitting height, with a surface larger than the base of the container and covered with Formica); and providing chairs or stools around the table. Plants need varying amounts of light and humidity, which must be considered in placing them in the room.

Other Areas. In addition to learning activity centers, a children's room should have private areas.[30] A private area serves as a place to "tune out," to enjoy being by oneself for a few minutes, or to reduce excitement. A private area also serves as a place to watch from, such as small block centers, a rocking horse, a window seat, playhouse, or a riding toy. A place to watch from should be close to ongoing activities, while providing the child with a sense of enclosure. Children also enjoy special interest areas, such as an aquarium or terrarium, rock, mineral, or shell collection, a garden seen from a window, a hanging basket, an arboretum, egg incubator, books, and displays connected with specific curriculum themes.

Before drawing a floor plan, these three steps may need to be taken:

1. Decide on the centers which best fit program goals and then calculate the number of center activity slots needed. To calculate the number of center activity slots needed, multiply the number of children by 1.5. (For example, twenty children require thirty activity slots.) Having more choices than children lessens waiting time and gives a reasonable number of options.
2. Next, list the centers and give the maximum activity slots (i.e., maximum number of children who can be in a center at the same time) for each center as shown in Figure 5–3.
3. Develop a matrix of centers and the requirements for each center. Requirements would need to be developed. (We used the Jones and Prescott dimensions and a few additional criteria as an example in Figure 5–4). Cluster-related activities which share compatible criteria, are shown in Figure 5–5.

Figure 5–6 is a floor plan for preschool and/or kindergarten (especially for three- through five-year-olds) children's activity room. Figure 5–7 is a floor plan for primary-level (especially six- through eight-year-olds) children's activity room. Figure 5–7 includes learning/activity centers devoted more directly to reading, writing, and mathematics while maintaining many of the centers in-

Center	Maximum Activity Slots
Cooking	3
Dramatic Play	4
etc.	etc.
	Total of 30 slots

FIGURE 5–3
Activity Center Maximum Activity Slots

Criteria	Centers		
	Block	**Art**	**Library**
open	X		
closed			
simple			
complex	X		
high mobility			
intermediate mobility	X		
low mobility			
individual			
small group	X		
intermediate group			
whole class			
soft	X (carpeted)		
hard			
intrusion			
seclusion	X		
risk			
safety	X		
electricity			
water			
quiet			
noisy	X		
open storage	X		
closed storage			
display			

FIGURE 5–4
Center Criteria

All of these centers need a water source.	cooking
	water play
	art
	snack
These centers are conceptually related and may be used together	dress up
	housekeeping

FIGURE 5–5

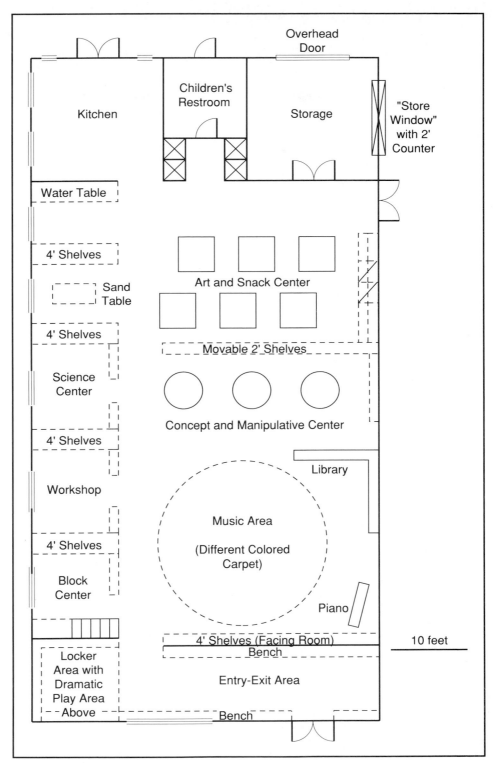

FIGURE 5–6
Preschool or Kindergarten Children's Activity Room

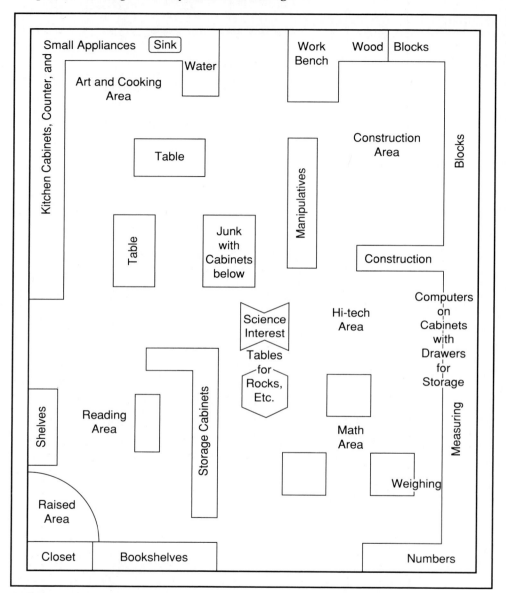

FIGURE 5–7
Primary Classroom

cluded in Figure 5–6. Because floor arrangements must fit the needs of the local program, the floor plans are intended for illustration of some of the principles just discussed.

School-Age Child Care Activity Centers

School-Age Child Care (SACC) activity centers are unique for three reasons. First, SACC programs must accommodate a wide age range (often five- through ten- or twelve-year olds). Second, programs are for shorter periods of daily time (average of two to three hours) during the school session and sometimes full day-care during holidays and summer vacation periods. And third, SACC programs are unique because they are often shared-space areas (i.e., space shared with regular school programs, church programs, or preschool day-care). It is too costly to set up a permanent, nonshared center for the fewer hours of the SACC program as compared with other early childhood programs.

Activity centers for SACC programs are often created by mobile shelves and dividers. A large storage closet or storage-workroom combination is most helpful. SACC programs are often designed with activities that are similar to quality home life for school age children. As shown in Figure 5–8, the centers can include: (1) quiet areas for reading, doing homework, listening to music with earphones, creative writing, or just resting; (2) creative area(s) for art/craft work, possibly including woodworking; (3) table games and manipulative area(s); (4) cooking and/or eating a snack area; and, (5) high technology areas such as computers and softwear, video cassette recorders (VCRs), and cassettes. Other fun areas are block construction, science centers, and larger table games such as Ping-Pong.

Additional Areas for Children

Learning is going on all the time in an early childhood program: in the shared activity area, the restrooms, the dining area, the napping area, and the isolation area as well as the children's activity room. The children use many additional areas to take care of their physical needs, and staff members emphasize the necessity for children's becoming self-reliant in taking care of these needs. Thus, designing additional areas must be done with as much care as planning the children's activity room.

Shared Activity Areas

In some early childhood programs, several rooms open into a shared activity area, usually a large room, an exceptionally long and wide hallway, or a covered patio. Shared activity areas are often used for physical education, music, rhythmic activities, and drama.

Resource Room

Early childhood programs involved in mainstreaming children with disabilities may have a resource room equipped with special education materials needed by children with disabilities who are enrolled in the program. Usually the special

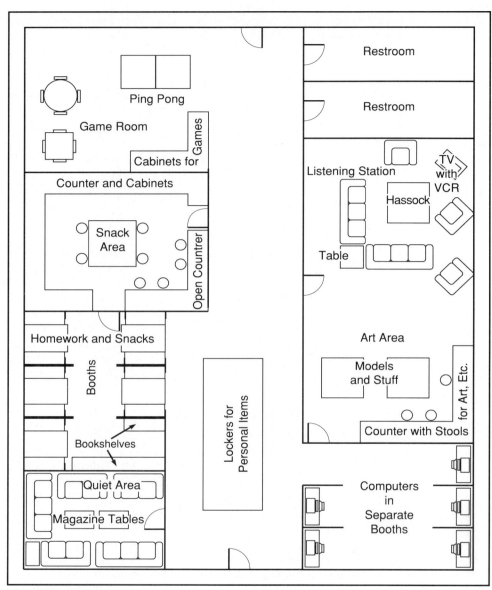

FIGURE 5–8
School-Age Child Care Activity Center

education teacher uses the resource room in working with the special child for part of the day.

Children's Lockers or Cubbies

Children should have their own individual cubbies for storing personal belongings because this emphasizes personal possessions, helps the children learn proper habits for caring for their belongings, and reduces the danger of spreading contagious disease. The locker or cubbie area should not be part of the entry-exit area, but should be close to this area and the outdoor space. The children's locker area should be large enough to facilitate easy circulation of staff members when they help children with wraps. The floor covering in the locker area should be easily cleaned because it will get quite dirty during inclement weather.

Various combinations of storage are possible for children's possessions. Outdoor garments, extra clothing and aprons, blankets or rest mats, and personal possessions, such as crayons, show-and-tell treasures, and art work to take home, may be stored together or separately. Lockers usually provide places to hang garments, and overshoes are placed on the floor of the locker. Such a locker may be modified by adding one or two top shelves to accommodate a shoe box or a tote tray (usually seven by eight by fifteen inches) for personal possessions, and a blanket or rest mat. Another shelf about ten inches from the bottom of the locker provides a place for the child to sit while putting on overshoes or changing clothes. Garment hooks are attached to the bottom of the lower top shelf or to the sides or back of the locker. The overall dimensions of this locker would be approximately fifty-six to sixty inches high, and twelve by fifteen inches wide and deep. Lockers seldom include doors as these catch little fingers, are always in the way, and are never closed.

Jefferson suggests creating inexpensive lockers by installing two parallel horizontal shelves about twelve inches apart, with upright partitions dividing the shelves into ten-inch compartments.[31] A hook is placed under each compartment for wraps. If there is no sitting place in the locker itself, stools or benches permit off-the-floor sitting.

Three other considerations need attention in planning children's lockers or cubbies:

1. If the lockers or cubbies are not designed with partitions between the wraps, hooks should be spaced so one child's wraps are not against those of another.
2. Hangers on clothing rods are difficult for children, as wraps have a tendency to fall off, and a child may, intentionally or unintentionally, use a hanger as a weapon.
3. Name tags or symbols on cubbies or tote trays further emphasize personal possessions and help staff members locate a child's cubbie when the child is sick and a parent comes to pick up a child's possessions. When straightening up the room after hours, a staff member can locate a child's misplaced possession.

Infants' Changing Areas and Children's Restrooms

The diapering area for infants should be spatially separated from the kitchen and feeding areas. The diapering table or counter should be adjacent to a sink with running hot and cold water for immediate staff handwashing.[32] A closed-closet storage for soap, washcloths, diapers, and counter disinfectants needs to be housed in the area. Diapers and other trash must be disposed of in containers inaccessible to both infants and older children. (See chapter 9 for further health standards.) The area should be interesting to infants with a mirror on the wall above the table and other displays on the wall or suspended from the ceiling. Washable toys may also be provided for infants to hold.

Children's restrooms should have two doors, one off the activity room and one into the outdoor area. Each restroom should be approximately five square feet per child when in maximum use. When a large building houses more than thirty-five children, there should be restrooms in different areas. Early childhood programs for children under school age do not generally provide separate restrooms for boys and girls. Because some children like privacy, unlocked, low partitions between and in front of toilets provide this feature and permit easy supervision. Partitions rather than doors are especially helpful for children who are physically disabled. The restroom should be cheerful, with windows for sunlight and ventilation, bright wall colors, and potted plants. The ratio of the number of toilets to the number of children should be approximately one to eight. Toilet seats should be between ten and thirteen inches from the floor. These toilet seat heights may be too high for the toddler or very young child; thus, the restroom may need portable "potties," a step installed to the child-sized toilets, or toilets set into the floor. For children who are disabled, the toilet tissue should be not more than six inches from the front of the toilet bowl. Handrails should be mounted on the wall for additional safety. Urinals, especially trough rather than floor-mounted types, keep the toilet seats and floors clean.

Lavatory bowls should be adjacent to, but outside of, toilet areas and placed near the door. The ratio of the number of bowls to the number of children should be one to ten or one to eight. Bowl heights should vary between one and one-half to two feet. A blade or lever rather than a knob water control should be used to help the child who is disabled become independent. The water heater should be set to provide lukewarm water, thus preventing scalded hands. (Because the thermostatic control must be set higher for the dishwasher, another water heater must be installed for kitchen water.) Bowls must be equipped with disposal drains to catch clay, sand, and so forth; mirrors, preferably of safety glass or metal, should be placed at child's height over them. If cloth towels are used, the hooks should be far enough apart so hanging towels do not touch each other; however, paper towels are more sanitary. To accommodate children who are disabled, the bottom edge of the paper towel dispenser should be mounted less than two feet from the floor. If the budget permits, a bathtub is helpful, especially in an all-day program or one serving younger children.

Drinking fountains should be located near the restrooms and out of the path of fast-moving traffic. They should be made of vitreous china or stainless steel and be between twenty and twenty-three inches high. Water-bubbling level should be controlled. It takes time for young children to learn to get enough water from a fountain to quench their thirst; thus, paper cups should be available for children learning to drink from a fountain.

Feeding and Dining Areas

The feeding area for infants and toddlers should be equipped with feeding chairs and some toddler-sized tables and chairs for family style eating. The feeding area should be near the kitchen, which can be equipped with a half-door (i.e., "Dutch" door) to provide visual supervision when staff members prepare or secure food or feeding items. Young children enjoy the contact between food preparation and eating, too. Pictures on the walls and soft music add to the feeding area.

Kitchen facilities need not be extensive for programs for older children serving snacks. A kitchen needs a few heating elements, a refrigerator with a small freezer compartment, a sink with hot and cold water, a dishwasher, work-counter space, and storage units. The Department of Agriculture publishes guides for the selection of food service equipment for programs serving main meals. Serving counters for children should be two feet or less in height and as close as possible to dining tables.

The dining area should be bright, cheerful, and airy, with screens on the windows. All surfaces should be made of materials that are soap-and-water scrubbable and resistant to water damage. In planning the dining area, allow plenty of space per child for manipulating trays, sliding chairs back, and so forth.

Napping Areas

Infant/toddler napping areas should be spacious with separate cribs for each child. The napping area should be adjacent to the playroom with an observation window in the sleeping room. The room should appear cozy with carpeting, shaded windows, and rocking chairs. A fan increases air circulation and masks outside noises. Soft music is also desirable.

For older children, a napping area should be considered for all-day programs. Sleeping areas should be isolated from noise in adjacent areas, and lighting should be controlled. If a separate napping room is used, efficient use of space can be achieved by placing cots end-to-end in rows, with an aisle approximately four feet wide between the rows. Small screens may be used to separate cots.

Programs that do not have separate napping areas must provide for resting in the children's activity room. The disadvantages of locating cots throughout the activity room are that more space is required, in comparison to placing cots head-to-toe; supervision is difficult; and cots must be moved at the beginning and end of each session. Cots must be stored in a well-ventilated storage unit, because stacked cots in the corner of the room make an attractive but dangerous climbing apparatus.

Isolation Area

An isolation area is necessary for caring for ill or hurt children until parents arrive. It should contain a bed or cot and have a small play space, because a cheerfully decorated room with a few toys reduces the hospital-like atmosphere. A small bathroom adjacent to the isolation area is helpful.

Adult Areas

Although the early childhood facility is planned primarily for young children, housing must also meet the requirements of staff members and parents. The two major criteria to meet in planning adult areas is that they be scaled to adult size and that the type and specific design of each area fit the needs of the program.

Parent Reception Area

A parent reception area should make parents feel welcome and encourage exchange of information between parents and staff members. A separate area adjacent to the children's activity room has these advantages: (1) a parent has a place to sit and wait until the child completes an activity or puts on her coat; (2) a parent does not have the feeling of being stranded in the middle of the children's room while waiting; (3) interruptions of children's activities are minimized; and (4) a parent can speak confidentially to a staff member. The parent reception area should be well-defined, comfortable, and invite the parent to view the materials arranged on the bulletin board, browse through the materials placed on various tables, or visit.

An observation room should be adjacent to or part of the parent receiving area. When the observation room is part of this area, one-way glass rather than screens should be used for the observation window because talking can be heard through a screen. If the observation room has a curtain drawn across the one-way glass, films can also be shown there. Observation rooms may also be balconies, which have the advantage of not taking up valuable floor space.

Staff/Parent Lounge

A staff/parent lounge should be provided for resting and visiting. Comfortable chairs and a place for preparing and eating a snack should be considered in designing a staff/parent lounge. For greater privacy, adult restrooms should not be part of the lounge but located nearby. The staff lounge may be combined with the parents' lounge; however, in all-day programs where the staff may need a period of relaxation, separate lounges should be considered.

Office and Workroom

When early childhood programs are housed with other programs under the same administrative control, office and workroom areas are usually shared. Conversely, early childhood programs housed in separate buildings or in buildings with other programs not under the same administrative control usually have office and workroom areas designed especially for their program.

The design of the office and workroom area should fit the needs of the local program. For most early childhood programs, space will be needed for desks or tables and chairs, cabinets for filing professional materials and records, office machines, large work tables, high stools, a sink, storage units for office supplies and other work materials. Additional offices are needed if the program employs special service personnel.

Environmental Control

An important consideration in constructing any early childhood facility is environmental control, including lighting, heating, cooling, ventilating, and acoustics. Lack of adequate environmental control results in a number of problems, such as eyestrain from glare or discomfort from heat or cold. It can also contribute to poor behavioral patterns, not only in children, but in adults as well. Adequate environmental control can also save money. Become familiar with good energy-saving practices by reading some of the many pamphlets on this topic.

Lighting

Illumination is highly important because of the amount of time spent on visual tasks. Also, approximately one-fifth of the enrolled children will have below-normal vision. Not only does lighting affect physical well-being, but it also has a psychological and aesthetic impact.

Diffused light, such as fluorescent bulbs above plastic diffusing panels, should be considered for use with young children, because it provides nonglare lighting with very little heat. Fluorescent lighting is less expensive to operate, although more expensive to install, than incandescent lighting. However, the "cool" shades of fluorescent lights should not be used; the best shades are the warm ones—"delux warm white," similar to light emitted by incandescent, or "vita lite," similar to light emitted by the sun. Because incandescent light is a concentrated source, it can spotlight learning/activity areas. Regulatory agencies frequently specify the minimum amount of light intensity for various parts of the facility. Usually fifty to sixty footcandles of glare-free illumination are recommended.[33] After fifty footcandles, the amount of light must be doubled or redoubled to increase visual efficiency; thus, task lighting is more efficient than general illumination when more than fifty footcandles of illumination is needed.

Because lighting should be tailored to the needs of children working in each center, variable light controls should be provided in each area. For example:

> the art area could have sun-free directional light from skylights or windows, the reading area could have soft incandescent light and a view of the window, and the plant area could be a small greenhouse.[34]

Local lighting in a learning/activity center should not be so bright as to make other centers appear dim and hence unattractive.

Window areas should be approximately one-fifth of the floor area.[35] Approximately 50 percent of the required window area should be openable, and those windows that open should be screened. A windowsill twenty-four inches high permits children to see out. Windows, when properly placed, help soften shadows cast by overhead lighting, provide a distant visual release, and allow for a link with the outside world.[36]

Reflective surfaces in the room determine the efficiency of illumination. Light-color shades on walls and ceilings are important reflecting factors. Walls should be light enough to reflect 50 percent of the light, and ceilings light enough to reflect 70 percent.[37] There should be as little contrast as possible between ceiling and light source. Tables and countertops should reflect 35 to 50 percent of the light.[38] Even light-colored floors increase the efficiency of illumination. Louvers, blinds, and overhangs control excessive light from windows and help prevent glare. Glare is also reduced by covering work surfaces with a matte finish. Peripheral lighting keeps the level of illumination uniform and thus prevents glare.[39]

Heating, Cooling, and Ventilating

The temperature of the room should be between 68 and 72 degrees Fahrenheit (20 to 22 degrees Celsius) within two feet of the floor.[40] Thermostats should be at the eye level of seated children. Many early childhood facilities are finding it necessary to have central air conditioning. Because it costs more to cool than to heat air, "there is a tendency to close in the space, make it more compact, increase the insulation, reduce the perimeter, and reduce the amount of window area."[41] There should be a circulation of ten through thirty cubic feet of air per child per minute.[42] For comfort, the humidity should be from 50 through 65 percent.[43] If a humidifying system is not installed, an open aquarium or water left in the pans at the water table will add humidity to the room.

Acoustics

A nearly square room has better acoustical control than a long narrow room.[44] Acoustical absorption underfoot is more effective, and thus more economical, than overhead.[45] Learning/activity centers that generate the greatest amount of noise should be designed and decorated for maximum acoustical absorption. Sand and grit on the floor increase noise as well as destroy the floor covering. Leeper, et al., suggest reducing noise by using tablecloths on luncheon tables, area rugs, padding on furniture legs, removable pads on tabletops when hammering, and doors to keep out kitchen noises.[46]

OUTDOOR SPACE

Outdoor play has been an integral part of early childhood programs and hence housing facilities. However, concepts about the values of certain types of play have changed over the years. Along with these changing concepts, there has been an evolution in playgrounds.

To Froebel, children's playgrounds "were nature itself." Children tended gardens, built stream dams, cared for animals, and played running games. By the 1900s, large apparatuses such as slides, swings, and stairs were added both to the indoor and outdoor areas of early childhood programs. Much of the equipment was not safe. The inadequate planning resulted in this so-called traditional playground coming to be referred to as the "sea of asphalt" or the "sterile square." The 1950s and 1960s saw innovative playgrounds designed by artists, recreational specialists, and commercial manufacturers. Two common types of playgrounds were the adventure playgrounds (discussed in Chapter 6) and theme playgrounds (e.g., boat-shaped sandbox in a nautical theme playground). In the 1970s and 1980s, modular wooden play structures became popular. More recently, these modular play structures have incorporated space-age plastics.[47]

Regardless of the type of program, outdoor space should meet these criteria:

1. Outdoor space should meet safety guidelines (as discussed in later sections of this chapter).
2. Outdoor space should preserve and enhance natural features (as described in later sections of this chapter).
3. The design should be based on the needs of children. Most early childhood professionals agree that play can enhance various aspects of development (i.e., physical, cognitive, social, and emotional) although the stress placed on various aspects of development will vary depending on the local program base. Frost and Wortham[48] summarize how each aspect of development is enhanced through play and list the types of materials suited for each developmental outcome. Frost's review of research shows that traditional playgrounds with their fixed equipment (e.g., swings, slides) are not good places for children to play from a developmental standpoint (as well as for safety reasons). Young children need both fixed, complex equipment (e.g., a play structure complex in design) and simple, readily transportable materials that can be manipulated by children (e.g., sand, water, lumber, and tires).[49] Similarly, Johnson, Cristie, and Yawkey found that two playground design features associated with high levels of play are: flexible materials (i.e., materials that children can manipulate, change, and combine) and materials providing a wide variety of experiences.[50] Playgrounds should also meet the needs of the child who is disabled.[51]
4. Outdoor space should provide opportunities for activities similar to those conducted in the indoor space. There should be places that challenge children's total development. Johnson, Christie, and Yawkey list four types of play experiences: (1) functional play or exercise which involves practice and repetition of gross motor activities; (2) constructive play which involves using materials such as paints or sand to create; (3) dramatic play or pretend play which is often conducted in enclosed places; and (4) group play or play which involves more than one child (e.g., seesaws, rule games, and often dramatic play.)[52] Howard discusses nine centers on playgrounds that can meet these four types of

play. These are (1) digging, (2) water play, (3) dramatic play, (4) climbing, (5) pushing/pulling or riding, (6) construction, (7) open running, (8) gardening, and (9) quiet.

Centers can integrate more than one type of play. For example, digging can be both constructive and dramatic.[53] Basically, the indoors is extended outside. However, there are some differences in the outside centers as compared to inside centers. Outside centers are often less structured; the divisions between centers are less clear (e.g., a "car wash" involves water play, dramatic play, and push/pull and riding toys); centers may be located in several areas (e.g., dramatic play may be in a playhouse under a play structure, in tents under the trees, or in the garden); there is more freedom to move; there are not as many restrictions on the number of children allowed per center; and there are more seasonal changes in outside centers (e.g., water play in warm weather) as compared to indoor centers.[54]

5. Outdoor space should be aesthetically pleasing. The outdoor space should appeal to all the senses. Talbot and Frost have proposed some design qualities (e.g., sensuality, brilliance, "placeness," and juxtaposition of opposites) that should be considered in designing playscapes which address the child's sense of wonder and awareness.[55]

Specifications for Outdoor Space

Specifications for the outdoor space should be sufficiently flexible to meet local needs and requirements and should include considerations such as location, size, enclosure, terrain, surface, and shelter.

Location

Outdoor activity areas should not surround the building because supervision becomes almost impossible. The area is best located on the south side of the building where there will be sun and light throughout the day. The outdoor space should be easily accessible from the inside area. To minimize the chance of accidents as children go from inside to outside, or vice versa, a facility should have (1) a door threshold flush with the indoor/outdoor surfaces, or a ramp, if there is an abrupt change in surface levels; (2) adjoining surfaces covered with material that provides maximum traction; (3) a sliding door or a door prop; and (4) a small glass panel in the door to prevent collisions.

Indoor restrooms and lockers should be adjacent to the outdoor area. If this is impossible, there should be one restroom opening off the playground. The sometimes difficult problem of managing clothing makes speedy access to a restroom important. A drinking fountain should also be easily accessible to children during outdoor play.

Size

Most licensing regulations require a minimum of seventy-five square feet per child for outdoor activity areas.[56] The Child Welfare League recommends two hundred square feet per child. For example, fifty feet by sixty feet (three thousand square feet) would be needed for fifteen children.[57] A minimum of fifteen square feet per child should be added for a sheltered area or terrace. Approximately one-third the square footage of the outdoor area should be used for passive outdoor play, as in a sand pit or outdoor art center, and the remainder for active outdoor play such as climbing and running. "Adventure" or junk playgrounds may be one-half to two and one-half acres in size.[58]

Enclosure

Enclosure of the outdoor area relieves the staff member of a heavy burden of responsibility, gives the child a sense of freedom without worry, and prevents stray animals from wandering in. A nonclimbable barrier approximately four feet high is adequate as boundaries that adjoin dangerous areas (parking lots, streets, or ponds), but minimal barriers such as large stones or shrubbery are adequate in areas where the outside has no potential dangers.

In addition to the entry from the building, the outdoor area should have a gate opening wide enough to permit trucks to deliver sand or large items of play equipment. If children are allowed to use the outdoor area for after-program hours, a small gate should be installed and benches placed on the periphery to give adults a place to relax while watching and supervising.

Terrain

Flat terrain with hard surfacing is dangerous because it provides no curb for random movement. A rolling terrain has several advantages. Mounds are ideal for active games of leaping and running and are a natural shelter for passive games such as sand or water play. Mounds can be used in conjunction with equipment; for example, slides without ladders can be mounted to a slope so children can climb the mound and slide down the slide. Ladders and boards can connect the mounds. Tricycle paths can wind on a rolling terrain.

Surface

Surface for infants and toddlers should be mainly grass, wood, sand, and dirt. Older children's outdoor activity area should also have a variety of surfaces and be well-drained, with the fastest-drying areas nearest the building. It is desirable to have one-half to two-thirds of the total square footage covered with grass, and about one-thousand square feet covered in hard surfaces for activities such as wheeled-toy riding and block building.[59] Some areas should be left as dirt for gardening and for realizing "a satisfaction common to every child—digging a big hole!"[60]

Safety is a primary concern when considering surfacing. Changes in types of surfacing should be level to prevent children from tripping. Special surfacing is needed under any equipment from which a child might fall. When a child falls, either the surface gives to absorb the impact or the child gives with a resulting bruise, broken bone, spinal injury, head injury, or even death. The American Society for Testing and Materials (ASTM) is the organization responsible for developing standards that are then adopted under federal law. ASTM has still not released the final surfacing standards.[61] The following are three types of surfaces, each with its disadvantages, used under equipment:

1. Organic loose material (e.g., pine bark and mulch) maintained at a depth of eight to twelve inches. Organic materials must be kept fluffed up and kept at the maximum depth to be effective. Unfortunately the material scatters and decomposes.
2. Inorganic loose material (e.g., sand, pea gravel, and shredded tires) maintained at a depth of eight to twelve inches. Animals may use sand as a litter box and it loses its resiliency in wet, freezing weather. Gravel is hard to walk on, and shredded tires stick to clothing.
3. Compact materials (e.g., rubber and foam mats). These materials require a flat surface and professional installation. These costly items are also subject to vandalism.

There should be a six-foot zone with protective surface in all directions as well as underneath stable equipment and a seven-foot zone with protective surface around and under equipment with moving parts (e.g., swings and gliders).[62]

Shelter

The building, trees and shrubs, or a rolling terrain should protect children from excessive sun and wind. Knowledge of snow patterns and prevailing winds may lead to the use of snow fences or other structures to provide snowy hills and valleys. A covered play area should be planned as an extension of the indoor area. The shelter's purpose is for passive play during good weather and for all play during inclement weather. It should be designed to permit a maximum amount of air and sunshine.

Outdoor Space Arrangement

As previously mentioned, the outdoor space should not be barren but should be aesthetically pleasing, safe, and designed to further the purposes of the early childhood program.

Outdoor Area for Infants and Toddlers

Many people think of playgrounds as areas for rough and tumble play. Thus, when one says an "infant and toddler playground," it almost sounds oxymoronic. However, we know infants and toddlers need fresh air and sunlight and delight in exploring their outside environment. Perhaps it would seem less strange to call the planned outdoor environment an *outdoor place* or *park*.

Although we have already discussed general specifications for outdoor space, three criteria are extremely important in planning an outdoor place for the infant and toddler. First, it must be scaled to the size of these very young children in order to be safe, comfortable, and rich for exploring. Second, it must be safe; that is, a gentle terrain for crawling, walking, running, and stepping up and down, no high play structures, no harmful materials if eaten (e.g., no gravel, only sand protected from animals, and plant life safe in all stages of growth),[63] and free from foreign objects. And third, the outdoor place must meet the sensory motor explorations of the very young.

For noncrawling infants, there should be an enclosed area with a surface that encourages reaching, grasping, and kicking. These infants also enjoy baby "sit-up swings" and "swinging cradles." The area should stimulate visual and auditory senses with colorful streamers, soft wind chimes, and natural sounds (e.g., breeze in the trees and bird songs). A stroller path would also be appropriate.

Unlike older preschool and primary grade children, toddlers either ignore or do not comprehend the function of separate play centers; thus, they will attempt to push a trike up a climber or pour sand on a crawling baby. A creative use of barriers will restrict children to developmentally appropriate areas by requiring certain skills to reach an area and will serve to help keep certain activities within an area. For example, two or three steps can lead to a fifteen-inch high platform, half-buried tires can form minitunnels around the sand area, a small gate can lead to the garden, and shrubs can curb the push/pull toy path.

Crawling and walking pathways in an infant and toddler outdoor place not only assist traffic flow but can serve as a means for exploring. The surfaces of these paths should be a mosaic—changing from dirt to grass with "cobblestones" of slatted plank squares, patterned rocks, colored bricks, and half logs buried along the way. Raised (fifteen-inch maximum) walkways with railings are also exciting.

Various structures are effective in an infant and toddler outdoor place, such as (1) set-in-the-ground ladders; (2) slides inset in a hill; (3) swings with baby seats, porch swings, and swinging platforms for looking at the "moving ground" or the clouds; (4) fourteen-inch or fifteen-inch raised platforms with rope or metal railings on one side and a boarded side with "shape holes" (e.g., squares, circles, and octagons) large enough to stick one's head and shoulders through in order to "survey one's world"; (5) minitunnels (i.e., half-buried tires) and longer tunnels to crawl through; (6) logs or low, anchored benches to straddle or climb over; (7) wobbly structures such as a board with springs or a low swinging bridge; (8) roofs for playhouses; (9) block building areas; (10) pathways for push/pull and ride-on toys; (11) sand areas—the favorite material; (12) elevated trough with moving water; (13) garden; (14) dirt-digging areas; and (14) objects that react with movement and sound to wind or touch such as colorful banners, canopies, tree branches, wind chimes, and pans for hitting. The safe natural environment—trees, shrubs, flowers, pine cones, and tree stumps—should be left. Finally, the outdoor place must have many benches for adult sitting and supervision and holding infants and toddlers.

Figure 5–9, a plan for an infant and toddler outdoor place, illustrates some of the principles discussed and is only one example of an outdoor activity area.

Outdoor Area for Older Children

Because the outdoor space is an extension of the indoor area, there must be areas for active and passive play. There is no clear-cut distinction between the two

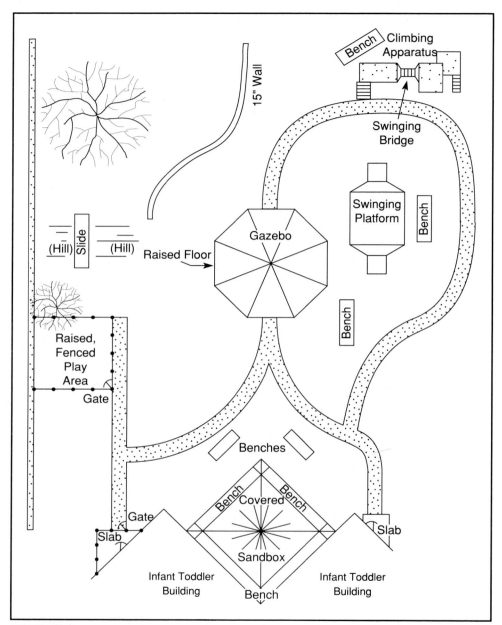

FIGURE 5–9
Outdoor Activity Area

types of play. Large-muscle play is usually active, but walking on a balance beam may be passive; water play is usually passive, but running from a squirting hose is active.

In passive play, children need protection from excessive wind or heat and from other fast-moving children. Passive play areas should be enclosed and protected from more active play areas. Enclosure may be accomplished with shrubbery or large stones, with small openings between these areas, by changing the terrain, or by providing a sheltered area. Additional protection may be obtained by building a slightly winding path or by separating the two types of play areas.

Play areas must be separated for safety reasons. Space around each piece of equipment must be equal to the child's potential action outward, or the maximum distance children can jump, slide, or swing forward from any position on the equipment. Children also need space to bypass a piece of equipment. Paths should be three to five feet wide, adjoin safety areas, and be slightly curving. If paths are too curvy, children tend to cut through one play area to reach another play area; and supervising staff members may not be able to adequately supervise all play areas.

Similar pieces of play equipment, such as climbing apparatus, should be scattered throughout the area rather than placed side-by-side or clustered. This arrangement has several advantages: (1) a child may be able to select a piece of equipment that is not in the hot sun; (2) it is aesthetically more pleasing; (3) children will have more contrasting types of muscle activity during one play session, because they tend to move from one play area to an adjacent one; and (4) daredevil competition may be lessened or eliminated. Complex play structures which are discussed in detail by Vergeront have almost totally replaced the separate, large muscle pieces of equipment (e.g., climbing frame, slides, and gliders) seen on "traditional playgrounds."[64]

Often in outdoor areas, there is a great deal of physical inactivity; thus, children need places to cluster and sit. Boulders or logs are perhaps more enjoyable than park or picnic benches.

The types of activities conducted in the outdoor area are often more extensive than those conducted in the indoor space. Because many of the interest centers are identical, factors to be considered in their outdoor arrangement would be similar to those suggested for the indoor design. The following suggestions should be considered in planning interest centers unique to the outdoor area.

1. *Road for vehicles.* A hard-surfaced area can form a tricycle, wagon, or doll buggy road extending through the outdoor space and returning to its starting point. The road should be wide enough to permit passing. A curving road is more interesting, but there should be no right-angle turns, as these cause accidents.[65]
2. *Sand pit.* Because the outdoor sand pit involves the child's whole body, a sand pit for twenty children must be approximately two hundred fifty

square feet. To prevent overlap of the sand area (and hence child aggression), the sand pit should be narrow. A winding river of sand is more aesthetically pleasing than an oblong-shaped box. Children should have flat working surfaces, such as wooden boards or flat boulders, beside or in the sand.

An outdoor sand pit should have a boundary element which "should provide a 'sense' of enclosure for the playing children, keep out unwanted traffic, protect the area against water draining from adjacent areas, and help keep the sand within the sand play areas."[66] Boundaries can be built or created by a rolling terrain.

The sand pit should be partially shaded, but with exposure to the purifying and drying rays of the sun. Water should be available so the sand is not bone dry, and the water source should be at the periphery of the sand pit with the runoff flowing away from the sand.

3. *Wading pool and water spray area.* Outdoor water play activities should allow for more energetic play than indoor water activities. Concrete wading pools must have slip-proof walking surfaces and a water depth of one-half foot. Water temperature should be between 60 and 80 degrees Fahrenheit (16 and 27 degrees Celsius). In colder weather, a drained wading pool makes an excellent flat, hard surface for passive play. For programs on a meager budget, an inflatable pool can be used and a garden hose with a spray nozzle or water sprinkler attached can serve as a water spray.

4. *Garden.* An outdoor garden should be fenced to protect it from animals or from being accidentally trampled. The garden should be narrow, perhaps two feet wide, to minimize the need for the child gardener to step into the garden (especially important when the plot is muddy). A narrow garden can take on an aesthetically pleasing shape as it parallels straight fences or encircles large trees.

5. *Outdoor animal cages.* Outdoor animal cages should be built to meet the specific needs of each animal; located in a well-drained area sheltered from excessive heat and wind; and near a water source and the delivery gate. Because of vandalism, programs should take animals on a one-day basis only.

Figure 5–10, a plan for an outdoor activity area, illustrates some of the principles discussed and is only one example of an outdoor activity area. For primary-grade and school-age child care programs, the grassy area could be free of the sand pit, dirt mound, storage/play structure, and play structure. The area could then be used for ball games.

Outdoor Storage

Outdoor storage can be attached to the main building, perhaps next to a terrace where the storage can provide shelter. If detached from the building, outdoor

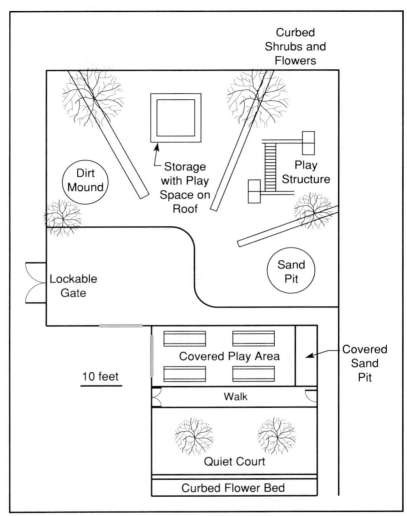

FIGURE 5–10
Preschool, Kindergarten, and Primary Outdoor Activity Area

storage should be of a design and material to fit and not detract from the main building. Also, if a separate building is used, it should serve as a windbreak to the outdoor activity area.

Outdoor storage twelve feet long, ten feet wide, and seven to eight feet high will be sufficient for most early childhood programs. The doorway should be six feet wide and should be a tilt- or roll-a-door garage-type. Hooks or pegs for hanging can be installed four and one-half feet above the floor along one side of the storage shed, and shelves for storing equipment in daily use can be built two or three feet above the floor along the back of the shed. A high shelf can be

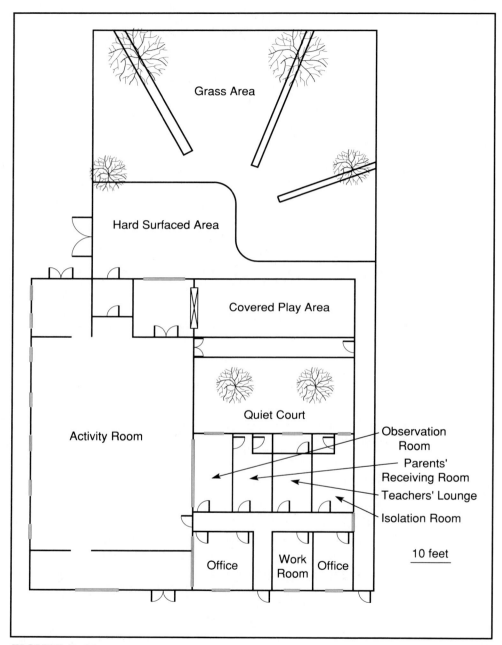

FIGURE 5–11
Early Childhood Facility

used for storing seasonal items or items for staff use. Outdoor storage areas should have slightly raised flooring to prevent flooding after a substantial rainfall. A ramp would facilitate moving equipment in and out of the storage shed and minimize tripping over different levels.

A storage shed can also serve as a prop for dramatic play. The roof might be fenced to serve as an additional play area, and the inside could serve as a place during inclement weather and for some daily play activities that require a firm surface.

Figure 5–11 illustrates the arrangement of the children's activity room, the outdoor activity area, and the other children's and adults' areas of an early childhood facility. The illustration of the physical plant layout shows only one possible arrangement of the various areas. Figure 5–11 is not intended as a model layout but is presented to graphically depict some of the ideas discussed in the chapter.

SAFETY

Safety of children, staff members, parents, and others is of maximum importance. A safe environment encourages children to work and play without heavy restrictions that wear on both children and adults and prevent maximum program benefit.

Safety can be provided by:

1. Providing physical supports such as soft landing areas, railings, and color-coding complex features (e.g., rungs of ladders that require spatial judgments).
2. Correcting or removing any damaged or unsafe structure or equipment.
3. Following all safety regulations and using additional guidelines such as:

   Frost, J. L., and Wortham, S. C. "The Evolution of American Playgrounds." *Young Children,* 43, 5 (1988): 19–21.

   Hogan, P. *The Playground Safety Checker.* Phoenixville: Playground Press, 1990.

   NAEYC Information Service. *Facility Design for Early Childhood Programs.* Washington, D.C.: National Association for the Education of Young Children, 1989, 13–16.

   U.S. Consumer Product Safety Commission. *A Handbook for Public Playground Safety,* Vol. 1: General Guidelines for New and Existing Playgrounds; Vol. 2: Technical Guidelines for Equipment and Surfacing. Washington, D.C.: U.S. Government Printing Office, 1981.

INSURANCE

Adequate insurance for a facility as well as equipment and materials is of utmost importance. Coverage is required for mortgaged buildings, and is recommended for all owned buildings and for the contents of rented buildings. Basically, fire insurance covers fire and lightning. Most policies can have an extended-coverage endorsement attached that covers such things as losses from wind, hail, explosion (except from steam boilers), civil commotion, aircraft, vehicles, smoke, vandalism, and malicious mischief. If the program moves equipment and materials to various buildings, the insurance should include a floater policy to protect against loss resulting from such transportation. In order to have adequate fire insurance (basic or extended coverage endorsement), the administrator must maintain up-to-date property records that reflect current values.

Three other types of insurance may be necessary. Boiler and machinery insurance is designed to protect against losses resulting from the explosion of pressure-type vessels or partial or complete breakdown of certain types of machinery. If the program owns vehicles, insurance should be secured to protect against losses from material damage or the destruction of the vehicle and its material contents. Theft insurance in some areas may be so high that it is unobtainable. To reduce rates, the federal government and some states have initiated a crime insurance program sold through regular insurance agents.

SUMMARY

To a great extent housing determines the quality of an early childhood program. Housing can be thought of as the stage upon which all interactions take place—child-child, child-adult, and child-material. Housing involves (1) the entry-exit area in which the child makes the transitions from home to program and from program to home and the area from which parents most frequently view the program; (2) the children's activity room, with its planned arrangement designed to meet the child's needs as defined by the program objectives; (3) the additional areas for children (i.e., shared activity areas, resource room, lockers, changing areas/restrooms, feeding/dining areas, napping area, and isolation area); (4) adult areas (i.e., parent reception area, lounge, and office/workroom); and (5) the outdoor space—an extension of the activity room.

Careful planning is required for housing an early childhood program. The program base and objectives of the local program should determine the housing facilities. Once housing facilities are constructed or selected, they determine the staff members' abilities to work with and supervise children, the types and convenience of activities, the accessibility of equipment and materials and of places to work and to play, and the safety of children. In short, one should never have to adapt the program to the building, rather, the building should always serve the purposes of the program.

NOTES

1. K. W. Brooks and C. Deen, "Improving Accessibility of Preschool Facilities for the Handicapped," *Young Children* 36, 3 (1981): 17–24.

2. D. E. Gardner, "An Ideal Environment for Learning," *Housing for Early Childhood Education,* ed. S. Sunderlin and N. Gray (Washington, D.C.: Association for Childhood Education International, 1968), 5.

3. D. E. Day and R. Sheehan, "Elements for a Better Preschool," *Young Children* 30, 1 (1974): 15–23.

4. C. D. Gibson, "Preschool Educational Housing," *Housing for Early Childhood Education,* ed. S. Sunderlin and N. Gray (Washington, D.C.: Association for Childhood Education International, 1968), 20.

5. R. G. Barker, *Ecological Psychology* (Palo Alto, CA: Stanford University, 1968).

6. D. E. Day, *Early Childhood Education: A Human Ecological Approach* (Glenview, IL: Scott, Foresman and Company, 1983).

7. T. Harms and R. M. Clifford, *Early Childhood Environment Rating Scale* (New York: Teachers College Press, Teachers College, Columbia University, 1980).

8. J. Vergeront, *Places and Spaces for Preschool and Primary—Indoors* (Washington, D.C.: National Association for the Education of Young Children, 1987).

9. S. Kritchevsky and E. Prescott, *Planning Environments for Young Children—Physical Space* (Washington, D.C.: National Association for the Education of Young Children, 1969), 5.

10. NAEYC Information Service, *Facility Design for Early Childhood Programs* (Washington, D.C.: National Association for the Education of Young Children, 1989), 2.

11. R. Lally, S. Provence, E. Szanton, and B. Weissbourd, "Developmentally Appropriate Care for Children from Birth to Age 3," *Developmentally Appropriate Practice in Early Childhood Programs Serving Children from Birth through Age Eight,* expanded edition, ed. S. Bredekamp (Washington, D.C.: National Association for the Education of Young Children, 1986), 17–33.

12. NAEYC Information Service, *Facility Design for Early Childhood Programs,* 2.

13. E. Prescott and T. G. David, "Effects of Physical Environments in Child Care Systems," ERIC ED 142 284 (New York: Paper presented at the Annual Meeting of the American Education Research Association, April 1977).

14. S. Shapiro, "Preschool Ecology: A Study of Three Environmental Variables," *Reading Improvement* 12 (1975): 236–241.

15. E. Prescott, E. Jones and S. Kritchevsky, *Day-Care as a Child-Rearing Environment, vol. 2* (Washington, D.C.: National Association for the Education of Young Children, 1972).

16. Day and Sheehan, "Elements for a Better Preschool."

17. Kritchevsky and Prescott, *Planning Environments,* 21.

18. L. W. Pluger and J. M. Zola, "A Room Planned by Young Children," *Young Children* 24, 6 (1969): 337–341.

19. S. Millar, *The Psychology of Play* (Baltimore: Penguin, 1968), 150.

20. *Environmental Criteria: Mentally Retarded Preschool Day-Care Facilities* (College Station, TX: Texas A and M College of Architecture and Environmental Design, 1971).

21. E. Prescott, "The Physical Setting in Day-Care," *Making Day Care Better,* ed. J. T. Greenman and R. W. Fuqua (New York: Teachers College Press, Teachers College, Columbia University, 1984), 44–65.

22. Ibid.

23. Shapiro, "Preschool Ecology."

24. A. P. Nilsen, "Alternatives to Sexist Practices in the Classroom," *Young Children* 32, 5 (1977): 53–58.

25. E. Jones and E. Prescott, *Dimensions of Teaching-Learning Environments II: Focus on Day-Care* (Pasadena: Pacific Oaks College, 1978).

26. F. Montes and T. R. Risley, "Evaluating Traditional Day-Care Practice: An Empirical Approach," *Child Study Quarterly* 4 (1975): 208–215.

27. C. Z. Cataldo, "Very Early Childhood Education for Infants and Toddlers," *Childhood Education* 58, 3 (1982): 149–154.

28. P. K. Adams and M. K. Taylor, "A Learning Center Approach to Infant Education," ERIC ED 253 315 (Columbus, GA: Columbus College, School of Education, 1985).

29. I. S. Stewart, "The Real World of Teaching Two-Year-Old Children," *Young Children* 37, 5 (1982): 3–13.

30. S. Bredekamp, ed., *Accreditation Criteria and Procedures of the National Academy of Early Childhood Programs* (Washington, D.C.: National Association for the Education of Young Children, 1984), 27.

31. R. E. Jefferson, "Indoor Facilities," *Housing for Early Childhood Education*, ed. S. Sunderlin and N. Gray (Washington, D.C.: Association for Childhood Education International, 1968), 41.

32. R. Highberger and M. Boynton, "Preventing Infant Illness in Infant/Toddler Day-Care," *Young Children* 38, 3 (1983): 3–8.

33. C. Stein, "School Lighting Re-evaluated," *American School and University* 48 (1975): 70–78.

34. F. Osmond, *Patterns for Designing Children's Centers* (New York: Educational Facilities Laboratories, 1971), 97.

35. N. E. Headley, *Education in the Kindergarten*, 4th ed. (New York: American Book, 1966), 80.

36. Osmond, *Patterns*, 98.

37. C. Wills and L. Lindberg, *Kindergarten for Today's Children* (Chicago: Follett, 1967), 111.

38. Educational Facilities Laboratory, *SER 2 Environmental Evaluations* (Ann Arbor: University of Michigan, Architectural Research Laboratory, 1965), 120.

39. F. K. Sampson, *Contrast Rendition in School Lighting* (New York: Educational Facilities Laboratory, 1970).

40. Wills and Lindberg, *Kindergarten for Today's Children*, 112.

41. Gardner, "Ideal Environment," 6.

42. Wills and Lindberg, *Kindergarten for Today's Children*, 112.

43. Ibid.

44. Jefferson, "Indoor Facilities," 44.

45. S. H. Leeper, R. L. Witherspoon, and B. Day, *Good Schools for Young Children*, 5th ed. (New York: Macmillan, 1984), 517.

46. Ibid.

47. For an interesting detailed history of the evolution of outdoor play areas for children, read J. L. Frost and S. C. Wortham's "The Evolution of the American Playground," *Young Children* 43, 5 (1988): 19–21.

48. J. L. Frost and S. C. Wortham, "The Evolution of the American Playground," *Young Children* 43, 5 (1988): 19–21.

49. J. L. Frost, "Children's Playgrounds: Research and Practice," *The Young Child at Play. Reviews of Research,* Vol. 4, ed. G. Fein and M. Rivkin (Washington, D.C.: National Association for the Education of Young Children, 1986), 195–208.

50. J. E. Johnson; J. F. Christie; and T. D. Yawkey, *Play and Early Childhood Development* (Glenview: Scott, Foresman and Company, 1987).

51. *An Adaptive Playground for Physically Disabled Children with Perceptual Deficits: The Mogruder Environmental Therapy Complex,* ERIC ED 036 941 (Orlando: Orange County Board of Public Instruction, 1969).

52. Johnson, Christie, and Yawkey, *Play and Early Childhood Development.*

53. A. E. Howard, *The Integrated Approach Design for Early Childhood Programs.* (Nacogdoches: Early Childhood Consultant Services, 1975).

54. E. Vaughn, "Everything Under the Sun: Outside Learning Center Activities," *Dimensions* 18, 4 (1990): 20–22.

55. J. Talbot and J. L. Frost, "Magical Playscapes," *Childhood Education* 66, 1 (1989): 11–19.

56. NAEYC Information Service, *Facility Design for Early Childhood Programs* 2.

57. *Child Welfare League of America Standards for Day Care Service,* revised edition (Edison: Child Welfare League of America, 1984).

58. F. C. Thompson and A. M. Rittenhouse, "Measuring the Impact," *Parks and Recreation* 9 (1974): 24–26, 62–63.

59. J. R. Foster and L. R. Rogers, *Housing Early Childhood Education in Texas* (College Station: Innovative Resources, 1970), 14.

60. K. R. Baker, "Extending the Indoors Outside," *Housing for Early Childhood Education,* ed. S. Sunderlin and N. Gray (Washington, D.C.: Association for Childhood Education International, 1968), 61.

61. For more information, write ASTM, 1916 Race Street, Philadelphia, PA 19103; tel. (215) 299–5487.

62. J. Vergeront, *Places and Spaces for Preschool and Primary—Outdoors* (Washington, D.C.: National Association for the Education of Young Children, 1988), 5.

63. C. A. Decker, *Children: The Early Years,* rev. ed., (South Holland: Goodheart-Willcox, 1990), 467.

64. Vergeront, *Places and Spaces for Preschool and Primary—Outdoors,* 5.

65. Baker, "Extending the Indoors," 61.

66. Osmon, *Patterns,* 77.

EXPERTISE CONTACT LIST

These individuals and organizations may be contacted for providing input on early childhood program housing.

Individuals

Joe L. Frost
244 Educational Building
Department of Curriculum and Instruction
University of Texas
Austin, Texas 78712

James Greeman
3854 Elliot Avenue South
Minneapolis, Minn. 55407

Elizabeth Jones
Pacific Oaks College
5 Westmoreland Place
Pasadena, Calif. 91103

Richard Katz
Richard Katz and Associates
1103 Westgate, Suite 304
Oak Park, Illinois 60301

Organizations

Center for Architecture and Urban Planning Research
University of Wisconsin-Milwaukee
Box 413
Milwaukee, Wisconsin 53201

Children's Environment Research Group
Center for Human Environments and Environmental
  Psychology Program
City University of New York
33 W. 42nd Street
New York, N.Y. 10036

ATTN: T. Wall
Council of Educational Facility Planners, International
1060 Carmack Road, Suite 160
Columbus, Ohio 43210

ATTN: T. Jambor
International Playground Association
American Association for the Child's Right to Play
University of Alabama at Birmingham
School of Education
Birmingham, Ala. 35294

FOR FURTHER READING

David, T., and Weinstein, C., eds. *Spaces for Children: The Built Environment and Children's Development.* New York: Plenum Press, 1987.

Eskensen, S. B. *The Early Childhood Playground: An Outdoor Classroom.* Ypsilanti: The High Scope Press, 1987.

Frost, J. L., and Klein, B. *Children's Play and Playgrounds.* Austin: Playgrounds International, 1983.

Frost, J., and Sunderlin, L., eds. *When Children Play.* Wheaton: Association for Childhood Education International, 1985.

Gibson, D. F. "Down the Rabbit Hole: A Special Environment for Preschool Learning." *Landscape Architecture* 68, 3 (1978): 211–216.

Greenman, J. *Caring Spaces, Learning Places: Children's Environments that Work.* Redmond: Exchange Press, 1988.

Hannah, G. G. *Classroom Spaces and Places.* Belmont: Fearon, 1982.

Houle, G. *Learning Centers for Young Children: To Be Built in Classrooms and Other Places Where Children Gather to Learn,* 3rd ed. West Greenwich: Tot-Lot Child Care Products, 1987.

Loughlin, K., and Suina, J. *The Learning Environment: An Instructional Strategy.* New York: Teachers College Press, Teachers College, Columbia University, 1982.

Moore, R. C.; Goltsman, S. M., and Iachofano, D. S. *Play for All Guidelines: Planning, Design, and Management of Outdoor Play Environments for All Children.* Berkeley: MIG Communications, 1987.

"Playground Improvement Rating Scale." *Young Children* 40, 3 (1985): 7–8.

Prescott, E. "The Physical Setting in Day Care." In *Making Day-Care Better: Training, Evaluation, and the Process of Change,* edited by J. T. Greenman and R. W. Fuqua. New York: Teachers College Press, Teachers College, Columbia University, 1984.

Sanoff, H., and Sanoff, J. *Learning Environments for Children: A Developmental Approach to Shaping Activity Areas.* Atlanta: Humanics, Ltd., 1988.

Walsh, P., Andersen, R., and Associates. *Early Childhood Playgrounds: Planning an Outside Learning Environment.* Victoria 3206, Australia: Albert Park, 1988.

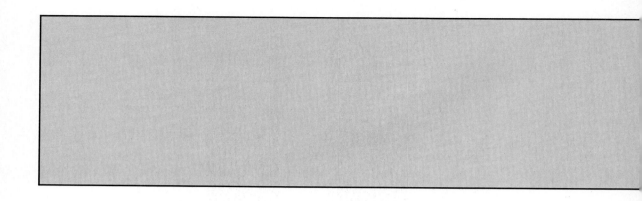

Chapter 6
Equipping

E quipment and materials have a major influence on both staff members and children; consequently, the educational objectives of the local early childhood program should determine what equipment and materials are used. These items should be planned and budgeted for at the conception of the early childhood program for two reasons. First, if budgeting for equipment and materials is an afterthought, these items may be purchased with what remains after other expenditures. Although the budget distribution in industries and schools should not necessarily be analogous, there is an interesting inverse relationship in their capital outlay budgets—industries use 10 percent of their capital outlay for structures and 90 percent for equipment, while schools spend 90 percent of their capital outlay for buildings and 10 percent for equipment.[1] A second reason for planning equipment and materials at the outset of a program proposal is that furnishing an architect with information about the types and quantities of equipment and materials can help the architect plan an adequate design.

PURCHASING EQUIPMENT AND MATERIALS

The purchasing of equipment and materials is of immeasurable significance. Items not meeting the needs of the program, or insufficient in quantity for activities planned, hamper rather than facilitate the program. Moreover, careful purchasing of equipment and materials helps insure quality items are chosen, which last longer. In today's inflationary world, careful planning is essential if the items are to be secured within budgetary limitations.

Purchasing Guidelines

Many considerations must be given to purchasing equipment and materials. The following suggestions are only minimal guidelines:

1. The buyer should purchase equipment and materials that will facilitate program objectives. For example, programs following the maturational and interactionist views use materials that encourage creativity, experimentation, and peer social interaction. In programs following the maturational view, materials are often organized into everyday themes. Interactionist-view programs use similar materials; however, they are somewhat more complex and symbolic in nature. Conversely, behavioral-environmental programs use task-directed, autotelic (self-rewarding) and self-correcting materials in the skill areas of reading readiness and mathematics. There are materials available to meet the needs of children with disabilities, and to teach multicultural, nonsexist concepts. These items include dolls and hand puppets with a range of skin tones or characteristic features, and books, puzzles, and pictures depicting various ethnic and racial groups and nontraditional sex-role behaviors. If program objectives are written in keeping with the ages and needs of the children to be served, the caregiving or teaching-learning methods to be employed, and the number and qualifications of the staff to be hired, the equipment and materials secured should be appropriate. Item usefulness is of prime importance.

2. The buyer should check on the amount of money available and the procedures for purchasing. The building administrator should have the budget and know the procedures regarding the use of moneys.

3. A perpetual inventory and list of items needed should be maintained. The inventory and list help insure that the most essential pieces of equipment and materials have priority and unwanted duplications will be avoided.

4. Building space for using and storing equipment, and any additional building specifications for use of the item (e.g., electrical outlet or water source) should be considered. Because equipment and materials require space for use and storage, the facility should be designed after the major pieces of equipment and materials are selected.

5. The buyer should be economical. He should price an item in several distributors' catalogs, negotiate prices with distributors, and put purchases of substantial amounts up for bids. The buyer should always ask the question, "Can the item be made or adapted from a previously purchased item?" The cost of making an item should be carefully calculated to include both raw materials and staff labor, and any plans for sharing equipment and materials in programs that have several groups of children under the care of various staff members should be worked out.

6. Consumable items (food, paste, paint, paper, and clay) should not be overbought. As a general rule, consumables are more susceptible to deterioration than permanent pieces of equipment and materials.

7. Buy only from reputable companies (See Appendix 6). Find out if you qualify for a quantity discount or a trial offer plan. Be sure that you are

ordering from the most recent catalog and that any items needed on a timely basis are currently available (i.e., do not require back ordering).

8. The buyer should check the various resources for purchasing suggestions. The "consumer's guide" for early childhood programs consists of the opinions of personnel employed by the state education or human resources departments and local universities, reports on research projects using the items, observations of displays at conventions, and discussions with other staff members.

9. The buyer should purchase safe equipment and materials. Standards for safety of equipment and materials are partially regulated by the Child Protection and Toy Safety Act (1969), the Child Safety Committee of the National Safety Council, and the Toy Manufacturers of America. Avoid equipment and materials with sharp edges and protrusions, brittle plastic parts, and parts easily pulled off, such as trimmings on doll clothes, squeakers that fall out of plastic toys, and so forth. Electrical equipment and materials should have the Underwriters' Laboratories (UL) seal; fabric products should be labeled nonflammable, flame retardant, or flame resistant; stuffed toys should be filled with hygienic, washable, and nonflammable materials; and painted items should have nontoxic paints. Some art materials are hazardous to one's health.[2] Choose the safest items. All playground equipment should be the right size for the children. Standing playground equipment should be firmly anchored in concrete, with anchoring devices placed below ground level (up to eighteen inches in depth is required by some licensing laws) to prevent equipment from falling or children from tripping. Equipment should be installed over soft materials; and bolt-ends on equipment should have protective end caps. Swing sets should be installed a minimum of six feet away from fences, other structures, walkways, and other play areas; moving parts of swing sets should have wide spaces to avoid pinching fingers or toys; swing chains should not have open-ended "S" hooks; swinging rings should have a diameter smaller than five inches or larger than ten inches to avoid entrapping a child's head; and climbing bars should not turn. Attachments at the fulcrum of a seesaw should be enclosed to protect hands, and a block should be placed under each end of the board to protect feet. Climbing nets should be in good repair, and adventure or junk playground equipment should be free from splinters and projecting nails.

10. Durable and relatively maintenance-free equipment and materials should be selected. Factors contributing to durability are the types and quality of raw materials, care given to fabricating the equipment and materials, and reliability of working parts.

11. As much as possible, comprehensive materials should be purchased. Because both budget and space are usually limited, staff members should consider equipment and materials that can be used in a variety of situations, that are suitable for individual differences, and that need

to be stored infrequently. Pragnell states: "Flexibility can be gained when each object has not only its obvious function but also a certain ambiguity, so that, in different circumstances it can be used in a variety of different ways."[3] Materials used in many ways also stimulate creativity. Of course, many pieces of equipment and types of materials are designed for specific purposes, and staff members must not overlook these items in making decisions.

12. Aesthetically pleasing equipment and materials should be selected. Young children are keenly aware of color, texture, size, form, brightness, sound, odor, and temperature; thus, equipment and materials should appeal to the senses.

13. Equipment and materials that actively involve the child should be chosen. They should not make the child a spectator, nor should all items call for the same repetitive activity.

Purchasing Procedures

Most early childhood programs, whether federal, public school, or private, have similar procedures for purchasing. However, publicly funded programs are subject to more restrictions than privately owned programs, and early childhood programs with large enrollments follow a more formal procedure for purchasing than programs with small enrollments. Because of the similarity in purchasing procedures, the following description of the basic purchasing procedure followed by public schools should generally apply to other early childhood programs.

The needs of each division within a school system, including food service, transportation, instructional, and personnel, are made known to the division administrators, who submit their budgetary needs to the superintendent. Using this information (and perhaps taking into account the demands of pressure groups), the superintendent develops a budget and offers it to the board of education. If the budget is approved by the board of education, the board authorizes the obligating of the school district funds for the purchase of equipment and materials, as well as for services and other goods. Adoption of the operating budget—which must be done within legal procedures, tax limitations, and the approved outline of the program—authorizes the superintendent to spend the funds allocated for the fiscal year. Various restrictions may be placed on the general authorization; for example, the superintendent cannot transfer funds allotted for purchases within one category to another category without authorization.

Specifications are prepared to determine whether bids on quotations should be secured or whether the item should be purchased by brand name. (Specifications can be helpful whether or not bidding will be the result.) Questions to answer include: Is the cost sufficiently high to justify bidding? Does the quantity of the single purchase or the possibility of repetitive purchases justify bidding? and, Is the item available from multiple sources? When purchases involve substantial amounts and are available from several manufacturers, companies are asked to submit bids. Requests for bids are announced publicly, extended to all companies that might have the specified items, and contain the rules that regulate receiving and approving such bids. On a specified date, the sealed bids are opened during the meeting of the local board. Bids are announced, and the contract awarded to the lowest bidder able to provide the items as specified. In cases where purchases do not involve substantial amounts or where there is no prospect of competition in the bidding, purchases are negotiated. If small centers in close geographic proximity would purchase as a group, they could probably obtain better prices and reduced shipping costs, and would have more clout in dealing with companies that sell inferior equipment. In comparing costs, the bottom line is total delivered costs. Differences in prices may be offset by freight charges. Also remember that service is as important as low prices.

In large school systems, purchased equipment and materials are stored in warehouses that must be free from moisture, insects, vermin, or extremes in temperature. Allocation of equipment and materials to each building is initiated by a requisition from an authorized staff member. When the items are delivered, a copy of the signed requisition form is placed on file and serves as a receipt.

The inventory record is an essential aspect of the purchasing procedure. This record should list and identify all equipment and materials that have been purchased and delivered. The inventory record should indicate date of acquisition, current cost of replacement (often more than the initial cost), and maintenance provided. The inventory serves as a record of the quantity of materials purchased and of the location of items; it becomes the basis for preventing duplication, determining what equipment and materials need to be replaced, deciding insurance needs, calculating loss or theft of items, and assisting in budget planning with yearly readjustments.

ARRANGING EQUIPMENT AND MATERIALS

If learning/activity centers are used, equipment and materials for daily use should be so arranged there. Portable objects should be placed on low shelves or in cabinets, so children can get them out and put them back. Open shelves encourage children to return their items. Heavy or nonportable objects should be placed on tables or shelves where they can be used without being moved; otherwise, children can hurt themselves or damage the items.

Many early childhood facilities lack enough shelf space. According to Osmon, economy of shelf use can be achieved by creating distinctiveness in the items placed on the shelves.[4] Distinctiveness is increased by using various types of shelving (inclined, slotted, stepped, and drawers) in one storage unit and by placing items with contrasting properties (color, size, shape, and texture) next to each other. Extensive use of contrasting properties as a criterion for placement of materials may be confusing to children. Finding the "homes" of various materials, both a self-help skill and visual discrimination skill, is aided by cues such as matching materials with color labels or shape labels provided on the storage unit.

Equipment and materials for regular but not daily use should be readily available and stored to prevent deterioration and damage. If space permits, they should be stored in or near the center where they will be used. Labeling also helps staff members locate equipment and materials quickly. Special care must be exercised in storing consumable items, such as food, paper, paste, and paints; audiovisual equipment; science materials; musical instruments; recordings; and any breakable objects.

CARING FOR EQUIPMENT AND MATERIALS

Caring for equipment and materials teaches children good habits and helps prevent expensive repairs and replacements. Keep the following suggestions in mind:

1. The room and shelves should be arranged to minimize the chance of accidents and to maximize housekeeping efficiency. Equipment and materials should be shelved close to the working space; objects susceptible to damage should be used in areas out of the main flow of traffic; breakable items or those likely to spill should be placed on shelves within easy reach (if there are frequent accidents involving the same item, try setting it in a different place). There should be enough open space to prevent accidents.
2. Children should be taught how to care for equipment and materials. Staff members should establish a routine for obtaining and returning equipment and materials and for using facilities. To establish a routine, every item must have a place, and time must be allowed for returning all items there.
3. Spilled materials should be cleaned up. In some cases, a teacher can create a science lesson on "how to clean it up."
4. Staff members should set good examples in caring for equipment and materials.
5. Staff members should station themselves properly for adequate supervision.
6. Children should be removed from an area when they deliberately destroy or damage equipment or materials.
7. Equipment and materials should be repaired as soon as possible. Items should not be used until they are repaired.
8. Equipment should be cleaned regularly. Toys for infants and toddlers should be cleaned daily with a disinfectant, and equipment for preschoolers cleaned weekly.
9. Staff members should periodically check equipment and materials. They should tighten loose nuts, bolts, clamps, and other hardware;

replace or sand rusted parts; repaint rusted tubing; oil metal parts; sand wooden equipment where splinters are found; paint or use clear protective coatings on wooden equipment and remove loose paint; repair torn fabric and secure fasteners on doll or dress-up clothes; and replace broken-off or sharp plastic equipment. To report a product one believes to be unsafe, write to

Standards Development Service Section
National Bureau of Standards
Washington, D.C. 20234
or
U.S. Consumer Product Safety Commission
Washington, D.C. 20207
(toll free, 800-638-2772, or Maryland residents only, call 800-492-2937)

10. Staff members should consider what heat, light, moisture, and storage methods may do to the equipment and materials.
11. Plenty of equipment and materials should be available, so each child has something to do and does not have to wait too long for a turn. Tempers flare and damage occurs when children are not constructively involved.
12. These items should be stored where children cannot get to them: ammonia, antifreeze, aspirin, bleach, camphor, cement and glue, detergent, drain cleaner, dry cleaning fluid, fabric softener, floor wax, furniture polish, gasoline, ink, insecticide, kerosene, kindling or prepackaged illuminating preparations, laundry bluing, leather polish and dye, lighter fluid, lye, metal polish, methanol, moth repellent, oil of wintergreen, oral prescription drugs, paint and thinner, putty and rust removers, rat poison, room deodorizer, rug cleaner, shoe cleaner, shoe polish, sulfuric acid, turpentine, typewriter cleaner, varnish, and washing soda. To request information about a product, call: Consumer Product Safety Hot Line 800-638-2666 (Maryland residents only, call 800-492-2937). The telephone number of the local poison control center should be posted.

SPECIFIC EQUIPMENT AND MATERIALS

Anderson and Gordon have discussed the method of assessing the complexity of children's materials following the simple-complex dimension developed by Kritchevsky, Prescott, and Walling used mainly with outdoor space (See Chapter 5, Table 5–1). Complexity of materials does not indicate difficulty but rather the possibilities for uses of materials. Simple materials have one obvious use (e.g., a single book). Complex materials have subparts (e.g., pegs and pegboards) or are two essentially different items used together (e.g., sand table with digging tools). Super-complex materials have three or more essentially different elements combined (e.g., magnet with metal and non-metal objects) or are a markedly different object already added to a complex material (e.g., unit blocks with animal figures).[5]

As described in Chapter 2, the interactionist psycho-philosophical position uses multidimensional materials that encourage exploration problem solving and are arranged in a way to convey the idea of a conceptual order. Hence, most of the materials used would be complex and super-complex. Conversely, the behavioral-environmental view uses more narrowly focused and unidimensional materials that meet program-selected objectives (i.e., objectives that are adult prescribed) and serve one mode of expression (e.g., language). Hence, more of the materials found in a program with the behavioral-environmental position would likely be simple. However, it is important to remember that teaching/learning strategy, which determines how materials are used, is much more directly related to program base than the materials themselves.

The materials used in early childhood programs should fit the objectives of the local program. Because this book follows the position statements concerning "appropriate practice," the materials described will more closely fit the interactionist psycho-philosophical view.

Furniture and Other Essentials

Furniture used in early childhood programs should be comfortable for both children and staff members and should be aesthetically pleasing. Furniture should also fit the objectives of the program. For example, programs for infants and toddlers and for older children following the interactionist psycho-philosophical view use fewer pieces of traditional school furniture and more soft pieces (e.g., pillows, hammocks, couches, beanbag chairs, and even carpeted floors). On the other hand, programs for older children, especially those following the behavioral-environmental psycho-philosophical view, are more apt to be equipped with traditional school furniture (i.e., tables and chairs, or desks).

For Infants and Toddlers
Infants and toddlers have some special needs. These include:

Feeding
car seats with trays
feeding chairs (high chairs and low chairs)
feeding implements (bibs, bottles, cups, plates, and spoons)
storage units
tables (about 15-$\frac{1}{2}$ inches high) and non-tip chairs
wastebasket (covered)

Changing and Toileting
changing table or counter
sink with spray nozzle
stools (small for toddlers)

storage units
toilet training chairs
wastebasket (covered)

Napping
bed linens (brightly colored patterned sheets, blankets, and stuffed
toys—no stuffed toys for very young infants)
cots (for toddlers)
cradles
cribs (for children under eighteen months)

Other furniture and essentials
barrels (carpeted)
chairs (infant seats, soft stuffed chairs, reclining baby chairs, and
rockers)
couches
cubbies (hooks at child's shoulder-level, not eye-level)
evacuation crib and mattress (or three by four foot canvas wheeled-cart
used in hotels and hospitals for collecting linen)
pillows (large, throw)
playpen or play yard (some are portable; some may be elevated for less
floor draft problems and for easier adult accessibility)
mattresses (including air)
storage cabinets (open and closed)
strollers
tables (for infants—14 inches high with raised edges; for toddlers—
$15\frac{1}{2}$ inches high) and chairs (8-inch seats)
toddler wagons (for transporting toddlers on "walking excursions")
walkers

For Older Children
Furniture for preschool (three- through five-year-olds) and primary-grade children (six- through eight-year-olds) should be of the proper height and proportions, durable and lightweight, and have rounded corners. If space is at a premium, furniture, especially children's chairs, should be stackable. Tables accommodating from four to six children are advisable. Although tables are designed in many geometric shapes, rectangular tables accommodate large pieces of paper for art and craft work, and round tables are attractive in the library center. Trapezoidal tables are quite versatile because they can be arranged in many configurations. All table surfaces should be "forgiving surfaces" (i.e., easy to clean and repair) due to children's intensive use.[6] Portable drawing and writing surfaces, such as clipboards and Formica-covered boards, can also be used. Formica countertops are excellent for art work (e.g., finger painting and play dough experiences) and cooking.

Children's chairs should have a broad base to prevent tipping and a full saddle seat with a back support approximately eight inches above the seat. So that chairs can be carried safely by children, chair weight should not exceed eight to ten pounds. The distance between the seat height of the chairs and the table surface should be approximately seven and one-half inches.[7] Chairs at tables should not have arms. In addition to regular school chairs, there should be soft furniture (e.g., couches, easy chairs, beanbag chairs, hammocks) and stools and benches. There must also be storage units and display facilities.

Some specific furniture includes

chairs (eight to twelve inch seat height)
children's rocking chairs, easy chairs, stools, and benches
dividers (bulletin boards, flannel boards, or screens)
storage units (portable and/or built-in and open and/or closed) and cubbies
tables (fifteen to nineteen inches high)

School-Age Child Care

Furniture for these older children must accommodate varying sizes of children. All types of furniture are needed for the many types of activities (e.g., arts and crafts, cooking, table games, homework, and watching videos). Most programs prefer the emphasis be placed on soft, home-like furniture, because many children have been at desks in hard chairs all day. Much storage space is needed for children's personal items and for program materials during non-program hours.

For Adults

Staff members and adults visiting the program need adult furniture for comfort. Children can also use some of the adult furniture. Some of the furniture includes

chairs (soft and wood)
desk and/or wood tables
filing cabinets
lockers and/or low cabinets (for personal possessions)

Audiovisual Equipment

Though early childhood programs have used audiovisual equipment for years, recent growth in both quantity and quality of material has broadened its use. Of course, "more" use is not necessarily better if vicarious experiences via audiovisual equipment are substituted for available real experiences. Audiovisual equipment that might be needed includes:

camera (35 mm and/or Polaroid)
filmstrip projector and filmstrips
headsets or earphones and listening stations
"Language Master"
loop (8mm)
movie projector (16 mm) and film
overhead projector and transparencies

projection table
record player and records
screen (thirty-six by forty-eight inches)
slide projector and slides
stereoscope and stereoscope reels (Viewmaster)
still pictures and graphic representations
storage cabinets for tapes, slides, and so on
tape recorders and blank tapes
television
three-dimensional models
videotape equipment

Microcomputers

In the past few years, many educators have recognized that computer literacy is no longer a skill needed only in certain professions; thus, they see the importance of infusing computer literacy objectives into the curriculum. Computers have become more and more integrated into school curricula.

Schools began using computers in the late 1960s. These were large computing systems. Then in 1979 the microcomputer came upon the educational scene. In the 1982–83 school year, 58 percent of the school districts in the United States reported the use of computers.[8] Today almost every school uses computers in their educational program.

Microcomputer Terminology

Understanding microcomputers involves learning the technical language. The following terms are frequently used in the literature concerning the availability, use, and evaluation of microcomputers:

1. **BASIC.** "Beginner's All-Purpose Symbolic Instruction Code," is the most commonly used microcomputer language.
2. **CAI.** "Computer-Assisted Instruction" is the direct use of the computer for instructional purposes.
3. **CMI.** "Computer-Managed Instruction" is the use of a computer to provide feedback (e.g., evaluate, diagnose, and prescribe) as the student uses noncomputerized materials.
4. **COBOL.** "Common Business-Oriented Language" is the computer language primarily used in business.
5. **Computer.** An electronic machine that follows directions.
6. **Computer literacy.** Awareness of the uses and limitations of computers—what they are, how they work, and their impact in our lives.
7. **Debug.** To correct "bugs" or errors in the computer program. The term *debug* actually came from the removal of a moth from a circuit in a glass enclosed computer in the 1940s.

8. **FORTRAN.** "Formula Translation" is the computer language primarily used in math and science.
9. **Hardware.** The physical components of a computer (e.g., mechanical, electrical and electronic devices).
10. **Keyboard.** The typewriter part of a microcomputer. There are two types of keyboards: (a) **live keyboards** permit response to be immediately entered into the memory without use of the "ENTER" key; and (b) **enter keyboards** that require the use of the "ENTER" key to enter responses into the memory.
11. **LOGO.** Developed by Seymour Papert and members of the Massachusetts Institute of Technology's Artificial Laboratory, LOGO is rooted in the theory of Piaget and is thus designed to enable young children to think by programming computers. In programming, children must plan and test ideas following a logical sequence. The language begins with graphics but extends through the entire range of mathematical and logic operations.
12. **Memory.** The storage area in the computer for both program and the data.
13. **Microcomputer.** A tabletop computer made up of a video display terminal (VDT) or television set, a keyboard, and memory circuits. The microcomputer is built around a **microprocessor,** and electronic circuits are engraved on silicon chips that are smaller than a postage stamp.
14. **Program.** A group of instructions designed to perform a task.
15. **Program documentation.** Materials accompanying the software (e.g., teacher's guide and student's workbook).
16. **Programmer.** A person who writes a computer program.
17. **Programming language.** The language used by the computer (e.g., BASIC, COBOL and FORTRAN).
18. **Software.** Stored computer programs (i.e., information and instructions).
19. **Storage device.** A component that stores information and instructions. Two storage devices are the **magnetic disk** (similar to a soft record) and a **magnetic tape** (similar to an audio recording tape).
20. **Video display type.** The type of display (e.g., color, black and white, or green) intended to be used with a particular system.

CAI Approaches to Instruction

Several approaches are used in computer assisted instruction in the classroom. Early childhood educators should be aware of the approaches to select programs that fit their needs. Computer assisted instruction (CAI) can take these forms:

1. **Drill and practice.** The common form of CAI. This approach is meant to be used to reinforce classroom learnings in areas such as spelling, math facts, and facts learned in subjects such as history and geography. This approach is practical for increasing speed and efficiency in routine learn-

ing situations, but it is not meant to replace classroom instruction for understanding.

2. **Tutorial approach.** This is designed so a child can test understanding of a topic. Materials are presented in a programmed learning format with the advantage of allowing a student to work through the materials at his own rate and with an introduction of remedial and review materials for students to gain mastery of the content.

3. **Games.** The CAI games approach often uses a problem-solving format, such as searching for a given number or alphabet letter. The computer gives clues, such as the number is greater than __ or less than __ or the letter comes before __ or after __. Such a game helps a young child learn the sequence of letters and numbers. Other games may be similar to Monopoly where the player must wisely deploy resources to achieve a goal.

4. **Simulation.** This approach uses the characteristics of a real situation (e.g., landing on the moon or an economic depression) where children can make decisions and note the consequences. Simulation programs are most often written for advanced students.

5. **Writing and graphics.** CAI can involve editing and revising writing and displays of graphic art.

6. **Computer programming.** CAI can involve computer programming where the child controls the machine and deals with model building. Seymour Papert developed LOGO to help young children learn programming with the help of robots, graphics, and sound. Papert studied with Piaget from 1958 to 1963 and thus developed ideas for children to use microcomputers to think creatively.[9]

Many of these approaches are combined in programs. Undoubtedly CAI approaches will continue to expand as educators become more familiar with computer usage and limitations.

Guidelines for Selecting Microcomputer Equipment

With the great variety of available microcomputer hardware and software, the microcomputer market must be carefully analyzed. As is appropriate for any equipment, selection must be based on goals and objectives of the local program. In addition, the technical skill of the staff members in using the microcomputer and the availability of dealers or service centers to provide in-depth maintenance must be carefully considered.

Once needs are determined, then specific selections can be made. Although hardware and software must be considered simultaneously because purchased programs are often machine-specific (i.e., fit a particular computer), for discussion purposes hardware and software are considered separately.

Hardware. In selecting hardware, one needs to develop a guide to compare the features of the various microcomputers. Check the local library for up-to-date computer shopping guides. Finally, in purchasing computer hardware, project future needs. Buying the model needed for current use and future expansion is the best consumer decision.

Software. Software is plentiful but presents more purchasing problems than hardware. First, poorly conceived microcomputer programs may be no more effective than a workbook page that costs less. Clements believes there needs to be more simulation, gaming, and problem solving software.[10] He believes the reason for the dearth of such software is that program developers have good knowledge in the technology of microcomputers and little knowledge of education. The second reason software must be purchased carefully is the reading ability, motor skills, and problem-solving abilities of the young child make much of the present software inappropriate. Papert's LOGO is a simplified language for the young child.[11] And, third, microcomputer software is proliferating at an amazing rate, making it almost impossible to keep up with the market. Reviews of software appear in both microcomputer journals and professional early childhood education journals.

Other Helpful Materials. Many articles appear in professional journals to help teachers become prepared to make decisions about microcomputers. *MicroNotes on Children and Computers* is an excellent source of information.[12] Teacher training programs on microcomputer use are available in many settings (e.g., in-service education, college courses, and professional meetings).

Materials for Very Young Infants

Very young, non-walking infants explore with their senses. Stimulation with materials is important. Items needed may include:

> bells (to firmly attach to wrist or shoes)
> faces (pictures and the live human face)
> objects (attached to cribs, playpens, including mobiles facing downward for infants to see)
> pictures and designs (on walls, crib linens, etc.)
> rattles
> recordings (of lullabies)
> rings and other objects (for grasping and mouthing)
> squeak toys
> squeeze toys

Materials for Activity Centers for Infants and Toddlers

A wide variety of materials are used in infant and toddler centers. Many of the items listed below can be used in various centers. Because of the differences in the types of centers provided in various infant/toddler programs and the wide variety of equipment and materials, it would be impossible to list all items available for learning/activity centers.

Listening
Items needed for listening may include:

> musical toys
> rattles
> record or cassette players
> recordings (records or tapes of books, rhymes, music, and animal sounds)
> rhythm instruments (e.g., drums, bells, wooden blocks, sticks, tambourines, and xylophones)
> windchimes

Seeing
Items needed for seeing may include:

> aquariums
> banners or streamers (especially for outside)
> books (picture books of cloth, vinyl, and cardboard)
> flannel boards with rather large pieces for placing on board
> mirrors (unbreakable; hand-held and hung on wall)
> mobiles (on eye level or with objects/pictures hung facing downward)
> pictures and wall hangings
> puzzles
> sponges (cut in different shapes)
> terrariums

Tactile
Items needed for touching may include:

> books (with "feely" pictures)
> cuddly toys
> "feely" balls/boxes
> teething toys
> textured cards and wall hangings

Manipulatives
Manipulative activity items may include:

> activity boards (e.g., "Busy Box" and latch and lock boards)
> beads (wooden beads, wooden spools, and snap beads)
> blocks (light-weight plastic or vinyl for stacking and large interlocking blocks such as "Lego" and "Bristle")
> block props (animals, people, and small vehicles)
> containers (pails, margarine tubs with lids, shoe boxes with lids, and muffin pans with items to fit in cups)
> cradle gyms
> dressing boards (button and zipper)
> hole punch

kitchen items (pots, pans, spoons, cups, and egg beaters)
peg boards with large pegs
push/pull toys
puzzles (simple with knobs)
rattles
sand and sand toys (pail, sieves and sifters, measuring cups and spoons, funnels, and sand wheels)
sewing/lacing cards, with yarn and laces
shape sorters
stacking/nesting toys
water and water play toys (for pouring, straining, and floating)

Fantasy

Fantasy items should fit the ongoing play. Some basic items may include:

bags (e.g., tote)
blankets
blocks (light weight)
cars/trucks/trains/planes
dolls (washable) with easy to dress clothes
dress-up clothes, especially hats
housekeeping furniture and other items—refrigerator, sink, stove, table and chairs, buggy, high chair, play food, empty (and clean) food containers, pots/pans, plastic dishes, and housekeeping tools (mop and broom)
miniature settings (doll house, farm, and airport)
mirrors
pillows
puppets
purses (including bags and suitcases)
scarves (to wave around)
shopping cart
stuffed animals
telephones

Creative

Items needed for creative play include:

crayons (large-size and non-toxic)
easel
glue
magazines (for cutting)
markers (water color and non-toxic)
paints (watercolors, fingerpaints, and tempera)
paint brushes
paper (construction, manila and white drawing paper, newsprint, and fingerpaint)

sand and sand toys
scissors (blunt-ended and soft-handled)
sponges (for painting)

Gross motor
Items for gross motor play may include:

balls (large rubber, soft beach, or balls designed for infants and toddlers)
bean bags and target
boxes, cardboard (to carry and crawl in)
bowling ball and pins (plastic)
bubble-making materials
climbers (low)
exercise mats
platform with railings (raised about fifteen inches off ground to make a bridge)
pounding bench
push/pull toys
ramps
riding toys (steerable, pedal, and scoot)
ring toss
rocking toys (rocking boat and rocking horse)
sand and sand toys (especially outside)
slide (low or placed on slightly inclined terrain)
steering wheels (attached to platforms with sides or other stable structures for pretend play)
steps (two or three not steep steps with railings)
swings (sling type that allows the child to swing sitting or "belly down")
troughs with moving water and floating objects
truck inner tube (only partially inflated)
tunnels
wagons
walking rails (attached fifteen inches off floor)
wheelbarrows

Toys, wall hangings, mirrors, and other interesting items should be available in the napping, feeding and dining, and changing and toileting areas.

Materials for Learning/Activity Centers for Older Children

Items included in learning/activity centers for older children should fit program objectives. Multicultural and nonsexist materials should be provided. The following lists name some basic equipment and materials available exclusive of textbooks, workbooks and instructional kits and sets.

Language Arts
The equipment and materials needed for language arts frequently envelop the specific curricular areas of listening, speaking, preparation for reading and writing, and literature. Although some early childhood programs have a language arts center, many place their language arts materials in several centers, such as the library, manipulative center, and concept-development center. Regardless of the arrangement of equipment and materials, items needed for language arts instruction include:

> alphabet letters (alphabet insets, kinesthetic letters, letters to step on, etc.)
> books and recordings of stories
> *filmstrips and/or slides of children's stories
> flannel boards
> lotto (covering many subjects)
> objects and pictures depicting rhyming words or initial sounds
> perceptual and conceptual development games (absurdities, missing parts, sequencing, go-togethers, opposites, and classification)
> picture dominoes
> *pictures and graphic representations of finger plays, poems, and stories
> *puppets and a puppet theater
> puzzles (jigsaw, sequencing, etc.) and puzzle rack
> recordings of sounds, such as animal, city, and home sounds
> signs and labels
> typewriter

Mathematics
Concepts frequently taught in mathematics include numbers, number combinations, and numerals; geometric concepts; size; position (i.e., ordinals); and patterns. Some early childhood programs have a mathematics center; others include mathematical equipment and materials in several centers, such as the concept-development center and the block center. Articles that help in children's mathematical development include:

> abacus (or counting frame)
> balance scales for developing an understanding of simple number operations
> beads for pattern work and for developing an understanding of geometric concepts
> "Broad Stair" for developing size concepts (Montessori)
> calendars, thermometers, clocks, scales, etc. that have numerals
> counting discs
> "Cuisenaire" materials for developing number and geometric concepts
> cylinders graduated in diameter and/or height (Montessori)

---

*Indicates multicultural and nonsexist materials.

design cubes
dowel rods in graduated lengths, for developing serial concepts
fabric, wallpaper, and cabinet- and floor-covering samples for pattern work
flannel board objects, numerals, and illustrations of finger plays and stories
    with mathematical concepts
fraction plates or cards
geometric shape insets and solids
"Golden Beads" for developing place value concepts (Montessori)
lotto (number and geometric shapes)
measuring cups and spoons for developing size concepts
number cards, dominoes, puzzles, and sorters
numerals (cards, insets, kinesthetic, puzzles, numerals to step on, etc.)
objects to count
pegboards and pegs for developing number and geometric concepts
*picture books, poems, and finger plays which have mathematical concepts
pictures of objects for grouping into sets and of geometric shapes
"Pink Tower" for developing size concepts (Montessori)
sorting box for geometric shapes
stacking and nesting blocks for developing size concepts
unit blocks and/or parquetry blocks for developing geometric and size
    concepts

Social Studies

Areas frequently covered in social studies include home and family; community
workers; concepts from geography, sociology, and economics; and holidays.
Though block and housekeeping centers can be considered social studies centers, they are usually arranged separately and their equipment and materials are
not listed here. Equipment and materials needed for social studies include:

books,* poems, and finger plays with the following themes: home and
    family, community workers, self-awareness (needs of security, self-
    confidence, achievement, belonging to groups, etc.), holidays, and fam-
    ily living in other parts of the world.
doll house, dolls, and miniature furniture
globes and maps (primary globe and a simple map of the area)
holiday decorations (although most decorations are child-made)
*pictures, posters, and flannel boards with the following themes: home
    and family, community workers, people in other parts of the country
    and the world, various geographical land and water areas, and holidays
*puppets (family, community workers, and holiday characters such as
    Santa Claus)
*puzzles and lotto: family, community workers, and holidays
village (miniature)

---

*Indicates multicultural and nonsexist materials.

100	units	1⅜"	x	2¾"	x	5½"
180	double units	1⅜"	x	2¾"	x	11"
200	quadruple units	1⅜"	x	2¾"	x	22"
36	ramps	1⅜"	x	2¾"	x	5½"
25	roof boards	⅜"	x	2¾"	x	11"
10	curves (elliptical)	1⅜"	x	2¾"	x	13¾"
10	curves (circular)	1⅜"	x	2¾"	x	7¾"
10	Y-switches	1⅜"	x	8¼"	x	11"
20	cylinders	2¾"	diam.		x	5½"
20	pillars	1⅜"	x	1⅜"	x	5½"
25	half-units	1⅜"	x	2¾"	x	2¾"
20	pairs triangles	1⅜"	x	2¾"	x	2¾"

FIGURE 6–1
Indoor Blocks

Blocks and Building Structures

Blocks and building structures may be set up in one center; however, small building materials such as Tinker Toys and Lego blocks, are often used in the manipulative center, and larger building materials such as hollow blocks, are placed in an outdoor activity center. Unit blocks, so named because each block is the size of the unit or a multiple or fraction of that unit, and larger floor blocks are most commonly placed in block and building centers. Materials to include in block and building centers are:

*accessories for block buildings, such as animals and people (wood, rubber, or plastic), wheel toys for pushing on floor, steering wheels, and block attachments

block bins or carts (unless shelves are used)

giant blocks (made of polyethylene and corrugated cardboard)

indoor blocks (See Figure 6–1.)[13]

interlocking planks

"Lego" blocks and other miniature interlockers (a wide assortment is available in wood and plastic)

outdoor hollow blocks (See Figure 6–2.)[14]

planks, boxes, wooden sawhorses, barrels, and so on

Tinker Toys (miniature and giant)

traffic sign set

---

*Indicates multicultural and nonsexist materials.

| 36 units | 12" | x | 12" | x | 6" |
| 36 double units | 12" | x | 24" | x | 6" |

FIGURE 6–2
Outdoor Blocks

Housekeeping and Dramatic Play

In dramatic play, children act out the roles of family members and community workers, reenact school activities and story plots, and learn social amenities such as table manners and telephone courtesy. Dramatic play may occur in almost any learning/activity center; however, one or more centers are usually arranged specifically for dramatic play. Necessary equipment and materials are:

cameras (toy and a "Polaroid" with film)
costumes, especially hats and tools of the trade of community workers (e.g., doctor's bag and stethoscope) and costumes for reenacting stories
doll items (table and two to four chairs; doll furniture—high chair, bed or cradle, carriage, chest of drawers, refrigerator, stove, sink, cabinet for dishes and washer-dryer; doll, wardrobes and linens; pots, pans, dishes, flatware (all items should be unbreakable); ironing board and iron; housekeeping articles—broom, dust mop, dustpan, and dust rag; artificial food; clothesline and clothespins; and dishpan).
*dolls (baby and teenage dolls)
dress-up clothes for men and women (long skirts, blouses, dresses, shirts, pants, shoes, caps, hats, boots, small suitcase, scarves and ribbons, flowers, jewelry, purses, neckties, and pieces of material)
fabric (several strips two or three yards in length, which can be used imaginatively)
gadgets, such as rubber hose, steering wheels, pipe, old faucets, door locks, springs, keys, pulleys, bells, scales, alarm clocks, cash registers and play money, cartons and cans, paint brushes, paper bags, light switches and paper punch (for tickets)
miniature doll house, community, farm, service station, and so on
mirrors (full-length and hand-held)
playscreens, cardboard houses, and so on
*puppets and stages
rocking chair
stuffed animals
telephone

---

*Indicates multicultural and nonsexist materials.

For specific prop equipment, see

> Bender, J. "Have You Ever Thought of a Prop Box?" *Young Children* 26, 3 (1971): 164–69.

In addition to the occupation props described by Bender, develop prop equipment for parent occupations.

Science

Both biological and physical science concepts are presented to young children. Because of the diversity of science equipment and materials, they are rarely housed in a single learning/activity center. Some of the equipment and materials include:

> animals and insect cages (container for small insects, cocoon holder, cage with treadmill, rabbit hutch, container for praying mantis, large walk-in cages, etc.)
> animals, insects, and fish
> aquarium (equipped with air pump and hose, filter, gravel, fish net, light, thermometer, medicine and remedies, and aquarium guide)
> balloons
> bird and suet feeders, and bird house
> books and pictures with the following themes: animals, plants, natural phenomena, and machinery
> bubble pipes and soap
> butterfly net
> chick incubator
> collections (rocks, bird nests, insects, sea shells, etc.)
> color wheel, color paddles (i.e., glass or plastic paddles in the primary colors), and prisms
> compass
> dry cell batteries, flashlight bulbs, bells, light receptacle, and electrical wire
> gardening tools (child-sized)
> kaleidoscope
> magnets (bar, horseshoe, and bridge)
> magnifying glasses (hand-held and tripod)
> measuring equipment (measuring cups and spoons; scales—balance, bathroom, postal; time instruments—sun dial, egg timer, clocks; thermometers (real indoor/outdoor and play); and linear measuring instruments (English and metric)
> miscellaneous materials (string, tape, hot plate, bottles of assorted sizes, pans, buckets, sponges, and hardware gadgets)
> models (animals, space equipment, machine, solar system, etc.)
> pinwheels
> plants, seeds, and bulbs (with planting pots, soil, fertilizer, and watering cans)
> pulleys and gears

puzzles with science themes
seed box
wheelbarrows (child-sized)
sound-producing objects
terrariums (woodland and desert)
vases and "frogs" for vases
weather vane

Water, Sand, and Mud
Water, sand, and mud learning/activity centers are found both in the indoor and outdoor areas. Some items are:

mops and sponges for cleanup
sand (white and brown)
sand and mud toys (trucks, jeeps, trains, bulldozers, tractors, cartons, cans, gelatin or sand molds, cookie cutters, spoons, pans, cups, dishes, strainers, watering cans, shovels, blocks, sand dolls, sieves, pitchers, sand pails, ladles, sifters, screens, sand combs, planks, and rocks)
sand table
siphon tubes
soap (floating) and soapflakes
straws
water play table
water play toys (small pitchers, watering cans, measuring cups, bowls of various sizes, plastic bottles, detergent squeeze bottles, medicine droppers, funnels, strainers, hose, corks, squeeze bottles, sponges, washable dolls, wire whisks, butter churns, and shaving brushes)
water pump for indoor water table

Cooking Few programs have a permanent cooking learning/activity center; however, most programs do provide children with occasional cooking experiences. If the facility has a kitchen or kitchenette, separate cooking equipment is not essential. Items that may be needed for cooking experiences include:

aprons (children and adult)
baking pans (cookie sheets, muffin pans, cake pans, and pie pans)
blender
cookie cutters
cooling racks
cutting board
dishcloth and dish towels
dishes and flatware
dish pan
electric countertop oven/broiler
floor cover (vinyl drop cloth)
grater
hot plate

kitchen utensils (stirring spoons, spatula, tongs, and knives)
measuring spoons and cups
microwave oven
mixing bowls
pantry items
placemats
popcorn popper
pot holder
pots, pans, and skillets
recipes written for young children
rolling pin
serving cart with wheels
serving dishes (trays, bowls, baskets, and pitchers)
sifter
strainer
supplies (paper plates, paper bowls, paper cups, napkins, paper towels, wax paper, toothpicks, straws, resealable plastic bags, dishwashing liquid, pot scrubber, paper bags, garbage bags, and air freshener)
tea kettle
thermometer
timer

Woodworking or Carpentry
The woodworking or carpentry learning/activity center may be set up in either the indoor or outdoor area. This is a popular center for young children. Equipment and materials needed for woodworking or carpentry are:

C clamps (variety of)
cloth, leather, styrofoam, cardboard, cork, bottle caps, and other scraps to nail on wood
drill (hand)
glue
hammers (claw) of differing weights and sizes
magnet (tied to a string for picking up dropped nails)
nails (thin nails with good-sized heads, because thick nails tend to split wood)
paints (water-base)
pencils (heavy, soft-leaded)
pliers
ruler and yardstick used as a straight edge more than for measuring
sandpaper of various grades (wrapped around and tacked to blocks)
sawhorses
saws (crosscut and coping)
scraps of wood (soft wood such as white pine, poplar, fir, and basswood with no knots), doweling, wood slats, and wooden spools

soap (rubbed across the sides of a saw to make it slide easier)
tacks
trisquare
vises (attached to workbench)
wire (hand-pliable)
worktable or workbench (drawers for sandpaper and nails are desirable)

Young children cannot handle and do not need a rasp, screwdriver and screws, a plane, a brace and bits, a file, an ax or hatchet, metal sheets, tin snips, or power tools.

Music
Young children respond to music by listening, singing, playing rhythm instruments, and dancing. Equipment and materials for music may include:

autoharp
capes and full skirts for dancing
chromatic bells
chromatic pitch pipe
headsets and listening stations
music books for singing, rhythms, and appreciation
music cart
piano and piano bench
pictures of musicians, musical instruments, and dancers
record player
record rack or cabinet and/or cassette rack
records and cassettes
rhythm instruments (drums, claves, triangles, tambourines, cymbals, tom-toms, handle bells, jingle sticks, wrist bells, ankle bells, shakers, maracas, rhythm sticks, tone blocks, castanets, sand blocks, sounder, finger cymbals, and gong bell)
scarves (five by three feet)
stories (e.g., picture books) about music and sound
tape recorder
xylophone

Art
Using various art media, children create graphic and three-dimensional works and learn concepts of color, form, texture, and size. Art equipment and materials include:

apron or smock (snaps preferred, because ties can knot)
chalk (various colors, $\frac{5}{8}$" to 1" diameter)
clay (powdered and/or "Play Doh" or "Plasticine")
clay boards
color paddles (three paddles—red, yellow, and blue)

crayons (red, yellow, blue, orange, green, purple, black, and brown)

design block sets

display boards and tables

drying rack

easels (two working sides with a tray for holding paint containers on each side)

erasers (art gum and felt for chalkboard)

geometric shapes (insets, etc.)

gummed paper in assorted shapes for making designs and pictures

junk materials for collage work (beads, buttons, cellophane, cloth, flat corks, wallpaper scraps, wrapping paper scraps, and yarn)

magazines for collage

markers (felt-tip, various colors)

mosaics

mounting board (twenty-two by twenty-eight inches)

pails (plastic with covers for storing clay)

paint (powdered or premixed tempera paint in various colors and finger paint)

paint jars (some are now made which do not spill)

paint and varnish brushes (camel hair or bristle, one-half and one-inch thick with long handles)

paper (corrugated paper; newsprint, twenty-four inches × thirty-six inches; finger paint paper or glazed shelf paper; construction, tissue, and poster papers of various colors; manila paper, eighteen inches × twenty-four inches; metallic paper, ten inches × thirteen inches; wrapping paper; and tag board, twenty-four inches × thirty-six inches)

paper bags

paper cutter

parquetry

paste brushes and sticks

paste and glue

pictures of children engaging in art activities and of famous artists

plastic canvas

printing blocks or stamps

recipes for finger paints, modeling materials, and so on

reproductions of famous paintings and pictures of sculpture and architecture

rulers

scissors (adult shears and right- and left-handed scissors for children)

scissors rack

sorting boxes for sorting colors and shapes

staff members' supplies (art gum erasers; masking, cellophane, and mystic tapes; shellac or a fixative; liquid starch; dishwashing detergent; straight pins; shears; stapler; paper punch; and cutter)

stories and poems with themes of color, shape, size, beauty of nature, and
so on
tape (masking, mending, and transparent)
textured materials
yarn (various colors)
yarn needles

Manipulatives

Manipulative activities help young children develop eye-hand coordination.
Equipment and materials for manipulative activities include:

art materials
beads for stringing
blocks (small, interlocking)
dressing dolls, dressing frames, and/or dressing vests (equipped with buttons, raincoat snaps, zippers, bows, snaps, and buckles)
insets (geometric shapes, numerals, and letters)
lacing boards (or cards)
latch frames
pegs and pegboards
pounding boards
puzzles
sewing cards

Large-Muscle

Because professionals concerned with young children are realizing the multifaceted benefits of large-muscle play, the equipment and materials designed for
vigorous activity have undergone several major changes. One change is the
emphasis on developing an outdoor area that takes advantage of and enhances
the beauty of the natural landscape.

A second change is the prevalent use of adventure (sometimes called "creative" or "junk") playgrounds. The idea of an adventure playground was first
conceived by C. T. Sorensen, a landscape architect in Copenhagen. Sorensen
noticed that children did not play on the playgrounds he designed; instead, they
played with discarded building materials. Disadvantages of traditional equipment are that it does not stimulate the imagination; children may use it in ways
other than those intended, so it becomes dangerous; children have to wait turns;
metal equipment is affected by weather and is expensive—from less than a
hundred to several thousand dollars per item. Although adventure playgrounds
are not without their problems (drainage, lack of enclosure, and unsightliness),
many writers feel these playgrounds will be prevalent in the future. A study by
Reid found that in comparing the enthusiasm of children, parents, school personnel, and people of the community for adventure playgrounds, children are
most enthusiastic and school personnel least enthusiastic.[15] Parents like the idea

of these playgrounds but are concerned about their children's clothing. Thompson and Rittenhouse show that social skills increase as children participate in adventure playgrounds.[16] All types of materials seem to have an irresistible fascination for children; thus, adventure playgrounds can include items to climb, such as ropes, rope nets, and walls; to crawl through, such as foxholes or culverts, with some opening straight up in an escape manhole; to balance on, such as balance logs or roll barrels; to walk or run on, such as stepping stones or tire walks; for stair-stepping or island hopping, such as stepping stones or log pieces; to swing on, such as tire swings and ropes; to slide on, such as boards or aluminum roofing; to stack, balance, and build, such as pieces of scrap lumber or plastic pipe; to bounce on, such as car springs with a platform or a used innerspring mattress; for water, dirt, and mud play; and for make-believe play, such as tree houses or forts, old cars, boats, or airplanes, and lookout towers or foxholes. It is interesting to note that manufacturers of play equipment are designing free-form climbing units and other structures somewhat like those of adventure playgrounds.

A third change is the increase in equipment and material available for large-muscle activity. Some items are:

> balance beams
> balls (inflatable: 14", 8 1/2", and 5" diameters)
> blocks (hollow and/or large floor blocks)
> dramatization materials
> gardening tools
> horse (broomstick variety)
> hula hoops
> inner tubes (partially inflated)
> kites
> mattresses for jumping (inner spring)
> musical game recordings and/or props
> pedal toys (e.g., tricycles)
> planks (cleats at ends to hold place on climbing structure, 6' × 10')
> play structures (provide place for large motor play and support dramatization; excellent criteria given by Vergeront)[17]
> ring toss game
> rocking boats
> ropes (jumping)
> sand pit (coverable)
> sand play toys
> sand substitutes (e.g., rice, wheat, oatmeal, cornmeal, popcorn, macaroni, varieties of beans, styrofoam packing materials, wood shavings)
> sand tables (types reviewed by Morris)[18]
> see saw
> swings (with sling type seats)
> wagons

water play toys
water tables (types reviewed by Morris)[19]
weather instruments (rain gauge, wind vane, thermometer)

Materials for School-Age Child Care Programs

School-age child care programs need a variety of materials to accommodate various ages and interests and needs.

Quiet
Items needed may include:

books (reference books for doing homework and a selection of trade books
    for leisure reading)
listening station (with earphones)
magazines (children's)
mazes
newspapers
recordings (music and stories)
word puzzles (e.g., crossword puzzles)

Games and Manipulatives
Items needed may include:

board games (e.g., Monopoly, Scrabble, chess, checkers, Chinese checkers,
    Life, Clue, bingo, and tic-tac-toe)
card games (decks of cards for fish, hearts, etc.)
jacks
interlocking blocks (e.g., Lego)
magnetic building sets
parquetry, design blocks, and design cards
puzzles (jigsaw with one hundred to five hundred pieces)

Woodworking
For items needed see list given for Older Children on p. 222–223.

Arts and Crafts
For items needed see list given for Older Children on p. 223–224.

Materials for Hobbies
Items needed would depend on hobbies.

Writing Supplies
Items needed may include:

chalk
chalkboards
marking pens
paper (various types)
pencils with pencil sharpeners
typewriter
wipe-off boards

High Tech

Items needed may include:

calculators
computers with selected software
filmstrips and projectors
typewriters
video cassette recorders with television and selected cassettes

Outside

Items needed may include:

ball game equipment (e.g., basketball, soft ball, dodge ball, kick ball, volley
   ball, and soccer)
marbles
riding equipment (e.g., bicycles, skates, and skateboards)
sand/water/mud (See list for "Older Children" on p. 221).

Equipment and Materials for Children with Disabilities

A growing number of materials are advertised as being designed for children with disabilities. Many types of disabilities require therapy with equipment and materials that can only be handled by a trained professional. Most regular early childhood equipment and materials are suitable for children with less severe disabilities, those most apt to be "mainstreamed." In fact, early childhood and "special education" equipment and materials are often listed in the same section of suppliers' catalogs. However, "special" children do need additional and sometimes different equipment and materials for their comfort and safety and for therapy. Specific equipment and materials can be chosen when individual education plans are developed for the children.

Children's Books and Magazines

Children's books are used extensively in most early childhood programs. Selection of books is important for two reasons: due to the varying quality of published books, it is possible for children to have a steady diet of poor to mediocre books; and books should enhance the specific goals of the local early childhood program. Books are usually selected using one or more of these criteria:

1. The book has a theme considered interesting to most young children (e.g., themes may be nature, machines, or holidays).
2. The book has a theme that can help young children overcome some general concerns (e.g., common fears, making friends, or cooperative play) or can help specific children cope with their particular problems (e.g., divorce, working mothers, minority-group membership, a disability or mobility). Using books from the viewpoint of children's needs is referred to as **bibliotherapy.**
3. The book has a theme that correlates with concepts taught in the classroom. Books are available to extend and enrich almost every curricular concept.
4. The book has a theme that can teach a value. Children's literature has traditionally been considered a good source for this.
5. The book is considered high quality literature (e.g., Caldecott Medal and Honor Books).

Early childhood educators may use several sources in finding titles of quality books:

Bulletin of the Center for Children's Books. University of Chicago, 5750 Ellis Ave., Chicago, Ill. 60637

Christian Science Monitor, One Norway St., Boston, Mass. 02115. (spring and fall reviews)

Council on Interracial Books, 1841 Broadway, New York, N.Y. 10023

Horn Book (bimonthly magazine), 585 Boylston Street, Boston, Mass. 02166

New York Times, 229 W. 43rd Street, New York, N.Y. 10036 (spring and fall reviews)

Notable Children's Books, Children's Service Division of the American Library Association, 50 E. Huron Street, Chicago, Ill. 60611

Saturday Review/World, Saturday Review Magazine Co., 214 Massachusetts Ave., NE No. 460, Washington, D.C. 20002 (spring and fall reviews)

To keep abreast of new publications of children's books, teachers may also note reviews in many professional journals.

In addition to books in early childhood education, there are some excellent magazines also available. These include:

Child Life
1100 Waterway Boulevard
Indianapolis, Ind. 46206

Children's Digest
1100 Waterway Boulevard
Indianapolis, Ind. 46206

Children's Playmate
1100 Waterway Boulevard
Indianapolis, Ind. 46206

Cricket
Carus Corporation
Box 300
Peru, Ill. 61354

Ebony, Jr.
820 S. Michigan Ave.
Chicago, Ill. 60605

Humpty Dumpty
1100 Waterway Boulevard
Indianapolis, Ind. 46206

Jack and Jill
1100 Waterway Boulevard
Indianapolis, Ind. 46206

Scienceland
Scienceland, Inc.
501 Fifth Avenue
New York, N.Y. 10017

Ranger Rick
National Wildlife Federation
1400 16th Street, NW
Washington, D.C. 20006

Your Big Back Yard
National Wildlife Federation
1400 16th Street, NW
Washington, D.C. 20006

Texts and Workbooks

Although textbooks and workbooks are not viewed as appropriate materials for those advocating the interactionist psycho-philosophical view, they are frequently used instructional materials. This text's authors feel that textbooks and workbooks are inappropriate below first grade level and should only be used with discretion at the primary-grade levels; however, early childhood teachers need to be familiar with these materials.

With the exception of reading textbook series, textbook series in the various curriculum areas, such as mathematics, social studies, science, spelling, English, and health, include one textbook (and possibly some supplementary materials) per grade or instructional level. Instructional materials for developing reading skills are usually referred to as **basal materials** and include children's readers covering all levels of reading, teachers' guides, workbooks, and supplementary materials such as word cards, pocket charts, tests, big charts, and various audiovisual aids. Instructional manuals or teachers' guides usually accompany each textbook and may include objectives of the materials; an itemized list of new vocabulary, concepts, and skills to be introduced; assessment questions or activities; a suggested sequence or time plan for presentation of materials; and supplementary enrichment activities. The manuals are printed in one of these forms:

1. The **teacher's annotated edition** (TAE) is a two-part manual. One part is an annotated edition of the children's textbook that includes the children's text with added comments printed in red in the margins, vocabulary words circled, and so forth. In short, the authors have made notes on the teacher's copy of the children's text—hence the name, teacher's annotated edition. Before or after the annotated part, another section describes objectives of the materials, assessment tasks, and supplementary activities.
2. Some instructional manuals are not annotated but contain two parts. One part is the children's textbook without annotations, and the other contains information for the teacher.
3. Some textbook series publish an instructional manual with information for the teacher but do not include the children's text. Because the size of the manual is reduced when the children's text is not included, the manual is often paperback.

Workbooks and worksheets provide paper-and-pencil activities for children. Although many professionals do not approve of these types of activities for young children, workbooks and worksheets that may not require reading are more often found in prekindergarten and kindergarten programs than textbooks. Characteristics of workbooks and worksheets are as follows:

1. Workbooks are published in paperback. Individual pages are occasionally perforated so children can handle them as worksheets rather than booklets. Worksheets are one page long and are sold in class-size packages of twenty-five or thirty copies. Some published worksheets are available as ditto masters.
2. Many textbook series have an accompanying children's workbook. If a textbook-workbook combination is not available, the publisher may suggest a particular workbook as supplementary instructional material.
3. Many workbooks and worksheets are written without reference to a textbook.
4. A workbook or worksheet may contain paper-and-pencil tasks for a curricular area at one instructional level, such as kindergarten mathematics, or for subcurricular areas at one instructional level, such as four kindergarten mathematics workbooks with one for each subarea: number concepts, spatial relationships, geometric concepts, and patterns.

Instructional Kits and Sets

The available kits and sets of early learning materials cover a range of psychomotor-, affective-, and cognitive-developmental tasks and embody the contents of various curricular areas. Kits and sets differ from singly packaged items in several ways: (1) the materials are collected and arranged to provide for a range of individual and group activities; (2) various learning methods are employed while working with materials (listening to records and stories, manipulating objects, viewing books, pictures, and filmstrips, and talking); (3) a manual or teacher's guide provides guidance in using the kit; (4) components of the kit or set are sold as a unit although components may be sold separately in kits that divide materials into distinct instructional units or that have consumable materials; (5) kits are rather expensive; and (6) the materials are encased in a drawer-, cabinet-, or luggage-type storage container. Some kits are published with staff-training materials, supplementary materials for children's activities, and evaluation materials.

As is true of all instructional materials, however, kits or sets should be carefully evaluated by the user. Before purchasing a kit or set, a person should ask:

1. How does the psycho-philosophical view of the program match the rationale of the kit or set in both content and methodology?
2. Are the materials in the kit or set appropriate for the methods and rationale stated in the accompanying manual?
3. Why were the materials gathered into a kit or set? Does it save the teacher time? Are the various components used together in such a way that some materials present concepts and other materials reinforce and extend the concepts?
4. Is the teacher's manual adequate and easy to handle? Are directions clear and easy to find? Are there suggestions for enrichment activities and for evaluation and diagnosis? How much teacher planning is necessary? Is the manual a "cookbook," a suggestion book, or both?
5. Can the local staff members use the kit or set without training?
6. How many kits or sets are required for the local program?
7. Are all the components sold only as a unit, or can replacement parts and consumable items be purchased separately?
8. Are other pieces of equipment necessary when using the kit or set? If so, are these additional items already owned by the local program or must they also be purchased?
9. Are special services, such as training of staff members, evaluation, installation, and maintenance, provided with the kit or set?
10. Are the materials, including storage case and manual, durable? Are the components safe for young children and easily maintained? Are they large enough and not easily lost?
11. How much physical space is required to use the kit or set? Is it easily stored and is storage space available?

12. What is the total cost of purchase, including tax and shipping charges, of replacement and consumable parts, of other equipment necessary for using the kit or set, and of maintenance and staff training?
13. How does the kit or set fare in terms of research results or subjective opinion by those using it in a similar program?
14. Are there other kits or sets on the market similar to this one? If so, how do they compare on all the above points?

Raw or Primitive Materials

Raw or primitive materials are any materials that do not duplicate reality—a lump of clay, a scrap of cloth, a bead, and so forth. Many programs employ such materials and many professionals see this type of material as excellent for instruction, because children with various degrees of competence and differing interests can work with them. Raw materials permit children to use various symbols to stand for a real object.

Other Equipment and Materials

Other equipment and materials that do not seem to fit under the foregoing headings but which should not be forgotten in equipping an early childhood program are:

> bathroom supplies
> clock (large, wall-mounted)
> first aid cabinet with recommended supplies
> flashlights
> food service equipment (information available through U.S. Department of Agriculture)
> housekeeping supplies
> office machines and supplies
> radio or television (for emergency information)

COMMUNITY RESOURCES

Since the early 1900s, early childhood programs have utilized community resources. Undoubtedly, with emphases on career education and use of parents as hired staff members and volunteers, community resources will be even more widely utilized by taking children to the community through field or study trips, by bringing the community to the children through resource people, and by getting families involved in community projects and services. Staff members should keep a perpetual inventory of local places to visit and of resource people suitable to their program's needs. In compiling such an inventory, one should list name of place, telephone number, person at location in charge of hosting visitors, age limitations, time of day visitors are welcomed, number of children the place can accommodate, how long a tour takes, and additional comments. Preferable apparel, whether advance notice is required, what children can see or do and what the host provides for the children, and number of adults requested to accompany the group should also be stated. The following list of places is provided only to start staff members thinking about local community resources:

airport
art and craft museum
bakery
bank
beauty shop
brick plant
building under construction
dairy
dentist's office
doctor's office
fast food chain
pizza shop
vocational high school (classes and equipment in cosmetology, mechanics, graphics, etc.)
dry cleaners
electric company
elementary school
farm (tree, animal, and crop)
feed store
fields
fire station
gas company
grocery store (corner market and supermarket)
hospital
ice cream plant
library
manufacturing company
milk processing plant
neighborhood walk
newspaper office
park (neighborhood, city, state, or national)
pet shop
photography studio
police station
post office
telephone company
television cable company
television studio
water plant
zoo

PROFESSIONAL LIBRARY

Early childhood program should have a professional library to keep staff members informed and to help them in planning. The library should contain:

1. Journals, newsletters, and special publications of professional organizations concerned with young children
2. Instructional manuals in addition to those regularly used
3. Curriculum guides printed by the state board of education, state department of public welfare, local school system, and other early childhood programs that have similar objectives
4. Professional books and audiovisuals concerned with various aspects of early childhood—child development, curriculum, guidance, and administration
5. Catalogs and brochures from distributors of equipment and materials
6. Newsletters or information on current legislation pertaining to child care and education (obtained by being on your congressman or senator's mailing list)
7. Information from local community resources—health department, dental association, March of Dimes, Heart Fund, Sickle Cell Anemia, and Sudden Infant Death Syndrome (SIDS) groups
8. Bibliographies of pertinent topics in child development, care and education, and parenting skills

SUMMARY

Because there is such a wide variety of equipment and materials available for use in early childhood programs, many may feel that the early childhood curriculum is entirely contained in such materials. Certainly, the uses of equipment and materials are powerful regulators of children's experiences. Thus, selection of the types of equipment and materials purchased and the ways in which they will be used must be carefully determined by the local program. Generally speaking, in the interactionist psycho-philosophical program base, equipment and materials are selected and arranged to allow children to explore and improvise. On the other hand, in the behavioral-environmental psycho-philosophical program base, the use of equipment and materials is often adult-prescribed and thus selected for one obvious use. This chapter listed specific equipment and materials for learning centers often used in interactionist early childhood programs.

Regardless of program objectives, all early childhood program administrators must know the basic procedures for purchasing and caring for equipment and materials. All early childhood programs must also include a professional library.

NOTES

1. H. Boles, *Step by Step to Better School Facilities* (New York: Holt, Rinehart and Winston, 1965), 190.

2. Contact the Arts and Craft Materials Institute (715 Boylston St., Boston MA 02116) or Art Hazards Information Center (5 Beekman Street, New York, N.Y. 10038).

3. P. Pragnell, "The Friendly Object," *Harvard Educational Review* 39 (1969): 39–40.

4. F. Osmon, *Patterns for Designing Children's Centers* (New York: Educational Facilities Laboratories, 1971), 48.

5. B. C. Anderson and S. L. Gordon, "Assessing the Complexity of Children's Materials," *Dimensions* 16, 4 (1988): 7–10.

6. J. Vergeront, *Places and Spaces for Preschool and Primary—Indoors* (Washington, D.C.: National Association for the Education of Young Children, 1987), 14.

7. N. Headley, *Education in the Kindergarten*, 4th ed. (New York: American Book, 1966), 96.

8. "Computer Corner," *Instructor* 92 (1983): 108.

9. S. Papert, *Mindstorms: Children, Computers, and Powerful Ideas* (New York: Basic, 1980).

10. D. H. Clements, "Computers and Young Children: A Review of Research," *Young Children* 43, 1 (1987): 34–44.

11. Papert, *Mindstorms*.

12. For information contact: ERIC Clearinghouse on Elementary and Early Childhood Education, University of Illinois, 805 W. Pennsylvania, Urbana, Ill. 61801.

13. E. B. Starks, *Blockbuilding* (Washington, D.C.: National Education Association, Department of Kindergarten-Primary Education, 1960).

14. Ibid.

15. M. J. Reid, *An Evaluation of Creative/Adventure Playgrounds and Their Use by Pupils of Elementary Schools*, ERIC ED 057 108 (Vancouver: Vancouver Board of School Trustees, 1971).

16. F. C. Thompson and A. M. Rittenhouse, "Measuring the Impact," *Parks and Recreation* 9 (1974): 24–26, 62–63.

17. J. Vergeront, *Places and Spaces for Preschool and Primary—Outdoors* (Washington, D.C.: National Association for the Education of Young Children, 1988).

18. S. Morris, "Sand and Water Table Buying Guide," *Childcare Information Exchange* (August 1990): 58–60.

19. Ibid.

FOR FURTHER READING

Buckleitner, W. *Survey of Early Childhood Software.* Ypsilanti: The High Scope Press, 1988.

Campbell, P. F., and Fein, G. G. *Young Children and Microcomputers.* Englewood Cliffs: Prentice-Hall, 1986.

Clements, D. H. *Computers in Early and Primary Education.* Englewood Cliffs: Prentice-Hall, 1985.

Feeney, S., and Magarick, M. "Choosing Good Toys for Young Children," *Young Children* 40, 1 (1984): 21–24.

Haugland, S., and Shade, D. *Developmental Evaluation of Software for Young Children*. Albany: Delmar Publishing, Inc., 1990.

Hoot, J. L. *Computers in Early Childhood Education: Issues and Practices*. Englewood Cliffs: Prentice-Hall, 1986.

Loughlin, C., and Suina, J. *The Learning Environment: An Instructional Strategy*. New York: Teachers College Press, Teacher's College, Columbia University, 1982.

Oppenheim, J. F. *Buy Me! Buy Me! The Bank Street Guide to Choosing Toys for Children*. New York: Pantheon, 1987.

Sinker, M. *Toys for Growing: A Guide to Toys that Develop Skills*. Chicago: Year Book Medical, 1986.

Sutton-Smith, B. *Toys Are Culture*. New York: Gardner, 1986.

Chapter 7
Financing and Budgeting

E arly childhood programs are expensive. The National Association for the Education of Young Children (NAEYC) has stated that the crisis facing early childhood programs is rooted in our nation's failure to recognize the antinomy of three basic needs—children's need for services, staff's need for adequate compensation, and parents' need for affordable programs. These needs are very difficult to fulfill simultaneously. In 1987, the NAEYC Governing Board adopted this position statement:

1. All children should have access to high quality early childhood programs. The key determinants of the quality of an early childhood program are:
   a. Trained teachers who have knowledge and ability to consistently implement developmentally appropriate curriculum.
   b. Group size and adult-child ratios based on the age and needs of the children served, to assure appropriate experiences for children.
2. Early childhood programs must be able to offer staff salaries and benefits commensurate with the skills and qualifications required in order to attract and retain qualified teachers and to assure the provisions of quality services.
3. High-quality early childhood programs must be available to any family wanting or needing their services, at a cost that families can afford.[1]

Both the scope and the quality of services are related to the financial status of a program. The exceptions to this rule are programs that rely heavily on volunteers' help and other in-kind contributions, that carefully budget meager funds, or that spend money wastefully. Although studies have shown that programs with similar hourly costs ranged in quality from poor to excellent,[2] even with careful budgeting, however, good programs cannot operate effectively for long depending on donations and volunteers without weakening the quality and quantity of their services and without damaging the morale of those involved. Although total budget may not be directly related to program quality, Olenick did find a positive relationship between program quality and budget allocations for teacher salaries and benefits (i.e., programs that spent approximately two-thirds of their budgets on salaries and staff benefits tended to be high quality and quality diminished considerably in programs spending less than one-half of their budgets on salaries and staff benefits).[3]

Few early childhood administrators receive adequate training in fiscal management. Such training is important because parents, funding agencies, and taxpayers who feel their early childhood programs are properly managed are more likely to subsidize the program. As is true of all other aspects of planning and administration, fiscal planning begins with the psycho-philosophical view of the local program. Unless the proposed services and the requirements for meeting those services, in the way of staff, housing or equipment, are taken into account, how can a budget be planned? And although program objectives should be considered first, probably no early childhood program is entirely free of financial limitations.

Fiscal planning affects all aspects of a program; consequently, it should involve input from all those involved in the program—board of directors or advisory board, director, primary program and support program personnel, and parents. By considering everyone's ideas, a more accurate conception of budgeting priorities, expenditure level, and revenue sources can be derived. Furthermore, planning and administering the fiscal aspects of an early childhood program should be a continuous process. Successful financing and budgeting will only come from evaluating current revenue sources and expenditures and from advance planning for existing and future priorities.

Fiscal affairs are probably the most surveyed aspect of an early childhood program. A central criterion used to evaluate the worth of a program is often economic; that is, using funds efficiently and showing benefits that exceed costs. Administrators can use evidence of economic worth from studies such as those presented in Chapter 2. Recently more early childhood administrators recognized the need to develop their own marketing programs.[4]

Not-for-profit programs are responsible to their funding agencies and for-profit programs are accountable to their owners, stockholders, or the Internal Revenue Service. Even if the average citizen doesn't understand the problems of fund management, any hint of fund misuse will cause criticism. Administrators must budget, secure revenue, manage, account for, and substantiate expenditures in keeping with the policies of the early childhood program in a professional and businesslike manner.

COSTS OF EARLY CHILDHOOD PROGRAMS

Reported costs of early childhood programs show extensive variation. Costs vary with the type of program, the level of training and size of staff, sponsorship (a federal program, public school, or parent cooperative), the delivery system (center-based, home visitor, or television), and with the children enrolled (age and disabled or nondisabled). Another factor contributing to variations in costs is whether the program is new or is offering new, additional services and thus has "start-up costs"—such as salaries of planning personnel and initial expenditures for housing, equipping, and advertising—or whether the program is already underway and has continuing costs. Geographic location, the amount of competition, and the general economy all contribute to the varying costs.

Estimates of Program Costs

Quality child care is labor intensive and expensive. Estimates are that good quality full-day programs cost a minimum of four thousand dollars per child per year.[5] However, there is a wide range in costs. In 1985, the average weekly (thirty-hour week) costs were: thirty-seven dollars per week for center care; thirty-five dollars per week for relative care; and thirty-nine dollars per week for family day-care. These figures were almost the same as the 1975 figures except for care by relatives which had risen dramatically; there was only a 5 percent increase from 1985 to 1987.[6] These averages would indicate that the average costs per child per year was nearer two thousand dollars. Costs of child care in major urban areas are closer to six thousand dollars per year.[7] Thus, a two-tiered child care system is developing—quality programs for those who can afford and inappropriate and even unsafe programs for those who cannot afford.[8]

Because of the estimated costs, this is the amount many government agencies will pay,[9] and thus, to some degree, circularity results. In other words, because agencies pay a certain number of dollars, program designers plan the program around the expected amount of money. If funded the first year, the designers write a similar program the next year in hopes of being refunded. Thus, the agency pays approximately the same amount again, and the cycle is continued. So the program is designed around a specific dollar value, whether or not it makes for the "best" program.

Different types of programs vary in their cost. Infant day-care is more expensive than care for older children due to the increased numbers of staff members in infant programs as compared to programs serving older children. Facilities in continuous use (e.g., preschool day-care) are cost-effective in comparison to facilities with "downtime" (e.g., half-day nursery schools and school-age child care (SACC) programs). Care in urban areas is more expensive than in rural areas of the country. And care that meets quality standards (e.g., accredited) is more expensive than that of other programs.

Mainstreaming increases the costs of early childhood programs. Frohreich found that certain expenditure categories contributed significantly to cost differences between exceptional-child programs and regular programs in these ways: (1) instruction was the largest single component of expenditure; (2) transportation, especially for physically-disabled children, was very high; (3) instructional support expenditures, for counselors, psychologists, and medical personnel, were major factors when the program used support personnel; and (4) regular classrooms converted to rooms for disabled and nondisabled students together resulted in fewer students per class, reduced square footage per pupil, and thus increased the cost.[10] A study to evaluate the costs of serving children with disabilities in Head Start indicated that in all categories of exceptionality (e.g., speech disabled, physically disabled, emotionally disabled) costs were more than those for a typical child. However, costs were a function of the type and degree of the exceptionality with intellectually gifted the least expensive and physically disabled the most expensive.[11]

Costs to Families

Half or more than half of families with young children cannot afford to pay for child care. For higher-income families, child care is less than 5 percent of their budgets; for middle-income families, child care is 10 percent of their family budgets (comparable to food), but for low-income families, child care is 20 to 26 percent of their family budgets (comparable to housing costs).[12] Day-care is the fourth largest expenditure for working families after food, clothing, and taxes.[13] It is estimated that only one percent of families can afford quality day-care program costs for one child, and even fewer can afford quality programs for more than one child.[14]

Costs to families may differ from absolute program costs because of "direct subsidies." There are several types of direct subsidies, such as:

1. Aid to Families with Dependent Children (AFDC). In October 1988, Congress passed the Family Support Act. The Act significantly expands the federal funds available for AFDC parents who are working or in school or training, and for parents leaving AFDC for employment.[15]
2. Project Head Start for families who qualify. Currently Head Start serves only one-fifth of all eligible four-year-old children and even fewer eligible younger children. There is now authorization for full funding of Head Start by 1994 for all eligible three- to five-year-old children.[16]
3. Federal income tax deduction allowed for day-care services (IRS Form 2441). Child-care tax credit can also now be claimed on Form 1040A, the short income tax form. Families can deduct 20 to 30 percent of their annual child-care expenses but this cannot exceed $2,400 for one child or $4,800 for more than one child from their income tax bill. There are three problems with this direct subsidy. First, this subsidy does not address the quality of early childhood programs. Second, poor families may not earn sufficient income to take advantage of this bill. And third, dependent care tax credit is not reimbursable; thus, poor families with little or no tax liability are unable to recoup any of their expenditures for child care.

The amount of foregone income when a family member provides child-care services rather than obtaining outside employment is another expense that varies from family to family. The income is considered foregone when a family member provides child-care services either without payment or on an intrafamilial income transfer. In either case, the amount of foregone income depends on the caregiver's employable skills and availability of employment, or on the caregiver's potential income. (Of course, one should consider costs of outside employment, such as transportation, clothing, organization or union dues, and higher taxes, in calculating foregone income.)

Cost Analysis of Programs

The decision to fund an early childhood program and the kind of investment to make depends on "answers" based on cost analyses. Given today's economic situation, programs applying for public moneys are reviewed in terms of costs versus savings (i.e., social benefits to the individuals involved and to society in general). Social benefits quantified in economic terms are always difficult to calculate and especially, in the case of early childhood programs, are made almost impossible due to the fact that many of the benefits cannot be measured until young children reach adulthood.

There are several types of cost analyses. The reason for doing a cost analysis determines the type of analysis employed. **Cost-effectiveness** analysis compares the costs of two or more programs that have the same or similar goals to find the least-cost method of reaching a particular goal. Programs that offer a low cost approach compared to other approaches to achieve certain objectives are referred to as cost-effective programs.

Cost-efficiency analysis usually follows cost-effectiveness analysis. Cost-effective programs can further reduce costs by developing a least-cost, within-program management plan. Cost efficiency is achieved when there is optimal use of all program components (e.g., staffing patterns, curriculum, scheduling). When the management of a single program is providing optimal desired outcomes, it is considered a cost-efficient program.

Cost-benefit analysis, the most difficult analysis, measures the value of the program to the child and his family and to society minus the costs of the program. As has been stated earlier in this chapter, it is hard to put a dollar value on benefits, and it is impossible to project benefits for fifteen or twenty years hence or for generations to come. However, a program is referred to as a cost-beneficial program when the monetarily calculated benefits exceed the monetarily calculated costs.

The cost analysis of a program varies greatly with the elements included in the analysis. For example, these distinctions must be made in making an analysis:

1. **Fixed and variable costs.** Fixed costs (e.g., program planning) do not vary with the number of children served, but variable costs (e.g., building, teacher salaries, equipment) vary with the number of children served.

2. **Marginal costs.** Marginal costs are the increased cost "per unit" (i.e., total program costs divided by the number of recipients) of expanding a program beyond a given size. Marginal costs may decrease to a given point and then increase when additional staff members or housing are required.
3. **Capital versus operating costs.** Capital costs (e.g., building) are basically one-time costs whereas operating costs (e.g., salaries, consumable materials) are recurrent.
4. **Hidden costs.** Hidden costs are costs free to a program, but paid by someone else (e.g., churches that permit "free" use of their facilities). **Joint costs** are somewhat "hidden" too, because they are shared costs (e.g., two separately-funded programs that share a staff workroom or audiovisual equipment). **Foregone income costs** (e.g., income foregone due to services or goods provided a program) are difficult to calculate.

Comparisons of costs must be made on the same basis, and cost analyses must include all of these costs to be accurate.

FINANCING EARLY CHILDHOOD PROGRAMS

Early childhood programs receive funds from local, state, and federal sources, as well as from foundations, fees and tuition, and miscellaneous sources. Various regulations govern (1) a program's eligibility to receive revenue from a source such as the federal government; (2) procedures for obtaining revenue; (3) use made of the revenue; and (4) which personnel are accountable for the expenditure. Because of the many types of programs and the intricacies and variations involved in funding, only a brief description of the sources of financing are given.

Public School Financing of Kindergartens and Primary Programs

Public school programs are supported by local, state, and federal moneys. Ninety percent of funding comes from state and local sources.[17] Taxation is the major source of moneys available for funding; consequently, revenues for public school programs are closely tied to the general economy of the local area, state, and nation.

Local Support

Tax funds are used to maintain and operate the schools, and the sale of bonds is used for capital improvements and new construction expenses. The local school board's authority to set tax rates and to issue bonds for school revenue purposes is granted by the state—that is, authority is *not* implied. When granted the power to tax, state laws concerning tax rates and procedural matters must be followed by the local school board in an exacting manner. In this way, the state protects the public from misuse and mismanagement of public moneys.

In most states, local school districts tax real and personal property based on some fraction of its market value. Only state laws can change the maximum tax rate for local schools. If a local board desires a tax rate increase, not in excess of maximum rates, it must follow state statutory procedures in presenting the tax increase issue to the voter. (Increases are usually requested when the budget exceeds the amount of revenue that will be collected under present tax rates or occasionally for accumulation of excess operating funds limited by statute.) If the board needs the revenue for the proposed budget and the tax referendum fails, the school board must trim its budget or borrow from future tax receipts.

The sale of bonds is the main source of revenue for major improvements of the school plant or for construction of new schools. **Bonds** are certificates documenting a debt by the school district. A special election is called for the purpose of approving the sale of bonds; if the referendum passes, the bonds are sold and the revenues used for the specified purposes.

State Support

The amount of state support for public schools varies widely from state to state. Almost every state has some form of foundation program designed to equalize the tax burden and educational opportunities among various school districts. Generally, the foundation program begins with a definition of minimum standards of educational service that must be offered throughout the state. The cost of maintaining the standards is calculated and the rate of taxation prescribed. The tax rate may be uniform or based on an economic index ability—the ability of a local school district to pay. If local taxes do not cover the cost of maintaining minimum standards, the balance of the costs is provided via state moneys.

These moneys come from three sources: (1) earnings from permanent school funds or lands; (2) taxes and fees specified for educational purposes, including license fees, occupational, inheritance and gift, and specific activity taxes; and (3) appropriations from the state's general revenue fund, the major source of support, obtained from state income and retail sales taxes.

States vary considerably in the machinery they use for channeling state moneys to local school districts, the most common plans being flat and equalization grants. States which have **flat grant** plans require that local school districts meet minimum standards for local taxation. The state sets the standards for determining a minimum (and maximum) tax rate, expressed in mills or cents, of assessed valuation of taxable property. Local school districts desiring flat grants from state revenues are then awarded moneys on the basis of average daily attendance (or on the basis of "per certified employee") in the local district and paid periodically during the fiscal year. **Equalization grants** are given on the basis of local need, in order to achieve some degree of equality in local district school funds throughout the state. States which use equalization grants have formulas that consider average daily attendance, local tax rates, and assessed property valuation.

Federal Support

Since the 1940s, the federal government has become the chief tax collector. Until recently, there has been a trend toward unprecedented expenditures for education. Consequently, public schools (as well as other institutions, agencies, and organizations) relied more and more on federal assistance programs to supplement their local and state resources. Federal funding of public schools is used for two purposes: (1) to improve the quality of education (e.g., research, experimentation, training, housing, and equipping); and (2) to encourage greater effort by state and local districts to improve the quality of education by providing initial or matching funds for a program. In the past few years, federal expenditures in education have declined due to reduction of types of programs funded or the amount of funds available in retained programs. The two major programs receiving federal support are Chapter 1, a compensatory education program formerly called Title 1, and the Individuals with Disabilities Education Act—P.L. 94-142.

State Financing of Early Childhood Programs

States are increasing their financing of programs for pre-kindergarten children. Most of the programs financed are center-based settings, including the public schools, although some include home-based components. None of the fifty states offers universal early childhood education, but the majority of states target their programs to three- and four-year-old children who have been identified as "at-risk" (i.e., economically disadvantaged, deficient in English, and/or identified as having academic difficulties that will lead to school failure).

The amount spent by the various states varies considerably. States also use various methods for dispersing early childhood funds. For example, some states allocate money to school districts based on school finance formulas (as previously discussed). Some states use a categorical aid system to allocate early childhood funds to school districts. The most common method of state funding of early childhood education, however, is through grants or contracts awarded by a state administrative agency, usually the department of education. Most of the grants are awarded through a competitive process. For example, grants may go to school districts or private agencies whose programs are approved by the state board of education or by other regulatory guidelines. In some states, grants are used for pilot programs only. A few states use non-competitive ways of awarding grants such as school districts that have high concentrations of low-income students or elementary students with low standardized achievement test scores. Several states require that state money be matched with local, federal (e.g., Chapter 1), or in-kind services. This matching is necessary in some states because of statutory restrictions on state spending for these programs.

Legislative support for early childhood programs is expected to grow. Future initiatives will undoubtedly address increased funding and methods of reducing costs by coordinating efforts with similar local programs (e.g., local day-care and Head Start).[18]

Federal Financing and Foundation Support

In addition to programs receiving some federal fiscal support, such as the public schools, the federal government remains the primary source of support for comprehensive early childhood programs for low-income children through Head Start programs. Because there is presently no federal centralized program of child care, the extent of federal involvement in early childhood programs is not easily determined. Programs are administered in many cabinet-level departments. And the lists of federally assisted early childhood programs may include direct subsidies, moneys to support local projects, and other miscellaneous types of support such as food subsidies. The purpose of most federal assistance programs is to accomplish particular educational objectives or meet the needs of specific groups. Most federal assistance programs have these characteristics: (1) require early childhood programs to meet specified standards; (2) give priority or restrict services to certain client groups; (3) require state and/or local support in varying amounts; and (4) specify funds to be used for certain purposes (e.g., food, program supplies), which in turn curtail a program's flexibility.

While federal support for social programs has declined in recent years, in dollar amounts, federal support for early childhood programs has remained rather constant. In 1990, for the first time in twenty years, comprehensive child-care legislation was passed by Congress and was signed into law. The new program is called the **Child Care and Development Block Grant.** This law will give states money to provide families assistance with their child-care expenses and to improve the availability and quality of early childhood programs. Tax credit (i.e., an increase in the Earned Income Tax Credit) and health credit are also included in the federal package.[19]

There has been a trend toward federal "deregulation." **Block grants** are considered a middle ground between the federal control of **categorical grants** (i.e., grants used for specified, narrowly defined purposes) and **general revenue sharing** (i.e., funds provided on a formula basis to state and/or local governments with few or perhaps no limits to how money is spent). In a block grant, federal aid is provided for more broadly defined activities so state or local groups can have greater discretion in designating programs to meet local needs. Recipients must comply with some federal regulations (e.g., fiscal reporting and nondiscrimination requirements). The new 1990 legislation is a block grant which contains strong state reporting requirements, such as supply and demand for early childhood programs, number of staff, and licensing standards and enforcement.

Funding Sources

Federal funding sources are in a state of constant change. Recently the changes have been more rapid than ordinary. The reader should refer to the latest edition or update of the *Catalog of Federal Domestic Assistance* (Washington, D. C.: Government Printing Office). This publication describes the federal agencies administering various assistance programs and some projects and services funded under these agencies. Some specific federal programs that provide funds for early childhood programs are listed in Appendix 7.

Obtaining Federal Funds

Several problems are associated with obtaining federal assistance. There is a bewildering array of funding agencies and assistance programs. Along with the problems of dealing with the number of federal sources, there is a jumble of rulings from agencies. Finally, assistance programs are constantly being deleted and added, and appropriations may fall below congressional authorization.

Most federal funds are obtained by writing and submitting a grant proposal and having the proposal approved and funded. One person on the early childhood staff should oversee the entire writing of the proposal although input should be obtained from all those involved in the program. In fact, early childhood programs that plan to seek regular federal assistance may find it advantageous to hire a staff member with expertise in the area of obtaining federal as well as other funds, such as foundation grants, that require proposal writing. Proposal writing can vary according to an assistance program's particular requirements, but most require a similar format.

A certain terminology is used in obtaining federal funds and must be understood by those involved in locating appropriate grants and writing proposals. The following terms are frequently used:

1. **Assets.** The amount of money, stocks, bonds, real estate, or other holdings of an individual or organization.
2. **Endowment.** Funds intended to be kept permanently and invested to provide income for support of a program.
3. **Financial report.** A report detailing how funds were used (e.g., listing of income and expenses).
4. **Grant.** A monetary award given a program. There are several types of grants:
   a. **Bricks-and-mortar grant.** An informal term for grants for building or construction projects.
   b. **Capital support.** Funds for buildings (construction or renovation) and equipment.
   c. **Declining grant.** A multiyear grant that grows smaller each year in the expectation that the recipient can raise other funds to compensate the difference.
   d. **General-purpose grant.** A grant made to further the total work of the program as opposed to assist a specific purpose.
   e. **Matching grant.** A grant with matching funds provided by another donor.
   f. **Operating-support grant.** A grant to cover day-to-day expenses (e.g., personnel salaries).
   g. **Seed grant** or **seed money.** A grant or contribution used to start a new project.

5. **Grassroots fundraising.** An effort to raise money on a local basis (e.g., raffles, bake sales, and auctions.)
6. **In-kind contribution.** A contribution of time, space, equipment, or materials in lieu of a monetary contribution.
7. **Proposal.** A written application for a grant.

Preproposal Planning. Preproposal planning is, in essence, research. And, as is true with any research, problem identification is the first step. What is needed? If the assistance program sends out a "Request for a Proposal"(RFP), the need is already defined in broad or general terms.

The next step is gathering documented evidence in the population or potential population served by the early childhood program. Also, assessment must be made as to how critical or extensive the need is. Most proposals require that needs, and the degree of these needs, be described in terms of demographic, geographic, and socioeconomic distribution as well as racial/ethnic makeup. Because proposals often have to be written quickly (perhaps two to four weeks), an up-to-date notebook should be kept with these data available. Data may be secured from these and other sources:

Community action associations (local)
Department of public welfare (local and state)
Federal publications (found in the *Monthly Catalog of U.S. Government Publications*)
U.S. Department of Commerce, Bureau of the Census
U.S. Department of Labor, Bureau of Labor Statistics
U.S. Department of Labor, Employment and Training Administration

The literature must be reviewed to see whether others have handled the problem, and with what results. To prevent duplication of services in a local area, one must also present evidence as to whether the same or similar needs are being met by other local programs. Check with local social service organizations, which can be identified through the telephone directory, the department of public welfare, and agencies served by the United Fund or Community Chest.

The final step is to write a two- or three-page preproposal prospectus. The prospectus should contain a statement of the proposed problem, what will be done about the problem, the target group to be served, the number of people to be served, and whether there is a need for the proposed early childhood program. The prospectus is helpful in clarifying one's thinking and in getting the opinion of others, including reviewers of funding agencies. (Some federal agencies require a prospectus before accepting a complete proposal.)

Funding sources must also be identified. Federal assistance sources may be found in the *Catalog of Federal Domestic Assistance Programs,* the *Code of Federal Regulations,* the *Commercial Business Daily,* and the *Federal Register.*

Writing the Proposal. Federal agencies have their own guidelines for writing a proposal; they differ from agency to agency, but the guidelines should be followed exactly. Most guidelines wish these points to be covered in the body of the proposal:

1. *Title page*—title of project, name of agency submitting application, name of funding agency, dates of project, and names, addresses, and signatures of the project director and others involved in fiscal management.
2. *Statement of problem*—general and specific objectives, documentation of needs and degree of needs, review of literature of programs that have tried to meet the specified needs, and description of any local programs currently involved in meeting specified needs.
3. *Program goals and objectives*—description of broad program goals and specific, measurable outcomes expected as a result of the program.
4. *Population to be served*—What qualifications will children and/or parents need for inclusion in the program? Will all who qualify be accepted? If not, how will the participants be chosen from those who qualify?
5. *Plan of procedure*—Were there several alternative approaches to solving the problem? If so, why was a particular alternative selected? How will each objective be accomplished?
6. *Administration of project*—What staffing requirements are being proposed? Indicate how the program will be managed by including an organization chart and writing brief job descriptions. Include a short vita of the program director. What is the program's capability to conduct the proposed project? Does it have community support? Show a time schedule of activities that will occur from the day of funding until project termination.
7. *Program evaluation*—What assessment devices will be used? Who will conduct the assessment? How and in what format will the evaluation be submitted?
8. *Future funding*—How will the operation of the program be continued at the conclusion of federal assistance?
9. *Budget* —must show sound fiscal management.
10. *Appendices*—job descriptions, director's vita, organizational structure of the early childhood program.

Some agencies also **require** completion of an application form, which usually asks for information about the general subject; to whom the proposal is being sumitted; the legal authorization; the project title; the name of the person submitting the proposal; the program director's name, address, and telephone number; the probable budget; the amount of funds requested; and the date the application is transmitted. Some agencies have a form for a proposal abstract, and usually agencies require that this summary be no longer than two hundred words. Forms assuring protection of human subjects and nondiscrimination may be required.

Foundation Support
Many fields, including education, have benefited from foundation giving. Foundations are one of several kinds of nongovernmental, not-for-profit organizations that promote public welfare, including that of young children, through the

use of private wealth. Other similar organizations are trusts and endowments. Foundation aid is typically given to support research. Because of increased federal support of education, foundation grants to education have decreased in the past few years. Nevertheless, administrators of early childhood programs should investigate foundations as potential sources of funds.

Similar to the process of obtaining federal funds, foundation funds are also obtained through submission and approval of a proposal. The foundation's board of directors determines the guidelines for submitting proposals, sets a deadline for application, reviews proposals, and selects recipients.

Fees, Tuition, and Miscellaneous Sources of Funds

For-profit programs operate almost exclusively on tuition and fees and are usually the most expensive. Although some parents pay up to 25 percent of their incomes for full-day care for one or more children, 10 percent of their combined gross incomes is a more reasonable and manageable figure. There are two ways to determine fees and tuition for early childhood programs. The first method is to draw up a budget and subtract moneys received from other funding sources. The remaining costs (and profit, if this is a for-profit program) are then distributed among the children. The second method is to determine the amount of money on a fixed fee, a sliding scale, or two fixed fees for different income bracket bases, and balance the budget with funds from other sources.

There are problems with both fixed fees and sliding-scale fees. Fixed fees may exclude lower-income families. Sliding-scale fees require obtaining information on family income.[20] Sliding-scale fees also require enough higher-income families to balance the lower-income families, and higher-income families would have to be willing to contribute more money.

Rowe and Husby explain that computing cost per child on the basis of enrollment underestimates the cost by 15 percent; most children are not in attendance every hour the early childhood program is open, and some children are enrolled part-time.[21] To remedy this underestimation, Ruoff et al., found that the baseline for determining cost should be cost per child-hour.[22] Morgan uses a more conservative projection by taking last year's actual income and dividing by maximum income from fees. The quotient is a percentage referred to as **utilization rate** (e.g., 95 percent). Utilization rates can be used to calculate expected fee income even if fees are increased.[23]

In addition to carefully calculating fees and tuition, an early childhood program must have definite policies on fee payment. Loss of income may occur as a result of absenteeism or child turnover. These suggestions might be considered in establishing a fee policy:

1. Set a deposit fee at time of enrollment, to be returned at time of withdrawal if all monetary policies have been met—two or three weeks' tuition or fees is reasonable.
2. Several weeks' notice should be given to withdraw a child. (The fee deposit covers this if notice is not given in advance.)

3. Children on the waiting list must be enrolled within a stated period of time after notification, or their place on the waiting list will be forfeited.
4. Payments may be no more in arrears than the amount of the initial deposit.
5. Payments must be made when a child misses a few days, or a withdrawal notice should be given for an extended absence.

There are several miscellaneous sources of funds for early childhood programs.

1. Public support via a community campaign can help balance the difference between the program's anticipated income and its expenses. For example, some programs qualify for United Way funds (which may be called by some other name). There are specific eligibility requirements for qualifying for such local funds.
2. In-kind contributions (that is, noncash contributions) are often available through some community resource, such as a charitable organization. In-kind contributions include program and support program volunteer services, free rent, and payment of utility bills.
3. Endowments may be given in someone's memory, or scholarships may be awarded.
4. The early childhood program may engage in fund-raising projects to supplement income from other sources. A cash-benefit analysis should be done before mounting a fund raiser. Yields from ten to twenty-five dollars per hour, after expenses, are of marginal value; raising funds above twenty-five dollars per hour is worthwhile. Scallan provides information on how to conduct a well-orchestrated fund-raising campaign.[24]

BUDGETING

A **budget** is a list of all goods and services for which payment may be made. Budgets are important because no matter how good a program is, it cannot continue to operate if it is not on a sound fiscal foundation. Limited funds require making decisions about priorities, and funding and regulatory agencies require information about monetary functions. No attempt will be made to project the expenditure level of a particular program because costs vary with types and quality of services, with the extent of a program, and with the geographical area, but features of budgeting that apply to most programs will be described.

Regulations Governing Budget Making and Adoption

Public school programs are subject to many budget regulations. In setting up a budget, a local school district is subject to constitutional or statutory limitations.

The superintendent of schools (or other administrative personnel directed by superintendent) determines the budget, estimates the assessed valuation of taxable property (minus an estimated amount for delinquent taxes), computes the tax rate and other sources of revenue needed to meet the proposed budget, and presents it to the school board. In most states, after the school board has tentatively approved a budget, a revised budget that includes the board's changes is made available to the public and hearings are held. (The budget is invalidated if state procedure is not followed exactly.) After the hearings, the board can adopt additional changes, if it desires. (States rarely give the public the right to mandate changes.) Unless the state requires fiscal control by other government agencies, such as the city government, the budget adoption process ends with the printing of the final draft. Fiscally dependent school districts (those that rely heavily on federal and/or state funds) must have their budgets reviewed by the designated government agencies before the adoption process ends.

Budgets of private and federally funded early childhood programs are developed by local program directors. Efforts are usually made to include the opinions of various personnel in the first draft of the proposed budget. The budgets are presented to their respective boards of directors or advisors for approval. In addition to the board's approval, regulations may require that the budget be presented to licensing and/or funding agency personnel before approval.

Developing a Budget

Budgets usually have three components: (1) a synopsis of the program; (2) specifically itemized expenditures for operating the program including direct costs (items attributed to a particular aspect of the program, such as personnel salaries) and indirect costs (overhead items not attributed to a particular aspect of the program, such as interest on bank loans, utility costs, and advertising); and (3) anticipated revenues and their sources, including in-kind contributions. Before writing the budget, the administrators should list the program's objectives and needs. The program and the fiscal plan should be carefully related and in writing. Although there are many ways of presenting data, an effective way is to present it under the same headings as the proposed expenditures.

The proposed expenditures are careful estimates of moneys required to operate the local program and should be organized under headings that fit the local program. These headings are referred to as the **budget format.** Two types of format are as follows:

1. **Functional classification.** This format assembles data in terms of categories for which money will be used, such as administration, child instruction, parent education, food and health services, and transportation. The advantage of the functional classification format is that one can readily link expenditure categories to program purposes. Disadvantages to this approach are that functional categories tend to be some-

what broad, raising questions as to expenditures within a classification, and there is not always a distinct classification for a particular item; for example, health services may be provided for within several other classifications.

2. **Line-item classification.** This format lists the sums allocated to specifics of the program (salaries of designated personnel, gas, electricity, water, telephone, postage, etc.). The major advantage of this approach is that it shows specific accountability of expenditures. On the other hand, if the categories are very fine, the director has little power to exercise changes in expenditures.

There are few estimates on what it costs to operate the various components of an early childhood program. The estimated costs are as follows: personnel—69 to 73 percent; housing, space, and utilities—10 to 12 percent; equipment—2 to 3 percent; supplies, excluding food—2 to 3.5 percent; food—11 to 15.5 percent; and miscellaneous—the remainder.[25,26,27] Income must increase dramatically to provide the recommended level of compensation for early childhood professionals.[28] This brings on the trilemma; that is, quality, staff compensation, and affordability are so interrelated that working on one problem makes it more difficult to solve the other two.[29] Examples of budgets are available for a family child-care system[30] and for an infant-care system.[31] There are also many computer-assisted finance programs that can be used in preparing a budget and in performing and recording financial transactions.[32]

After the expenditure section the administrators should furnish actual figures for the current fiscal year. Any significant difference between current services and expenditures and those proposed should be explained. In planning the expenditure section, administrators should keep in mind that:

1. Wages or salaries must be paid on time;
2. A desirable inventory level is one that will carry a program through two months of operation; and[33]
3. A program may have cash flow problems. Federal funds do not pay ahead of time for expenses; receipts and proof of money spent are required for reimbursement, and even reimbursement checks may come irregularly.

To prevent cash flow problems an administrator should follow these practices:

1. Initial enrollment should not be overestimated.
2. All equipment should not be purchased at the beginning. Equipment estimates should be calculated on cost per use rather than on the purchase price. For example, it is more expensive to spend one hundred dollars on equipment and then not use it than to spend five hundred dollars on equipment that will be in constant use.
3. The number of staff members hired should correspond to initial enrollment.

4. Enrollment variations—for example, a summer lull—should be expected.
5. The administrator should check with the government agency for its reimbursement schedule, which may be six months or longer. He should determine whether the local bank will give credit or a short-term loan to state or federally funded centers that receive government reimbursements.

The third part of the budget is an estimate of income or receipts. This section should clearly indicate moneys from specified sources, such as tuition fees, contributions, and fund-raising projects. An excellent source of useful budgeting information is:

Morgan, G.G. *Managing the Day-Care Dollars: A Financial Handbook.* Cambridge: Steam Press, 1982.

There are many ways to write a budget with only one absolute rule of budget formulation—planned expenditures cannot exceed projected income.

SUMMARY

Programs for young children are expensive. A quality program will cost four thousand dollars or more per child per year. Although families seldom pay the absolute costs, early childhood programs can be a large expenditure of the family budget—especially for middle- and lower-income families. And, for many families, quality early childhood programs are simply not affordable.

Public early childhood programs are financed through local, state, and federal funding sources. For-profit early childhood programs are supported primarily through tuition and fees.

Budgets must be carefully made in keeping with program goals; that is, expenditures should reflect the goals of the program. Fiscal planning is important for several reasons. First, the quality of a program is determined to a great extent by expenditures, expecially staff compensation. Unfortunately, inadequate staff compensation has resulted in a staffing crisis in day-care programs. Furthermore, the central criterion for evaluating a program is often economic (i.e., benefits should exceed costs). Finally, administrators must show fiscal responsibility. Not-for-profit programs are responsible to their funding agencies and for-profit ones are accountable to their owners, clients, and the Internal Revenue Service.

NOTES

1. "NAEYC Position Statement on Quality, Compensation, and Affordability in Early Childhood Programs, "*Young Children* 43, 1 (1987): 31.

2. E. Prescott and E. Jones, *The "Politics" of Day-Care* (Washington, D.C.: National Association for the Education of Young Children, 1972), 78.

3. M. Olenick, "The Relationship Between Day-Care Quality and Selected Social Policy Valuables"(Unpublished dissertation, University of California, Los Angeles, 1986).

4. M. Frank and B. M. Caldwell, *Marketing Child Care Programs: Why and How* (New York: Haworth, 1985).

5. A. Mitchell, "Old Baggage, New Visions Shaping Policy for Early Childhood Programs," *Phi Delta Kappan* 70, 9 (1989): 670.

6. S. L. Hofferth and D. A. Phillips, "Child Care in the United States, 1970 to 1995," *Journal of Marriage and the Family* 49 (1987): 559-571.

7. E. F. Zigler, "Policy Recommendations on Child Care," (Testimony presented to the United States Senate Subcommittee on Children, Families, Drugs, and Alcoholism on June 11, 1987).

8. A. J. Kahn and S. B. Kamerman. *Child Care: Facing the Hard Choices* (Dover: Auburn House, 1987).

9. M. P. Rowe, "Economics of Child Care," Hearings on S.20003 before the Committee on Finance, United States Senate, 92nd Congress, 1st Session, 22–24 September 1971, 280.

10. L. Frohreich, "Costing Programs for Exceptional Children: Dimensions and Indices," *Exceptional Children* 39 (1973): 517–18.

11. Division of Special Education and Rehabilitation, *Costs in Serving Handicapped Children in Head Start: An Analysis of Methods and Cost Estimates, Final Report*, ERIC ED 108 443 (Syracuse: Syracuse University, Division of Special Education and Rehabilitation, 1974).

12. S. L. Hofferth, "What is the Demand for and Supply of Child Care in the United States?" *Young Children* 44, 5 (1989): 28–33.

13. W. Winget, "The Dilemma of Affordable Child Care," *Day-Care: Scientific and Social Policy Issues*, ed. E. Zigler, and E. Gordon (Boston: Auburn House, 1982).

14. M. Stephen, Policy Issues in Early Childhood Education, ERIC ED 008 595 (Menlo Park: Stanford Research Institute, 1973), 30.

15. A very complete discussion of the Family Support Act is found in H. Blank's "Child Care and Welfare Reform: New Opportunities for Families," *Young Children* 44, 4 (1989): 28–30.

16. "101st Congress: The Children's Congress," *Young Children* 46, 2 (1991): 78–80.

17. L. J. Schweinhart and D. P. Weikart, "Evidence that Good Early Childhood Programs Work," *Phi Delta Kappan* 66, 8 (1985): 545–51.

18. A state-by-state analysis of the population served, the resources, and methods of funding are provided for FY 1987 in C. Warger's *A Resource Guide to Public School Early Childhood Programs* (Alexandria, Va: Association for Supervision and Curriculum Development, 1988), 14–21.

19. "101st Congress: The Children's Congress."

20. Information on a community's income distribution is available from the Bureau of Labor Statistics; the Child-Care Employee Project (see Appendix

5) can provide information on how to conduct a salary survey and how to report and use the survey information.

21. M. P. Rowe and R. D. Husby, "Economics of Child Care: Costs, Needs, and Issues," *Child Care: Who Cares?* ed. P. Roby (New York: Basic Books, 1973), 98–122.

22. R. Ruoff, et.al., *A Day-Care Guide for Administrators, Teachers, and Parents* (Cambridge: Massachusetts Institute of Technology Press, 1973).

23. G.G. Morgan, *Managing the Day-Care Dollars* (Cambridge: Steam Press, 1982).

24. P. Scallan, "Ask and Ye Shall Receive: A Primer for Large-Scale Fundraising," *Child Care Information Exchange* (December, 1988), 19–21.

25. T. Keener and D. Sebestyen, "A Cost Analysis of Selected Dallas Day-Care Centers," *Child Welfare* 60, 2 (1981): 87–88.

26. J. W. Seaver and C. A. Cartwright, *Child-Care Administration* (Belmont, Calif.: Wadsworth, 1986), 299.

27. Abt Associates, Inc., "Day-Care Centers in the U.S.: A National Profile, 1966–77, sponsored by the U.S. Department of Health, Education, and Welfare, Administration for Children, Youth, and Families." Reprinted from *The Conditions of Education.* (Washington, D.C.: Department of Education, 1980).

28. For an overview of staff compensation problems and recommendations, read R. C. Granger's "The Staffing Crisis in Early Childhood Education," *Phi Delta Kappan* 71, 2 (1989): 130–134 and "NAEYC Position Statement on Guidelines for Compensation of Early Childhood Professionals," *Young Children* 46, 1 (1990): 30–32.

29. J. Greenman, "Living in the Real World," *Child-Care Information Exchange* (August, 1990): 29–31.

30. P. Lauritzen, "Sample Budget for a Family Child-Care System," *Setting Up for Infant Care: Guidelines for Centers and Family Day-Care Homes,* ed. A. Godwin and L. Schrag (Washington, D.C.: National Association for the Education of Young Children, 1988), 69–71.

31. L. Schrag, E. Khokha, and E. Weeks, "Sample Budget for an Infant Care Center," *Setting Up for Infant Care: Guidelines for Centers and Family Day-Care Homes,* ed. A. Godwin and L. Schrag (Washington, D.C.: National Association for the Education of Young Children, 1988), 51–52.

32. R. Neugebauer, "Child-Care Center Management Software Buying Guide Update," *Child-Care Information Exchange,* (November, 1987), 43–47.

33. M. S. Host and P. B. Heller, *Day-Care Administration, no. 7, Child Development Series* (Washington, D.C.: Office of Child Development, 1971), 156.

FOR FURTHER READING

Evaluating Service Programs: A Guide for Policymakers and Funders. Washington, D.C.: National Center for Clinical Infant Programs, 1987.

Haller, L. *Financial Resource Management for Nonprofit Organizations.* Englewood Cliffs: National Academy Press, 1982.

Isensee, L. C., and Campbell, N. D. *Dependent Care Tax Provisions in the States: An Opportunity for Reform*. Washington, D.C.: National Women's Law Center, 1987.

Kagan, S. L., and Glennon, T. "Considering Proprietary Child Care." In *Day Care: Scientific and Social Policy*, edited by E. F. Zigler and E. W. Gordon. Boston: Auburn House, 1982.

Modigliani, K. "Twelve Reasons for the Low Wages in Child Care." *Young Children* 43, 3 (1988): 14–15.

Morgan, G. G. *Managing Day-Care Dollars: A Financial Handbook*. Cambridge, Steam Press, 1982.

Weikart, D. P. "Hard Choices in Early Childhood Care and Education: A View to the Future." *Young Children* 44, 3 (1989): 25–30.

Willer, B., ed. *Reaching the Full Cost of Quality in Early Childhood Programs*. Washington, D.C.: National Association for the Education of Young Children, 1990.

Part 3
Implementing the Children's Program

Chapter 8

**Planning and Scheduling
Children's Activities**

The focus of planning and administering an early childhood program is on planning and scheduling children's activities. All other major administrative tasks, such as determining criteria for housing design, choosing equipment, and hiring staff as well as judgments made in regard to assessment, parental partnership, and expenditures are performed in reference to planning and scheduling of children's activities.

The role of the administrator is to serve as the local program leader in defining the program base (i.e., combining knowledge of children and the concerns of parents and staff members), in defending the pedagogy (i.e., being knowledgeable and sensitive to program implementation), and in working in collaborative efforts with those agencies in the community that provide support services (e.g., health care, family support, and social services).

The psycho-philosophical position of the local program should determine the curriculum, the teaching strategies, and the scheduling. More specifically, these three questions are raised and answered through the psycho-philosophical position taken by the local program:

1. What should children learn, in what scope and sequence, in each area of development?
2. How should children learn skills, information, values, and attitudes—through drill or game-like tasks, through prescribed or free-choice activities, or through individual effort or group work?
3. How will staff members determine whether a child has learned the skill—that is, what type of assessment will be used?

Regardless of the program's psycho-philosophical view, careful planning and scheduling are essential. When programs take on a laissez-faire posture, goals are not met, stress occurs in children and staff, and chaos is inevitable.

Part of planning and scheduling is determining how children will be grouped. Grouping arrangements help to provide the best ways to meet the needs of individuals and of the group via scope and sequence of content, methodology, and assessment.

GROUPING

Our society recognizes the importance of the individual by encouraging and recognizing individual achievement and by granting and protecting the individual right to think, speak, and act in accordance with personal beliefs; yet, a chaos-free society must have some conformity—some group-mindedness. From birth until a child enters an early childhood program, his individuality is fostered, tempered only to some extent by the "group needs" of his family. In contrast, because of the numbers of children involved and the time limits imposed, the program is forced to put greater emphasis on group needs. In fact, we often say that a child enrolling in an early childhood program is entering a "group setting."

Size of Group

The term **group** is difficult to define, because groups may refer to the number of children in a room, a given space (e.g., learning-activity center), or assigned to an adult.[1] The National Association for the Education of Young Children defines **group** as the number of children assigned to a staff member or to a team of staff members occupying an individual classroom or a well-defined physical space within a larger room.[2]

Teachers have lauded the benefits of smaller classes, while administrators have emphasized the higher costs associated with reductions in class size. Some problems of large groups include: (1) it is more difficult to give individual attention;[3] (2) teachers are restricted in range of teaching strategies;[4] (3) teachers cannot adequately accommodate children's characteristics (e.g., short attention span, constant movement, and emotional outbursts);[5] (4) instructional time is directly affected by the extent to which a teacher is able to meet children's needs;[6] and (5) children only begin to become adjusted to a group setting.[7] Children taught in small classes show increased achievements and better attitudes; teacher satisfaction is also greater.[8]

Group Size for Infants and Toddlers
The National Academy of Early Childhood Programs recommends the group size and adult-child ratio detailed in Table 8–1.

TABLE 8–1

	Group Size	Adult-Child Ratio
Infants	6	1:3
	8	1:4
Toddlers (12 to 24 months)	6	1:3
	8	1:4
	10	1:5
	12	1:4[9]

The National Association for the Education of Young Children recommends a maximum group size of eight for infants and ten for toddlers. The Association recommends an increase in staff when special-needs children are included and during feeding or other more difficult times of the day.[10]

Group Size for Preschool Children
The National Academy of Early Childhood Programs recommends the group size and adult-child ratio detailed in Table 8–2.

TABLE 8–2

	Group Size	Adult-Child Ratio
2-year-olds (24–36 months)	8	1:4
	10	1:5
2- and 3-year olds	10	1:5
	12	1:6
3-year-olds	14	1:7
	16	1:8
	18	1:9
4-year-olds	16	1:8
	18	1:9
4- and 5-year-olds	16	1:8
	18	1:9[11]

The National Association for the Education of Young Children states that the maximum group size for three- through five-year-olds is twenty with two adults.[12]

Group Size for Kindergartens and Primary-Grade (level) Children
The National Academy of Early Childhood Programs recommends the group size and adult-child ratio detailed in Table 8–3.

TABLE 8–3

	Group Size	Adult-Child Ratio
5-year-olds	16	1:8
	18	1:9
	20	1:10
6- through 8-year-olds	20	1:10
	22	1:11
	24	1:12[13]

The National Association for the Education of Young Children states that the maximum class size for a primary-level teacher should be fifteen.[14]

Grouping Patterns

Grouping, or organizing children for learning, is an attempt to aid individual development in a group setting. Grouping has been devised to make caring for and teaching children more manageable and effective. There is no consensus as to the "best" grouping practice. However, instructional and scheduling plans are determined to a great extent by grouping patterns.

Vertical Grouping

Vertical grouping is concerned with how children move from year to year, in either a **graded** or **nongraded** approach. At the turn of the century, a uniform age of school entry was established and progress through the grades on the basis of age became a regular practice.[15] The graded system is based on the concept that children of similar ages are homogeneous in ability. Thus, a child enters the graded system at a specified age (usually six years for first grade) and, at the end of a year's instruction, is promoted to the next level. A variant of this practice is to "double promote" children who far exceed age and grade expectations, and to retain children who fail to meet the expectations. Although this approach has been and is the most typical practice of elementary schools, nursery schools and other programs for the younger child have also admitted children on an age basis and "promoted" some of them on the same basis, rather than according to developmental gains.

Because children of similar ages are not necessarily homogeneous in achievement, nongraded approaches have been used at the preprimary and primary levels. The "traditional" nursery schools of the 1950s, Montessori schools, the British Infant Schools (which divide children into three year groups—four-, five-, and six-year-olds; five-, six-, and seven-year-olds; and six-, seven-, and eight-year-olds), and the New Zealand schools (which children enter on the day of their fifth birthday and then move through cycles at their own pace) all use this approach. Goodlad and Anderson define the nongraded approach as a plan that enables children to advance in the sequenced curriculum at their own rate.[16] Children's learning becomes more continuous because children take up where they left off the preceding year.

Horizontal Grouping

Horizontal grouping is concerned with how students are assigned to instructional groups. The two types of horizontal grouping are homogeneous "ability" grouping and heterogeneous "family" grouping.

Homogeneous Ability Grouping. Ability grouping is really achievement-level grouping and is widely practiced in the primary grades in elementary schools for such subjects as reading and mathematics. Ability grouping is also common in early childhood programs adhering to the behaviorist position. In this approach the teacher prescribes objectives and activities, usually in reading and mathematics, to ability-grouped children. (Children are placed in ability groups as determined by test scores and teacher judgments.)

Furthermore, ability or achievement-level grouping is practiced in early childhood programs which screen upon entrance or within a few weeks after entrance and then place children in "developmental" kindergartens if they appear to lag in tested developmental areas, and similarly, ability grouping is practiced in programs which have a transitional level between kindergarten and first grade for children who are considered at-risk for failure in the formal academic subjects of the first grade (See Chapter 2).

Ability grouping is based on the assumption that both children and teachers profit from a homogeneous-achievement group. Several problems with ability grouping are that (1) there is still a wide range of abilities after grouping (e.g., dividing a class into two ability groups on the basis of IQ reduces the total variability of the class by only seven percent, and dividing a class into three ability groups reduces heterogeneity by only 17 percent);[17] (2) such grouping may be associated with lower achievement scores on the part of slower students;[18] (3) the quality of instruction may be inferior in lower groups;[19] (4) children are likely to remain in the same ability group to which they are originally assigned;[20] and (5) slow learners may feel the stigma associated with such placement. Placement practices based on screening for abilities have a backlash effect causing the curriculum to become even more difficult (See Chapter 2).

Heterogeneous "Family" Grouping. Heterogeneous "family" grouping is defined as placing children who are at least one year apart in age in the same classroom group. Thus, it is also called **multi-age grouping**. Unlike ability grouping which purports that instruction is more effective in homogeneous groups, multi-age grouping is intended to optimize what can be learned from interactions in a heterogeneous group.

Although there has been a movement toward removing heterogeneity in early childhood programs by screening and tracking, there has also been a resurgence of interests in multi-age grouping.[21] The nongraded approach, a vertical approach to grouping, uses multi-age or "family" grouping. Multi-age grouping is also used in early childhood programs adhering to the interactionist position. In this approach children do mostly individual work or small group work in which peer interactions occur. Instead of prescribing objectives and activities teachers look for ways to enrich the environment as children refine their present skills and move to more advanced developmental levels. In short, planning is done according to children's interest and developmental stage rather than to their age-grade levels.

A great deal of research has been conducted on family-versus-ability grouping. The advantages of family grouping over ability grouping are:

1. Teachers accept a wider range of behaviors and plan activities and schedules for individuals and small groups.[22]
2. Children who lag behind children who are the same age find it less stressful, because the interactions with younger children enhance self confidence.[23]
3. Social advantages can be noted. Friendships transcend age-mates,[24] older children use facilitative leadership tactics (e.g., use organizing statements and solicit opinions in play);[25] older children take more responsibility for task completion;[26] older children become more self-regulated when put in the role of rule-enforcer;[27] and, older children who are behind developmentally become leaders in groups of younger children rather than becoming isolated.[28]
4. Some cognitive advantages are also noted. Older children create complex play for younger children and structure play roles for themselves and the younger children.[29] In learning tasks, older children often become the "experts" who assist their "novices."[30] Older children refine the skills they have learned when they play with younger children.[31]

In comparison to homogeneous groups, family grouping does have some difficulties that must be worked out. Family grouping requires more teacher skill as a diagnostician of what children need to enhance their development, more planning in terms of managing schedules and equipment-materials, and a greater ability to operate in a team-teaching situation. Family grouping also requires parent education because many parents feel that their older children are not being stimulated due to the presence of younger children in the group. There are several excellent readings on strategies for programs implementing mixed-age groups.[32]

CURRICULUM PLANNING

Curriculum is a way of helping teachers think about children and organize the child's experience in the program setting. The long-range goals contained in a program's rationale are explicitly defined in terms of curriculum planning. These plans, including the activities, teaching-learning approaches, and materials used in implementation, become the tools in realizing these goals. Because young children learn from every experience, curriculum for young children includes such things as "discipline techniques, recess, individual and group activities, routines such as snack time, and all other aspects of the child's day at school, as well as the activities we think of as educational."[33] In short, the curriculum we select is the "actual membrane between the world and the child."[34]

Basing Curriculum on Program's Rationale

Planning the curriculum is essential regardless of the type of early childhood program. However, the program's rationale determines the curriculum and hence the way activities are planned.

Psycho-Philosophical Differences in Curriculum

Two major psycho-philosophical views have evolved. One way to look at curriculum is to design it on the basis of requisites for success in adult society. These requisites have to be based on current knowledge of society and rather narrowly defined. Education is seen as skill development for meeting cultural demands. This way of thinking supports "continuity in the educational enterprise as it currently exists."[35] In this view, early childhood curriculum is designed to facilitate young children's success in later school programs—a top-down orientation. In order to accomplish academic success, this curriculum focuses on teacher-prescribed and narrowly defined basic skills, often in the academic areas of reading and mathematics. Systematic and direct tuition teaching-learning strategies are frequently used. Commercially developed and published programs which often include segmented verbal and paper-and-pencil activities are used to drill homogeneous "ability-grouped" children. This curriculum view is held by the behaviorists.

A second way to look at curriculum is the nurturance view of early education. In this view, successful adulthood is seen as being achieved by a fully enriched, child-centered curriculum. Curriculum planning begins with the analysis of children's developmental characteristics—a bottom-up design. Thus, the early childhood curriculum, instead of being determined by later school content, is seen as possibly promoting later school reform. This approach supports the child's construction of knowledge through child-initiated learning. This curriculum view is held by the interactionists.

Professional Position Statements

As explained in Chapter 2, there are a variety of concerns regarding the recent trends in early childhood education and more especially on the formal academic emphasis of the curriculum. For example, the Public School Early Childhood Study[36] found that most public school kindergartens were highly academic, teacher-directed, tightly scheduled, and heavily reliant on workbooks (i.e., 78 percent of the observed kindergartens had workbooks). These trends are also occurring in day-care programs for preschool children.

Early childhood education and child development experts criticize these trends as inconsistent with our knowledge of how young children learn best.

"The language of early childhood education is the language of the 'whole child' and of integrated learning."[37] Thus, one cannot foster cognitive development without involving all aspects of development.

Many have called formal academic practices an escalated curriculum. However, scholars in education find these practices are not helping children to take on appropriate roles as literate and problem-solving adults. The National Association of State Boards of Education stated the academic curriculum is "shockingly unstimulating to children and fails to stimulate their thinking."[38]

Finally, there has been concern about the social results of academic programs. Weikart pointed out that in his ten-year follow-up study of children in various types of early childhood programs that the different types of curriculum produced essentially the same academic results but very different social results. He found that children who were in programs with child-initiated curriculums were able as adolescents to maintain their own goals and organize their own futures. Conversely, children who were taught what to do and who learned within teacher-prescribed objectives, developed as adolescents a sense of alienation from home and school and even society at large.[39]

These concerns and many more led to a broadened base of consensus and support for a curriculum developed from a clear child development theory. Such a curriculum came to be referred to as a "developmentally appropriate curriculum." A developmentally appropriate curriculum focuses on practices based on knowledge of how children develop, and thus, the curriculum is viewed as a continuum from birth through age eight.[40]

Using Appropriate Components

Many early childhood programs are rethinking the developmental appropriateness of their curriculums. Play, whole language, and manipulatives are in, and didactic instruction is out. These programs are also considering the importance of social skills, cooperative learning, and differences in development in their planning. This section will focus on curriculum from the interactionists' position, the developmentally appropriate curriculum.

Age/Stage Appropriate Components

Child development theory and research are the major sources of information that guide planning for the developmentally appropriate curriculum. Developmental theory views children as active learners in a rich environment and teachers as facilitators of their experiences. For programs with the developmental approach, these questions need to be considered: What are the children's ages? What understandings, skills, and attitudes do they have? How long are their attention spans and what are their degrees of perseverance? Are they having to cope with special problems or excitement?

Curriculum must always be planned with specific children in mind. However, a general overview of some of the major competencies and the appropriate types of experiences is given for these age/stage groups in Tables 8–4, 8–5 and 8–6.

TABLE 8–4
Sample Curriculum for Infants/Toddlers

Needed Competencies	Sample Curriculum for Infants/Toddlers	
Infants and toddlers need to:	For *infants* adults need to:	For *toddlers* adults need to:
Develop a sense of trust and a loving relationship.	Read infant cues and meet their physical and psychological needs quickly and warmly.	Support attempts to accomplish tasks, comfort when tasks are frustrating, and express joy at successes.
		Respect security objects such as a favorite toy.
Develop a sense of self.	Call infant by name.	Name body parts.
	Place mirrors on eye level including near the floor.	Respect children's preferences (e.g., toys and food).
		Support attempts at self-care.
Have social contact.	Engage in face-to-face contacts, use physical contact, and have vocal interactions.	Help children control negative impulses and comfort when they fail.
		Help children become aware of others' feelings.
		Model interactions for children to imitate.
Explore their world.	Take children to their world of experience or bring objects and activities to them.	Provide support for active exploration (i.e., be near but refrain from too many adult suggestions for play).
Sample sensory experiences.	Provide pictures and objects to touch, taste, and smell.	Place books and objects on shelves.
		Decorate room with pictures and objects.
Undertake motor experiences.	Provide safe places for movement.	Provide safe places and equipment and materials that aid large muscle development (e.g., stairs, ramps, large balls, and push/pull toys).
	Encourage movement (e.g., place objects slightly beyond reach).	
	Express joy at successes.	Express joy at successes.

TABLE 8–4   (cont.)

Needed Competencies	Sample Curriculum for Infants/Toddlers	
Infants and toddlers need to:	For *infants* adults need to:	For *toddlers* adults need to:
Express themselves vocally and listen to the speech of others.	Talk to, read to, sing to, and play games with language (e.g., peek-a-boo). Imitate infant's vocalizations in a turn-taking manner.	Talk to, read to, sing to, tell and dramatize little stories. Encourage toddlers to ask for things and tell you things.
Express themselves creatively.		Encourage children to explore and manipulate art media and musical instruments (e.g., drum, xylophone, bells); do not expect finished products such as a picture.
Become familiar with symbols.	Talk to infants (e.g., call them by name and carry on a conversation taking both roles). Provide books and pictures. Encourage imitation of gestures such as waving "bye."	Encourage make-believe by providing props. Show picture books and talk about pictures. Encourage imitation of gestures such as beckoning. Encourage the making of animal and other sounds.
Make choices and implement their own ideas.	Provide a variety of toys.	Provide many materials for play. Allow freedom to choose play interests. Permit food choices. Permit the toddler to sleep or just lie quietly with a book or toy. Comfort toddler when choice is not feasible (e.g., mother leaves, play inside but not outside, or change diaper).

TABLE 8–5
Sample Curriculum for Preschoolers

Needed Competencies	Sample Curriculum for Preschoolers
Preschoolers need to:	**For *preschoolers* adults need to:**
Feel reassured when fearful or frustrated.	Use positive statements.
	Provide comfort when frustrated and demonstrate needed rules repeatedly.
Become more independent.	Provide opportunities for practicing self-help skills such as having dressing dolls and providing time and just the needed assistance in toileting and eating.
Make friends.	Permit children to form their own play groups.
	Encourage onlookers to join a play group by suggesting roles for them (e.g., a grandmother in housekeeping center in which the other roles are already taken).
	Model positive social interactions for them to imitate.
Explore their world.	Provide many materials that children can manipulate (e.g., water, sand, blocks, and latches) in order to discover relationships.
	Provide dramatic play props for children to use in trying on roles.
Exercise their large muscles and control their small muscles.	Provide equipment to climb on, "vehicles" to ride on, and balls to throw and catch.
	Provide materials to manipulate (e.g., art tools, puzzles, pegs and pegboards, and beads to string).
Engage in language experiences.	Talk to, read to, sing to, tell and dramatize stories, and play singing games (e.g., Farmer in the Dell).
	Write children's dictated stories.
	Have classroom charts and other print in view.
	Provide materials (e.g., paper and writing tools) for children to draw, scribble, write, and copy signs, etc.
Express themselves creatively.	Provide a variety of art media and various forms of music for creative expression.

TABLE 8–5 **(cont.)**

Needed Competencies	Sample Curriculum for Preschoolers
Preschoolers need to:	**For *preschoolers* adults need to:**
Develop concepts of themselves and the world around them.	Provide opportunities to learn skills (e.g., mathematics) and content areas (e.g., social studies and science) in integrated ways (i.e., while working on projects instead of times set aside to concentrate on each area).*
Become familiar with symbols.	Provide props for dramatic play.
	Provide books for "reading."
	Write children's dictated stories.
	Provide art and writing materials.
Make choices and implement their ideas.	Permit children to select many of their own activities.
	Provide a physical setting which encourages individual or small, informal groups most of the time.

TABLE 8–6
Sample Curriculum for Children in Kindergartens and Primary Grades

Needed Competencies	Sample Curriculum for Children in Kindergartens and Primary Grades (Levels)
Children in kindergartens and primary grades (levels) need to:	**For children in *kindergartens* and *primary grades (levels)* adults need to:**
Show more self-control.	Prevent overstimulation when possible and help children deal with fears and excitements (e.g., talking about them).
	Set clear limits in a positive way and involve children in rule-making.
	Use problem solving to manage discipline problems.
Gain more independence.	Permit children to identify areas needing improvement.
	Support children in their work toward mutually established goals.
Work with other children.	Provide opportunities through small groups for children to cooperate with and help other children.

TABLE 8–6 (cont.)

Needed Competencies	Sample Curriculum for Children in Kindergartens and Primary Grades (Levels)
Children in kindergartens and primary grades (levels) need to:	For children in *kindergartens* and *primary grades (levels)* adults need to:
Explore their world.	Provide materials that are concrete and relative to on-going projects.
	Plan for field trips and resource people to enhance classroom projects.
Use large and small muscles.	Provide appropriate materials.
Use language as a way of both communicating and thinking.	Provide materials for both reading and writing that will enhance on-going projects.
	Provide quality literature.
	Read aloud stories and poems each day and ask child readers to share in the oral reading.
	Plan projects such as preparing a class newspaper or making books.
Express themselves creatively.	Plan ways to integrate art, music, dance, and drama throughout the day.*
Develop concepts.	Integrate curriculum (i.e., skill and content areas) in such a way that learnings occur through activities such as projects rather than in an isolated format.*
Use symbol systems.	Provide manipulatives.
	Assist children in developing skills in reading, writing, and mathematics when these are needed to explore or solve meaningful problems.*
Make choices.	Provide opportunities to work individually and in small groups with self-selected projects and materials for a greater part of the time.
	Involve children in their own self-management (e.g., setting their own goals, budgeting their time, evaluating their own efforts, and cooperating with others).

*Key readings on the content of and teaching strategies for skill and content curricular areas are listed following the Notes under the heading, "Readings on Curriculum Planning" on p. 291.

Other Considerations

Other considerations which need to enter into curriculum planning include:

1. Preparing children for increased complexities and future uncertainties. Hartman[41] suggests ways to help young children develop (a) focusing skills necessary to deal with a highly stimulating world, (b) decision-making skills, (c) independence, and, (d) curiosity.
2. Exposing children to a multiplicity of heritages. Multicultural education should be integrated into all aspects of the curriculum; however, the Public School Early Childhood Study[42] found that even in schools serving predominately minority students that culturally relevant activities were usually isolated (i.e., special events). The *Anti-Bias Curriculum*[43] challenges traditional methods of eliminating barriers based on race, sex, or ability by posing that different methods be used to achieve these goals. (See Appendix 1 for further readings.)
3. Using computers and related technologies in ways that serve the goals of quality programs such as exploring the computer environment as part of one's world, manipulating (as opposed to being manipulated by) the computer, and using the computer to broaden other learnings.[44,45]

Making Daily Plans

Daily plans come from the basic curriculum chosen for a program. Daily plans involve objectives and themes, delivery systems, and other basic considerations.

Objectives and Themes

All early childhood programs must plan for two basic components: activities related to children's physical care and other activities that may be called the "developmental," "interest," "learning," or "educational" component (i.e., any activities not directly related to physical care). The psycho-philosophical approaches give a different emphasis to these components.

1. The behaviorist approach helps children follow set procedures in physical care activities (e.g., children gather for snacks at a given time; children are seated; snacks are distributed in a predetermined way; and clean-up procedures are followed). Staff plans all other activities. Children are encouraged to stay on task and use materials in a specified way. Formal group lessons are often a part of the daily plans.
2. In the interactionist view physical care activities are used for socialization (e.g., table manners are emphasized during eating) and cognitive enrichment also takes place (e.g., children discuss nutrition and properties of foods—color, size, texture, and shape of foods). Staff plans and arranges materials for the educational component. Children are free to select activities, but staff try to find ways to stretch children's thinking in chosen activities and expand interests in other activities. Some formal group times are also planned.

This section will focus on objectives and themes from the interactionist position, the developmentally appropriate curriculum. Objectives in the developmentally appropriate curriculum are rather broad (in comparison to objectives used in the behaviorist-based programs). Broad objectives permit the offering of a wide range of activities. Varying levels of skills and interests are accommodated, and a variety of performance criteria are valued. Also, objectives are not adult-prescribed in the interactionist approach.[46] An example of one strategy for planning without pre-determined objectives is as follows:

1. Step 1. Recognize by observation the developmental level of the child or group of children.
2. Step 2. Decide the next step. One of three steps can be taken:
   a. Child or group may continue with no change in environment or materials in order that the children may engage in more thorough exploration. This is called a **constant.**
   b. Child or group may continue with the activity but in a different environment (e.g., indoor sand table to outdoor sand pit) or with different materials (e.g., sifters are added to sand play materials) in order that children may improve or refine skills. This is called a **horizontal movement.**
   c. Child or group may move from a simpler to a more complex level or from a concrete to a more abstract level, because child or group is felt to be ready for the next developmental level. This is called **vertical movement.**
3. Step 3. State why the step is important and what the teacher is to do.[47]

Elkind feels that daily plans should be locally determined. He states that curriculum publishers fail to do research and fail to field-test items, and thus, teachers in a program need to determine the objectives to be accomplished.[48]

Position statements on developmentally appropriate practice call for an integrated curriculum. The curriculum may be planned around themes and projects and/or facilitated by providing learning areas. Many materials are available with ideas on themes and some call for more innovative themes.[49]

Delivery System
In addition to planning objectives and themes, the staff must plan the delivery system. Staff may prearrange activities using learning centers or may design learning episodes. **Learning centers** are places where equipment and materials are usually arranged, such as for dramatic play, library, science, art, and music (see Chapters 5 and 6 for more detail). In contrast, **learning episodes** are any form of direct teaching involving one child, a small group, or the entire class.

The psycho-philosophical view will determine not only the objectives but also the delivery system. The behaviorist approach places heavy emphasis on learning episodes. The interactionist approach often uses both learning centers and episodes, but the emphasis is on learning centers. Spodek suggests that the **unit of instruction** is the **activity.** "Activity" differs from the "lesson" in that: it does not have a formal beginning, middle, and end; it is often open-ended; and it is not teacher-prescribed. Children carry an activity forward and determine its content.[50] For simplicity, the following discussion is an example of the delivery system using a single objective. In most programs, several objectives would be used in daily planning.

Prearranging Activities for Learning Centers. In a few early childhood programs, no activities are planned for the learning centers. Each child is permitted to use any materials and equipment not being used by other children. Because plans have not been made, children's needs are likely to go unmet.

Planning activities for the learning centers should begin with the specific objectives of the program. For example, one or more specific objectives are chosen for several days' work, the appropriate equipment and materials are selected and arranged in learning centers, and all unneeded supplies are stored until they are needed to accomplish other objectives. Consequently, regardless of which learning center a child chooses in spontaneous play, she will be working with equipment and materials that will help achieve the objectives. For example, if a specific objective is for the children to be able to name a circle, rectangle, and triangle, the following materials could be prearranged in the learning centers:

1. In the art center, precut construction paper circles, rectangles, and triangles are provided. The child may make a collage with these geometric shapes.
2. In the manipulative center, sorting boxes for geometric shapes are placed on the table.
3. In the block center, blocks of various geometric shapes are available for building.
4. In the mathematics center, materials for fishing for shapes, lotto games using shapes, and a flannel board with felt shapes for making or extending patterns are arranged.
5. In the active or physical play center, bean bags of different geometric shapes are tossed at geometrically shaped targets.

Designing a Learning Episode. In designing a learning episode, the teacher could read a children's book, perhaps *Shapes*, by M. Schlein, teach a game, use a piece of equipment, or develop a modified activity based on the Cuisenaire Geoboard, for example. Learning episodes can serve several purposes: (1) teachers do not have to wait to take advantage of children's spontaneous activities; (2) it is easier for inexperienced teachers to become familiar with a concept in a learning episode rather than in a spontaneous learning situation; (3) learning episodes can be used to introduce something new to the children and to evaluate their progress; and (4) they can be used to determine the appropriateness of equipment and materials.[51]

Using Learning Centers and Learning Episodes. Programs may use both learning centers and episodes to achieve specific objectives. Often learning episodes introduce new content and/or materials and evaluate progress. Learning centers explore the introduced content in depth and give needed individual practice.

Additional Considerations

Regardless of the program rationale, several other points need to be considered in planning. One consideration is the staff. Does each staff member understand and accept the program's basic rationale? Does each staff member recognize the rationale of each activity as a step in realizing long-range goals? Is the program adequately staffed in terms of the number and needs of the children, the physical layout of the building and grounds, and the nature of the activities?

A second consideration is the amount and arrangement of indoor and outdoor space. Is it adequate for the planned activities? Is supervision of children difficult because of the vastness of space or its arrangement? Is much time spent in moving equipment and materials between each activity? Do accidents occur frequently because of the amount or arrangement of space?

Availability of resources is a third consideration. Are appropriate equipment and materials available in sufficient quantity for the activities? Are community resources available?

The fourth consideration is time. Are too many or too few activities planned? How much time is involved in getting out and putting away, in going to the restroom or to lunch, and in conducting administrative duties such as attendance and lunch counts? Are the blocks of time suitable for the various types of activities?

A final consideration is the planning of backup or alternative activities. These kinds of activities forestall problems that result from a lack of interest, inclement weather conditions, unforeseen scheduling changes, or breakage of materials or equipment. What other activities can be used to help children achieve the planned goals and objectives? Can other personnel or material resources be used if needed? Can the same topic be approached using a different learning modality? Does the planner know where the activity fits within the sequence of skills in case the "match" is not appropriate—the activity is too easy or too difficult?

SCHEDULING

Scheduling and planning are equally important because decisions about scheduling greatly influence the children's feelings of security, the accomplishment of objectives, and the staff's effectiveness. **Scheduling** involves planning the length of the session and timing and arranging activities during the session.

Length of Session

Early childhood programs have traditionally been half-day sessions. Exceptions have been full-day sessions in day nurseries and day-care programs that are becoming increasingly popular because more mothers have jobs outside the home and because of the awareness of the needs of disadvantaged children.

Some day-care programs have incorporated kindergarten objectives and activities into their programs because parents cannot leave work to transport their children to and from kindergartens that operate on half-day sessions.

There is a great deal of controversy concerning the length of the session. Advocates of half-day sessions cite these advantages: (1) children do not get as tired; (2) staff members have more time for planning, evaluating, and working with parents (unless teachers are employed for two half-day sessions), and half-day sessions help prevent staff "burnout"; and (3) young children have an opportunity to be with their parents for part of the day. Supporters of full-day sessions enumerate these advantages: (1) fewer transportation problems, (2) longer blocks of time for lengthy activities, (3) care for children whose parents work, (4) staff members can get to know the children better, and (5) more time for academic experiences or more time for emphasis on play (a point of disagreement among those advocating a full-day session). There is no evidence that a full-day academic program is more academically beneficial over the short or long term than a developmentally appropriate full-day program.[52] There is some evidence that there are academic advantages for children who are in full-day sessions, as compared with those in half-day sessions.[53] However it is obvious that the quantity of time spent in school is not as significant as the quality of the kindergarten experience.[54] Other individuals, rather than advocating a half-day or a full-day session for all children, support an individualized schedule to meet the needs of each child. Berson states: "Kindergartens and their timetables are not sacred; children are."[55]

Timing and Arranging Activities

Regardless of whether the session is half- or full-day, good schedules for early childhood programs have certain characteristics:

1. A good session begins with a friendly, informal greeting of the children. Staff members should make an effort to speak to each child individually during the first few minutes of each session. A group activity such as a greeting song also helps children feel welcome.
2. Children's physical needs, such as toileting and eating, should be cared for at regular intervals in the schedule. Special times should be set aside for toileting early in the session, before and after each meal or snack, and before and after resting. Meals should be served every four or five hours, and snacks should be served midway between each mealtime; however, each child's individual needs must be considered.
3. The schedule must provide a balance between physical activity and rest. Young children are prone to become overtired without realizing their need for relaxation.
4. The schedule should fit the psycho-philosophical view of the program and the needs of the children as individuals and as a group. There should be a balance between indoor and outdoor activities, group and individual times, and child-selected and staff-determined activities.

5. The schedule must be flexible under unexpected circumstances, such as inclement weather, children's interests not originally planned for, and emergencies.
6. A good schedule should be readily understandable to the children so they will have a feeling of security and will not waste time trying to figure out what to do next.
7. A good session ends with a general evaluation of activities, straightening of indoor and outdoor areas, a hint about the next session, and a farewell. Children need to end a session with the feeling they have achieved something and with a desire to return. These feelings are important to staff members, too!

Every program should devise its own schedule. Programs that serve children of different age groups, such as infants or toddlers, must prepare more than one schedule so each group's needs will be met.

Schedules must fit the length of the program day, week, and year. However, scheduling usually refers to the timing of daily activities. In general, schedules are often referred to as flexible or as fixed. **Flexible schedules** allow for individual children to make some choices as to how to spend their time and require children to conform to the group for only a few routine procedures such as the morning greeting and short periods of group "instruction" such as music and listening to stories. Infant programs have perhaps the most flexible schedules of all early childhood programs because infants stay on their own schedules, regardless of adult needs. Day-care programs often have flexible schedules due to their longer hours of operation, the children's staggered arrivals and departures, and the varying ages of the children the center serves. Programs adhering to the interactionist view also have long, flexible time periods. For an excellent example of a flexible schedule, see the schedule used in Nimnicht, McAfee, and Meier's program.[56]

Other programs place more emphasis on group conformity by having **fixed schedules,** by expecting children to work and play with others at specified times, and by taking care of even the most basic human differences—appetites and bodily functions—at prescribed times except for "emergencies." Often programs for primary-grade (level) children have fixed schedules (open education is the exception). Behaviorist programs are very time-oriented. An excellent example of a fixed schedule is that used in Bereiter and Englemann's program.[57] The National Association for the Education of Young Children states that flexible schedules are developmentally appropriate.[58]

The following schedule examples for different age groups are only suggestions; they are not prescriptive. Examples are not given for infants who follow their own schedules or public school programs adhering to state regulations regarding scheduling (i.e., state departments of education/instruction often specify the total length of a school day and the number of minutes of instruction in each of the basic subjects).

Toddler schedules usually revolve around the children's feeding and sleeping periods, but should include some manipulative activities, outside play, cre-

7:00-8:30 A.M	Arrival, changing or toileting, and dressing babies who are awake, and individual activities
8:30-9:00 A.M.	Breakfast snack, songs, stories, and fingerplays
9:00-10:00 A.M.	Manipulative toy activities conducted by staff, and changing or toileting
10:00-11:00 A.M.	Naps for those who take morning naps and outside play for others. (Children go outside as they awaken.)
11:00-11:45 A.M.	Lunch and changing or toileting
11:45-1:00 P.M.	Naps
1:00-2:00 P.M.	Changing or toileting as children awaken and manipulative toy activities
2:00-2:30 P.M.	Snack, songs, stories, and fingerplays
2:30 P.M. until departure	Individual activities

FIGURE 8–1
Full-day Toddler Schedule

ative activities, and storytime. An example of a schedule for a full-day session is described in Figure 8–1.

Nursery schools serve pre-kindergarten-age children (usually exclusive of infants) and are frequently operated for half-day sessions. Children arrive and depart at approximately the same times. Generally, nursery school schedules have short group times and longer blocks of time for active work and play periods. An outline of a nursery school schedule is shown in Figure 8–2.

Day-care centers have perhaps the most flexible schedules of all early childhood programs because of their longer hours of operation, the children's stag-

9:00-9:15 A.M.	Arrival, group time activities, such as attendance count, greeting song, and brief exchange of experiences
9:15-10:15 A.M.	Active work and play period with child-selected activities in the activity centers
10:15-10:30 A.M.	Toileting and snack
10:30-10:45 A.M.	Group time for story, finger play, music, or rhythmic activities
10:45-11:15 A.M.	Outdoor activities
11:15-11:30 A.M.	Rest
11:30-11:45 A.M.	Cleaning up and discussing the next session; "What we will do tomorrow . . ."
11:45-12:00 NOON	Quiet activities and farewells as children depart

FIGURE 8–2
Nursery School Schedule

7:00-9:00 A.M.	Arrival, breakfast for children who have not eaten or who want additional food, sleep for children who want more rest, and child-initiated play (which should be relatively quiet) in the activity centers
9:00-9:30 A.M.	Toileting and morning snack
9:30-11:45 A.M.	Active work and play period, both indoor and outdoor. Field trips and class celebrations may be conducted in this time block.
11:45-12:00 NOON	Preparation for lunch, such as toileting, washing, and moving to dining area
12:00 NOON-1:00 P.M.	Lunch and quiet play activities
1:00-3:00 P.M.	Story, rest, and quiet play activities or short excursions with assistants or volunteers as children awaken from naps
3:00-3:30 P.M.	Toileting and afternoon snack
3:30 P.M. until departure	Active work and play periods, both indoor and outdoor, and farewells as children depart with parents
5:00 P.M.	Evening meal for those remaining in center, and quiet play activities until departure

FIGURE 8-3
Day-Care Center Schedule

gered arrivals and departures, and the varying ages of the children the center serves. An example of a day-care center schedule is shown in Figure 8–3.

Kindergartens are usually half-day programs with children arriving and departing at approximately the same times. Kindergartens usually schedule longer group times than nursery schools because kindergartens have more structured activities. An example of a half-day kindergarten schedule is shown in Figure 8–4.

Some kindergartens have full-day sessions. An example of a schedule for a full-day session is shown in Figure 8–5.

School-age day-care programs usually follow very flexible schedules. An outline of a school-age day-care program is shown in Figure 8–6.

Toileting was placed in the foregoing schedules. However, toileting should be conducted on an "as needed" basis, unless building plans do not permit, as when the toilet is "down the hall," or when toilets may not be available for a short period of time, such as when the children are leaving to go home or on a field trip. Also, the feeding and resting schedule must be flexible enough to meet the needs of a hungry or sleepy child.

Determining the Responsibilities of Program Personnel

In making daily plans, coordination of the responsibilities of program personnel is essential. Without careful planning, there will be duplication of tasks, omis-

8:15-8:30 A.M.	Arrival and greeting of individual children
8:30-9:00 A.M.	Greeting of group, opening exercises, such as good morning song and flag salute, sharing of experiences, and planning for the day
9:00-10:00 A.M.	Active work and play in activity centers (with small-group learning episodes in some kindergarten programs) and cleanup
10:00-10:30 A.M.	Music and rhythmic activities
10:30-10:45 A.M.	Toileting and snack
10:45-11:15 A.M	Group time for stories and other quiet activities (with full-class learning episodes in some kindergarten programs)
11:15-11:45 A.M.	Outdoor activities
11:45 A.M.-12:00 NOON	Evaluation of the day, preparing for next session, straightening of room, and farewells

FIGURE 8–4
Half–Day Kindergarten Schedule

8:15-8:30 A.M.	Arrival, greeting of individual children, and toileting
8:30-8:45 A.M.	Greeting of group, opening exercises, sharing of experiences, and planning for the day
8:45-9:45 A.M.	Active work and play in activity centers (with small group learning episodes in some kindergarten programs) and cleanup. Field trips and class celebrations may be conducted during this time block.
9:45-10:15 A.M.	Outdoor activities
10:15-10:45 A.M.	Music and rhythmic activities
10:45-11:00 A.M.	Toileting and preparing for lunch
11:00-11:45 A.M.	Lunch
11:45 A.M.-12:15 P.M.	Rest and toileting
12:15-12:45 P.M.	Outdoor or indoor activity
12:45-1:30 P.M.	Active work and play in activity centers and cleanup
1:30-1:45 P.M.	Toileting and snack
1:45-2:00 P.M.	Evaluation of day, preparing for next session, cleanup of room, and farewells

FIGURE 8–5
Full–Day Kindergarten Schedule

6:30-7:00 A.M.	Arrival, and activities such as quiet games or reading
7:00 A.M. until departure from school	Breakfast, grooming, and activities such as quiet games or reading
3:00-3:15 P.M.	Arrival from school
3:15 until departure	Snack, and activities such as homework, tutorials, outdoor play, craft projects, table games, and reading

FIGURE 8–6
School–age Day Care Schedule

sions in services, and a general lack of staff efficiency. Criteria to consider in planning the responsibilities of the staff are: (1) the psycho-philosophical view of the program as it reflects the needs of the children; (2) specific organizational policies (i.e., the way children are grouped for care or instruction); (3) the number of program personnel involved and the qualifications and skills of each individual; (4) the layout of the building and grounds and the nature of equipment and materials, and (5) the specific plans for the day.

The responsibilities of program personnel must be in keeping with legal authorizations and with the policies of the board of education or board of directors. The director usually determines the responsibilities of program personnel; however, in some cases, teachers may assign duties to assistant teachers and to volunteers. Specific responsibilities may be delegated by the director or ''lead'' teacher, but mutually agreed-upon responsibilities in keeping with the basic job descriptions are usually more satisfactory. Both people will understand the plans for the day, and the day's program will thus function more coherently and smoothly; a periodic exchange of some duties lessens the likelihood of staff ''burnout'' and the frustration of always having less popular responsibilities, such as straightening the room; and staff morale will be higher when all personnel are involved in the program from planning to execution.

Special Plans

Special plans must be suitable to children's needs and must be as carefully developed as daily plans. Although daily plans should be changeable, special plans require even more flexibility. Certain routines—especially eating, toileting, and resting—should always be followed as closely as possible. Planning for first days, field trips, and class celebrations are discussed in this chapter because of the almost universal need for making special plans for these situations.

First Days
Whether the first days represent a child's first experience in an early childhood program or denote her entry into a different program, the child views the first days with a mixed

feeling of anticipation and anxiety. The first days should be happy ones, for they may determine the child's feeling of security and attitude toward the program.

Initiation of children into an early childhood program is often done gradually. Preliminary orientation of the children to the staff and routine may be handled in several ways:

1. If the group is small, all the children may attend for half the normal session.
2. If it is a large group, two plans could be used: the daily session could be divided into two sections, with half the children coming to each; or two evenly divided groups could attend alternate-day sessions, full- or half-time.
3. A few children may come the first day for the full session or for half the session. Each day additional children are added. This plan works well with multiage groups. Children who know the routine assist the staff in helping new children make initial adjustments.
4. If all children enter on the same day, additional paraprofessional or volunteer assistance should be secured for the first days.

Generally speaking, planning for first days requires that more time and individual attention be given to greeting children and their parents, to establishing regular routines, and to familiarizing the children with teachers and with the physical plant. These suggestions will facilitate children's orientation to an early childhood program:

1. Name tags help staff members become acquainted with the children.
2. For the first days, use equipment and materials and have activities that most children of that age are familiar with and enjoy and that require minimum preparation and cleanup time.
3. Begin to make mental notes (if not written) on strong and weak points in your plans. Also, begin to note the children's strengths and problems, but be careful not to pass judgment too fast or compare a fall group to last year's spring group.
4. Plan what to do about children who will not leave their parents or who cry after their parents leave.

Field Trips

A field trip is a planned journey to somewhere outside the school building or grounds, although teachers sometimes use the term in reference to journeying on foot to a destination on the school property, such as the carpenter's room or the kitchen area of the cafeteria. Thoughtful planning of field trips is important both because of their benefits to children's learning and because of the added dangers of taking children beyond the building and grounds.

Field trips require a great deal of planning and supervision. The teacher must:

1. Develop specific objectives that help children achieve the goals of the program.

2. Make arrangements with those in charge at the point of destination. Know the rules of the host: date and time preferred, size of group recommended, safety rules, and parking space. Furnish all needed information to the host, such as the purpose of the trip, age and number of children, date and time of proposed arrival, and time of proposed departure. Arrange for children to see and hear the designated functions of the place visited; if the host is to give explanations to the children, be sure he can communicate with them. Make arrangements for care of the physical needs of children, staff, and other adults assisting with the field trip, such as locations of places to eat and restrooms. One staff member should visit the destination before making final plans.

3. Provide enough qualified supervisors. Good judgment and experience in working with young children are qualities to look for in supervisors. There should be one adult for every four or five children. Supervisors should have a list of the names of children under their care; when they do not know the children, name tags should be worn for easier identification.

4. Obtain written parental consent for each field trip and keep the signed statement on file. Note the example of a field trip form in Figure 8–7. The signed form is essential because the signature serves as evidence that the parent has considered the dangers of his child's participating in

---

Dear Mom and Dad,

    Our class will be making a field trip to the _____ bakery on May 13. A baker will take us on a tour of the bakery. We hope to learn how bread and rolls are made. We will be leaving school at 9:00 a.m. and will be returning in time for lunch. We will ride on a bus to the bakery and back to our school. We all think it will be fun to ride on the bus with our teacher, Mrs. Smith, and three mothers. Please sign the form below to give your permission for me to take the trip.

Jody

- -

I, _____, give my permission for
          (name of parent)

_____ to attend a field trip to
          (name of child)

_____.
          (destination)

My child has permission to travel _____.
                                 (in a parent's car, on a school bus)

I understand that all safety precautions will be observed.

Date _____ Signature _____

FIGURE 8–7
Field Trip Form

the field trip experience. There should be no statement on the form relieving the teacher and director of any possible liability for accidents. Such a statement is worthless because a parent cannot legally sign away the right to sue (in the child's name) for damages, nor can the staff escape the penalty for its own negligence.[59, 60]

5. Obtain permission for the children to participate in the field trip from the director or building principal. Policies of early childhood programs often require that teachers complete forms giving the specifics of the field trip.

6. Become familiar with the procedures to follow in case of accident or illness. Take children's medical records and emergency information records along, in case an accident or illness requiring emergency treatment occurs during the field trip.

7. Make all necessary arrangements for transportation, and determine whether all regulations concerning vehicles and operators are met.

8. Prepare the children by helping them understand the purposes of the field trip and the safety rules to be observed. In some cases, the host may send information or may come and talk to the children before they make the field trip. After the field trip, provide follow-up activities.

9. Evaluate all aspects of planning the field trip and the field trip itself.

Class Celebrations

Class celebrations of birthdays and holidays are traditional in early childhood programs and require special planning. Celebrations should relate to the program's objectives, because "tacked on" celebrations may be counterproductive. A policy should be written to cover the following points:

1. The specific celebrations the children will observe should be determined. Which celebrations are most appropriate to the program's objectives and learning activities? Will children's birthdays be celebrated? Which holidays will be celebrated?

2. The amount of time during the session that can be used for the celebration should be regulated by policy.

3. The number of celebrations to be observed during one session should be included in the policy. Can there be two or more birthday celebrations, or a birthday and a holiday celebration, during one session? If there are two or more celebrations during one session, are they to be conducted jointly, successively, or with a time interval? The foregoing decision may affect the amount of time alloted for each celebration.

4. If birthdays are observed, these decisions should be made: the nature of and responsibility for birthday celebrations; whether a parent is responsible or can help; the policy on treats, favors, decorations, and entertainment; type and quality (homemade or purchased) of food; advance notice needed by the staff; and use and cleanup of kitchen and dishes. If the staff has full or part responsibility, the foregoing decisions, plus the amount of money to be spent, also need to be noted.

5. If holidays are to be observed, all policy decisions mentioned for birthday celebrations need to be considered; for example, the type of exchange (card or gift) and who participates in the exchange (children or staff members) need to be decided. If a gift exchange is appropriate, a limit on the number of gifts and amount spent per gift should be specified. If a program has room parents, decisions need to be made concerning their responsibilities.

6. The places where celebrations can take place should be regulated. Are certain areas of the building more suitable for celebrations than others? Can the outdoor space be used, or can children be taken to places beyond the organization's property for celebrations?

SUMMARY

With only a few exceptions, our schools, including our programs for young children, have used many inappropriate practices in planning children's activities. More specifically, programs have used a narrow age range for grouping children. Adult-chosen activities in these programs were often prescribed to teach **homogeneous** children selected skills and concepts—especially the knowledge deemed important by publishers of curriculum materials and standardized tests. Such program planning has been referred to as the **factory model** of education.[61]

When one looks at how young children grow and develop, it becomes clear why early childhood education must be viewed as a continuum from birth to eight years of age. Professionals called for educators to focus on young children's development in planning children's programs and referred to programs which applied knowledge of child development as **developmentally appropriate**. Developmentally appropriate programs are age/stage designed but are implemented to fulfill the special needs of each child. This chapter highlighted these developmentally appropriate practices for grouping, curriculum planning, and scheduling:

1. Groups which are smaller in size permit not only safety in care but also the implementation of appropriate practices. Groups should be multi-aged in composition, because age grouping is based "upon physical time, whereas children grow on biological time and operate on psychological time."[62] Multi-age groups allow teachers to plan for and accept the "range" of physical, cognitive, and social behaviors and permit children to progress at their own rate, rather than "fit" the average rate of the class.

2. Curriculum is planned to foster natural development. Skills and concepts are age/stage appropriate, integrated (as opposed to separate subject offerings), and presented as meaningful activities centered on themes or projects. Individual needs are met as children choose among the many and varied activities and work for most of the day in small groups or individually.

3. Schedules are flexible, fitting the age/stage of the group and the needs of individual children within the group. All good schedules, however, do provide a balance in activities (e.g., active/passive, indoor/outdoor, and small group/large group).

NOTES

1. "Three Components of High Quality Early Childhood Programs: Administration, Staff Qualifications and Development, and Staff-Parent Interaction," *Young Children* 38, 4 (1983): 51–56.
2. "Progress Report on the Center Accreditation Project," *Young Children* 39, 1 (1983): 35–48.
3. G. V. Glass and M. L. Smith, "Meta Analysis of Research on the Class Size and Its Relation to Attitudes and Instruction," *Educational Evaluation and Policy Analysis* 1 (1979): 2–16.
4. D. W. Leitner and S. M. Tracy, "The Meta Analysis of the Effect of Class Size on Achievement: A Secondary Analysis" (Paper presented at the Annual Meeting of the Mid-Western Educational Research Association in Chicago, September 27–29, 1984).
5. Ibid.
6. E. Phyfe-Perkins, *Effects of Teacher Behavior on Preschool Children: A Review of Research* (Champaign: ERIC Clearinghouse on Elementary and Early Childhood Education, 1981).
7. D. Scott-James, "Family Influences on Cognitive and School Achievement," *Reviews of Research in Education*, ed. The American Research Association (Washington, D.C.: The American Research Association, 1984).
8. Glass and Smith, "Meta-Analysis of Research."
9. S. Bredekamp, ed. *Accreditation Criteria and Procedures of the National Academy of Early Childhood Programs* (Washington, D.C.: National Association for the Education of Young Children, 1984), 24.
10. "Progress Report."
11. Bredekamp, *Accreditation Criteria and Procedures of the National Academy of Early Childhood Programs*.
12. "Making Schools Ready," *Young Children* 46, 1 (1990): 39.
13. Bredekamp, *Accreditation Criteria and Procedures of the National Academy of Early Childhood Programs*.
14. "Making Schools Ready."
15. D. Pratt, "Age Segregation in Schools," ERIC ED 231 083 (Paper presented at the Annual Meeting of the American Educational Research Association, Montreal, 1983).
16. J. Goodlad and R. H. Anderson, *The Nongraded Elementary School*, rev. ed. (New York: Harcourt Brace and Jovanovich, 1963).
17. Ibid.

18. G. Heathers, *Organizing Schools Through the Dual Progress Plan* (Danville: Interstate Press, 1966).
19. Ibid.
20. J. C. Daniels, "Effects of Streaming in the Primary School II: A Comparison of Streamed and Unstreamed Schools," *British Journal of Educational Psychology* 31 (1961): 119–127.
21. Note that J. I. Goodlad and R. H. Anderson's book *The Non-graded Elementary School* was published in 1959 and reissued in 1987 (New York: Teachers College Press, Teacher's College, Columbia University).
22. J. M. Gallagher and J. Coche, "Hothousing: The Clinical and Educational Concerns Over Pressuring Young Children," *Early Childhood Research Quarterly* 2 (1987): 203–210.
23. C. Mobley, *A Comparison of the Effects of Multi-Age Grouping versus Homogeneous Age Grouping in Primary School Classes of Reading and Mathematical Achievement*, ERIC ED 128 102 (unpublished doctoral dissertation, 1976).
24. G. H. Brody, Z. Stoneman, and C. E. MacKinnon, "Role Asymmetries in Interactions Among School-Aged Children, Their Younger Siblings and Their Friends," *Child Development* 53 (1982): 1364–1370.
25. D. C. French, "Children's Knowledge of the Social Functions of Younger, Older, and Same Age Peers," *Child Development* 55 (1984): 1429–1433.
26. W. G. Grazinano, D. French, C. A. Brownell, and W. W. Hartup, "Peer Interactions in the Same-Age and Mixed-Age Triads in Relation to Chronological Age and Incentive Condition," *Child Development* 47 (1976): 707–714.
27. M. D. Lougee, R. Grueneich, and W. W. Hartup, "Social Interactions in Same-Age and Mixed-Age Dyads of Preschool Children," *Child Development* 48 (1977): 1353–1361.
28. W. Furman, D. F. Rahe, and W. W. Hartup, "Rehabilitation of Socially Withdrawn Preschool Children through Mixed-Age and Same-Age Socialization," *Child Development* 50 (1979): 915–922.
29. C. Howes and S. A. Farver, "Social Pretend Play in Two-Year-Olds: Effects of Age of Partner," *Early Childhood Research Quarterly* 2 (1987): 305–314.
30. R. E. Slavin, "Developmental and Motivational Perspectives on Cooperative Learning: A Reconciliation," *Child Development* 58 (1987): 1161–1167.
31. N. S. Mounts and J. L. Roopnairne, "Social-Cognitive Play Patterns in Same-Age and Mixed-Age Preschool Classrooms," *American Educational Research Journal* 24, 3 (1987): 463–476.
32. For practical suggestions, see: L. G. Katz, D. Evangelou, and J. A. Hartman's *The Case for Mixed-age Grouping in Early Education* (Washington, D.C.: National Association for the Education of Young Children, 1990), 41–47; and R. R. Nachbar's "A K/1 Class Can Work—Wonderfully!" *Young Children* 44, 5 (1989): 67–71.
33. J. T. Peck, G. McCaig, and M. E. Sapp, *Kindergarten Policies: What Is Best for Children?* (Washington, D.C.: National Association for the Education of Young Children, 1988), 33.

34. D. P. Weikart, "Hard Choices in Early Childhood Care and Education: A View to the Future," *Young Children* 44, 3 (1989): 25–30.

35. L. D. Miller and J. L. Dyer, "Four Preschool Programs: Their Dimensions and Effects," *Monographs of the Society for Research in Child Development*, serial no. 162, 40 (1975): 199.

36. F. Marx and M. Seligson, *The Public School Early Childhood Study: The State Survey* (New York: Bank Street College, 1988).

37. S. L. Kagan, "Early Care and Education: Beyond the Schoolhouse Doors," *Phi Delta Kappan* 71, 2 (1989): 107–112.

38. National Association of State Boards of Education, *Right From the Start. The Report of the NASBE Task Force on Early Childhood Education* (Alexandria, VA.: National Association of State Boards of Education, 1988), 4.

39. Weikart, "Hard Choices in Early Childhood Care and Education."

40. For major position statements see: S. Bredekamp, ed., *Developmentally Appropriate Practice in Early Childhood Programs Serving Children from Birth Through Age Eight*, expanded edition (Washington, D.C.: National Association for the Education of Young Children, 1987); *Right From the Start. The Report of the NASBE Task Force on Early Childhood Education* (Alexandria, VA: National Assocation of State Boards of Education, 1988); and *Continuity of Learning for Four-to-Seven-Year-Old Children* (Little Rock: Southern Association on Children Under Six, 1990).

41. K. Hartman, "How Do I Teach in a Future-Shocked World?" *Young Children* 32, 3 (1977): 32–36.

42. Marx and Seligson, *The Public School Early Childhood Study.*

43. L. Derman-Sparks and A.B.C. Task Force, *Anti-Bias Curriculum: Tools for Empowering Children* (Washington, D.C.: National Association for the Education of Young Children, 1989).

44. *Appropriate Uses of Computers on the Early Childhood Curriculum: Position Statement* (Little Rock: Southern Association on Children Under Six, 1989).

45. M. Kaden, "Issues on Computers and Early Childhood Education," *Continuing Issues in Early Childhood Education*, ed. C. Seefeldt (Columbus: Merrill, 1990), 261–275.

46. K. E. Smith, "Developmentally Appropriate Education or the Hunter Assessment Model: Mutually Incompatible Alternatives," *Young Children* 45, 2 (1990): 12–13.

47. D. J. Cassidy, B. K. Myers, and P. E. Benion, "Early Childhood Planning: A Developmental Perspective," *Childhood Education* 64, 1 (1987): 2–8.

48. D. Elkind, "Developmentally Appropriate Practice: Philosophical and Practical Implications," *Phi Delta Kappan* 71, 2 (1989): 113–117.

49. J. C. Nunnelley, "Beyond Turkeys, Santas, Snowmen, and Hearts: How to Plan Innovative Curriculum Themes," *Young Children* 46, 1 (1990): 24–29.

50. B. Spodek, *Teaching in the Early Years*, 3rd ed. (Englewood Cliffs: Prentice-Hall, 1985), 217–218.

51. G. Nimnicht, "Planning a Head Start or Kindergarten Classroom," *Curriculum Is What Happens*, ed. L. Dittmann (Washington, D.C.: National Association for the Education of Young Children, 1970), 10–11.

52. D. Elkind, "Full-Day Kindergarten," *Young Children* 42, 5 (1987): 2.
53. R. H. Nieman and J. F. Gastright, "The Long-Term Effects of Title I Preschool and All-Day Kindergarten," *Phi Delta Kappan* 63, 3 (1981): 184–185.
54. M. R. Jalongo, "What Is Happening to Kindergarten?" *Childhood Education* 62, 3 (1986): 154–160.
55. M. P. Berson, "The All-Day Kindergarten," *Today's Education* 57 (1968): 29.
56. G. Nimnicht, O. McAfee, and J. Meier, *The New Nursery School* (New York: General Learning, 1969), 148–149.
57. C. Bereiter and S. Englemann, *Teaching Disadvantaged Children in the Preschool* (Englewood Cliffs: Prentice-Hall, 1966), 67.
58. S. Bredekamp, ed. *Developmentally Appropriate Practice*, 8.
59. School District No. 23 v. McCoy, 30 Kan. 268, 1 Pac. 97, 46 Am St. Rep. 757.
60. Meiler v. Jones, 224 NC 783 32 SE (2nd) 594.
61. G. Katz, D. Evangelou, and J. A. Hartman, *The Case for Mixed-Age Grouping in Early Education* (Washington, D.C.: National Association for the Education of Young Children, 1990), vii.
62. D. Elkind, "Multiage Grouping," *Young Children* 43, 1 (1987): 2.

READINGS ON CURRICULUM PLANNING

Language

Ferrerio, E., and Tekerosky, A. *Literacy Before Schooling*. Portsmouth, Heinemann, 1982.

Genishi, C. "Acquiring Language and Communication Competence." In *Early Childhood Curriculum: A Review of Current Research*, edited by C. Seefeldt, 75–106. New York: Teachers College Press, Teachers College, Columbia University, 1987.

Goodman, K. *What's Whole in Whole Language?* Portsmouth: Heinemann, 1986.

Hall, N. *The Emergence of Literacy*. Portsmouth: Heinemann, 1987.

Newman, J. *Whole Language: Theory in Use*. Portsmouth: Heinemann, 1985.

Schickedanz, J. *More Than ABCs*. Washington, D.C.: National Association for the Education of Young Children, 1986.

Math and Science

Carlin, A., and Sund, R. B. *Teaching Science Through Discovery*. Columbus: Merrill, 1980.

Forman, G., and Kaden, M. "Research on Science Education for Young Children." In *Early Childhood Curriculum: A Review of Current Research*, edited by C. Seefeldt, 141–164. New York: Teachers College Press, Teachers College, Columbia University, 1987.

Ginsburg, H., ed. *The Development of Mathematical Thinking*. New York: Academic Press, 1983.

Holt, B. *Science with Young Children.* Washington, D.C.: National Association for the Education of Young Children, 1977.

Kamii, C. *Number in Preschool and Kindergarten.* Washington, D.C.: National Association for the Education of Young Children, 1982.

Kamii, C. *Young Children Reinvent Arithmetic.* New York: Teachers College Press, Teachers College, Columbia University, 1985.

McCracken, J. B. *More than 1, 2, 3: The Real Basics of Mathematics.* Washington, D.C.: National Association for the Education of Young Children, 1987.

McIntyre, M. *Early Childhood and Science.* Washington, D.C.: National Science Teachers Association, 1984.

Social Studies

Kendall, E. *Diversity in the Classroom.* New York: Teachers College Press, Teachers College, Columbia University, 1983.

Ryan, F. *The Social Studies Sourcebook.* Boston: Allyn and Bacon, 1980.

Saracho, O. N., and Spodek, B. *Understanding the Multicultural Experience in Early Childhood Education.* Washington, D.C.: National Association for the Education of Young Children, 1983.

The Arts

Carpenter, J. *Creating the World: Poetry, Art, and Children.* Seattle: University of Washington Press, 1986.

Lasky, L., and Mukerji, R. *Art: Basic for Young Children.* Washington, D.C.: National Association for the Education of Young Children, 1980.

Play

Bergen, D. *Play as a Medium for Learning and Development.* Portsmouth: Heinemann, 1987.

Fein, G., and Rivkin, M., eds. *The Young Child at Play: Reviews of Research,* Vol. 4. Washington, D.C.: National Association for the Education of Young Children, 1986.

Frost, J., and Sunderlin, S. *When Children Play.* Wheaton: Association for Childhood Education International, 1985.

Monighan-Nourot, P.; Scales, B.; Van Hoorn, J.; and Almy, M. *Looking at Children's Play.* New York: Teachers College Press, Teachers College, Columbia University, 1987.

Rogers, C., and Sawyers, J. *Play in the Lives of Children.* Washington, D.C.: National Association for the Education of Young Children, 1988.

FOR FURTHER READING

Bredekamp, S., ed. *Developmentally Appropriate Practice in Early Childhood Programs Serving Children from Birth through Age Eight,* expanded edition. Washington, D.C.: National Association for the Education of Young Children, 1987.

Caruso, D. A. "Play and Learning in Infancy: Research and Implications." *Young Children* 43, 6 (1988): 63–70.

Cassidy, D. J., Kimes, B.; and Benion, P. E. "Early Childhood Planning: A Developmental Perspective." *Childhood Education* 64, 1 (1987): 2–8.

Connell, D. R. "The First Thirty Years Were the Fairest: Notes from the Kindergarten and Ungraded Primary (K–1–2)." *Young Children* 42, 5 (1987): 30–39.

Greenberg, P. "Why Not Academic Preschool?" *Young Children* 45, 2 (1990): 70–80.

Honig, A. S. "Quality Infant/Toddler Caregiving: Are There Magic Recipes?" *Young Children* 44, 4 (1989): 4–10.

Kagan, S. L. "Readiness 2000: Rethinking Rhetoric and Responsibility." *Phi Delta Kappan* 72, 4 (1990): 272–279.

Peck, J. T.; McCaig, G.; and Sapp, M. E. *Kindergarten Policies: What Is the Best for Children?* (Washington, D.C.: National Association for the Education of Young Children, 1988).

Right From the Start. The Report of the NASBE Task Force on Early Childhood Education (Alexandria: National Association of State Boards of Education, 1988), 4.

Schickendanz, J. A.; Chay, S.; Gopin, P.; Sheng, L. L.; Song, S.; and Wild, N. "Preschoolers and Academics: Some Thoughts." *Young Children* 46, 1 (1990): 4–13.

Seefeldt, C., ed. *Continuing Issues in Early Childhood Education.* Columbus: Merrill, 1990.

Short, V. M., and Burger, M. "The English Infant/Primary School Revisited." *Childhood Education* 64, 2 (1987): 75–79.

Williams, L. R. "Diverse Gifts: Multicultural Education in the Kindergarten." *Childhood Education* 66, 1 (1989): 2–3.

Chapter 9
Providing Nutrition, Health, and Safety Services

Increasing emphasis on health and safety in our society has resulted in expanded programs for young children. Today's emphasis is on total health rather than only control of contagion. One aspect of today's health and safety services is the provision for a healthful school environment, which was discussed in Chapter 5. In addition, young children need many other such services. A comprehensive approach to high quality child health and safety services requires the cooperative involvement of administrators, medical consultants, staff members, and parents.

NUTRITION

Because of the effects of hunger and malnutrition on young children, early childhood programs are becoming more concerned about nutrition. Adequate nutrition is essential for the fulfillment of one's potential for physical or biological growth and development and for maintenance of the body. This is accomplished via providing for biological needs (nutrition, rest, exercise, etc.) and prevention of harmful agents (diseases, harmful chemicals, "binding" of feet to prevent growth, etc.).

During periods of rapid growth, a child is especially unprotected against malnutrition. The permanent effects of malnutrition on brain size and composition would most likely occur before four-and-a-half years of age and especially before one year of age.[1] The effects of malnutrition depend not only on the point at which deprivation occurs but on its severity and the nutrients involved. Because malnutrition interferes with development of the central nervous system, it also affects mental functioning; it can impair learning during critical periods and can change motivation and other aspects of behavior.[2,3] And nutrition habits, like many others, are formed early in life.

Developing Objectives for a Nutrition Program

Current nutrition programs are very broadly based, encompassing more than food preparation, serving, and cleanup. The comprehensive approach is evidenced in the Nutrition Education and Training Act of 1966 (P. L. 95–166) that provides funds to states for meeting these objectives: (1) to instruct students on the nutrition values of foods and the relationships between nutrition and health; (2) to train food service personnel in the principles of food service management; (3) to instruct teachers in nutrition education; and (4) to develop and use classroom materials and curricula in nutrition.

Objectives for Early Childhood Nutrition Programs

Based on the Nutrition Education and Training Act and other sources, four broad objectives seem to be an integral part of the early childhood nutrition programs. These objectives are: (1) planning food service; (2) identifying children's nutrition problems; (3) implementing nutrition education for children, and (4) assisting parents in meeting children's nutrition needs.

Planning Food Service

Planning food service for an early childhood program is comprehensive. It involves providing and serving nutritious meals and snacks, hiring staff, providing facilities and equipment, purchasing food, and meeting sanitation requirements.

Providing and Serving Nutritious Meals and Snacks. First, a program must provide for a nutritionally adequate diet. Specific nutrition requirements depend upon the type of early childhood program. Each state's licensing requirements prescribe the fraction of the recommended daily food allowances a child must receive. This is often one-half to two-thirds of the recommended daily allowance during the six- to eight-hour period a child spends in the program. Although licensing regulations contain minimum nutrition requirements, a 1969 White House Conference on Food, Nutrition, and Health recommended that day-care programs provide 80 percent of the child's total nutrition requirements. Having a quality breakfast is important. A study designed to examine the effects of improved breakfast nutrition on learning resulted in findings that showed a greater gain on standardized tests for the experimental group (who had a varied breakfast menu with high density carbohydrates and protein) as compared to the control group (who had a nonvaried breakfast menu of fruit or juice, milk, and prepackaged cereals).[4] Snacks are also important, making up approximately 22 percent of all the foods young children consume daily.[5]

Furthermore, a nutrition program should expose children to a wide variety of foods, so they will develop a taste for many foods; should provide for direct dietary consultation to meet the needs of children; and should provide menus to parents to aid in food selection for the remaining part of the child's diet.

Finally, providing and serving nutritious meals and snacks not only feed the child's body and mind, but meals and snacks provide an opportunity for the child to learn about new foods, new ways foods can be served, and social amenities. These objectives will be discussed in greater detail in later sections of this chapter.

Medical advice should be followed in providing foods for infants. Typical menus for infants are given in Table 9–1. There are some other practices to follow in feeding infants.

1. Wash hands before getting formula, food, or items used in feeding.
2. Change infant's diaper. Wash hands again.
3. Before feeding, place a bib or similar article under infant's chin.
4. Hold infants under six months of age comfortably in a semi-sitting position. Eye contact and cuddling are essential to affective develop-

TABLE 9–1
Regulations of the Special Food Service Program for Infants

Pattern	Infants Birth– 4 months	Infants Ages 4– 8 months	Infants Ages 8– 12 months
Breakfast			
Infant formula (iron-fortified)	4–6 ounces	6–8 ounces	6–8 ounces
Infant cereal (iron-fortified)	0	1–3 tablespoons	2–4 tablespoons
Snack (supplement)			
Infant formula (iron-fortified)	4–6 ounces	2–4 ounces	2–4 ounces
or full-strength fruit juice	0	2–4 ounces	2–4 ounces
or whole fluid milk	0	0	2–4 ounces
Enriched or whole grain bread	0	0–1/4 slice	0–1/4 slice
or cracker-type product (suitable for infants)	0	0–2 crackers	0–2 crackers
Lunch or Supper			
Infant formula (iron-fortified)	4–6 ounces	6–8 ounces	6–8 ounces
Infant cereal (iron-fortified)	0	1–2 tablespoons	
Strained fruit and/or vegetable (to total)	0	1–2 tablespoons	3–4 tablespoons
Strained meat, fish, poultry,			
or egg yolk	0	0–1 tablespoon	1–4 tablespoons
or cheese	0	0–1/2 ounce	1/2–2 ounces
or cottage cheese,			
cheese food,			
or cheese spread	0	0–1 ounce	1–4 ounces

Source: *A Planning Guide for Food Service in Child Care Centers,* Washington, D.C.: U.S. Department of Agriculture, Food and Nutrition Services 1981.

ment. Bottles are never propped. Babies taking bottles in a reclining position are more prone to choking and developing ear infections and dental caries than infants who take their bottles in a semi-sitting position. Older infants may be fed in high chairs or feeding tables. Adults must supervise at all times.

5. If solid foods are to be offered, present them before the major portion of the formula or breast milk is given.
6. Discard opened or leftover formula.
7. Keep infants upright for fifteen minutes after feeding to help avoid regurgitation of formula, breast milk, or food.
8. When returning young infants to bed, place them on their right sides to prevent aspirating formula or breast milk.
9. Introduce solid foods gradually—no more than one each two or three days. (Many physicians do not recommend any solid foods prior to six months of age.)
10. Use great patience in beginning spoon feeding. Babies push food from their mouths as a reflexive action of the tongue.
11. Clean infants' hands, faces, and necks after feeding.

Meal and snack patterns for young children are often based on the four basic food groups: meat (two or more servings), vegetables and fruits (four or more servings), milk and milk products, and bread and cereal (four or more servings). Young children must learn to eat a variety of nutritious foods. Table 9–2 is an example of a typical meal and snack plan. For other suggestions, see *A Planning Guide for Food Service in Child-Care Centers* (Washington, D.C.: U.S. Government Printing Office, 1981).

The following are some other practices for planning enjoyable meals and snacks:

1. Large portions of food are overwhelming to children; serve food in small portions and permit second helpings.
2. When serving a new or unpopular food, try the following: (a) serve a tiny portion with a more generous portion of a popular food, (b) introduce only one new food at a time, (c) introduce new food when children are hungry, (d) eat the food yourself, (e) have children prepare the food, and/or (f) keep offering the food (the Birch study found the more often children are offered a food, the more children are inclined to try it.)[6]
3. Plan special menus for holidays and birthdays, but avoid junk foods.[7]
4. Do not serve the same food, or virtually the same food, such as meatballs and hamburgers, on consecutive days.
5. Consider children's ethnic backgrounds and plan meals to include familiar foods.
6. Take advantage of children's likes and dislikes as to how foods are prepared and served. Young children generally like a variety of foods (different sizes, shapes, colors, textures, and temperatures); foods prepared in different ways; foods served in bite-sized pieces or as finger

TABLE 9–2
Regulations of the Special Food Service Program for Children

Pattern	Children 1–3 years	Children 3–6 years	Children 6–12 years
Breakfast			
Milk, fluid	½ cup	¾ cup	1 cup
Juice or **fruit** or **vegetable**	¼ cup	½ cup	½ cup
Bread and/or **cereal,** enriched or			
whole grain bread or	½ slice	½ slice	1 slice
cereal: Cold dry or	¼ cup[1]	⅓ cup[2]	¾ cup[3]
Hot cooked	¼ cup	¼ cup	½ cup
Midmorning or Midafternoon Snack (Supplement)			
(Select 2 of these 4 components)			
Milk, fluid	½ cup	½ cup	1 cup
Meat or **meat alternate**	½ ounce	½ ounce	1 ounce
Juice or **fruit** or **vegetable**	½ cup	½ cup	¾ cup
Bread and/or **cereal,** enriched or			
whole grain bread or	½ slice	½ slice	1 slice
cereal: Cold dry or	¼ cup[1]	⅓ cup[2]	¾ cup[3]
Hot cooked	¼ cup	¼ cup	½ cup
Lunch or Supper			
Milk, fluid	½ cup	¾ cup	1 cup
Meat or **meat alternate**			
Meat, poultry, or fish, cooked (lean meat without bone)	1 ounce	1½ ounces	2 ounces
Cheese	1 ounce	1½ ounces	2 ounces
Egg	1	1	1
Cooked dry beans and peas	¼ cup	⅜ cup	½ cup
Peanut butter	2 tablespoons	3 tablespoons	4 tablespoons
Vegetable and/or **fruit** (two or more)	¼ cup	½ cup	¾ cup
Bread or **bread alternate,**			
enriched or whole grain	½ slice	½ slice	1 slice

[1]¼ cup (volume) or ⅓ ounce (weight), whichever is less.
[2]⅓ cup (volume) or ½ ounce (weight), whichever is less.
[3]¾ cup (volume) or 1 ounce (weight), whichever is less.
Source: A Planning Guide for Food Service in Child-Care Centers. Washington, D.C.: U.S. Department of Agriculture, Food and Nutrition Services, 1981.

foods; vegetables with mild flavors; strong-flavored vegetables served only occasionally and in small portions; fruit (but not vegetable) combinations; good texture (fluffy, not gooey, mashed potatoes); and foods that are not too hot or cold.

7. Provide a good physical and emotional climate by having adults set a good example of eating; by having an attractive room setting with furniture, dishes, silverware, and serving utensils suited to young children; by either avoiding serving delays or by using activities such as singing and simple games while waiting; by providing a quiet time before meals; by making meal time pleasant; by permitting the child to have choices and recognizing that young children occasionally go on food sprees (wanting the same food every day or even several times a day); and by understanding that young children do not have an adult's sense of time and are not prone to hurry to finish.

In providing and serving nutritious meals and snacks, the program must meet the special needs of a child with a disabling condition. For example, children with delayed feeding skills may need special help, and children with metabolic problems and food allergies will need a carefully planned diet.

Hiring Staff. Foods may be prepared at either an early childhood facility that complies with health standards or at another approved facility and transported to the program using appropriate sanitary containers and temperatures. Programs with a large enrollment that serve a main meal should have a staff dietitian registered with the American Dietetic Association. If a full-time dietitian is not available, one should be hired as a consultant. Enough personnel should be employed so meals and snacks can be prepared in the time allowed. Each state's licensing standards for private programs or state and federal regulations for public programs indicate the qualifications necessary for food service personnel.

Providing Facilities and Equipment. Meals and snacks must be prepared and served with the available facilities and equipment. A registered dietitian can help plan the equipment and kitchen layout. An excellent publication concerning food service equipment is the booklet *Equipment Guide for Preschool and School Age Child Service Institutions*, published by the U.S. Department of Agriculture. Some equipment, such as the automatic dishwasher, must meet local and state health agency regulations.

Purchasing Food. Planning food purchases helps control costs and reduces waste. The following suggestions should be considered when purchasing food:

1. Check several food companies or stores in the area for quality food at reasonable prices and for services such as credit or delivery.
2. Know food products. Purchase government inspected meats, fish, and poultry; pasteurized, Grade A milk and milk products; properly sealed breads and pastries; and frozen foods that are kept hard-frozen and perishable foods that are kept under refrigeration. Notice which brand names prove most satisfactory.

3. Carefully calculate quantities of food needed. Use standardized recipes that always yield a specific quantity. Two sources are the U.S. Department of Agriculture's publications: *Quantity Recipes for Child-Care Centers* and *Quantity Recipes for Type A School Lunches*. A standardized recipe can be adjusted to provide the number of servings needed for a meal or snack.
4. The types of food (perishable or nonperishable) and the amount of storage space must be carefully considered in determining when to purchase food.
5. Keep accurate records of type and quality of food purchased, when and how food was used in program, cost, and any other notes useful for other purchases.

Meeting Sanitation Requirements. All sanitation requirements must be rigidly enforced to avert disease. Sanitation must be considered in all aspects of food service.

1. All food service employees must meet state and local health requirements, must be free of infections on the skin and contagious diseases, and must be clean.
2. Preparation and serving utensils and dishes must be thoroughly washed, sterilized, and properly handled. A dishwasher should be set for a water temperature of 160–165 degrees Fahrenheit (66–74 degrees Celsius), using 0.25 percent detergent concentration or one ounce of detergent per three gallons of water.
   Follow these four steps if washing by hand:
   a. Wash with soap or detergent in hot water (110–120 degrees Fahrenheit);
   b. Rinse in warm water;
   c. Sanitize by immersing for at least one minute in clean hot water (at least 170 degrees Fahrenheit) or by immersing for at least three minutes in a sanitizing solution of one tablespoon household bleach per two gallons of water; and
   d. Air—do not wipe—dry.
3. Foods should be checked upon delivery, protected in storage, used within the specified time, and kept at appropriate serving temperatures: hot foods at 140 degrees Fahrenheit (60 degrees Celsius) or above and cold foods at 40 degrees Fahrenheit (4 degrees Celsius) or below.
4. Wash raw foods carefully and cook other foods properly.
5. Dispose of all foods served and not eaten.
6. Help children develop habits of cleanliness.

Identifying Children's Nutrition Problems

There has been much concern about the role of nutritional problems in physical health[8, 9, 10, 11] and in learning disabilities and behavioral disorders.[12] Nutrition assessment is part of the final regulations of the Department of Health and Human Services' Early and Periodic Screening, Diagnosis and Treatment (ESDPT) program for individuals under twenty-one years.[13] Referral for medical and dental examinations and laboratory tests reveals nutrition conditions that need remediation such as overweight, underweight, iron deficiency anemia, food allergies, and faulty food habits. If treatment is necessary, staff members should follow the recommendations while the child is in the program; if necessary, they should assist the family in carrying out the care plan ascertaining whether the child has received follow-up assessment. Staff members should have in-service training in awareness of specific nutrition problems.

Implementing Nutrition Education for Children

A program should include nutrition education for young children. In the past, nutrition has been a part of the health component of the curriculum or has centered on specific food activities rather than being an integral part of the total curriculum. Children should talk about foods and good diets, and learn about food origins, storage, and preparation. Cooking experiences will help them learn to measure, follow directions, cooperate with others, coordinate eye-hand movements, use language as a means of expression, recognize differences in food preferences of the various ethnic groups, and eat foods prepared in different ways. Children also need to develop socially acceptable eating behavior and adaptability to various meal settings—at home, in restaurants, or on picnics. Herr and Morse provide a good example of how to integrate one nutrition concept throughout the early childhood curriculum.[14] The following is a list of other available resources.

Brody, J. *Jane Brody's Nutrition Book,* DesPlaines, Ill.: Bantam Books, 1987.

Church, M. "Nutrition: A Vital Part of the Curriculum." *Young Children* 35, 1 (1979): 61–65.

Cooking and Eating with Children—A Way to Learn. Washington, D.C.: Association for Childhood Education International, 1976.

Endres, J. B., and Rockwell, R. E. *Food, Nutrition, and the Young Child.* New York: Merrill, 1985.

Ferreira, N. "Teachers' Guide to Educational Cooking in the Nursery School—An Everyday Affair." *Young Children* 29, 1 (1973): 23–32.

Food–Early Choices: A Nutrition Learning System for Early Childhood. Rosemont, Ill.: National Dairy Council, 1980.

Food—Your Choice, Level 1. Rosemont, Ill.: National Dairy Council, 1980.

Galen, H. "Cooking in the Curricula." *Young Children* 32,2 (1977): 59–69.

Gooch, S. *If You Love Me Don't Feed Me Junk.* Reston, Va.: Reston Publishing Company, 1983.

Good Times with Good Foods: Classroom Activities for Young Children. Greensboro: Center for Action-Based Leadership Experiences Publications, 1978.

Goodwin, M., and Pollen, J. *Creative Food Experiences for Children.* rev. ed. Washington, D.C.: Center for Science in the Public Interest, 1980.

Greene, K. *Once Upon a Recipe.* New Hope, Pa.: New Hope Press, 1987.

Kamen, B., and Kamen, S. *Kids Are What They Eat: What Every Parent Needs to Know about Nutrition.* New York: Arco Publishing, 1984.

Lappe, F. M. *Diet for a Small Planet.* New York: Random House, 1982.

Little Ideas. Rosemont, Ill.: National Dairy Council, 1980.

Marback, E.; Plass, M.; and O'Connell, L. *Nutrition in a Changing World: A Curriculum for Preschool.* Nursery-Kindergarten. Provo: Brigham Young University, 1979.

McAfee, O. *Cooking and Eating with Children: A Way to Learn.* Washington, D.C.: Association for Childhood Education International, 1974.

McWilliams, M. *The Parents' Nutrition Book.* New York: Wiley, 1986.

Nutrition Source Book. Rosemont, Ill.: National Dairy Council, 1981.

Oliver, S. D., and Musgrave K. O. *Nutrition: A Sourcebook of Integrated Activities.* Boston: Allyn and Bacon, 1984.

Puryear, A. *Exploring Foods with Young Children: A Recipe for Nutrition Education.* Tallahassee: Early Childhood And Elementary Education, State Department of Education, 1977.

Randell, J.; Olson, C.; Jones, S.; and Morris, L. *Early Childhood Nutrition Program.* Ithaca: Distribution Center, Cornell University, 1980.

Richert, B. *Getting Your Kids to Eat Right.* New York: Cornerstone, 1981.

Vonde, D. A. S., and Beck, J. *Food Adventure for Children.* Redondo Beach, Calif.: Plycon, 1980.

Wagner, P. A.; Allen, J.; and Canal, J. A. *A Guide to Nutrition Education for the Preschool Teacher.* Gainesville: University of Florida, 1980.

Wanamaker, N.; Hern, K.; and Richarz, S. *More than Graham Crackers: Nutrition Education and Food Preparation with Young Children.* Washington, D. C.: National Association for the Education of Young Children, 1979.

Weiner, M. A., and Goss, K. *The Art of Feeding Children Well.* New York: Warner Books, 1982.

Whitener, C. B., and Keeling, M. H. *Nutrition Education for Young Children: Strategies and Activities.* Englewood Cliffs: Prentice-Hall, 1984.

Many cookbooks are available for children. Some contain recipes children prefer, while others are designed to teach children how to cook:

Ackerman, D. *Cooking with Kids*. Mt. Rainier, Md.: Gryphon House, 1981.

Baxter, K. M. *Come and Get It: A Natural Foods Cookbook for Children*. 3rd ed. Ann Arbor: Children First, 1981.

Bruno, J., and Dakam, P. *Cooking in the Classroom*. Belmont, Calif.: Lear/Siegler/Fearon, 1974.

Catron, C. E., and Parks, B. C. *Cooking Up a Story*. Minneapolis: T. S. Denison and Company, Inc., 1986.

Cristenberry, M. A., and Stevens, B. *Can Piaget Cook?* Atlanta: Humanics Limited, 1984.

Edge, N. *Kids in the Kitchen*. Port Angeles, Wash.: Peninsula Publishing Company, Inc., 1975.

Faggella, K. *Concept Cookery*. Bridgeport: First Teacher Press, 1985.

Harms, T. *Learning from Cooking Experiences*. Menlo Park: Addison-Wesley Publishing Company, 1983.

Jenkins, K. S. *Kinder-Krunchies*. Pleasant Hill, Calif.: Discovery Toys, 1982.

Johnson, B. *Cup Cooking Starter Set: Single Step Charts for Child Portion Picture Recipes*. Mt. Rainier, Md.: Gryphon House, Inc., 1978.

McClenahan, P. and Jaqua, I. *Cool Cooking for Kids: Recipes and Nutrition for Kids*. Belmont, Calif.: Fearon Pitman, 1976.

Ontario Science Center. *Foodworks*. Reading, Mass.: Addison-Wesley, 1987.

Palmer, M., and Edmonds, A. *Vegetable Magic*. Storrs, Conn.: Connecticut State Board of Education, 1981.

Stori, M. T. *I'll Eat Anything If I Can Make It Myself*. Chicago: Chicago Review, 1980.

Veitch, B., and Harms, T. *Cook and Learn*. Menlo Park: Addison-Wesley Publishing Company, 1981.

Warren, J. *Super Snacks/Sugarless*. Everett, Wash.: Warren Publishing House, Inc., 1982.

Wilms, B. *Crunchy Bananas*. Salt Lake City: Gibs M. Smith, 1984.

Wishik, C. S. *Kids Dish It Up Sugar-Free*. Port Angeles, Wash.: Peninsula Publishing, 1982.

Zubrowski, B. *Baking Chemistry*. Boston: Little Brown, 1981.

Serving Parents' Needs

Parents as well as early childhood educators have an impact on children's nutritional habits. Although children decide on *how much* (or even *whether*) to eat, adults are responsible for *the foods* children are offered. Researchers indicate that parents are less reliable food providers today than they were in previous generations.[15] Parents can help their children develop appropriate nutrition concepts and attitudes. Parents need to be informed on various topics concerning nutrition for children, including: (1) foods needed for a healthy child; (2) planning, buying, storing, preparing varieties of foods; (3) common eating problems of children; (4) children who need special diets; and (5) money savers.

Staff members need to know the social realities of the families with whom they work, or they may make nutrition demands that families cannot meet. Parents can be reached in parents' meetings, demonstration classes, home visits, and through newsletters. Some specific suggestions are:

1. Staff members can aid parents in planning nutritious meals using the basic four food groups. A list of foods in each of the four groups may help parents plan adequate meals or may help those who are already planning adequate meals see how they can vary their food choices.
2. Newsletters can contain information about food planning and preparation and recipes as a way of developing the young child's interest in foods and snacks.
3. Menus should be posted for parents.
4. Other information on nutrition should be made available, such as the nutrient content of foods in relation to cost, the nutrient content of food after storage and preparation, and the relationship between nutrition and health of infants and young children.
5. Using volunteers in food education may be helpful in informing parents.

HEALTH

Attention to health issues in programs for young children dates back to 1945.[16] Research concerning health has been sporadic until recently. Today there is concern about children's health status in early childhood programs, practices aiding children's health, and staff members' health. Administrators of early childhood programs must develop health policies for children and staff members in keeping with current information. Some health policy categories were suggested in Chapter 3.

Children's Health Status

Concern about the problems of disease spread in early childhood programs, especially in day-care centers, is increasing. Children in day-care are highly vulnerable due to: (1) close physical contacts among children and adults—

feeding, diapering and toileting, sharing objects including moist art media and water tables, and affection giving and receiving; (2) children's lack of immunity; (3) children's small body structures such as the distance between the nose and throat and the middle ear; (4) children's bumps and scrapes on the skin that afford entry of infectious agents into the body; and (5) children's lack of understanding of how to protect themselves from infectious agents.

Clarke-Stewart states that attendance in early childhood programs is not detrimental to the physical growth of children, but children in early childhood programs may "catch" more diseases than those raised at home.[17] Children in programs, however, are not at a substantially increased risk of developing infectious disease compared with others kept at home.[18] When young children spend time with peers or have older siblings who themselves are with nonhousehold children in groups, preschool illness patterns are more like those of children who attend early childhood programs. Evidence indicates that except for infants under one year of age and a greater incidence of runny noses in large centers (i.e., those with over fifty children), children reared at home have the same type or number of respiratory infections as those in early childhood programs.[19]

Practices Aiding Children's Health

Early childhood program staff can play important roles in aiding children's health. They serve in liaison roles as they work with parents in maintaining children's complete and up-to-date health records and aiding parents in securing health services. They also work directly with children to maintain good health.

Health Records

Licensing and other regulations usually require that each child has a recent medical examination and an up-to-date immunization record before admission to a program. Most regulations require that the medical examination be given within the last six months before entry; however, an examination one month prior to entry provides maximum protection for all children. Health records should contain: (1) record of immunizations, (2) pertinent health history, and (3) a signed physician's statement concerning the child's ability to participate in the program's activities and any special health needs, such as food allergies or restrictions of physical activities (see Appendix 9). Parents may want to add information on health habits, such as dental hygiene and foods preferred.

Because children are being cared for more and more frequently in early childhood programs, it is important for staff members to work with the children's physicians. A staff member may have important information to convey to the physician or may wish to obtain the physician's advice on handling a particular health problem in the center. Dixon[20] provides some guidelines which make communication easier.

Health Services

All children need to receive high-quality health services. Early childhood programs are required by various regulatory agencies to provide some health services (e.g., employ health consultants).[21] In addition, early childhood administrators need to locate available resources and obtain their criteria for assistance for the children and families served by the early childhood program. For starters, administrators need to check city, county, state, and regional health departments; clinics operated by hospitals and medical schools; voluntary groups such as United Fund, American Red Cross, civic clubs, religious groups, and family service associations; medical assistance under Medicaid (Title XIX); armed forces medical services; and insurance and other prepayment plans.

Basic Health Practices

Safer environments for both children and adults can be achieved by following certain health practices. Some of the basics are listed below:

1. Safer environments are programs with fewer than fifty children, with small groups of nontoilet-trained infants and toddlers,[22] and that separate children in diapers.[23]
2. As discussed in this chapter, food service must meet health standards.
3. The diapering area in an infant center is the most dangerous for the growth of illness-causing microorganisms. These practices reduce risks in diapering:
   a. Change child on a table with a plastic covered pad that has no cracks and has a restraint device.
   b. Place newspaper, paper bags, computer paper, or wax paper squares under each child before changing. Paper is also used to pick up diaper.
   c. Use disposable gloves to augment handwashing procedures.
   d. Wash diapering surface twice daily and after any diaper leaks. Scrub with detergent and water. Rinse with clean water treated with a disinfectant (i.e., one-fourth cup chlorine bleach to one gallon water) kept in a spray bottle. The disinfectant must be made fresh daily, and stored away from children.
   e. Wash hands after diapering, using running water. Sinks with elbow controls are desirable in this area or use a paper towel to turn off faucet.
   f. Post procedures for diapering in area.[24]
4. Require consistent attention to handwashing. Children and adults should wash hands before serving or eating food, after each diaper change or use of restrooms, and after wiping a nose. Proper handwashing requires:
   a. Use of soap in soft water areas and detergent in hard water areas. Liquid soap is more sanitary than bar soap. Liquid soap dispensers should be cleaned and refilled on a regular basis. If bar soaps are

used, the bar should be rinsed before and after use and kept dry. An antiseptic form made from alcohol and lanolin (e.g., "Alcare" manufactured by Vestal Labs) is effective in place of soap.

b. Work soap in hands for two to three minutes; rinse with running water; clean under nails; keep elbows higher than hands; turn off faucet with a paper towel; and dry hands with a disposable paper towel.

c. For handwashing of infants and young toddlers, wipe hands with damp towels moistened with a liquid soap solution, wipe with towels moistened with clean water, then dry with paper towels. For older children, squirt drops of liquid soap on their hands from a squeeze bottle; children rinse hands under running water, drying them with a paper towel.

5. Wear disposable gloves when cleaning wounds and augment with thorough handwashing.

6. The facility and equipment must be cleaned regularly. The following are suggestions for cleaning:

a. General cleaning of the building should be done daily when children are gone.

b. Clean cribs, strollers, and tables daily using the same procedure and cleaning materials as described for cleaning the diapering table. This should also be done with wooden toys and laminated books.

c. Wash high chair trays in dishwasher.

d. Wash toys that are put in the mouth daily. This can be done more quickly if toys are placed in nylon mesh bags (used for hosiery), washed, rinsed, and hung to dry.

e. Rinse rattles and other dishwasher-safe mouth toys before placing in dishwasher. (Saliva forms a film when heated, aiding in the growth of microorganisms.).

f. Use bedding with one child only; wash weekly or after soiling.

g. Clean and disinfect bath fixtures daily or after soiling.

h. Remove trash daily.

i. Soiled diapers should be disposed of or held for laundry in a closed container.

j. Never place dishes or bottles on the floor.

k. Clean floors and other surfaces after feeding.

7. Use a sanitation checklist where health practices are checked off by date and time and initialed by person fulfilling the requirement. (See *Sanitation Checklist* prepared by K. Albrecht and staff at the Department of Home Economics, Child and Family Development Center, Southwest Texas State University, San Marcos, Texas.)

Child Care for Infectious Diseases

About half of all state and other regulations require that children with communicable diseases be sent home. Today such policies are being debated, centering on these questions:

1. Does removing an ill child reduce the spread of infection? Programs with stringent policies for excluding ill children compared with less strict programs showed no difference in the amounts or kinds of illnesses. For many illnesses, it is difficult to diagnose the risk of spread of infectious diseases for these reasons: (*a*) children with no symptoms may spread infection; (*b*) children often spread infection several days before and after symptoms; and, (*c*) the presence or absence of certain symptoms including fever is not correlated with the amount of infectious disease a child is spreading. Exclusion is recommended for infectious diarrhea, infectious conjunctivitis (until the next day after treatment initiated), Hepatitis A, vaccine-preventable diseases (measles, etc.), and strep throat (until next day after treatment initiated). For illnesses such as Acquired Immune Deficiency Syndrome (AIDS) and Kawasaki Syndrome (an infectious disease agent which does not appear to be contagious), each case should be considered individually with medical consultation.[25]

2. Can family members afford to stay home with a mildly ill child? Parents may feel unable to lose work time and thus leave an ill child at home alone, under the care of an older sibling, or under the care of a neighbor who is to "check" on the child. Parents may try to cover the illness by trying to cover the symptoms. Parents may also feel guilty about not providing total care of their child and supposedly exposing the child to an illness spread in the program.

3. What is best for ill children? Ill children do not need to feel guilty about the inconvenience their illness causes their parents or their caregivers. Ill children may need more comfort, but often not much more care than well children. If the child is to be kept in the program, staff members need to: (*a*) maintain information on onset of and current symptoms, possible contributing factors (e.g., vaccinations), complicating illnesses (e.g., chronic illnesses), intake (i.e., food and drink) and output (i.e., times urinated and number of bowel movements), and care given; (*b*) follow basic health practices, especially handwashing; (*c*) follow approved practices for caring for children with fever, vomiting, or diarrhea; and (*d*) provide place and play materials suited to an ill child.

4. Can parents pay for short-term special care when their children are ill? Aronson has given these special care options for program administrators: (*a*) hiring additional staff for ill children; (*b*) providing a "get well room" with a familiar caregiver; and/or (*c*) forming a linkage with nearby families to provide temporary family home care or with a sick child center. (See Chapter 1 on alternative care centers.) In each of these options, the parents pay for the special care.[26]

Administrators of programs must develop policies for specifying limitations on attendance of ill children, provisions for notification of parents, and plans for the comfort and care of ill children. Parents need to be informed of program policy and any available special care options.

Child Care for Noninfectious Chronic Illnesses and Disabilities
Many children who are chronically ill and disabled are eligible for services under Public Law 94–142. Planning needs to be done prior to accepting these children. Some points to consider include: (1) prognosis of illness or disability; (2) adaptations in program activities or in schedule; (3) special housing arrangements needed; (4) special equipment needed; (5) special dietary needs; (6) coordination of home and program administration of medication; and (7) possible special care and emergency procedures. Although some children require intensive services beyond the usual early childhood program, most children who are chronically ill and disabled will require only minor adaptations.

Medication Administration
Legally speaking, the administration of medication is an act by an adult that can alter the metabolism of a child in a way not always susceptible to immediate control. Before making a policy, check licensing or other regulations. In writing a policy, these points should be considered: (1) parent provides the written order of a physician authorizing the use of the medication for a specified length of time for a particular child; (2) parent provides a written request that a staff member administer the medication; (3) medication is labeled with child's name, name of drug, and directions for its administration; (4) staff members maintain a written record of date and time of each administration and name of the staff member administering medication; and (5) safe storage places for medications are designated. (See Appendix 9 for an example of a medication administration form.)

Protecting Staff Members' Health

The health of adults is a key element in the quality of an early childhood program. A staff member's illness can become a health hazard to children and other staff members, is costly to a program in which substitutes must be hired, and can cause a lack of consistent child care.

Medical examinations are an important means of protecting staff members' health. Programs need standard requirements and policies to include: content of examination, which can differ for the various staff positions; the criteria for "passing" the examination; when examinations are indicated (e.g., prior to employment, after a severe illness); where the examination may be given; who receives the findings; and who pays for the examination. More suggestions on establishing policy are given by Aronson.[27]

In addition to medical examinations, adequate paid sick leave protects the health of adults. When sick leave is not available, staff members might not leave when they are ill or may return before they should resume their duties.[28]

SAFETY

Safety is no longer seen as sheltering the child. Safety includes safety consciousness, safety practices, and environmental care. Children will take risks—many of which are good learning experiences. At other times, though, an adult must stop or redirect a child in a potentially harmful situation. Children must begin learning how to predict hazards and choose safe alternatives.

Safety, including transportation safety, needs to be an integral part of the daily early childhood program. Staff members need training in observing children for safety practices. Not only is the well-being of the child involved, but the courts have ruled there is no contributory negligence by the young child.[29] Staff members must also receive training in handling potentially harmful situations, and in modeling and teaching practices. Suggestions are available in many general curriculum texts on early childhood education as well as from specialized sources such as:

American Academy of Pediatrics
141 Northwest Point Blvd.
P. O. Box 927
Elk Grove Village, Ill. 60009

National Child Passenger Safety
P. O. Box 841
Ardmore, Pa. 19003

Physicians for Automotive Safety
P. O. Box 430
Armonk, N.Y. 10504

Consumer Product Safety Commission
Washington, D.C. 20206
Hotline: 1–800–638–CPSC

Environmental safety needs close attention. General environmental safety practices are given in Chapters 5 and 6. Each program needs to establish environmental safety guidelines to fit its own special needs. Procedures also need to be developed for following through on the established safety guidelines.

Some regulations require disaster plans. Each program must develop plans for evacuating children in the event of fire or explosion and measures to take during tornadoes, flash floods, smog alerts, and civil defense emergencies.

PROCEDURES FOR EMERGENCIES AND NONEMERGENCY ILLNESSES

Emergencies and nonemergency illnesses arise even when early childhood programs take every possible measure to protect children's health and safety. To minimize the risks to children, procedures for handling them must be developed.

The key elements in handling emergencies and other illnesses include:

1. One or more employees of a program should be trained in first aid. Some states' licensing regulations require that at least one staff member have a current American Red Cross Standard First Aid Certificate or its equivalent. Regardless of the regulations, such knowledge is important.
2. First aid supplies and equipment are available including references on handling childhood emergencies such as

> Aronson, S. *First Aid in Child-Care Settings.* Washington, D.C.: American Red Cross, 1988.

> Green, M. *A Sigh of Relief—The First Aid Handbook for Childhood Emergencies.* 2nd ed. New York: Bantam, 1984.

> Rovertson, A. A. *Health, Safety, and First Aid: A Guide for Training Child Care Workers.* White Bear Lake, MN: Toys 'n Things Press, 1980.

3. Employees should be informed of their responsibility to administer first aid. This information should be covered in staff meetings and posted in conspicuous places throughout the facility.
4. Parents or legal guardians must be notified. They should be given the opportunity, if possible without endangering the child, to participate in making decisions and aiding in the treatment procedure.
5. An early childhood program should have a consent form on file authorizing emergency medical treatment and transportation if parents cannot be reached. The emergency information form usually includes names, addresses, and phone numbers of parents and other persons who can accept responsibility for the child when parents cannot be contacted; name and phone number of the physician to be contacted; and name and address of the hospital to which the child may be taken (see Appendix 9). This form should be updated every six months and should be taken on each field trip. Forms should also be available for staff members to document the procedures they followed in handling an emergency or illness. Careful documentation helps prevent mistakes in caring for children and also lessens potential liability to the program.

HEALTH AND SAFETY TRAINING FOR STAFF MEMBERS

Staff members often are very aware of their responsibilities to protect children. However, most staff members are deficient in health and safety information. Information is needed in many areas such as: (1) relationship of health to total well-being, (2) characteristics of the child's development associated with health problems and safety hazards, (3) nutrition for the growing child, (4) injury prevention, (5) managing and detecting symptoms of the common infectious diseases of childhood, (6) detection of other medical conditions and child abuse/neglect, (7) health and safety education and resources, and (8) emergency preparedness.

Training must be provided in these and other areas of need and interest. Staff training on various topics must be repeated so new staff members can receive training and all other staff members can replenish their knowledge and skills.

Suggestions are available in many texts on health education as well as from specialized sources such as:

American Public Health Association
1015 15th Street, N. W.
Washington, D.C. 20015

Center for Chronic Disease Prevention and Health Promotion
1600 Clifton Road, N. E.
Atlanta, Ga. 30333

National Center for Health Education
30 East 29th Street
New York, N.Y. 10016

SUMMARY

Health and safety are essential ingredients of quality early childhood programs. Nutrition is highly important in programs for young children for these two reasons: (1) early childhood programs need to provide up to 80 percent of the young child's total nutrition requirements; and (2) children develop lifelong eating habits as a result of early eating experiences. Thus, staff members of early childhood programs need to know the nutritional requirements of young children, how to provide a nutritious diet, and how to create an appropriate meal and snack environment.

Health affects each area of a person's development. Adults' health also affect their state of well-being. The health goals in early childhood programs are to provide routine health care, to prevent health problems, and to coordinate health plans with parents and children's physicians. Similar to health, safety includes safety consciousness, safety practices, and environmental care. Staff members must also respond effectively and efficiently to emergencies.

NOTES

1. M. Winnick, *Malnutrition and Brain Development* (London: Oxford University, 1976).

2. G. R. Norwood, *The Relationship of Health and Nutrition to the Learning Process,* ERIC ED 248 955 (1984).

3. D. L. Pertz and L. R. Putnam, *What is the Relationship Between Nutrition and Learning?* ERIC ED 220 797 (1982).

4. A. Stein, R. Foucar-Szock, and S. Kauffman, *Nutrition and Learning: the Breakfast Role.* ERIC ED 241 463 (1984).

5. N. R. Beyer and P. M. Morris, "Food Attitudes and Snacking Patterns of Young Children," *Journal of Nutrition Education* 6, 4 (1974): 131–134.

6. L. L. Birch, D. W. Marlow, and J. Rotter, "Eating as the 'Means' Activity in a Contingency: Effects on Young Children's Food Preference," *Child Development* 55 (1984): 431–439.

7. F. Wardle, "Bunny Ears and Cupcakes for All—Are Parties Developmentally Appropriate?" *Child Care Information Exchange* (August, 1990), 39–42.

8. Committee on Nutrition, American Academy of Pediatrics, "Prudent Life Style for Children: Dietary Fat and Cholesterol," *Journal of Pediatrics* 12 (1986): 521–525.

9. C. S. Rogers and S. S. Morris, "Reducing Sugar in Children's Diets," *Young Children* 41, 5 (1986): 11–16.

10. M. D. Lebow, *Child Obesity* (New York: Springer, 1984).

11. C. F. Schactele, "Changing Perspectives on the Role of Diet in Dental Caries Formation," *Nutrition News* 45, 4 (1982): 13–14.

12. D. J. Rapp, *The Impossible Child in School—at Home: A Guide for Caring Teachers and Parents* (Buffalo: Practical Allergy Research Foundation, 1986). Also see Notes 2 and 3.

13. *Federal Register* 44 (May 18, 1979), 28424–26.

14. J. Herr and W. Morse, "Food for Thought: Nutrition Education for Young Children," *Young Children* 38, 1 (1982): 3–11.

15. N. W. Jerome, "Changing Nutritional Styles within the Context of the Modern Family," *Family Health Care,* vol. 1, eds. D. P. Hymolvich and M. U. Bernard (New York: McGraw-Hill, 1979), 194–203.

16. *Day-Care: A Partnership of Three Professions* (Washington, D.C.: Child Welfare League of America, 1945).

17. K. A. Clarke-Stewart, "The Day-Care Child," *Early Childhood Education 85/86.* ed. J. S. McKee (Guildford, Conn.: Dushkin, 1985).

18. M. Howell, "Is Day-Care Hazardous to Health?" *Early Childhood Education 85/86.* ed. J. S. McKee (Guildford, Conn.: Dushkin, 1985).

19. S. S. Aronson, "Infection and Day-Care," *Child-Care Information Exchange* (1983): 10–14.

20. S. Dixon, "Talking to the Child's Physician: Thoughts for the Child-Care Provider," *Young Children* 45, 3 (1990): 36–37.

21. S. H. Schuman, "Day-Care Associated Infection: More than Meets the Eye," *Journal of the American Medical Association* 249 (1983): 76.

22. S. C. Hadler, et al., "Risk Factors for Hepatitis A in Day-Care Centers," *The Journal of Infectious Diseases* 145 (1982): 255–61.

23. L. K. Pickering and W. E. Woodward, "Diarrhea in Day-Care Centers," *Pediatric Infectious Disease* 1 (1982): 47–52.

24. Aronson, "Infection and Day-Care."

25. S. S. Aronson, "Exclusion Criteria for Ill Children in Child Care," *Child Care Information Exchange* (1986): 14, 16.

26. Ibid., 15.

27. S. S. Aronson, "Why Is Adult Health an Issue in Day-Care?" *Child Care Information Exchange* (1984): 26–28.

28. A. D. Peters, "Children, Communications, Communities: Enhancing the Environment for Learning," *American Journal of Orthopsychiatry* 52 (1982): 646–54.

29. *Fowler* v. *Seaton* 61 C 2d 681, 39 Cal. Rpts. 881, 394 p. 2d 697.

FOR FURTHER READING

Andersen, R. D., Bale, Jr., J. F., Blackman, J. A., and Murph, J. R. *Infections in Children: A Sourcebook for Educators and Child-Care Providers*. Rockville: Aspen Publications, 1986.

Deitch, S. R. *Health in Day-Care: A Manual for Health Professionals*. Elk Grove Village, Ill.: American Academy of Pediatrics, 1982.

Kane, D. N. *Environmental Hazards to Young Children*. Phoenix: Oryx Press, 1985.

Kendrick, A. S., Kaufmann, R., and Messenger, K. P., eds. *Healthy Young Children—A Manual for Programs*. Washington, D.C.: National Association for the Education of Young Children, 1988.

Metzger, M., and Whittaker, C. P. *The Childproofing Checklist: A Parent's Guide to Accident Prevention*. New York: Doubleday, 1988.

NAEYC Information Service. *Child Care and Ill Children and Healthy Child Care Practices*. Washington, D.C.: National Association for the Education of Young Children, 1989.

Sleator, E. K. *Infectious Diseases in Day-Care*. Urbana, Ill.: ERIC Clearinghouse on Elementary and Early Childhood Education, 1986.

Chapter 10
Assessing, Recording, and Reporting Children's Progress

Assessing, recording, and reporting children's progress is one of the most controversial aspects of program development for young children. Among the various types of early childhood programs, there is perhaps greater diversity in the area of assessment than in almost any other aspect of the programs. The controversy revolves around (1) the purposes of evaluation and the methods used in assessment; (2) the staff time spent in recording children's progress, the possibility that records will negatively typecast children, and the indiscriminate release and use of information about children and their families; and (3) the problem of what and how much to communicate to parents who are not professionally trained in interpreting assessment results and who are emotionally involved in their children's development. At the same time, assessing, recording, and reporting children's progress serves as a basis for many worthwhile functions, such as planning and implementing all program services, guiding each child's development, and communicating with parents, the public, and regulatory agencies.

ASSESSING

Assessing goes beyond measurement, grading, or classifying. **Assessment** involves four separate processes. First is determining the need and thus, the purpose of assessment. (Broad purposes of assessment are discussed in the next section.) Second is the gathering of qualitative and quantitative evidence by the appropriate method. Recently, many concerns have been raised about appropriate assessment instruments; thus, these concerns and the professional position statements stemming from these concerns are discussed in detail in this chapter. Third is processing the information so as to permit the formation of judgments. Processing may be as simple as converting raw scores into local stanines or as involved as using many types of data collected over time to form an individual profile. And fourth is the making of professional judgments. At this point assessment is simply a tool in the decision-making process. As professionals we never remove ourselves from the assessment process for only well-trained humans can make the "call"—the value judgment.

There are some additional considerations in planning an assessment program. Some questions that must be answered include:

1. How willing and knowledgeable are staff members to administer the assessment instruments and interpret the scores?
2. How much time and money are budgeted for assessment? What intrusions on staff members, children, and parents can be accommodated for collecting, analyzing, recording, and preparing the data for use?
3. Who will coordinate the assessment program?
4. Will the services of resource persons such as psychologists and guidance workers be needed?
5. How will children's progress be interpreted to parents and to the community?

Purposes of Assessment

In early childhood programs assessment is currently being used for many purposes. These three purposes are the most common:

1. Assessment is being used as *a* factor or *the* factor in placement and retention practices. In a national survey of public school testing of prekindergarten and kindergarten children, it was found that: (a) thirty states report the use of readiness tests prior to kindergarten, and seven of these states mandate such testing; (b) forty-three states use readiness tests prior to first grade, and six of these states require such testing; and (c) forty states have developmental kindergartens and transitional first-grade programs in at least some of their schools.[1]
2. Assessment is being used for curriculum planning. This form of assessment is used to determine the child's progress in attaining program goals/objectives and to serve as a tool in parent-staff communication. Assessment used to modify curriculum, to determine methodology, and to provide feedback in a mastery-learning strategy is called **formative assessment.**[2]
3. Testing is also used in program evaluation. Program evaluation permits the planning of additions to or revisions of services and even determines changes in program rationale. Assessment used to determine the effectiveness of curriculum and methodology and to provide a product measurement is called **summative evaluation.**[3]

Concerns in Assessment

Although assessment can serve many useful functions, assessment also has the potential for doing harm. Some of the recent concerns should be taken seriously by early childhood program administrators.

Matching the Assessment Instrument to Purpose

Because assessment is not a supplementary activity but an integral aspect of a program, the assessment instrument must match the program's rationale. Kamii and Elliott state that there must be a match between program objectives and instructional content, between instructional content and assessment instruments, and between program objectives and assessment instruments.[4] One of the greatest dangers is that assessment itself can determine a program, rather than a program determining the how and why of assessment. It is almost as though the cart is placed before the horse. For example, some program planners take the content of standardized tests and plan activities to teach these items. Teaching to a test encourages a narrow academic program. "Curriculum based on tests is narrow and fails to embed knowledge in meaningful contexts, thus making it virtually unusable for the learner."[5] The order should be reversed. A program should be rationally planned, based on current and accurate information about children; then tests should be selected to fit the program's goals and objectives.

Assessment instruments may not reflect current theory. For example, the whole language approach to reading instruction is advocated by many, but reading achievement tests focus on narrow subskills.[6] Likewise, achievement tests in mathematics look at subskills rather than the construction of number concepts.

Finally, tests may be used for purposes other than those for which they were designed. In many early childhood programs, readiness tests instead of developmental screening tests are used supposedly to assess the child's ability to acquire skills. (Readiness test results often lead to placement and retention decisions.) Readiness and screening tests can never be used interchangeably.[7]

Assessing for Placement/Retention Decisions

As we previously discussed, testing for placement and retention decisions is becoming commonplace. Results of testing just prior to kindergarten are used to determine whether children are ready to begin kindergarten. If children are deemed "not ready," they usually wait a year or enter a pre-kindergarten program (often called a **developmental kindergarten**) and then enter kindergarten the following year. Test scores at the end of kindergarten determine whether children are retained in kindergarten, sent to a pre-first (often called **transitional class**), or promoted to first grade. Children who are labeled "not ready" at either testing point always end up one or more years older than the "ready" children for first-grade entrance and may spend one or two extra years in school.

There are several problems with this assessment/placement package:

1. Teachers and administrators are not aware or are not acting on the evidence which shows that such placements and retention practices are not beneficial (see Chapter 2). Kindergarten teachers "believe that the pupil career should be driven by competence or readiness—and for the most part they act according to these beliefs."[8] Thus, children in early childhood programs are being retained in increasing numbers.[9]

2. Placement/retention decisions based on testing may be faulty due to the inherent cultural and linguistic biases of tests.[10] Reasons for "holding children back" or retaining them go beyond low academic achievement to such reasons as low socioeconomic status, gender (i.e., boys more than girls), and minority status.[11]

3. Placement/retention decisions are often based on the results of *one test* and that one test may even be a test designed for other purposes. A single developmental screening test only identifies children who need further diagnostic assessment before making education program plans. Smith states that "none of the available tests are accurate enough to screen without a 50 percent error rate."[12] Such an error rate demands additional assessment. Weikart feels direct observations, case studies over time, and developmental records are all steps in the right direction.[13] It may even be illegal to use one test for placement.[14]

   Furthermore, placement/retention decisions are often based on tests designed for other purposes. Nomothetic methods which involve standardized testing are designed to search for general laws of child development rather than give an in-depth view of children. Idiographic methods, as opposed to nomothetic methods, focus on the individual. In idiographic methods normative data are considered only as data promote a better understanding of the individual and are used as one piece of information along with many others. And, as previously discussed, often the chosen standardized test does not match the purpose. **Developmental screening tests** focus on the child's ability to acquire skills and thus attempt to locate children who need further evaluation; **readiness tests** focus on current skill acquisition. However, schools tend to use readiness tests such as the *Gesell School Readiness Test* or the *Metropolitan Readiness Test* instead of developmental screening tests for screening children as a first step. (Meisels states that currently there are only four valid screening tests for young children: *Denver Developmental Screening Test, Early Screening Inventory, McCarthy Screening Test,* and *Minnesota Preschool Screening Instrument*.[15]) Following screening, children who seem to have "problems" would then undergo thorough diagnostic assessment which would determine whether or not there was a disability and identify specific areas of strengths and weaknesses.

   Finally, administrators must remember to consider the environments (i.e., early childhood programs) in which they expect their predictions to be actualized. Fedoruk states that schools often screen children without considering the curriculum and teaching strategies of their programs, and this is just as futile as predicting the plant growth of a seedling without knowing the nature of the environment (e.g., soil and weather conditions) in which the seedling will be planted.[16]

Selecting Quality Instruments

Tests should meet the standards given in *Standards for Educational and Psychological Testing*.[17] Some of the major concerns have been tests which did not undergo appropriate validity and reliability studies or which do not have acceptable levels of validity and reliability.[18] Appropriate technical data must be provided. In addition to validity and reliability, other recommended criteria for judging a test are relevance (i.e., Does the test meet a given purpose?); importance (i.e., Is the purpose really important?); scope (i.e., Is the information broad enough to be useful?); credibility (i.e., Do the users have faith in the data the test will yield?); timeliness (i.e., Is the information coming at the right time?); and efficiency (i.e., Is there an appropriate alternative in terms of time, cost, etc.?).[19]

Using Appropriate Statistics

Raw scores on tests are converted into certain derived scores. Although test manuals often discuss these statistics of testing, many staff members fail to read the information carefully. For example, grade-level equivalency, the most commonly used achievement test derived score, is the most misleading. To derive the grade-level equivalency score, the test makers assign the median score of a norm population a grade-level equivalency (e.g., the median of a test given to second graders would be 2.0). Scores above and below are simply extrapolations, a statistical construct. Grade-level equivalency does not really suggest that a second-grader who scores 3.9 on a reading test is reading as well as a child completing third grade, because third-graders do not take tests constructed for second graders and vice versa. Grade-level equivalency scores are so imprecise that a raw score of only two points difference can result in a reported grade-level difference of two grades (and yet the stanine remains the same). In essence, derived scores cannot be understood without understanding the test as a whole, the types of items, and the norms to which the score refers.

Sampling Children's Progress for Program Evaluation

Bredekamp and Shepard point out that programs have been evaluated at the expense of children. Although early childhood programs need to be evaluated, they make these recommendations:

1. Do not use standardized achievement testing of all children before third grade.
2. Choose children for testing using sampling techniques. For program evaluation, sampling avoids labeling of children and is cost-effective.
3. Develop means other than children's test performance for program evaluation such as systematic observations.[20]

Showing Sensitivity to Those Involved

For children, testing may be stressful. Testing itself is always a problem with young children, because young children do not have a repertoire of test-taking skills. Some of the problems these children have are inadequate motor skills for taking paper and pencil tests, short attention spans, problems in following directions, and the problem of being influenced by the tester and/or the physical setting. Staff members need to be aware of children's feelings.

Parents are also under a great deal of stress when their children are being tested. Many parents are apprehensive of decisions based on testing and on labels which may be placed on their children if "inadequacies" are noted. Commercial publishers are "feeding" on parent anxieties by selling kits on test-taking skills for pre-kindergarten, kindergarten, and first graders.[21] Some states are also offering "CAT Academies" for these young children.

Staff members may also be under stress. Testing drains learning time and funds. In some schools, children's achievement test scores are used as the predominant indicator of a teacher's and/or a program's accountability. Unfortunately, this situation has led to teachers' basing their curriculum on certain tests and, in some instances, teaching the test items themselves, helping children with the answers during the testing session, and even tampering with recorded responses. These pressures should be removed immediately.

Position Statements on Standardized Testing

Because of these concerns in assessment practices, two professional associations have issued strong statements about standardized testing of young children.[22,23] The goal is not to prohibit all standardized testing. The goal is for early childhood administrators to recognize that:

1. Assessment instruments should be used only for their intended purposes.
2. The assessment instruments should meet acceptable levels of quality (e.g., validity and reliability).
3. Placement/retention decisions should be made from multiple sources of data.
4. Assessment instruments should be used only if children will benefit, and benefit does not come from reduced group variation. (Schools must be more adaptive to normal variance.)

Informal Methods

For purposes of this book, **informal methods** of assessing children's progress include all methods of assessment except standardized tests. Because the definition is broad, these informal methods may range from general observation of children while they engage in activities to staff-constructed tests designed to measure specific knowledge and skills. In early childhood programs, informal assessment is preferred over the use of standardized tests.

Observations

Undoubtedly, observation is the most frequently used informal method of assessing young children's progress. Observations are also the most rewarding method of assessing children's growth and development. The National Association for the Education of Young Children calls for more systematic observations of student performance.[24]

The observer must be unobtrusive. There should be no observer interactions with or reactions to children's activities. Observers must never discuss their observations casually if the children can be identified or professionally if any child or any adult (except adults involved with the child in the program) is within hearing distance. Written records must also be kept secure.

There are at least nineteen different types of observations and a number of different systems for recording and storing observations as well as analyzing the data.[25] The purposes of the observations determine the method of observation and the recording system. Three popular methods of observing young children and some of the recording possibilities used by teachers (and researchers) are described.

Naturalistic Observations. Naturalistic observations are observations of the child in the child's natural setting engaged in regular day-to-day activities. These open-ended observations allow the child options which, in turn, permit the teacher (or researcher) to see the uniqueness of the child.

Naturalistic observations may be recorded as an anecdotal record or a running record. An **anecdotal record** is a record of an incident in a child's life during participation in program activities or made during a home visit. Characteristics of a good anecdote are:

1. It gives the date, the place, and the situation in which the action occurred. We call this the **setting**.
2. It describes the actions of the child, the reactions of other people involved, and the responses of the child to these reactions.
3. It quotes what is said to the child and by the child during the action.
4. It supplies "mood cues"—postures, gestures, voice qualities, and facial expressions that give cues to how the child felt. It does not provide interpretations of his feelings, but only the cues by which a reader may judge what they were.
5. The description is extensive enough to cover the episode. The action or conversation is not left incomplete and unfinished but is followed through to the point where a little vignette of a behavioral moment in the life of the child is supplied.[26]

Below the narrative account there should be space for comments. These comments may be interpretive (i.e., what the observer believes about the incident) and evaluative (i.e., what the observer believes should be done to help the child developmentally). See example in Figure 10–1 on page 324.

A **running record** is similar to an anecdotal record except that it is more detailed with a total sequence of events. See example in Figure 10–2 on page 325.

A **specimen-description** is a method in which the observer records all the events within a given situation. One records the entire "stream of behavior" which is so complete it can be dramatized. Because one cannot observe/record this very complete running record and teach at the same time, specimen-descriptions are usually written by researchers.

Child's name ___*Susie*___   Date ___*2/12/92*___

Setting: _Block center in a day-care center; activity child-chosen._

Incident: _Susie was building a block tower. When the 7-block tower fell, she tried again. This time she only succeeded in getting 6 blocks stacked before they fell. She kicked her blocks and walked over to John's 9-block tower and knocked it over. When the teacher approached, she cried and refused help with the tower. (John left the center after his tower was knocked over.)_

Comments: _Susie is showing more patience by rebuilding–a patience not seen last month. However, her crying and destructive responses are not as mature as they should be for a 5-year-old. She must be shown ways to cope with these common frustrations._

FIGURE 10–1
Anecdotal Record of Behavior

Structured Observations. Structured observations are structured in terms of bringing children into contrived environments (e.g., how infants react when a stranger is present, while the mother is present, or while the mother is absent) or identifying a specific, defined behavior, observing it in the natural environment, and keeping quantitative records (e.g., Sarah had two biting episodes on Monday and one biting episode on Tuesday).

Two structured types of observations are **event-sampling** and **time-sampling.** In event sampling a behavior is preselected (called a **target behavior**), defined very specifically, and then observed. In order to record, the observer usually knows when to expect the behavior (e.g., time of day, during a certain activity, in a certain grouping pattern, and/or with a given adult). In event sampling, the observer is trying to confirm a hypothesis about what triggers the behavior. Thus, three items are recorded: (1) the antecedent behavior (i.e., what led to the target behavior); (2) the targeted behavior (i.e., complete description of the incident); and (3) the consequent event (i.e., reactions of child such as crying). See example in Figure 10–3 on page 326.

In time-sampling, a target behavior is pre-selected, carefully defined, and then observed at specified intervals. For discrete behaviors a simple frequency tabulation is recorded. See example in Figure 10–4 on page 326.

Because the amount of writing is reduced, the observer can record observations on several children in one session by rotating observations in a predetermined and consistent manner among the children. Using the time periods in the above example, Child A would be observed during the first minute of each time frame—9:00–9:01, 9:05–9:06, et cetera; Child B would be observed during

Child's name ___*Susie*___   Date ___*2/12/92*___

Setting: *Block center in a day-care center; activity child-chosen.*

	Incident	**Comments**
9:25	*Susie watches three or four children play with the blocks.*	*Susie is interested in the blocks.*
9:30	*She calls to John, "What are you doing?" John replies, "I'm building a tall, tall building, the biggest one ever." Susie says, "I can build a big one."*	*She especially likes John's tower.* *Susie is apparently challenged.*
9:31	*Susie stacks 7 blocks. They fall. (She counts the blocks in John's tower.) She again starts stacking blocks—with the sixth block, they fall.*	*Susie knows she almost got the same height tower again.* *Susie is willing to try again.*
9:35	*She kicks at her blocks three times and then walks over to John's tower and strikes it with her hand.*	*Her aggression spreads to John.*
9:37	*Mrs. Jones approaches Susie. Susie turns her back on Mrs. Jones and cries. Mrs. Jones kneels down and talks to Susie. Then Mrs. Jones picks up a block, but Susie runs away. (John left the center earlier.)*	*She is not yet willing to be comforted or helped.* *Teacher's approach was calming—no more aggression.*

FIGURE 10–2
Running Record of Behavior

the second minute of each time frame—9:01–9:02, 9:06–9:07, et cetera; and in a similar way three other children would be observed.

For nondiscrete behaviors (e.g., crying, clinging to adult, and wandering around the room) the length of occurrence or duration is often recorded. See example in Figure 10–5 on page 327.

Both frequency and duration recordings may be summarized in graphs which give visual representations. Even two complementary behaviors may be plotted on the same graph for a better picture of a child (e.g., daily totals of aggressive and sharing acts).

Child's name ___Mike___   Date ___2/1/92___

Behavior: _Biting a child on exposed skin areas_

Time	Antecedent	Behavior	Consequent Event
8:00	Children eating breakfast as they arrive. Ann has finished breakfast but takes a piece of apple off of Mike's plate.	Mike tries to get it back. When un-successful, bites Ann's hand.	Ann cries, and Mike calls out, "I didn't bite."

NOTE: Other behaviors are recorded as they occur.

FIGURE 10–3
Event-Sampling Behavior Record

　　　Both naturalistic and structured observations are profitable with young children for two reasons: (1) observations are appropriate for young children who have a limited test-taking repertoire; and (2) observations of children are more accurate with younger than with older children, because young children are incapable of hiding feelings. Other reasons for the popularity of observation may be these factors: an individual can simultaneously work and observe children (unfortunately, many look and do not see!); observations may be conducted by skilled and unskilled observers; they may be conducted for long or short

Child's name _____   Date _____

Time 1	Time 2	Time 3	Time 4	Time 5
9:00	9:05	9:10	9:15	9:20
V+	V+	NV–	V–	0

V   =   verbal interaction
NV =   non-verbal interaction
0   =   no interaction
+   =   positive
–   =   negative

FIGURE 10–4
Time-Sampling Behavior Record

Child's name _____ Date _____

Behavior: *Wandering from center to center. (Child stays less than 2 minutes at an activity in one "stretch.")*

Days	Time	Total
1	*9:04–9:08*	*4*
	9:12–9:20	*8*
2		
3		
4		

Average: 21.5 minutes per day

FIGURE 10–5
Duration Record of Behavior

intervals of time; observations may be used in conjunction with any other assessment methods—both informal methods and standardized tests; and observation is suitable for use in any type of program, because one child or a group of children may be observed, and any aspect of development can be assessed. Disadvantages in using observations for assessment are that the validity of observation depends on the skill of the observer; the observer's biases are inherent in the observation; the soundness of the observation may depend upon the behavior observed, because some aspects of development, such as motor skills, are easier to observe than others, such as thinking processes; when an individual is simultaneously working with children and observing them, it can be difficult to "see the forest for the trees"; and one-way mirrors used in observation rooms and hidden audio- or videotapes may not be ethical.

Interviews
Because of the emphasis on parental involvement, **interviews with parents** are now used with greater frequency in early childhood programs. The interview method permits a more comprehensive picture of the child's life at home and with peer groups. The interview method of assessment generally has these characteristics:

1. Questions used in an interview are usually developed by staff members, although interviews are available in publications such as the *Vineland Adaptive Behavior Scales—Classroom Edition.* (See Appendix 8.)
2. Parents of the child are usually interviewed; others familiar with the child are occasionally interviewed.
3. Specific questions in the interview commonly include background information about the child: birth history; self-reliance; development, especially affective development and motor skills; previous experiences

that aid concept development, such as places the child has visited in the community, trips he has taken, and previous group experiences; problems, such as disabilities and illnesses, fears, and accident proneness; and interests, such as television shows, books, toys, pets, and games. Occasionally, questions are asked about the family situation, family relationships, and parental attitudes, and may encompass family income, housing, occupations, educational level, aspirations for their children, and views of child rearing. Answers to these questions help in assessing needs and potential program services.

Interviews with children may be structured as in the **psychometric method**, or semistructured, as in the **exploratory method.** In the *psychometric method,* the examiner must follow a standard set of procedures specified in a manual without any deviation. On the other hand, with the *exploratory method,* the examiner tests her hypothesis by following the child's train of thought in a conversational way (i.e., the examiner tries to understand and make herself understood by the child).[27]

Advantages of the interview as an assessment technique are that valuable information—both verbal and emotional—may be gleaned; interviews can be used in conjunction with other informal assessment methods and with standardized tests; they are suitable for use in any type of early childhood program; and interviews can help clarify and extend information found on written forms. The interview method also has disadvantages: the information obtained may not be comprehensive or accurate because the questions were unclear or not comprehensive and/or because the interviewee was unable or unwilling to answer; the interviewee's and interviewer's biases are entwined in the information given and in the interpretation of the information, respectively; and the interview method is very time consuming.

Samples of Children's Work

Samples of children's work serve as an excellent informal method of assessment if they meet the following criteria:

1. Samples of various types of children's work should be collected: dictated or tape-recorded experiences told by children; drawings, paintings, and other two-dimensional art projects; photographs of children's projects (for example, three-dimensional art projects, block constructions, or a completed science experiment); tape recordings of singing or language activities; videotapes of any action activities; and samples of writing or math worksheets if this type of formal activity is conducted in the program.
2. Samples are collected on a systematic and periodic basis.
3. Samples are dated with notes on the children's comments and attitudes.

Advantages to using samples of children's work as an assessment technique are that the evidence is a collection of children's real, ongoing activities or products of activities, and not a contrived experience for purposes of assessment; collecting samples is not highly time-consuming; collecting samples works for all aspects of all programs; samples can be used as direct evidence of progress; if samples are dated and adequate notes taken about them, interpretations can be made later by various people; some samples can be analyzed for feelings as well as concepts; and samples can be used in conjunction with other informal methods of assessment and with standardized tests. Disadvantages are that samples may not be representative of the children's work; samples of ongoing activities are more difficult to obtain than two-dimensional art work; some children do not like to part with their work; storage can be a problem; photographs, magnetic tapes, and videotapes are expensive; and staff members often try to read too much into the samples.

Staff-Constructed Tests

Many **staff-constructed tests** are administered to children in early childhood programs; however, most of these tests are not the conventional paper-and-pencil variety that are administered to all children at the same time. Characteristics of staff-constructed tests are

1. Most tests are administered to individual children, although a few tests are given to small groups or to the entire class at one time.
2. Administration of the tests is usually conducted by observing the skills and concepts exhibited as children engage in the program's activities, by asking questions, and by requesting demonstrations of skills and concepts. For example, a staff member might note which children can measure during a cooking experience; point to a red ball and ask, "What color is this ball?"; or request that a child skip or count beads set out on a table.
3. In most staff-constructed tests, the content of each test covers one skill, or a group of related skills, and is administered for the purpose of assisting staff members in planning activities. Some staff-constructed tests are inventories of many skills and concepts, with the information used for referral, placement, or retention.
4. Scoring of staff-constructed tests usually consists of checking the skills and concepts each child has mastered, or by rating the level of mastery achieved.

The advantages of staff-constructed tests are that if the tests are carefully constructed, there will be a match between test items and program goals, and between test items and developmental levels; they are more adaptable to the program's time schedule than are standardized tests; they lend themselves to many types of responses, such as gross-motor, manipulative, and verbal; they can be used in conjunction with other assessment methods and tests; and they are inexpensive and do not require the services of a psychometrist for administering, scoring, and interpreting. Some disadvantages of staff-constructed tests are that the match between the program goals and test items depends on the skill of the staff members; developing adequate test items is highly time consuming; and, with the exception of a few locally normed tests, no normative data are available. The use of computers now helps to overcome some of these problems. Microcomputers can be used to make and print tests, to generate all or part of a test used before, to change the format of a test, to score test responses, and to analyze responses.

Standardized Testing

Standardized tests are formal methods of assessing children's progress and have these characteristics:

1. Specific directions for administering the test are stated in detail, usually including even the exact words to be used by the examiner in giving instructions, and specifying exact time limits. By following the directions, teachers and counselors in many schools can administer the test in essentially the same way.
2. Specific directions are provided for scoring. Usually a scoring key is supplied that reduces scoring to merely comparing answers with the key; little or nothing is left to the judgment of the scorer. Sometimes carefully selected samples are provided with which a student's product is to be compared.
3. Norms are supplied to aid in interpreting scores.
4. Information needed for judging the value of the test is provided. Before the test becomes available for purchase, research is conducted to study its reliability and validity.
5. A manual that explains the purposes and uses of the test is supplied. It describes briefly how the test was constructed, provides specific directions for administering, scoring and interpreting results, contains tables of norms, and summarizes available research data on the test.

There are some advantages in using standardized tests. The tests are developed by people familiar with test construction, and before marketing, research is conducted to study test reliability and validity; specific instructions are given for administering and scoring; the manuals contain quick methods for converting raw scores into normative data; the examiner can compare a child's most recent performance with an earlier one; one can compare the performance of children in the local program against that of other children of similar ages and backgrounds; scores provided by good standardized tests are usually reliable and stable although the younger the child, the more unstable the score; some tests provide diagnostic information; test manuals usually summarize available research data on the test; and the tests may be used with any other form of assessment. We have discussed many of the concerns about standardized testing and the positions taken by the professional associations. These concerns are the major disadvantages in using standardized tests. There are other disadvantages, too. Most standardized tests now available do not encompass far-ranging behaviors in all areas of development, particularly affective development. The services of a psychometrist may be required for administering the test and interpreting results, particularly some of the individual aptitude and personal-social adjustment tests.

There has been a staggering proliferation of new assessment instruments, most of which are conventional. Several trends in standardized testing may be considered innovative:

1. Because of the emphasis on identifying disabilities at an early age, there are more screening procedures used at entry level (e.g., pre-kindergarten). Some screening devices are developed by the local school district while others are standardized procedures. Standardized screening tests usually look at such areas as: (a) visual-motor/adaptive (e.g., fine motor control, remembering visual sequences, and drawing two-dimensional forms and reproducing three-dimensional forms); (b) language and communication (e.g., language comprehension, verbal expression, and ability to reason and repeat auditory sequences); and (c) gross-motor/body awareness (e.g., balance tasks and imitation of body positions from visual clues).[28]

2. With growth of infant programs, there has been a corresponding development of assessment instruments for measuring cognitive and sensory-motor development in infants.

3. Because of increased emphasis on the desirability of culturally fair tests, more tests are available for measuring individual differences along cultural-linguistic dimensions.

4. More assessment instruments are available for evaluating children's language.

5. There has been an obvious gap in assessment instruments for measuring the affective domain; however, more instruments are now available.

The specific standardized tests described in Appendix 8 are not evaluated, because the values of a test depend on the objectives of the local program, the children involved, and the use made of the test. However, those persons proposing to use a test should carefully evaluate its appropriateness for local use. Questions to consider before using a standardized test include:

1. For what purpose do we need to administer this test? Will it help us meet the objectives of our program? Is the test required by the funding agency? Is the test to be given for research purposes?

2. How will the test data be used?

3. Is the rationale of the test appropriate to the objectives of our program?

4. What is the degree to which this test measures our objectives accurately and reliably?

5. Is the response form required by the test (paper-and-pencil, verbal, manipulative, or gross-motor performance) familiar to the children?

6. Is the printed matter in the test of good quality?

7. Is the norming population similar to the children in our program?

8. Will the children be penalized because of their cultural orientation?

9. Which children need the test?
10. Does the test have diagnostic cues, such as subscale scores or other pattern data?
11. Is the information as to mental age or grade equivalent yielded by the test appropriate for our purposes?
12. Is the test an individual or group test? Will additional staff be needed when the tests are administered?
13. Who can administer the test? Will an expert be needed to interpret the scores?
14. Are the directions clear and sufficient for administering and scoring the test?
15. What is the length of the test and is it appropriate for the children? What schedule will be followed on testing days?
16. What facilities are needed for administering the test? Using the present facilities, how will this be arranged?
17. Will there be any foreseeable negative attitudes on the part of the children, staff, or parents as a result of administering this test? If so, how will these be handled?
18. What is the cost of the test?
19. Are there other services, such as scoring or training, provided with the test?
20. Are there other tests on the market similar in rationale to this test? If so, how do they compare to this one on all of the above points?

Because young children may find a standardized test situation strange, staff members may find testing somewhat difficult. Although specific directions for administration are given with each test, the following suggestions may help alleviate children's uneasiness: (1) make the testing area attractive and comfortable; (2) keep materials not in immediate use out of sight; (3) be completely familiar with the test; (4) develop a rapport with the child before testing; (5) encourage the child throughout the testing situation; and (6) make sure the child's responses reflect his full cooperation, because valid test results can only be obtained when the child actively engages in the tasks.

Scores on standardized tests and the normative data supplied to aid in interpreting the scores are given in technical terms used in educational and psychological measurement. The following terms are frequently used in reporting or interpreting scores on standardized tests for young children:

1. **Age equivalent.** The age equivalent score is expressed as a year and month of chronological age; for example, 5.11 is five years, eleven months. The age equivalent for a raw score represents the year and month of chronological age for which that raw score is the median for the norming group for the same year and month. Some of the age equivalents reported on various tests are language, psycholinguistic, attainment, and social.

2. **Anticipated achievement.** Anticipated achievement is a predicted score on an achievement test. When the predicted score is compared with the child's actual score, children who are falling significantly below levels of achievement attained by students with similar sex, age, and grade characteristics can be identified.

3. **Battery.** A battery consists of several tests standardized on the same population so that the results of the group of tests are comparable. The most common kinds of batteries are those of school achievement.

4. **Bias.** Bias is a systematic difference in the way a test functions for different groups (e.g., gender and majority/minority groups).

5. **Ceiling.** A ceiling is the upper limit of ability that can be measured by a test. A test is said to have too low a ceiling for a person who scores at or near the highest possible score.

6. **Composite score.** A composite score is a score derived from several subscores; a total of subscores.

7. **Criterion-referenced measure.** A criterion-referenced measure is one in which an individual's behavior is interpreted by comparing it to a pre-selected or established standard or criterion of performance. Because minimum absolute standards of competence have been established, the performance of others is irrelevant. Scores are translated into statements of behavior typical of people with that score. The test should be relevant to children from different backgrounds and abilities who are represented in the local program.

8. **Culture-fair test.** A culture-fair test is constructed with an attempt to provide equal opportunity for success by persons from various cultures. Some test designers use the term *culture-free test*, which would seem to be a misnomer, because culture is involved in all experiences.

9. **Diagnostic profile.** This is a graphic representation of the child's performance on test items or categories of test items. The profile permits easy identification of areas of strength and weakness.

10. **Class record sheet.** The class record sheet provides an analysis of an individual's performance and a description of the group's performance.

11. **Equivalent forms.** Equivalent forms of a test will yield similar means and measures of variability for a given group due to similar content and the number and difficulty of items on the various forms.

12. **Extrapolation.** Extrapolation is estimating values beyond those actually obtained (e.g., extrapolated values are usually given for extremes in a scoring range).

13. **Grade equivalent.** The grade equivalent score is expressed as a year and month of school; for example, 2.3 is second grade, third month. The grade equivalent for a raw score represents the year and month of school for which that raw score is the median for the norming group for the same year and month. Because a grade equivalent is based solely on the number of items answered correctly, it does not mean the child has mastered all concepts taught in his school up to the year and

month indicated by the grade equivalent. Language and reading tests are likely to have a wider range of scores than mathematics tests.

14. **Grade level indicator.** The grade level indicator is read or interpreted in much the same way as the grade equivalent. To determine grade equivalents, the publishers make interpolations (that is, set grade equivalents for the months that fall between the times the test was actually given) and extrapolations (that is, inferences of grade equivalents above and below the grades in which the test was given). The grade level indicator is based on more empirical evidence, as opposed to statistical charting, because students used in norming actually take the tests on a range of levels, and the tests are normed several times per year.

15. **Group test.** A group test is administered to several individuals at one time by one examiner.

16. **Growth scale value.** Growth scale value is an equal interval standard score on a scale that provides continuous measurement of student performance over successive grade levels. Growth scale values are often plotted on a chart.

17. **Individual test.** An individual test can be administered to only one individual at a time.

18. **Intelligence quotient.** The intelligence quotient, referred to as IQ, is a measure that takes into account the raw score on the intelligence test and the child's chronological age. Specifically:
    a. The **ratio intelligence quotient** is the ratio of an individual's mental age (MA) to his chronological age (CA), or the ratio of an individual's mental age to the mental age normal for chronological age. In both cases, the ratio is multiplied by 100 to eliminate the decimal.
    b. The **deviation intelligence quotient** is a measure of mental capacity based on the difference (i.e., deviation) between an individual's score and the score that is normal for that individual's chronological age.
    c. The **verbal, performance,** or **full-scale intelligence quotients** measure an individual's mental capacity on language, nonlanguage, or all test items, respectively.

19. **Intelligence quotient equivalent.** The intelligence quotient equivalent is an expression of a comparable score on other intelligence tests.

20. **Interpolated norms.** Interpolated norms are values that result from the process of estimating a value that falls between two known or computed values so that the norms table will cover the range. (For example, interpolated percentiles are sometimes available for each quarter month of the school year and are calculated from the fall and spring standardized periods.)

21. **Inventory.** An inventory is a questionnaire or checklist, usually in the form of a self-report. Inventories are usually concerned with interests, attitudes, and personality traits rather than mental abilities.

22. **Key.** The key is the correct answers to a test and is used to score the test.
23. **Local norms.** Local norms are test norms that are based on groups tested locally (e.g., a school district).
24. **Mental age.** Mental age (MA) is the performance on an intelligence scale which is typical of a given chronological age group.
25. **Normal Curve Equivalent (NCE).** NCE is a score based on an equal increment standard of measurement, on a scale from 1 to 99, with a mean of 50, and a standard deviation of 21.06.
26. **Normal distribution.** Normal distribution is a symmetrical distribution of scores that forms a bell-shaped curve. Each half of the distribution (curve) is a mirror image of the other half.
27. **Norming sample.** Norming sample is a representative sample drawn from the total population with which the test is intended to be used. (Also called **reference group**.)
28. **Norm-referenced measure.** A norm-referenced measure is one in which an individual's behavior is interpreted against the behavior of others (hopefully, but not always of similar background) on the same testing instrument. This type of measure is designed to spread people out along some dimension of behavior.
29. **Norms.** Norms are statistics that describe the average performance on a specified test for a particular age, socioeconomic level, geographic area, grade, or sex group.
30. **Percentile.** A percentile is a value on a scale of 100 that indicates the percent of a distribution that is equal to or below it. (A percentile score of 25 is a score equal to or better than 25 percent of the scores.)
31. **Percentile rank.** A percentile rank is the percentage of scores in a distribution equal to or lower than the score gained. Thus, a child's percentile rank may be explained as the percentage of children in the norm group who scored equal to or lower than he scored. A scale of percentile ranks is not a scale of equal measuring units; in terms of raw score units, a given percentile difference is greater near the extremes of the distribution than it is near the middle.
32. **Performance test.** A performance test involves motor or manual responses as opposed to paper-and-pencil tasks.
33. **Profile.** A profile is a graphic representation of results expressed in comparable terms (i.e., results of each test reported as percentiles, etc.) for an individual on a group of tests or on a group of individuals (e.g., class profile).
34. **Projective technique.** A projective technique is a method used in many personality measures in which a person responds to ambiguous stimuli (e.g., ink blots, words).
35. **Raw score.** A raw score is a quantitative but uninterpreted, unconverted result obtained in scoring a test. It usually represents the number of items on the test answered correctly.

36. **Scaled scores.** Scaled scores are any derived scores.
37. **Standard score.** A standard score is usually used as a general term denoting several varieties of converted scores. Examples of converted scores include percentile rank, age and grade equivalents, and so forth.
38. **Stanine.** A stanine is a standard score from a scale of nine units (STAndard score—NINE units; hence STANINE). The mean stanine of the norming population is 5.0 and the standard deviation is 2.0. The scale ranges from 1.0 through 9.0 with 1.0 as the lowest level and 9.0 as the highest level. The units are equal, with each representing approximately one half a standard deviation.

The following delimitations should be noted in reading the descriptions of the standardized tests described in Appendix 8:

1. These tests represent only some of the many available standardized tests; consequently, staff members of an early childhood program will want to review the latest edition of the *Mental Measurements Yearbook*, edited by Oscar K. Buros, for a more comprehensive listing. However, examples of both typical and atypical types of items included in standardized tests for young children may be readily discerned by reading test descriptions in Appendix 8.
2. No attempt is made to evaluate or compare the tests. There are critical reviews available in such sources as the latest edition of the *Mental Measurements Yearbook*.
3. The tests described are classified on the basis of content. The test classifications are *(a)* aptitude, *(b)* achievement and diagnostic, and *(c)* personal social adjustment. However, not all tests fit into one of these categories; there are other bases for classifying tests.

Aptitude Tests

An individual's aptitudes (capacities for learning) are the result of innate abilities and environmental learning—both direct experiences and social transmissions. **Aptitude tests** are designed to evaluate an individual's ability to progress in cognitive activities; they may measure an aggregation of abilities or one or more discrete abilities. Items on aptitude tests are "(1) *equally unfamiliar* to all examinees (that is, novel situations) or (2) *equally familiar* (in the sense that all students have had equal opportunity to learn, regardless of their pattern of specific courses)."[29] There are aptitude tests of (1) general mental ability, (2) special aptitudes (for example, motor performance or articulation), and (3) screening tests. Appendix 8 describes some standardized tests for use with young children.

Achievement and Diagnostic Tests

Achievement tests measure the extent to which an individual has mastered certain information or skills as a result of specific instruction or training. Readiness tests focus on current skill acquisition. Diagnostic components of achievement tests pinpoint specific areas of weakness based on item analysis of achievement tests. Achievement and diagnostic tests are given most frequently in the areas of reading, language, and mathematics. Appendix 8 describes some standardized tests for assessing young children's achievements and specific weaknesses.

Personal-Social Adjustment Tests

Personal-social adjustment tests are, in reality, tests of good mental health. Generally, an individual is considered to have good mental health if his behavior is typical of his own age and cultural group. Appendix 8 describes some standardized tests for assessing the personal-social adjustment of young children.

Documentation

Documentation is an approach to assessment that builds on observational records, samples of children's work, and any other form of assessment that is valid in terms of child development and hence program practices. Documentation is based on the premise that such information is more interpretable than the results of formal tests. The ideas underlying documentation are old, but there is a growing knowledge base supporting this approach to assessment.

Procedures for data collection are adapted from the research literature and from teachers' practices. Recordings are collected over time. Both primary and support staff must aid in data collection and review.

Early childhood staff members must have in-service training on assessment in order to address the various questions on assessment and provide for the necessary continuity. More information on documentation may be received through the Educational Testing Service.[30]

RECORDING

Record keeping, the developmental record of a child or a group of children, has always been an important aspect of a staff member's duties; today, record keeping is becoming even more important and prevalent. Most early childhood programs have a philosophy of providing for children's individual differences, and record keeping allows the program to assess and improve the services it provides. There is also greater involvement with parents and increasing mobility of both children and staff members. In addition, funding agencies, citizens' groups, boards of directors or school boards, and parents often require "proof" of the early childhood program's effectiveness in meeting its stated objective so the evidence is often best demonstrated by the records that have been kept. There are possible disadvantages to record keeping:

1. A staff member can spend more time keeping records than in planning and working with children.
2. A staff member can make a prejudgment based on records and become positively or negatively biased towards a child.

3. Records may cause staff members to mentally picture a particular chronological age group homogeneously. For example, a staff member may notice that his records indicate that most five year olds can count by rote to ten and thus assume that all five year olds can do so.
4. Parents can challenge inaccurate, inappropriate, misleading, and irrelevant information and unsubstantiated opinions (see section on P.L. 93–380, p. 344–345).
5. Record keeping may become a meaningless activity because the types of data required to be kept may not be congruent with the objectives of the local program or because records may be filed and forgotten or may not be used effectively.

Computers are helping overcome some of these problems. For example, microcomputers can store information, maintain and generate files, and ensure privacy of records (by coding the computer so that only specified people have access to certain parts of a student's file). Producers of software have noted teachers' needs for quick and accurate record keeping.

Uses of Records

There are many effective uses for records. They are especially valuable to staff members as guides for planning the types of experiences each child needs. By studying a child's records, a staff member can find evidence of strengths and weaknesses, and can better judge when to push, when to step aside, when to go back, or even when to look further. Developmental records of a child's progress are like medical records that contain information about what has been done in the way of examinations and treatment and form the basis for further diagnosis and prescription. Again, records should not be used as instruments for typecasting children; rather, they should help staff members formulate a realistic but open-ended picture of a child. Good records also permit independent evaluation of a child by more than one individual. Codes used in recording should be meaningful to others.

The process of recording data causes staff members to think about each child more profoundly. Staff members are forced to consider each child, not just categories like "children with problems," "extra-bright children," or "creative children." Their records thus make the work of specialists (guidance counselors, physicians, or caseworkers) more efficient by helping them determine whether a problem is transient or continuous, in knowing when a problem began, in ascertaining how pervasive its effects are in the child's development, and in suggesting possible solutions to the problem.

Records can help staff members see each child's progress; because staff members work daily with a child, they may not be able to see progress except through a review of the records. The child can also see his progress in records—especially in collected samples of his work. Samples should be dated so that sequences and patterns are revealed.

Records can also be used as a basis for discussion with parents and can become a defense in dealing with a dissatisfied parent. In working with parents, it is the staff member's use of records that determines their value.

Records can be invaluable in home-school contacts if the school personnel know how to use its records wisely and constructively in dealing with parents. No school device is more effective when wisely used, but no material is more likely to antagonize parents if wrongly used. On the whole, no school record should just be handed to parents for them to look over. Selected parts of records should be shown to parents by a member of the school staff who is competent to interpret this material constructively.[31]

Recent legislation, permitting parents to view the records of their children, should make staff members more aware of their responsibilities in determining the nature of records to be kept. (A more comprehensive discussion of P.L. 93–380 appears later in this chapter.)

Records are beneficial to children who change programs frequently. Records of a recently transferred child make it easier for staff members to assist the child in the new situation. The local program's regulatory agency requires various records. These records of children's progress toward a program's stated goals may determine whether subsequent funding will be forthcoming. Other uses for records are referral conferences, to help teachers see results of new teaching techniques or services, and as data for research.

Types of Records

The information contained on records may be classified (1) on an objective-subjective information continuum; (2) on the basis of written information about children or samples of children's work; (3) according to the individual who provided the information (child, parent, staff member, physician, or psychometrist); (4) according to the contents of the record (whether social behavior, medical information, or cognitive achievement); or (5) in keeping with the purposes of the records, such as grouping, placement, referral, reporting to parents, or information for a regulatory agency. The types of records—background information, observational, achievement, guidance and placement, referral, and cumulative—are used in a variety of situations.

Background Information Records

Boards of directors or local school boards and staff members are realizing that home background, early experiences in the home and neighborhood, and language experiences all affect what a child can accomplish in an early childhood program. Many programs now ask for considerable information from parents. Sometimes these records are supplemented by additional information obtained by a caseworker or are volunteered at a later date by the parents or the child.

Basic information about the child and her family is always part of background information records, including the child's legal name, home address, and telephone number; birth date, birthplace, and birth certificate number; number of siblings; marital status of parents, and whether both parents are living; and the father's and mother's or guardian's legal names, home address and telephone number, occupation, place of business, and business telephone number.

Medical information is also included in the background information records, and completion of medical information records is required before a child is admitted to a program. (See the section entitled "Forms" in the Parents' Handbook found in Appendix 9 on pages 565–571.) Usually, parents complete a health history form, which asks for a general evaluation of the family's health, a history of the child's illnesses (especially communicable diseases); frequent illnesses or complaints, such as colds, headaches, or sties; and any physical or personal-social disabilities that might affect the child's participation in the program. Medical professionals must complete records of recent physical and dental examinations and immunization records. These records may call for comments on any significant medical findings concerning eyes, ears, nose, throat, glands, heart, circulation, lungs, bones, joints, reflexes, and so forth; a statement as to whether the child can participate in the regular program or needs an adjusted program; the condition of teeth and gums; and dates of immunizations.

Finally, records on the child's personal-social history are frequently included as part of the background information records. This information may be supplied by a parent or by another adult who knows the child. Parents may record the information on forms, or a staff member may record the information during an interview. The child's personal-social history is likely to include information about self-reliance, development, previous experiences, problems, interests, and family situation, relationships, and attitudes toward child rearing. The records may also ask parents to report guidance methods they have found effective.

Observational Records
Observational records include anecdotal records, running records, specimen-description records, event-sampling records, and time-sampling records. These records were discussed under informal methods, because they are often not used as an entity but rather as professional notes in documentation assessment and recording. However, any of these records may be used as an entity, and observational records can also include check sheets, rating scales, and semantic differential scales (all of which is discussed in the next section).

Achievement Records
These are invaluable for planning activities to assist the child in development. **Achievement records** include facts, general understanding and skills the child has developed, a prognosis of readiness for the next stage of development, and an indication of how the child compares with others in various areas of devel-

Sept. 27. Tim and two other boys (David and Tom) were in the sand box using dump trucks for hauling sand. David remarked that his lot needed more sand than the lot to which they had just delivered one dump-truck load. Tim looked and asked, "How much more sand?" "Twice as much," replied David. "Then I'll drive my truck up once and give them a load and come back for one more load of sand," Tim commented.

FIGURE 10–6
Anecdotal Achievement Record

opment (a comparison of the child's score with available normative data). Achievement records can take several forms:

1. They may be written as anecdotes. See example in Figure 10–6.
2. Achievement may be recorded on check sheets. See example in Figure 10–7.
3. Rating scales may be used. See example in Figure 10–8 on page 342.

_____
(Child's name)

Art Concepts

Can recognize these colors: red   _____

yellow   _____

blue   _____

green   _____

orange   _____

purple   _____

black   _____

brown   _____

Can arrange four varying grades
of sandpaper from rough to smooth.   _____

Can name the colors and point
to rough and smooth fruit in a
reproduction of Cezanne's painting
Apples and Oranges.   _____

FIGURE 10–7
Check Sheet Achievement Record

```
_____
         (Child's name)

1. Can put on his outdoor clothes.


                                    _____
                                    Not          Sometimes      Always
                                    Yet
```

FIGURE 10–8
Rating Scales for Achievement

4. Semantic differential scales, which are similar to rating scales, may be used. See example in Figure 10–9.
5. Collected samples of children's work may be used. These records are more valuable if they are dated and contain comments regarding the situations under which the samples were collected.
6. Achievement records may consist of the raw or converted scores of staff-constructed or standardized tests. The scores may be recorded in a class record or grade book, a cumulative record form, an individual profile sheet, or a diagnostic profile sheet.
7. Achievement records may be in the form of a list. For example, a staff member may list songs a child can sing or nursery rhymes he can recite.

Guidance and Placement Records

Guidance and placement records per se have not generally been used in pre-kindergarten and kindergarten programs. These records are more frequently used in early childhood programs that enroll school-age children (sometimes including kindergarten-age children), or in programs with academic objectives. Early childhood programs serving children younger than school-age and programs that are primarily care-giving customarily group children by chronological

```
_____ can be seen as
              (Child's name)

        happy — — — — — — — — — sad

        active — — — — — — — — — passive
```

FIGURE 10–9
Semantic Differential Scales for Achievement

age. (Licensing requirements frequently specify such grouping.) Placement records are used when children with disabilities are mainstreamed.

Guidance and placement records are used for ability groupings for learning or instruction in a graded system, or for placement in an appropriate learning or instructional level in a continuous progress approach. More specifically, placement and guidance records are used for initial placement in a group, for moving a child from group to group, and for keeping track of a child's present level of work. Certain dated records should be kept for guidance and placement:

1. Scores on aptitude tests.
2. Present level of work in academic areas in which children are grouped (usually skill areas of reading, mathematics, and writing). The level of work may be indicated by specific skills mastered or by books completed in a series, such as reading readiness, preprimer, or primer, and by other materials completed, such as labs or workbooks.
3. Achievement test scores.
4. Staff members' comments about developmental characteristics and problems.

Referral Records

All early childhood programs that employ specialists for purposes of working with children who need unique assistance need **referral records**. Specialists hired as full-time staff members or as part-time consultants may include medical professionals, psychometrists, guidance counselors, speech pathologists, and remedial reading specialists. If the program does not employ specialists for support services, it will be necessary to develop a community resource directory. In some cases, a directory may be available through the local Chamber of Commerce, the United Fund, the Community Council, or the State Department of Social Services. Administrators who must compile their own file of community resources should include in each description the basic service, whether it is health, mental health, or recreation; the name of the agency, its address and phone number; the days and hours of operation; and a detailed explanation of the services it provides, the eligibility requirements, and the name of the person to contact.

Local early childhood programs should develop a separate referral form for each type of referral, for example, a form for medical referral, or a form for referral to a psychometrist or to a speech pathologist. The items on each form differ, but each type should include the signed permission for referral from parent or legal guardian; date and person or agency to which referral is being made; the name of the staff member who is referring the child; specific reasons for referral; either a digest of, or the complete reports from, other referrals; comments or attitudes of parents, peers, or the child himself if these are available; length of time the staff member has been aware of the problem; and what staff members or parents have tried and with what success. Many referral records allow space for the specialist's report after he evaluates or works with the child.

Cumulative Records/Portfolios

Cumulative records are permanent records of the child's progress in a program. The purpose of cumulative records is to get a total picture of the child.

The contents of the records should fit the program's requirements. For example, if a birth certificate is required to verify each child's age, the cumulative record form should contain a space for recording the birth certificate number. The contents of the cumulative record form should also meet the program's objectives. Some categories frequently found in the cumulative record are background information, such as personal family data; attendance records; records of assessment (aptitude, achievement, and personal-social adjustment); reports of special interests and goals; a digest of, or reference to, other records of the child's progress and adjustment; and objective specific comments of staff members. The form should be reviewed and revised periodically and should require minimal clerical work.

A more popular term for cumulative records in early childhood programs is **portfolios.** Portfolios are constructed in documentation assessment. Portfolios include such items as records of teacher observations, check sheets, samples of children's work, notes from parent-teacher conferences, major test results (if any are given), and notes from psychological evaluative sessions including referral/placement decisions.

Public Law 93–380

Children's records are now protected under The Family Educational Rights and Privacy Act of 1974, P.L. 93–380. This law provides that:

1. Parents of children who attend a school receiving federal assistance may see information in the school's official files. This information includes test scores, grade averages, class rank, intelligence quotient, health records, psychological reports, notes on behavioral problems, family background items, attendance records, and all other records except personal notes made by a staff member solely for his own use.
2. Records must be made available for review within forty-five days of the request.
3. Parents may challenge information irrelevant to education, such as religious preference, or unsubstantiated opinions.
4. Contents of records may be challenged in a hearing. If the school refuses to remove material challenged by parents as inaccurate, misleading, or inappropriate, the parent may insert a written rebuttal.
5. With some exceptions (e.g., other officials in the same school, officials in another school to which the student has applied for transfer, some accrediting associations, state educational officials, some financial aid organizations, and the courts), written consent of parents is required before school officials may release records. Schools must keep a written record as to who has seen, or requested to see, the child's records.
6. Parents have the right to know where records are kept and which school officials are responsible for them.

7. Unless a divorced parent is prohibited by law from having any contact with the child, divorced parents have equal access to official records.
8. Most of the foregoing rights pass from parent to child when the child is eighteen years of age.
9. School districts must notify parents (and the eighteen-year-olds) of their rights.

REPORTING

Reporting is becoming a more important aspect of early childhood programs, as programs seek to involve parents in their children's development and as they become more accountable to parents, citizens' groups, and funding and regulatory agencies.

As is true of all aspects of an early childhood program, reporting practices should be based on program objectives. The first step in developing a reporting practice is to determine the purposes of reporting. Once these have been determined, the second step is to clarify ambiguous objectives (that is, objectives that cannot be assessed and for which progress cannot be reported) and put program objectives into categories. The third step is to determine reporting methods—whether informal reports, individual conferences, report letters, check sheets, or report cards—that best convey information about children's progress, that are understood and accepted by those receiving the reports, and that suit staff members' abilities and time. The final step is to experiment with the reporting practices and revise them if necessary.

Purposes of Reporting

For most early childhood programs, the major purpose of reporting is to provide information to parents about their children's progress. Parents and staff jointly discuss each child's strengths and needs and plan the next steps in the educative process. In addition to parent-staff communication, there are other purposes of reporting:

1. Evaluating the evidence of each child's progress helps staff members plan experiences the child should have and sometimes shows gaps in their knowledge about a child's progress.
2. Reporting progress helps obtain support for the program from parents and citizens' groups.
3. Reporting progress, especially by group, is often required by regulatory and funding agencies.

Methods of Reporting

One trend in reporting children's progress is the great diversity of methods. Common methods include informal reports, individual conferences, report letters, check sheets, and report cards. Many programs use more than one method.

Informal Reports

Informal reports are perhaps the most common way of reporting; so common that staff members may not even be aware they are communicating information about children's progress. This kind of report may be a casual conversation with a parent in which the staff member mentions that, "Lori excels in mathematical concepts" or "Mark can't tie his shoes"; it might be a paper carried home by the child with corrections marked on it, or a star or a smiling or sad face; it might be praise or corrections of a child while a parent visits the program; or it might be reports from the child himself, such as, "I learned to skip today."

Individual Conferences

Many programs schedule **individual conferences** with each child's parents. Conferences permit face-to-face communication between parents and staff members. A staff member must plan intensively for a successful conference. First, she needs to send out a newsletter explaining the purposes of the conference and inviting parents to make an appointment during specified times; she then makes a schedule of appointments and confirms them; provides a place for the conference; secures a babysitter for enrolled and younger children; and plans a waiting area for early-arriving parents. (See "Individual Conferences" in Chapter 11.) The next task is to develop a guide sheet for reporting the child's progress. This sheet outlines points the staff member plans to cover in the conference. Although the staff member should concentrate on those items felt to be most significant, she will want to present a well-rounded picture of the child, not just problem areas. The staff person should consult all records on the child and carefully transfer to the guide sheet any information to be shared with parents. A report card or check sheet given to parents at the conference can be used as the guide sheet although some supplemental material may need to be gathered. The third step in preparing for an individual conference is to gather samples of the child's work. A collection of samples that represents all or most areas of development gives parents a more comprehensive picture of their child's progress. The final step is to duplicate reports to give to parents and to plan a method for documenting the conference.

Report Letters

Programs using **report letters** usually provide forms on which staff members write a few brief comments about a child's progress under each of several headings, such as psychomotor development, personal-social adjustment, cognitive development, language growth, work habits, problem-solving growth, aesthetic growth, self-reliance, and general evaluation. An example of a report letter form is shown in Figure 10–10. The advantages of report letters are that the staff member can concentrate on a child's specific strengths and needs without ranking by letter grade or satisfactory/unsatisfactory ratings or checking progress in highly specific areas, such as "knows his address" or "ties his shoes." The disadvantages are that they are highly time-consuming, and staff members may

Your Child's Progress
Name _____ Level _____
Psychomotor development (motor skills): George can gallop, skip, run, and throw and catch a rubber ball. He enjoys all games that use movement and his skills indicate that his attainment is high in this area of development.
Personal-social adjustment: George does not initiate many aggressive acts; however he still has trouble keeping his hands to himself. He responds to negative overtures from his classmates by hitting.
Language growth: George appears to enjoy new words. He uses rhyming words and makes up words to fit the rhymes. He has not been able to express his negative feelings toward others with words, however.
General evaluation: George is progressing nicely. More opportunities to talk to others would help him learn to express himself. He performs well in the room and on the playground as long as he is kept busy and as long as others leave him alone.

FIGURE 10–10
Progress Report Letter

develop stereotypical comments, especially after writing the first few letters. Microcomputers can be programmed to produce letters to parents.

Check Sheets

Check sheets contain lists of desired achievements. The staff member indicates that the child has developed a particular skill or shown understanding of a particular concept by a check mark—hence the name. Some programs use check sheets as the only method of reporting, but check sheets are more frequently used in conjunction with other methods of reporting. These sheets may be given to a parent during an individual conference or enclosed in the report card. Check sheets generally differ from report cards in these ways:

1. They are usually printed on sheets of paper rather than on cards.
2. Categories of items on check sheets are similar to those on report cards, but the items on check sheets tend to be more specific. An item on a report card might read as shown in Figure 10–11. The same category listed on a check sheet might look like the example in Figure 10–12.
3. Items on report cards may rate a child as to degree of accomplishment— for example, satisfactory, progressing, and needs improvement—while

	Always	Sometimes
Shows self-reliance by putting on his own outdoor clothing.		

FIGURE 10–11
Progress Report Card

check sheets indicate whether or not the child has accomplished a specific task.

Report Cards
The **report card** is more frequently used in early childhood programs that enroll kindergarten or primary children (programs that have an educational focus) than in programs that enroll pre-kindergarten age children. Because the predominant marking system on report cards presents evaluations of work habits, reading readiness, and mathematics readiness, report cards are used mainly in programs with the behaviorist perspective. Programs following an interactionist's view would not use the report card. Although there are rumors that the report card is dead, or at least dying, it in fact survives, finding its way into homes at monthly to semiannual intervals. (It is being discussed in this text because it is so common.)

Report cards usually list items such as academic subjects or activities and areas of personal-social adjustment, and have a blank space opposite each item for recording a symbol denoting progress. A key on the report card interprets the symbols, whether they are the traditional *A, B, C, D,* and *F* symbols (rarely used) or others. Other specifics frequently included are the child's attendance record, a space for comments, and a parent's signature line for each reporting period.

Because the items selected for inclusion on the report card should fit program objectives, the items vary. The following list, compiled from a nationwide

Can button clothes .... _____

Can put on overshoes .... _____

Can zip a coat .... _____

Can lace and tie shoes .... _____

FIGURE 10–12
Progress Check Sheet

sampling of kindergarten report cards, indicates the wide range of evaluated achievements:

1. General well-being (e.g., alertness and ability to rest)
2. Identity (e.g., writes name and knows address)
3. Social maturity (e.g., friendly, shares, and controls temper)
4. Eye-hand coordination (e.g., able to use art and hand tools and able to trace shapes)
5. Perception of direction (e.g., shows consistent handedness and knows right-left)
6. Work habits (e.g., has adequate attention span and follows directions)
7. Language development (e.g., speaks clearly, has adequate vocabulary, and makes up stories)
8. Reading readiness (e.g., understands sequence, shows interest in stories, and recognizes likenesses and differences both visually and aurally)
9. Mathematics (e.g., counts rationally and recognizes numerals)
10. Science (e.g., shows curiosity and classifies)
11. Music (e.g., enjoys listening and singing and participates in rhythmic activities)
12. Art (e.g., enjoys arts and crafts, recognizes colors, and handles tools correctly)
13. Health, safety, and physical education (e.g., practices good health habits, obeys safety rules, participates in physical activities, and shows good sportsmanship)

There are various styles for report cards; one style may require the staff member to check a child's achievements. An understanding or skill the child has not developed is left unchecked. This style closely resembles the check sheet and is shown in Figure 10–13.

Another style may require staff members to mark both understandings and skills the child has achieved and not achieved. A report card style that might be used for a program that serves children of bilingual families is shown in Figure 10–14.

The examples in Figures 10–15a (page 351) and b (page 352) require the staff member to denote each child's progress by marking one of three or one of four choices, respectively. Another style calls for the staff member to evaluate both effort and progress on each item as shown in Figure 10–16 on page 353. Yet another style requires the staff member to evaluate progress on each item on an inferior-superior continuum; such a style is actually a rating scale as shown in Figure 10–17 on page 354.

Staff members must recognize that regardless of the method of reporting, the report is only as accurate and comprehensive as the assessment devices and recording. When the assessment plan matches program objectives and recording is accurate and thorough, reporting becomes a valuable facet of the early childhood program.

A Message to Parents,

   In kindergarten your child lives, works, and plays with other children of his age. He has learning experiences that are a foundation for all that follows in later school years.   This card is a description of your child's development at this time.   Each quality checked is evident in your child.   You, as a parent, will help and encourage him by your interest in his growth.

BEHAVIOR	Participates with confidence	
IN LARGE	Usually follows others	
GROUP	Participates in activities	
SITUATIONS	Gets along well with others	

RESPONSE	Cooperates when encouraged	
TO	Accepts group decisions	
RULES	Follows rules of the school	

FIGURE 10–13
Report Card with Achievements Checked

Name (Nombre) _____

S   Satisfactory growth at this time.
     Desarrollo satisfactorio al presente.

N   Not yet.
     Todavia no es satisfactorio el desarrollo.

Can hop Puede saltar		Puts on wraps Se pone el abrigo	
Knows age Sabe su edad		Knows address Sabe su domicilio	

FIGURE 10–14
Bilingual Report Card

Progress Report

Name _____

A check shows the child's performance	1st Semester			2nd Semester		
	Most of the time	Part of the time	Not at this time	Most of the time	Part of the time	Not at this time
Work habits						
Takes care of materials						
Has good attention span						
Is able to work independently						
Follows group instruction						

FIGURE 10–15a
Level of Progress Checked

SUMMARY

Assessment, recording, and reporting are integral parts of an early childhood program. Thus, these components must be thoughtfully and carefully planned in keeping with program objectives. Providing quality assessment, recording, and reporting is not a simple matter but requires a highly trained staff and leadership by administrators.

Similar to the professional concerns about inappropriate curriculum content and teaching strategies are concerns about standardized test results being used to make decisions about placement and retention and to measure "progress" on academic subskill tasks. Many changes are being called for, such as:

1. The use of more informal (not casual) methods of assessing (e.g., continuous observations in children's natural environments and samples of children's work).
2. The construction of anecdotal records, running records, and some check sheets to record these appropriate assessments and the collection and organization of all assessments using a portfolio format.
3. The employment of reporting practices which adapt to the needs of young children rather than model versions used with older children (e.g., using conferences with parents at the school and in the home rather than traditional report cards).

THIS PRESCHOOL PROGRAM is designed to help each child: build self-confidence, sharpen his senses, learn to work with others, and enlarge his span of experiences.	COMMENDABLE	SATISFACTORY	NEEDS TO MAKE GREATER EFFORT	NEEDS MORE TIME TO DEVELOP
READING READINESS First reporting period				
Is interested in learning to read				
Sees and hears likenesses and differences in words				
Follows directions most of the time				
Is becoming acquainted with books				
READING READINESS Second reporting period				
Can distinguish right and left				
Hears rhyming sounds				
Hears beginning sounds				
Knows the letters of the alphabet				
Can write most letters clearly				

FIGURE 10–15b
Level of Progress Checked

EDUCATIONAL GROWTH	EFFORT		PROGRESS	
	Adequate	Needs to Improve	Shows Development	Shows Strength
PERSONAL ATTITUDES AND SKILLS				
Is interested and contributes				
Can put on outdoor clothing				
Can tie shoes				
Can wait his or her turn				
Keeps hands to himself or herself (doesn't bother others)				
STORY PERIOD				
Retells stories and rhymes				
Refrains from disturbing others				
Sits quietly				
Shows interest in story				
Listens while story is read				

FIGURE 10–16
Effort and Progress Checked

NOTES

1. M. T. Gnezda and R. Bolig, *A National Survey of Public School Testing of Pre-Kindergarten and Kindergarten Children* (Paper commissioned by the National Forum on the Future of Children and Their Families of the National Academy of Sciences and the National Association of the State Boards of Education, 1989).
2. J. H. Block, ed. *Mastery Learning: Theory and Practice.* (New York: Holt, Rinehart and Winston, 1971).

Your Child's Progress

_____   _____
Name of child   Year and class

_____   _____
School   Teacher

GROWTH AND DEVELOPMENT   RARELY .... CONSISTENTLY

A. Considers ideas and
   points of view of others   .   .   .   .   .

B. Associates with a variety
   of people   .   .   .   .   .

C. Respects the feelings of
   each human being   .   .   .   .   .

D. Practices conservation of
   living things   .   .   .   .   .

E. Practices safety habits   .   .   .   .   .

F. Demonstrates good health
   habits   .   .   .   .   .

FIGURE 10–17
Progress Rating Scale

3. M. Scriven, "The Methodology of Evaluation," *Perspectives of Curriculum Evaluation,* ed. R. Tyler, R. Gagne, and M. Scriven (Chicago: Rand McNally, 1967), 39–93.

4. C. Kamii and D. L. Elliott, "Evaluation of Evaluations," *Educational Leadership* 28 (1971): 827–31.

5. B. Bowman, "Child Care: Challenges for the '90's," *Dimensions* 18, 4 (1990): 30.

6. W. Teal, E. Hiebart, and E. Chittenden, "Assessing Young Children's Literacy Development," *The Reading Teacher* 40 (1987): 772–776.

7. S. J. Meisels, *Developmental Screening in Early Childhood: A Guide,* 3rd ed. (Washington, D.C.: The National Association for the Education of Young Children, 1989).

8. M. L. Smith and L. A. Shepard, "Kindergarten Readiness and Retention: A Qualitative Study of Teachers' Beliefs and Practices," *American Educational Research Journal* 25 (1988): 330.

9. D. J. Walsh, "Changes in Kindergarten: Why Here? Why Now?" *Early Childhood Research Quarterly* 4 (1989): 377–391.

10. L. A. Shepard and M. L. Smith, *Boulder Valley Kindergarten Study: Retention Practices and Retention Effects* (Boulder: Boulder Valley Public Schools, 1985).

11. P. Mantzicopoulos, D. C. Morrison, S. P. Hinshaw, and E. T. Corte, "Nonpromotion in Kindergarten: The Role of Cognitive, Perceptual, Visual-Motor, Behavioral, Achievement, Socioeconomic, and Demographic Characteristics," *American Educational Research Journal* 26, 1 (1989): 107–121.

12. D. Smith, *California Kindergarten Practices* (Fresno: California State University—Fresno, School of Education, Office of Research, 1987).

13. D. P. Weikart, "Hard Choices in Early Childhood Care and Education: A View to the Future," *Young Children* 44, 3 (1989): 25–30.

14. Center for Law and Education, Inc., "Parents Win Challenge to Kindergarten Exam," *NewsNotes* (August 1988): 2–3.

15. Meisels, *Developmental Screening in Early Childhood*, 31–39.

16. G. M. Fedoruk, "Kindergarten Screening for First-Grade Learning Problems: The Conceptual Inadequacy of a Child-Deficit Model," *Childhood Education* 66, 1 (1989): 40–42.

17. *Standards for Educational and Psychological Testing* (Washington, D.C.: American Educational Research Association, American Psychological Association, and the National Council on Measurement in Education, 1989).

18. **Validity** is the measure of how well a test accomplishes its purposes. (Validity can be determined by correlating it with some other test index and is referred to as **concurrent validity** or by noting the correctness of a decision based on the test and is referred to as **predictive validity**.) **Reliability** is a quantitative index of the consistency of results using the instrument. Reliability is estimated by some form of **reliability coefficient** or by the **standard error of measurement.** (Reliability is referred to as the measure of confidence that can be placed in a test when it is used by different examiners, when the same test and procedure are repeated after a specified period of time, and the "sameness" of different forms of the test.)

19. *Standards for Educational and Psychological Testing* American Educational Research Association, American Psychological Association, and National Council on Measurement in Education.

20. S. Bredekamp and L. Shepard, "How Best to Protect Children from Inappropriate School Expectations, Practices, and Policies," *Young Children* 44, 3 (1989): 22–23.

21. J. Robinson, *The Baby Boards: A Parents' Guide to Preschool and Primary School Entrance Tests* (New York: Arco, 1988).

22. National Association for the Education of Young Children, "NAEYC Position Statement on Standardized Testing of Young Children 3 Through 8 Years of Age," *Young Children* 43, 3 (1988): 42–47.

23. National Council of Teachers of English, "On Testing Young Children," *Language Arts* 67 (1990): 92–93.

24. Bredekamp and Shepard, "How Best to Protect Children from Inappropriate School Expectations, Practices, and Policies."

25. G. Fassnacht, *Theory and Practice of Observing Behavior* (London: Academic Press, 1982).

26. D. A. Prescott, *The Child in the Educative Process* (New York: McGraw-Hill, 1957), 153–54.

27. C. Kamii and R. Peper, *A Piagetian Method of Evaluating Preschool Children's Development in Classification*, ERIC ED 039 013 (Washington, D.C.: Office of Education, Bureau of Elementary and Secondary Education, 1969).

28. Meisels, *Developmental Screening in Early Childhood*, 8.

29. G. S. Adams, *Measurement and Evaluation in Education, Psychology, and Guidance* (New York: Holt, Rinehart & Winston, 1965), 182.

30. Contact Edward Chittenden or Rosalea Courtney, Educational Testing Service, Princeton, N.J. 08541 (609–921–9000).

31. E. Kawin, "Records and Reports, Observations, Tests, and Measurements," *Early Childhood Education 46th Yearbook*, National Society for the Study of Education (Chicago: University of Chicago, 1947), 290.

FOR FURTHER READING

Anrig, G. R. "Educational Standards, Testing, and Equity." *Phi Delta Kappan* 66, 9 (1985): 623–25.

Beaty, J. J. *Observing Development of the Young Child*, 2nd ed. Columbus: Merrill, 1990.

Bennett, R. E., and Maher, C. A., eds. *Emerging Perspectives on Assessment of Exceptional Children*. New York: Haworth, 1986.

Freeman, E. B., and Hatch, J. A. "What Schools Expect Young Children to Know and Do: An Analysis of Kindergarten Report Cards." *Elementary School Journal* 89 (1989): 595–605.

Gibbs, E. D., and Teti, D. M. *Interdisciplinary Assessment of Infants: A Guide for Early Intervention Professionals*. Baltimore: Paul H. Brookes, 1990.

Kamii, C., ed. *Achievement Testing in the Early Grades: The Games Grown-Ups Play*. Washington, D.C.: National Association for the Education of Young Children, 1990.

McLoughlin, C. S. *Parent-Teacher Conferencing*. Springfield, Ill.: Charles C. Thomas, 1987.

Meisels, S. J., and Shonkoff, J. P., eds. *Handbook of Early Childhood Intervention*. New York: Cambridge University Press, 1990.

"National Association for the Education of Young Children 3 through 8 Years of Age." *Young Children* 43, 3 (1988): 42–47.

Rosetti, L. M. *Infant-Toddler Assessment: An Interdisciplinary Approach*. Boston: Little Brown, 1990.

Standards for Educational and Psychological Testing. Washington, D.C.: American Psychological Association, American Educational Research Association, and National Council on Measurement in Education, 1985.

Woodrich, D. L., and Kush, S. A. *Children's Psychological Testing: A Guide for Nonpsychologists.* Baltimore: Paul H. Brookes, 1990.

Wortham, S. C. *Tests and Measurement in Early Childhood Education.* Columbus: Merrill, 1990.

Chapter 11
Working with Parents

Families have always been involved in the education of their children. Where there were no schools available, education of the young was a family function. The public school system of the United States was founded by parents and other citizens of the community. Schools were not only established by parents and other community members, they were run by them, which resulted in local schools and school boards with a membership comprised of lay people. The Parent-Teacher Association (PTA) has had a long history in public school education.[1]

Historically, many early childhood programs had parent involvement.[2] Frederich Froebel, founder of the kindergarten, developed activities for mothers to do with their infants. From the late 1800s through the early 1900s, kindergarten teachers in the United States taught children in the mornings and spent the afternoons visiting parents in their homes.[3] Nursery schools valued and promoted parent involvement.[4] Nursery schools operated in the prestigious academic institutions of the United States involved parents. And parents were dependent on the nursery school programs under the Works Progress Administration of the Depression years and the Lanham Act Centers during World War II. More recently, the Head Start program has performance standards that mandate parent participation. Also, laws for children with disabilities (i.e., P.L. 94–142 and P.L. 99–457) require parental involvement in decisions about a child's educational placement and treatment plan (See Chapter 3).

VALUES AND PROBLEMS IN WORKING WITH PARENTS

Although families have been involved in children's programs, the nature of the involvement has changed. As schools became more organized, professionals were put in control and parents, especially mothers, were asked to: get children to school regularly, on-time, clean, fed, and ready to learn; oversee children's homework; and help with money-raising projects (e.g., making products for bake sales and school carnivals), escorting children on field trips, and correcting papers (in the back of a classroom). Even these activities were given to parents hesitantly, because many staff members have responded with alarm to parent involvement. These staff members have seen home teaching of academics as confusing to the child, parent visits to the program disruptive, and parents' critiques of the program's curriculum and methodology as unqualified judgments of professionals by nonprofessionals. Thus, before the 1960s, working with parents was primarily parent education—the school communicating to parents but parents not involved in major decisions. Parents began to feel as though they were "friendly intruders."[5]

By the 1960s intervention programs such as Head Start mandated parent involvement. Parents were seen as allies, and the benefits of parent involvement began to appear in the research literature. With the inclusion of children, infants, and toddlers with disabilities in early childhood programs, parents' views, abilities, and difficulties had to be considered in program decisions and parents themselves became more vocal.[6, 7]

Benefits of Working with Parents

Many benefits stem from parent involvement in early childhood programs. Henderson, in an annotated bibliography, reported on thirty-five studies showing that various types of parental inclusion had positive results, including measurable gains in pupils' performance.[8] A 1987 update of this report summarized eighteen additional studies with similar findings.[9] These benefits affect the program, the child, and the parent.

Benefits for Program
Early childhood programs can benefit from parent involvement. Benefits for the program include the following:

1. Parent involvement frequently enables the school to comply with federal and/or state guidelines. For example, the Head Start program mandates that the local advisory boards have parent representatives and that parents serve in the classroom as paid employees, volunteers, and observers. Federal guidelines established by Public Law 94–142 and Public Law 99–457 require parents to be involved in the writing of the Individual Educational Plan (IEP) for their exceptional children.
2. Through parent involvement, schools achieve a better adult-child ratio. Parent assistance often enables teachers to conduct program activities which would be impossible without such assistance.
3. Parents can serve as resource people. Their special talents and interests can be useful to the program.

4. Parents have a unique empathy in explaining the program's services and problems to other parents. Some early childhood programs have had a parent educator component in which parent educators (a) trained new parents in specific activities (e.g., toy making); (b) modeled language patterns to be used with activities; (c) explained the program rationale; and (d) stressed the importance of parent involvement.
5. In addition to sharing teaching responsibilities with professionals in the classroom and in the home, parents can serve as program decision makers. Many early childhood programs have parent advisory councils (which are discussed in a later section of this Chapter).
6. When parents are available to "explain" the child's culture to the teacher, the teacher may become more empathetic.
7. Parents have a chance to see other children of the same age and gain a more realistic picture of their child's strengths and weaknesses.

Benefits for Child

A major premise is that goals for children are best achieved if parents and teachers agree on these goals and the basic ways of achieving them. Caldwell has suggested that early childhood programs function as an extended family.[10] Some benefits for the child include the following:

1. More quality adult attention increases the chance for greater achievement. Parents who interact, participate in intellectually stimulating activities, foster independence, and read and discuss stories with their children have children who show cognitive gains in language, concepts, and problem-solving skills.[11] Zigler points out that children who do not receive enough adult attention from parents have such a high need for attention that they are not motivated to solve intellectual problems; these children put effort into attention-seeking behavior rather than into intellectual tasks.[12] Parent involvement in an early childhood program is motivating.
2. Children see their parents in new roles and can see that parents and staff are working together for them. This relationship impacts on children's affective functioning such as a positive self-image and a productive orientation to social relations.[13, 14]
3. Parent assistance in the early childhood program can enhance program quality, a benefit to the child.

Benefits for Parent

Planned parent participation in early childhood programs is viewed as a means of enhancing parents as adults and as parents. Benefits for parents include the following:

1. Participation in early childhood programs can enhance the parents' feelings of self-worth and contribute to increased education and employment.[15, 16]

2. Parent-education programs can help parents gain confidence as a parent. Self-image as a parent leads to confidence in the "parent as an educator" role.[17] White found effective parents were nurturing, had clear and consistent discipline, and were skilled at designing home learning activities.[18] Parents can profit from the educational expertise the early childhood program offers in child development and guidance, bringing it into the home. Effective parents also become more involved within the total family.[19]

3. As parents become more effective with their children and within their families, they become more involved in the schools.[20] Parents learn their importance in their children's education and how to help schools maximize educational benefits.

4. Parents may even become an early childhood program's strongest advocates.[21]

Problems of Working with Parents

Many benefits have been stated; however, parent involvement in an early childhood program may present some problems. These include the following:

1. Sociologists theorize that there is an optimal social distance between home and school. The distance protects the unique characteristics of each.[22] However, it is difficult to find the balance in early childhood education, because teachers must do traditional parenting-type tasks.[23] Studies have confirmed a tension between parents and teachers.[24] Some examples are Kontos' findings that teachers saw parents as having far poorer parenting skills than the parents felt they had[25] and Galinsky's findings that mothers who expressed guilt about working were more likely to be seen as inadequate parents than those who did not express guilt.[26] Parents and teachers felt possessive about children and there was often jealousy.[27]

2. Parents and teachers may have different goals for children. Prescott noted differences in values, goals, and discipline techniques in parents and teachers.[28] Greenberg states that when families feel alienated children often feel that they must choose between home and school or "compartmentalize" their two worlds. These children often become major discipline problems.[29]

3. Some parents, particularly those from lower socioeconomic classes, feel inhibited or even inferior around staff personnel because of their limited and unsuccessful school experiences and because of the socioeconomic distance between themselves and staff members. Communication with staff can be difficult or embarrassing for parents who cannot read or write English; do not have paper or pencil; or cannot get to school because of work hours, transportation, or babysitting problems. Similarly, racial minority parents may feel inferior, especially around staff members who come from the majority race. Teachers respond nega-

tively to lower socioeconomic class and minority parents, often discounting what they do for their children.[30] Kontos and Wells concluded that the parents needing the most staff support were least likely to get it.[31]

4. Staff members can feel threatened by parents, especially those who are highly educated. Staff members see these children coming to programs already "knowing," having been taught by uncredentialed parent-educators.[32]

5. Parents may feel helpless about their ability to contribute in a meaningful way to a program. The demographics of family structure leave little time to support program activities.[33] For example, Greenberg has stated that only one-half of the elementary schools now have Parent-Teacher Associations.[34] The lack of time also translates into a general anxiety about childrearing.[35]

6. Parents and staff bring their stress to the relationship.[36] This results in conflict over program policies. For example, parents expect staff to take into account the lack of anyone to care for sick children at home, getting to the center by bus before closing time, and their need to "pay later." On the other hand, staff members expect parents to understand limitations of group care (e.g., caring for individual children, payment of fees, and hours of operation).

Some problems may be overcome. A few suggestions are given:

1. Time must be built into staff members' schedules to work with parents.

2. Staff members must truly listen to parents and convey the idea that the parent is the leader of the parenting team comprised of all those who support the development of the child. The roles of both the parent and teacher must be defined. Teachers are supportive of, not substitutes for, parents. Powell has identified these four teacher roles in working with parents: child-rearing information and advice, emotional support for parents, role modeling, and referrals.[37] Parents do seem to prefer distinctions between the role of the parent and the professional; for example, Powell found that almost 85 percent of parents believed they should discuss center goals and expectations with the staff; however, over 61 percent of the parents did not want to share information about the family.[38]

3. Programs should implement an involvement program tailored to the needs of parents. For example, Seefeldt has suggested parent participation in the curriculum of an early childhood program. She suggests sending home stories about school life dictated by children and written by staff members; booklets with lists of favorite stories, songs, and poems; and snapshots, tape recordings, and samples of children's work.[39] Other ideas include flexible hours and babysitting and transportation services for school conferences.

4. Programs need to work for total support of parents such as advocating before and after school child care. Seefeldt has suggested that the Foster

Grandparent Program offers companionship to all members of the family rather than just to the child.[40]

5. Those working in early childhood programs need to be trained to work with parents. This is basically a neglected area in many teacher-training programs and in-service activities. More and more work is being done. For information, contact professional early childhood education associations (see Appendix 4) and the National Coalition for Parent Involvement in Education, the National Committee for Citizens in Education, and the National Congress of Parents and Teachers (see Appendix 5 for addresses).

LEGAL RIGHTS OF PARENTS

The legislative and judicial branches of our government have recognized the need for parent involvement. Consequently, legislation and litigation have been a part of the history of parent involvement in schools for young children. Because of the extent of this history, only a few key examples of parents' legal rights will be discussed.

Public schools are funded and advised by the local school district. The concept of local control is fundamental to public school organization, and parents, as citizens and taxpayers, have a right to be involved in the decision-making process.

All educational agencies that receive funds under any federal program administered by the U.S. Office of Education must allow parents access to their child's official records. Due process is also granted if parents wish to challenge the records on the grounds that they are inaccurate, misleading, or inappropriate. Parents must give written permission for the release of their child's records to a third party. Under this law, commonly referred to as the "Buckley Amendment," parents must be informed of their rights to access, to use the due process provision, and to determine whether a record may be released.[41]

As discussed in Chapter 3, parents have specific rights under P.L. 94–142, including a role in yearly diagnosis, in placement decisions, and in development of the Individual Educational Plan (IEP). A due process provision is also a part of P.L. 94–142.

In the statutes of most states, the teacher stands *in loco parentis* to the child. This legal terminology is replaced in some state statutes by another phrase meaning the same thing, such as teachers "stand in the relation of parents and guardians to pupils."[42] In states without such a provision, the court affirms the *in loco parentis* position of the teacher. To more appropriately assume this role, teachers should know what parents want for their children.

PARENT INVOLVEMENT

The movement toward greater parent involvement in programs for young children has come about for several reasons. In a democracy, all citizens have the right to be involved in the operation of their social institutions, including the schools. Throughout the history of public education in the United States, citizens have professed and defended the benefits of community control over educational policy and decision making.

Second, the importance of the role of the family in a child's overall development is more fully understood. The school working in isolation is likely to be impotent. Cooperation between parent and school gives children a sense of security, knowing that both institutions are working together for their welfare. It also helps both parties to recognize each other's competencies and weaknesses and thus be able to help each other meet the common goal of a successfully functioning child.

Early childhood educators promote the early involvement of parents in programs for maximum impact. Also, when parents cooperate from the beginning, there is a chance for lasting program concern and identification. Professional associations and many local parent groups work for parent involvement in the schools.

Involvement with parents includes parent-staff communication and parent participation. Maximum returns in the area of parent-staff communication require the use of various information channels: conferences, home visits, and written communication; various ways of promoting dialogue, such as individual and small-group conferences, demonstrations, and formal programs; and plans for acting upon the information received—that is, methods of adjusting the services of the program to fit the needs of the child and procedures for making referrals. Parent participation includes parents serving in various planning and advisory capacities and parents working as volunteers, either program or support program, and as resource people.

Parent-Staff Communication

Because parents and teachers are concerned with the optimal development of the child, they are important allies. Communication centers on exchanging information about individual children and the principles of child development for the benefit of each child in the program. In addition, parents must be well-informed about the program and welcome as observers and contributors.

Parent Reception Area

This area helps parents feel welcome and encourages an exchange of information between parents and staff members. Such an area should be well-defined and inviting, with adequate lighting and ventilation, comfortable chairs, a place to write, and materials with information about child development and about the early childhood program. Suggested materials are:

1. Periodicals published by organizations concerned with young children
2. Guidelines for helping parents choose appropriate literature, toys, and other materials for young children

3. Suggestions for good movies, television shows, local events, and any community happenings designed for children and/or parents
4. Information about the program's services, basic schedule, names of staff members, special events, and vacation periods
5. Directions for making things, such as finger paint, flannel boards, and bulletin boards
6. Materials that serve as preparation for or follow-up to parents' meetings—for example, if a teacher is introducing a new mathematics approach in the program, some books and materials about this new approach may be displayed
7. Information of concern to all parents on childhood diseases, safety in home and other play areas, warnings on products used by children, and discipline and guidance. Free or inexpensive booklets can be secured from the American Red Cross, local pediatricians, and insurance companies.

The parent reception area should invite relaxed communication among parents and between parents and staff members, in addition to providing information. Some other suggestions for a parent reception area are as follows:

1. If there is an observation room for parents, it should be adjacent to or part of the parent reception area.
2. Photographs of the children engaged in the program's activities and samples of the children's art and other work can be displayed in this area.
3. Items for viewing, such as the photographs and samples of children's work, and informational materials should be changed frequently. Each child's work should be displayed from time to time, rather than only "the best" work.
4. Refreshments may be placed in the parent reception area on special occasions (at holiday seasons and at the beginning and end of the term).

Spring or Autumn Orientation

Many early childhood programs have an orientation meeting for parents who will be enrolling children. This is an excellent means of establishing a cooperative relationship between parents and staff. Although the orientation meeting is usually held in late spring, it can be held in early autumn. The purpose of the meeting is to orient parents to the services and requirements for admission to the program and to the techniques they can use in preparing their children for entrance.

Parents should be greeted as they arrive. An orientation meeting that begins with an informal presentation, such as songs, finger plays, rhythmic or other typical activities by the children presently enrolled, gives insight into the program. If enrolled children are not available for a presentation, a slide-tape presentation is most effective. If children are invited to come with their parents, a presentation of a few activities by young children is not only entertaining but also gives the new children something to look forward to. Following the presentation, the new children should be asked to join the enrolled children and several staff members or volunteers in activities to be conducted in another room or in the outdoor area. Reluctant children may remain with their parents.

The director and other program and support program personnel should explain the program's services in an interesting way. Written, take-home materials are usually appreciated by the parents, who should be given an opportunity to ask questions about the program's services.

Requirements for admission to the program should be carefully described and included in a parent's handbook; if the handbook is not distributed at the orientation, the requirements should be in written form for parents to take home. Requirements for admission usually include: (1) age requirements and verification of age through presentation of a birth certificate or an acceptable alternative; (2) residence in a certain attendance area (often required by public school early childhood programs); (3) fees; (4) proof of adequate immunizations and tuberculosis test; (5) medical statement concerning the child's ability to participate in the program; (6) emergency information form completed and signed by each child's parents; and (7) parental needs for and ability to pay for the child's enrollment (sometimes required by government-subsidized programs). In addition to admission requirements, parents should be informed about what kind of clothing the child should wear and whether he is to bring a change of clothing, along with suggestions about what kinds of clothing children can most easily manage. Finally, a list of supplies to be purchased by the parent should be included. The supplies can be displayed so parents can see exactly what to purchase. A note on the supply list can remind the parent to put the child's name on each article, thus reducing loss of property. Some programs provide a list with children's and parents' names, addresses, and telephone numbers, so parents can get acquainted and arrange car pools, if they wish.

Parents often want to know how to prepare the child for an early childhood program. They should be discouraged from engaging in a "crash course" of academic preparation, because young children are less likely to gain long-lasting knowledge and may develop an unfavorable attitude toward learning. The staff member, to allay parents' fears of no longer being needed in helping their children's development, should give parents a list of suggestions. These would help prepare the children for the program and include places to visit, home experiences that would be beneficial, techniques and activities for developing listening skills and oral expression, and ways to encourage independence. The staff member can also indicate some materials that will be used in the early weeks of the session, so the parents can familiarize their children with them.

The informal meeting should last no longer than an hour. A social time following the meeting gives parents a chance to visit with each other and with staff members. A tour of the facility is appropriate during this time.

Parent's First Individual Visit
The first individual visit to an early childhood program is often to register the child. The initial, individual contact between parent and staff member must go

beyond the mechanics of registration, however. The parent's first visit to the program's facility is a time of direct learning and impressions for both parent and staff member.

The parent should bring the child. The conference room should contain a child-sized table and chair; books, crayons, and drawing paper; and manipulative toys. In order that the parent may observe the child and the child may watch the parent, the child's table should be close to the table provided for parent and staff member. Also, the close proximity of the child allows the staff member to observe the child informally.

From the parent, a staff member should obtain (1) an impression of the relationship between parent and child, (2) an impression of how the child reacts to the new situation and how the parent feels about putting the child in the program, (3) a personal and social history of the child, (4) all necessary admission forms, and (5) tuition fees. The parent should obtain from the staff member (1) an impression of the staff member, (2) an overview of the philosophy of the program and of the facility and equipment, (3) a handbook or mimeographed information sheet, (4) a list of items (clothing and supplies) needed before the child begins attending, and (5) receipts for tuition and fees paid.

Handbook for Parents

The major purposes of the handbook are to help the parent become oriented to the program and serve as a reference during the child's first year of enrollment. In planning a handbook, there are several points to consider:

1. Information in the parent's handbook should be consistent with the program's philosophy and policies. If the program is based on a specific model, this should be stated. Because philosophy and policies differ from program to program, the staff of each program must develop its own handbook.
2. At a minimum, the handbook should contain an introduction to the philosophy and the services of the program; information about the program's policies that directly concern parents, such as hours of operation, fees, and children's celebrations; and information on requirements that must be met before admission to the program, such as proof of age, record of immunizations, completion of the emergency information, the personal information, and the health history forms. Other information the handbook might contain includes developmental characteristics of young children; ways parents can help their child's development; health and safety guidelines for young children; methods the staff members will use to report the child's progress; a list of supplies parents need to purchase; ways parents can be involved in the center; and dates of scheduled meetings, such as board and parent meetings.
3. Before writing the handbook, the frequency of revision should be determined. If annual revisions are not planned, a minimum of variable

information, such as names of staff members, fees, and hours of operation should be included. Because much of the variable information is essential, blank spaces can be left in the handbook and completed in handwriting each year. An example is shown in Figure 11–1. For partial revision, a plastic spiral binding or a stapled handbook can be easily dismantled.

4. Information in the handbook should be arranged logically. Having a table of contents, printing each section on a different-colored paper, and cutting each section longer or wider than the preceding section for a tab effect are ways to facilitate locating specific information.

5. Information in the handbook should be concise. The handbook is a reference—not a novel!

6. The parents' level of understanding should be considered in wording the handbook. Wording should not sound condescending, nor should it be educational jargon. Bilingual handbooks should be available if the program serves children in a multicultural area.

7. The handbook should be attractive and the writing style interesting. Various colors of paper, readable printing, photographs, cartoons, or children's drawings help make it attractive. The writings might be in various styles or "voices"; for example, a staff member may "talk" to the parents as in the example in Figure 11–2. The child may "talk" to his parents as shown in Figure 11–3. The parent may "talk" to the child as shown in Figure 11–4. A previously enrolled child may "talk" to a new child as shown in Figure 11–5. Or the wording may be impersonal as shown in Figure 11–6. Although different styles of wording are usually not combined, some combinations add to the cleverness of the writing as seen in Figure 11–7.

8. In designing a handbook, costs must be considered. Since the handbook can become expensive, various typesetting and printing techniques, including typewritten camera-ready copy should be explored. Several estimates should be obtained. Ditto or mimeograph may be least expensive and more than adequate for the program's needs. If a computer is available, word processing is also cost-effective.

Lunch period

A hot lunch will be served in the cafeteria every day. It costs _____¢ a day, or you may pay $___.___ a week. (Checks may be made payable to _____.) If your child wishes to bring his lunch, milk will cost _____¢ a day. Those who wish to know whether their children qualify for free or reduced-cost lunches may secure forms in the central office.

FIGURE 11–1
Early Childhood Program Handbook (A)

Dear Parents:

We wish to extend a warm welcome to you and your child. We want to make this kindergarten year a pleasant one for parents as well as for children. You, as parents, will influence, to a large degree, your child's success in this venture.

Your help and cooperation will assist us in helping your child. Please feel free to talk with us anytime you feel it is necessary. You are welcome to visit and to get to know us and the program better.

Sincerely,

_____
(Staff member's signature)

FIGURE 11–2
Early Childhood Program Handbook (B)

I am ready, if . . .

I know my name and address.
I know the safest way to school.
I know how to put on and take off my clothes.

FIGURE 11–3
Early Childhood Program Handbook (C)

I will keep you home, when you have . . .

Fever
Sore throat
Pain
Chills
Diarrhea
Rash
Earache
Vomiting

FIGURE 11–4
Early Childhood Program Handbook (D)

In kindergarten, you'll draw and paint. The teacher told my mom that drawing and painting help children symbolize their everyday world, express their feelings, develop creativity, and coordinate eyes and hands. It sounds serious, but drawing and painting are fun.

FIGURE 11–5
Early Childhood Program Handbook (E)

A child is eligible to enroll in the kindergarten of the Hubbard Suburb's Public School if he is five years old on September 1 of the year he enters.

FIGURE 11–6
Early Childhood Program Handbook (F)

I can enter, if . . .

    I have my birth certificate.
    I have all my immunizations.

P.S. To parents:

*If you do not have a birth certificate, write to:
    Bureau of Vital Statistics
    State Capitol Building

    _____   _____   _____
    (Capital city)   (State)   (Zip Code)
*All immunizations are available from your doctor or the Public Health Center, _____

_____.
                    (Address)

To request information or an appointment call _____.

FIGURE 11–7
Early Childhood Program Handbook (G)

The staff of each early childhood program should develop a handbook to fit its unique program objectives and policies. Appendix 9 presents an example of a parent's handbook for a kindergarten program.

Large-Group Conferences

Although individual conferences are most common, large-group conferences may be conducted. A popular type is the "get acquainted" and "preview of what's to come" conference. Unlike the spring or autumn orientation, the "get acquainted" conference is held a few weeks after the beginning of the term. It is especially important when staff members do not conduct an orientation meeting. For a "get acquainted" conference, these suggestions should be followed:

1. Send invitations to parents. If you include an RSVP, you can follow up on parents who do not respond, perhaps by telephone for a personal touch. A night meeting is preferable to an afternoon one, because it permits working parents to attend. Tuesdays, Wednesdays, and Thursdays are usually the best days for meetings, but check the community calendar before setting a date. Plan a conference to last a maximum of one hour, followed by a social period.
2. Set the conference date after you know the children, so you can associate parents with children.
3. Plan simple refreshments and ask volunteer parents to serve.
4. Arrange the room to show your program to best advantage; for example, put the program's schedule on the chalkboard, arrange materials and equipment around the room, and display some of the children's work.
5. Make a specific outline of your presentation; for example:
   a. When most of the guests have arrived, greet them as a group.
   b. Introduce other staff members.
   c. Briefly describe your background and express confidence in the year ahead.
   d. Outline the purpose of the conference. Explain that there will be individual conferences scheduled and that parents can call anytime about their own child.
   e. Explain the purposes of the program, using specific examples. An excellent way to communicate objectives and activities is to take parents through a "typical day."
   f. Review the policies of the program. Parents may be asked to bring their "Parent's Handbook" for reference.
   g. Suggest ways parents can help their children.
   h. Have a short question and answer period, but remind parents that a child's particular problems are discussed in individual conferences.
   i. Circulate paper or ask for parents who will serve as resource people, etc.
   j. Invite parents to have refreshments, visit with each other, and look around the room. Thank them for coming.

In addition to the get-acquainted conference, a large-group conference is an appropriate setting for explaining new policies and changes in previous policies, for introducing new program services, and for outlining and explaining new methods or curricular content. The large-group conference is also an excellent medium for sampling parents' opinions about and attitudes toward the program.

Small-Group Conferences

Three or four parents may be invited to a small-group conference, for which a topic may or may not be predetermined. In small-group conferences without predetermined topics, each parent might describe a situation that bothers him in relation to his own child. The staff members and other parents can discuss the situation and make suggestions. The director might invite an authority to lead the discussion on a topic selected by interested parents or the program director. Observation of the program before the conference is another stimulus to discussion. Small-group conferences help parents who feel uneasy in an individual or large-group conference and reassure them that others have similar problems.

Scheduled Individual Conferences

Based on the point of view that parent rights and responsibilities must not be usurped or violated by the early childhood program, individual parent-staff conferences help the parent know what is going on in the program and how the child is developing. Although the conference setting may be informal, parents can expect staff members to discuss the program's objectives and methodology in depth and how the child relates to the program. If the question or problem is not under the staff member's jurisdiction, she should direct the parent to appropriate channels. Suggestions for preparing and conducting individual conferences are as follows:

1. Send out a brief newsletter explaining what individual conferences are, what parents can contribute, and what staff members hope to accomplish as a result of the conferences. The point of the conference is to share with parents the ways the staff is helping the child meet program objectives and to elicit parental concerns for the child. If certain topics are to be covered, inform the parents. It is not necessary to send a newsletter if information about scheduled individual conferences is included in the handbook.
2. Specify appointment times and invite parents to make an appointment. An example is shown in Figure 11–8.
3. Construct a schedule of appointments, allowing a few minutes' break between each conference to jot down notes and prepare for the next conference. Although the example schedule is designed for twenty-minute conferences, many teachers find thirty minutes minimal to cover the purposes of the conference and to avoid an assembly-line appearance.

Dear _____ ,

Let's get together and talk. I would like to discuss with you:

1. Bedtime _____   5. Sharing toys _____

2. Breakfast _____   6. General
                                        adjustment _____
3. Bathroom habits _____

4. Crying _____   7. _____

Please list below some of the things you would like to talk to me about.

_____

_____

_____

   A baby-sitter will be available for your enrolled child and younger children. Please indicate the day(s) and time(s) you could come for a twenty-minute conference by circling one or more of the following time periods:

Oct. 7 Mon.	Oct. 8 Tues.	Oct. 9 Wed.	Oct. 10 Thurs.	Oct. 11 Fri.
3:00–3:20	3:00–3:20	3:00–3:20	3:00–3:20	3:00–3:20
3:30–3:50	3:30–3:50	3:30–3:50	3:30–3:50	3:30–3:50
4:00–4:20	4:00–4:20	4:00–4:20	4:00–4:20	4:00–4:20
4:30–4:50	4:30–4:50	4:30–4:50	4:30–4:50	4:30–4:50
5:00–5:20	5:00–5:20	5:00–5:20	5:00–5:20	5:00–5:20
5:30–5:50	5:30–5:50	5:30–5:50	5:30–5:50	5:30–5:50

I will confirm a time for your appointment.

Sincerely,

_____
(Staff member's signature)

FIGURE 11–8
Invitation to Parent-Teacher Conference

4. Confirm the conference time with each responding parent.
5. In your letter requesting parents to make appointments, explain whether they are to bring their enrolled child and other young children. If an aide or volunteer can babysit, more parents may be able to participate in an individual conference.
6. Provide an attractive, private place for the conference. The staff member should not sit behind a desk. It might be advantageous to hold the conference in one of the parents' homes rather than in the school.

(Individual conferences with all parents in one home are not to be confused with the home visit.)

7. Provide early arriving parents with a place to wait and have an aide or parent volunteer chat with them until time for the conference. If no one can wait with them, provide professional or popular reading material.

8. Have a clear picture of the child in terms of the objectives of your program. Also, list information to collect from parents; for example, you may want to obtain a developmental history of the child. Plan to elicit parental concerns for the child early in the conference. Morgan has helpful insights into "reading" parent concerns.[43]

9. Greet parents cordially. Explain what you are doing with and for the child. In talking about the child, use your file of anecdotal and achievement records and samples of the child's work. Point out strengths or positive areas first, then weaknesses.

10. Never put the parent on the defensive. Negative expressions will often do so; for example, instead of calling a child a "troublemaker," say he "disturbs others by. . . ." A staff member needs to recognize the attitudes a parent may take when his child is having problems, so the staff member does not respond argumentatively. The most frequent defensive attitudes a parent has are projection and denial. In projection, the parent insists the problem must be that the staff member doesn't know how to handle the child. In denial, the parent considers the problem small or feels the child is just active or going through a stage. With either defensive attitude, the parent is protecting himself from the possibility that he has failed in some way, or that he doesn't know what to do.

11. Be careful about talking down to parents, using educational jargon, or giving long-winded, complicated explanations. Conduct conferences in the parent's native tongue, using a translator, if necessary.

12. Do not expect to have an answer to every problem or parents to solve all problems. Decisions should be reached during the discussion by listening to parents' suggestions for solving the problem; by offering suggestions; by suggesting referral to special services, if necessary; and by making arrangements to follow through. Follow-up is most important. If the parent knows she has your help she will not feel helpless.

13. Practice professional ethics. Respect parents' confidences and do not belittle the director of the program, other staff members, other families, or other children.

14. Do not make the parent feel rushed; however, in fairness to other waiting parents, conferences must end on schedule. If necessary, the parent can make another appointment to continue the discussion.

15. Make notes on the conference and file them in the child's folder.

A new trend in parent-teacher conferences is the "child-parent-teacher" conference. Young children are usually excluded from parent-teacher conferences. Including children in conferences where objectives for their education are being determined is helpful in securing their cooperation in meeting present goals for development as well as becoming increasingly skillful in self-evaluation and decision making. Several excellent reports address the techniques of incorporating children in conferences.[44]

Nonscheduled Individual Conferences

Unlike large-group, small-group, and scheduled individual conferences that are usually staff-initiated and noted on the program calendar, nonscheduled conferences may be initiated by parent or staff member and held when the need arises. These conferences should be encouraged for any number of reasons: learning more about the program, questioning the meaning of activities observed, or discussing a present or foreseeable problem.

Most communication between parent and staff occurs at the transition point when parents leave and pick up their children. However, one study found that one-third of the parents could not identify a staff member with whom they had a significant relationship and a few parents did not know the names of any staff members. Thus, if nonscheduled individual conferences are to be meaningful, there needs to be a consistent person to reach out to parents during transition times and staff must receive training in parent-staff communication.

If the staff member initiates the conference to discuss a child's problems (and certainly many conferences have been initiated for that reason only!), he should give parents suggestions to solve the problem. The staff member must begin and end the conference on a positive note. In discussing a problem, the staff member should show evidence to support statements and use tact. Finally, the staff member and parent should concentrate on one or two suggestions, not a long list.

Home Visits

Home visits demonstrate acknowledgment of the home as a source of change in children's lives. Jones identifies four roles or combinations of roles a staff member can use in making home visits: (1) the *teacher-expert*, who enlists parental help by teaching the parent how to teach the child; (2) the *teacher-learner*, who seeks information from the parent about the child, such as the child's abilities and interests; (3) the *student-researcher*, who questions parents about their beliefs about child rearing; and (4) the *bringer of gifts*, who, like the teacher-expert, enlists parental help in the educative process but who brings, in addition to instructional procedures, materials such as games, books, and toys.[45] There are several advantages to home visits: (1) the staff member is seen as a person who cares enough about a child to visit the family; (2) the staff member may obtain valuable information about the child that will help in meeting program objectives for that child; (3) children are proud because their teacher came to see them; (4) the staff member sees the child in the home environment; (5) at home, the parent is more likely to do the talking, conversely, at the program's facility the staff member is more likely to do the talking; (6) the staff member can note alternative courses of child rearing open to the parents rather than just criticizing; (7) if a home visit is made prior to enrollment, there may be fewer tears shed on the first day; and (8) the staff member is seen as "just an individual" when she makes home visits. (Home visitation for the purpose of parent education will be discussed later in the chapter.)

Parent Visitation

Parent visitation helps make parent-staff conferences more meaningful. The parent has the opportunity to observe the program and to see the child functioning with peers and adults. The staff member has the opportunity to observe parent-child interaction in the program setting and the parent's expressed attitudes toward the program. When a parent visits the room, the staff member or a volunteer and the visitor's child should greet the parent. The parent can watch various groups of children engaging in activities or may even initiate an activity, such as reading a story. If a parent wants to see the child in action without the child's knowledge, invite the parent to use the observation room or gallery.

Parents should be encouraged to visit the program; however, many parents do not visit unless their children have special problems. Sending a special invitation often results in more visitations and may even initiate greater involvement in the program. A sample invitation is seen in Figure 11–9.

During an "Open House," parents and other family members view samples of the children's work, (e.g., art work, stories children have written, and block structures they have built), examine equipment and materials, and visit with staff members and other guests. It is held at a time when the program is not in session. An example of an invitation to an Open House is shown in Figure 11–10.

Telephone Conversations

These may be initiated by either parent or staff member. A parent may use telephone conversations to help staff members better understand the child during the day. Perhaps the child was sick during the night, is worried, or is excited.

Dear Parents,

The PTA will meet on Tuesday, October 8, at 3:00 P.M. Won't you try to attend? The program will be on "Children's Phobias." Before the PTA meeting, our kindergarten class would like you to visit us at 2:00 P.M. Won't you please visit our class, and then we can attend PTA as a group? A baby-sitter will be available for your enrolled child and younger children.

Sincerely,

_____

(Teacher's signature)

FIGURE 11–9
Invitation for Parent Involvement

Dear Parents,

　　We are having Open House, Thursday, October 24, at 7:30 P.M. Examples of your child's work will be on display. We hope you will come and see some of the things your child has done in school.

　　We will be looking forward to visiting with you. Refreshments will be served in the auditorium.

　　　　　　　　　　　　　　　　　Sincerely,

　　　　　　　　　　　　　　　　　_____

　　　　　　　　　　　　　　　　　(Staff member's signature)

FIGURE 11–10
Open House Invitation

Some parents may be more at ease talking over the telephone than in a face-to-face encounter.

　　Staff members can use telephone conversations as a means of making a positive contact, which can serve as a pleasant event for the child, too. These are examples of positive telephone contacts:

1. The staff member explains to the parent something interesting or successful the child did; parents are then able to reinforce the child immediately.
2. The staff member can call to inquire about the health of family members.

Newsletters

Newsletters can be sent home on a regular or irregular basis. The newsletter can be duplicated and sent to each parent via the child. A newsletter helps the parent communicate with his child and develops a liaison between staff members and parents. Information that might be included in newsletters are announcements about the program or about daily or special activities in the program; suggestions for home learning activities and methods that may be conducive to learning; information on new books, play materials, and television shows for children; articles to help parents; announcements about community events; and ideas for summer fun. An example of a newsletter to parents about television is shown in Figure 11–11. An excellent example of a newsletter format is found in the following:

　　Harms, T. O., and Cryer, D. "Parent Newsletter: A New Format." *Young Children* 33, 5 (1978): 28–32.

Other Methods

Several other methods aid parent-staff cooperation. A short note praising a child's effort, a "happy note," can be sent to the parent. An example is shown in Figure 11–12.

Dear Parents,

   Television plays a big part in your child's life. He enjoys watching television in his spare time. Of course, it is important that he does not stay "glued" to the TV. Playing outside in the fresh air, visiting with his friends, looking at books, and getting to bed early are important.

   Because there are many TV shows which are educational and enjoyable, television can be a wise use of some leisure time. Each week I will send home a schedule of some shows from which your child might profit. Your child might tune in these shows if they are convenient for your family.

                                    Sincerely,

                                    _____
                                    (Staff member's signature)

FIGURE 11–11
Newsletter

   When staff members have casual contacts with parents outside of school, the contacts should be friendly and never used for serious conferences. A shopping center or a community affair is not the place for a conference. If a parent wants to talk about his child, the staff member should suggest an appointment time.

   Some schools have tried materials workshops for parents and staff members. In a materials workshop, parents and staff members analyze instructional materials for concepts and develop original equipment and material for presenting these instructional concepts. Workshops may also be held in the evening for doing repair jobs on the building and grounds or on equipment and materials. Social meetings, such as picnics for the whole family, a coffee for parents, or a mother's or father's recognition night stimulate good relationships between parents and staff members. Sending cards or notes when a child has a birthday or is ill or when a parent is ill show that staff members care. Parents can be given feedback on the child's progress when they drop off or pick up their children; this is also a good time for staff and parents to get to know one another as people.

_____ was a good helper. She helped a friend pick up the spilled pegs.

FIGURE 11–12
"Happy Note"

Parent Participation

Involvement with parents includes parental participation in the program. The early childhood program must initiate and maintain programs that enlist the worthwhile services and resources of the community. Parents and other community citizens must feel the program is their own, and not off limits. Early childhood programs must revise the old conception of the parent's role as exclusively a guest at a holiday presentation, homeroom mother, or field trip supervisor.

Parents as Members of Policy Advisory Committees and Boards of Directors

Many early childhood programs include parents as members of planning and advisory groups; for example, parents serve as members of Head Start policy groups. Including parents in planning and advisory groups is in accordance with the democratic principles of citizen's rights and responsibilities in formulating public policy, works as a two-way public relations committee, and constitutes a partnership between professional and nonprofessional persons.

Parent Advisory Committees (PACs) work with the director and staff of a program in generating tasks and in resolving problems. PACs are often used as a "think tank" or as a sounding board for program-parent issues. For parents to be effective members of planning and advisory groups, these committees and councils must have the following characteristics:

1. The committee or council must be an educational group, not a pressure group. Although politically minded individuals may serve on the committee or advisory council, their input should not necessarily be considered the thinking of the majority.
2. The director must show members of the committee or council how a decision will affect the program and make sure parents have appropriate information on which to base their decisions. Parents must then have input into the decision-making process, because one cannot convince parents to become involved if the most important decisions have already been made—for example, decisions regarding goals of the program, the program's delivery system, staffing policies, fiscal matters, and program evaluation.
3. The parents and all other board members must be trained. Programs have failed because of problems at the committee or council level. Training must be given in identifying problems, investigating possible solutions, understanding regulations, learning decision-making processes, and communicating recommendations to the power structure.
4. The committee or council must be small enough to be manageable (twelve or fewer members), and membership should be rotational.

Most state licensing laws require that a not-for-profit, private early childhood organization operate under a governing board composed, at least in part, of the people it serves. Public school early childhood programs are under the jurisdiction of the local board of education or trustees, an elected, policy-making group representing the community's interests. Programs may operate under two boards—one at the program level and the other at the agency level if the program is part of a community service agency. The ultimate form of parent involvement occurs when parents serve on the board of directors.

Parents as Volunteers

Parents can also participate as volunteers, on a regular, semiregular, or occasional basis. For a volunteer program to work, the administrator must support the program by providing general guidance in planning, although parents can organize and operate the program itself. In effective programs, all parents are given a chance to participate, a choice of roles, and the freedom to determine the extent of their participation. Some parents will choose not to participate. Galen[46] reports on how a New Jersey school used an eight-step procedure for expansion of parental involvement.

Program and Support Program Volunteers. Parents are valuable as program volunteers because they know and understand parents' working hours, transportation situations, and community mores; they can serve as cultural models for the children; help staff members understand the children's likes and dislikes, strengths and weaknesses, and home successes and failures; act as interpreters in bilingual programs; and assist staff members in program activities such as storytelling, art, music, and gardening. Parent volunteers also assist in positive control of children by understanding the values of positive guidance, by using consistent, positive reinforcement and kindness, and by solving minor concerns before they develop into major disciplinary problems; accompany staff members in home-visiting programs; and serve as ambassadors to the neighborhood. Specific expectations of volunteers should be determined by the program's needs and the volunteers' abilities. Some basic considerations are as follows:

1. Volunteers should have an orientation to the program's facility and staff, to professional ethics, and to state and local laws regarding personnel qualifications and activities. Orientation could include a broad overview of the program's philosophy and objectives, rules and regulations, specific tasks and limits of responsibility, classroom management (if involved with children), and a "hands on" experience with materials. Their response to the orientation will benefit future programs.
2. Staff members should be oriented toward using volunteers. After orientation, staff members should be given a choice of whether or not to use volunteers.
3. A handbook is helpful for staff and volunteers, reiterating much of the information given during the orientation program.
4. Staff members should plan specific activities for volunteers. Karnes and Greenberg reported that when parents are given menial jobs or are asked to perform tasks no one else wants to do, they may develop a negative attitude and become less involved.[47] Teaching activities require careful planning; staff members should set up the activities for the volunteers so that only one child or a small group of children works with a parent

---

Dear Parents,

We are planning a trip by bus to the zoo on Thursday, April 4.

We need at least four parents to go with us as guides. Would you please help us? We will be leaving the building at 9:00 A.M. and will return at 1:30 P.M. If you can go with us, please let us know by April 2.

Yours truly,

_____

(Staff member's signature)

FIGURE 11–13
Invitation for Parent-Volunteers

volunteer at one time; and, before demonstrating teaching techniques, a staff member should briefly explain the rationale for and the plan of the activity, the material to be used, and the expected learnings.
5. Volunteers must be evaluated by the administration and staff and should be encouraged to discuss their involvement.

Parents can serve as support program volunteers such as lunchroom workers, aides to program nurses, aides in the library-media center, assistants in distributing equipment and materials, workers in transportation services, office workers, and as resource people to locate or gather services or items.

Occasional Volunteers. Many parents cannot serve as volunteers on a regular or semiregular basis; however, they often can and are willing to help on several occasions during the year. They may be needed for transportation or supervisory services on field trips and can be invited to volunteer by letter as shown in Figure 11–13. Parents often help with class celebrations, if invited. See Figure 11–14. They can also help with money-raising projects. See Figure 11–15.

Dear Parents,

Our kindergarten class is planning five parties this year. The parties will be for Halloween, Thanksgiving, Christmas, Valentine's Day, and Easter. I hope that you will be able to help with one of them. We will need refreshments consisting of cupcakes or cookies and something to drink. If you want to help with a party, please indicate which one.

Sincerely,

_____

(Staff member's signature)

FIGURE 11–14
Invitation for Parent-Volunteers

Dear Parents,

Our kindergarten will be having a bake sale on Friday, April 26, from 10:00 A.M. until noon. The sale will be at the end of the hall in our school. The money made from the sale will be used to buy materials for our room.

We need our parents to make cookies, fudge, cupcakes, brownies, popcorn balls, and just anything else that is good to eat. Your children will love to help you prepare the goodies. Everything must be cut in servings and wrapped individually. If you can help, will you please send a note to me stating "what type" and "how many" goodies you plan to make.

We also need several parents to help sell our goodies. If you will be able to help, please send a note to me at school. You will need to be at the school around 9:15 A.M. to help prepare for the bake sale.

Thanks so much for helping in any way you can.

Sincerely,

(Teacher's signature)

FIGURE 11–15
Invitation for Parent-Volunteers

Parents can serve as resource persons, because they frequently enjoy sharing their talents with young children. Staff members should survey parents for their special talents and encourage them to participate in the program. They should ask parents to serve as resource persons representing various occupations and hobby groups.

PARENT EDUCATION AND FAMILY RESOURCE AND SUPPORT PROGRAMS

Parent education has had a long and exciting history.[48] Parent education and home visitations began early in the century as a way to help immigrants. The Children's Bureau was founded in 1913 to eradicate some child labor practices but began to publish materials on child rearing, most of it middle-class oriented.

Parent education for the middle class thrived in the 1920s with the development of the Progressive Education Movement. Many parent and lay programs were developed during this period, such as the child study movement, the Parent-Teachers Association, mental health associations, and parent cooperative nursery schools. In the 1960s, the shift of emphasis was away from the middle class. Similar to the early-intervention programs, in fact, often directly connected with these programs, parent education programs began to focus on low-income parents. Parent education programs grew rapidly in the 1970s, because data from early intervention programs showed increased effectiveness when there was a parent education component.[49] In addition to federally funded parent education programs (e.g., Parent and Child Center Program), over one-third of the states have some form of parent education.[50] And today a great deal of effort is expended on evaluating parent education programs.

Purposes of Parent Education and Family Resource and Support Programs

The basic assumption of parent education is that if the parent's role as a teacher is enhanced, the parent will be able to maximize the child's level of functioning. Several attributes seem to be critical to quality parenting such as a positive view about the future,[51] a willingness to take a proactive stance in dealing with family issues,[52] knowledge of child development[53] plus the use of personal experiences in guiding children's development,[54] a positive work-role attitude along with a view that work and family are harmonious,[55] and a sense of support from a spouse or friend.[56] It is believed that this positive self-image as a parent leads to confidence in the parent-educator role.[57]

Thus, specific purposes of parent education are to

1. Become more positive about oneself as a change agent within the family.
2. Learn more about child growth and development.
3. Develop general concepts of effective child-rearing practices.
4. Acquire an understanding of the local early childhood program's rationale, program content and methodology, and support services.
5. Become an important part of the educative process by expressing good attitudes about the program and staff and about education in general; by reinforcing the child's achievement; by providing continuity between activities at home and in the program; and by extending the child's knowledge and skills.

There has been a major movement toward family resource and support programs in the 1980s. Family resource and support services differ from the more traditional education programs in that they offer a wide array of services such as a *support system* for families rather than as a *change agent* and work to prevent problems rather than repair damage in parent-child relations.[58]

Types of Parent Education and Family Resource and Support Programs

There are many types of parent education programs. Their nature depends on program needs, parental needs and wishes, and program philosophy. For example, programs that use many parent volunteers need more emphasis on parent education, Spanish-speaking parents may need bilingual education, and some early childhood programs may want to train parents to reinforce the program's concepts and language models. Techniques may vary as well. Services for parents may be either staff-directed or parent-initiated; they may have one focus or be multifaceted; and they may be direct, using organized classrooms, or indirect, with parents observing teaching and guidance techniques during program visitations. Programs may be sponsored by school systems, universities, various community agencies, or handled through a cooperative, interagency approach.

Orientation Programs

Perhaps the most common service for parents of children enrolled in an early childhood program is orientation—through handbooks, by attending meetings, and by becoming members of parent-teacher associations. Orientation programs are designed by the staff in local programs.

The Parent and Child Center (PCC) Program

The PCC was developed in response to research on the importance of prenatal and infancy periods on a child's later development. The program, financed by the Office of Economic Opportunity and administered by the Washington office of Project Head Start, was designed to provide services to low-income families with children under three years and to expectant mothers. The PCC objectives were to overcome physical, cognitive, and affective deficits; to improve parent skills, motivations, and confidence; to strengthen family organization; to encourage a community spirit; to provide training and experience for professionals and nonprofessionals; and to conduct research and evaluation of progress toward these objectives. Four major program components were developed: (1) programs for children including a home-visiting program, a home-care program, and a center-based program; (2) programs for parents in areas such as home economics, child development, adult education, and job counseling; (3) health and nutrition services, including medical services for children and their parents, classes in child care, safety, and nutrition; and (4) social services, such as referral, recreational, and assistance in finding adequate housing and in providing food and clothing.

Home Visiting Programs

Home visiting programs were designed to help parents learn how to teach their young children, including how to prepare and collect educational materials. In home visiting programs, a paraprofessional, often a trained parent, or a professional models the teaching/reinforcing style to parents in the home. The parent may later plan to teach the activities, because many program planners feel that parents should learn to set their own goals for their children. In some home visiting programs, parents are taught in groups without children present. After the group consultation, parents return home and present activities to their children. The exact nature of home visiting programs depends on program objectives, the number of families to be visited, the number and frequency of visits per family, and the program's financial resources. Other specifics were discussed in Chapter 1.

Parent Discussion Programs

The basic goals of parent discussion groups are to clarify misconceptions of the functions of parenthood, to define the role of parents in child development, and to extend parents' knowledge and understanding of the needs of children.[59] The resource person must be able to relate information from theory and research to practice. Guidelines for developing structured parent discussion groups include *The Bowdoin Method*,[60] Gordon's *Parent Effectiveness Training*,[61] and Dinkmeyer and McKay's *Systematic Training for Effective Parenting*.[62]

Parents can also identify an area of concern, and a knowledgeable resource person leads the discussion group. Parent discussion groups can be particularly beneficial to parents of children who are disabled, chronically or critically-ill, deceased, or abused. Peer support helps these parents adjust as well as provides needed information.

Resource Centers

A rather popular type of resource center for children is the toy-lending library. These help parents provide intellectual stimulation for their children and offer guidelines in using toys. Nimnicht set up a toy-lending library to develop concepts and verbal fluency in children ages three to nine years.[63] The toys were loaned to parents who enrolled in an eight-week course. Specifics on establishing and operating a toy-lending library may be found in

> McNelis, J. R. *A Practical Guide for Planning and Operating a Toy-Lending Library*, ERIC ED 145 962. Washington, D.C.: American Institute for Research, 1974.

Parent-Child Learning Centers for parents and their children were established in the Johnson County, Kansas, libraries. Materials such as common, everyday objects; puzzles; art media; and stories with suggestions for activities can be found there.[64]

Adult resource centers have also been used for parent education. For example, in Montgomery County, Maryland, the Adult Education Department has established a Parent Education Resource Center. The facility has four areas: (1) a children's discovery corner with books and toys, (2) an adult area with publications of interest to parents, (3) an area for using multimedia equipment, and (4) a record and toy-lending library.[65] Materials are needed in the resource centers to explain concepts of child development and early childhood education. For example, parents need to understand something of what children are like physically, cognitively, and affectively; what tasks the children are trying to accomplish; what experiences retard and facilitate development; and what evidence is indicative of progress. Parents are also concerned about the normality of certain behaviors or stages and the length of time each should last.

Parents need to understand the interacting influences of various aspects of development. Certain behaviors are incompatible; for example, toilet training is most difficult when a toddler is at the peak of the runaround stage and doesn't want to sit. Other behaviors are compatible; for example, when the young child begins to imitate sounds in his physical environment, like those of motors and animals, he enjoys hearing stories and poems that have onomatopoeic words like "buzz" and "hiss."

Parents need knowledge about several approaches to guiding a child based on the developmental stage. If parent demands are not geared to development, disharmony between adult and child results. If parent expectations are too low, the child sometimes shows permanently dependent behavior; if too high, the child displays agonizing frustration. Parents also need to understand the child's interests, what types of experiences are meaningful, and which play equipment and materials help the child develop. As parents become more enlightened, they can reinforce the practices of the early childhood program and can become more discriminating consumers of equipment and materials, movies and television shows, and other things marketed for children. Parents also need help with the specific skills children should develop; with teaching techniques, such as activities, language models, questioning techniques, and reinforcement methods; and with teaching equipment and materials.

Parent Self-Improvement Programs

Parent self-improvement programs were designed to empower parents as individuals to improve their own lives. Services can include instruction for parent self-improvement in the areas of basic adult education, English for speakers of other languages, consumer education, nutrition, clothing, health, community resources, home repairs, and family life. Such instruction may be in the form of formal courses for high school credit or informal workshops, and are usually offered by the public school system for the benefit of all adult residents of a community.

Family Resource and Support Programs

Family resource and support programs are programs that offer services for parents such as parent education, job training, respite care, employment referral, and emotional support and services for children such as health and developmental screening, home-based programs, and center care. Family resource and support programs have their roots in the research that supports the role of families in the educative process and in the parent self-improvement and parent involvement/education programs. Unlike the more traditional programs, parent resource and support programs are based on these premises: (1) there should be a recognition and acceptance of the validity of a variety of parenting styles and of the significances of the contexts (e.g., community and special relations) in which families are embedded; and (2) parent behaviors do not affect children in a unilateral way.[66]

Family resource and support programs are for all parents. However, to be effective, the services must be individualized to support different stages in the family life cycle and to meet other concerns (e.g., work/family issues and family crises). These programs must also stress an egalitarian relationship between parents and early childhood program staff.[67] A leading force in family resource and support programs is the Family Resource Coalition. (See Appendix 5.)

Effects of Parent Education and Family Resource and Support Programs

Vast amounts of research have emphasized the importance of parent-child relationships in the early years of a child's life. Such research suggests parental involvement at early ages significantly contributes to achievement motivation and other factors associated with educational success. The objectives of recent parent education and family support programs are now being studied in terms of impact on child and parent, comparisons of delivery systems, and directions for future studies.

Impact on Child and Parent

Some studies indicate a short-term impact on intelligence,[68, 69] infant responsiveness,[70] and school achievement.[71] The impact of programs on parents has not been studied as often as the effects on the child. However, studies do show the following program impacts on parents: (1) maternal behavior is more positive;[72] (2) parental language interactions with children are improved;[73] (3) parents have better conceptions of their importance in their children's lives;[74] and (4) parental attitudes toward childrearing become more flexible.[75] Parents also report that feelings of control over their own lives increased as a result of program participation.[76]

Comparison of Delivery Systems

In general, one type of parent education or family support program does not seem more effective than another. Some specific findings are as follows:

1. Radin found that a parent education component is important if the child is to benefit from a compensatory preschool program.[77] Similarly, Bronfenbrenner's study indicated that a parent education component is important if the child is to continue to benefit from a compensatory preschool program.[78]
2. Positive effects of parent education programs have been found for both programs that used home visits and also for those that used small-group work as the delivery systems.[79, 80]
3. Three home-based programs that emphasized various curricula (i.e., social, language, and play) were equally effective in raising toddlers' intelligence quotients.[81]

4. Comparisons of popular parent education programs (i.e., PET, Adlerian, and behavioral) did not find one approach more effective than another.[82]

Negative results have been found in several cases. For example, Chilman[83] has noted that traditional parent programs involving casework and community organization strategies have not been very effective. Lambie, et al., argue that "canned" objectives and activities must not be used; rather, objectives must be based on the needs and knowledge of specific groups of parents.[84] There should also be a "match" to the existing parent-child relationship; for example, fathers were included in some activities of the Houston Parent Child Development Center because of the father's instrumental role in the Chicano family. Lambie, et al. summarized their research by stating that negative results occurred in programs with minimal treatment (no match between the objectives of the program and the needs of the children and their parents), high turnover rate of visitors, little supervision, and no or inappropriate objectives.

Directions for Future Studies

One problem concerns matching the content and structure of parent education and family support programs to the needs and developmental levels of parents. For example, Powell found some parents focus on other parents while others focus on staff trainees.[85] Mothers with many ties to families and friends were more responsive to home-based educators than mothers with fewer emotional support systems.[86] The Child and Family Resource Program was more successful with self-confident mothers than with those who were less self-confident.[87] Program effects seem to vary greatly in relation to ethnic group.[88, 89]

Educators do not know how extensive parent education and family support programs must be to yield maximum and lasting results. Long-term consultation (i.e., a minimum of eighteen to twenty-four months) seems to produce the most significant effects.[90, 91] In the Florida Parent-Infant Education Project, home visitation programs of less than two years were found to be ineffective. Two years of home visitation and one year of participation in the home learning center were most effective in changing maternal attitudes toward schooling.[92] These findings lead to the problem of how to retain parents.[93, 94]

Finally, questions need to be answered concerning possible negative effects of programs. Powell has raised some questions about how parents deal with information conflicting with their ideas of child rearing.[95]

SUMMARY

Working with parents has had a long history in early childhood education. The early kindergartens and nursery schools had parent education as one of their program services. Early childhood kindergartens and primary grades (levels) housed in the public schools became more involved in communicating with parents and having parents occasionally assist in the classroom than having parents as close allies in the educative process. However, by the 1960s research-ers involved in the intervention programs found that a parent involvement and education program-component was necessary for maximum benefits to the child. Since the 1980s, there has been a movement toward parent resource and support programs which serve not as agents of family change but rather as a support system for preventing problems while accepting family diversity.

The field of parent involvement/education and support represents consid-erable diversity. Vital components of quality parent-school programs include the following:

1. A fully interactive communication network between home (parent) and program (staff) has long been recognized. Early childhood educators have devised many ways to share their knowledge resources with par-ents and receive valuable information on each child from the parent. Some of the ways of sharing are: parent reception areas, group and individual conferences, handbook for parents, home visits, parent vis-itations to program, and newsletters.
2. A sharing-based involvement through which parents make program decisions (e.g., advisory council membership), assist in classroom teaching, serve as resource people, and help with program support services (e.g., food services, transportation, and clerical).
3. A mutual concern and support system for well-functioning families through one or more of the many types of programs.

Despite the long history and the values of working with parents, many questions remain. Among these questions are:

1. What program approaches are most effective (i.e., sustain participation, have short-term benefits, and have long-term benefits)? Should there be a "match" between program content and structure and the characteris-tics of parents?
2. Are there negative effects to program participation?
3. Can a real alliance among parents and teachers protect the unique charac-teristics of each? Resolve different goals for children without compartmen-talizing the child's world? Avoid negative overt and covert judgments of each other? Allow for the stress of family life and job responsibilities?

NOTES

1. J. E. Butterworth, *The Parent Teacher Association and Its Work* (New York: Macmillan, 1928).
2. G. Epstein, "School Policy and Parent Involvement: Research Results," *Ed-ucational Horizons* 62 (1984): 70–72.
3. E. Weber, *The Kindergarten: Its Encounter with Educational Thought in America* (New York: Columbia University Teachers College, 1969).
4. M. McMillan, *The Nursery School* (London: J. M. Dent and Sons, 1919).

5. C. E. Joffe, *Friendly Intruders* (Berkeley: University of California Press, 1977).

6. M. Fantini, *Community Control and the Urban School* (New York: Praeger, 1970).

7. J. P. Comer, *Maggie's American Dream: The Life and Times of a Black Family* (New York: Penguin, 1988).

8. A. Henderson, *The Evidence Grows* (Columbia, Md.: National Committee for Citizens in Education, 1981).

9. A. Henderson, *The Evidence Continues to Grow: Parent Involvement Improves Student Achievement* (Columbia, Md.: National Committee for Citizens in Education, 1987).

10. B. Caldwell, "What Is Quality Child Care?" *What is Quality Child Care?*, eds. B. Caldwell and A. Hillard (Washington, D.C.: National Association for the Education of Young Children, 1985), 1–16.

11. J. Comer, "Parent Participation in the Schools," *Phi Delta Kappan* 67, 6 (1986): 442–446.

12. E. Zigler, "The Environmental Mystique: Training of the Intellect versus Development of the Child," *Childhood Education* 46, 8 (1970): 402–12.

13. E. Schaefer, "Parent and Child Correlates of Parental Modernity," *Parental Belief Systems: The Psychological Consequences for Children*, ed. I. Sigel (Hillsdale, N.J.: Erlbaum, 1985), 287–318.

14. G. Spivack and N. Cianci, "High Risk Early Behavior Patterns and Later Delinquency," *Prevention of Delinquent Behaviors*, eds. J. Burchard and S. Burchard (Newbury Park, Calif.: Sage, 1987), 44–74.

15. D. T. Slaughter, "Early Intervention and Its Effects on Maternal and Child Development," *Monographs of the Society for Research in Child Development* 48 (1983): serial no. 202.

16. E. Zigler and W. Berman, "Discovering the Future of Early Childhood Intervention," *American Psychologist* 38 (1983): 894–906.

17. K. Swick, "Teacher Reports on Parental Efficacy/Involvement Relationships," *Instructional Psychology* 14 (1987): 125–132.

18. B. White, *Educating Infants and Toddlers* (Lexington: Lexington Books, 1988).

19. G. Rekers, *Family Building: Six Qualities of a Strong Family* (Ventura: Regal Books, 1985).

20. Swick, "Teacher Reports on Parental Efficacy/Involvement Relationships."

21. L. Latlimore, "Parent Involvement in the Classroom: Good Grief!" *Thrust for Educational Leadership* 6 (1977): 18–19.

22. E. Litwak and H. Meyer, *School, Family, and Neighborhood: The Theory and Practice of School-Community Relations* (New York: Columbia University Press, 1974).

23. L. G. Katz, "Mothering and Teaching: Some Significant Distinctions," *Current Topics in Early Childhood Education*, vol. 3, L. G. Katz (Norwood, N.J.: Ablex Publishing Corp., 1980), 47–63.

24. S. Kontos, "The Attitudinal Context of Family—Day-Care Relationships," *Continuity and Discontinuity of Experience in Child Care, vol. 2: Annual Advances in Applied Developmental Psychology*, eds. D. Peters and S. Kontos (Norwood, N.J.: Ablex Publishing Corp., 1987), 91–113.

25. S. Kontos, "Congruence of Parenting and Early Childhood Staff Perceptions of Parenting," *Parenting Studies* 1, 1 (1984): 5–10.

26. E. Galinsky, "Why Are Some Parent/Teacher Partnerships Clouded with Difficulties?" *Young Children* 45, 5 (1990): 2–3, 38–39.

27. Ibid.

28. E. Prescott, *A Pilot Study of Day-Care Centers and Their Clientele*, Children's Bureau, pub. no. 428 (Washington, D.C.: Government Printing Office, 1965).

29. P. Greenberg, "Parents as Partners in Young Children's Development and Education: A New American Fad? Why Does It Matter?" *Young Children* 44, 4 (1989): 61–75.

30. Ibid., 69.

31. S. Kontos and W. Wells, "Attitudes of Caregivers and the Day Care Experiences of Families," *Early Childhood Research Quarterly* 1 (1986): 47–67.

32. Greenberg, "Parents as Partners in Young Children's Development and Education," 69.

33. S. B. Heath and M. W. McLaughlin, "A Child Resource Policy: Moving Beyond Dependence on School and Family," *Phi Delta Kappan* 68, 8 (1987): 576–580.

34. Greenberg, "Parents as Partners in Young Children's Development and Education," 67.

35. E. Galinsky and W. Hooks, *New Extended Family* (Boston: Houghton Mifflin, 1977).

36. E. Galinsky, "Parents and Teacher-Caregivers: Sources of Tension, Sources of Support," *Young Children* 43, 3 (1988): 4–12.

37. D. Powell, "Day-Care as a Family Support System," *America's Family Support Programs: Perspectives and Prospects* (New Haven: Yale University Press, 1987), 115–132.

38. D. R. Powell, "The Coordination of Preschool Socialization: Parent Caregiver Relationships in Day-Care Settings" (Paper presented at the Conference of the Society for Research in Child Development, New Orleans, March 1977).

39. C. Seefeldt, "Parent Involvement: Support or Stress?" *Childhood Education* 62, 2 (1985): 98–102.

40. Ibid.

41. Title IV of P.L. 90–247 (The General Education Provision Act), Sec. 438, added by Sec. 513 P.L. 93–380 (August 21, 1974) and amended by Senate Joint Resolution (Sen. J. Res. 40) (1974).

42. *The School Code of Illinois*, 1967, sec. 23–24, 253.

43. E. L. Morgan, "Talking with Parents when Concerns Come Up," *Young Children* 44, 2 (1989): 52–56.

44. C. A. Readdick, et al., "The Child-Parent-Teacher Conference: A Setting for Child Development," *Young Children* 39, 5 (1984): 67–73.

45. E. Jones, "Involving Parents in Children's Learning," *Childhood Education* 47, 3 (1970): 126–130.

46. H. Gallen, "Increasing Parental Involvement in Elementary School: The Nitty-Gritty of One Successful Program," *Young Children* 46, 2 (1991): 18–22.

47. Greenberg, "Parents as Partners in Young Children's Development and Education," 66.

48. S. M. Gruenberg, "Parent Education in Six White House Conferences," *Child Study* 37 (1959–1960): 9–15.

49. U. Bronfenbrenner, *Is Early Intervention Effective? A Report on Longitudinal Evaluations of Preschool Programs* (Washington, D.C.: Office of Child Development, Department of Health, Education, and Welfare, 1974).

50. F. Marx and M. Seligson, *The Public School Early Childhood Study: The State Survey* (New York: Bank Street College of Education, 1988).

51. I. Sigel, ed., *Parental Belief Systems: The Psychological Consequences for Children* (Hillsdale, N.J.: Erlbaum, 1985).

52. Schaefer, "Parent and Child Correlates of Parental Modernity."

53. R. LaRossa, *Becoming a Parent* (Newbury Park, Calif.: Sage, 1986).

54. B. Bettelheim, *A Good Enough Parent* (New York: Alfred A. Knopf, 1987).

55. P. Voyanoff, *Work and Family Life* (Newbury Park, Calif.: Sage, 1987).

56. E. Galinsky, *The Six Stages of Parenthood* (Reading, Mass.: Addison-Wesley, 1987).

57. Swick, "Teacher Reports on Parental Efficacy/Involvement Relationships."

58. E. Zigler and W. Berman, "Discerning the Future of Early Childhood Intervention," *American Psychologist* 38 (1983): 894–906.

59. S. R. Slavson, *Child Centered Group Guidance* (New York: International Universities, 1974).

60. R. Bowdoin, *The Bowdoin Method* (Nashville: Webster's International Tutoring Systems, 1976).

61. T. Gordon, *Parent Effectiveness Training* (New York: Peter H. Wyden, 1970).

62. D. Dinkmeyer and G. D. McKay, "Systematic Training for Effective Parenting," *Leader's Manual* (Circle Pines, Minn.: American Guidance Service, 1976).

63. G. P. Nimnicht and E. Brown, "The Toy Library: Parents and Teachers Learning with Toys," *Young Children* 28, 2 (1972): 110–117.

64. S. Vartuli and P. Rogers, "Parent-Child Learning Centers," *Dimensions* 14, 1 (1985): 8–10.

65. P. Edmister, "Establishing a Parent Education Resource Center," *Childhood Education* 54, 2 (1977): 62–66.

66. B. Weissbourd, "The Family Support Movement: Greater Than the Sum of Its Parts," *Zero to Three* 4 (1983): 8–10.

67. S. L. Kagan, "Early Care and Education: Beyond the Schoolhouse Doors," *Phi Delta Kappan* 71, 2 (1989): 107–112.

68. S. R. Andrews, et al., "The Skills of Mothering: A Study of Parent Child Development Centers," *Monographs of the Society for Research in Child Development* 47 (1982): serial no. 198.

69. Slaughter, "Early Interventions."

70. J. R. Dickie and S. C. Gerber, "Training in Social Competence: The Effect on Mothers, Fathers, and Infants," *Child Development* 51, 4 (1980): 1248–1251.

71. M. Cochran and C. Henderson, *Family Matters: Evaluation of the Parental Empowerment Program. Final Report to the National Institute of Education* (Ithaca: Cornell University, 1985).

72. Andrews, et al., "Skills of Mothering."

73. D. Z. Lambie, J. T. Bond, and D. P. Weikart, "Home Teaching with Mothers and Infants," *Monographs of the High/Scope Educational Research Foundation* no. 2 (Ypsilanti: High/Scope, 1974).

74. J. Travers, M. J. Nauta, and N. Irwin, *The Effects of a Social Program: Final Report of the Child and Family Resource Program's Infant Toddler Component* (Cambridge: Abt, 1982).

75. Slaughter, "Early Interventions."

76. Travers, Nauta, and Irwin, *Effects of a Social Program.*

77. N. Radin, *Three Degrees of Parent Involvement in a Preschool Program: Impact on Mother and Children* (Ann Arbor: University of Michigan, School of Social Work, 1971).

78. U. Bronfenbrenner, *A Report on Longitudinal Evaluations of Preschool Programs, vol. 2: Is Early Intervention Effective?* pub. no. OHD 74–25 (Washington, D.C.: Department of Health, Education, and Welfare, 1974).

79. M. B. Karnes, et al., "Educational Intervention in the Homes of Disadvantaged Infants," *Child Development* 41 (1970): 925–35.

80. E. Badger, S. Elssas, and J. M. Sutherland, *Mother Training as a Means of Accelerating Childhood Development in a High Risk Population,* ERIC ED 104 522 (Paper presented at the Meeting for Pediatric Research, Washington, D.C., 1974).

81. W. Kessen, et al., *Variations in Home-Based Infant Education: Language, Play, and Social Development. Final Report to the Office of Child Development, U.S. Department of Health, Education and Welfare* (New Haven: Yale University Press, 1975).

82. M. Pinsker and K. Geoffrey, "Comparison of Parent Effectiveness Training and Behavior Modification Parent Training," *Family Relations* 30 (1981): 61–68.

83. C. S. Chilman, "Programs for Disadvantaged Parents," *Review of Child Development Research,* vol. 3, ed. B. M. Caldwell and H. N. Ricciuti (Chicago: University of Chicago Press, 1973), 403–465.

84. Lambie, Bond, and Weikart, "Home Teaching."

85. D. R. Powell, "Stability and Change in Patterns of Participation in a Parent-Child Program," *Professional Psychology: Research and Practice* 16 (1985): 172–180.

86. Kessen, et al., *Variations in Home-Based Infant Education.*

87. Travers, Nauta, and Irwin, *Effects of a Social Program.*

88. Lambie, Bond, and Weikart, "Home Teaching."

89. Cochran and Henderson, *Family Matters.*

90. I. J. Gordon and B. J. Guinagh, *A Home Learning Center Approach to Early Stimulation, Final Report,* ERIC ED 115 388 (Gainesville: University of Florida, Institute for Development of Human Resources, 1974).

91. P. Levenstein, *A Message from Home: A Home-Based Intervention Method for Low-Income Preschoolers,* ERIC ED 095 992 (Mineola, N.Y.: Family Services Association of Nassau County, 1974).

92. Gordon and Guinagh, *Home Learning Center.*

93. D. L. Johnson and J. N. Breckenridge, "The Houston Parent-Child Development Center and the Primary Prevention of Behavior Problems in Young Children," *American Journal of Community Psychology* 10 (1982): 305–316.

94. J. E. Lochman and M. V. Brown, "Evaluation of Dropout Clients and of Perceived Usefulness of a Parent Education Program," *Journal of Community Psychology* 8 (1980): 132–139.

95. D. R. Powell, "Enhancing the Effectiveness of Parent Education: An Analysis of Program Assumptions," *Current Topics in Early Childhood Education*, vol. 5, ed. L. Katz (Norwood, N.J.: Ablex, 1984).

FOR FURTHER READING

Bjorklund, G., and Burger, C. "Making Conferences Work for Parents, Teachers, and Children." *Young Children* 42, 2 (1987): 26–31.

Bundy, B. F. "Fostering Communication between Parents and Preschools." *Young Children* 46, 2 (1991): 12–17.

Cataldo, C. Z. *Parent Education for Early Childhood: Child-Rearing Content for the Student and Professional.* New York: Teachers College Press, Teachers College Columbia University, 1987.

Herrera, J. F., and Wooden, S. L. "Some Thoughts About Effective Parent-School Communication." *Young Children* 43, 6 (1988): 78–80.

Musick, J. S., and Weissbourd, B. *Guidelines for Establishing Family Resource Programs.* Chicago: National Committee for the Prevention of Child Abuse, 1988.

Powell, D. R. *Families and Early Childhood Programs.* Washington, D.C.: National Association for the Education of Young Children, 1989.

Powell, D. R. "Home Visiting in the Early Years: Policy and Program Design Decisions." *Young Children* 45, 6 (1990): 65–72.

Powell, D. R. ed. *Parent Education as Early Childhood Intervention: Emerging Directions in the Theory, Research, and Practice.* Norwood, N.J.: Ablex Publishing Corp., 1988.

Stone, J. G. *Teacher-Parent Relationships.* Washington, D.C.: National Association for the Education of Young Children, 1987.

Swap, S. M. *Enhancing Parent Involvement in Schools: A Manual for Parents and Teachers.* New York: Teachers College Press, Teachers College Columbia University, 1987.

Chapter 12
Contributing to the Profession

The role of the early childhood administrator, regardless of his official title, is one of leadership. As a leader, the administrator must be concerned with the quality of early childhood care and education. The concern for quality must go beyond the local program to an interest in the overall excellence of early childhood programs. Consequently, administrators as leaders can contribute to their profession by promoting professionalization of early childhood education, attempting to influence public policy, becoming involved in research, and helping others find a place in the profession.

PROMOTING PROFESSIONALIZATION

Professionalization is defined as the dynamic process whereby an occupation can be observed to change certain crucial characteristics in the direction of a profession.[1] The word **profession** is defined in terms of certain characteristics occupational such as (1) having an existing knowledge base; (2) focusing on service; (3) performing a unique function for clients and society; (4) having a monopoly of knowledge in the field; (5) internally determining standards of education and training; (6) having professional practice recognized by some form of license or certification; (7) shaping most legislation of the profession by the profession; (8) gaining in power, prestige, and income; (9) identifying with the profession individually and as a group through a national association; and (10) seeing the profession as a lifelong occupation.[2] Houle notes these characteristics of a profession: (1) clarification of the occupation's defining functions; (2) mastery of theoretical knowledge; (3) capacity to solve problems; (4) use of practical knowledge; (5) self-enhancement; (6) formal training; (7) credentialing; (8) creation of subcultures (e.g., awareness of history of the profession and its role in the culture, staff titles reflecting current nomenclature, and understanding of terminology used in the profession); (9) legal reinforcement; (10) public acceptance; (11) ethical practice; (12) penalties; (13) relations to other vocations; and (14) relations to users of the service.[3] Radomski developed a series of questions that focuses on each of Houle's characteristics. A rating form is provided for local early childhood programs to assess their level of progress toward professionalization.[4]

Caldwell states that the early childhood education field suffers from a lack of conceptual clarity and standard terminology. She has identified five issues critical to the professional identity of early childhood education, namely, to determine, "just what we do," "what we cannot (or should not) do," "how we should do that which we do," "where we should do what we do," and "how we communicate what we do."[5] Hostetler and Klugman state that the field needs to identify commonalities among all who work with young children while simultaneously allowing for diversity.[6] Dresden and Myers discuss three myths that impede our own valuing of what we do and how we conduct our business. The myths are: (1) the hierarchical model of power and working relationships is the only model for productive behavior, (2) the only way to pursue a career seriously is via a career ladder, and (3) genuine career commitment needs to exclude other commitments and connections.[7]

A **code of ethics**, a statement of professional conduct, is another sign of a mature profession. Moore calls a code of ethics "a private system of law which is characteristic of all formally constituted organizations."[8] Practitioners share a code of ethics highlighting proper relations and responsibilities to each other and to clients or others outside the profession. Katz gives four reasons why the early childhood education needs a code of ethics:

1. Practitioners of education have almost unlimited power over children whose self-protective repertoire is limited. How shall children be protected?
2. The professional staff serves a multiplicity of clients—children, parents, regulatory/funding agencies, and the community. Who makes the final decisions?
3. Because of the unavailability and unreliability of empirical findings, there are gaps in knowledge of what is best. How can educators avoid the seemingly "functional" orthodoxies or ideologies and remain open-minded?
4. Educators are responsible for the whole child, yet there are limits to their expertise and power. Parents, for example, are gaining more power in the decision-making process. What are the educators' limits?[9]

The issue of professional ethics was raised with the National Association for the Education of Young Children (NAEYC) members. The 1985 survey was funded by NAEYC and the Wallace Alexander Gerbode Foundation.[10] Feeny and Kipnis stated the survey showed that early childhood educators were in "ethical pain."[11] Ninety-three percent of all respondents (and 100 percent of specialists) agreed or strongly agreed that attention to ethical issues and the development of a code of ethics should be an important priority in the field. Data also showed that relationships with parents and with staff and administrators are the areas of greatest concern among early childhood educators. The major ethical problems reported were unprofessional behavior, information management, child abuse and neglect, and referrals to outside agencies.[12] Following workshops and another survey of the membership, a final document was approved by NAEYC's Governing Board in July, 1989. The adopted Code of Ethics sets forth professional responsibilities in four areas of professional relationships: children, families, colleagues, and community and society.[13] The Ethics Commission decided that the Code should be "encouraged" rather than "enforced" at this time and should be incorporated into the ongoing projects of the Association. The Code will be reviewed in 1991 and then at regular intervals, possibly every five years.[14]

INFLUENCING PUBLIC POLICY

Advocacy is the process of maintaining, extending, or improving services to children, families, and staff. Advocacy brings together all the significant people in the child's life and tries to approach the needs of the child through interdisciplinary teamwork. There are two types of advocacy—case and class advocacy. **Case advocacy** refers to a situation where a particular child or family is not receiving services or benefits for which it is eligible. The advocate takes the necessary steps to right the situation. **Class advocacy** involves more than an isolated incident; rather it is advocacy on behalf of a group—migrants, the disabled, or minority groups—that needs help in working with the agencies established for it. Advocacy may also be viewed as an immediate action (e.g., lobbying on behalf of specific legislation or a particular regulation or coalitions built around a specific focus) or as setting goals for later initiatives (i.e., networks publicizing needs, demonstrating cost-effectiveness of specific programs, contributing to political action campaigns, or voting for candidates concerned about children).

Major advocacy efforts in early childhood began in the 1930s and 1940s when teacher educators on the President's Advisory Committee on the WPA Nursery Schools campaigned to keep the nursery schools in operation. Early childhood educators seemed less active in advocacy in the 1950s and 1960s. When the Child Development Act of 1971 was vetoed, the need for effective advocacy was noted. The federal government recognized the importance of child advocacy when the Office of Child Development established a Center for Child Advocacy in 1971. In 1980, the Center for the Study of Public Policies for Young Children, a part of High/Scope Educational Research Foundation, was founded by the Carnegie Corporation of New York. The goal of the Center was to communicate with the federal and state policymakers about implications of research findings for policies affecting young children. Not only are advocacy efforts increasing but training for public policy and advocacy is on the rise.[15]

Roles in Influencing Public Policy

Takanishi indicates three roles in public policy formulation:

1. An **expert** assesses the research literature pertinent to some issue and evaluates the likely efficacy of a proposed procedure for achieving a goal. The expert makes judgments based on consideration of alternatives, costs and benefits of alternatives, and analyzes the techniques necessary to bring about and maintain policy change.
2. The **advocate** pursues or defends a program believed to be in the best interest of the child or his family. The advocate stays close to the data base of the expert, but his main role is one of action. In a sense, professional practice itself is advocacy.
3. **Community members** must also be involved in policy making, in order to prevent encroachment on local autonomy. Services should respond to the needs expressed by people of the local community. Community involvement also increases accountability; thus, administrators must devise a process for community participation.

Becoming an Effective Advocate

There are several steps to becoming an effective advocate:

1. Know about the problems and the number of people in the area affected by a problem. The Child Care Information Service of the National Association for the Education of Young Children provides demographic fact sheets, information kits, bibliographies, and directories. Another source is

   Frank, M. *Child Care: Emerging Legal Issues.* New York: Haworth, 1983.

2. Determine the appropriate congressional committee, subcommittee, or agency responsible for correcting the problem. Know what authority each level of government has. Those responsible may try to deny responsibility. Two good sources are

   Ebert Flattau, P. *A Legislative Guide.* Washington, D.C.: Association for the Advancement of Psychology, 1980.

   Jewett, P.A. *Kids and Politics Do Mix: The Role of the Early Childhood Professional in the Influencing of Public Policy,* ERIC ED 207 690. Springvale, Maine: New England Association for the Education of Young Children, 1980.

3. Note legislative issues. Examine the Association for the Advancement of Psychology's *APA Monitor.* Know the congressional representatives and how lobbies are formed. Information on forming state lobbies is found in . . . .

> Hass, E. "Getting Support for Children's Programs: Organizing Child Advocacy." In *Rationale for Child-Care Services: Programs vs. Politics*, vol. 1 edited by S. Auerback, 125–135. New York: Human Sciences, 1975.

4. Translate ideas into concrete terms. According to Fink and Sponseller child advocacy can be learned through simulation.[16] Simulation can help in testing various alternatives and clarifying thinking.
5. Write to members of Congress. Some excellent tips for contacting elected officials are found in . . .

> Allen, E. "Children, the Congress, and You," *Young Children* 38, 2 (1983): 71–75.

6. Do not duplicate the work of other child advocacy groups.
7. Practice patience, but take the offensive. Advocacy is more than defensive in nature.
8. Follow through on plans for correcting a situation. Many plans have been delayed for further study or for lack of budget at the expense of child and family.
9. Enlist more child advocates by informing others. See . . .

> Dittmann, L. L. "Affecting Social Policy in Community and Nation." *Childhood Education* 55, 4 (1979): 194–204.

> Duff, R. E., and Stroman, S. H. "Mobilizing Community Agencies in Coalitions for Child Advocacy." *Childhood Education* 55, 4 (1979): 210–212.

> *Organizing Your Community for Child Advocacy: The 4C Approach*, Lansing: Michigan Community Coordinated Child Care (4-C) Council, 1976.

> White, J. A., and Vernon, L. "Parents, Teachers and the Legislative Process—Texas Style!" *Childhood Education* 55, 4 (1979) 207–210.

> Wingfield, L. G. A. "How to Get Involved." *Childhood Education* 55, 4 (1979) 205–207.

10. Join groups that assume an advocacy role and professional organizations listed in Appendices 4 and 5.

BECOMING INVOLVED IN RESEARCH

Research has come to occupy a position of major importance in society. Tremendous advances have been made in business, industry, and medicine. Some businesses and industries allocate more than 50 percent of their budgets for research. Although advancement in education lags behind some other areas and educational research has been conducted on a shoestring budget, research is now recognized as a major way to effect improvements in education. For example, research on Head Start changed public policy. More groups are now interested in and financially support research. Contributing to research and interpreting data for the benefit of children, their families, and those working on behalf of children have become recognized as part of administration.

Early childhood education is involved in both psychological and pedagogical research. Prior to the 1960s, research focused on developmental characteristics of children.[17] After that, research continued to focus on child development. The cultural context of early childhood education was examined more precisely.[18] From the mid-1960s through the early 1970s, research centered on cognitive and linguistic "deprivation" and the effects of "compensatory action."[19]

Almy[20] and Katz[21] have denounced the distance between researcher and teacher. Takanishi believes that this distance began when earlier child development researchers wanted to establish their field as more "pure" science untainted by any practical considerations.[22] Sears believes that child development research must turn back to relevancy—social problem-solving research.[23] For example, Caldwell has identified areas needing more research. According to Caldwell, some of the questions needing answers are: What happens to the gains made in the early years? What is the proper balance between group- and individual-oriented teaching? How do we help children who do not have parental support? What do we do about gifted children who are often not served prior to third grade? Where should our early childhood programs operate and who should control them? How should we communicate what we do?[24] Weikart calls for better instruments and research methodologies to supply adequate assessment procedures for areas which are in need of research (e.g., affective development and curriculum methodologies). He also says that we need to know about the consequences of our work with children below three years of age.[25] In order for research to become more relevant, differences between the practitioner's and researcher's perspectives must be narrowed.[26]

All early childhood educators should become involved in research efforts. One effort to resolve the dilemma between formal research and functional practice is the Teachers' Research Network.[27] Teachers might begin by volunteering or cooperating with those conducting research when requested. (One example of collaborative research was reported by Rogers, Waller, and Perrin.[28]) Guidelines for cooperation have been proposed by Allen and Catron,[29] and Jolongo and McCracken have provided suggestions for writing a publishable manuscript.[30]

HELPING OTHERS FIND A PLACE IN THE PROFESSION

Helping others find a place in the profession of early childhood education is a major leadership responsibility. This is certainly a form of advocacy, as others are encouraged to contribute. Early childhood educators can:

1. Provide places for student teachers, interns, and others in their programs.[31]

2. Write and verbally consult with others on careers in early childhood education, beginning by including childhood education as a career along with the other careers introduced to young children in the program.
3. Share skills and knowledge with others who work with young children.[32]
4. Encourage others to continue their education through independent study, conferences, short courses, formal degrees, and participation in professional organizations, and set an example by continuing their own education.

With the contributions of others, the education profession grows and improves for the benefit of all young children.

SUMMARY

There have been many calls in recent years for professionalism in early childhood education. Professionalism is linked to many processes such as defining early childhood education, developing a knowledge base, abiding by a code of ethics, and focusing on service and maintaining, extending, and improving that service.

Children, the clients of early childhood educators, are dependent upon adults who know their needs and who can make their needs visible to decision makers. If we as early childhood educators fail to raise our collective voice on behalf of children and their families, the problems faced by children and their families will never be solved and our commitment will be broken. Thus, advocacy is the way we actualize our professional responsibility.

As a profession our knowledge base is created through research. Researchers in psychology and education and teachers in the field need to be working on more joint projects. Researchers need to be aware of the many concerns of daily practice, and teachers need to use the eye of the researcher as they practice.

Early childhood educators need to confirm their professionalism in helping others become involved. Encouragement and assistance are needed in helping others develop a sense of identity within the profession. We need more of the dauntless men and women who carry the banner of early education at every level of involvement.

Professionalism is dynamic in nature. Early childhood education will continue to change in positive ways as all of us who call ourselves professionals become involved in promoting professionalization, influencing public policy, becoming involved in research, and helping others find a place in the profession. And, in this profession, we need administrators who take the leadership role in seizing opportunities to make a difference in young children's lives.

NOTES

1. H. W. Vollmer and D. L. Mills, *Professionalization* (Englewood Cliffs: Prentice-Hall, 1966).

2. D. S. Thompson, *The Professionalism of Early Childhood Educators and Administrators: Problems and Prospects,* ERIC ED 256 468 (1984).

3. C. O. Houle, *Continuing Learning in the Profession* (San Francisco: Jossey-Bass, 1981).

4. M. A. Radomski, "Professionalization of Early Childhood Educators," *Young Children* 41, 5 (1986): 20–23.

5. B. M. Caldwell, "Educare: A New Professional Identity," *Dimensions* 16, 4 (1990): 3–6.

6. L. Hostetler and E. Klugman, "Early Childhood Job Titles: One Step Toward Professional Status," *Young Children* 37, 6 (1982): 13–22.

7. J. Dresden and B. K. Myers, "Early Childhood Professionals: Toward Self-Definition," *Young Children* 44, 2 (1989): 62–66.

8. W. E. Moore, *The Profession: Roles and Rules* (New York: Russell Sage Foundation, 1970), 116.

9. L. G. Katz, *Ethical Issues in Working with Young Children,* ERIC ED 144 681 (Washington, D.C.: Department of Health, Education, and Welfare, National Institute of Education, 1977).

10. S. Feeney and K. Kipnis, "Public Policy Report: Professional Ethics in Early Childhood Education," *Young Children* 40, 3 (1985): 54–58.

11. Ibid.

12. S. Feeney and L. Sysko, "Professional Ethics in Early Childhood Education: Survey Results," *Young Children* 42, 1 (1986): 15–20.

13. S. Feeney and K. Kipnis, "Code of Ethical Conduct and Statement of Commitment," *Young Children* 45, 1 (1989): 24–29.

14. S. Feeney, "Update on the NAEYC Code of Ethical Conduct," *Young Children* 45, 4 (1990): 20–21.

15. J. Lombardi, "Training for Public Policy and Advocacy," *Young Children* 41, 4 (1986): 65–69.

16. J. Fink and D. Sponseller, "Practicing for Child Advocacy," *Young Children* 32, 3 (1977): 49–54.

17. E. M. Fuller, et al. "Practices and Resources in Early Childhood Education," *Forty-sixth Yearbook of the National Society for the Study of Education, Part 2: Early Childhood Education,* ed. N. S. Light (Chicago: University of Chicago, 1947).

18. I. J. Gordon, ed. *Seventy-first Yearbook of the National Society for the Study of Education, Part 2: Early Childhood Education* (Chicago: University of Chicago, 1972).

19. R. Takanishi-Knowles, *Federal Involvement in Early Childhood Education (1933–1973): The Need for Historical Perspectives,* ERIC ED 097 969 (Los Angeles: University of California, Department of Education, 1974).

20. M. Almy, *The Early Childhood Educator at Work* (New York: McGraw-Hill, 1975).

21. L. Katz, *Talks with Teachers* (Washington, D.C.: National Association for the Education of Young Children, 1977).

22. R. Takanishi, "Early Childhood Education and Research: The Changing Relationship," *Theory into Practice* 20 (1981): 86–93.

23. R. R. Sears, "Your Ancients Revisited: A History of Child Development," *Review of Child Development Research, vol. 5,* ed. E. M. Hetherington (Chicago: University of Chicago, 1975), 1–73.

24. Caldwell, "Educare: A New Professional Identity."

25. D. P. Weikart, "Hard Choices in Early Childhood Care and Education: A View to the Future," *Young Children* 44, 3 (1989): 25–30.

26. A. S. Bolster, Jr., "Toward a More Effective Model of Research on Teaching," *Harvard Educational Review* 53 (1983): 294–308.

27. J. Chattin-McNichols and M. H. Loeffler, "Teachers as Researchers: The First Cycle of the Teachers' Research Network," *Young Children* 44, 5 (1989): 20–27.

28. D. L. Rogers; C. B. Waller; and M. S. Perrin, "Learning More about What Makes a Good Teacher Good through Collaborative Research in the Classroom," *Young Children* 42, 4 (1987): 34–39.

29. J. Allen and C. Catron, "Researchers at the Early Childhood Center: Guidelines for Cooperation," *Young Children* 45, 4 (1990): 60–65.

30. M. R. Jalongo and J. B. McCracken, "Writing for Professional Publication in Early Childhood Education," *Young Children* 41, 2 (1986): 19–23.

31. F. Funk, "The Cooperating Teacher as the Most Significant Other: A Competent Humanist," *Action in Teacher Education* 4 (1982): 57–64.

32. S. C. Raines, "Who Are We in the Lives of Our Children?" *Young Children* 39, 3 (1984): 9–12.

FOR FURTHER READING

Clapp, G. *Child Study Research: Current Perspectives and Applications.* Lexington, MA: Lexington Books, 1988.

Dresden, J., and Myers, B. K. "Early Childhood Professionals: Toward Self-Definition." *Young Children* 44, 2 (1989): 62–66.

Fennimore, B. S. *Child Advocacy for Early Childhood Educators.* New York: Teachers College Press, Teachers College Columbia University, 1989.

Goffin, S. G., and Lombardi, J. *Speaking Out: Early Childhood Advocacy.* Washington, D.C.: National Association for the Education of Young Children, 1988.

Howes, C. *Keeping Current in Child Care Research,* Washington, D.C.: National Association for the Education of Young Children, 1986.

Jensen, M. A., and Chevalier, Z. W. *Issues and Advocacy in Early Education.* Needham Heights, MA: Allyn and Bacon, 1990.

Melton, G. B. *Child Advocacy: Psychological Issues and Interventions.* New York: Plenum, 1983.

Ornstein, A. C. "The Trend Toward Increased Professionalization for Teachers." *Phi Delta Kappan* 63, 3 (1981): 196–98.

Radomski, M. A. "Professionalization of Early Childhood Educators." *Young Children* 41, 5 (1986): 20–23.

Seefeldt, C. *Continuing Issues in Early Childhood Education,* Columbus: Merrill, 1990.

Simmons, J. M. *Exploring the Relationship between Research and Practice: The Impact of Assuming the Role of Action Researcher in One's Own Classroom.* Paper presented at the annual meeting of the American Educational Research Association, Chicago, April 1985.

Spodek, B.; Saracho, O. N.; and Peters, D. L., eds. *Professionalism and the Early Childhood Practitioner.* New York: Teachers College Press, Teachers College Columbia University, 1988.

Wilkins, A., and Blank, H. "Child Care: Strategies to Move the Issues Forward." *Young Children* 42, 1 (1986): 68–72.

Appendix 1
Resources for Program Planning

Infants and Toddlers

Adcock, D., and Segal, M. *From One to Two Years*. San Diego: Oak Tree, 1980.

Belsky, J. "The 'Effects' of Infant Day-Care Reconsidered," *Early Childhood Research Quarterly*, 3 (1988): 235–272.

Bowlby, J. *A Secure Base: Parent-Child Attachment and Healthy Human Development*. New York: Basic Books, 1988.

Caldwell, B. M. "Professional Child Care: A Supplement to Parental Care." In *Group Care for Young Children: Considerations for Child Care and Health Professionals, Public Policy Makers, and Parents*, edited by N. Guzenhauser and B. M. Caldwell. Skillman, N.J.: Johnson and Johnson Baby Products, 1986.

Cataldo, C. *Infant and Toddler Programs: A Guide to Very Early Childhood Education*. Reading: Addison-Wesley, 1982.

Chase-Landsdale, I., and Owen, M. T. "Maternal Employment in a Family Context: Effects on Infant-Mother and Infant-Father Attachment." *Child Development* 58 (1988): 1505–1512.

Clarke, J. I.; Davenport, G.; Houtz, N.; and Lawrence, M., eds. *Help! For Parents of Children Eighteen Months to Three Years*. San Francisco: Harper and Row, 1986.

Clarke, J. I.; Kemp, S.; Nordeman, G.; and Peterson, E., eds. *Help! For Parents of Infants from Birth to Six Months*. San Francisco: Harper and Row, 1986.

Clarke, J. I.; Montz, D.; Popp, J. L.; and Salts, J. A., eds. *Help! for Parents of Children Six to Eighteen Months*. San Francisco: Harper and Row, 1986.

Cryer, D.; Harms, T.; and Bourland, B. *Active Learning for Infants*. Reading: Addison-Wesley, 1987.

Dittman, L. L., ed. *The Infants We Care For*, rev. ed. Washington, D.C.: National Association for the Education of Young Children, 1984.

Eheart, B. K., and Leavitt, R. L. "Supporting Toddler Play." *Young Children* 40, 3 (1985): 18–22.

Evans, J., and Illfield, E. *Good Beginnings*. Ypsilanti, Mich.: High/Scope, 1982.

Field, T.; Masi, W.; Goldstein, S.; Perry, S.; and Silke, P. "Infant Day-Care Facilitates Preschool Social Behavior." *Early Childhood Research Quarterly* 3 (1988): 341–359.

Gordon, I. J. *Baby to Parent, Parent to Baby: A Guide to Loving and Learning in a Child's First Year*. New York: St. Martin's Press, 1978.

Gordon, I. J. *Child Learning Through Child Play: Learning Activities for Two and Three Year Olds*. New York: St. Martin's Press, 1972.

Greenfield, P. M., and Tronick, E. *Infant Curriculum, the Bromley Heath Guide to Care of Infants in Groups*. Santa Monica: Goodyear Publishing, 1980.

Hass, C. B. *Look at Me: Activities for Babies and Toddlers*. Glencoe, Ill.: CBH, 1985.

Honig, A. S. "The Eriksonian Approach: Infant/Toddler Education." In *Approaches to Early Childhood Education,* edited by J. Roopnarine and J. Johnson. Columbus: Merrill, 1987.

Honig, A. S. "Evaluation of Infant/Toddler Intervention Programs." In *Studies in Educational Evaluation,* Vol. 8, edited by B. Spodek. London: Pergamon Press, 1983.

Honig, A. S. "High Quality Infant/Toddler Care: Issues and Dilemmas." *Young Children* 41, 1 (1985): 40–46.

Honig, A. S. "Meeting the Needs of Infants." *Dimensions* 11, 4 (1983): 4–7.

Honig, A. S. "Quality Infant/Toddler Caregiving: Are There Magic Recipes?" *Young Children* 44, 4 (1989): 4–10.

Honig, A. S., and Lally, J. R. "Behavior Profiles of Experienced Teachers of Infants and Toddlers." *Early Child Development and Care* 33 (1988): 188–199.

Howes, C. "Quality Indicators in Infant and Toddler Child Care: The Los Angeles Study." In *Quality in Child Care: The Education of Young Children,* edited by D. A. Phillips. Washington, D.C.: National Association for the Education of Young Children, 1987.

Howes, C.; Rodnig, C.; Galluzzo, D. C.; and Meyers, L. "Attachment and Child Care." *Early Childhood Research Quarterly* 3 (1988): 403–416.

Lally, J. R., and Gordon, I. J. *Learning Games for Infants and Toddlers.*

ERIC ED 149 860. Syracuse: New Readers, 1977.

Levenstein, P. *Messages from Home: The Mother-Child Program and the Prevention of School Disadvantage.* Columbus: Ohio State University Press, 1988.

Lourie, R., and Nuegebauer, R., eds. *Caring for Infants and Toddlers: What Works and What Doesn't,* Vol. 2. Redmond, Wash.: Child Care Information Exchange, 1982.

Moss, H. A.; Hess, R.; and Surft, C., eds. *Early Childhood Intervention Programs for Infants.* New York: Haworth, 1982.

Neugebauer, R., and Lurie, R., eds. *Caring for Infants and Toddlers: What Works, What Doesn't.* Summit, N.J.: Summit Care Center, 1980.

Nuba-Scheffler, H.; Sheiman, D. L.; and Watkins, K. P. *Infancy: A Guide to Research and Resources.* New York: Garland, 1986.

Richters, J. F., and Zahn-Waxler, C. "The Infant Day-Care Controversy: Current Status and Future Directions." *Early Childhood Research Quarterly* 3 (1988): 319–336.

Segal, M. *Your Child at Play, Birth to One Year.* New York: Newmarket, 1985.

Segal, M., and Adcock, D. *Your Child at Play, One to Two Years.* New York: Newmarket, 1985.

Segal, M., and Adcock, D. *Your Child at Play, Two to Three Years.* New York: Newmarket, 1985.

Stewart, B., and Vargas, J. S. *Teaching Behavior to Infants and Toddlers:*

A Manual for Caregivers and Parents. Springfield: Charles C. Thomas, 1990.

Stewart, I. S. "The Real World of Teaching Two-Year-Old Children." *Young Children* 37, 5 (1982): 3–13.

Weiser, M. G. *Group Care and Education of Infants and Toddlers.* St. Louis: C.V. Mosby, 1982.

Weissbourd, B., and Musick, J., eds. *Infants: Their Social Environment.* Washington, D.C.: National Association for the Education of Young Children, 1981.

White, B. L. *The First Three Years of Life,* rev. ed. Englewood Cliffs: Prentice-Hall, 1985.

Wilson, L. C. *Infants and Toddlers: Curriculum and Teaching.* Albany: Delmar, 1986.

Young Children—Interactionist View

Althouse, R. *The Young Child: Learning with Understanding.* New York: Teachers College Press, Teachers College Columbia University, 1981.

Ashton-Warner, S. *Teacher.* New York: Simon and Schuster, 1986.

Barbour, N. "Curriculum Concepts and Priorities." *Childhood Education* 63, 5 (1987): 331–336.

Biber, B. *Early Education and Psychological Development.* New Haven: Yale University, 1984.

Biber, B.; Shapiro, E.; and Wickens, D. *Promoting Cognitive Growth: A Developmental-Interaction Point of View.* Washington, D.C.: National Association for the Education of Young Children, 1971.

Clift, R. T.; Houston, W. R.; Pugach, M. C., eds. *Encouraging Reflective Practice in Education: An Analysis of Issues and Programs.* New York: Teachers College Press, Teachers College Columbia University, 1990.

Day, D. E. *Early Childhood Education: A Human Ecological Approach.* Glenview: Scott, Foresman, 1983.

Dialogues on Development for the Developmental Approach to Education. Rosemont: Programs for Education, Inc., 1986.

Dittmann, L. L., ed. *Curriculum Is What Happens: Planning Is the Key,* rev. ed. Washington, D.C.: National Association for the Education of Young Children, 1977.

Elkind, D. "Formal Education and Early Childhood Education: An Essential Difference." *Phi Delta Kappan* 67, 9 (1986): 631–636.

Elkind, D. *Miseducation: Preschoolers at Risk.* New York: Knopf, 1987.

Fein, G., and Rivkin, M., eds. *The Young Child at Play: Reviews of Research,* vol. 4. Washington, D.C.: National Association for the Education of Young Children, 1986.

Forman, G. E., and Hill, F. *Constructive Play: Applying Piaget in the Preschool.* Monterey: Brooks/Cole, 1980.

Forman, G., and Kuschner, D. *The Child's Construction of Knowledge: Piaget for Teaching Children.* Washington, D.C.: National Association for the Education of Young Children, 1983.

Fromberg, D. P. *The Full-Day Kindergarten.* New York: Teachers College Press, Teachers College Columbia University, 1987.

Hendrick, J. *The Whole Child: Developmental Education for the Early Years,* 4th ed. Columbus: Merrill, 1988.

Hendrick, J. *Total Learning: Developmental Curriculum for the Young Child,* 3rd ed. Columbus: Merrill, 1990.

Kamii, C. K., and DeVries, R. *Group Games in Early Education: Implications of Piaget's Theory.* Washington, D.C.: National Association for the Education of Young Children, 1980.

Katz, L. G.; Raths, J. D.; and Torres, R. T. *A Place Called Kindergarten.* Urbana: ERIC Clearinghouse on Elementary and Early Childhood Education, University of Illinois, 1987.

Lavetelli, C. S. *Piaget's Theory Applied to an Early Childhood Curriculum,* 2nd ed. Boston: American Science and Engineering, 1973.

Montessori, M. *The Montessori Method.* New York: Schocken, 1964.

Peterson, R., and Felton-Collins, V. *The Piaget Handbook for Teachers and Parents: Children in the Age of Discovery, Preschool-Third Grade.* New York: Teachers College Press, Teachers College Columbia University, 1986.

Raths, J.; Wasserman, S.; Jonas, A.; and Rothstein, A. *Teaching for Thinking: Theory, Strategy, and Activities for the Classroom.* New York: Teachers College Press,

Teachers College Columbia University, 1986.

Read, K. *The Nursery School: A Human Relationships Laboratory,* 6th ed. Philadelphia: W. B. Saunders, 1976.

Read, K.; Gardner, P.; and Mahler, B. C. *Early Childhood Programs: Human Relationships and Learning,* 8th ed. New York: Holt, Rinehart, and Winston, 1987.

Rosenshine, B. V. "Synthesis of Research on Explicit Teaching." *Educational Leadership* 43, 7 (1986): 66–69.

Schweinhart, L.; Weikart, D.; and Larner, M. "Consequences of Three Preschool Curriculum Models Through Age Fifteen." *Early Childhood Research Quarterly* 1, 1 (1986): 15–46.

Seefeldt, C., ed. *The Early Childhood Curriculum: A Review of Current Research.* New York: Teachers College Press, Teachers College Columbia University, 1987.

Spodek, B. "Conceptualizing Today's Kindergarten Curriculum." *The Elementary School Journal* 89, 2 (1988): 203–212.

Uphoff, J. K., ed. *Changing to a Developmentally Appropriate Curriculum Successfully: Four Case Studies.* Rosemont: Programs for Education, Inc., 1989.

Wasserman, S. *Serious Players in the Primary Classroom.* New York: Teachers College Press, Teachers College Columbia University, 1990.

Weber, E. *Ideas Influencing Early Childhood Education: A Theoretical*

Analysis. New York: Teachers College Press, Teachers College Columbia University, 1984.

Weikart, D. P.; Rogers, L.; Adcock, C.; and McClelland, D. *The Cognitively Oriented Curriculum.* Washington, D.C.: National Association for the Education of Young Children, 1971.

Young Children—Behavioral-Environmental View

Anderson, V., and Bereiter, C. "Extending Direct Instruction to Conceptual Skills." In *The Preschool in Action: Exploring Early Childhood Programs*, edited by R. K. Parker. Boston: Allyn and Bacon, 1972.

Becker, W.; Englemann, S.; and Thomas, D. R. *Teaching: A Course in Applied Psychology.* Chicago: Science Research Associates, 1971.

Bushnell, D., Jr. "The Behavior Analysis Classroom." In *Early Childhood Education*, edited by B. Spodek. Englewood Cliffs: Prentice-Hall, 1973.

Cohen, M. A., and Gross, P. J. *The Developmental Resource: Behavioral Sequences for Assessment and Program Planning*, vols. 1 and 2. New York: Grune and Stratton, 1979.

Gewitz, J. L. "Stimulation, Learning, and Motivation Principles for Day Care Programs." In *Day Care: Resources for Decisions*, edited by E. H. Grotberg. Washington, D.C.: Office of Economic Opportunity, 1971.

Hom, H. L., and Hom, S. L. "Research and the Child: The Use of

Modeling, Reinforcement/Incentives, and Punishment." In *Aspects of Early Childhood Education: Theory to Research to Practice*, edited by D. G. Range, J. R. Layton, and D. L. Roubinek. New York: Academic, 1980.

Resnick, L. "Instructional Psychology." In *Annual Review of Psychology*, edited by M. R. Rosenzweig and L. W. Porter. Palo Alto: Annual Reviews, 1981.

Sherman, J. A., and Bushnell, D., Jr. "Behavior Modifications as an Educational Technique." In *Review of Child Development Research*, vol. 4, edited by F. D. Horowitz. Chicago: University of Chicago, 1975.

Thoreson, C. E., ed. *Behavior Modification in Education. The Seventy-second Yearbook of the National Society for the Study of Education*, part 1. Chicago: University of Chicago, 1973.

Family Day-Care

Seefeldt, C., and Dittmann, L. L., eds. *Day Care 9: Family Day-Care.* Washington, D.C.: Department of Health, Education and Welfare, Office of Child Development, 1973.

Squibb, B. *Family Day Care: How to Provide It in Your Home.* Cambridge: Harvard Common Press, 1980.

West, K., ed. *Family Day-to-Day Care*, rev. ed. Mound, Minn.: Quality Child Care, 1980.

School-Age Child Care

Alexander, N. P. "School-Age Child Care: Concerns and Challenges." *Young Children* 42, 1 (1986): 3–10.

Baden, R.; Genser, A.; Levine, J.; and Seligson, M. *School-Age Child Care: An Action Manual.* Boston: Auburn House, 1982.

Coleman, M.; Rowland, B. H.; and Robinson, B. E. "School-Age Child Care: The Community Leadership Role of Educators." *Childhood Education* 66, 2 (1989): 78–82.

Coolsen, P.; Seligson, M.; and Garbarino, J. *When School's Out and Nobody's Home.* Chicago: National Committee for Child Abuse, 1985.

Powell, D. R. "Research in Review. After-School Child Care." *Young Children* 42, 3 (1987): 62–66.

Robinson, B. E.; Rowland, B. H.; and Coleman, M. *Home Alone After School: The Working Parent's Complete Guide to Providing the Best Care for Your Child.* Lexington: Lexington, 1989.

School-Age Child Care. Boston: Massachusetts Office for Children, 1988.

Seefeldt, C., ed. *The Early Childhood Curriculum: A Review of Current Research.* New York: Teachers College Press, Teachers College Columbia University, 1987.

Spodek, B. "Conceptualizing Today's Kindergarten Curriculum." *The Elementary School Journal* 89, 2 (1988): 203–212.

Uphoff, J. K., ed. *Changing to a Developmentally Appropriate Curriculum Successfully: Four Case Studies.* Rosemont: Programs for Education, Inc., 1989.

Multicultural

Chez, M. *Globalchild: Multicultural Resources for Young Children.* Ottawa: Child Care Initiatives, 1990.

Chud, G. and Fuhlman, R. (with R. Baker and P. Wakefield). *Early Childhood Education for a Multicultural Society: A Handbook for Educators.* Vancouver: Western Education Development Group, The University of British Columbia, 1983.

Derman-Sparks, L., and the A. B. C. Task Force. *Anti-Bias Curriculum: Tasks for Empowering Young Children.* Washington, D.C.: National Association for the Education of Young Children, 1989.

Froschel, M., and Sprung, B. *Resources for Educational Equity: A Guide for Grades Pre-K–12.* New York: Garland, 1988.

Hale-Benson, J. *Black Children: Their Roots, Culture, and Learning Styles,* rev. ed. Baltimore: Johns Hopkins University Press, 1986.

Kendall, F. E. *Diversity in the Classroom: A Multicultural Approach to the Education of Young Children.* New York: Teachers College Press, Teachers College Columbia University, 1983.

Neugebauer, B., ed. *Alike and Different: Exploring Our Common Humanity with Young Children.* Redmond: Exchange Press, 1987.

Ramsey, P. G. *Teaching and Learning in a Diverse World: Multicultural Education for Young Children.* New York: Teachers College Press, Teachers College Columbia University, 1987.

Ramsey, P. G.; Vold, E. B.; and Williams, L. R. *Multicultural Education: A Source Book.* New York: Garland, 1989.

Williams, L. R.; De Gaetano, Y.; Sutherland, I. R.; and Harrington, C. H. *Alberta: A Multicultural, Bilingual Approach to Teaching Young Children.* Menlo Park, Calif.: Addison-Wesley, 1985.

Integration of Exceptional and Nonexceptional Young Children

Bailey, D., Jr., and Worley, M. *Assessing Infants and Preschoolers with Handicaps.* Columbus: Merrill, 1989.

Bailey, D., Jr., and Worley, M. *Teaching Infants and Preschoolers with Handicaps.* Columbus: Merrill, 1984.

Baum, D., and Wells, C. "Promoting Handicap Awareness in Preschool Children." *Teaching Exceptional Children* 17 (1985): 282–287.

Charting Change in Infants, Families, and Services: A Guide to Program Evaluation for Administrators and Practitioners. Washington, D.C.: National Center for Clinical Infant Programs, 1987.

Cook, R. E.; Tessier, A.; and Armbruster, V. B. *Adapting Early Childhood Curricula for Children with Special Needs,* 2nd ed. Columbus: Merrill, 1987.

Early Intervention: Consideration for Establishing Programs. Chicago: National Easter Seal Society, 1986.

Fuller, N., and Umansky, W. *Young Children with Special Needs.* Columbus: Merrill, 1985.

Infants Can't Wait: The Numbers, Washington, D.C.: National Center for Clinical Infant Programs, 1987.

Johnson-Martin, N. M.; Attermeier, S. M.; and Hacker, B. *The Carolina Curriculum for Preschoolers with Special Needs.* Baltimore: Paul H. Brookes, 1990.

Peterson, N. L. *Early Intervention for Handicapped and At-Risk Children.* Denver: Love Publishing Company, 1987.

Pueschel, S. M.; Bernier, J. C.; and Weidenman, L. E. *The Special Child: A Source Book for Parents of Children with Developmental Disabilities.* Baltimore: Paul H. Brookes, 1988.

Spodek, B.; Saracho, O. N.; and Lee, R. C. *Mainstreaming Young Children.* Belmont, Calif.: Wadsworth, 1984.

Zeitlin, S., and Williamson, G. G. "Promoting Programs: Early Intervention for Infants and Toddlers." *Teaching Exceptional Children* 19 (1986): 57–59.

Appendix 2
State Licensing and Certification Agencies

State	State Dept. Responsible For Licensing	State Dept. Responsible For Certification
Alabama	State of Alabama Dept. of Human Resources Office of Day-Care and Child Development S. Gordon Persons Building 50 Ripley Street Montgomery, Ala. 36130	State of Alabama Dept. of Education Montgomery, Ala. 36130
Alaska	Dept. of Health & Social Services Division of Family & Youth P.O. Box H–05 Juneau, Alas. 99811	Dept. of Education P.O. Box F Juneau, Alas. 99811
Arizona	Dept. of Economic Security Box 6123 Phoenix, Ariz. 85005	Dept. of Education 1535 West Jefferson Phoenix, Ariz. 85007
Arkansas	Dept. of Human Services Division of Children and Family Child Care Licensing P.O. Box 1437, Slot 720 Little Rock, Ark. 72203	Dept. of Education 4 State Capitol Mall Little Rock, Ark. 72201
California	Dept. of Social Services Children's Day-Care Bureau 3701 Branch Center Road Sacramento, Calif. 95812	Commission on Teacher Credentialing Licensing Branch Box 944270 Sacramento, Calif. 94244
Colorado	Dept. of Social Services 1575 Sherman Street Denver, Colo. 80203	Dept. of Education 201 East Colfax Ave. Denver, Colo. 80203
Connecticut	Dept. of Children and Youth Services 170 Sigourney Street Hartford, Conn. 06105	Dept. of Education Box 2219 Hartford, Conn. 06145
Delaware	Child Support Office Office of Secretary 1901 Dupont Hwy. New Castle, Del. 19720	Dept. of Public Instruction The Townsend Building P.O. Box 1402 Dover, Del. 19903
Florida	Dept. of Health and Rehabilitative Services Family Support Services 1317 Winewood Blvd. Tallahassee, Fla. 32301	Dept. of Education Office of Certification Tallahassee, Fla. 32399
Georgia	Dept. of Human Resources Room 606 Atlanta, Ga. 30309	Dept. of Education Twin Towers East Atlanta, Ga. 30334

State	State Dept. Responsible For Licensing	State Dept. Responsible For Certification
Hawaii	Dept. of Human Services Public Welfare Division Program Development P.O. Box 339 Honolulu, Hi. 96809	Dept. of Education P.O. Box 2360 Honolulu, Hi. 96804
Idaho	Dept. of Health and Welfare Division of Field Operations 4355 Emerald Boise, Id. 83706	State Dept. of Education Boise, Id. 83720
Illinois	Dept. of Children and Family Services 406 East Monroe Springfield, Ill. 62701	State Board of Education 100 North First Street Springfield, Ill. 62777
Indiana	Dept. of Public Welfare Child Welfare/Social Services Division 141 South Meridian Street 6th Floor Indianapolis, Ind. 46225	Dept. of Education Room 229, State House Indianapolis, Ind. 46204
Iowa	Dept. of Human Services Hoover State Office Building Des Moines, Ia. 50319	Dept. of Education Grimes State Office Building Des Moines, Ia. 50319
Kansas	Dept. of Health and Environment Bureau of Adult and Child Care Landon State Office Building 900 Southwest Jackson Topeka, Kan. 66612	State Dept. of Education Kansas State Education 120 East 10th Street Topeka, Kan. 66612
Kentucky	Cabinet for Human Resources Office of Inspector General 275 East Main Street Frankford, Ky. 40621	Dept. of Education Capital Plaza Frankfort, Ky. 40621
Louisiana	Dept. of Health & Hospitals Bureau of Health Services Financing Health Standards Section P.O. Box 3767 Baton Rouge, La. 70821	Dept. of Education P.O. Box 94064 Baton Rouge, La. 70804
Maine	Dept. of Human Services State House, Station 11 Augusta, Me. 04333	Dept. of Education & Cultural Services State House, Station 23 Augusta, Me. 04333

State	State Dept. Responsible For Licensing	State Dept. Responsible For Certification
Maryland	Office of Child Care Licensing and Regulation 311 West Saratoga Street Baltimore, Md. 21201	State Dept. of Education 200 W. Baltimore Street Baltimore, Md. 21201
Massachusetts	Office for Children Licensing 10 West Street Boston, Mass. 02111	Dept. of Education 1385 Hancock Street Quincy, Mass. 02169
Michigan	Dept. of Social Services 300 South Capitol Ave. P.O. Box 30037 Lansing Mich. 48909	Dept. of Education P.O. Box 30008 Lansing, Mich. 48909
Minnesota	Dept. of Human Resources 1060 East Kellogg St. Paul, Minn. 55101	Dept. of Education Capitol Square 550 Cedar Street St. Paul, Minn. 55101
Mississippi	State Dept. of Health Child Care and Special Licensing P.O. Box 1700 Jackson, Miss. 39215	State Dept. of Education P.O. Box 771 Jackson, Miss. 39205
Missouri	Dept. of Social Services Division of Family Services P.O. Box 88 Jefferson City, Mo. 65102	Dept. of Elementary and Secondary Education P.O. Box 480 Jefferson City, Mo. 65102
Montana	Dept. of Family Services P.O. Box 8005 Helena, Mont. 59604	Office of Public Instruction State Capitol Helena, Mont. 59620
Nebraska	State of Nebraska Dept. of Social Services P.O. Box 95026 Lincoln, Neb. 68509	Dept. of Education 301 Centennial Mall Box 94987 Lincoln, Neb. 68509
Nevada	Dept. of Human Resources Bureau of Services for Child Care 505 East King Street Room 606 Carson City, Nev. 89710	Nevada Dept. of Education Capital Complex Carson City, Nev. 89710
New Hampshire	Div. of Public Health Services Bureau of Child Care Standards & Licensing Health and State Building Hazen Drive Concord, N.H. 03301	Dept. of Education State Office Park South 101 Pleasant Street Concord, N.H. 03301

State	State Dept. Responsible For Licensing	State Dept. Responsible For Certification
New Jersey	Division of Youth and Family Services Mercer District Office Princess Road, Bldg. 9–F CN 717 Lawrenceville, N.J. 08648	Dept. of Education 225 West State Street Trenton, N.J. 08625
New Mexico	Health and Environment Dept. P.O. Box 968 Santa Fe, N.Mex. 87504	Department of Education Education Building Santa Fe, N.Mex. 87501
New York	Dept. of Social Services Ten Eyck Building 40 North Pearl Street Albany, N.Y. 12243	State Education Dept. The University of the State of New York Albany, N.Y. 12234
North Carolina	Office of Child Day-Care Licensing 701 Barbour Drive Raleigh, N.C. 27605	Dept. of Public Education 116 W. Edenton Street Raleigh, N.C. 27603
North Dakota	Dept. of Human Services State Capitol Building Bismarck, N.Dak. 58505	Dept. of Public Instruction State Capitol, 9th floor 600 East Boulevard Ave. Bismarck, N.Dak. 58505
Ohio	Bureau of Child Care Services Dept. of Human Services 30 East Broad Street, 30th Floor Columbus, O. 43266	Dept. of Education 65 South Front Street Columbus, O. 43266
Oklahoma	Dept. of Human Services Sequoyah Memorial Office Building P.O. Box 25352 Oklahoma City, Okla. 73125	State Dept. of Education 2500 North Lincoln Blvd. Oklahoma City, Okla. 73105
Oregon	Children's Services Division 198 Commercial Street, S.E. Salem, Ore. 97301	Dept. of Education 700 Pringle Parkway, S.E. Salem, Ore. 97310
Pennsylvania	Dept. of Public Welfare Office of Children, Youth, & Families Bureau of Child Day-Care Services P.O. Box 2675 Harrisburg, Pa. 17105	Dept. of Education 333 Market Street Harrisburg, Pa. 17126
Rhode Island	Dept. for Children and Their Families Licensing Day Care Services 610 Mount Pleasant Ave. Providence, R.I. 02908	Dept. of Education 22 Hayes Street Providence, R.I. 02908

State	State Dept. Responsible For Licensing	State Dept. Responsible For Certification
South Carolina	Dept. of Social Services Children and Family Services P.O. Box 1520 Columbia, S.C. 29202	State Dept. of Education Rutledge Office Building Columbia, S.C. 29201
South Dakota	Dept. of Social Services Richard F. Kneip Building 700 Governors Drive Pierre, S.Dak. 57501	Dept. of Education and Cultural Affairs 700 Governors Drive Pierre, S.Dak. 57501
Tennessee	Dept. of Human Services 400 Deaderick Street Nashville, Tenn. 37219	Dept. of Education 125 Cordell Hall Building Nashville, Tenn. 37219
Texas	Dept. of Human Services 701 West 51st Street P.O. Box 149030 MC 550-W Austin, Tex. 78714	Texas Education Agency W. B. Travis Building 1701 North Congress Ave. Austin, Tex. 78701
Utah	Dept. of Social Services Division of Family Services 120 North, 200 West Rm. 324 Salt Lake City, Ut. 84103	State Office of Education 250 East, 500 South Salt Lake City, Ut. 84111
Vermont	Dept. of Social & Rehabilitation Services Children's Day-Care Licensing Division of Licensing & Registration 103 South Main Street Waterbury, Vt. 05676	Dept. of Education State Office Building 120 State Street Montpelier, Vt. 05602
Virginia	Dept. of Social Services Blair Building 8007 Discovery Drive Richmond, Va. 23229	Dept. of Education P.O. Box 60 Richmond, Va. 23216
Washington	Dept. of Social and Health Services 5000 Capital Blvd. Olympia, Wash. 98504	Dept. of Public Instruction 600 South Washington Olympia, Wash. 98504
West Virginia	Dept. of Human Resources 1900 Washington Street, East Charleston, W.Va. 25305	State Dept. of Education Building 6—Room B–337 Capitol Complex Charleston, W.Va. 25305
Wisconsin	Dept. of Health and Social Services Division of Community Services 1 West Wilson Street P.O. Box 7851 Madison, Wis. 53707	Dept. of Public Instruction 125 South Webster Street P.O. Box 7841 Madison, Wis. 53707

State	State Dept. Responsible For Licensing	State Dept. Responsible For Certification
Wyoming	Dept. of Health and Special Services Hathaway Building Cheyenne, Wyo. 82002	State Dept. of Education Hathaway Building Cheyenne, Wyo. 82002

Appendix 3
Accreditation Criteria Examples

ACCREDITATION BY THE NATIONAL ACADEMY OF EARLY CHILDHOOD PROGRAMS*

Each component (i.e., interactions among staff and children; curriculum; staff-parent interaction; staff qualifications and development; administration; staffing; physical environment; health and safety; nutrition and food service; and evaluation) begins with a goal statement. For example, the goal statement for the component interactions among staff and children is:

> **Goal.** Interactions between children and staff provide opportunities for children to develop an understanding of self and others and are characterized by warmth, personal respect, individuality, positive support, and responsiveness. Staff facilitate interactions among children to provide opportunities for development of social skills and intellectual growth.

The goal statement is followed by the rationale. For example:

> **Rationale.** All areas of young children's development—social, emotional, cognitive, and physical—are integrated. Optimal development in all areas derives from positive, supportive, individualized relationships with adults. Young children also develop both socially and intellectually through peer interaction.

The criteria for the component follow. These criteria indicate whether a goal is being achieved.* For example:

> A–1. Staff interact frequently with children. Staff express respect for and affection toward children by smiling, touching, holding, and speaking to children at their eye level throughout the day, particularly on arrival and departure, and when diapering or feeding very young children.

> A–2. Staff are available and responsive to children; encourage them to share experiences, ideas, and feelings; and listen to them with attention and respect.

> A–3. Staff speak with children in a friendly, positive, courteous manner. Staff converse frequently with children, asking open-ended questions and speaking individually to children (as opposed to the whole group) most of the time.

> A–4. Staff equally treat children of all races, religions, and cultures with respect and consideration. Staff provide children of both sexes with equal opportunities to take part in all activities.

> A–5. Staff encourage developmentally appropriate independence in children. Staff foster independence in routine activities such as picking up

---

* S. Bredekamp, ed., *Accreditation Criteria and Procedures of the National Academy of Early Childhood Programs* (Washington D.C.: National Association for the Education of Young Children, 1984), 8–10, 40.

toys, wiping spills, personal grooming (toileting, hand washing), obtaining and caring for materials, and other self-help skills.

A–6. Staff use positive techniques of guidance, including redirection, anticipation of and elimination of potential problems, positive reinforcement, and encouragement rather than competition, comparison, or criticism. Staff abstain from corporal punishment or other humiliating or frightening discipline techniques. Consistent, clear rules are explained to children and understood by adults.

A–7. The sound of the environment is primarily marked by pleasant conversation, spontaneous laughter, and exclamations of excitement rather than harsh, stressful noise or enforced quiet.

A–8. Staff assist children to be comfortable, relaxed, happy, and involved in play and other activities.

A–9. Staff foster cooperation and other pro-social behaviors among children.

A–10. Staff expectations of children's social behavior are developmentally appropriate.

A–11. Children are encouraged to verbalize feelings and ideas.

Finally, there are interpretive statements for each criterion. For example, for A–5 above, the interpretive statements are:

A–5. Staff encourages independence in children as they are ready.
For example:
Infants: finger feeding self.
Toddlers: washing hands, selecting own toys.
Three- and four-year-olds: dressing, picking up toys.
Five-year-olds: setting table, cleaning, acquiring self-help skills.
School-agers: performing responsible jobs, participating in community activities.

ACCREDITATION BY THE CHILD WELFARE LEAGUE OF AMERICA*

Each standard is classified by a numbering system. For example:

D.2.06
The agency has a policy regarding access to and content of case records, whether open or terminated.

---

*Excerpts from *Agency Accreditation Manual of the Council on Accreditation of Services for Families and Children, Inc.* (Washington, D.C.: Child Welfare League of America, Inc., 1990), D9-D10.

The manual states the evidence of compliance sought which must be presented in the document of self-study and which must be available for the on-site visit. For example:

> Evidence of Compliance (D.2.06, D.2.07, D.2.08)
> Provide policies and procedures that govern record access, location, and safe maintenance.
>
> (DOCUMENT)
>
> Observation of record storage.
>
> (ON–SITE)

Finally, rating indicators are given. For example:

Rating Indicators (D.2.06)

1. Policy exists and is explicit and detailed.
2. Policy is very general, but provides some guidance.
3. Policy has been violated in rare instances.
4. No policy and/or careless procedures exist. There is the potential for breach of confidentiality or actual breach.

NATIONAL COUNCIL FOR ACCREDITATION OF TEACHER EDUCATION*

Each component (i.e., curriculum; instructional methods; resources; faculty qualifications; professional relationships; cultural diversity; enrollment; administrative structure; and, evaluation and constituent responsiveness) begins with a general statement concerning the nature of the component. For example, the general statement for Component 6—Cultural Diversity is:

> This component addresses the need for sensitivity to and recognition of cultural pluralism.

Program objectives follow. For example:

Program Objectives

A. The early childhood teacher education program prepares candidates to function in a pluralistic society.
B. All areas of the program reflect respect and appreciation for cultural diversity.
C. Candidates are prepared to eliminate practices and materials that discriminate against children and their families on the basis of race, sex, ethnic origin, language, religion, or physical handicap.

Early Childhood Teacher Education Guidelines—Basic and Advanced. Position Statement of the National Association for the Education of Young Children. (Washington, D.C.: National Association for the Education of Young Children, 1991), 34.

Standards, given for both undergraduate and graduate programs, are listed under "Standards." Because graduate programs must be of an even higher quality, other standards are given—"Additional Standards for Advanced Programs." For example:

Standards

A. Cultural pluralism is reflected in the faculty, candidates, program philosophy, and institutional policies.
B. Faculty regularly examine the content of courses, instructional materials, and field placements to ensure that they reflect the cultural diversity of society.
C. Cultural diversity is integrated into all program components and, when appropriate, addressed as a separate topic for study.
D. Candidates are instructed in methods of fostering respect and appreciation for cultural diversity in early childhood settings.
E. Candidates are made aware of various forms of discrimination and develop skills in identifying discriminatory practices and implementing methods to counteract discrimination in education.

Additional Standards for Advanced Programs

F. Minority candidates and faculty members are actively recruited for early childhood education programs.
G. Candidates develop awareness and sensitivity to issues of cultural diversity and discrimination; and are prepared to work in programs serving culturally diverse populations.

Appendix 4
**Professional Organizations
Concerned with Young Children**

History	Purposes	Publications	Membership Requirements
American Montessori Society (AMS) **150 Fifth Ave.** **New York, N.Y. 10011** The American Montessori Society was founded in 1960. Although Montessori's ideas held great interest for the American public between 1912 and 1918, there was no central organization to support them, and her psychological principles were dissonant with the times and frowned on by leaders of the educational community. It was not until 1958, when Nancy McCormick Rambusch opened a Montessori program at the Whitby School, and the first American Montessori teachers training course was offered in 1960, that the Montessori movement experienced an American revival.	The basic purposes of the Society are to promote better education for all children through teaching strategies consistent with the Montessori system and to incorporate the Montessori approach into the framework of American education. The purposes are implemented by: 1. Serving as a clearinghouse for information about Montessori methods, materials, teachers, and schools. 2. Affiliating programs for the training of Montessori teachers in preprimary, primary, and secondary levels, and issuing credentials to persons	1. *Montessori Life* (journal published quarterly) 2. *Annual Report* 3. *Teaching Opportunities,* a list of staff openings in AMS affiliates. The list is reserved for teacher members. 4. *Directory of Affiliated Montessori Schools* 5. *Directory of AMS, Affiliated Teachers Preparation Programs* 6. Newsletter for Heads of Schools	The Society is comprised of and supported by public, private, and parochial schools, Montessori teachers, and concerned individuals. Membership classes are: 1. Organizational Affiliates a. Schools: furnish documentation of Montessori training of teachers, details of their organization, and evidence of compliance with state and local requirements. School affiliates are required to have a consultation the first or second year of affiliation and every four years thereafter. b. Subscribers: an interim membership for ongoing programs to

successfully completing accredited course requirements.

3. Maintaining a consultation/resource service to assist member schools.
4. Conducting one annual seminar/conference and three regional seminars per year.
5. Assisting research projects.
6. Providing assistance to those interested in starting Montessori schools.
7. Maintaining a materials/publications center, with a full selection of Montessori and Montessori-oriented teaching aids and literature.
8. Maintaining communication with and assistance to State Departments of Education in relation to Montessori and early childhood education legislation.

assist and encourage them in converting to full Montessori programs.

   c. Associates: any group, or individual interested in starting a Montessori School.
   d. Corresponding: overseas Montessori schools meeting full requirements

2. Individuals
   a. Teachers' Section: open to teachers furnishing copies of a recognized Montessori credential and details of their academic background
   b. General: no restrictions
   c. Heads of Schools
   d. Lifetime

History	Purposes	Publications	Membership Requirements

Association for Childhood Education International (ACEI)
11141 Georgia Avenue, Suite 200
Wheaton, Md. 20902

History	Purposes	Publications	Membership Requirements
During the 1892 meeting of the National Education Association, the International Kindergarten Union (IKU) was founded. In 1915, thirty representative educators in the kindergarten and primary fields met in Cincinnati, Ohio, and formed another association, the National Council of Primary Education. The IKU's official journal, *Childhood Education*, was launched in 1924. In 1930, the International Kindergarten Union and the National Council of Primary Education united under the title the Association for Childhood Education. The word "International" was added to the name in 1946. Today, the association is a not-for-profit, professional organization which is supported by dues and income from sale of publications. The national headquarters of the association is in Wheaton, Md.	ACEI's purposes are: 1. To promote desirable living conditions, programs, and practices for children from infancy through early adolescence. 2. To support the raising of standards of professional preparation. 3. To bring into active cooperation all organizations concerned with children in the home, the school, and the community. 4. To inform the public of the needs of children and how the educational program must be organized and operated to meet those needs.	1. *Childhood Education* (journal, published five times a year) 2. *ACEI Exchange* (newsletter, published six times per year) 3. *Journal of Research in Childhood Education* (journal, published two times a year) 4. Other special publications	Membership is open to all concerned with the well-being and education of children. Three types of membership: (1) Institution; (2) Professional; and (3) Student and retiree.

432

History	Purposes	Publications	Membership Requirements
Association Montessori Internationale (AMI) **161 Koninginneweg** **1075 CN Amsterdam** **The Netherlands**			
In 1929, a Montessori congress was held in Helsingor, Denmark. At the Congress, the idea of the Association Montessori Internationale was born. From 1935, the organization has had its seat in Amsterdam, Holland.	AMI's purposes are: 1. To further the study, application, and propagation of the Montessori ideas and principles for education and development. 2. To propagate knowledge and understanding of the conditions necessary for full development from conception to maturity both at home and in society. 3. To accredit centers where people may be trained according to the principles and practices of education as envisioned by Dr. Maria Montessori. 4. To create a climate of opinion and opportunity for the full development of the potential of all young people so humanity can work in harmony for a higher and more peaceful civilization.	*Communications* (quarterly journal)	Membership includes (1) Ordinary members, such as individuals or unincorporated groups, incorporated societies or institutions; (2) Legal persons; (3) Life members; and (4) Honorary members.

History	Purposes	Publications	Membership Requirements
Association Montessori Internationale (AMI)—(cont'd) **161 Koninginneweg** **1075 CN Amsterdam** **The Netherlands**	5. To promote general recognition of the child's fundamental rights as envisioned by Dr. Maria Montessori irrespective of racial, religious, political, or social environment. 6. To cooperate with other bodies and organizations that promote the development of education, human rights, and peace.		

History	Purposes	Publications	Membership Requirements
Child Welfare League of America, Inc. (CWLA) **440 First Street, N.W. Suite 310** **Washington, D.C. 20001**			
The league was founded in 1920. It is a nonsectarian federation of affiliated agencies in the United States and Canada. The League is financed from (1) dues paid by member agencies, (2) restricted grants, (3) foundations, (4) United Way allocations, (5) bequests and contributions, and (6) publication sales.	CWLA's purposes are: 1. To devote its efforts to improvement of child welfare services for deprived and neglected children. 2. To develop standards for services. 3. To conduct research and to publish professional materials. 4. To provide consultation to agencies and communities and to maintain a literary information service. 5. To cooperate with other organizations in an effort to improve child welfare services for deprived and neglected children.	1. *Child Welfare* (journal, published bimonthly) 2. *Children's Voice* (newsletter, published nine times per year) 3. Books and monographs 4. *Washington Social Legislation Bulletin* (bulletin, published semimonthly) 5. *Children's Monitor* (newsletter, published monthly) 6. *News From the Children's Campaign* (newsletter, published quarterly)	Not applicable.

435

History	Purposes	Publications	Membership Requirements
Day-Care Council of America **1602 17th Street N.W.** **Washington, D.C. 20009**			
The Council began when a small group of interested individuals organized in 1959 at the National Conference on Social Welfare. In 1960, this group incorporated as the "National Committee for the Day-Care of Children." The committee published a newsletter and held two national day-care conferences (1960, 1965). In 1967, the committee reorganized to become a broad-based citizen action agency to work on behalf of children. It thus became known as the Day-Care and Child Development Council of America, Inc., with national headquarters in Washington, D.C. The name was changed to Day-Care Council of America in 1982. The Council is private, not-for-profit, and membership supported.	The Council's purposes are: 1. To promote development of a locally controlled, publicly supported, and universally available child-care program. 2. To formulate public child-care policies. 3. To render assistance to local communities establishing child-care programs. 4. To improve the life of the child, family, and community through a child-care system.	1. *Voices for Children* (published bimonthly). 2. *Resources for Day Care* (publication list). 3. *Bulletin* (published when need indicates). 4. *Day Care Journal.* 5. Other special publications. The Council published *4–C* from March-April, 1970 through January-February, 1971 and published four or five issues of *Action for Children* which came to an end in July, 1971. Between 1980 and 1982, it adopted the *Human Science Press Magazine, Day Care and Early Education* as its journal. This was replaced by the *Day Care Journal.*	Membership is open to those interested in all facets of child care—parents, staffs of child care centers, and professionals in the field of child development. Three levels of membership: (1) individual, (2) agency, and (3) library.

History	Purposes	Publications	Membership Requirements
National Association for the Education of Young Children (NAEYC) 1834 Connecticut Ave., N.W. Washington, D.C. 20009			
The organization began in 1926 as the National Committee on Nursery Schools. In 1931 it was organized under the title of the National Association for Nursery Education (NANE). The NANE became the National Association for the Education of Young Children in October, 1966, with national headquarters in Washington, D.C. The association has focused on enhancing the development and advancement of programs for children under eight years of age and facilitating the professional growth of people working for and with young children.	The expressed purpose of NAEYC is to serve and act on behalf of the needs and rights of young children, with primary focus on the provision of educational services and resources to adults who work for and with children. This purpose is accomplished through a variety of services—publications, training videos, and conferences—designed to expand the understandings and skills of adults working with and for children; sponsorship of the Week of the Young Child; dissemination of public policy information to assist members in speaking on behalf of the developmental needs of young children; and affiliate group activities that provide advocacy and growth opportunities in communities and states.	1. *Young Children* (journal, published bimonthly). The official journal changed its title from the *Journal of Nursery Education* (begun in 1945–46) to *Young Children* in 1964–65. 2. NAEYC books—The Association offers more than seventy titles reflecting a broad base of information in the field of early childhood education. 3. National Academy of Early Programs—administers a voluntary accreditation system that recognizes high quality in centers and schools. 4. Information Service distributes child care information to the public, media, and government.	Membership is open to persons engaged in work with or for young children. Two categories of membership: (1) independent—membership through the national headquarters, and (2) affiliate—membership through one of the state or local affiliated groups.

History	Purposes	Publications	Membership Requirements
National Association of Early Childhood Teacher Educators (NAECTE)			
Dr. Doris Bergen, Miami University, Dept. of Educational Psychology, 201 McGuffey Hall			
Oxford, Oh. 45056			
The organization was started in 1977 by a group of early childhood professors from four-year colleges under the leadership of Michael Davis. The first meeting was held in Chicago at the annual Fall NAEYC Conference. A steering committee was formed with Mary Elizabeth York serving as chairman. In the second year, the name Early Child Teacher Educators was selected, purposes formulated, and dues levied. In 1980, a steering committee was elected and Marlis Mann served as chairman. In 1980, the bylaws were adopted and "National" added to the title. Officers and a governing board of representatives took office in 1981.	The purposes of the association are to promote the professional growth of its membership and discuss the educational issues specific to members. To this end, it shall 1. Provide a forum for consideration of issues and concerns of special interest to educators of early childhood teacher institutions that grant bachelors, masters, and doctoral degrees; and 2. Provide a communication network for early childhood teacher educators.	*NAECTE Bulletin* published three times per year (fall, winter, and spring)	Membership is open to persons subscribing to the purposes of the organization. Regional early childhood teacher education groups and student memberships may form affiliate groups.

438

History	Purposes	Publications	Membership Requirements
Society for Research in Child Development (SRCD) **5720 S. Woodlawn Avenue** **Chicago, Ill. 60637** In 1922, a subcommittee was appointed on child development under the Division of Anthropology and Psychology of the National Research Council. The subcommittee became the Committee on Child Development in 1925. In 1933, the Committee was dissolved and replaced by the Society for Research in Child Development. The headquarters of the Society are located in Chicago, Illinois, at the University of Chicago Press.	SRCD's purposes are: 1. To advance research in child development. 2. To encourage interdisciplinary consideration of problems in the field of child development. 3. To encourage study of the implications of research findings. 4. To enable specialists to share research tools and techniques. 5. To sponsor national and regional conferences.	1. *Child Development* (journal published bimonthly) 2. *Child Development Abstracts and Bibliography* (journal, published triannually) 3. *Monographs of the Society for Research in Child Development* (journal, published two to four times annually) 4. Newsletter 5. A membership directory	Membership application may be made by an individual engaged in research in child development or a related field, who teaches undergraduate and graduate courses in child development, and who has published in the field of child development; or by an individual who actively promotes the purposes of the society. All applications are considered by the governing board of the society. Three types of memberships: (1) individual, (2) graduate or medical student; and (3) emeritus.

History	Purposes	Publications	Membership Requirements
Southern Association on Children Under Six (SACUS) **Box 5403 Brady Station** **Little Rock, Ark. 72215 (501) 663-0353**			
SACUS began as the Nashville Council for the Education of Children Under Six in September 1948. During the third meeting of the group, the participants voted to become the Southern Regional Association on Children Under Six and adopted a constitution. At the 1954 conference in Biloxi, Mississippi, the constitution was amended to delete "Regional," and the official organization became the Southern Association on Children Under Six (SACUS).	The basic purposes of SACUS are to work on behalf of young children and their families and provide opportunities for the cooperation of individuals and groups concerned with the well-being of young children. Particular concerns are: 1. To further the development of knowledge and understanding of young children and the dissemination of such information. 2. To contribute to the professional growth of persons working with and for young children. 3. To encourage the provision of educational and developmental resources and services for young children. 4. To improve the standards for group care and education of children and their quality of life. 5. To provide support for state associations in their work for these objectives.	1. *Dimensions*, the quarterly journal, began as a regular publication in 1973. 2. *Proceedings*, the proceedings of the annual conference were published each year except 1966. 3. Other special publications	Membership is open to all persons concerned with infants and young children. Two classes of membership: (1) affiliate (a members of a state affiliate association) and (2) individual.

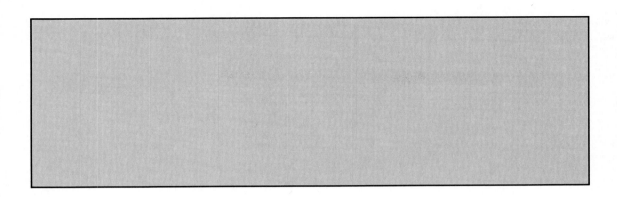

Appendix 5
Additional Organizations of Concern to Early Childhood Educators

Organizations

AAUW Educational Foundation
1111 16th Street, N.W.
Washington, D.C. 20036

Action for Children's Television
46 Austin Street
Newtonville, Mass. 02160

American Academy of Pediatrics
141 Northwest Point Blvd.
P.O. Box 927
Elk Grove Village, Ill. 60009

American Bar Association
National Legal Resource Center for
   Child Advocacy and Protection
1800 M St., N.W., Suite 20005
Washington, D.C. 20036

The American Dietetic Association
216 West Jackson, Suite 800
Chicago, Ill. 60606

American Federation of State,
   County and Municipal
   Employees, AFL-CIO
1626 L Street, N.W.
Washington, D.C. 20036

American Home Economics
   Association
1555 King Street
Alexandria, Va. 22314

American Library Association
50 East Huron Street
Chicago, Ill. 60611

American Medical Association
535 North Dearborn Street
Chicago, Ill. 60610

American Psychiatric Association
1400 K Street, N.W.
Washington, D.C. 20005

American Speech-Language-Hearing
   Association
10801 Rockville Pike
Rockville, Md. 20852

Association for the Care of
   Children's Health
7910 Woodmont Avenue, Suite 300
Bethesda, Md. 20814

Association for Retarded Citizens
National Headquarters
2501 Avenue J
P.O. Box 6109
Arlington, Tex. 76005

Association for Supervision and
   Curriculum Development
1250 Pitt St.
Alexandria, Va. 22314

Bananas
6510 Telegraph Avenue
Oakland, Calif. 94609

Cease
17 Gerry St.
Cambridge, Mass. 02138

Center for Law and Social Policy
1616 P Street, N.W.
Suite 350
Washington, D.C. 20036

Center for the Study of Evaluation
Graduate School of Education
145 Moore Hall
405 Hilgard Avenue
Los Angeles, Calif. 90024

Child Care Action Campaign
330 Seventh Ave, 18th Floor
New York, N.Y. 10001

Child Care Employee Project
6536 Telegraph Avenue
Suite A–201
Oakland, Calif. 94609

Child Care Law Center
625 Market Street
Suite 195
San Francisco, Calif. 94105

Child Care Support Center
1340 Spring Street, N.W. Suite 200
Atlanta, Ga. 30309

Child Welfare League of America
440 First Street, N.W., Suite 310
Washington, D.C. 20001

Children's Book Council, Inc.
568 Broadway, Suite 404
New York, N.Y. 10012

Children's Defense Fund
128 C Street, N.W.
Washington, D.C. 20005

The Children's Foundation
725 Fifteenth Street, N.W., Suite 505
Washington, D.C. 20005

The Conference Board
845 Third Avenue
New York, N.Y. 10022

Council for Early Childhood
   Professional Recognition
1718 Connecticut Avenue, N.W.
Suite 500
Washington, D.C. 20009

The Council of State Governments
P.O. Box 11910 — Iron Works Pike
Lexington, Ky. 40548

Department of Health and Human
   Services
Public Health Service
Centers for Disease Control
Atlanta, Ga. 30333

Education Commission of the States
707 17th Street, Suite 2700
Denver, Colo. 80202

ERIC Clearinghouse on
   Elementary and Early
   Childhood Education
805 West Pennsylvania Avenue
Urbana, Ill. 61801

ERIC Clearinghouse on
   Handicapped and Gifted
   Children
Council for Exceptional Children
1920 Association Drive
Reston, Va. 22091

Family Resource Coalition
Suite 1520
200 South Michigan Avenue
Chicago, Ill. 60604

Family Service America
11700 West Lake Park Drive
Park Place
Milwaukee, Wis. 53224

The C. Henry Kempe National
   Center for the Prevention and
   Treatment of Child Abuse and
   Neglect
Department of Pediatrics
1205 Oneida Street
Denver, Colo. 80220

High/Scope Educational Research
   Foundation
600 North River Street
Lafayette, Ind. 47902

Institute for Women's Policy
   Research
1400 20th Street, N.W., Suite 104
Washington, D.C. 20036

Jean Piaget Society
Center for Applied Cognitive
   Science
The University of Toledo
Toledo, Oh. 43606

John Tracy Clinic
806 West Adams Boulevard
Los Angeles, Calif. 90007

Learning Disabilities Association of
   America
4156 Library Road
Pittsburgh, Pa. 15234

Legal Defense and Education Fund
99 Hudson Street
New York, N.Y. 10013

March of Dimes Birth Defects
   Foundation
1275 Mamaroneck Avenue
White Plains, N.Y. 10605

Military Early Childhood Alliance
c/o Olga Borden
934 Avenida del Sol, N.E.
Albuquerque, N. Mex. 87110

National Association for Family Day
Care
725 Fifteenth Street, N.W., Suite 505
Washington, D.C. 20005

National Association of Child Care
Resource and Referral Agencies
2116 Campus Drive, S.E.
Rochester, Minn. 55904

National Association of Children's
Hospitals and Related Institutions
401 Wythe Street
Alexandria, Va. 22314

National Association of Elementary
School Principals
1615 Duke Street
Alexandria, Va. 22314

National Black Child Development
Institute, Inc.
1463 Rhode Island Avenue, N.W.
Washington, D.C. 20005

National Center for Clinical Infant
Programs
733 Fifteenth St., N.W., Suite 912
Washington, D.C. 20005

National Coalition for Campus
Child Care, Inc.
Box 258
Cascade, Wis. 53011

National Coalition for Parent
Involvement in Education
National Education Association
1201 16th St., N.W., Rm. 810
Washington, D.C. 20036

National Commission on Working
Women of Wider Opportunities
for Women
1325 G Street, N.W., Lower Level
Washington, D.C. 20005

National Committee for Citizens in
Education
10840 Little Patuxent Parkway #301
Columbus, Md. 21044

National Committee for Prevention
of Child Abuse
332 South Michigan Avenue, Suite
1600
Chicago, Ill. 60604

National Conference of State
Legislatures
444 North Capitol Street, N.W.,
Suite 500
Washington, D.C. 20001

National Congress of Parents and
Teachers
700 N. Rush St.
Chicago, Ill. 60611

National Council of the Churches of
Christ in the United States of
America
475 Riverside Drive
New York, N.Y. 10115

National Council of Jewish
Women
53 West 23rd Street
New York, N.Y. 10010

National Easter Seal Society
2023 West Ogden Avenue
Chicago, Ill. 60612

National Governors' Association
Hall of the States
444 North Capital Street, Suite 250
Washington, D.C. 20001

National Head Start Association
1220 King Street, Suite 200
Alexandria, Va. 22314

National Institute of Health
Department of Health and Human
Services
Public Health Service

Bldg. 31, Room 2A32
Bethesda, Md. 20892

National League of Cities Institute
1301 Pennsylvania Avenue, N.W.
Washington, D.C. 20004

National PTA
700 North Rush Street
Chicago, Ill. 60611

National Society to Prevent
  Blindness
500 East Remington Road
Schaumburg, Ill. 60173

Nine-to-Five, National Association
  of Working Women
614 Superior Avenue, N.W.
Cleveland, Ohio 44113

Office of Information Services
John F. Kennedy Center for
  Research
Box 40, Peabody College
Vanderbilt University
Nashville, Tenn. 37203

Parents Anonymous
National Office
6733 South Sepulveda Blvd.,
  Suite 270
Los Angeles, Calif. 90045

Resources for Child Caring
450 North Syndicate, Suite 5
St. Paul, Minn. 55104

Spina Bifida Association of America
343 South Dearborn, Suite 310
Chicago, Ill. 60604

United Cerebral Palsy Association,
  Inc.
66 East 34th Street
New York, N.Y. 10016

U.S. House of Representatives
Select Committee on Children,
  Youth, and Families
H2–385 House Office Bldg.
Annex 2
Washington, D.C. 20515

Wellesley College
School-Age Child Care Project
Center for Research on Women
Wellesley, Mass. 02187

Work/Family Directions
930 Commonwealth Avenue, South
Boston, Mass. 02215

Appendix 6
Suppliers of Early Childhood Equipment, Books, Tests, and Materials

ABC School Supply, Inc.
P.O. Box 100019
Duluth, Ga. 30136

Addison-Wesley Publishing Co.
2725 Sand Hill Road
Menlo Park, Calif. 94025

AFRO-AM Incorporated
819 South Wabash Avenue
Suite 610
Chicago, Ill. 60605

American Guidance Service
Publisher's Building
P.O. Box 99
Circle Pines, Minn. 55014

American Playground Corporation
Box 2599
Anderson, Ind. 46018

Angeles Toys, Inc.
9 Capper Drive
Dailey Industrial Park
Pacific, Mo. 63069

E. J. Arnold, Inc.
105 Thompson Park Drive
Mars, Pa. 16046

The Australian Council for
  Educational Research, Ltd.
P.O. Box 210
Hawthorn, Victoria 3122, Australia

Barnell Loft, Ltd.
P.O. Box 5380
Chicago, Ill. 60680

Beckley-Cardy
1 East First Street
Duluth, Minn. 55802

Breakfall, Inc.
759 North Milwaukee Street
Milwaukee, Wis. 53202

Britannica
Encyclopaedia Britannica
Educational Corporation
310 South Michigan
Chicago, Ill. 60604

Carroll Publishing Co.
P.O. Box 1200
Palo Alto, Calif. 94302

Carlisle Tire & Rubber Co.
P.O. Box 99
Carlisle, Pa. 17013

Channing L. Bete Co, Inc.
200 State Road
South Deerfield, Mass. 01373

Chapman Brook & Kent
555 Dover Ct.
Arrowhead, Calif. 92352

Childcraft Educational Corporation
20 Kilmer Road
Edison, N.J. 08817

Childlife Play Specialties, Inc.
55 Whitney Street
P.O. Box 527
Holliston, Mass. 01746

Children's Book & Music Center
2500 Santa Monica Blvd.
Santa Monica, Calif. 90404

Children's Defense Fund
122 C Street, N.W.
Washington, D.C. 20001

The Child's World
P.O. Box 989
Elgin, Ill. 60120

Chime Time
934 Anderson Drive
Homer, N.Y. 13077

Classic School Products
174 Simoran Commerce
  Place, A106
Apopka, Fla. 32703

Claudia's Caravan
P.O. Box 1582
Alameda, Calif. 94501

Community Playthings
Route 213
Rifton, N.Y. 12471

Constructive Playthings
1227 E. 119th Street
Grandview, Mo. 64030

CTB Macmillan/McGraw-Hill
2500 Garden Road
Montery, Calif. 93940

Cuisenaire Company of America,
  Inc.
12 Church Street, Box D
New Rochelle, N.Y. 10802

Delta Education, Inc.
P.O. Box 915
Hudson, N.H. 03051

Demco
P.O. Box 7488
Madison, Wis. 53707

Early Learning Book Club
Delran, N.J. 08075

The Education Center, Inc.
1410 Mill Street
P.O. Box 9753
Greensboro, N.C. 27429

Educational Activities, Inc.
P.O. Box 392
Freeport, N.Y. 11520

Educational Development
  Corporation
10302 E. 55th Place
Tulsa, Okla. 74146

Educational Productions, Inc.
4925 S.W. Humphrey Park Crest
Portland, Oreg. 97221

Educational Products Division
Binney & Smith, Inc.
1100 Church Lane, P.O. Box 431
Easton, Pa. 18044

Educational Insights
19560 S. Rancho Way
Dominquez Hills, Calif. 90220

Educational Teaching Aids
199 Carpenter Avenue
Wheeling, Ill. 60090

Educators Publishing Source. Inc.
75 Moulton Street
Cambridge, Mass. 02238

Environments, Inc.
P.O. Box 1348
Beaufort, S.C. 29901

Exchange Press, Inc.
P.O. Box 2890
Redmond, Wash. 98073

The Fiber Group
141 Halstead Ave.
Mamaroneck, N.Y. 10543

Field Publications
4343 Equity Drive
Columbus, Oh. 43216

Films for the Humanities & Science
P.O. Box 2053
Princeton, N.J. 08543

Gleason Corporation
P.O. Box 343
Milwaukee, Wis. 53201

Good Apple
Box 299
1204 Buchanan St.
Carthage, Ill. 62321

Goodheart-Willcox
123 West Taft Drive
South Holland, Ill. 60473

Gryphon House, Inc.
Early Childhood Books
P.O. Box 275
Mt. Rainer, Md. 20712

J. L. Hammett Company
P.O. Box 9057
Braintree, Mass. 02184

Harcourt Brace Jovanovich, Inc.
1250 Sixth Ave.
San Diego, Calif. 92101

Heinemann, Boynton, & Cook
70 Court Street
Portsmouth, N.H. 03801

Harper and Row, Publishers
10 East 53rd Street
New York, N.Y. 10022

Holt, Rinehart and Winston
301 Commerce Street, Suite 3700
Ft. Worth, Tex. 76102

Humanics Learning
P.O. Box 7447
Atlanta, Ga. 30309

Insight Media
121 West 85th Street
New York, N.Y. 10024

Institute for Personality and Ability
  Testing, Inc.
P.O. Box 188
Champaign, Ill. 61824

Irwin Publishing
1800 Steeles Ave. West
Concord, Ontario L4K 2P3

Judy/Instructo
4325 Hiawatha Avenue South
Minneapolis, Minn. 55406

Kaplan
1310 Lewisville-Clemmons Road
Lewisville, N.C. 27023

Kendall/Hunt Publishing Co.
2460 Kerper Boulevard
P.O. Box 539
Dubuque, Ia. 52004

Kenner Parker Toys, Inc.
1014 Vine Street
Cincinnati, Oh. 45202

Kids Rights
3700 Progress Blvd.
Mount Dora, Fla. 32757

Kimbo Educational
10 North Third Avenue-A
Long Branch, N.J. 07740

Kompan, Inc.
80 King Spring Road
Windsor Locks, Conn. 06096

Kinworthy Educational Source, Inc.
Ellicott Station, P.O. 60
138 Allen St.
Buffalo, N.Y. 14205

Lakeshore Curriculum Materials Co.
2695 E. Dominquez Street
P.O. Box 6261
Carson, Calif. 90749

Learning Products, Inc.
700 Fee Fee Road
St. Louis, Mo. 63043

The Learning Seed
330 Telser Road
Lake Zurich, Ill. 60047

Learning Things, Inc.
68A Broadway
Arlington, Mass. 02147

Lego Systems, Inc.
555 Taylor Road
Enfield, Conn. 06082

Longman Publishing
95 Church Street
White Plains, N.Y. 10601

Love Publishing Co.
1777 South Bellaire St.
Denver, Colo. 80222

Mat Factory, Inc.
1378 East Edinger
Santa Ana, Calif. 92705

Mattel Toys
Mattel, Inc.
Consumer Affairs
5150 Rosecrans Ave.
Hawthorne, Calif. 90250

Mayfield Publishing Co.
1240 Villa Street
Mountain View, Calif. 94041

McGraw Hill Publishing Co.
1221 Avenue of the Americas
New York, N.Y. 10020

Media Materials
1821 Portal Street
Baltimore, Md. 21224

Melody House Publishing Co.
819 N.W. 92nd Street
Oklahoma City, Okla. 93114

Meridian Education Corporation
236 E. Front St.
Bloomington, Ill. 61701

Mitchell Rubber Products
491 Wilson Way
City of Industry, Calif. 91744

Modern Curriculum Press
13900 Prospect Road
Cleveland, Oh. 44136

Morrison School Supplies, Inc.
304 Industrial Way
San Carlos, Calif. 94070

Nasco
901 Janesville Ave.
P.O. Box 901
Fort Atkinson, Wis. 53538

National Geographic Society
Educational Services
Washington, D.C. 20036

Nystrom Division of Herff Jones,
    Inc.
3333 Elston Avenue
Chicago, Ill. 60618

Open Court Publishing Co.
P.O. Box 599
315 Fifth Street
Peru, Ill. 61354

Opportunities For Learning, Inc.
20417 Northoff St. Dept. Y
Chatsworth, Calif. 91311

PCA Industries Inc.
5642 Natural Bridge
St. Louis, Mo. 63120

Peninsula Publishing, Inc.
P.O. Box 412
Port Angeles, Wash. 98362

The Perfection Form Company
1000 North Second Avenue
Logan, Ia. 51546

Persenaire Park & Playground
    Products
9818 Whethorn Dr.
Houston, Tex. 77095

Play Designs
P.O. Box 427
New Berlin, Pa. 17855

Playsafe Surfaces, Inc.
240 West Bristol Lane
Orange, Calif. 92665

J. A. Preston Corporation
60 Page Road
Clifton, N.J. 07012

Pro Ed
8700 Shoal Creek Blvd.
Austin, Tex. 78758

The Psychological Corporation
Test, Products, and Services
Harcourt Brace Jovanovich, Inc.
555 Academic Court
San Antonio, Tex. 78204

The Putnam & Grosset
    Corporation
200 Madison Avenue
New York, N.Y. 10016

Reese Industries, Inc.
P.O. Box 912
Prospect Heights, Ill. 60070

Research Concepts
A Division of Test Maker, Inc.
1368 East Airport Road
Muskegon, Mich. 49444

Rhythms Productions
Tom Thumb Records/Books
Whitney Building, Box 34485
Los Angeles, Calif. 90034

The Riverside Publishing Co.
8420 Bryn Mawr Avenue
Chicago, Ill. 60631

Robert Godfrey, LTD
141 Halstead Avenue
Mamaroneck, N.Y. 10543

Safety Soil
2909 Garfield Avenue
Carmichael, Calif. 95608

S. C. Distributing Company
Journal Square Station
P.O. Box 16234
Jersey City, N.J. 07306

Scholastic Book Clubs, Inc.
2931 E. McCarty Street
P.O. Box 7502
Jefferson City, Mo. 65101

Scholastic Testing Service, Inc.
480 Weyer Road, P.O. Box 1056
Bensenville, Ill. 60106

Science Research Associates, Inc.
155 North Wacker Drive
Chicago, Ill. 60606

The Sesame Street Catalog
2515 East 43rd Street
P.O. Box 182228
Chattanooga, Tenn. 37422

Stepping Stones
P.O. Box 830058
Richardson, Tex. 75080

Stoelting Co.
Oakwood Centre
620 Wheat Lane
Wood Dale, Ill. 60191

Teachers College Press
Teachers College, Columbia
  University
New York, N.Y. 10027

Tire Turf Systems
P.O. Box 186
Harlan, Ind. 46743

Tonka Products
6000 Clearwater Drive
Minnetonka, Minn. 55343

Toys 'n Things Press
450 North Syndicate, Suite S
St. Paul, Minn. 55104

Travelin' Magazine
P.O. Box 23005
Eugene, Ore. 97402

Trend Enterprises, Inc.
P.O. Box 64073
St. Paul, Minn. 55164

Troll Associates
100 Corporate Drive
Mahwah, N.J. 07430

Unimat Industries
121 East Alton Ave.
Santa Ana, Calif. 92707

United Learning, Inc.
6633 West Howard Street
Miles, Ill. 60648

Wadsworth Publishing Co.
Ten Davis Drive
Belmont, Calif. 94002

Wake Forest University
Dean of the Graduate School
Box 7487 Reynolds Station
Winston-Salem, N.C. 27109

Warren Publishing House, Inc.
P.O. Box 2250
Everett, Wash. 98203

Waveland Press, Inc.
P.O. Box 400
Prospect Heights, Ill. 60070

Webster's International, Inc.
5729 Cloverland Place
Brentwood, Tenn. 37027

Weekly Reader Skills Books
4343 Equity Drive
P.O. Box 16618
Columbus, O. 43216

Whitney Bros. Co.
P.O. Box 644
Keene, N.H. 03431

Wood Designs of Monroe, Inc.
P.O. Box 1308
Monroe, N.C. 28110

Zaner-Bloser
1459 King Avenue
P.O. Box 16764
Columbus, Oh. 43216

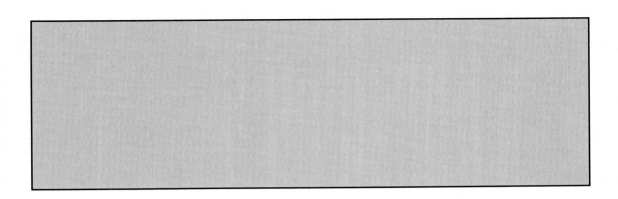

Appendix 7
Federal and Philanthropic Assistance

Federal Assistance

Department of Agriculture
Fourteenth Street and Independence
Avenue, S.W.
Washington, D.C. 20250
(202–447–2791)
   School Breakfast Program
      10.553*
   School Lunch Program 10.555
   Special Milk Program 10.556
   Women, Infants, and Children
      10.557
   Child Care Food Program
      10.558
   Summer Food Service 10.559
   State Administrative Expenses
      for Child Nutrition 10.560
   Nutrition Education and Train-
      ing Program 10.564

Department of Health and Human
   Resources
200 Independence Avenue, S.W.
Washington, D.C. 20201
(202–245–6296)
   Maternal and Child Health
      13.110
   Child Immunization Grants
      13.268
   Administration for Children,
      Youth, and Families—Head
      Start 13.600
   Administration for Children,
      Youth, and Families—Child
      Welfare Research and Dem-
      on   stration 13.608

Department of the Interior
1800 C Street N.W.
Washington, D.C. 20240
(202–343–3171)

Indian Social Services—Child
   Welfare Assistance 15.103
Indian Education—Assistance
   to Schools 15.130
Indian Child Welfare Grant—
   Title II Grants 15.144

Appalachian Regional Commission
1666 Connecticut Avenue, N.W.
Washington, D.C. 20235
(202–673–7893)
   Appalachian—Child Develop-
      ment 23.103

Action
1100 Vermont Avenue, N.W.
Washington, D.C. 20525
(202–634–9380)
   Foster Grandparent Program
      72.001

Department of Education
400 Maryland Avenue, S.W.
Washington, D.C. 20202
(202–245–3192)
   Bilingual Education 84.003
   Educationally Deprived
      Children—Local Educational
      Agencies 84.010
   Migrant Education—Basic State
      Formula Grant Program
      84.011
   Educationally Deprived
      Children—State Administra-
      tion   84.012
   Follow Through 84.014
   Handicapped Early Childhood
      84.024
   Handicapped Preschool 84.173
   Transition Program for Refugee
      Children 84.146

*As listed in the *Catalog of Federal Domestic As-
sistance Programs* (the first two digits of the program number identify the department or
agency).

For additional help write for: *Guide to
Federal Assistance to Education* (New
Century Education Corporation, 440
Park Avenue South, New York, NY
10016).

Philanthropic Assistance

Help in locating foundation sources includes:

College and University Reporter
Commerce Clearing House, Inc.
4025 W. Peterson
Chicago, Ill. 60646

The Foundation Center
79 Fifth Avenue
New York, N.Y. 10003

Foundation Research Service
Lawson Williams Associates, Inc.
39 East 51st Street
New York, N.Y. 10022

The Grantsmanship Center
1030 South Grand Avenue
Los Angeles, Calif. 90015

The Oryx Press Grant Information
  System
The Oryx Press
3930 East Camelback Road
Phoenix, Ariz. 85018

Taft Information System
Taft Products
Suite 600
1000 Vermont Avenue, N.W.
Washington, D.C. 20005

Appendix 8
Tests

Aptitude

ADMINISTRATION	CONTENT	MATERIALS	TEST DATA
*ACER Checklists for School Beginners, 1974, 1977 Rowe, H.A.H.			
The Australian Council for Research Limited P.O. Box 210 Hawthorn, Victoria 3122 Australia			
Administrator: teacher	ACER Checklists for School Beginners is a sixty-two-item checklist covering the areas of social development, emotional development, motor skills, memory, attention, and language skills.	Administrator: manual checklist class record sheet Parent: thirty-eight-item parent checklist	Research results relating to the validity, reliability and stability of the Checklists
Grade range: preschool through first grade			
Time required: approximately fifteen minutes			
Teacher checklist			

ADMINISTRATION	CONTENT	MATERIALS	TEST DATA

ACER Early School Series 1981
Rowe, H.A.H.
 	
Australian Council for Educational Research Limited
P.O. Box 210
Hawthorn, Victoria 3122
Australia
 	
Administrator:
    teacher
 	
Grade range:
    school beginners
 	
Time required:
    approximately fifteen
    minutes
 	
Group and individual test
	ACER Early School Series is a diagnostic and screening test to provide estimates of cognitive development and maturity. The ten tests, based on a criterion-referenced model of measurement, include:
	
	1. Auditory Skills Analysis—auditory discrimination
	2. Conceptual Skills—number test and a figure-formation test
	3. Language Skills—five syntactic-structured tests and a word-knowledge test
		Administrator:
		    manual
		    booklet for each test
		    score key
		    "Early Identification and Intervention"
		Each child:
		    test booklet
		    pencil
			Rasch Scale ability estimates

461

ADMINISTRATION	CONTENT	MATERIALS	TEST DATA
Arizona Articulation Proficiency Scale (Revised) (AAPS)			
Fudala, J.B.			
Western Psychological Services			
Publishers and Distributors			
12031 Wilshire Blvd.			
Los Angeles, Calif. 90025			
Administrator: speech clinician	AAPS uses numerical scale to test articulatory proficiency (i.e., numerical values for sounds are related to probable frequency of occurrence in American speech). Scale may be used for screening and for determining progress. Picture Test Cards are used with younger children; the Sentence Test is used with older children and adults.	Administrator: manual	Total consonant score
Age range: three through twelve years		Picture Test Cards	Total vowel score
		The Sentence Test	Total sound score
Time required: ten minutes		The Protocol Booklet	AAPS total score (percentage of individual's articulation which is correct)
Individual test		The Survey Form	
Verbal			Average AAPS score for each age level
			Interpretive values of AAPS total scores

ADMINISTRATION	CONTENT	MATERIALS	TEST DATA
Basic School Skills Inventory-Screen (BSSI-S) Hammill, D. D., and J. E. Leigh			
Pro-ed **8700 Shoal Creek Blvd.** **Austin, Tex. 78758**			
Administrator: teacher	The *BSSI-S* is used to locate children who are "high risk" for school failure, who need more in-depth assessment, and who should be referred for additional study.	Administrator: manual answer sheets	Raw score Scaled scores Standard scores Age equivalent
Age range: four years through six years, eleven months			
Time required: five to eight minutes			
Individual test			
Oral and observation			

ADMINISTRATION	CONTENT	MATERIALS	TEST DATA
The Bayley Scales of Infant Development Bayley, N. **The Psychological Corp.** **Harcourt Brace Jovanovich, Inc.** **1250 Sixth Ave.** **San Diego, Calif. 92101** Administrator: psychometrist Age range: two to thirty months Time required: not timed, approximately forty-five minutes Individual test Manipulative	*The Bayley Scales of Infant Development* are divided into three parts: 1. Mental Scale designed to measure child's sensory responses, understandings of "object constancy," ability to learn and remember, vocalizations and verbal communication, and ability to generalize and classify. 2. Motor Scale is designed to assess child's general body control and large and small muscle skills. 3. Behavior Record contains ratings of child's social and object orientation, goal directedness, general emotional tone, and interest in sensory areas.	Administrator: kit of materials record forms for each of the three scales manual	Raw score Mental Development Index Psychomotor Development Index Infant Behavior Record (descriptive rating scales)

ADMINISTRATION	CONTENT	MATERIALS	TEST DATA
Bruininks-Oseretsky Test of Motor Proficiency **Bruininks, R.H.** **American Guidance Service** **Publishers' Building, P.O. Box 220** **Circle Pines, Minn. 55014** Administrator: teacher, occupational therapist, psychologist Age range: four-and-a-half through fourteen-and-a-half years Time required: Complete battery—forty- five to sixty minutes; short form—fifteen to twenty minutes Individual test Motor activities	The *Bruininks—Oseretsky* *Test of Motor Proficiency* measures gross and fine motor development. Subtests are: 1. Running speed and agility 2. Balance 3. Bilateral coordination 4. Strength 5. Upper-limb coordination 6. Response speed 7. Visual-motor control 8. Upper-limb speed and dexterity	Administrator: manual individual record form equipment for testing children	*Complete battery* Raw scores Standard scores (Gross Motor Composite; Fine Motor Composite; Battery Composite) Percentile ranks (Gross Motor Composite; Fine Motor Composite; Battery Composite) Stanines (Gross Motor Composite; Fine Motor Composite; Battery Composite) Age equivalents *Short form* Raw scores Standard scores Percentile rank Stanines

ADMINISTRATION	CONTENT	MATERIALS	TEST DATA
Cognitive Skills Assessment Battery, 2nd ed. (CSAB) Boehm, A. E., and B. R. Slater **Teachers College Press** **Teachers College, Columbia University** **1234 Amsterdam Ave.** **New York, N.Y. 10027**			

Administrator:
school psychologist,
teacher, teacher's aide
Grade range:
pre-kindergarten through
kindergarten
Time required:
twenty to twenty-five
minutes
Individual test
Verbal and paper-and-pencil
	CSAB was developed to
	provide teachers of
	prekindergarten and
	kindergarten children with
	information regarding
	children's progress relative to
	teaching goals in the
	cognitive and physical-motor
	areas. *CSAB* provides
	information in five areas:
	1. Orientation toward one's
	   environment
	2. Discrimination of
	   similarities and differences
	3. Comprehension and
	   concept formation
	4. Coordination
	5. Immediate and delayed
	   memory
		Administrator:
		card easel
		manual
		pupil response sheet
		class record sheet
		eight blocks of same
		   color, shape, and size
		watch with "seconds"
		   shown
		pencils (primary size)
		paper clipboard
		Each child:
		pupil response sheet
		   (handled by child for
		   copying shapes)
		pencil
			Percentages of children
			responding to each
			option by grade and
			socioeconomic status
			Level of response (e.g.,
			elaborated statements,
			partial descriptions, and
			incorrect or irrelevant
			responses)

ADMINISTRATION	CONTENT	MATERIALS	TEST DATA
Comprehensive Identification Process (CIP) Zehrbach, R. **Scholastic Testing Service, Inc.** **400 Meyer Road** **P.O. Box 1056** **Bensenville, Ill. 60106** Administrator: teacher or trained paraprofessional Age range: two-and-a-half through five-and-a-half years Time required: approximately thirty minutes Individual test Paper-and-pencil, verbal, and manipulative	*CIP* is a screening instrument for identifying preschool disabled children. Areas screened include fine motor, gross motor, cognitive-verbal, speech and expressive language (articulation, voice fluency, and expressive language), social-affective behavior, medical history, hearing, and vision.	Administrator: screening administrators' and interviewers' manuals Parent Interview Form Child Record Folder Speech and Expressive Language Record Observation of Behavior Form Screening booklet Symbol booklet	Manual refers to three possibilities for each area screened: (1) Pass—normal for age; (2) Refer or rescreen—for a specific problem such as hearing, vision, speech or check for temporary or minimal problem; and (3) Evaluate—a complete diagnostic evaluation by medical specialist or a professional interdisciplinary team.

ADMINISTRATION	CONTENT	MATERIALS	TEST DATA
Detroit Tests of Learning Aptitude—Primary Hammill, D. D., and B. R. Bryant **Pro-ed** **8700 Shoal Creek Blvd.** **Austin, Tex. 78758** Administrator: psychometrist Age range: three-and-a-half through nine years Time required: fifteen to forty-five minutes Individual test Verbal and paper-and-pencil	The *Detroit Tests of Learning Aptitude-P* is designed to measure young children's intellectual abilities. More specifically, it measures linguistics, cognition, attention, and motor domains.	Administrator: *Administration and Picture Book* Response form Each child: response form pencil	Raw score Standard score Percentile rank Deviation intelligence quotient Profile

ADMINISTRATION	CONTENT	MATERIALS	TEST DATA
The Development Activities Screening Inventory—II **Fewell, R. R., and M. B. Langley** **Pro-ed** **8700 Shoal Creek Blvd.** **Austin, Tex. 78758**			

Administrator:
  teacher
 	
Age range:
  birth through sixty months
  (functioning age)
 	
Time required:
  thirty to sixty minutes
 	
Individual test
 	
Verbal and manipulative
	The *Developmental Activities Screening Inventory—II* was designed as an informal developmental assessment for young children or children with auditory impairments or language disorders.	Administrators:
		  manual
		  response form
		  kit of materials
		  additional common
		    household items
			Raw score
			Developmental age
			Developmental quotient
			  (ratio)
			Instructional program for
			  remediation purposes

ADMINISTRATION	CONTENT	MATERIALS	TEST DATA
Developmental Test of Visual-Motor Integration Beery, K. E. **Modern Curriculum Press** **13900 Prospect Road** **Cleveland, Ohio 44136** Administrator: teacher Age range: approximately two through fifteen years (designed for preschool and early primary grades) Time required: not timed, approximately fifteen to twenty minutes Group and individual test Paper-and-pencil	*Developmental Tests of Visual-Motor Integration* determines degree to which visual perception and motor behavior are integrated in young children. Short test form (with fifteen geometric figures) is suitable for ages two to eight. Long test form (with twenty-four figures) intended for children ages two to fifteen. Child copies the following geometric figures: 1. Vertical line 2. Horizontal line 3. Circle 4. Vertical-Horizontal cross 5. Right oblique line 6. Square 7. Left oblique line 8. Oblique cross 9. Triangle	Administrator: manual Each child: test booklet (short form or long form) pencil	Raw score Age equivalent Percentile Standard score equivalent Recommended instructional methods (Monographs & Stimulus Cards and Assessment Worksheets) Developmental comments given for purposes of making scorer aware of certain developments and deviations

ADMINISTRATION	CONTENT	MATERIALS	TEST DATA
Early Screening Inventory (ESI) **Meisels, S. J., and M. S. Wiske** **Teachers College Press, Teachers College** **Columbia University 1234 Amsterdam Avenue** **New York, N.Y. 10027** Administrator: teacher or person familiar with early childhood behavior and development Age range: four through six years Time required: fifteen to twenty minutes Individual test Verbal	*ESI* is a brief developmental screening instrument that is designed to identify children who may need special educational services in order to perform well in school. *ESI* examines Visual-motor Adaptive, Language and Cognition, and Gross Motor/Body Awareness development in children. *ESI* also includes Draw a Person Task and Letter Writing.	Administration: manual cards with drawings cubes objects for verbal expression *ESI* Score Sheets Parent questionnaires manila paper eight 2" × 2" squares of colored paper large pencil white drawing paper piece of 8-½" × 11" cardboard	Raw Score Cut-off scores given for age ranges to recommend the child as *OK, rescreen,* or *refer*

ADMINISTRATION	CONTENT	MATERIALS	TEST DATA
Early Screening Profiles (ESP) Harrison, P. **American Guidance Service** **Publishers' Building** **P.O. Box 99** **Circle Pines, Minn. 55014** Administrator: teacher and parent Age range: two years through six years, eleven months Time required: fifteen through forty minutes	*ESP* assesses cognitive language, motor, and self-help and social development. It also surveys the child's articulation, home environment, health history, and test behavior (i.e., behavior during the cognitive language and motor profiles).	Administration: manual Motor Administration Manual Test Plates in Easel Test records Self-Help/Social Profile Questionnaires score summaries Home/Health History Survey tape measure beads carrying case	Screening Index Standard Scores

ADMINISTRATION	CONTENT	MATERIALS	TEST DATA
Extended Merrill-Palmer Scale **Ball, R. S., P. Merrifield, and L. H. Stott** **Stoelting** **Oakwood Centre: 620 Wheat Lane** **Wood Dale, Ill. 60191**			
Administrator: psychometrist Age range: three to five years Time required: approximately forty-five minutes Individual test Manipulative	The sixteen tasks of the *Extended Merrill-Palmer* *Scale* lead to a differentiation of these four dimensions of a child's thought processes: 1. Semantic production 2. Figural production 3. Semantic evaluation 4. Figural evaluation	Administrator: manual task record forms scoring forms manipulatives	Percentile ranges of the four abilities at six age intervals during the years three to five

ADMINISTRATION	CONTENT	MATERIALS	TEST DATA
The Gesell Preschool Assessment	The *Gesell Preschool Assessment* includes a series of individual test situations that, taken together, reveal the child's relative maturity ratings in four basic fields of behavior: motor, adaptive, language, and personal-social.	Administrator: manual recording sheets developmental schedules kit *The Gesell Institute's Child From One to Six*	Developmental age
Programs Modern for Education Learning Press			
RRB 167			
Rosemont, N.J. 08556			
Administrator: teacher psychologist			
Age range: two and one-half through six years			
Time required: forty minutes			
Individual test			
Verbal, manipulative, and paper-and-pencil			

ADMINISTRATION	CONTENT	MATERIALS	TEST DATA
Goldman-Fristoe Test of Articulation **Goldman, R., and M. Fristoe** **American Guidance Service** **Publishers' Bldg., P.O. Box 220** **Circle Pines, Minn. 55014** Administrator: speech clinician Age range: two to sixteen-plus years Time required: approximately ten to fifteen minutes for "Sounds-in-Words" subtest; time variable on other two subtests Individual test Verbal	The *Goldman-Fristoe Test of Articulation* assesses articulation. The test includes three subtests: 1. "Sounds-in-Words" assesses child's articulation of major speech sounds in initial, medial, and final position. 2. "Sound-in-Sentences" appraises child's articulation of connected speech. 3. "Stimulability" yields information about the relative ease with which a child can correctly articulate the sounds known to be most difficult for him or her, given the contexts of syllables, words, and sentences.	Administrator: test plates manual response forms (filmstrip available as alternative testing method)	Raw score Percentile rank (for survey use) Record of articulation errors (for diagnostic use by clinician)

ADMINISTRATION	CONTENT	MATERIALS	TEST DATA
Goldman-Fristoe-Woodcock Test of Auditory Discrimination **Goldman, R., M. Fristoe, and R. W. Woodcock** **American Guidance Service** **Publishers' Bldg., P.O. Box 220** **Circle Pines, Minn. 55014**			
Administrator: individual with minimum preparation (see list of materials) Age range: three years to eighty years Time required: approximately fifteen minutes including training Individual test Pointing response	The *Goldman-Fristoe-Woodcock Test of Auditory Discrimination* measures speech-sound discrimination ability. Auditory discrimination measured under ideal listening conditions and in presence of controlled background noise.	Administrator: manual training and test plates, spiral-bound into an easel kit magnetic tape recording response forms Large training plates (for training a group of children—optional)	Raw score Standard score Age equivalent Age-based percentile rank Stanine

ADMINISTRATION	CONTENT	MATERIALS	TEST DATA
Goodman Lock Box **Goodman, J. F.** **Stoelting** **Oakwood Centre: 620 Wheat Lane** **Wood Dale, Ill. 60191**			
Administrator: psychometrist Age range: preschool age children Time required: approximately six-and-a-half minutes Individual test Manipulative	The *Lock Box* provides a three-dimensional task for assessing fine motor skills. The task determines whether a child is systematic and organized or poorly focused and distractible.	Administrator: manual record forms Lock Box	Age range command to normal children

ADMINISTRATION	CONTENT	MATERIALS	TEST DATA
Hiskey-Nebraska Test of Learning Aptitude **Hiskey, M. S.** **Hiskey-Nebraska Test (Lincoln, NB)** **Marshall S. Hiskey** **5640 Baldwin** **Lincoln, Neb. 68507** Administrator: psychometrist Age range: three through eighteen years Time required: approximately fifty to sixty minutes Individual test Manipulative test	The *Hiskey-Nebraska Test of Learning Aptitude* is a nonverbal scale designed especially for the deaf and language disabled (e.g., bilingual, learning disabled). Separate standardizations are provided for deaf and hearing. There are twelve subtests that sample widely divergent abilities.	Administrator: manual kit pencil stop watch record booklet	Learning age (deaf) Mental age (hearing) Deviation I.Q. (hearing)

ADMINISTRATION	CONTENT	MATERIALS	TEST DATA
Houston Test for Language Development **Crabtree, M.** **Stoelting Company** **Oakwood Centre: 620 Wheat Lane** **Wood Dale, Ill. 60191** Administrator: psychometrist Age range: birth to six years Time required: approximately thirty minutes Individual test Verbal and manipulative	The *Houston Test for Language Development* assesses linguistic and nonverbal communication ability which involves such areas as self-identity, vocabulary, gestures, sentence length, imitation, and linguistic structure.	Administrator: manual record forms objects and vocabulary cards	Communication age

ADMINISTRATION	CONTENT	MATERIALS	TEST DATA
Illinois Test of Psycholinguistic Abilities **Kirk, S. A., J. J. McCarthy, and W. D. Kirk** **University of Illinois Press** **Stoelting** **Oakwood Centre: 620 Wheat Lane** **Wood Dale, Ill. 60191**			
Administrator: psychometrist Age range: two to ten years Time required: not timed, approximately one hour Individual test Verbal	*Illinois Test of* *Psycholinguistic Abilities* evaluates abilities in: 1. Channels of communication (auditory-vocal and visual-motor) 2. Psycholinguistic processes (receptive, organizing, and expressive) 3. Organization levels (automatic, representational) The twelve subtests are: auditory reception, visual reception, auditory association, visual association, verbal expression, manual expression, grammatic closure, visual closure, auditory sequential memory, visual sequential memory, auditory closure, and sound blending.	Administrator: manual kit of materials record forms	Raw score Composite Psycholinguistic age Estimated mental age Scaled scores on each subtest

Ipat-Culture Fair Intelligence Test, Scale I

Institute for Personality and Ability Testing, Inc.
P.O. Box 188
Champaign, Ill. 61824

ADMINISTRATION	CONTENT	MATERIALS	TEST DATA
Administrator: teacher	Ipat-Culture Fair Intelligence Test is designed to eliminate "pseudointelligence" carried largely by language and scholastic skills as measured by some intelligence tests. Scale not wholly nonverbal. Four subtests administered individually, four to the group. IQ estimate can be obtained from the group administered subtests alone.	Administrator: handbook scoring key Classification Test Cards test booklet	Raw score Mental age Deviation IQ
Age range: four to eight years		Each child: test booklets pencils	
Time required: forty to sixty minutes gross time; twenty-two minutes testing time			
Group and individual test (four subtests each)			
Verbal, manipulative, and paper-and-pencil			

ADMINISTRATION	CONTENT	MATERIALS	TEST DATA

Kaufman Assessment Battery for Children (K-ABC)
Kaufman, A. S., and N. L. Kaufman
 	
American Guidance Service
Publishers' Bldg., P.O. Box 220
Circle Pines, Minn. 55014
 	
Administrator:
  psychometrist
 	
Age range:
  two-and-a-half through
  twelve-and-a-half years
 	
Time required:
  approximately thirty-five to
  eighty-five minutes
 	
Individual test
 	
Verbal, paper-and-pencil,
manipulative
	The sixteen subtests of the
	K-ABC provide measures of
	sequential processing,
	simultaneous processing, and
	achievement.
		Administrator:
		  three test easels
		  test record
		  pencil
		  watch that indicates
		    seconds
		  manipulatives
		  administration and scoring
		    manual
		  interpretive manual
		
		Each child:
		  pencil with eraser
			Raw score
			
			Standard score
			
			National percentile rank
			
			Age equivalent
			
			Grade equivalent
			
			Sociocultural percentile rank

ADMINISTRATION	CONTENT	MATERIALS	TEST DATA
Kaufman Infant and Preschool Scale (KIPS) Kaufman, H. Stoelting Company Oakwood Centre: 620 Wheat Lane Wood Dale, Ill. 60191 Administrator: teacher Age range: one month to four years Time required: approximately thirty minutes Individual test Manipulative	The *KIPS* provides a measure of early high-level cognitive thinking in general reasoning, storage, and verbal communication. All items assessed are maturational prototypes that can be taught to enhance maturation.	Administrator: manipulatives stimulus cards evaluation booklets	Functioning age (Mental age) Functioning Quotient

ADMINISTRATION	CONTENT	MATERIALS	TEST DATA
Kindergarten Behavioural Index, 1972 Banks, E. M.			
Australian Council for Educational Research, Ltd. P.O. Box 210 Hawthorn, Victoria 3122 Australia			
Administrator: teacher	The *Index* consists of a checklist of thirty-seven behavioral responses that a teacher may observe in the normal classroom situation to assist in identifying children whose readiness for formal tasks such as reading is doubtful.	Administrator: manual teaching guide individual record form class record sheet	Predictive Index
Grade range: preschool through first year of school			
Time required: checked by teacher on basis of day-to-day observations			
Teacher checklist			

ADMINISTRATION	CONTENT	MATERIALS	TEST DATA
Knox's Cube Test, Junior Version Stone, M. H., and B. D. Wright **Stoelting** **Oakwood Centre: 620 Wheat Lane** **Wood Dale, Ill. 60191**			
Administrator: psychometrist Age range: two to eight years Time required: approximately thirty minutes Manipulative	Knox's *Cube Test* is a nonverbal mental test that measures the attention span and short-term memory of children and adults. The test consists of a tapping series that must be accurately reproduced by the child.	Administrator: manual record form blocks	Age compared to norms

ADMINISTRATION	CONTENT	MATERIALS	TEST DATA
Kohs Block Design Test **Kohs, S. C.** **Stoelting** **Oakwood Centre: 620 Wheat Lane** **Wood Dale, Ill. 60191**			

Administrator:
    psychometrist
 	
Age range:
    three to nineteen years
 	
Time required:
    thirty to forty-five minutes
 	
Individual test
 	
Manipulative
	Kohs Block Design Test uses design cubes to obtain intelligence quotient; eliminates language factor involved in most intelligence tests.	Administrator:
		    sixteen blocks
		    seventeen design cards
		    score cards (examiner records time and number of moves)
			Raw score
			Mental age equivalent

ADMINISTRATION	CONTENT	MATERIALS	TEST DATA
Kuhlmann-Anderson Test (8th ed.) Kuhlmann, F., and R. G. Anderson **Scholastic Testing Service, Inc.** **480 Meyer Road** **P.O. Box 1056** **Bensenville, Ill. 60106**	*Kuhlmann-Anderson Test* measures intelligence. Level K includes: 1. Verbal (story completion, vocabulary, number concepts, and auditory patterns). 2. Nonverbal (missing parts of pictures, form completion, visual discrimination, and memory drawing).	Administrator: test booklet manual class record sheet keys for scoring technical manual Each child: test booklet pencil	Raw score Standard score National and local percentile ranks Cognitive Skills Quotient National and local stanines
Administrator: teacher Grade range: levels K and A: grades K–1 Time required: timed, approximately forty to sixty minutes (several sittings) Group and individual test Paper-and-pencil Verbal			

488

ADMINISTRATION	CONTENT	MATERIALS	TEST DATA
Leiter International Performance Scale **Leiter, R. G.** **Stoelting** **Oakwood Centre: 620 Wheat Lane** **Wood Dale, Ill. 60191**			
Administrator: psychometrist Age range: two through eighteen years Time required: approximately forty-five minutes Individual test Manipulative	The *Leiter International Performance Scale* is a noncultural, nonverbal test. The test does not require a spoken word from either the examiner or the child. It is ideal for non-English speaking subjects, disadvantaged persons, illiterates, and children with speech and hearing disabilities. Testing is performed by the child matching blocks with corresponding-characteristic strips positioned with the sturdy wooden frame. Difficulty increases at each age level.	Administrator: manual record cards three trays of blocks and strips carrying case	Intelligence Quotient Mental age

ADMINISTRATION	CONTENT	MATERIALS	TEST DATA
Lincoln-Oseretsky Motor Development Scale **Sloan, W.** **Stoelting** **Oakwood Centre: 620 Wheat Lane** **Wood Dale, Ill. 60191**			
Administrator: psychometrist Age range: six to fourteen years Time required: approximately thirty to forty-five minutes Individual test Manipulative	The *Lincoln-Oseretsky Motor Development Scale* has thirty-six test items involving a wide variety of motor skills. These include static coordination, dynamic coordination, speed of movement, asynkinesia (finger dexterity), eye-hand coordination, and gross activity of the hands, arms, legs, and trunk. Both unilateral and bilateral motor tasks are involved in the scale.	Administrator: manual manipulatives record blanks	Percentage passing each time at each age level Correlations of each item score with age Tentative percentiles for sexes, separately and combined

ADMINISTRATION	CONTENT	MATERIALS	TEST DATA
The Merrill-Palmer Scale of Mental Test Stutsman, R. **Stoelting** **Oakwood Centre: 620 Wheat Lane** **Wood Dale, Ill. 60191**			

Administrator:
  psychometrist
 	
Age range:
  eighteen to sixty-five
  months
 	
Time required:
  total test approximately
  forty-five minutes; certain
  items timed
 	
Individual test
 	
Verbal and manipulative
	The Merrill-Palmer Scale of Mental Test measures mental ability in such areas as language and gross and fine motor skills. Designed as supplement to or substitute for Stanford-Binet. (Does not contain any items from the Binet, as does the *California Preschool Mental Scale* and the *Minnesota Preschool Scale*.)	Administrator:
		  manual
		  kit materials (nested cubes,
		  form boards, scissors,
		  pegboard, etc.)
		  record blanks
			Raw score
			Percentile rank
			Mental age
			Ratings of personality traits in mental test situation

ADMINISTRATION	CONTENT	MATERIALS	TEST DATA
Peabody Picture Vocabulary Test (Revised) Dunn, L. M., and L. M. Dunn American Guidance Service Publishers' Bldg. P.O. Box 220 Circle Pines, Minn. 55014			
Administrator: teacher Age range: two-and-a-half years to adulthood Time required: not timed, approximately ten to fifteen minutes Individual test Points to indicate answer	The *Peabody Picture Vocabulary Test—Revised* provides an estimate of verbal intelligence by measuring hearing vocabulary.	Administrator: series of plates (form L or M) manual individual test records	Raw score Percentile rank Standard score Age equivalent Stanine Graphic representation of an individual's derived score

ADMINISTRATION	CONTENT	MATERIALS	TEST DATA
Preschool Screening Instrument (PSSI)	The *PSSI* evaluates developmental status in the following areas:	Administrator: manual record books wooden blocks story card primary pencils	Levels that relate to months behind age-level (Level 1 —within age level; Level 2 —six to eleven months behind age level, etc.)
Cohen, S. P.	1. Visual-motor perception		
Stoelting	2. Fine-motor development		
Oakwood Centre: 620 Wheat Lane	3. Gross-motor skills		
Wood Dale, Ill. 60191	4. Language development		
Administrator: teacher	5. Verbal fluency		
Age range: 4.0 to 5.3 years with tables extending down to three years	6. Conceptual skills		
Individual test	7. Speech and behavioral difficulties		
Verbal, manipulative, and drawing			

493

ADMINISTRATION	CONTENT	MATERIALS	TEST DATA
Psycholinguistic Rating Scale (PRS) **Hobby, K. L.** **Western Psychological Services** **Publishers and Distributors** **12031 Wilshire Blvd.** **Los Angeles, Calif. 90025**			
Administrator: teacher Grade range: Level I—kindergarten through grade 1.4; Level II—grades 1.5–2.9; Level III—grades 3–5.9; Level IV—grades 6–8.9 Time required: five minutes Individual test Paper-and-pencil	*PRS* is a brief rating scale, completed by teachers, that measures psycholinguistic behaviors in ten areas: 1. Auditory reception 2. Auditory association 3. Auditory memory 4. Auditory closure 5. Verbal expression 6. Visual reception 7. Visual association 8. Visual memory 9. Visual closure 10. Manual expression These areas are further categorized by channels, processes, and levels of communication.	Administrator: manual rating book	Subscale scores Combined scale scores Total score T-Scores Verbal descriptor of classroom psycholinguistic functioning

ADMINISTRATION	CONTENT	MATERIALS	TEST DATA
Quickscreen **Fudala, J. B.** **Western Psychological Services** **Publishers and Distributors** **12031 Wilshire Blvd.** **Los Angeles, Calif. 90025** Administrator: teacher Grade range: separate tests for kindergarten, grade one, and grade two Time required: fifteen to twenty-five minutes Group test Verbal and paper-and-pencil	*Quickscreen* is a classroom screening procedure to identify students who may have speech, language, or learning problems. The test consists of three sections: visual-motor tasks, auditory-vocal tasks, and auditory-comprehension tasks. For second grade, a cognitive task is added.	Administrator: manual test booklet score sheet scoring summary card stopwatch Each child: test booklet pencil	Subtest score Total score "High Risk" or "Possible Risk" classifications

ADMINISTRATION	CONTENT	MATERIALS	TEST DATA
The Riley Articulation and Language Test (Revised) Riley, G. O. **Western Psychological Services Publishers and Distributors 12031 Wilshire Blvd. Los Angeles, Calif. 90025**			
Administrator: psychometrist Age range: four through seven years Time required: three minutes Individual test Verbal	*The Riley Articulation and Language Test* estimates language proficiency and intelligibility; provides objective articulation loss score, standardized language loss score, and language function score.	Administrator: manual Protocol Booklet	Articulation loss score (index of speech loss and speech function) Language loss score Language function score Cutting scores

ADMINISTRATION	CONTENT	MATERIALS	TEST DATA
Rockford Infant Developmental Evaluation Scales (RIDES) **Project RHISE Children's Developmental Center, Rockford, IL** **Scholastic Testing Service, Inc.** **480 Meyer Road** **P.O. Box 1056** **Bensenville, Ill. 60106**			
Administrator: trained professional Age range: birth to forty-eight months Time required: time is variable since it is an observational instrument Individual test Observations	*RIDES* is used for educational assessment with young children for fine motor/adaptive, gross motor, expressive language, receptive language, personal-social/self-help activities arranged in developmental order within the areas listed.	Administrator: manual checklist	Developmental profile Developmental age (approximation)

ADMINISTRATION	CONTENT	MATERIALS	TEST DATA
Sensory Integration and Praxis Tests (SIPT) Ayres, A. J. **Western Psychological Services** **12031 Wilshire Blvd.** **Los Angeles, Calif. 90025** Administrator: trained occupational or physical therapist Age range: four through eight years Time required: individual test—about ten minutes full battery—about two hours	The *SIPT* measures visual, tactile, and kinesthetic perception and motor performance. It is composed of seventeen tests: Space Visualization, Design Copying, Postural Praxis, Motor Accuracy, Kinesthesia, Graphesthesia, Sequencing Praxis, Oral Praxis, Postrotary Nystagmus, Figure-Ground Perception, Standing and Walking Balance, Bilateral Motor Coordination, Manual Form Perception, Finger Identification, Localization of Tactile Stimuli, Praxis on Verbal Command, and Constructional Praxis.	Administration: manual kit of test equipment test forms computer scored answer and transmittal sheets	Raw score Z-scores Interpretive report

ADMINISTRATION	CONTENT	MATERIALS	TEST DATA
Screening Test of Educational Prerequisite Skills (STEPS) Smith, F. **Western Psychological Services** **12031 Wilshire Blvd.** **Los Angeles, Calif. 90025** Administrator: teacher Grade level: kindergarten Time required: twelve to fifteen minutes Individual Paper-and-pencil, manipulative, and verbal	*STEPS* is a screening test for kindergarten. The test screens in five major areas with seventeen tasks and observations: Fine/Gross Motor (two tasks), Verbal Information (eight tasks), Intellectual Skills in writing and drawing (three tasks), Attitude towards school/learning (one task), and administrator observations (three ratings). *STEPS* identifies children as either likely to adapt and cope with a kindergarten curriculum or likely to need follow-up. Follow-up need is further specified in order of severity: teacher monitoring in Intellectual Skills, teacher monitoring in Verbal Skills, close monitoring in both areas, or recommendation for a multidisciplinary diagnostic assessment. An optional Home Questionnaire assesses parental concerns.	Administration: manual administration and scoring book self-report picture booklet Teddy-bear counter toys Home Questionnaire pencil (primary)	Categorical screening recommendations

ADMINISTRATION	CONTENT	MATERIALS	TEST DATA
Stanford-Binet Intelligence Scale Terman, L. M., and M. A. Merrill **The Riverside Publishing Company** **8420 Bryn Mawr Ave.** **Chicago, Ill. 60631**	*Stanford-Binet Intelligence Scale* measures general mental ability. Items included for ages two to five are identification of parts of the body, picture vocabulary, delayed response, identifying objects by name and by use, repeating digits, obeying commands, block building, paper folding, and geometric figures, comprehension of sentences, sorting objects, size comparisons, analogies, memory for sentences, pictorial similarities and differences, discrimination of forms, and stringing beads.	Administrator: kit materials (includes manual and printed card material) record booklets, forms, and objects	Raw scores Mental age Deviation IQ
Administrator: certified examiner			
Age range: two years through adult			
Time required: not timed, approximately thirty to forty minutes for young children			
Individual test			
Verbal			

ADMINISTRATION	CONTENT	MATERIALS	TEST DATA
System to Plan Early Childhood Services (SPECS) **Bagnato, S. J., and Neisworth, J. T.** **American Guidance Service** **Publishers' Building** **Box 99** **Circle Pines, Minn. 55014**			
Administrator: Psychologist, teacher, parent, or others (social worker) Age range: two years through six years, eleven months Time required: several weeks to do individual assessment and conduct team meetings Individual Observation with tests and interviews	*SPECS* is an assessment instrument and a system for making decisions about early childhood special services required by P.L. 99–457. Child is assessed in six domains: "Communication," "Sensorimotor," "Physical," "Self-regulation," "Cognition," and "Self/Social."	Administration: manual Developmental Specs Team Specs Program Specs *Linking Developmental Assessment and Early Intervention:* *Curriculum-based Prescriptions*	Developmental Specs Team Specs Program Specs

ADMINISTRATION	CONTENT	MATERIALS	TEST DATA
Test of Cognitive Skills (TCS) **CTB Macmillan/McGraw-Hill** **2500 Garden Road** **Monterey, Calif. 93940**			
Administrator: teacher	*TCS* has these four subtests:	Administrator: manual	Raw score
Grade range: Level 1: grades two to three	1. Sequences measure the ability to comprehend a rule or principle implicit in a pattern or sequence of figures, letters, or numbers.	scoring key individual record sheet class record sheet	Age or grade percentile rank Stanine Scale score
Time required: timed, Level 1 —forty-seven minutes	2. Analogies measure the ability to see relationships and to classify.	Each child: test booklet pencil with eraser	Cognitive Skills Index
Group and individual test	3. Memory test measures the ability to recall previously presented materials.		
Paper-and-pencil	4. Verbal reasoning measures the ability to discern relationships and reason logically.		

ADMINISTRATION	CONTENT	MATERIALS	TEST DATA
Test of Concept Utilization (TCU) **Crager, R. L.** **Western Psychological Services** **Publishers and Distributors** **12031 Wilshire Blvd.** **Los Angeles, Calif. 90025**			

Administrator:
  teacher
Age range:
  five through eighteen years
Time required:
  ten to twenty-five minutes
Individual test
Verbal
	The *TCU* contains fifty plates, each composed of a pair of common-object pictures. The child is asked to tell how the pictures are alike or how they go together. Responses are scored for concept categories of equivalence (e.g., color, shape, homogeneous function), relational (e.g., relational function, minor relational), and qualitative (e.g., infusion, creation).	Administrator:
		  manual
		  test plates
		  protocol sheet
		  scoring booklet
		  short scoring form
			Scale raw scores
			T-scores

ADMINISTRATION	CONTENT	MATERIALS	TEST DATA
Test of Early Language Development (TELD) **Hresko, W. P., D. K. Reid, and D. D. Hammill** **Pro-ed** **8700 Shoal Creek Blvd.** **Austin, Tex. 78758**			
Administrator: teacher Age range: three years through seven years, eleven months Time required: fifteen minutes Individual test Oral	*TELD* measures the spoken language abilities of children. It gives information that is directly related to semantic and syntactic aspects of language.	Administrator: manual pictures record forms	Raw score Scaled scores Percentile rank Age equivalent

ADMINISTRATION	CONTENT	MATERIALS	TEST DATA

Test of Gross Motor Development
Ulrich, D. A.
 	
Pro-ed
8700 Shoal Creek Blvd.
Austin, Tex. 78758
 	
Administrator:
  teacher
 	
Age range:
  three through ten years
 	
Time required:
  fifteen minutes
 	
Individual test
 	
Movement (e.g., jump, bounce ball)
	The *Test of Gross Motor Development* evaluates gross motor functioning of children. The test measures twelve gross motor skills frequently taught to children in preschool, early elementary, and special education.	Administrator:
		  manual
		  Student Record Book
		  common play equipment
			Raw score
			
			Standard score
			
			Percentile rank
			
			Gross Motor Developmental Quotient
			
			Profile

ADMINISTRATION	CONTENT	MATERIALS	TEST DATA
Test of Language Development-Primary (TOLD-P) **Newcomber, P. L., and D. D. Hammill** **Test of Language Development-2-Primary (TOLD-2-P)** **Newcomber, P. L., and D. D. Hammill** **Pro-ed** **8700 Shoal Creek Blvd.** **Austin, Tex. 78758** Administrator: speech pathologist Age range: four through eight years Time required: approximately forty minutes Individual test Oral	The *TOLD-P* has seven subtests that measure different components of spoken language. "Picture Vocabulary" and "Oral Vocabulary" assess the understanding and meaningful use of spoken words. "Grammatic Understanding," "Sentence Imitation," and "Grammatic Completion" assess different aspects of grammar. "Word Articulation" and "Word Discrimination" measure the abilities to say words correctly and to distinguish between words that sound similar.	Administrator: manual picture book answer sheets	Raw score Standard scores Percentile rank Age equivalent Language Quotient (deviation)

ADMINISTRATION	CONTENT	MATERIALS	TEST DATA
Thinking Creatively in Action and Movement Torance, E. P. **Scholastic Testing Service, Inc.** **480 Meyer Road** **P.O. Box 1056** **Bensenville, Ill. 60106**			
Administrator: 　teacher Age range: 　three to eight years Time required: 　approximately ten to thirty 　minutes depending upon 　the number of creative 　activities performed Individual test Verbal/Physical	*Thinking Creatively in Action and Movement* includes four items or activities that each child describes. For example, the child is asked to behave like a particular animal.	Administrator: 　manual 　scoring guide and key 　booklets for writing 　descriptions of child's 　behavior	Raw score Standard score

ADMINISTRATION	CONTENT	MATERIALS	TEST DATA
Torrance Tests of Creative Thinking Torrance, E. P. **Scholastic Testing Service, Inc.** **480 Meyer Road** **P.O. Box 1056** **Bensenville, Ill. 60106**	*Torrance Tests of Creative Thinking* consists of a verbal and figural test. Measures following aspects of creative thinking:	Administrator: test booklets scoring worksheets manual examiner's kit booklet of norms and technical information	Raw score Scores for fluency, abstractness of title, originality, elaboration, resistance to premature closure, and creativity index (total score) are obtained
Administrator: teacher	1. Fluency—aptitude in originating ideas about and solutions to problems		National and local percentiles
Age range: five years to adult	2. Flexibility—adaptability to changing directions, emancipation from normal constraints in thinking, and capability of using several means of access to solutions		Standard scores
Time required: verbal test: forty-five minutes figural test: thirty minutes	3. Originality—talent for providing uncommon answers and ingenious or clever calculations		
Group and individual test	4. Elaboration—knack of executing and embellishing an idea		
Verbal and paper-and-pencil			

ADMINISTRATION	CONTENT	MATERIALS	TEST DATA
Vineland Adaptive Behavior Scales—Classroom Edition Sparrow, S. S., D. A. Balla, and D. V. Cicchetti American Guidance Service Publishers' Bldg., P.O. Box 220 Circle Pines, Minn. 55014			
Administrator: skilled interviewer Age range: three years through twelve years, eleven months Time required: approximately twenty minutes Individual test Interview of parent or questionnaire completed by teacher	The *Vineland Adaptive Behavior Scales—Classroom Edition* measures four domains: 1. Communication 2. Daily living skills 3. Socialization 4. Motor skills	Administrator: manual questionnaire booklet (Levels I and II) report to parents	Standard score National percentile rank Age equivalent Stanine Adaptive level

ADMINISTRATION	CONTENT	MATERIALS	TEST DATA
Wechsler Preschool and Primary Scale of Intelligence Wechsler, D. **The Psychological Corp.** **Harcourt Brace Jovanovich, Inc.** **1250 Sixth Ave.** **San Diego, Calif. 92101**			
Administrator: psychometrist Age range: four through six-and-a-half years Time required: not timed, time ranges between forty-five and seventy-five minutes (two or more sittings) Individual test Verbal and manipulative	*Wechsler Preschool and Primary Scale of Intelligence* has two subtests: 1. Verbal tests include information, vocabulary, similarities, comprehension and arithmetic. Sentences is a supplementary test. 2. Performance tests include animal house, picture completion, mazes, geometric design, and block design.	Administrator: kit of materials manual record forms maze test geometric design sheets	Raw score Verbal, performance, and full-scale IQs

ADMINISTRATION	CONTENT	MATERIALS	TEST DATA
Wesman's Auditory Discrimination Test (ADT) Second Edition **Wesman, J. M., Second Edition by Reynolds, W.** **Western Psychological Services** **12031 Wilshire Blvd.** **Los Angeles, Calif. 90025**			
Administrator: trained professional	*ADT* is a forty-item test of a child's ability to discriminate commonly used phonemes in English.	Administrator: manual test sheet	Raw score T-scores Percentile equivalents
Age range: four through eight years			
Time required: five to ten minutes			
Individual test			
Verbal			

Achievement

Anton Brenner Developmental Gestalt Test of School Readiness
Brenner, A.

Western Psychological Services
Publishers and Distributors
12031 Wilshire Blvd.
Los Angeles, Calif. 90025

ADMINISTRATION	CONTENT	MATERIALS	TEST DATA

Administrator:
  teacher
 	
Age range:
  five through six years
 	
Time required:
  ten minutes or less
 	
Individual test
 	
Verbal and paper-and-pencil
	The Anton Brenner Developmental Gestalt Test of School Readiness is a qualitative and quantitative test of school readiness; measures perceptual and conceptual differentiation.	Administrator:
		  manual
		  BGT Protocol Booklet
		  number recognition forms
		  fifteen to twenty ½-inch
		    cubes of the same color
		
		Each child:
		  pencil
		  black or blue crayon
			Raw score
			
			BGT total score
			
			Readiness evaluation based on BGT total score

ADMINISTRATION	CONTENT	MATERIALS	TEST DATA
Basic School Skills Inventory-Diagnostic (BSSI-D) **Hammill, D., and J. E. Leigh** **Pro-ed** **8700 Shoal Creek Blvd.** **Austin, Tex. 78758**			
Administrator: teacher Age range: four years through six years, eleven months Time required: twenty minutes Individual test Oral	The *BSSI-D* measures these six areas of school performance: 1. Daily living skills 2. Spoken language 3. Reading readiness 4. Writing readiness 5. Math readiness 6. Classroom behavior (Teacher fills out checklist-tests for child only if uncertain of skill level.)	Administrator: manual picture cards answer sheets Each child: checklist-test	Raw score Standard score Scaled score Age equivalent

513

ADMINISTRATION	CONTENT	MATERIALS	TEST DATA
Bilingual Syntax Measure—I (BSM) **Burt, M. K., H. C. Dulay, and E. H. Ch.** **The Psychological Corp.** **Harcourt Brace Jovanovich, Inc.** **1250 Sixth Ave.** **San Diego, Calif. 92101**	*BSM* identifies child's control over basic oral syntactic structures in both English and Spanish. Cartoon-type pictures and simple questions elicit responses. May be used for placement decisions as well as summative and formative evaluation.	Administrator: manual picture books response booklets class record technical handbook	Level of language proficiency
Administrator: teacher Grade range: kindergarten through grade twelve Time required: ten to fifteen minutes Individual test Verbal			

ADMINISTRATION	CONTENT	MATERIALS	TEST DATA
Boehm Test of Basic Concepts Boehm, A. E. **The Psychological Corp. Harcourt Brace Jovanovich, Inc. 1250 Sixth Ave. San Diego, Calif. 92101** Administrator: teacher Grade range: kindergarten through second grade (difficult for prekindergarten children) Time required: not timed, approximately thirty to forty minutes Group and individual test Paper-and-pencil	*Boehm Test of Basic Concepts* evaluates child's knowledge of terms selected from directions and other portions of curriculum materials in reading, arithmetic, and science. Terms selected: 1. Those which occurred with considerable frequency; 2. Those which were seldom clearly defined, or defined in simpler forms than used in complex forms without adequate transitions; and 3. Those which were abstract.	Administrator: manual demonstration copy of both test booklets class record form Each child: booklets one and two pencil or crayon	Raw score Percentile Class record sheet Recommended instructional methods Percentage passing for each item Class average

ADMINISTRATION	CONTENT	MATERIALS	TEST DATA
California Achievement Tests, Level 10	In the *California Achievement Tests* the "Total Prereading" score comprises six test scores:	Administrator: manual practice book test book Class Management Guide norms books Test Coordinator's Handbook Technical Bulletin Student diagnostic sheets	Raw scores Percentile ranks Stanines Scale scores Grade equivalent Normal curve equivalents
CTB Macmillan/McGraw-Hill 2500 Garden Road Monterey, Calif. 93940			
Administrator: teacher	1. Listening for information 2. Letter forms 3. Letter names 4. Letter sounds 5. Visual discrimination 6. Sound matching	Each child: practice test test book pencils with erasers scratch paper place marker	
Grade range: Level 10: K.0–K.9 Level 11: 1.0–1.9 Level 12: 1.6–2.9	There is also a mathematics test that assesses early basic familiarity with number systems, operations, and measurements.		
Time required: Level 10: two hours, four minutes Level 11: one hour, fifty-three minutes Level 12: two hours, thirty-three minutes			
Group test			
Paper-and-pencil			

516

ADMINISTRATION	CONTENT	MATERIALS	TEST DATA
Comprehensive Tests of Basic Skills (CTBS and new revision CTBS/4)			
CTB Macmillan/McGraw-Hill **2500 Garden Road** **Monterey, Calif. 93940**			

Administrator:
  teacher
	The *CTBS* (levels A through D) includes:	Administrator:
		  manual
		  test booklet
			Raw score
			Scale scores

Grade range:
  Level A: K.0–K.9
  Level B: K.6–1.6
  Level C: 1.0–1.9
  Level D: 1.6–2.9
	1. Reading tests that measure visual and sound recognition of letters, words, vowels, and consonants. Vocabulary and comprehension skills are assessed.	Norms Book
		  class record sheet
		  locator test
		  practice test
		  Test Reviewer's Guide
		  stopwatch
			Grade equivalents
			National percentiles
			Normal curve equivalents
			Individual test record
			Class record sheet

Time required:
  Level A—one hour, eight minutes
  Level B—one hour, nine minutes
  Level C—one hour, fifty-nine minutes
  Level D—three hours, thirty-eight minutes
	2. Spelling tests that measure application of rules for consonants, vowels, and various structural forms.	Each child:
		  practice test
		  test book
		  pencil with eraser
		  place marker	

Group and individual test	3. Language tests that measure the mechanics of writing, the use of various parts of speech, and formation and organization of sentences.		
Paper-and-pencil	4. Mathematics tests that measure the four operations and the application of mathematical concepts.		
	5. Science tests that reflect content from the physical and life sciences.		
	6. Social Studies tests that reflect the areas of geography, economics, history, political science, and sociology.		

ADMINISTRATION	CONTENT	MATERIALS	TEST DATA
Developing Skills Checklist (DSC)	*DSC* evaluates the full range of skills children develop during this grade range.	Administration:	Raw score
CTB Macmillan/McGraw-Hill		Administration and Scoring	Percentile
2500 Garden Road		Interpretation Manual	Stanine
Monterey, Calif. 93940		Three Item Books	
	DSC measures these skills:	manipulatives	
Administrator:	Language, Visual, Auditory,	Concepts of Print and	
teacher	Mathematical concepts and	Writing Administration	
	operations, Social and	Manual	
Grade range:	Emotional, Fine and Gross	A Day at School	
prekindergarten through	Motor, and Print and Writing	Writing and Drawing	
kindergarten		Book	
		DSC Score Sheet	
Time required:		Class Record Book	
no time stipulated		Parent Conference Form	
Individual test		Each child:	
		Writing and Drawing Book	
Verbal, manipulative, and		Social-Emotional	
paper-and-pencil		Observational Record	
		Each parent:	
		Parent Conference Form	

518

ADMINISTRATION	CONTENT	MATERIALS	TEST DATA
Doren Diagnostic Reading Test of Word Recognition **Doren, M.** **American Guidance Service** **Publishers' Bldg., P.O. Box 220** **Circle Pines, Minn. 55014** Administrator: teacher Grade range: primary grades Time required: approximately one to three hours Group test Paper-and-pencil	The *Doren Diagnostic Reading Test of Word Recognition* diagnoses reading difficulties regardless of basic reading program used. The test assesses: 1. Letter recognition 2. Beginning sounds 3. Whole word recognition 4. Words within words 5. Speech consonants 6. Ending sounds 7. Blending 8. Rhyming 9. Vowels 10. Discriminate guessing 11. Spelling 12. Sight words	Administrator: manual test booklet class composite sheet key Each child: test booklet pencil	Raw score Recommended remedial activities Individual skill profile Class composite record

ADMINISTRATION	CONTENT	MATERIALS	TEST DATA

Early Identification Screening Program
Baltimore City Public Schools
 	
Modern Curriculum Press
13900 Prospect Road
Cleveland, Ohio 44136
 	
Administrator:
  teacher
 	
Grade range:
  beginning of kindergarten
  or first grade
 	
Time required:
  approximately twenty
  minutes in three sessions
 	
Individual test
 	
Verbal and paper-and-pencil
	Early Identification Screening Program tests:
	1. Eye-hand coordination when using a pencil
	2. Ability to imitate a pattern
	3. Ability to count
	4. Ability to name letters
	5. Ability to match colors
	6. Ability to name picture symbols of objects
	7. Auditory discrimination and locating body parts
	8. Ability to reproduce letters
	9. Ability to name numbers
		Administrator:
		  manual
		  stopwatch
		  class record sheet
			Raw score
			
			Average score for Hear-Write, See-Write, and See-Say

ADMINISTRATION	CONTENT	MATERIALS	TEST DATA
Early School Assessment (ESA)			
CTB Macmillan/McGraw-Hill			
2500 Garden Road			
Monterey, Calif. 93940			
Administrator:	The *ESA* measures skills that	Administration:	Raw score
teacher	are characteristic of	manual	Scaled score
	kindergarten children and	Practice Book	Percentile
Grade level:	prerequisite to instruction in	Test Book	Stanine
Level I: Prekindergarten	reading and mathematics.	Teacher's Guide	Normal curve equivalent
through middle of	The skills and concepts	Class Record Sheet for	
kindergarten	measured are: language,	Hand Scoring	
	visual, auditory, mathematical	Norms Book for ESA	
Level II: Middle of	concepts and operations,	Parent Conference Form	
kindergarten to the	memory, total mathematics,	Technical Report	
beginning of first grade	and total prereading.	CTB Test Organizer	
		Each child:	
		Practice Book	
		Test Book	
		pencil	
		eraser	
		2″ × 8-½″ bar markers	
		Each parent:	
		Parent Conference Form	

ADMINISTRATION	CONTENT	MATERIALS	TEST DATA
Educational Development Series—Level 10A			
Anderhalter, O. F., R. H. Baurenfeind, M. E. Greig, C. Mallinson, J. Mallison, J. F. Papenfuss and N. Vail			
Scholastic Testing Service, Inc. **480 Meyer Road** **P.O. Box 1056** **Bensenville, Ill. 60106**			
Administrator: teacher	The *Educational Development Series—Level 10A* comprises ability (nonverbal and verbal cognitive skills) and achievement tests (reading, language arts, and mathematics). A single report based on norms is published.	Administrator: manual test booklet	Raw score
Grade range: kindergarten through first grade			National and local percentile
		Each child: test booklet	Local stanine
Time required: approximately three hours (five sittings)			Grade equivalent
			Performance and growth profile
Group test			Identifies prime counseling problems
Paper-and-pencil			

ADMINISTRATION	CONTENT	MATERIALS	TEST DATA
Gates-MacGinitie Reading Tests—Second Edition	The *Gates-MacGinitie Reading Tests* measure important knowledge and skills that are common to most school reading curricula. Vocabulary and comprehension are measured at each level. Basic R, the earliest test for students just beginning to read also includes these skills that are widely taught in beginning instruction: sounds of initial and final consonants, sounds of vowels, word analysis, word families, letter recognition, and letter matching.	Administrator: teacher's manual student test booklet	Raw score
MacGinitie, W. H.			Percentile rank
The Riverside Publishing Company		Each child: test booklet pencil	Normal curve equivalent scores
8420 Bryn Mawr Ave.			Stanine
Chicago, Ill. 60631			Grade equivalent
Administrator: teacher			Scaled scores
Grade range:			
Level R: 1–1.9			
Level A: 1.5–1.9			
Level B: 2			
Level C: 3			
Time required: about sixty minutes (two sittings)			
Group test			
Paper-and-pencil			

ADMINISTRATION	CONTENT	MATERIALS	TEST DATA

Key Math-Revised
Connoly, A. J.
 	
American Guidance Service
Publishers' Building,
P.O. Box 99
Circle Pines, Minn. 55014
 	
Administrator:
  teacher
 	
Grade Range:
  Kindergarten through ninth
  grade
 	
Time required:
  thirty to fifty minutes
 	
Individual test
 	
Verbal
	In *Key Math-R* three content
	areas are assessed by
	thirteen subtests as follows:
	1. Basic Concepts
	   Numeration
	   Rational Numbers
	   Geometry
	2. Operations
	   Addition
	   Subtraction
	   Multiplication
	   Division
	   Mental Computation
	3. Applications
	   Measurement
	   Time and Money
	   Estimation
	   Interpreting Data
	   Problem Solving
		Administrator:
		  manual
		  test records
		  test books
		    (composed of test plates
		    in a wire-bound easel)
			Raw score
			Standard score
			Grade equivalent
			Age equivalent
			Percentile rank
			Stanine
			Normal curve equivalency

ADMINISTRATION	CONTENT	MATERIALS	TEST DATA
Metropolitan Readiness Tests **Nurss, J., and M. E. McGauvran** **The Psychological Corp.** **Harcourt Brace Jovanovich, Inc.** **1250 Sixth Ave.** **San Diego, Calif. 92101** Administrator: teacher Grade range: Level I, beginning through kindergarten Level II, end of kindergarten through beginning first grade Time required: Level I, eighty minutes (seven sittings) Level II, ninety minutes (five sittings) Levels I and II, Practice Booklet, fifteen minutes Copying Test (optional), five minutes Group and individual test Paper-and-pencil	Level I of the *Metropolitan Readiness Tests* assesses prereading skill development in: 1. Auditory memory—tests ability to remember and associate sounds with visual symbols. 2. Rhyming—evaluates ability to discriminate among medial and final sounds in rhyming context 3. Letter recognition—evaluates ability to recognize upper- and lowercase letters 4. Visual matching—assesses visual-perceptual skills in matching words, numerals, etc. 5. School language and listening—measures basic concepts and grammatical structure 6. Quantitative language—evaluates size, shape, number-quality relationships.	Administrator: practice booklet test booklet manual (parts I and II) copying sheet class analysis chart Each child: practice booklet test booklet copying sheet crayon or pencil without eraser Other materials: *The Handbook of Skill Development Activities for Young Children* *Parent-Teacher Conference Report* *Early School Inventory*	Raw score Percentile rank Stanine Performance Ratings, such as high, average, and low, based on stanines Scaled scores

Level II of the *Metropolitan Readiness Tests* assesses skills needed in beginning reading and math:

1. Beginning consonants— assesses ability to discriminate among initial sounds of words
2. Sound-letter correspondence— evaluates ability to associate sound-symbol relationship in words
3. Visual matching—assesses ability to match letters, numerals, and letter-like forms
4. Finding patterns—measures ability to locate letter-groups, words, and numerals embedded in layer groupings of similar content
5. School language—tests basic concepts and grammatical structure
6. Listening—evaluates ability to integrate and reorganize information, to draw inferences, and to analyze material
7. Quantitative operations— measures ability to do rational counting and simple operations (adding, subtracting) (optional).

Levels I and II "Copying"— measures fine visual-motor coordination needed in writing (optional)

ADMINISTRATION	CONTENT	MATERIALS	TEST DATA
Monroe Diagnostic Reading Test Monroe, M. **Stoelting** **Oakwood Centre; 620 Wheat Lane** **Wood Dale, Ill. 60191** Administrator: reading specialist Grade range: Grades one through ten Time required: approximately two hours Individual test Verbal	The *Monroe Diagnostic Reading Test* diagnoses special reading difficulties. Test includes: 1. Alphabet Repeating and Reading 2. Iota Word Test 3. b, d, p, q, u, n Test 4. Recognition of Orientation 5. Mirror Reading, Mirror Writing 6. Number Reversal 7. Word Discrimination 8. Sounding 9. Handedness	Administrator: manual test cards record blanks	Grade Score

527

ADMINISTRATION	CONTENT	MATERIALS	TEST DATA
Peabody Individual Achievement Test—Revised (PIAT-R) Markwardt, Jr., F. C. **American Guidance Service Publishers' Building P.O. Box 99 Circle Pines, Minn. 55014**			
Administrator: teacher Grade range: level 1: K–1 level 2: 2–12 Time required: seventy-five minutes	*PIAT-R* measures general information, reading recognition, reading comprehension, spelling, mathematics, and written expression.	Administration: manual test plates test records pronunciation guide cassette ASSIST software carrying bag Each child: response booklet	Raw score Age-based standard score Grade-based standard score Grade equivalent Percentile rank Stanine Normal curve equivalency

ADMINISTRATION	CONTENT	MATERIALS	TEST DATA
Prescriptive Reading Inventory (PRI)			
CTB Macmillan/McGraw-Hill			
2500 Garden Road			
Monterey, Calif. 93940			
Administrator:	*PRI* is a criterion-referenced	Administrator:	Raw score
teacher	testing system that measures	manual	Objectives Mastery Report
Grade range:	student mastery of reading	test book	Individual Diagnostic Map
Level: K.0–1	objectives commonly taught	practice exercises	Classroom Diagnostic Map
Level II: K.5–2	in the elementary school.	pretests	Individual Study Guide
Time required:		interpretive handbooks	Class Grouping Report
Level 1: approximately		technical reports	Program Reference Guide
seventy-five minutes		examiner's cassettes	
Level II: approximately		checklist of observable	
seventy-five minutes		behaviors	
Individual test			
Paper-and-pencil			

ADMINISTRATION	CONTENT	MATERIALS	TEST DATA

Ready or Not?
Austin, J. J., and J. C. Lafferty
Research Concepts
A Division of Test Maker, Inc.
1368 East Airport Road
Muskegon, Mich. 49444
 	
Administrator:
    parent
 	
Grade range:
    kindergarten through first
    grade
 	
Time required:
    approximately one-half
    hour, unless parent has
    already observed the skills
    and concepts in the child
 	
Individual test
 	
Paper-and-pencil
	"*Ready or Not?*" assists
	parents in determining child's
	readiness for kindergarten
	(The School Readiness
	Checklist) and for first grade
	(The First Grade Readiness
	Checklist). Readiness
	checked in counting, drawing,
	motor skills, taking care of
	oneself, and general
	knowledge.
		Administrator:
		    Handbook for the School
		      Readiness Checklist and
		      The First Grade
		      Readiness Checklist
		    The School Readiness
		      Checklist
		    The First Grade Readiness
		      Checklist
		    paper for drawing shapes
		    additional booklets and
		      articles on readiness
		
		Each child:
		    pencil
		    paper for drawing shapes
			Based on raw score, an
			approximate state of
			readiness for kindergarten or
			first grade is given and some
			suggestions for possible
			action.

ADMINISTRATION	CONTENT	MATERIALS	TEST DATA
School Readiness Test **Anderhalter, O. F., and Jan Perney** **Scholastic Testing Service, Inc.** **480 Meyer Road** **P.O. Box 1056** **Bensenville, Ill. 60106** Administrator: teacher Grade range: kindergarten or during second week of first grade (no "repeaters") Time required: approximately one hour (two sittings); items timed Group test Paper-and-pencil	*School Readiness Test* measures readiness in word recognition, identifying letters, visual discrimination, auditory discrimination, comprehension and interpretation, vocabulary, number knowledge, handwriting ability, and developmental spelling ability.	Administrator: manual test booklet Each child: test booklet pencil crayon	Raw score Percentile rank Class record sheet Verbal rating based on total score

ADMINISTRATION	CONTENT	MATERIALS	TEST DATA
Stanford Early School Achievement Test (Level I) **Madden, R., E. F. Gardner, and C. S. Collins** **The Psychological Corp.** **Harcourt Brace Jovanovich, Inc.** **1250 Sixth Ave.** **San Diego, Calif. 92101** Administrator: teacher with assistant Grade range: kindergarten through end of first grade Time required: approximately 130 minutes (five sittings) Group and individual test Paper-and-pencil	*Stanford Early School Achievement Test* measures achievement in environment, mathematics, language arts, and reading. Level 1: 1. Environment items—measure child's knowledge of social and natural environments. 2. Mathematics items—evaluate conservation of number, space, and volume; measurement; numeration; counting; classification; algorithms 3. Letter and Sound items—appraise ability to recognize upper and lower case letters and auditory perception of initial sounds 4. Aural Comprehension items—evaluate ability to pay attention to, organize, interpret, infer, and retain verbal communication	Administrator: test booklet manual scoring key class record sheet chart of practice sheet Each child: test booklet pencil	Raw score Percentile Stanine Grade equivalent Scaled score

ADMINISTRATION	CONTENT	MATERIALS	TEST DATA
Stanford Early School Achievement Test (Level II) Madden, R., and E. Gardner **The Psychological Corp.** **Harcourt Brace Jovanovich, Inc.** **1250 Sixth Ave.** **San Diego, Calif. 92101** Administrator: teacher Grade range: K.5 through last month of first grade Time required: approximately two hours and twenty minutes (seven sittings) Group and individual test Paper-and-pencil	*Stanford Early School Achievement Test* measures achievement in environment, mathematics, language arts, and reading. Level II: 1. Environment items—taken almost equally from social and natural sciences 2. Mathematics items—measures conservation of number and space, counting, measurement, numeration, classification, simple operations 3. Letter and Sound items—measures recognition of printed symbols and auditory perception of beginning sounds 4. Aural Comprehension items—requires ability to pay attention to, organize, interpret, infer, and retain verbal communication 5. Word Reading items—requires child to recognize words from reading tests 6. Sentence Reading items—requires child to identify sentence that tells about a picture (Three sentences about each picture are read before child identifies appropriate sentence.)	Administrator: test booklet class record sheet manual scoring key Each child: test booklet pencil	Raw score Percentile rank Stanine Grade equivalent Scaled score

ADMINISTRATION	CONTENT	MATERIALS	TEST DATA
Test of Basic Experiences (2nd ed.) Moss, M. H. **CTB Macmillan/McGraw-Hill** **2500 Garden Road** **Monterey, Calif. 93940** Administrator: teacher Grade range: overlapping levels—K and L—covering preschool through grade one Time required: not timed, approximately forty-five minutes for each of the four tests Group and individual test Paper-and-pencil	*Test of Basic Experiences* is comprised of four curriculum-oriented tests: 1. Mathematics test—measures fundamental mathematical concepts, terms used, and ability to see relationships between objects. 2. Language tests—assess vocabulary, sentence structure, verb tense, sound-symbol relationships, letter recognition, listening skills, and the concept that symbols carry meaning 3. Science test—measures scientific observations 4. Social studies test—has items concerning social groups, social roles, social customs, safety, and human emotions Each item consists of a verbal stimulus and four pictured responses.	Administrator: User's Guide Instructional Activities kit Class Evaluation Record Each child: practice test test book pencil with eraser	Raw and standard scores Percentile rank Stanine Normal curve equivalents

534

ADMINISTRATION	CONTENT	MATERIALS	TEST DATA

The Test of Early Mathematics Ability—Second Edition
Ginsburg, H. P., and A. J. Baroody
 	
Pro-ed
8700 Shoal Creek Blvd.
Austin, Tex. 78758
 	
Administrator:
  teacher
 	
Age range:
  four through nine years
 	
Time required:
  approximately thirty
  minutes
 	
Individual test
 	
Verbal, paper-and-pencil, and
manipulative
	The *Test of Early*
	Mathematics Ability, second
	edition, measures children's
	informal mathematics (i.e.,
	concepts of relative
	magnitude, counting skills,
	and calculation skills) and
	formal mathematics (i.e.,
	knowledge of conservation,
	number facts, calculation,
	and base-ten concepts).
		Administrator:
		  manual
		  scoring form
		
		Each child:
		  Student Worksheet
		  pencil
			Raw score
			Standard score
			Percentile rank
			Math Quotient (deviation)
			Profile

ADMINISTRATION	CONTENT	MATERIALS	TEST DATA
Test of Early Reading Ability, second edition (TERA–2) Reid, D. D., W. P. Hresko, and D. D. Hammill	The two alternate forms of the TERA–2 can be used to document early reading ability. Review of its items will also yield diagnostic information about three areas related to early reading: (1) knowledge of alphabet, (2) comprehension, and (3) the conventions of reading (e.g., book orientation and format).	Administrator: manual picture book record forms	Raw score Reading Quotient (deviation) Percentile rank
Pro-ed 8700 Shoal Creek Blvd. Austin, Tex. 78758			
Administrator: teacher			
Age range: three years through seven years, eleven months			
Time required: approximately twenty minutes			
Individual test			
Oral			

ADMINISTRATION	CONTENT	MATERIALS	TEST DATA
Woodcock Reading Mastery Tests—Revised (WRMT-R) Woodcock, R. W. **American Guidance Service Publishers' Building,** **P.O. Box 99** **Circle Pines, Minn. 55014**			
Administrator: teacher	*WRMT-R* offers two areas of readiness testing: Visual Auditory Learning and Letter Identification (with a Supplementary Letter Checklist) as well as four tests of reading achievement: Word Identification, Word Attack, Word Comprehension, and Passage Comprehension	Administration: manual test plates on easel test record forms (for G form and H form) Pronunciation Guide Cassette Compact shelf box (storage) Report to parents Microcomputer scoring program	Raw score Percentile rank Standard score Grade equivalent Age equivalent Normal curve equivalency Relative Performance Index (replaces the Relative Mastery Score of the WRMT) Instructional level profile Percentile rank profile
Age range: five through adult			
Time required: thirty to forty minutes			
Individual test			
Verbal			

Personal-Social Adjustment

ADMINISTRATION	CONTENT	MATERIALS	TEST DATA
Brief Index of Adaptive Behavior (BIAB) **McCallum, R. S., M. S. Herrin, J. P. Wheeler, and J. R. Edwards** Scholastic Testing Service, Inc. 480 Meyer Road P.O. Box 1056 Bensenville, Ill. 60106			
Administrator: teacher Age range: five through seventeen years Time required: varies Individual test Verbal and manipulative	The *BIAB* assesses a student in independent functioning, socialization, and communication. The *BIAB* screens and identifies those who may need a complete evaluation of behavior disorders, including areas where the student behaves differently from the norm.	Administrator: manual response sheet	Raw score Standard score Estimated functioning age

ADMINISTRATION	CONTENT	MATERIALS	TEST DATA
Burks' Behavior Rating Scales **Burks, H. T.** **Western Psychological Services** **Publishers and Distributors** **12031 Wilshire Blvd.** **Los Angeles, Calif. 90025** Administrator: teacher or parent but must be scored by professional other than parent Grade range: preschool and kindergarten grades one through nine Time required: approximately twenty minutes Individual test Paper-and-pencil	*Burks' Behavior Rating Scales* is a rating scale for identifying patterns of behavior problems in children. This norm-referenced instrument measures excessive self-blame, anxiety, withdrawal, dependency, suffering, sense of persecution, aggressiveness, and resistance, as well as poor ego strength, physical strength, impulse control, coordination, intellectuality, academics, attention, reality contact, sense of identity, anger control, and social conformity.	Administrator: manual administration booklet profile form	Category scores

ADMINISTRATION	CONTENT	MATERIALS	TEST DATA
California Test of Personality* Thorpe, L. P. **CTB Macmillan/McGraw-Hill** **2500 Garden Road** **Monterey, Calif. 93940** Administrator: teacher Grade range: Primary form, kindergarten through third grade Time required: forty-five minutes Individual (if children cannot read) or group (if children can read) test Paper-and-pencil	*California Test of Personality* determines effectiveness with which individual meets personal and social problems. Also indirectly measures how child impresses peers. "Personal Adjustment" subtest measures self-reliance, sense of personal worth, sense of personal freedom, feeling of belonging, withdrawing tendencies, and nervous symptoms. "Social Adjustment" subtest measures social standards, social skills, antisocial tendencies, family relations, school relations, and community relations.	Administrator: manual test booklet profile sheet class record sheet Each child (if children are mature enough to mark their own tests) test booklet pencil	Raw score Percentile rank (test and subsections) Recommended guidance methods

*As this is an extremely old test, the publishers recommend it for research purposes *only.*

ADMINISTRATION	CONTENT	MATERIALS	TEST DATA
Child Anxiety Scale (CAS) Gillis, J. **Institute for Personality and Ability Testing, Inc.** **P.O. Box 188** **Champaign, Ill. 61824**			
Administrator: 　teacher Age range: 　Five through twelve years Time required: 　approximately twenty 　minutes Group test Paper-and-pencil	The *CAS* is a brief screening instrument based on the *Early School Personality Questionnaire.*	Administrator: 　manual 　answer sheet 　taped instructions Each child: 　answer sheet 　pencil	Raw score Standard score Percentile

ADMINISTRATION	CONTENT	MATERIALS	TEST DATA
The Child Behavior Rating Scale (CBRS) **Cassel, R. N.** **Western Psychological Services** **Publishers and Distributors** **12031 Wilshire Blvd.** **Los Angeles, Calif. 90025** Administrator: someone familiar with child Grade range: preschool through third grade Time required: approximately thirty minutes Individual test Teacher check list	CBRS is standardized for objective assessment of personality adjustment. Ratings on specific child can be compared with typical children and emotionally disabled children. Measures adjustment in five areas: self-adjustment, home adjustment, social adjustment, school adjustment, physical adjustment and total personality adjustment. Each item rated on six-point scale that indicates degree to which child presents a specific behavior to the rater.	Administrator: manual rating book	Weighted score for each area of adjustment Personality total adjustment score (sum of weighted scores in self, home and school adjustment) T-scores Profile — compares scores with T-scores of typical children and with atypical children

ADMINISTRATION	CONTENT	MATERIALS	TEST DATA

Children's Apperception Test (CAT)
Bellak, L., and S. S. Bellak
	CAT measures personality adjustment. Based on *Thematic Apperception Test* (TAT).	Administrator:
		  manual
		  stimulus pictures
		  scoring key
			Projective pictures

C.P.S., Inc. P.O. Box 83 Larchmont, N.Y. 10538			
Administrator: psychometrist	However, Bellak and Bellak believe children respond to the situations in the pictures of the *CAT* more readily than to those in the *TAT*. For each stimulus picture, child expresses her conception of interpersonal relationships.		
Age range: three through ten years			
Time required: approximately thirty minutes	The *CAT-H-Human Version (CAT-H)*. Some children prefer human stimuli over animals, and these preferences are associated with specific personality variables. Furthermore, high-IQ children between the ages of seven and ten sometimes consider animal pictures below their intellectual dignity. Thus, the *CAT-H* lends itself especially well to an upward extension of the usefulness of the *CAT* and helps close an age gap between applicability of the *CAT* and *TAT*. Nevertheless, equivalence of the *CAT* and *CAT-H* has been experimentally established and they can best be used for testing-retesting.		
Individual test			
Verbal and manipulative			

ADMINISTRATION	CONTENT	MATERIALS	TEST DATA
Children's Apperception Test (CAT)—(cont'd) Bellak, L., and S. S. Bellak C.P.S., Inc. P.O. Box 83 Larchmont, N.Y. 10538	The *CAT-S-Supplement (CAT-S)* was designed to illuminate frequently occurring situations not necessarily pertaining to "universal problems." For example, an additional picture might be given from the *CAT-S* to a child with a physical disability and another to a child whose mother is pregnant. The *CAT-S* consists of cutout figures for use as a play technique for nonverbal or poorly verbalizing children.		

ADMINISTRATION	CONTENT	MATERIALS	TEST DATA
Coping Inventory Zeitlin, S. **Scholastic Testing Service, Inc.** **480 Meyer Road** **P.O. Box 1056** **Bensenville, Ill. 60106**			
Administrator: teacher Age range: three to sixteen years Time required: varies Individual test Verbal and manipulative	The *Coping Inventory* assesses the behavior patterns and skills used to meet personal needs and adapt to environmental demands.	Administrator: manual observation form	Coping Profile Coping with Self-Score Coping with Environment Score Adaptive Behavior Index List of Most and Least Adaptive Behaviors

ADMINISTRATION	CONTENT	MATERIALS	TEST DATA
Early Coping Inventory **Zeitlin, S., G.G. Williamson, and M. Szczepanski** **Scholastic Testing Service, Inc.** **480 Meyer Road** **P.O. Box 1056** **Bensenville, Ill. 60106** Administrator: teacher or person familiar with early childhood development Age range: four through thirty-six months Time required: Need to see child in several settings; thus requires three to four weeks. Individual inventory Observation with documentation of specific behaviors	The *Early Coping Inventory* is an observation instrument to assess the coping-related behaviors that are used by infants and toddlers in their everyday living. There are 48 items divided into three categories: 1. *Sensorimotor Organization* refers to the behaviors used to regulate psychophysiological functions and to integrate sensory and motor processes; 2. *Reactive Behaviors* are actions to respond to demands of the physical and social environments; 3. *Self-Initiated Behaviors* are autonomously generated, self-directed actions used to meet personal needs and to interact with objects and people.	Administrator: manual *Early Coping Inventory*	Raw scores Level of Effectiveness scores for each of 3 categories Coping Profile List of "Most" and "Least" Adaptive Coping Behaviors

ADMINISTRATION	CONTENT	MATERIALS	TEST DATA
Early School Personality Questionnaire **Institute for Personality and Ability Testing, Inc.** **Institute for Personality and Ability Testing, Inc.** **P.O. Box 188** **Champaign, Ill. 61824**			
Administrator: teacher Age range: six to eight years Time required: approximately thirty to forty minutes Group and individual test Paper-and-pencil	*Early School Personality Questionnaire* predicts development in thirteen factor-analytically defined dimensions.	Administrator: test manual with norms and questions answer booklet scoring stencils Each child: Two answer booklets	Raw score Profile Standard Ten Score (STEN) Ability to identify clinical problems Identification, prediction, and understanding of disciplinary problems Prediction of academic potential

ADMINISTRATION	CONTENT	MATERIALS	TEST DATA
Holtzman Inkblot Technique **Holtzman, W. H.** **The Psychological Corp.** **Harcourt Brace Jovanovich, Inc.** **1250 Sixth Ave.** **San Diego, Calif. 92101** Administrator: psychometrist Age range: five years through adult Time required: untimed Individual and group test Verbal	*Holtzman Inkblot Technique* helps clinician in diagnosis of behavior pathologies. A set of forty-five inkblots is used to elicit and appraise projective-expressive responses.	Administrator: manual scoring guide inkblots record forms materials for group administration	Percentile norms

ADMINISTRATION	CONTENT	MATERIALS	TEST DATA
Joseph Preschool and Primary Self-Concept (JPPSST) Screening Test			
Joseph, J.			
Stoelting			
Oakwood Centre, 620 Wheat Lane			
Wood Dale, Ill. 60191			
Administrator: teacher	The *JPPSST* derives a child's self-concept regarding significance and competence, as well as level of satisfaction with these perceptions. The test requires the child to draw his own face on a figure of the corresponding sex which has a totally blank head area. The child is also asked to respond to a series of fifteen questions, thirteen of which are illustrated by dichotomous sets of pictures.	Administrator: manual stimulus cards referenced drawings record forms	Global self-concept score is based on five dimensions, and provides high-risk cut-off points.
Age range: three-and-a-half through nine years			
Time required: approximately five to seven minutes			
Individual test			
Verbal and paper-and-pencil			

ADMINISTRATION	CONTENT	MATERIALS	TEST DATA
Preschool Self-Concept Picture Test (PS-CPT) Woolner, R. B. **Dr. Rosestelle Woolner 3551 Aurora Circle Memphis, Tenn. 38111**	*PS-CPT* is a picture test composed of four separate subtests for black and Caucasian children. Child is presented plates with paired pictures representing characteristics preschool children recognize as sharing and not-sharing, etc. Examines opinions children have of themselves: (1) as they perceive themselves to be (self-concept); (2) as they think they would prefer to be (ideal self-concept). Also provides measure of degree of variability between the foregoing. Positive and negative characteristics selected for use on picture plates related to needs, concerns, characteristics, and developmental tasks.	Administration: manual answer sheets pencil	The child is compared to himself or herself and not to others.
Administrator: teacher Age range: four through six years Time required: approximately twenty minutes Individual test Verbal or nonverbal			

550

ADMINISTRATION	CONTENT	MATERIALS	TEST DATA
Rosenzweig Picture-Frustration Study: Children's Form Rosenzweig, S. **Psychological Assessment Resources, Inc.** **P.O. Box 998** **Odessa, Fla. 33556** Administrator: teacher with supervision Age range: four through thirteen years Time required: fifteen through twenty-five minutes Individual (if verbal) or group (if paper-and-pencil) Paper-and-pencil or verbal	*Rosenzweig Picture-Frustration Study* involves response to twenty-four cartoon-like pictures, representing an everyday frustrating situation involving two persons. One cartooned character is shown saying something; subject is asked to complete caption box or balloon above the second character. Half the cartoons involve an adult frustrating the child, other half involve frustration by a peer.	Administrator: basic manual supplementary manual scoring sheet examination leaflet Each child: examination leaflet pencil (if group, paper-and-pencil exam)	Raw score based on type of aggression and direction of aggression Percentiles by age

ADMINISTRATION	CONTENT	MATERIALS	TEST DATA
Personality Inventory for Children (PIC) **Wirt, R. D., D. Lachar, J. K. Klinedinst, and P. D. Seat** **1990 Edition by Lachar, D.** **Western Psychological Services** **12031 Wilshire Boulevard** **Los Angeles, Calif. 70025** Administrator: trained professional Age range: three through sixteen years Time required: twenty-five to sixty minutes, depending on number of sections completed Individual test Paper-and-pencil	*PIC* is a 420-item, true-false, standardized questionnaire completed by parent or adult familiar with the child. The revised format divides items into four sections: completion of each additional section provides more scale information. Three validity scales and thirteen clinical scales are scored including adjustment, development, achievement, intellectual screening, somatic concern, depression, family relations, delinquency, withdrawal, anxiety, psychosis, hyperactivity, and social skills.	Administrator: manual scoring keys profile form Parent: administration booklet answer sheet	Scale raw scores T-scores

ADMINISTRATION	CONTENT	MATERIALS	TEST DATA

Primary Test of Cognitive Skills (PTCS)
Huttenlocher, J., and S. C. Levine
 	
CTB Macmillan/McGraw-Hill
2500 Garden Road
Monterey, Calif. 93940
 	
Administrator:
teacher
 	
Grade range:
Level 1: end of prekindergarten through middle of kindergarten
 	
Level 2: middle of kindergarten through beginning of first grade
 	
Time required:
approximately thirty minutes for each of the four tests
 	
Group test
 	
Paper-and-pencil
	PTCS measures sequencing, spatial integration, spatial memory, associative memory, category concepts, spatial concepts, object naming, and syntax comprehension.	Administration:
		manual
		Spatial Memory Stimulus
		   Book
		Associative Memory
		   Stimulus Book
		extra test books
		extra bar markers
		extra pencils
		clock
		
		Each child:
		PTCS Practice Book
		PTCS Test Book
		pencil
		eraser
		two-by-eight-inch bar
		   marker
			Raw score
			Percentile rank
			Grade percentile rank
			Stanine
			Cognitive Skills Index
			Anticipated Achievement
			   Score

ADMINISTRATION	CONTENT	MATERIALS	TEST DATA
School Behavior Checklist **Miller, L. C.** **Western Psychological Services** **Publishers and Distributors** **12031 Wilshire Blvd.** **Los Angeles, Calif. 90025**			
Administrator: teacher but must be interpreted by mental health worker Age range: four through thirteen years Time required: eight to ten minutes Individual test Paper-and-pencil	*School Behavior Checklist* is an inventory of behaviors covering a wide range of social and emotional behaviors from social competence to moderate social deviance. Form A–1 is for ages four through six, and Form A–2 is for ages seven through thirteen. Norms by sex and age are available for Form A–1, and by sex for Form A–2. The inventory covers such areas as need achievement, aggression, anxiety, cognitive deficit, hostile isolation, extraversion, and total disability.	Administrator: questionnaire answer sheet manual	Scale raw scores Standard scores Percentiles

554

ADMINISTRATION	CONTENT	MATERIALS	TEST DATA
Sex Attitude Measure (SAM) **Williams, J. E., and D. L. Best** **Department of Psychology, Wake Forest University** **Box 7778, Reynolder Station** **Winston-Salem, N.C. 27109**			
Administrator: teacher Age range: five to twelve years Time required: twenty minutes Group and individual test Verbal or paper-and-pencil	The *(SAM)* has been developed to assess children's attitudes or evaluative bias toward male and female persons, independent of their stereotyped knowledge. The *SAM* stories employ positive and negative adjectives. The *SAM* is generally given as an adjunct procedure to the *SSM II* and thus follows the administration of the *SSM II*.	Administrator: manual stories thirty-two silhouettes record sheet	Female Positive score Female Negative Score Male Positive Score Male Negative score Total Attitude score

555

ADMINISTRATION	CONTENT	MATERIALS	TEST DATA
Sex Stereotype Measure II (SSM II) Williams, J. E., and D. L. Best			
Department of Psychology, Wake Forest University **Box 7778, Reynolder Station** **Winston-Salem, N.C. 27109**			
Administrator: teacher	The (SSM II) assesses children's knowledge of adult-defined, conventional, sex-trait stereotypes. Brief stories presented with human figure silhouettes are designed to represent traits that adults define as descriptive of the male and female stereotypes.	Administrator: manual stories thirty-two silhouettes record sheet	Female Stereotype score Male Stereotype score Total Stereotype score
Age range: five through twelve years			
Time required: twenty minutes			
Group or individual test			
Verbal or paper-and-pencil			

ADMINISTRATION	CONTENT	MATERIALS	TEST DATA
Stamp Behavior Study Technique (BST) Stamp, I. M. **Australian Council for Educational Research Limited** P.O. Box 210 Hawthorn, Victoria 3122 Australia Administrator: teacher describes behavior, psychometrist scores Age range: three through five years Time required: approximately forty-five minutes Individual test Teacher checklist	*Stamp BST* describes and evaluates behavior. Screens behavioral problems in (1) attitudes toward self and others, (2) expression of negative feelings, (3) use of powers, and (4) integration of home and kindergarten life. Form is multiple choice questionnaire, requiring observer to select behavior most typical of the child in different situations.	Administrator: teacher: teacher's guide questionnaire psychologist: manual questionnaire scoring key	Percentages of children described in various categories

557

ADMINISTRATION	CONTENT	MATERIALS	TEST DATA
Test of Early Socioemotional Development (TOESD) **8700 Shoal Creek Blvd.** **Austin, Tex. 78758**			

Administrator:
  teacher
Age range:
  three through seven years
Time required:
  ten minutes
Three rating scales and one sociogram
	The *TOESD* evaluates children's affective behavior as seen by the child himself or herself, teacher, parent, and peers.	Administrator:
		  Student Rating Scale
		  Teacher Rating Scale
		  Parent Rating Scale
		  Sociogram
		Each child:
		  Student Rating Scale
		  Sociogram
		Each teacher:
		  Teacher Rating Scale
		  pencil
		Each parent:
		  Parent Rating Scale
		  pencil
			Raw score
			Standard score
			Percentile rank
			TOESD Profile

Appendix 9
Parent's Handbook

1. Our School

Dear Mom and Dad,

It's going to be four months before I can start kindergarten. I went to see my school today, so I can find out about kindergarten. That way I'll be ready to go in September.

My school is in a big building with very few interior walls. I like that, because I can see just about everything. I've never seen so many toys, books, and records. And, they even have hamsters and lots of other animals—almost like a zoo!

My teacher's name is _____. I asked her lots of questions and found out all about kindergarten. My school is a kindergarten-primary school. The kids will be five, six, seven, and eight years old. My teacher said there will be plenty of things for all of us to do. At first, I'll have easy things to do. Then as I learn, I'll get harder things to do. My teacher said that most children go to school here four years, but a few go three years and a few stay five years. It's called a "continuous progress" approach. I don't understand what that means, but you will hear about it in the Spring Orientation meeting tomorrow.

2. Entrance Requirements

Age

Little kids can't go to kindergarten. I'm big now. I'm five! This was printed in our newspaper:

Note: Because of space limitations, sections of the Parent's Handbook are indicated by numbers and headings. In making your school's handbook, arrange materials attractively on each page, a short paragraph can be centered; drawings, and so forth, can be added.

A child may attend kindergarten if he or she is five years old on or before November first.

Birth Certificate

Our state requires that children have a legal birth certificate to enter school. I have to bring it when I register. You have mine, but the teacher said that Mary's parents will have to write to:

The Bureau of Vital Statistics

State Capitol Building

_____,   _____   _____
(Capital City)   (State)   (Zip Code)

The charge is $_____.

Emergency Information Form

You always give me lots of good food, put me to bed early, and let me play outside. I'm very careful because skinned knees hurt. My teacher will take care of me while I'm at school and will need an "emergency information form," in case I get sick or hurt. It's in the back of this book. I'll get your pen and you can give my teacher the information.

Health History
Physical Examination
Immunizations
Dental Examination

My teacher says that I must be healthy and strong in kindergarten. You will have to call my doctor and dentist soon, because they're so busy. They have to write on all the other forms in the back of this handbook. Will I need to get a pen for the doctor and the dentist? I'll bring one, just in case.

3. Registration, Supplies, and Clothing

Registration

I am assigned to the school in the school attendance area in which I live. You found out where my class was by calling the Elementary School Director's Office. About two weeks before school starts, our town's newspaper will tell all about the school attendance areas and when to register.

The newspaper will also tell you about bus routes and the times the bus will pick me up and bring me back home, if I am to ride the bus.

Supplies

My teacher gave me a list of supplies. Here is a copy.

One box of large washable crayons.

One 20 in. × 48 in. plastic mat stitched crosswise in several sections.

One terry cloth apron with snap fasteners.

These supplies are sold in our three variety stores and our two discount stores.

Clothing

With so many children and with so much for each of us to do in kindergarten, the teacher says these are good qualities for school clothes:

1. Labeled for identification
2. Easy to handle (large buttons and buttonholes; underwear convenient for toileting; boots the child can put on and remove; loops on coats and sweaters for hanging)
3. Washable
4. Sturdy
5. Not too tight
6. Shoes with composition or rubber soles

4. Attendance, Session Times, and Early Dismissal

Attendance

Our school has attendance regulations. My teacher says it is important that I go to school every day, so I'll get to do all the fun things with my friends.

Session Times

Our kindergarten starts at _____ and closes at _____. I should arrive at school no more than ten minutes before school starts. If you bring me to school in the car, we should drive in the circular driveway and I should enter the school at the side door. I should never leave our car at the curb by the street. You can pick me up at the same place right after school.

Early Dismissal

My teacher says that I'm not to leave early unless there is an emergency. These are the rules parents have to follow:

1. Only the principal can dismiss a student.
2. A student cannot be excused by a telephone call without verification of the telephone call.
3. A student can be dismissed only to a parent or a person properly identified.

5. Lunch and Milk

I want to eat lunch and drink milk with the other kids. Here's a note that tells all about it.

A hot lunch will be served in the cafeteria every day. It costs _____¢ a day or you may pay $_____ a week. Checks may be made payable to _____. If your child wishes to bring his lunch, milk will cost him _____¢ a day. Those who wish to inquire whether their children qualify for free or reduced-cost lunches may secure forms in the central office.

When sending money to school, place it in an envelope and write the child's name and the teacher's name on the envelope.

6. A Child Stays Home

When Ill

I'm supposed to stay home if I'm sick. Here is a list of reasons.

chills	fever
communicable disease	headache, severe
coughing	joints, red or swollen
diarrhea	listlessness
earache	nausea or vomiting
eyes, inflamed or swollen	skin rash or sores
face, flushed or unusual pallor	sore throat

During Family Emergency

I may stay home if there is a death or serious illness in our family.

During Extremely Inclement Weather

Mom and Dad, you must decide if the weather is too bad for me to go to school. Sometimes there will be no school during bad weather. Local radio and TV stations carry school closing announcements are WKID, WKDG-TV, and WBUG-TV.

Bring a Note

I'm supposed to bring a note when I come back to school telling my teacher why I've been absent. If I've been to the doctor, he must sign my note before I return.

7. Everyday Experiences

When I visited the kindergarten at my school, I saw children doing many things in the building and outdoors. Some of the children were singing in the music room, two boys were feeding the hamsters, a girl was walking on a balance beam, and one big boy was reading a story to a little boy. My teacher said that in the kindergarten-primary school we do all those things and much more, like counting, painting, working with clay, reading books, learning about ourselves and people near and far, and visiting places in our town. We even eat together at lunch and get two snacks, one in the morning and one in the afternoon.

8. Special Experiences

Field Trips

When our class plans a field trip, the school asks our parents if we can go. The teacher will send a note to you each time we go on such a trip, and you will have to sign it. If I forget to get it signed, the teacher says I can't go *even if you call*. I'll have to be very careful not to lose the notes.

Parties and Treats

Birthdays are a lot of fun. When it is my birthday, I can share some treats with my class. My teacher will give you a list of all the rules about birthday treats. Even grown-ups have rules!

We will have five holiday parties. My teacher will send a note to you. Maybe you can sign-up to help with a party.

At our school we do not exchange gifts at Christmas (or on any holiday). We just say, "Merry Christmas!" We can give cards on Valentine's Day. My teacher will send you a list of names.

Bringing Things to School

Sometimes I can share one of my books, games, pictures, objects from nature and souvenirs from trips. You can help me choose what to bring so that I don't bring fragile, valuable (i.e., expensive or family treasure), or sharp-edged objects.

9. How Parents Can Help

Guess what? My teacher at school says that all the kids' parents are teachers, too! There are lots of teachers. Here is a letter from my school teacher to my parent teacher.

Dear Parents,

As parents you have been responsible for the early teaching of your child. Although he/she is now old enough for school, you will still be the most important teachers in your child's life. Here are some ways you can help your child in school.
1. Attend individual and group conferences as often as you can.
2. Read and answer all notes from the school.
3. Give special help to your kindergartener by:
   Promoting good health and safety habits
   Praising your child for things done well
   Talking about everyday experiences
   Planning family activities
   Reading stories
   Watching children's television shows with your child
   Providing materials for cutting, coloring, and building
   Helping your child start a collection
   Teaching your child to take care of toileting needs, to dress (outdoor clothing), and to put away toys.

---

10. Your Child's Progress

Our school doesn't send home report cards, but you can find out how I'm doing in school. My teacher will get together with you several times this year, and you will talk about how I'm doing in just about everything.

You can talk with my teacher anytime, and you can see me in school too. My school will also have some special meetings for you. I've got a list of the meetings the teacher planned. There's a blank space by each one. You can write the time in when you get a note or telephone call from my teacher.

Get-acquainted conference (approximately
    two weeks after the beginning of school) _____

Fall individual conference (November) _____

Spring individual conference (April) _____

11. Parent's Check List

Here's a "Parent's Check List" to make sure everything is done.

Have you read this handbook?   _____
Does your child have a legal birth certificate?   _____
Have you completed and signed the emergency information form?   _____
Have you completed and signed the health history form?   _____
Has your physician completed and signed the physical examination form?   _____
Has your physician completed and signed the immunization record form?   _____
Has your dentist signed the dental report?   _____
Do you know the date of registration?   _____
Have you obtained the school supplies?   _____
Are all outdoor clothes labeled?   _____
Does your child have the right type of school clothes?   _____
Are you following the suggestions given in the section "How Parents Can Help"?   _____
List any questions you would like to discuss with the staff.

_____
_____
_____

---

12. Forms

Remember those forms* that are part of the entrance requirements? Here they are, and you will have to take them when I go to school the first day.

_____

*Forms from the state should be used if provided.

Emergency Information

Child's name _____

Home address _____ Phone number _____

Father's name _____

Place of business _____ Phone number _____

Mother's name _____

Place of business _____

Phone number _____

Give name of another person to be called in case of emergency, if parents cannot be reached:

Name _____ Phone number _____

Address _____ Relationship _____

Physician to be called in case of emergency:

1st choice: _____ Phone number _____

2nd choice: _____ Phone number _____

Name of hospital to be used in emergency:

1st choice: _____

2nd choice: _____

Other comments: _____

_____

_____

_____

Date _____ Signed _____

(Parent or guardian)

Health History

Child's name _____

General evaluation of family's health: _____

_____

Family deaths (causes): _____

_____

Child's illnesses. If your child has had any of these diseases, please state the age at which he had them.

_____ measles		_____ smallpox
_____ mumps		_____ diabetes
_____ whooping cough		_____ heart disease
_____ poliomyelitis		_____ Chorea (St. Vitus Dance)
_____ rheumatic fever		_____ epilepsy (convulsions)
_____ scarlet fever		_____ chicken pox
_____ diphtheria		_____ pneumonia
_____ serious accident		_____ asthma, hay fever

Has your child ever had tests for tuberculosis? _____

Skin test? _____ Date _____ Chest X-ray? _____ Date _____

Please check any of the following which you have noted recently.

_____ frequent sore throat		_____ shortness of breath
_____ persistent cough		_____ frequent nose bleed
_____ frequent headaches		_____ allergy
_____ poor vision		_____ frequent urination
_____ dizziness		_____ fainting spells
_____ frequent styes		_____ abdominal pain
_____ dental defects		_____ loss of appetite
_____ speech difficulty		_____ hard of hearing
_____ tires easily		_____ four or more colds per year

Describe your child socially and emotionally _____

_____

_____

Are there any matters which you would like to discuss with the school staff?

_____

Date _____ Signed: _____
(Parent or guardian)

Physical Examination

Child's name _____

Comment on any significant findings:

Eyes: Right _____ Left _____ Squint _____

Ears: Right _____ Left _____ Discharge _____

Nose _____ Throat _____

Glands _____ Tonsils _____

Heart and Circulation _____

Lungs _____

Abdomen _____

Bones and joints _____

Reflexes _____

Nutrition _____

Posture _____

Hernia _____ Neurological _____

Hemoglobin (if physician indicates) _____

Urinalysis (if physician indicates) _____

Does the school program need to be adjusted for this child? _____

_____

_____

Date _____ Signed: _____ M.D.
D.O.

Immunization Record

Child's name _____

Diphtheria-Tetanus (since age 3)

_____   _____   _____
     (1st date)   (2nd date)   (Booster)

Poliomyelitis (since age 3)

_____ _____ _____ _____
  (1st date)   (2nd date)   (3rd date)   (Booster)

Measles (Rubeola): Disease or Immunization _____
                                                        (date)

T.B. Test

   Tine _____   Reaction: Pos. _____   Date: _____

   Mantoux _____   Neg. _____   Date: _____

   Chest X-Ray _____   Results: _____   Date: _____

Date _____ Signed: _____ M.D.
                                                                 D.O.

Dental Report

Child's name _____

Cavities _____ Gums _____

Malocclusion _____

Please explain any abnormal findings or deformities _____

_____

_____

Please indicate care given:

Prophylaxis _____ Cavities filled _____

Extractions _____ Orthodontics _____

What additional care do you plan for this child? _____

_____

_____

_____

Date _____ Signed: _____ D.D.S.

Medication Permission Form

Medications for children can be administered only when requested by the prescribing physician. Each container shall be childproof and carry the name of the medication, the name of the person for whom it was prescribed, the name of the prescribing physician, and the physician's instructions. Each child's medication shall be stored in its original container. This is in compliance with state and federal laws.

Child's Name _____

Prescription Name and Number _____

Pharmacy Name _____

Physician's Name _____ Phone # _____

Description of Medication (i.e., white liquid, red capsules) _____

Illness/Condition _____

Dosage _____ Time(s) of day to be given _____

Precautions _____ Date prescribed _____

Date to be discontinued _____

_____   _____
Signature of physician   Date

_____   _____
Signature of parent   Date

Medications Given

	Date	Time	By whom		Date	Time	By whom
1.				8.			
2.				9.			
3.				10.			
4.				11.			
5.				12.			
6.				13.			
7.				14.			

Index